ISONZO

—ISONZO—

The Forgotten Sacrifice
of the Great War

JOHN R. SCHINDLER

Westport, Connecticut
London

Library of Congress Cataloging-in-Publication Data

Schindler, John R.
    Isonzo : the forgotten sacrifice of the Great War / John R. Schindler.
      p. cm.
    Includes bibliographical references and index.
    ISBN 0–275–97204–6 (alk. paper)
    1. Isonzo, Battles of the, Italy, 1915–1917. I. Title.
    D569.I69S35 2001
    940.4′145—dc21   00–061108

British Library Cataloguing in Publication Data is available.

Library of Congress Catalog Card Number: 00–061108
ISBN: 0–275–97204–6

First published in 2001

Praeger Publishers, 88 Post Road West, Westport, CT 06881
An imprint of Greenwood Publishing Group, Inc.
www.praeger.com

Printed in the United States of America

The paper used in this book complies with the
Permanent Paper Standard issued by the National
Information Standards Organization (Z39.48–1984).

10 9 8 7 6 5 4 3 2 1

**For the soldiers of all nationalities
who were sacrificed on the Isonzo**

CONTENTS

An unnumbered photo section follows chapter 9.

Acknowledgments

This book is the result of several years' work in a half-dozen countries, four archives, and more than two dozen libraries and museums, not to mention much up-close, old-fashioned investigation of forgotten battlefields. To cite, and thank, all the institutions and individuals that assisted me in my research would be impossible. That said, several people and places cannot justly go unnoted.

Among institutions, the Austrian *Staatsarchiv* in Vienna, particularly its famed *Kriegsarchiv*, was preeminent in my piecing together of the Isonzo story; two of its officials, *Hofrat* Dr. Peter Broucek, Deputy Director, and *Rat* Mag. Dr. Wolfgang Kuderma, *Referent* for First World War records, assisted me considerably. Acknowledgments are likewise due to several people who helped me at various points in the research and writing of this project, with everything from archival and linguistic matters to more mundane but no less vital computing and editorial issues. In North America: the ever encouraging Dr. John P. Campbell, Dr. Gabriele Erasmi, my friend and factotum G. Bruce Strang, my most helpful editor Heather Staines, and Dr. Geza Schay, not to mention Dr. Mark R. Peattie, who dispatched me down this road several years ago; in Europe: Vera Ivančič, Luigi Berlot, Dr. Klaus Schäfer, and Dragan Meržan, as well as countless Slovenes and Italians who helped a wayfaring scholar trying to track down long-forgotten mountains, monuments, trenches, and cemeteries.

No less, I would like to express my gratitude to my mother, Dawn, for her unfailing support of this undertaking. Thanks are likewise due to my late father, Richard, who instilled in me a love of history and scholarship, as well as a healthy interest in the subject of war—composed of equal parts fascination and loathing—that he learned during three tours in Vietnam. And my wife, Tracey, deserves special thanks for her kind support of me and this book through many long months, during which she doubtless felt she was the last victim of the Isonzo battles. Last, but assuredly not least, I wish to thank B.D.M., who made everything possible.

John R. Schindler

INTRODUCTION

The Isonzo River flows through one of the loveliest valleys in Europe. The cold and fast-moving Isonzo begins high in the Julian Alps, in Slovenia's forbidding Triglav National Park, barely more than an azure-hued mountain stream. As the winding blue-green water follows its course south to the Adriatic Sea, between snowy Alpine peaks and densely forested hills, past a dozen sleepy Slovene towns and villages long forgotten to history, it slowly widens and darkens in color. Once the river has reached the Italian border at the city of Gorizia, fifty miles downstream from its source, the Isonzo's pace has slowed, its depth has doubled, and its width has trebled. On its banks, the mountains have become mere hills, and the Slovene towns have been replaced by bustling Italian industrial cities. The last miles of the Isonzo's course before it reaches the head of the Adriatic take the river west, to the edge of the Friulian plain. Where the Isonzo disappears into the sea, the city of Trieste and its surrounding hills are clearly visible to the east.

The almost unknown Isonzo is notable for several reasons. Geologically, the Julian Alps, which overlook and give birth to the river, are the European watershed between the Mediterranean and the Black Sea. Ethnically, the Isonzo has served as the dividing line between Latin and Slavic Europe for centuries; the population to the west of the river is mostly Italian, and to the east it is largely Slovene. Politically, the Isonzo valley has divided Italy from several of its northeastern neighbors throughout the twentieth century: Habsburg Austria, followed by Tito's Yugoslavia, and now the Republic of Slovenia. Yet the Isonzo is hardly well known because of these attributes. Instead, the river is now noted, if at all, for its beautiful color and its excellent white water sports, particularly in its mountainous upper half. The stunning scenery attracts a modest number of Italian tourists, especially in the summer. The tourists come, often for only a day, to enjoy the Isonzo's beauty and the affordable prices of newly independent Slovenia. Tourism is an overwhelmingly local phenomenon; it is difficult to encounter a visitor who is not Italian, Slovene, or Austrian. Even fewer tourists still will notice the faded monuments perched by the roadside, the overgrown trenches hiding behind houses, or the occasional partially obscured cemetery near the river's edge. The Isonzo's tragic recent past has been all but totally forgotten.

Earlier in the twentieth century, the river's name evoked horror and sorrow. Throughout Europe and North America, the name Isonzo stood alongside Verdun and the Somme in the collective memory of needless sacrifice of the First World War. The terrible bloodletting that scarred France and Flanders and shattered the lives of millions did not spare the Isonzo. From May 1915 to October 1917, the Italian Army attempted to break the Austro-Hungarian defensive line on the Isonzo and to advance deep into the Central European heartland. A series of eleven major Italian offensives proved futile, winning only a few miles of worthless trenches and hills. Countless regiments of both armies were sacrificed in pointless battles for useless objectives. The cost was unprecedented. Twenty-nine months of fighting on the Isonzo cost Italy 1,100,000 soldiers dead and wounded. The Austrians, desperately holding on to every inch of ground, lost 650,000. The Italians finally crossed the Isonzo in triumph only in November 1918, at the Great War's end, following Austria-Hungary's complete political collapse. It was at best a Pyrrhic victory. More than any other front of the Great War, the war on the Isonzo was noted for the harshness of the terrain, the viciousness of the fighting, and the relentless cycle of disastrously failed offensives. For Italians and Central Europeans of a dozen nationalities, the Isonzo symbolized the terrible cost and utter futility of the First World War. The bloody battles fought on the Isonzo's banks, the centerpiece of the Austro-Italian struggle, constituted a needless campaign in a needless war. The Isonzo's impact on twentieth-century Italy and Central Europe has been politically, socially, and culturally immense.

Yet, surprisingly, the Isonzo has almost entirely disappeared from historical consciousness. The handful of impressive war memorials in the valley have few visitors today, and the dozens of smaller cemeteries are now mostly forgotten. For the Italians, the horrible cost and sad futility of the fighting on the Isonzo represent an inglorious, and perhaps embarrassing, chapter in the history of Italian arms; the political use of the memory of the Isonzo by Mussolini's Fascist regime has further obscured the bloody river's legacy in modern Italy. For the Slovenes, on whose territory most of the fighting took place, the Great War inevitably seems part of an increasingly distant historical past. And the Austrians and other Central Europeans pay little attention to the Isonzo fighting today, viewing it as a legacy of a defunct empire and an irrevocably lost age. Who in the age of the European Union and continental unity can imagine Italians and Central Europeans killing each other in the hundreds of thousands for a minor Alpine river? Across the Atlantic, the memory of the Isonzo, never strong, has disappeared entirely. Few historians, much less average citizens, have ever heard of the river or the terrible events that happened there more than eight decades ago. The river is remembered vaguely, if at all, for its fictional appearance in Hemingway's *A Farewell to Arms*. Even specialists in military history and the history of twentieth-century Europe make little mention of the Isonzo or its impact on the modern world. For most English-language historians, battles and campaigns of the Great War that did not happen on the Western Front or involve English-speaking troops apparently are not worth exploring. Thus the Isonzo, the worst campaign of the First World War, not to mention one of the most historically significant, has been forgotten.

No doubt this historical neglect of the Isonzo fighting is in part attributable to the widely lamented martial achievements of the Italian and Austrian armies. Italy's military reputation, once among the finest in Europe, has not survived the twentieth century intact. The dismal performance of Mussolini's Fascist legions in the Second World War, including defeats at the hands of not just the British and the Russians, but also the French and Greeks, has left an enduring blemish on the record of Italian arms. Often this image of military incompetence, even cowardice, has been unfairly presumed to encompass all of Italian history. Yet Italian soldiers can fight bravely, and the heroic performance of the Italian Army in a dozen battles of the Isonzo stands as a poignant reminder of the truth of the old cliché that there are no bad soldiers, only bad officers.

In a similar vein, Austria's once-renowned martial reputation has declined precipitously, and apparently permanently, since the Great War. From the perspective of the twenty-first century, the era of universal nationalism and self-determination, the multinational empire and army of the Habsburgs appear as part of an unimaginably distant European past, more akin to feudalism than to modern Europe. Had not Napoleon, surely an expert witness, declared Austria to be *"toujours en ritard d'une année, d'une armée et d'une idée?"* Indeed, progressive European opinion had predicted the imminent demise of the Habsburg realm since the Thirty Years' War, so when at last the empire crumbled, three centuries later, it seemed like a long foregone conclusion. And there was the ethnic question. Austria, a confusing jumble of ten different—and often mutually hostile—nationalities, looked doomed to fail in an era of nation-states; in retrospect, its demise at the end of the Great War appears all too predictable. Surely the fictional, yet unforgettable, *Good Soldier Švejk* has not helped Austria's modern martial reputation either. However, the steadfast performance of Austrian arms on the Isonzo serves as a reminder that Habsburg battlefield efforts were not inevitably failures, and that multinationalism, per se, has little to do with military effectiveness.

This book seeks to remedy the pervasive historical amnesia that has allowed the Isonzo front to be forgotten. It is intended to bring the river and the battles fought there back to their rightful place in the history of the First World War and modern Europe. To achieve these aims, the book relies upon many sources in several languages: archival documents and records, official historical accounts, memoirs, unit histories, and numerous secondary sources. It tells the untold story of the Isonzo front chronologically, from the road to the Great War, through the twelve battles of the Isonzo, to the war's end and aftermath; for the benefit of adventurous explorers, a guide to the battlefield today follows the book's conclusion. The book covers the fighting in operational detail, as well as in its wider military, political, and social contexts. Throughout, the battles will be illuminated through identifiable units and men, including many notable characters, rather than in abstract historical terminology: wars are ultimately won—or lost—by men, not by organizations or bureaucracies. One hopes that the legacy of valor and horror, forgotten for so many decades, will thus come alive again, and the epic European tragedy of the Isonzo and the men who were needlessly sacrificed there will justly reenter the history of the twentieth century.

THE ROAD TO WAR

ONE

ITALIA IRREDENTA

On the eve of the First World War, the Isonzo valley was securely Austrian terri- tory. Since the Middle Ages, the river and its environs had belonged to the House of Habsburg. In 1914, the Isonzo ran through the western edge of the Austrian Littoral, the province of Küstenland. The Littoral, one of the smallest Habsburg dominions, consisted of the province of Trieste and the margravate of Istria, 938,000 subjects in all. The population of the Littoral was highly diverse, like Austria herself: by language, 46 percent Italian, 31 percent Slovene, 21 percent Croatian, and only 2 percent German-Austrian. As varied geographi- cally as it was ethnically, Küstenland extended from the snow-capped Julian Alps to the head of the sunny Adriatic and down to the end of the Istrian Penin- sula, including several scenic islands.

The province's capital was Trieste, its only large city. A natural port well po- sitioned at the head of the Adriatic, Trieste had been established in Roman times, during the reign of Augustus. It voluntarily entered the Habsburg realm in 1382 and enjoyed modest prosperity; its more successful and much larger Adriatic rival, Venice, had for centuries been Trieste's main competitor for trade and prominence. Trieste was made a free port in the eighteenth century to help commerce, but the city's economic takeoff came with the extension of the Vienna railway in 1857. The arrival of the *Südbahn*, coupled with a high Aus- trian protective tariff, made Trieste a major port, bringing new business and prosperity to the city; by the eve of the First World War, it was the eighth busiest port on earth. Its great shipping company, Lloyd Triestino, was world re- nowned. With economic expansion came jobs and unprecedented immigration.

By 1914 Trieste boasted a population of 243,000 to match its new-found wealth.

The Littoral's other city was the much smaller and less bustling Gorizia, on the east bank of the Isonzo little more than twenty-five miles northwest of Trieste. It, too, had been settled in the Roman era, and had belonged to the Habsburgs since the Renaissance. It was a successful market town as early as the fifteenth century, and became a local textile center a hundred years after that. Even so, Gorizia, bounded on the west by the Isonzo and on the east by the last of the Julian Alps, was noted more for its pleasant climate and scenic vistas than for its riches. Its population, 31,000 in 1914, had not expanded greatly in past decades. The "City of Violets," in fact, was regarded as a pensioners' colony, particularly for retired Austrian Army officers, who enjoyed its comfortable Mediterranean atmosphere, relaxed charm, and affordability.

Except for the port of Pola at the tip of the Istrian Peninsula, the headquarters of Austria's fleet, the rest of the Littoral was mostly poor and agricultural, dotted with small farming villages and trading towns. At the province's southern end, Istria included numerous fishing villages living off the natural wealth of the Adriatic, as well as many peasant settlements in the peninsula's more mountainous inland region. Moving north along Istria's Adriatic coast, passing the small ports of Pirano and Capodistria, Trieste arose where the mountains disappeared. Just north of the capital, the impressive Miramare Castle jutted into the Adriatic. Commissioned in 1856 by Emperor Franz Joseph's ill-fated younger brother, Archduke Maxmilian, the magnificent Miramare was only briefly enjoyed by Maxmilian and his family before their voyage to Mexico. Beyond the castle, a dozen miles north of Trieste, lay the Carso, the unique and desolate "world of rock" that stretched to the banks of the Isonzo and the edge of Gorizia. The Carso was a plateau of naked limestone, nearly devoid of vegetation and marked by countless depressions and crevasses. The depressions, known as *dolinas*, were formed by centuries of chemical erosion of the rock, and served as occasional oases. There plants could take root, including vines that produced the region's sharp *terrano* wines.[1] The *dolinas* also offered protection against the Carso's often harsh climate. The summer months were typically pleasant, with cool, clean breezes, although the limestone could become extremely hot; indeed, many Triestine families retreated to the plateau during July and August to escape the city's lowland heat. Winter on the Carso, however, was far less welcoming. Then it was buffeted by the *bora*, a fierce, cold wind from the north caused by the meeting of the high pressure fronts of southeastern Europe and the low pressure of central Italy. The relatively few inhabitants of the Carso endured the annual arrival of the *bora*, eking out a meager existence farming the rocky fields, living off a diet of *jota*, a staple soup of barley, beans, pork, and whatever else might be at hand. In the half century before the war, the Austrian forestry service had made heroic efforts to make the Carso bloom, partly to moderate the effects of the *bora*. Despite the planting of fifteen million trees by 1914, most of them black pines, the stony Carso remained a harsh, uninviting place to live.

North of the Carso, across the Vipacco River, a tributary of the Isonzo, Gorizia lay between the limestone plateau and the Julian Alps farther to the north. On the Isonzo's west bank were Gorizia's few factories and workshops, in the shadow of Podgora hill. East of the city the heavily forested Ternova plateau, dotted by occasional villages, dominated Gorizia with mountains up to 2,200 feet. North along the Isonzo, against its current, the fashionable suburb of Salcano stood at the mouth of a considerable river gorge, with Mt. Sabotino (2,010 ft.) to the west and Mt. Santo (2,250 ft.) to the east. The latter mountain was particularly noted for a medieval monastery at its peak that overlooked Gorizia and the entire lower Isonzo. After Salcano the river passed between steep Alpine peaks and gradually narrowed. At the town of Plava, five miles upstream, the Isonzo shifted eastward, its course taking it past several quiet villages of white stucco houses with red tile roofs, perched on the river's east bank, that stood out against the green forests of the Bainsizza plateau. With peaks as high as 2,400 feet, the sparsely populated Bainsizza was the main topographical feature of the central Isonzo valley. Four miles farther north, at the town of Tolmein, just beyond the Bainsizza, the river shifted westward again, becoming the fast-running upper Isonzo, surrounded on all sides by the high Julian Alps. Tolmein and the town of Karfreit, eight miles upstream, were overlooked from the east bank by the 7,410-foot Mt. Krn, snow-capped year-round, the highest peak in the valley. The ever narrower and bluer Isonzo turned east again at Saga before reaching the market town of Flitsch, the last settlement of any size in the valley, at the foot of the imposing Mt. Rombon (7,290 ft.). Northeast of Flitsch, the river disappeared into the high Julian Alps and the snows that gave it birth.

The Littoral was one of the most beautiful and tranquil regions of the Habsburg realm, indeed of all Europe. Yet even after decades of peace, stability, and increasing prosperity, particularly in Trieste, the province was plagued by a seemingly intractable problem. Like so much of Europe in 1914, and the Habsburg lands in particular, the Littoral was sharply divided by ethnicity and nationalism. The national question loomed large in all areas of life in the Isonzo valley and Trieste. The Italian majority saw itself increasingly threatened by the province's large and growing Slav population. Trieste and Gorizia remained majority Italian, but the countryside was overwhelmingly Slav. Outside the cities, Italians outnumbered Slavs only along the lower Isonzo near Gorizia. The province's hinterland was otherwise Slovene and Croatian. The villages and countryside of the upper Isonzo were entirely Slovene, as was much of the Carso. The Istrian Peninsula was Italian only along the coast; its interior was Croatian. Even the Italians of Trieste and Gorizia felt threatened. The smaller city was by language half Italian and almost a third Slovene, with German-Austrians making up most of the rest. The Slovene percentage was growing every year in Gorizia, but the City of Violets was not large or important enough to be a major rallying point for Italian nationalists. Trieste, however, was another matter entirely.

Trieste had always been an unquestionably Italian city, even if it was subject to Vienna rather than Rome. For centuries it had served as a distant outpost of Italian culture, the northeastern frontier of an ancient Latin civilization. Trieste had produced its share of Italian literary and artistic successes, most recently the novelist Italo Svevo; it was something of an international writers' mecca in the years before the war, receiving visits from well known literati, including Rainer Maria Rilke and more notably James Joyce, who spent several pleasant years with his family in Trieste. In 1914, the Italian majority of Trieste (65 percent of the city's population, versus 24 percent Slovene) should have felt secure. The city's elite, including the powerful mercantile class, remained solidly Italian, whereas the Slavs, mostly recent arrivals from the countryside, were confined to the proletarian and servant classes and some minor positions in the civil service. No less significantly, the Austrian government had historically favored the Italians, giving them substantial political privileges not shared by the Habsburg realm's other minorities.

Still, for many *triestini* the Slav threat seemed only too real. The burgeoning Slav population—the numbers of Slovenes in Trieste grew 130 percent in the first decade of the twentieth century, and the suburbs were already majority Slav—forecast a dire future for Trieste as a uniquely Italian city. Trieste was unquestionably a Slovene city too: there were more Slovenes living in Trieste than in Ljubljana, the capital of Slovenia after 1918. To the city's Italian upper and middle classes, the "Slav peril" endangered their entire way of life. Their Slavophobia grew every year, with each revelation of ever increasing numbers of Slovenes leaving peasant farming for modest employment in the city, particularly after 1907, when Austria introduced universal male suffrage. The high Slav birthrate only increased Italian paranoia. The Littoral's Italians saw themselves as urban defenders of an ancient civilization imperiled by masses of primitive, priest-ridden Slav peasants.

Trieste's reality was inevitably more complex than Italian nationalist fears portrayed it. Latins and Slavs had lived side by side in the Littoral quite peaceably for centuries. The Slavs, though undeniably mostly peasants, were by no means newcomers: the ancestors of the Slovenes arrived in the Isonzo region in the early Middle Ages. More tellingly, many of Trieste's elite were Italians by language and culture, not by ethnicity. A substantial number of the city's "Italians" were, in fact, Italian-speaking Greeks, Armenians, Jews, and other minorities who had assimilated linguistically and culturally with the majority Italians, often quite recently. In a typical case, the Trieste Jew Aron Schmitz transformed himself into Italo Svevo, thus becoming a successful Italian writer whose *italianità* was never questioned. The assimilation of the non-Slav minorities was total and enthusiastic. Indeed, many of the most ardent Italian nationalists in Trieste and the Littoral were of distinctly non-Latin descent; they compensated for their foreign origins with the zeal of converts, and were among the loudest denouncers of "Slav barbarism." Additionally, the advancement of some Slavs from the working class into the lower ranks of the province's civil service, a rise that mortified the Italians, was attributable largely to Italian arrogance. Even the lowest-paid position in the state bureaucracy required fluency in both Italian and Slovene (or Croatian): any educated Slav knew Italian, whereas few Italians could be bothered to learn Slav languages, despised as "peasant tongues." Thus the rise in the Slovene population in Trieste was a complex phenomenon, politically and ethnically. Nevertheless, the Littoral's Italian elite lived in fear of the eventual overwhelming of their Austrian province by Slavs. At the least, educated Italians wanted special state protection for their privileged economic and cultural position. In the last decade of peace, the Italian nationalists' tone grew increasingly alarmist. Many of them saw union with neighboring Italy as the only relief from the ever growing Slav threat.

For many Italians living west of the Isonzo, across the border in the Italian nation-state, the specter of Slavs overwhelming their conationals in the Littoral was simply intolerable. The possible cultural extinction of an ancient Italian city by Slovene peasants was no longer merely an internal Austrian matter; it was becoming an international issue of major proportions. Italian nationalists had always hated the Habsburgs anyway. Italy was still a very young state, dating only to 1861, and its unity had to be wrested from the Austrians step by step, and always at considerable cost. The national revolutions of 1848 to force the occupying Austrians out of northern Italy had been crushed unexpectedly and bloodily by the octogenarian Field Marshal Joseph Radetzky and his army of Slavs, Germans, and Hungarians. The Italians were more successful in 1859, pushing the Austrians out of Lombardy, although only with considerable French help. In 1866, the Italians attacked the Austrians while the Prussians distracted most of the Habsburg Army in Bohemia. In the peace settlement Vienna gave Rome its last wholly Italian province, Venetia, leaving relatively few Italians under Habsburg authority. It was therefore an unshakable tenet of Italian nationalist faith that Austria was Italy's mortal enemy, and that all Italians living under Habsburg mistreatment had to be liberated.

There were other compelling reasons why Austria and all it represented were so detested by patriotic Italians of all political denominations. Unified Italy was a modern, liberal-minded nation-state, strongly anticlerical in outlook (it had occupied the Papal States in 1870, leaving the pope effectively a prisoner in his Vatican enclave). In stark contrast, Austria-Hungary was an anachronism, the last Catholic great power, a throwback to premodern Europe in an age of secularism and nationalism; it remained a highly diverse multinational empire, conservative in politics and clerical in matters of faith. For these reasons the Habsburg possession of any ethnically Italian territory was anathema to nationalists of all stripes. To them, the Austrian frontier provinces were *Italia irredenta*, "unredeemed Italy."

The Littoral was the nationalists' primary objective, the land most in need of redemption by Rome. It was there that *italianità* was most threatened. The entire province was claimed by irredentists, who saw its union with Rome as the only way to complete Italy's natural borders and to save Trieste from the Slav threat. The province's Slav majority was not worthy of consideration. Irredentist claims also included the Trentino, the southern part of the Austrian province of Tyrol. The Tyrol, overall nearly two-fifths Italian, was divided by high mountain ranges that had served as an ethnic boundary for more than a thousand years. The land south of the mountains, the Trentino, was over 95 percent Italian, whereas the territory to its north was equally German. The irredentists' ethnic claim to the Trentino was therefore very good. However, very few Tyrolean Italians desired union with Italy. Conservative and devoutly Catholic farmers, they had lived peacefully and moderately prosperously under the Habsburgs for centuries, and felt no need to be redeemed by their liberal and secular neighbor.

Even so, the political movement to unite the Littoral and the Trentino with Italy dated to the early years of the Italian nation-state. In 1877, a leading nationalist formed the Association for *Italia irredenta*, with the aim of agitating against Austria. More peacefully, the Dante Alighieri Society was established in 1889 to spread Italian culture and the cause of irredentism among Austria's Italian minority. In the end, the objective of both organizations—union of the Littoral and Trentino with Italy—was identical. The irredentist cause soon also had a cause célèbre. In 1882 the Austrian government executed Guglielmo Oberdan, a twenty-four-year-old Austrian citizen, for attempting to assassinate Emperor Franz Joseph during an official visit to Trieste. The Triestine Oberdan (born Wilhelm Oberdank—like so many ardent nationalists from the Littoral, he was ethnically a Slav), a former student at the University of Vienna, was serving as an officer cadet in the Austrian Army when Vienna invaded Bosnia in 1878. Outraged by the invasion, Oberdan deserted and fled to Italy, becoming a devout irredentist. He sneaked back into Austria to kill the emperor, but his plan was foiled. Franz Joseph reluctantly condoned the death sentence. Oberdan's death gave the irredentist cause its first martyr.

The idea of wresting *Italia irredenta* from Austrian control appealed to many Italians in senior military and civil positions, for both nationalist and strategic reasons. However, until the First World War irredentism was destined to remain a private and unofficial enthusiasm. Officially, Italy was committed to Austria's territorial integrity. More than that, the Habsburg Empire was Italy's main ally. In 1882, Rome, Vienna, and Berlin agreed to form the Triple Alliance, a defensive pact that bound the three states together militarily. Italy, afraid of being diplomatically and militarily isolated, had allied herself with her traditional enemy. The three powers even undertook considerable secret military planning to put Italian armies in the field alongside their former adversaries. Relations between the Latin and Teutonic powers, though sometimes strained, remained cordial. The only way for Italy to gain *Italia irredenta* was through conquest—Vienna would never part with her provinces without a fight—but there was no point in contemplating war against an ally. Up to 1914, irredentism was a strident voice in Italian national life, but always one well removed from the centers of power.

It was just as well that Rome gave little thought to winning the Littoral and the Trentino on the field of battle, for the Italian military was widely considered to be weak and ineffective. Certainly the recent record of Italian arms left ample room for doubt. Although Italian soldiers often fought bravely, the army's leadership at all levels had failed to distinguish itself in battle. In 1848, Radetzky's outnumbered, ragtag army bested the Piedmontese, and in 1859 the Italians generally performed poorly compared with their French allies and their Austrian adversaries. In 1866, the Austrians, although quickly defeated by the Prussians in Bohemia, made short work of the Italians both on land and at sea, winning stunning and unexpected victories at Custozza and Lissa. Four years later, the Italians dared occupy Rome only because the French were busy resisting the Prussian invasion of 1870. Italy's fighting record in the colonies was hardly better. An attempt to conquer Ethiopia in 1896, at the height of the European scramble for Africa, led to the slaughter of several Italian brigades at Adua, the only significant defeat of a European army by a native force during the nineteenth century. The performance of the Italian Army in Libya in 1911–1912, although somewhat better, still left considerable doubt about the professional competence of the officer corps. The Italian military seemed consistently badly organized, poorly trained and led, and shabbily equipped. The army was far more effective at breaking strikes and suppressing peasant uprisings—missions assigned to it all too frequently—than at defeating foreign adversaries. Its performance inspired little confidence among Italy's political leadership.

The military could not convincingly claim that financial neglect had caused its poor reputation. The army and navy consumed a large proportion of Rome's finances—from 1861 to 1913, a total of 17.4 percent of state spending, a percentage that grew rapidly in the last half-decade of peace. Italian military spending, although not proportionally as high as German or French, nonetheless consumed a larger part of the budget than in several other European countries, Austria included. The last peacetime budget devoted 650 million lire to military spending, but only 150 million to education. The army was indeed poorly equipped, but this was attributable to Italy's economic backwardness, not to governmental parsimony. Italian industry staged impressive gains in the last decade of the nineteenth century and the first decade of the twentieth: between 1896 and 1914, industrial output rose by nearly 90 percent, and steel production grew tenfold. That said, Italy remained an overwhelmingly agricultural country. Little more than a sixth of the workforce was employed in manufacturing and industry, whereas 60 percent lived off the land. Eighty percent of those were landless peasants, and an alarming 54 percent were casual day laborers. The North in particular had begun to industrialize impressively, but Italy on the whole remained a poor, underdeveloped country. It thus had no hope of competing with major European powers in the arms race that engulfed the continent before the First World War. Worse, Italy had depressingly few natural resources, and was overwhelmingly dependent on foreign fuels and raw materials; in a typical year, 90 percent of Italian coal was imported from Britain. Even the impressive increases in steel output amounted to little progress: Italy produced 90,000 tons of steel annually, whereas Germany and Austria together produced 20 million. Economic weakness placed strong limits on Italy's military potential.

The military and industrial bureaucracies only made matters worse. By 1898, it was evident that the army's main field gun was obsolete, and that an entirely new model was required. The domestic arms industry was small and outmoded, so the army looked for a foreign model to produce under license. The process of choosing a gun took fourteen years. The cumbersome bureaucracy further delayed the production of new guns. The industrial consortium of twenty-seven firms contracted to build the new 75mm cannon proved so awkward and slow that the army did not receive deliveries of the gun until mid-1915, seventeen years after it decided to acquire new artillery.

Yet the Italian Army's material weaknesses were perhaps not its most serious defects. The army's problems as an institution were potentially even more ominous. Italy, although a nation-state, was in truth a collection of widely varying, and often mutually hostile, regions. The economic, political, and cultural disparities between North and South appeared unbridgeable; the widespread particularism of cities and districts within regions was hardly less notable. Beyond a flag, a Piedmontese and a Calabrian, or a Venetian and a Sardinian, had little else to unite them. The Italian language was divided into so many dialects that communication was sometimes impossible. As a truly national institution, the army offered the state a unique opportunity to unite Italy and to build a loyalty to the nation that would supersede regional identity. Italy, like all continental European powers, introduced conscription by the 1870s, sending fit young men to the military for three years' mandatory service. Conscription was implemented to bring more recruits to the army, but also to foster national unity. It was to be a "school of national education" for the millions of young Italian men who passed through its ranks. The army offered the first—and frequently, the only—chance for peasants to leave the fields and see the world beyond their villages, meeting young men of other regions. The army, the only truly national institution, was well placed to help unite a very divided country.

Sadly for nationalists, the army on the whole failed to produce a united nation. In the first place, the army was barely united itself. The Royal Italian Army was an amalgam of different forces with unique traditions—Piedmontese, Neapolitan, Sicilian, Venetian, and others. These regional armies were proud of their heritage, including a history of fighting each other. The marriage was not always a happy one, and the *Regio Esercito* was not as united as its founders had hoped. As in Italy generally, Piedmontese custom dominated the army, to the frustration of other regions. The favoritism shown toward Northern, and especially Piedmontese, officers in promotion, particularly marked in the higher ranks, was a perpetual sore point. The army did try to act as the school of the nation, but its policies were frequently cumbersome and ineffectual. It was not recruited regionally, as in most European armies, but through a complex system that placed political concerns over military ones. Each regiment drew its recruits from two different regions and sent them to a third. (The *Alpini*, elite mountain troops recruited in the Alpine North, were an exception.) This entailed uniting men who sometimes had little in common—if their dialects were too varied, simple communication was a problem—and dispatching them to a "safe" region of the country. For example, conscripted Sicilians were sent far from home, usually up north, while their island was garrisoned by men from distant regions; this ensured that soldiers would not be overly sympathetic to the local population, a practical consideration, given how frequently the army was called upon to quell domestic disturbances. This policy, although politically astute, did not contribute to unit cohesion and morale. It made mobilization slow and cumbersome, and the supply of replacements complicated.

The building of regimental spirit and national identity was the mission of the officer corps. Unfortunately for the army, its officers frequently were not up to the peacetime tasks assigned them. Although the army enjoyed some prestige in Italian society, it still had trouble recruiting intelligent, hardworking young men for the officer corps. Too often it got those unsuitable for other professions who were interested neither in soldiering nor in their men. Worse, the army tended to promote timeservers and bureaucrats to its highest ranks. As former Prime Minister Giovanni Giolitti noted on the eve of the First World War, "The generals are worth little, they came up from the ranks at a time when families sent their most stupid sons into the army because they did not know what to do with them." This judgment, though harsh and indicative of the politicians' low opinion of the army, was largely valid. Too few officers took an active interest in tactics or strategy, and fewer still seemed concerned with their men. The relationship between officers and men was invariably distant; the bourgeois officers were no more likely to show concern for their peasant recruits than their civilian counterparts were. This was worsened by the fact that the army was chronically short of professional sergeants. The NCO corps was smaller than in most European armies—Italy did not produce enough educated men of the lower middle class, the backbone of the noncommissioned ranks—with the result that most training had to be undertaken by officers, who rarely showed sufficient interest in their men. The army's nation-building mission was further complicated by Italy's high illiteracy rate—37.6 percent nationally, and far higher in the rural areas that provided most of the infantry—which made political indoctrination difficult.

Unsurprisingly, military service was widely unpopular. Many peasants and workers considered the army an instrument of political oppression, associating it more with the protection of the upper classes than with the defense of the nation against foreign threats. They also rejected its harsh discipline. Draft avoidance was a chronic problem, particularly in Sicily. In 1914, Italy's last year of peace, more than 10 percent of conscripts failed to report for duty, just short of an all-time absentee record. To sum up, the condition of the Italian military on the eve of the First World War was an unenviable one.

The assassination of the Austrian Archduke Franz Ferdinand and his wife Sophie in Sarajevo on June 28, 1914, by Serbian terrorists plunged Europe into an unprecedented international crisis. While Vienna and Berlin solidified their alliance, and London, Paris, and St. Petersburg discussed their common concerns, and Europe divided into armed camps, Rome was unsure how to respond to the escalating crisis. Few Italians of any political persuasion favored going to war over the Austrian-Serbian dispute, and many nationalists and irredentists were adamant that Italy not fight on the side of hated Austria. Still, the Triple Alliance committed Italy to come to her allies' side in their hour of need. Long-standing diplomatic arrangements had placed Rome in a difficult predicament. Domestic problems further complicated matters. In early June, Italy was shaken by a series of violent urban strikes and peasant uprisings. The crisis, known as "Red Week," was so serious that the army had to deploy 100,000 soldiers, many of them recalled reservists, before order was restored. By the time the cities and countryside were again tranquil, seventeen rioters were dead and more than a thousand were injured. Italy was still reeling from the shock of Red Week and its bloody aftermath when the Sarajevo crisis unfolded. Never had national unity seemed so lacking. A decision for war would have been unwise, given the country's recent domestic trauma.

Prime Minister Antonio Salandra, in office only since March, had no desire to launch a divided Italy into a major war on the side of Austria and Germany. Rome's treaty obligations seemed to dictate intervention, however. Foreign Minister Antonino di San Giuliano wanted to fight alongside Austria no more than Salandra did. He noted that the Triple Alliance treaty did not require Italy to come to her allies' aid in an offensive war, which Vienna's ultimatum to Serbia seemed to indicate; furthermore, Article VIII of the treaty promised Italy adequate territorial compensation for any Austrian advances. On these grounds, di San Giuliano argued that Italy was not committed to backing her allies. On July 31, 1914, the cabinet decided in favor of neutrality in the impending war. The decision was formally announced on August 2, sending shock waves throughout Europe. At once, Rome had decisively shifted the balance of power in favor of the Triple Entente—France, Britain, and Russia—at the expense of her allies. It was a momentous decision politically and militarily, helping to determine the early course of the coming conflict. It was also an act of betrayal that Austria and Germany would not soon forget.

In Italy, however, the decision for neutrality was met with nationwide celebration. The threat of an unpopular war had been averted. Salandra's abandonment of Italy's allies was greeted enthusiastically by virtually all political parties and interests. Disappointment was heard from only some archconservatives, who were pro-German, and ultranationalists, who favored war for its own sake. The military was also happy not to be going to war. The army and navy both had doubts about their ability to wage war effectively. The army in particular was in a state of disarray at the highest level. The army's professional head, Chief of the General Staff General Alberto Pollio, died on July 1, as the international crisis was unfolding. His replacement, General Luigi Cadorna, did not assume his new position until three weeks later, leaving the army effectively without a high command while Europe girded for war. Upon becoming chief of the General Staff, Cadorna began to prepare the army for war against France, as the Triple Alliance had mandated. Due to the complete lack of communication between the politicians and generals that was all too common, Cadorna was not informed that the government was contemplating abandoning its allies. On July 31, the day that the cabinet opted for neutrality, Cadorna sent his war plan, which called for the dispatch of an entire Italian field army to assist Germany against France, to King Vittorio Emanuele III. On August 2, the day neutrality was officially declared, the king—as unaware as his top general of the politicians' decision—approved Cadorna's plan! The chief of the General Staff and the monarch were completely surprised when Italy formally opted for nonintervention.

As soon as Italy had formally renounced its obligation to its allies, Cadorna encouraged Foreign Minister di San Giuliano to declare war on Austria. The general saw a perfect opportunity to attack Italy's historic foe in its unprotected rear while Habsburg armies were busy fighting Serbia and Russia. Fortunately cooler heads prevailed in Rome, despite Cadorna's repeated proddings throughout August to invade Austria. This radical overnight shift in positions, from invading France to assaulting Austria's undefended border, should have given rise to doubts in Rome about Cadorna's professional judgment. Instead, Cadorna's counsel was ignored, his odd behavior overlooked. Yet the general's poor judgment was a portent of things to come. He was a typical highflier in the

Italian military system, boasting good personal connections and solid career credentials. Born into a Piedmontese family with a long military tradition—his father was a successful general, famed for conquering the Vatican in 1870—the sixty-four-year-old Count Luigi Cadorna had spent virtually his entire life in uniform. He was sent at age ten to Milan's prestigious military college, and at fifteen to Turin's military academy, and was commissioned in the field artillery at eighteen. He attended and excelled at all the right schools to secure promotion, including the all-important Staff College, which opened the doors of higher command to the young officer. Like most successful products of the Staff College, Cadorna spent most of his career at headquarters and on staffs, away from field units. His experience actually commanding soldiers was therefore limited. Significantly, although Cadorna was considered an astute student of tactics, he had missed both the Ethiopian and the Libyan wars. He had never heard a shot fired in anger. This in no way hurt his career. He achieved general rank at the age of forty-eight, young by Italian standards, rising to command a division in 1905 and a corps in 1910. When appointed chief of the General Staff, Cadorna was serving as commander of the 2nd Army, one of the most senior positions in the army.

Although he was well connected in Rome, Cadorna had accumulated enemies during his career due to his personality, which was as unattractive as his short and squat stature. His temperament was cold, reserved, even harsh, wholly predictable; Cadorna was, in fact, the exact opposite of the stereotypical gregarious, extroverted, and impulsive Italian. Methodical and authoritarian in demeanor, he was a hard driver, ruthless with subordinates who did not meet his standards. He was always completely sure of himself and his decisions, and tolerated no dissent from his staff, which he ruled absolutely. He expected success and unfailing personal loyalty from those who served under him, and dealt harshly with those he felt had failed him. In all, the unappealing Cadorna represented much of the bad side of the Italian officer corps. He was undoubtedly an unfortunate choice to lead Italy in the greatest war ever seen.

Cadorna should have known that the army was sadly unprepared for war, but he was poorly informed about the real condition of the fighting forces. In truth, the army had barely recovered from the recent Libyan war, which consumed half of the government's annual revenue and required the dispatch of 100,000 troops to defeat the desert tribes. In August 1914, there were still 50,000 soldiers garrisoning Libya, and the army had not yet replaced the stocks of guns, ammunition, and other vital supplies expended in North Africa. Financial stringency meant that the army was still replenishing its depleted arsenals, and Finance Minister Rubini threatened to resign if Italy entered another conflict so soon after the Libyan war. The army lacked adequate numbers of weapons of all types, including artillery, machine guns, and even rifles. Due to the great delays in procuring new guns for the artillery, ten of the army's thirty-six field artillery regiments simply did not exist. Worse, shortages of equipment meant that of the 1,260,000 soldiers of all classes that Italy could mobilize in the event of war, only 732,000 could be equipped for battle; some 200,000 of them would not even receive uniforms. In addition, the training of reservists had always been accorded a low priority, so many reservists were woefully unprepared for combat, a serious defect, considering that the standing army totaled only 380,000 soldiers. The territorial militia, which the army depended on to flesh out its field forces, frequently was totally untrained for war. The army did not have enough officers either; in the summer of 1914 the High Command discovered the army was short 13,500 officers, a serious deficit, particularly for fighting units. The government wisely ignored Cadorna's call for a general mobilization in August and an invasion of Austria soon to follow. Despite Cadorna's fanciful planning, the army was not ready to fight.

The chief of the General Staff contented himself with a limited mobilization, including the increase of troops on the Austrian border to 142,000. He and his staff started to plan for the invasion of Austria that Cadorna was sure would eventually come. True to form, the generals did not consult with the politicians, and the politicians did not inform the army of their plans. The army's numerous weaknesses appeared insurmountable, yet the Piedmontese count was absolutely sure that victory was guaranteed if his orders were followed. To start with, he had to create an offensive strategy because all Italy's prewar planning had been defensive. Before 1914, the army had been preoccupied with an invasion from the north by France or perhaps Austria. Military planning had therefore focused on fortifications and strong defenses to repel any invaders. Plans for invading Austria simply did not exist. Cadorna therefore set about constructing a strategy to defeat the Habsburg Empire.

He assumed that the Austrian Army would be wholly preoccupied with the Russian and Balkan fronts, where in the late summer and fall of 1914 Habsburg arms were suffering notable defeats, and that Vienna could spare few troops to guard its southern border with Italy. Cadorna envisioned an invasion of Austria to coincide with Russian and perhaps also Serbian offensives, which would inflict a decisive and fatal defeat on the Habsburgs. He saw the Isonzo valley as the best avenue for his grand offensive. To be sure, the mountainous Isonzo offered difficult terrain that favored the defender, but it was also the quickest, most direct route to Trieste, as well as Ljubljana, Budapest, and Vienna. It was impossible to avoid the Alps: 90 percent of Italy's border with Austria consisted of high Alpine terrain, and the other fronts were even more forbidding to an attacker. The Carinthian and Tyrolean frontiers had even higher mountains than the Isonzo, as well as fewer roads and relatively unimportant military and political objectives. A successful invasion of the Tyrol might gain the Trentino for Italy, but a victorious drive across the Isonzo could knock Austria out of the war. Further strategic options—a Balkan intervention to save Serbia or a landing on Austria's Dalmatian coast—appeared even less attractive. In the first place, Cadorna favored a direct assault on Austria; second, any movement across the Adriatic required close cooperation with the navy, which feared the Austrian fleet and was barely on speaking terms with the army. There was, in fact, no coordinated war planning between the army and the navy during the months before the war. Each service intended to fight its own war against Austria without consulting the other.

Cadorna's grand strategy, first drafted at the beginning of September and completed in late December 1914, called for an Italian offensive across the Isonzo by two reinforced armies, the bulk of Italy's field forces. While the 1st and 4th Armies undertook secondary supporting attacks on the Tyrolean and Carinthian fronts, respectively, the 3rd Army would attack Austrian positions on the Carso, and the 2nd Army would assault the Isonzo line from Gorizia to Flitsch. Cadorna expected little resistance and a rapid breakthrough, with the 3rd Army securing Trieste and the 2nd taking Ljubljana; Vienna and Budapest would soon be threatened. As Cadorna planned it, his offensive would redeem *Italia irredenta* within a week, and the Habsburg Empire would be on its knees in less than two months. He hoped to launch his victorious blow by the late spring of 1915.

Before Austria could be defeated, however, the Italian Army had to be readied for conquest. Cadorna soon learned that the army needed far more arms, munitions, and supplies than it possessed in August 1914, and he attempted to remedy the pervasive shortages of virtually all war matériel that rendered his army ineffective. In early October he made a trusted subordinate, General Vittorio Zupelli, responsible for readying the army for war in the coming year. Although the task before him was daunting, Zupelli set about fleshing out the army's ranks with trained men and arming them with modern weapons. He improved industrial productivity, fought waste, and enjoyed some notable successes; by December he intended to have an army of 1,400,000 ready for Cadorna to mobilize by the late spring. He even substantially remedied the officer shortage. Zupelli could not perform miracles—Italy's economic backwardness and Byzantine bureaucracy prevented that—but he did make notable strides toward having Italy's army ready to fight in 1915. There was still much work to be done.

While Cadorna planned for an aggressive war and Zupelli prepared the army to wage it, the Italian people watched the European catastrophe unfold from a safe distance, behind a shield of neutrality. Most educated Italians, liberal, anticlerical Western Europeans, were sympathetic to the Entente, particularly to beleaguered France. Sentiment against the Central Powers, especially Austria, ran deep. Italians generally cheered little Serbia's defiant stand against Vienna, and few greeted the possibility of a Hohenzollern-Habsburg victory with anything but gloom; a Teuton-dominated Europe would inevitably be a threat to Italy. As the opening campaigns of August and September ebbed, the Central

Powers had not inflicted a total defeat on the Entente, but Belgium and much of northern France were occupied by Germany. Paris was narrowly saved at the Battle of the Marne. Austria's humiliating failure to subdue Serbia and her thrashing at the hands of the Russians in Galicia brought hope to all Italians who gleefully anticipated a Habsburg demise. Yet Russia's defeat in East Prussia evened out the odds on the Eastern Front. The casualties for both the Allies and the Central Powers were enormous: by the onset of the autumn the war had claimed more than a million dead and wounded. The vast majority of Italians were relieved not to be a party to the bloodletting.

A dedicated and vocal minority in Italy, however, wanted Rome to abandon neutrality and enter the fray. Particularly for some on the Left, the war was nothing less than a fight for progress against reaction, democracy against autocracy, freedom against Teutonic enslavement. Many radical democrats and republicans, freemasons and other political heirs of the legendary Garibaldi—the outstanding hero of the Risorgimento—ardently advocated entering the war on France's side. One of their leaders, Peppino Garibaldi, grandson of the revolutionary icon, did more than merely agitate, leading 4,000 Italians to France. The contingent enlisted in the Foreign Legion and served as a unit at the front in the autumn of 1914, distinguishing itself in battle and suffering many killed, including two of Peppino's four brothers who went to France with him. Many supporters of intervention saw in Garibaldi's deeds an example for the nation to follow. Needless to say, Italy's numerous irredentists looked forward with enthusiasm to the coming day when their nation would liberate the Littoral and the Trentino. Their ranks were swelled by several hundred Italians who fled their native Austria rather than fight Serbs and Russians. They received a warm welcome in Italy, where their message of impending doom for the Habsburg Empire was received with anticipation. Other radicals, including extreme nationalists, advocated intervention to revolutionize Italy. To these interventionists, many of them Futurist artists and writers, Italy was enslaved by a staid, unheroic bourgeois political and economic culture that needed to be cast off. War and the upheaval it produced offered the best possibility to achieve their goal, *velocizzare l'Italia* (speeding Italy up).

In 1914, interventionists remained a small but vocal minority. The main political parties, including the Socialists, opposed entering the war. Although they may have found little redeeming in Italy's socioeconomic fabric, the Socialists were against all "imperialist wars," and did not believe anyone—least of all the workers and peasants who filled the ranks of the army—would benefit from Italy's joining the conflict on the side of the Allies. The government was inclined to agree. Neutrality offered Italy the best opportunity to protect her interests without great risks. In truth, the neutral, uncommitted position profited Rome far more than intervention could. For although a German-Austrian victory would be an alarming threat to Italy—a strong, victorious Habsburg Empire across the Adriatic, intent on avenging Italy's betrayal, was a possibility too dreadful for Rome to contemplate—an Allied victory appeared not much less threatening; a triumphant France would represent a major problem for Italy, particularly in the Mediterranean, where the Italian Navy feared French intentions. As Foreign Minister di San Giuliano expressed Italy's predicament in early September, "The ideal situation would be if Austria and France were both beaten." Neutrality represented Italy's best possible diplomatic and military position, despite what the generals and the interventionists believed.

As 1914 drew to a close, however, the mood in Italy slowly began to change. With Austria reeling from more defeats in the East, with Habsburg armies repulsing the Russians with great difficulty and suffering further setbacks in Serbia, the chance to liberate *Italia irredenta* had never seemed closer. One of the most strident new voices in favor of war was a that of a leading Socialist, the popular journalist Benito Mussolini. The thirty-one-year-old Mussolini had a well developed reputation for incendiary rhetoric and rabble-rousing, yet he had never been considered a nationalist, much less a warmonger; indeed, he had vehemently denounced the "imperialist" Libyan war of 1911–1912. His abrupt conversion to intervention was therefore as surprising as it was total. In November 1914 he broke party ranks and founded a newspaper, *Il Popolo d'Italia*, dedicated to espousing the interventionist and radical nationalist line. Mussolini argued that the surest and fastest way to transform Italy and bring about a revolution was by waging war: only war would unite the Italian people and bring all Italians into a single state. His rhetoric was dramatically bellicose, beginning with the November 15 premier issue of *Il Popolo d'Italia*: "This appeal, this cry, is a word that I would never have uttered in normal times, but which I give out today clearly and vigorously, without reservations, and with full confidence: that one forceful and fascinating word—WAR!" Mussolini cited numerous historical antecedents of his position, including Napoleon's dictum "Revolution is an idea that has found bayonets." The renegade Socialist's militancy, with its fusion of nationalism and radicalism, soon found an audience. Mussolini's Socialist colleagues, however, were appalled by their former comrade's heresy. Mussolini was quickly expelled from the party and denounced for encouraging imperialist war. Several leading Socialists found his sudden conversion suspect, and questioned his sources of funding for his new journal. Rumors (well founded, as it turned out) spread that French interests were financing him to agitate for Italian intervention on the side of the Allies. The allegation neither diminished Mussolini's influence nor stemmed the growing tide of interventionism.

As 1914 drew to a close, the Italian government's appraisal of the international situation had also begun to change, due largely to the influence of Baron Sidney Sonnino. In October, Foreign Minister di San Giuliano, a leading advocate of neutrality, died and was replaced by Sonnino. The new minister was less inclined to neutrality. In August he had argued for honoring Italy's alliance commitments to Germany and Austria. The French victory at the Marne, which prevented a quick German victory and ensured that the war would drag on, changed Sonnino's mind, and he began to consider Italy's diplomatic options, including joining the Allies. Rome was searching for the best offer from either side, the most territorial concessions to be gained, preferably without having to fight for them. The government was acting in defense of what Prime Minister Salandra, in October, in an unfortunate and unforgettable phrase, called *sacro egoismo* (sacred egotism). On December 9, Italy and Austria opened secret negotiations: Rome wanted land and Vienna wanted Italy to stay out of the war. The Austrians were desperate, their armies reeling from defeats in Galicia and the Balkans, and could not fight a three-front war. Emperor Franz Joseph and his new foreign minister, István Burián, were willing to trade land for Italian nonintervention. Italy demanded the entire Littoral and the Trentino as a minimum, and also desired parts of Dalmatia and other smaller Austrian possessions. The terms were simply too high, no matter how much Vienna wanted peace. Surrendering the Trentino, which was admittedly almost entirely ethnically Italian, presented little difficulty, but the loss of the entire Littoral and much of Dalmatia was unacceptable. This was not just dynastic pride, but a practical political consideration. Burián, supported by Hungarian Prime Minister István Tisza, a fellow member of Hungary's ruling elite, believed that handing land to Italy as a ransom for peace would establish a dangerous precedent of extortion for the multinational Habsburg Empire: How long would it be before neutral Romania demanded Hungary's ethnically Romanian districts? Carving up Austria-Hungary on national lines, even for a good cause, could signal the death knell of the empire. The Italian representatives left the negotiations empty-handed and frustrated.

In the new year, as Cadorna's armies girded for war and the interventionists' cries approached a fever pitch, Sonnino, supported by Prime Minister Salandra, continued to explore Italy's diplomatic options. On February 16, 1915, Rome dispatched a secret courier to London to explore the possibility of joining the Allies in exchange for generous territorial gains. Sonnino correctly assumed that the British and French would be more willing to surrender Habsburg provinces than the Austrians had been. The Italian claims to the Littoral and the Trentino presented few problems for the Allies. Rome's designs on Dalmatia and some Adriatic islands posed diplomatic difficulties, however, because not only did they have virtually no Italian populations, but they also were claimed by Serbia, Britain and France's ally. The secret negotiations continued for weeks, with the Italian and Entente delegations arguing over territorial concessions. The issue nevertheless soon became not whether Italy would join the war on the Allied side, but how high her price of admission would ultimately be.

While Sonnino's negotiators were busy arguing Italy's claims in London, at home the interventionist campaign continued to expand. In the spring, there were large demonstrations demanding war in major cities throughout Italy. Although the vast majority of Italians, peasants and workers, remained oblivious to the war fever, the interventionist cause had won many converts among the educated. War against Austria now appealed to radicals, progressives, and nationalists of all sorts. The Habsburg Empire appeared to be in its death throes, and the redemption of the Littoral and the Trentino seemed imminent. Mussolini, always provocative, publicly warned the king that he would lose his throne if he did not accept the will of the people and lead Italy to war. The interventionists did not need to worry: their militant call to arms would soon be answered, with the full approval of the monarch and the government.

On April 26, 1915, Italy signed the secret Treaty of London, which committed her to an invasion of Austria in a month's time in exchange for considerable territorial concessions: all of the Littoral, including Gorizia, Trieste, and the Istrian Peninsula; all of the South Tyrol, not just the Trentino; Slovene lands deep in the Julian Alps; a southern corner of the province of Carinthia; and northern Dalmatia and several Adriatic islands. This was beyond *Italia irredenta*, even more land than demanded from Vienna in December 1914; significantly, much of the promised territory was not even Italian by ethnicity. In the end, for London and Paris, Italy's claims outweighed those of Serbia or any other ally. The policy of pursuing *sacro egoismo* had evidently paid off, and Sonnino was justly pleased with his negotiators. The agreement was kept secret for a time, even from Cadorna. Italy formally left the Triple Alliance on May 4, but the General Staff was not informed of the treaty until the next day. Cadorna, anticipating the onset of war in May anyway, had ordered a secret partial mobilization on April 23, three days before the treaty's signing. Eight of Italy's fourteen army corps were placed on war footing, and the remaining six soon followed. Even before it was ordered by the government to mobilize for war, the army was readying for the invasion of Austria by the end of May.

The Austrian government panicked when Italy formally abandoned the Triple Alliance. Desperate to prevent an Italian invasion, on May 7 Vienna promised Rome not just the Trentino but concessions in the Littoral, including the establishment of Trieste as a free city. But it was too little, too late. The Austrians could no longer hope to compete with the Entente's generous promises of land. In an attempt to avert catastrophe, Italy's former Prime Minister Giolitti, a consistent proponent of neutrality, visited Rome on May 9 and met with Salandra and King Vittorio Emanuele. He argued that the Italian people did not want war, the army and the generals were not up to the task, the tide of the war had turned in the Germans' favor, and the war would not be brief and victorious. Giolitti's wise and prophetic counsel was dismissed. The irrevocable decision had already been made: Italy was going to war, ten months after the rest of Europe had opted for the sword. Cadorna spent the month of May making last-minute preparations and getting his armies into position for the invasion.

The government was so confident of a quick victory and of Austria's collapse that it requested only a few months' financial assistance from the Allies to help finance the war effort. All the military movements did not go unnoticed, but the government did not formally declare its intentions until May 23, Pentecost Sunday. The Italian ambassador to Vienna visited the Austrian Foreign Ministry at the Ballhausplatz and informed his former allies that a state of war now existed between Italy and the Habsburg Empire.

The news was greeted with rapturous enthusiasm in Italy. Spontaneous demonstrations in support of the government's decision broke out in numerous cities. After so many months of waiting, the interventionists had gotten what they had so consistently and forcefully demanded. Mussolini announced that the declaration of war was "the victory of the people," and added that the fight against ailing Austria would be short and victorious. Gabriele D'Annunzio, the bellicose and celebrated poet and vehement interventionist, in an irredentist Sermon on the Mount promised that war with Austria would bring national transformation: "Blessed be the pure of heart, blessed be those who will return victorious, for they will see Rome's new visage, Dante's forehead crowned anew, Italy's triumphant beauty." Of course, the majority of the Italian people did not want war, a fact that Prime Minister Salandra well knew. Italy's millions of peasants and workers, who would be called upon to bear the brunt of the impending war, had no interest in diplomatic agreements and exactly which territory Rome had been promised. They shared none of the enthusiasm of the educated nationalists and radicals who jumped at the chance to fight for Italy. Regardless, within three days Italian forces would be engaging Austrian regiments on the frontiers. The hour to wrest *Italia irredenta* from Austrian domination, the irredentist dream born decades earlier, had finally arrived. All that remained was actually to do it.

TWO

A HOPELESS STRUGGLE

On April 26, 1915, the day Italy signed the Treaty of London, the Austrian Army was near the end of its catastrophic winter in the Carpathian mountains. Virtually the entire strength of Austria's forces—five armies with fifty-three infantry and eight cavalry divisions—stood deep in the Carpathians, defending the vital mountain passes from Russian attacks. The late summer and autumn Habsburg débâcle in Galicia brought the Tsar's armies to the gates of Cracow and deep into northern Hungary. Throughout the winter, Russian armies threatened to break through the frozen Carpathian passes and pour onto the Hungarian plain, endangering Budapest—indeed, the entire Habsburg war effort. The empire had lost almost all of Galicia, and although the army prevented the enemy from breaking out of the mountains, its repeated offensives in the depths of the harsh winter had failed to dislodge the Russians. The cost for both sides had been exorbitant. The Carpathian winter cost the Austrians at least 600,000—and perhaps as many as 800,000—soldiers killed, wounded, captured, or seriously ill. The casualties were so enormous that the army had lost effective count of its losses. It can be reliably estimated that the Habsburg Empire lost 6,600 soldiers every day during the winter on the Carpathian front. An appallingly high percentage of the casualties was due to illness, particularly frostbite and cholera. The frigid winter in the high mountains had taken its toll on the poorly equipped Austrian Army as surely as the Russians had. Thousands of Austrian infantrymen, including entire units lacking winter uniforms, froze to death in the mountain passes. Even more alarming for the Austrian High Command, the army's morale was crumbling. There were consistent reports of units of certain Slav minorities—principally Czechs, Ukrainians, and Serbs—refusing to resist the Russians, in some cases of whole regiments going over to the "brother Slav" enemy. The Habsburg Army, after only nine months of war, appeared to be coming apart at the seams.

In truth, that the army had survived so long in the field was something of a surprise. Such longevity and durability in the face of repeated battlefield disasters had not been anticipated. In the decades before the First World War, the Habsburg Empire appeared to most outside observers, as well as to many of its subjects, to be a dying anachronism, a throwback to premodern Europe. In an age of nationalism and nation-states, when the rise of united Germany and Italy inspired smaller nations to follow suit, multinational, dynastic Austria seemed hopelessly out of date and probably doomed. Its ethnic diversity was breathtaking. According to the last census, taken just before the war, the Habsburg lands, with a population of nearly fifty-three million subjects, comprised 25 percent Germans, 17 percent Magyars (i.e., ethnic Hungarians), 13 percent Czechs, 11 percent Serbs and Croats, 9 percent Poles, 8 percent Ukrainians, 7 percent Romanians, 4 percent Slovaks, 3 percent Slovenes, and 2 percent Italians. The last decades of peace had been a period of rising ethnic tension and rivalry, particularly among the Slav minorities. Increasingly shrill political agitation led to seemingly unending crises in Vienna, and by the eve of the war, Austria's parliament had grown so unruly that it was suspended. The empire was effectively ruled by government ministers and the monarch. The Habsburg monarchy had existed for centuries, and had been a great power since the beginning of the modern age, a consistent feature of European geography, politics, and diplomacy. It had defended Christendom against the Ottomans for centuries, and had served as the bulwark of the coalition opposed to Napoleon. That the ancient and apparently interminable monarchy and empire would disappear was to many inconceivable. Still, by 1914 the fate of Austria seemed bleak, and numerous foreign and domestic observers anticipated its imminent demise. How much longer could the troubled multinational Habsburg Empire survive in a twentieth-century Europe of nation-states?

Much of the widespread pessimism about Austria's future was caused by the empire's internal disputes, not by foreign worries. Certainly Vienna's domestic concerns were serious enough on their own. In the last half-century of its existence, the Habsburg realm was divided into separate Austrian and Hungarian halves.[1] The Compromise (*Ausgleich*) of 1867 split the empire into independent Austrian and Hungarian realms united by the monarchy itself. Vienna and Budapest, each with its own national parliament, had complete sovereignty in virtually all areas: finance, justice, internal commerce, education, transportation, and the like. Austria and Hungary were politically united only in the emperor himself, as well as in common defense and foreign ministries, and a joint finance ministry to fund them. As an attempt to purchase the loyalty of Hungary's powerful and strongly nationalist Magyar political elite, the *Ausgleich* was largely successful; as a remedy for the empire's political ailments, it proved a disaster.

The essential problem with the compromise was that although it satisfied many of the demands of Hungarian nationalists, it ignored several other ethnic groups advancing claims to self-government, or at least greater autonomy within the empire. This was less of a problem in the Austrian half. There, although the German-Austrians, 36 percent of the population, unquestionably were dominant both politically and economically, the state was reasonably tolerant of regional diversity and ethnic rights. The Austrian half was not run as a specifically German state, relying instead on a degree of provincial autonomy; the Poles of Galicia and the Italians of the Littoral were as politically favored as the Germans were in their Alpine home provinces. The Austrian arrangement was by no means ideal—the Czechs in particular were dissatisfied with the German predominance in Bohemia—but on the whole it functioned well enough. Hungary, however, was another matter. The Magyar political ruling class, exhibiting a cultural arrogance equal to that of Trieste's Italian elite, ran Hungary as a Magyar nation-state, ignoring the half of the population that did not happen to be Magyar. The Romanians, Germans, Slovaks, Serbs, Croats, and Ukrainians who lived in Hungary were treated not as members of ethnic groups but as would-be Magyars. The state used every possible means, including the bureaucracy, the judiciary, and particularly the schools, to convert the minorities into Magyars. Through these coercive measures, Budapest expected to achieve its goal of a united Magyar Hungary, a state without minorities, within a few generations. It must be noted that these policies, although authoritarian and detested by Hungary's minorities, were not violent, and that Magyar nationalists were interested in language and culture, not race. Anyone who learned the Magyar tongue and entered Magyar society was considered a Magyar, regardless of ethnic or religious background. Indeed, Hungary's large Jewish population proved particularly susceptible to Magyarization, and new Jewish converts to the Magyar cause—like the numerous Triestine Jews, Slavs, and other non-Latins who "became" Italians—were among the most vocal Hungarian nationalists.

All the same, Budapest's internal policies were hated by most of Hungary's minorities. They also served as an endless irritant in Vienna. The Romanians, Slovaks, and other persecuted ethnic groups had little political recourse because Hungarian voting and electoral districts were gerrymandered to guarantee Magyar dominance in parliament; however, the fate of Hungary's minorities did not go unnoticed in Austria. The Czechs in particular took up the cause of their Slovak neighbors deprived of a voice in Hungary. Austrian Serbs and Croats similarly spoke out on behalf of their South Slav brethren living in Hungary. For many of the Habsburg Empire's Slavs, the Compromise of 1867 was an injustice that had to be overturned: Why should Hungary's ruling Magyars enjoy rights and privileges denied other ethnic groups? Yet for the Magyar elite, the *Ausgleich* represented its minimum demands. There was to be no turning back, and no concessions to minorities; in fact, within a few years of the agreement, Budapest was clamoring for even more independence from Vienna. Therein lay the essence of the problem. Every ten years after 1868, the joint provisions of the compromise, military and foreign policy, were brought up for review, and any changes had to be approved by both Vienna and Budapest. Thus every ten years the defense of the empire was held hostage to Hungarian demands. As a result, nothing ever got done. Budapest's intransigence increased while military spending remained stagnant and the minorities grew increasingly frustrated with the political system. There seemed to be no way to remedy the obvious injustices of the compromise. Indeed, forcing Budapest to back down would have meant a civil war. By the early twentieth century, the Habsburg Empire's political problems appeared insoluble.

That said, the empire enjoyed several notable forces of unity to counter the increasing ethnic disharmony which tore at its political fabric. In the first place, the aged Emperor Franz Joseph, symbol of the dynasty and realm, was genuinely popular with his subjects of all nationalities, not least because of his astonishing longevity. He had come to the throne in 1848, at the age of eighteen, and his reign had seen generally increasing prosperity at home and, after 1866 at least, peace abroad. As the emperor grew older, the tumult of his early reign, including the suppression of the 1848 revolutions and the military defeats of 1859 and 1866, disappeared from memory. Franz Joseph was a man of decidedly unaristocratic tastes who understood his people, sharing their piety and delight in simple pleasures. His popularity increased every year, and by the turn of the century Franz Joseph was regarded sympathetically by most of his subjects, who knew of the emperor's numerous personal traumas. His marriage had not been a happy one, and he had endured a series of painful family deaths: the execution of his brother Maxmilian in Mexico; the mysterious death of Archduke Rudolf, his only son and heir to the throne, in a bizarre murder-suicide pact with his teenage mistress in 1889; and the assassination of his beloved if unstable wife, the Empress Elizabeth, by a deranged anarchist in 1898. The emperor's silver jubilee, celebrating a half-century of his reign, was an impressive spectacle, and by the eve of the First World War, after six and a half decades on the throne, Franz Joseph was the unchallenged grand old man of European royalty. His personal popularity could not erase his empire's numerous political problems, but he served as an invaluable symbol of unity in a dividing realm.

The Roman Catholic Church was another important force for cohesion in the Habsburg Empire. Although Austria had many religious minorities, including Orthodox Christians, Jews, and even Muslims, the vast majority of its citizens were adherents of the Church of Rome. A common faith helped bridge the deep ethnic divisions in the empire. Millions of pious peasants accepted the Church's teachings unquestioningly, and the Church helped inculcate a loyalty to the Habsburg throne in countless schools and sermons. For the Vatican, the empire was the last Catholic great power, the successor to the Holy Roman Empire, and the only remaining major secular defender of Catholicism. The church therefore consistently supported the Habsburgs both domestically and internationally, and Vienna reciprocated by defending the Vatican and its interests (Austria never recognized Italy's annexation of the Papal States in 1870), an especially sore point with Rome.

An even greater source of unity in the empire, perhaps even more significant than Franz Joseph himself, was the Austrian Army. The Habsburg standing army dated to the early seventeenth century, and enjoyed a reputation for steadfast loyalty to the dynasty. The army won many wars and lost others—it helped defeat the Turks at the gates of Vienna in 1683, bested Frederick the Great at Kolin in 1757, lost to Napoleon at Austerlitz in 1805, and helped defeat him at Leipzig eight years later—but it was first and foremost a dynastic instrument. As "the strongest pillar of the Habsburg fortification," it had defended Franz Joseph and his many predecessors against all foes, foreign and domestic, in the end always saving the dynasty and realm. Indeed, the army had sometimes been the only force for unity. In 1848, with most of the empire in revolt, it alone remained loyal (though some of its units joined the rebel Hungarians), in the end restoring the Habsburg throne by force of arms. Its officers and men swore allegiance not to governments in Vienna or Budapest, but to the Habsburg dynasty.

Unsurprisingly, the Habsburg Army was as complicated as the empire it served. In the first place, by 1914 there was technically not one army but three (nevertheless, for the sake of simplicity they will be referred to together as the Austrian or Habsburg Army). The main force, or "common" army, was the Imperial-and-Royal Army, the *kaiserlich- und königliche*—hereafter, *k.u.k. Armee*, the traditional force recruited from all regions of the empire. But the Compromise of 1867 created two national armies as well, a concession to Hungarian pride: the Austrian *Landwehr* and the Hungarian *Honvéd*. These smaller armies, controlled by Vienna and Budapest, were originally intended to be second-line reserve forces, but by the eve of the war they were equipped with artillery and other supporting services, and their field units were pretty much the equal of those of the common army.

The army's ethnic makeup was even more complex. Because the army conscripted young men from all regions of the empire for two years' service, it faithfully mirrored the wider society. Of every hundred soldiers, there were twenty-five Germans, twenty-three Magyars, thirteen Czechs, nine Serbs or Croats, eight each Polish and Ukrainians, seven Romanians, four Slovaks, two Slovenes, and one Italian. Such unparalleled ethnic diversity meant that the Habsburg Army could not function like the other, national armies of Europe.

Unlike the Italians, the Austrians recruited their regiments regionally, from specific provinces and cities, so that each unit had a distinct ethnic character. Hence Vienna's 4th Infantry Regiment was almost entirely German; Prague's 28th was exclusively Czech; Trieste's 97th was almost half Slovene, a quarter Croatian, and a fifth Italian; and the 61st Regiment, recruited in the city of Temesvár in south Hungary, was a mix of Romanians, Germans, Magyars, and Serbs. German was the language of command and service (it was Magyar in the *Honvéd*), the language used by officers for parade ground drill and technical matters, and to communicate with each other. But otherwise officers had to use the soldiers' own languages. The army recognized ten "regimental languages" (those of the nationalities listed earlier): in each unit, a language was accorded official status if 20 percent of its soldiers spoke it as their native tongue, and all officers had to learn it. Taking the army as a whole, only 142 units had one regimental language; 163 had two; 24 had three, and a few had four or even five.

Despite this daunting degree of ethnic diversity, the Austrian Army on the whole functioned rather well, going to considerable lengths to accommodate the linguistic needs of its soldiers. It generally dealt with ethnic difficulties in a tactful and delicate manner, and as a result the army was much less plagued by national antagonism and inefficiency than most Habsburg institutions. Although the officer corps was disproportionately German—79 percent of the regular officer corps and about half of the reserve officer cadre—this was the result of tradition much more than prejudice. Ethnic and religious minorities were well represented in the officer ranks of the reserve, including many Jews. (Jews, just 5 percent of the empire's population, made up 17 percent of the reserve officer corps; there were, in fact, six Jewish officers for every Jewish rank-and-file soldier in the Austrian Army.)

Nationality or religion played no role in admission to the officer corps or in career advancement, and many senior officers were non-Germans, including numerous Magyars, Croats, Czechs, and Poles. Promotion was solely by merit, and the Habsburg officer corps was generally efficient and well accustomed to dealing with the complexities of the polyglot army. The elite General Staff, which ran the army, in particular was well trained and professionally competent. To be sure, the army had its share of deadwood in the officer corps, but the notable shortcomings of the Austrian military were found not in poor leadership, and still less in its ethnic diversity, but rather in the results of decades of inadequate funding.

As previously noted, any increases in the joint military budget had to be approved by both the Austrian and the Hungarian parliament. Getting increased appropriations through Vienna was relatively easy, but Budapest kept the military budget hostage to Hungarian political demands. The Hungarian political elite had no interest in increasing funding for the *k.u.k. Armee*, which it saw as a foreign army; if any greater military outlays were required, Budapest perhaps would be willing to make modest increases in its own home guard, the *Honvéd*, but it refused to provide more funds to the joint forces. Therefore, during the first decade of the twentieth century, while Europe turned into a armed camp and the international situation grew dangerously unstable, the Habsburg Empire's relative military potential decreased dramatically. In 1903, the citizens of Austria-Hungary actually spent three times as much on beer, wine, and tobacco as on national defense, and a decade later the ratio had hardly changed. Austria's military spending in 1911 was one-quarter that of Germany or Russia, and was even lower than Italy's. Aware that Austria's military was rapidly falling behind its potential adversaries, the generals grew pessimistic. When asked about Austrian participation in the Hague disarmament conference (Second International Peace Conference) of 1907, the chief of the General Staff replied, echoing a common sentiment in the officer corps, "The present condition of our army has already an appearance of permanent limitation of armament." The Hungarian government agreed to significant budget increases only during the Balkan Wars of 1912–1913, on the eve of the world war, when it became obvious that the fighting on Austria's southern frontier represented a serious threat to the empire's security. By then it was too late.

The effects of decades of parsimonious funding for the army were all too evident. The army simply did not have enough soldiers. Although the joint defense ministry first requested more troops in 1898, Budapest refused to approve a greater annual conscript levy until 1912. Thus, while the empire's population rose from forty million in 1890 to fifty-two million in 1910, the number of conscripts essentially remained the same. Due to financial pressures, only one Austrian male in eight was drafted, a rate far lower than in any of the other European powers. Because the conscript levy was so small, Austria's reserve cadres also were inadequate, and the lack of funds meant that reservists received little annual training. When the Habsburg Army mobilized for war in 1914, calling up all classes of reservists as well as the militia, it fielded a force of 2,265,000 soldiers. Yet France, with ten million fewer citizens than Austria, mobilized an army of four million in August 1914.

The effect of low funding on the army's weaponry was equally alarming. Although Austria enjoyed a reasonably well developed arms industry, and was a recognized leader in artillery development, the field units went to war woefully ill-equipped. The army was short of virtually everything, including rifles and machine guns, but the lack of modern artillery represented the most serious defect. The majority of the army's artillery was outmoded, dating to the late nineteenth century. As a result, the army went to war badly outgunned by its adversaries. It counted its forces by divisions, the smallest self-contained force of all combat arms capable of acting independently on the battlefield. The Austrian infantry division of 1914 adhered to the standard continental European pattern: two infantry brigades, each of two regiments, with three battalions of a thousand men per regiment; a field artillery brigade; plus detachments of cavalry, engineers, signal troops, and logistical and medical units as required, a total of 12,000 to 18,000 soldiers at full strength. Cavalry divisions consisted of splendidly uniformed mounted, rather than infantry, regiments, and possessed lighter artillery and about 5,000 fewer soldiers. The standard Austrian infantry division boasted at most fifty-four guns and howitzers, and few divisions had anywhere near that many. In contrast, the German division had as many as seventy-two artillery pieces, and the Russian had sixty; of all the types of divisions to enter combat in 1914, the Habsburg contained the least firepower. The army had designed several new and promising field guns, howitzers, and mountain guns, but there had been no funding to put them into production. Further, the prewar training budgets were also inadequate, and the army entered the war with limited ammunition reserves, particularly for the artillery. In all, the Habsburg Army was sadly unprepared to fight a major war.

On mobilization in July 1914, the Habsburg Army, including *Landwehr*, *Honvéd*, and militia troops, fielded a force of forty-eight infantry and eleven cavalry divisions. Against the forty-eight Austrian infantry divisions, Russia and Serbia, Vienna's two opponents, mobilized ninety-three and eleven infantry divisions, respectively. On paper, the Habsburg war effort appeared doomed from the outset, a fact quietly acknowledged by the Austrian Army's leadership. Indeed, the Habsburg High Command entered the First World War with a profound and justified sense of pessimism. The army's professional head, General Franz Conrad von Hötzendorf, believed that victory was impossible even in August 1914. Chief of the General Staff since late 1906, Conrad was regarded as an intelligent, forward-looking officer with considerable staff experience; he enjoyed an excellent reputation and a considerable following in the officer corps. He was acutely aware of the empire's severe, and worsening, political vulnerabilities and military deficiencies. Indeed, he was perhaps too sensitive to the forces, both foreign and domestic, arrayed in opposition to the Habsburg throne. Imbued with a sense of impending disaster for Austria and an acceptance of the inevitability of conflict, Conrad believed passionately that the empire could survive only if it proved willing to wage aggressive wars for ostensibly defensive political purposes.

From his appointment as chief of the General Staff until the outbreak of the First World War eight years later, Conrad repeatedly urged Franz Joseph to launch preventive wars against neighboring states; Serbia and especially Italy were his bugbears. He considered the crushing of Italy or Serbia—particularly the former, but ideally both—to be the only way to save the dying empire from internal collapse. He desperately wanted to invade Serbia during the Bosnian annexation crisis of 1908–1909. Conrad likewise recommended an invasion of Italy during the 1911–1912 Libyan war, writing to Franz Joseph, "Austria's opportunity has come, and it would be suicidal not to use it." The old monarch, cautious in such matters after several serious military defeats early in his reign, dismissed Conrad, only to bring him back at the end of 1912. After the conclusion of the Balkan Wars in 1913, the reinstated Conrad grew increasingly pessimistic. He feared that Austria's military position had so deteriorated compared with her adversaries that it might be too late to stem the tide of collapse. In his "Summation of the Situation at the Beginning of the Year 1914," Conrad concluded that the time for preventive war had passed. After the assassination of Archduke Franz Ferdinand, he mobilized his army for battle according to well laid plans, but he faced the impending war with resignation, even fatalism. He wrote privately as the war began, "It will be a hopeless struggle, but nevertheless it must be, because such an ancient monarchy and such an ancient army cannot perish ingloriously."

To the astonishment of Conrad and the other senior generals, mobilization went smoothly; in particular, there were no incidents of ethnic disloyalty, even among suspect nationalities like the Czechs and Ukrainians. To the contrary, soldiers of all ethnic groups reported for duty punctually, in most cases with unexpected enthusiasm. In Austria, as in all Europe that summer, volunteers, conscripts, and reservists alike went to war not with foreboding but with eager anticipation. Austria soon had its outgunned and outnumbered army ready to march to war. Actually getting the troops into combat proved less successful than calling them to duty, however. The movement of units by rail, vital to all military operations, was a muddle, with divisions often arriving at the front behind schedule and sometimes in the wrong places. As a result, the start of Conrad's planned offensives against Serbia and Russia had to be delayed, giving Austria's enemies precious time to prepare for battle.

Habsburg arms first entered combat against Serbia. On August 12, General Oskar Potiorek, commander on the Balkan front, began his offensive, leading the Austrian 2nd, 5th, and 6th armies across the Drina and Danube rivers into Serbia. Potiorek, governor-general of Bosnia-Hercegovina when the heir to the throne was assassinated, was anxious to redeem his stained reputation with a quick victory. Unfortunately for Potiorek, the experienced and tough Serbian Army was determined to defend its homeland, and Austrian progress was slow due to the difficult terrain, the lack of good roads, and the stiffer than expected Serbian resistance. Worse, in the predawn hours of August 16, regiments of the Serbian 2nd Army, veterans of tough fighting in the recent Balkan Wars, struck the weak defenses of the untried Austrian VIII Corps, which had just crossed into Serbia. The Austrians' forward positions were soon overwhelmed by the enemy counteroffensive, forcing a retreat by the mostly Czech VIII Corps. The strategic situation was worsened by the planned withdrawal of the Austrian 2nd Army, Potiorek's strongest. Because Conrad simply did not have enough divisions to attack Serbia and Russia simultaneously, he intended to use the 2nd Army in the Balkans to inflict a rapid defeat on Serbia, and then send it by train across Austria to the Russian frontier, where it was needed for his other offensive. Thus Potiorek lost the 2nd Army on August 18, before it could play a major role in his plan. Its dispatch to Galicia decisively weakened the Austrian forces in the face of the Serbian counteroffensive. Potiorek's 5th Army was retreating to Bosnia, and he reluctantly had to order a general withdrawal from Serbian territory. By sunset on August 24, no Habsburg units remained on Serbian soil. Little Serbia had delivered the Entente its first victory of the war. The *k.u.k. Armee*'s anticipated "brief autumn stroll" to Belgrade had ended disastrously. At a cost of 28,000 men, including 4,500 prisoners in Serbian hands, Potiorek and his forces had gained little but an appreciation of Serbian fighting prowess. In less than two weeks of fighting, the ancient army of the Habsburgs had been defeated by a Balkan peasant kingdom, an immense humiliation for Austria's military and dynasty.

The rapidly unfolding events in Galicia, however, would soon make Potiorek's failure seem a minor setback. Conrad was committed to attacking Russia, in support of Austria's German ally while the bulk of Berlin's forces were invading France and Belgium. The concept, laid out by the von Schlieffen plan, was for Austrian forces to inflict a temporary defeat on the slow-mobilizing Russians, buying the Germans six weeks to finish off France. Then the Austrians and Germans together would concentrate in the East, inflicting a decisive defeat on Russia. Unfortunately for Conrad, his armies were not strong enough to accomplish their mission, even temporarily: his thirty-two divisions marshaling in Galicia faced more than fifty Russian divisions. The bulk of Russia's field forces were deployed against Austria, and planned to invade East Galicia. When the great Habsburg offensive began in earnest on August 20, Conrad's 1st and 4th Armies were ready, but the 3rd—delayed by rail problems—had arrived late and was not yet in position, and the 2nd was still on the way to Galicia.

Conrad, unwilling to wait for the arrival of the 2nd Army, sent his forces into battle. The 1st and 4th armies initially made good progress into Russian Poland, defeating several Russian probes in a series of battles that lasted until the end of August. The 3rd Army, just arriving in East Galicia, was not so fortunate. On August 23, its divisions collided with the advancing Russians near Lemberg. Several days of ferocious fighting followed, and the 3rd Army's advance was stalled. Further Russian attacks forced the Austrians to retreat across Galicia, and Conrad did not have enough units to stem the tsarist tide; even the belated arrival of the 2nd Army could not save the situation. Conrad had to call off the 1st Army's successful drive into Poland and order a general retreat. By the time the great withdrawal halted, Austrian armies had retreated 150 miles across Galicia and were on the outskirts of Cracow. Except for a considerable garrison left besieged in the fortress city of Przemyśl, nearly all of Galicia was in Russian hands. The cost of Conrad's dismally failed offensive had been appallingly high. In just three weeks of fighting in Galicia, his force lost 400,000 men, including 100,000 prisoners, a total of one-third of the Austrian Army's combat effectives. Fully half of the Habsburg force that attacked the Russians on August 20 was dead, wounded, captured, or missing.[2] Russian casualties of 250,000 had also been excessive, but the Tsar's armies could replace their fallen and maimed soldiers relatively easily; Austria, lacking sufficient trained reserves, could not. The catastrophe in Galicia wiped out Austria's standing army, and there was nothing available to take its place in the field. It was a stunning blow from which the Habsburg Army would never fully recover.

The Austrian strategic situation deteriorated further throughout the autumn and into the winter. Efforts to evict the Russians from Galicia inevitably failed, even with German assistance. By the time the first snows fell, the Austrians had been forced to retreat even farther into the Carpathian Mountains, Hungary's natural frontier. A Russian offensive to breach the Carpathian passes and invade north Hungary in early December was thwarted, but at a heavy cost. Before 1914 ended, the Russians tried again to seize the mountain passes. The weak Austrian 3rd and 4th Armies were pushed deeper into the Carpathians by the enemy assault, but in the end they held their ground and repulsed a Russian breakout attempt. The war's first Christmas brought little peace to the Austrian armies holding the frozen Carpathian line; they could expect more of the same in the new year.

Habsburg troops on the Serbian frontier that Christmas were a bit more fortunate. A second offensive into Serbia in mid-September had gained more ground than the first, but it soon stalled, and the Serbian front remained quiet from late September to late October. In the last week of October, Potiorek ordered a breakout from his armies' footholds in Serbia. This time, the Austrians made considerable progress against the tired Serbian forces. By mid-November, the Serbs were in full retreat, and Potiorek's armies had finally advanced out of the mountains onto the Serbian plain. Habsburg divisions marched across northern and central Serbia, taking Belgrade on December 2. The depleted Serbian Army was in disarray, and the long-awaited Austrian defeat of the Balkan kingdom appeared at hand. But Potiorek's armies were tired and understrength from their six-week advance, and the winter weather made supply difficult. Radomir Putnik, Serbia's senior general, ordered a last-ditch counteroffensive with his few remaining reserves. The spirited surprise attack cut through weakened Austrian divisions like a scythe, and within days Potiorek had to order another general retreat from Serbian soil. By mid-December, Habsburg forces had abandoned Belgrade and all Austrian soldiers had left Serbia. The year ended on a dismal note for Austria's armies in the Balkans and for Potiorek, who was soon sacked for repeated failures in battle. His forces had suffered another humiliation. Still, they had destroyed the Serbian Army; in that highly limited sense Potiorek and his divisions had succeeded. The little kingdom could not replace its crippling losses of men and matériel. Putnik's small but fierce army had successfully defended its homeland, but it had been sacrificed in the process. It certainly no longer represented any threat to the Habsburgs. As 1914 drew to a close, therefore, Austria's southern frontier was quiet again.

The cost of the war's opening campaigns had been immense for Austria. In just four months of fighting, its army had lost 1,269,000 soldiers—a total greater than the entire army's rifle strength on mobilization in August— three-quarters of them on the Eastern front. The prewar army had been annihilated. Losses among officers had been especially heavy: 22,000 of the total of 50,000 active and reserve officers became casualties by the end of the year. The army was thus deprived of its vital cadre of trained leaders, particularly at the small unit level. Austria would never recover from this tremendous and unprecedented loss of men. During the winter of 1914–1915, the Austrian Army was rebuilt with whatever men were available. They included teenaged recruits, middle-aged recalled reservists, and masses of almost untrained militia, often without proper uniforms and armed with whatever obsolete weapons the army could scrape together. This improvised army, thrown haphazardly into the line, held the strategic Carpathian passes against repeated Russian offensives. The raw recruits, aging reservists, and untried militiamen made up in determination what they lacked in training and firepower.

This new, war-raised army's trials were just beginning. The Carpathian winter of 1915—the dreaded *Karpathenwinter*—would put it fully to the test. Despite his army's weakness, the winter conditions and the forbidding terrain, Conrad was determined to push the enemy out of the Carpathians to prevent a Russian advance onto the Hungarian plain. No less, he wanted to recapture Galicia and lift the siege of beleaguered Przemyśl, where 120,000 Austrian soldiers were trapped sixty miles behind Russian lines. He could muster only seventeen understrength divisions to execute his plan, but he began the first Carpathian offensive on January 23 anyway, in the middle of a harsh winter. The Austrian 3rd Army attacked vigorously despite the appalling weather but made little headway in the face of stiff Russian resistance, made worse by deep snow, ice storms, and fog- and snow-induced blindness. In retrospect, it is remarkable that the 3rd Army made any progress whatsoever. By the end of January, Conrad's offensive had petered out after suffering heavy casualties, attributable as much to the weather as to the enemy. The Russians launched an immediate counteroffensive to overturn the modest Austrian advances. By the second week of February, the Russians had regained their lost ground and pushed the 3rd Army even deeper into the frozen Carpathians.

For the next six weeks the Austrians and Russians dueled for the Carpathian passes, with no significant effect except heavy losses on both sides. Conrad's second Carpathian offensive in late February was no more successful than the first, but similarly costly and futile. And the Russian March offensives bled their armies badly, too, for no decisive return. On March 23, the isolated fortress of Przemyśl, without hope of relief or reinforcement, capitulated to the Russians: a loss of nine generals, 2,500 officers, and 117,000 soldiers. Buoyed by this success, the Russians went on the offensive in the Carpathians in April, achieving notable local victories over the ailing Austrians. As was so often the case in the First World War, however, and particularly in the terrible Carpathian conditions, the Russians were unable to exploit their tactical advances to achieve strategic gains. The Habsburg Army survived because the Russians were by now equally battered, weakened, and exhausted.

Three months of tug-of-war in the Carpathians cost the Austrians between 600,000 and 800,000 soldiers. Barely recovered from the Galician disaster of 1914, the army had been subjected to another dreadful series of hopeless offensives; indeed, for the soldiers, freezing in the high Hungarian mountains in midwinter, the *Karpathenwinter* was far worse than even the nightmarishly intense Galician maneuver battles of August and September 1914. It is therefore hardly surprising that the army began to display serious cohesion problems during the winter of 1915. Morale on the Eastern Front plummeted after Conrad's disastrous attacks, particularly in Slav units. Ethnic disharmony started to appear, especially in Czech, Ukrainian, and Serb units, as desertions increased and units fought with little spirit; Russian propaganda, urging Austria's Slav troops—half the army—to surrender to their "brother Slav" enemy, was having an effect. Almost an entire Czech regiment, Prague's 28th, surrendered to the Russians en masse without a fight in early April. The battered multinational army was starting to crumble. Conrad's failed Carpathian offensives finished off what little had remained of the Austria's trained prewar cadres, and dealt the army a further blow from which it could never fully recover.

In late April, while the bulk of the Austrian Army was starting to come apart in the Carpathians, the few units fortunate enough to be guarding the Italian frontier were preparing to greet the return of spring. Austria's long border with Italy had been tranquil since the outbreak of the war. On August 13, 1914, General Franz Rohr was appointed commander of the districts bordering Italy, but he had only a handful of units at his disposal. The army, fighting for its life in the Carpathians, had few battalions to spare, and defending a neutral border was a low priority. Hence Rohr's command consisted of an odd collection of training battalions, replacement and militia units, and gendarmerie detachments. His command had no first-line regiments, and was equipped with a strange mix of obsolete weaponry: his infantrymen were armed with five types of rifles, including captured Russian weapons and rifles built for export to Mexico. An actual defense of the Littoral or the Trentino against a determined Italian offensive was out of the question. Many Austrian officers, from Conrad down, considered an Italian attack on the beleaguered empire's virtually undefended "back door" a distinct possibility. The chief of staff concluded in August 1914 that such an opportunistic assault would be "completely in the spirit of the Italian mind-set." Conrad, like most Austrian officers—and a great many civilians—considered Rome's refusal to back her allies in July 1914 an act of unforgivable betrayal. He wanted revenge, to be sure, but now was a very inopportune time for Austria to fight a three-front war. Punishing Italy for her perfidy would have to wait.

The Isonzo valley had been quiet since Austria went to war the previous summer. The little villages and surrounding fields were even more tranquil than usual. There were few military-age men to be seen, only boys and old men: the army had sent those fit to fight to Galicia and the Carpathians, where many met an unenviable fate. The militia companies manning the nearly nonexistent frontier defenses had little to do except watch for sporadic movement by neighboring Italian frontier guard units. There had not been any shooting, much less real fighting. The only gunfire anyone could remember was the unfortunate killing of Countess Lucy Christalnigg. In the second week of August, just as the war was starting, the countess, a Red Cross official, was driving from Gorizia back to Carinthia along the main Isonzo road. She passed a checkpoint near Karfreit, failing to heed the sentries' order to stop. The two nervous Slovene guards, worried about permitting a possible enemy agent to drive past their checkpoint, opened fire. A well aimed rifle bullet struck the countess in the head, killing her instantly. A minor scandal ensued, and the two soldiers were court-martialed; they were acquitted, however, for after all, they were following orders. The death of Countess Lucy was the only noteworthy event in the valley since the war started.

Trieste was similarly quiet. There was much griping about the war, particularly the inflation and the rationing of foodstuffs. Still, Trieste, like Gorizia and the Isonzo valley, had not yet been directly touched by the war. Many native sons were dead or missing on unpronounceable Eastern battlefields, but Trieste had not endured the suffering of so many cities all across Europe—shelling, bombing, enemy occupation. There was unpleasantness, of course, notably when returning wounded soldiers of Trieste's 97th Regiment brought with them two horrors from the Carpathians: stories of appalling losses and a cholera epidemic. The city suffered a cholera outbreak that further irritated its citizens during the winter of 1915, but Trieste was comparatively fortunate. Some *triestini* looked enviously at nearby neutral Italy, spared the war's tumult and indignities; a few no doubt wanted to join Italy, but they were a minority. Most were pleased that the war had not yet touched Trieste and the Littoral directly. By late April, their happiness would be short-lived.

In the weeks before Italy formally declared war on Austria, there were clear signs of Italian military moves. Luigi Cadorna's early mobilization of eight corps on April 23, although secret, did not go unnoticed by Austrian intelligence. Even the border posts on the Isonzo observed increasing troop movement across the frontier. Every day the possibility of war grew more likely, particularly after Rome abandoned the Triple Alliance. Still, there was little Conrad and his generals could do. Until Vienna was certain that an Italian invasion was imminent, the army could not afford to dispatch its emaciated reserves to the Isonzo; every available soldier was needed in the East. In early April, Conrad, growing increasingly suspicious of Italian intentions, had wanted to withdraw seven divisions from the Carpathians and deploy them on the Italian border. But General Erich Falkenhayn, Berlin's chief of staff and the senior partner in the German-Austrian alliance, refused Conrad's request. So the Austrians did the best they could, scraping together a few additional units for the Littoral, including replacement battalions sent from regimental depots without completing their training.[3] By mid-May, the entire Littoral was garrisoned by three understrength divisions, hastily cobbled together formations with little artillery. On May 23, when Italy declared war, the unfortified Isonzo line from Mt. Krn to the Adriatic, a distance of thirty-five miles, was held by just twenty-four Austrian battalions, 25,000 rifles supported by 100 guns. Most of these units were recently arrived replacement battalions, collections of half-trained teenagers, middle-aged family men, and wounded veterans returning to the front. These men would have to hold back the bulk of Italy's might, the reinforced 2nd and 3rd Armies. On paper, the odds looked hopeless. Admiral Anton Haus, commander in chief of the Habsburg Navy, fearing that the Isonzo line would soon collapse, prepared to move the navy's headquarters and fleet from the Istrian port of Pola to Cattaro, at the other end of Austria's Adriatic coastline. Cadorna's "walk to Vienna," and the collapse of the Habsburg Empire, appeared imminent.

1915

THREE

"The Hour of the Triumph of the Finest Values"

Once Italy declared war, General Luigi Cadorna quickly moved his headquarters and staff close to the front. He settled the *Comando Supremo* in the Friulian city of Udine, only a dozen miles from the Austrian frontier and just seventeen from the banks of the Isonzo. There Cadorna intended to direct the execution of his grand strategy, to see his well laid plans brought to fruition. He expected his 2nd and 3rd Armies, marshaling in eastern Friulia, to cross soon into Austria for the decisive battle on the Isonzo. Cadorna anticipated that his divisions would easily break through the weak Austrian defenses and advance rapidly eastward toward the Ljubljana gap, the major pass through the Julian Alps to the flatlands of Central Europe. Once there, his forces would threaten the Austrian capital. *Italia irredenta* would be liberated, and the Austrian Empire would be on its knees. By midsummer, it would all be over.

Everything seemed to be in Cadorna's favor. On May 23, the first day of the war, his legions were fully mobilized. Months of secret preparations, as well as the partial mobilization in late April, meant that Italy's official mobilization on May 22 was a mere formality. The army was ready to enter battle immediately. By any standards, the forces at Cadorna's disposal were impressive. His field army totaled 900,000 soldiers. Counting second-line reserves, the army included thirty-five infantry divisions, a dozen divisions of militia, and four cavalry divisions, as well as a division of *Bersaglieri*, elite light infantry. There were also fifty-two battalions of *Alpini*, crack mountain troops, and fourteen battalions of combat engineers. The field artillery boasted 467 batteries, almost 2,000 guns and howitzers. There were also numerous battalions of paramilitary police, *Carabinieri*, and Finance Guards to support the field army. Cadorna's months of readying the army for war had borne fruit. Certainly the Italian Army was far larger, better trained, and better equipped than it had been the previous summer.

Still, there were notable weaknesses in Cadorna's order of battle. On paper, Italy's infantry divisions were organized pretty much like Austria's: two infantry brigades, each of two three-battalion regiments; a field artillery regiment; supporting units of engineers and cavalry; and service and medical units to sustain the division in the field. Yet despite General Vittorio Zupelli's months of reorganizing the field forces and procuring modern weaponry for them, combat units still lacked badly needed modern guns, machine guns, and even rifles. The artillery had the greatest shortfalls. The light field artillery, which did most of the work, was outfitted well enough, but the army was short of mountain guns, vital in the Alpine fighting Cadorna was about to initiate. Worse, the heavy artillery hardly existed: there were only 112 heavy guns in the entire army. In the siegelike conditions that would soon prevail on the Isonzo, this lack of heavy firepower would prove a serious shortcoming. Cadorna's armies were also short of machine guns, the dominant weapons of the First World War. There were only 618 machine guns on strength in late May, an average of only two per infantry regiment—one-third the Austrian rate. Hand grenades, dangerous and useful new weapons in 1915, were all but unknown in the Italian Army. There were not even enough modern rifles to go around. Italian arsenals produced only 2,500 M.1891 rifles per month, nowhere near enough to equip reserve and militia units, and woefully inadequate to replace battle losses once the fighting began. The army's artillery shell reserve was limited, adequate only for a very short war, and daily shell output from Italy's factories—seven rounds per gun—could not sustain prolonged fighting. Italy's forces, although large, were thus unprepared for a long campaign. If the fighting lasted more than a few weeks, the army would run out of guns and munitions. Fortunately for Cadorna, his numerical superiority was so overwhelming than Austria's rapid collapse seemed guaranteed.

Italy's legions had a major factor in their favor to counteract some of their material deficiencies. Austria's military, unready for war even in 1914, had already suffered two million casualties and was on its last legs. Habsburg regiments were understrength and weak from the war, and morale was plummeting in the Carpathians. How long could Austria's badly bloodied army sustain a third front? In stark contrast, Italy's forces were fresh, eager, and untried. They displayed no war weariness; indeed, quite the opposite. Cadorna's regiments were marching to war enthusiastically, as Austria's had almost a year earlier. Their ranks were bolstered by thousands of ardent young volunteers, eager to enter battle and liberate Austria's Italian provinces. For such young men, fired by romantic nationalism, the Habsburgs' long-awaited day of reckoning and Italy's hour of glory had finally arrived. As one young poet pronounced, "This is the hour of the triumph of the finest values." Italy's unblooded regiments marched to the Isonzo with an enthusiasm not witnessed in Europe since doomed ranks of jubilant volunteers departed Vienna for Serbia and Galicia ten months before.

Of course, firepower had defeated mere numbers on all fronts of the war. In Flanders, Galicia, Alsace, and Serbia, weight of shell had annihilated whole divisions of enthusiastic volunteers. The will to fight was all-important, the most basic need in any army; yet it alone could not overcome superior gunnery, and it was not an adequate substitute for realistic training and preparation. This surely was the lesson of the terrible carnage on all fronts in 1914. Austria's weary army had learned this. Never again would Habsburg regiments go into battle as naively unprepared as in the previous summer. At the cost of two million soldiers lost in battle, the Austrian Army had learned that modern weapons—especially machine guns and artillery—dominated the battlefield and determined the outcome of combat. Cadorna's armies massing for battle remained untaught.

Italian tactical doctrine—that is, the army's official instructions about how to deploy units on the field of battle—in fact remained untouched by the fighting that had plagued Europe for the past ten months. Italian doctrine betrayed no awareness of the lessons of the costly fighting on either the Western or the Eastern front. At Cadorna's direction, the army prepared for war without examining the new patterns of combat that had emerged in the past year, particularly trench warfare. All over Europe, most notably in France and Flanders, the armies had burrowed deep into the earth to escape the lethal effects of artillery and machine gun fire. The fighting had become static and entrenched, a condition that strongly favored the defense. This was a rude shock for everyone—in fact, the precise opposite of the tactics taught throughout Europe before the war, which had preached that future combat would be mobile and decisive, and that modern weapons favored the attacker. However, Cadorna still planned to fight a mobile offensive war of a kind that had disappeared from the other fighting fronts. The Italian Army was preparing to fight the Austrians with the same tactics—mass infantry assaults without direct artillery support—that had such horrifying results everywhere in 1914.

There was ample evidence that such methods would lead to disaster. Italy had officers serving as observers at all the fighting fronts who witnessed the growing carnage as well as the complete change in tactics. The army's attachés serving in foreign capitals had ample opportunity to note the rise of trench warfare. Indeed, by May 1915 there was a great deal of information available to Cadorna and his staff which indicated plainly that something had gone dreadfully wrong on the Western front. In December 1914 and February 1915, Lieutenant Colonel Breganzi, military attaché in Paris, submitted detailed reports concerning the fighting in France. His first report noted the strength of the defense, the dominant role of artillery and fortifications, the tremendous casualties, and the great expenditure of ammunition; the second concluded that it was impossible for either side to reach a battlefield decision in such conditions. In March, Cadorna received an even more in-depth analysis from Colonel Bongiovanni, attaché in Berlin. The perceptive colonel described in great detail all aspects of the new siegelike trench warfare that prevailed everywhere on the Western front: the dominance of artillery and machine guns, the need for infantry-artillery cooperation, the construction of trenches, and the impact of barbed wire and new weapons like hand grenades and mortars. Bongiovanni warned Cadorna that huge amounts of artillery and even greater quantities of shells would be required for any offensive to be successful. The chief of staff simply ignored these and many other revealing and cautionary reports. The stubborn and closed-minded Cadorna believed that the Austrians were weak, indeed collapsing, and that his forces would cross the Isonzo without a prolonged fight. His vague doctrine called for a mass artillery barrage followed by waves of infantry to overwhelm the enemy. Cadorna remained supremely confident of victory; the troops' enthusiasm and high morale would prevail against any merely physical obstacles: "This will depend on their energy, their tenacity, and their conviction of their own material and moral superiority."

In the last days of May, the much reinforced 2nd and 3rd Armies, now on the Austrian border, made their final preparations for battle. The 3rd Army, commanded by the king's handsome and popular cousin, Emanuele Filiberto di Savoia, the Duke of Aosta, had the politically significant mission: securing the western edge of the Carso and marching on Trieste. General Pietro Frugoni's 2nd Army was to take Gorizia and the upper Isonzo. Before the main assault could begin, however, Frugoni's divisions had a very important preliminary task: seizing several important towns and mountains before the Austrians could reinforce their weak garrisons. In the last days of May and the first days of June, the 2nd Army was to cross the upper Isonzo and occupy the town of Karfreit and several strategic peaks, including Mt. Krn and Kolovrat ridge. Frugoni readied his units, particularly his elite *Alpini* mountain battalions, for the war's opening engagements.

While the 2nd Army made last-minute preparations, Cadorna and his staff waited in Udine for the war to get going. The chief of staff was undoubtedly frustrated that the movement of troops into the battle zone was slower than expected, despite the months of planning. There had been a few minor penetrations across the border soon after the declaration of war, but no major advances yet. And supplies were somewhat delayed. There were six rail lines to the Piave River, but only two went beyond it to the Austrian frontier, so each of Cadorna's field armies had only a single rail line to carry all its munitions and supplies. Still, Cadorna was unconcerned. He had been joined in the field by the king, who had come to observe his army's imminent triumph. Although Vittorio Emanuele III was the titular head of all Italy's fighting forces, he came to the Isonzo as a spectator: Cadorna exercised all real control. Short and unmilitary in bearing, Vittorio Emanuele was an unlikely and unimposing commander in chief. Yet he was an avid military enthusiast; military history was his favorite conversation topic, and he had always preferred military men to civilians. Since coming to the throne in 1900, the king had displayed considerable interest in military affairs, and fully supported the war; he was fond of saying, "Italy was unified not by Dante but by bayonets." Like almost everyone else, he was confident of victory. Yet ironically it was Vittorio Emanuele alone who voiced a degree of caution, or at least realism, as his armies marched into battle. In his order of the day for May 27, the king stated his faith in his troops but admitted that the Austrians would not be as easy to defeat as Cadorna and the generals had imagined: "Favored by the terrain and by careful preparation, they will put up a tough resistance, but your unquenchable dash will, without doubt, overcome them."

Vittorio Emanuele's more sanguine assessment of the fighting soon to engulf the Isonzo valley was possibly due to the recent unwelcome news from the Eastern front. Between Italy's signing of the Treaty of London on April 26 and her official declaration of war on May 23, the fighting in the East had shifted decisively in favor of the Central Powers. Just one day before Italy denounced the Triple Alliance, a combined German-Habsburg offensive opened in Galicia and the Carpathians. The push, spearheaded by the German 11th Army, was intended to take the pressure off the ailing Austrian forces in the Carpathians. The Gorlice-Tarnów offensive soon succeeded beyond all expectations. A dozen veteran German divisions, attacking on a front of less than fifteen miles and well supported by heavy artillery, quickly overran the weak Russian 3rd Army; the disorganized defenders were soon in headlong retreat. By the second week of May, Austrian divisions had fought their way out of the Carpathians, and the Russians were hastily withdrawing eastward. By early June, the Austrians had retaken the fortress of Przemyśl, and by the end of the month nearly all of Galicia was again in Habsburg hands. The Russians suffered an unprecedented defeat, losing the better part of a million men. All the Allied gains of the previous autumn had been overturned; the strategic balance on the Eastern front had been altered decisively in favor of the Central Powers. Significantly, Austria now had some breathing room, and the Habsburg Army had been saved from apparent annihilation. The expected Russian victory in the Carpathians, and the resulting Austrian collapse—the root strategic assumptions of Italian entry into the First World War—had evaporated.[1]

With the mortal Russian threat in the Carpathians lifted, Austria could concentrate more forces on her exposed Italian frontier. Conrad could now shift reserve divisions to the Isonzo to hold off the expected Italian invasion. On May

23, within hours of Italy's declaration of war, the chief of staff ordered the XV and XVI Corps from the quiet Serbian front to the Isonzo. These corps (each of two or more infantry divisions and supporting troops) totaled five understrength divisions, forty veteran mountain battalions in all. Their experience and equipment made them ideal for holding the Alpine terrain on the Isonzo's east bank. The divisions were dispatched to the Littoral on the first available trains in a race to reach the Isonzo before Cadorna launched his great push. Franz Conrad von Hötzendorf also created a new command, the 5th Army, to hold the Isonzo line and to control the defense of the entire Littoral, from Triglav to Pola.

The new army was placed under the command of an experienced leader, General Svetozar Boroević von Bojna, whose name would be irrevocably associated with the war on the Isonzo. The fifty-eight-year-old Boroević was a born warrior, the son of a Serbian *Grenzer* family from Croatia. The Habsburg Army's *Grenzer* regiments had defended the empire's southern border against the Ottomans since the early sixteenth century. Until its disbandment in 1881, the unique Military Border, as it was known, provided the Habsburgs with their fiercest soldiers, wild Serbian and Croatian irregulars renowned for their loyalty to the emperor and their brutality toward all foes. All men in the border regions could be called out to defend the frontier in an emergency. The *Grenzer* farmer-warriors lost their unique status in 1881, their local regiments being amalgamated with the regular army. But their spirit lived on in the border region's soldiers, like Svetozar Boroević. The general was descended from *Grenzers* on both sides of his family, and his father had fought the Italians in 1859 and 1866. He was a Serb from Croatia's harsh frontier, the region more recently known as the Krájina,[2] and he had spent nearly his entire life serving Franz Joseph.

Boroević, like Cadorna, entered cadet school at age ten, and succeeded at every school he attended. He served as a junior officer in the infantry, fought in several battles during the occupation of Bosnia in 1878, and was decorated for bravery at the capture of Sarajevo. Soon after, he attended the War School, where he excelled, and then entered the elite General Staff. He thereafter divided his assignments between staffs and field commands, performing well in both roles. Before the war Boroević commanded Croatia's home guard, the 42nd *Honvéd* Division, known as the "Devil's Division" for its martial prowess. He distinguished himself as a corps commander in the Galician battles of 1914, and rose to command the 3rd Army during the terrible Carpathian winter. His army suffered appallingly high losses, but Boroević was considered an effective leader nevertheless. He was physically unimposing, a small, almost petite man, but his appearance belied a stern character; Boroević had a well earned reputation for determination and toughness, which was sometimes taken out on rival generals and subordinates. On the whole, however, Conrad felt him to be a skilled defensive general, an astute tactician, and a cool-headed officer, able to hold ground at any cost—an ideal commander for the 5th Army.

General Boroević arrived in Ljubljana on May 27, accompanied by four staff officers from the 3rd Army. The small headquarters began the confusing process of sorting out the tasks before it. Newly arriving units had to be deployed, defenses improved, logistical details arranged, and the new command structure established—all before the Italian blow fell. The result was often chaotic, with reinforcements and supplies going to the wrong units—the headquarters' "Carpathian tempo" was much criticized by the High Command—but the new 5th Army command was in place and functioning by the end of May. By May 28, reinforcements had begun to arrive from the Balkans, the XV Corps on the upper Isonzo and the XVI Corps at Gorizia. Before the June fighting commenced, Boroević had at his disposal a total of eight divisions. In the week between the Italian declaration of war and the first notable Italian moves, while Cadorna waited to unleash his armies, the strength of the Austrian forces on the Isonzo more than doubled.[3]

The arrival of fresh troops was not the only movement in the Isonzo valley in late May. Half of Gorizia's residents voluntarily evacuated the city after the Italian declaration of war. Villages on the Carso likewise emptied before the Italians started shelling. On the middle and upper Isonzo, soon to be a battlefield, the entire population was evacuated by the Austrian Army. In a considerable logistical undertaking, some 80,000 Slovenes, most of them women, children, and the elderly, were removed from their villages west of the river and on its east bank. Many were sent to Slovene areas farther from Italy, but thousands of less fortunate Slovenes were collected in refugee centers near Vienna, where they sat out the fighting in crowded barracks, waiting for the war to end.

The entry of Italy into the war had an unanticipated impact on the Austrian war effort. Although the addition of a third front was a strategic liability, the impending Italian invasion gave a tremendous boost to morale. Even among common Austrian soldiers, there existed a sincere sense of outrage against a former ally that had attacked beleaguered Austria on its exposed frontier. Habsburg subjects of all nationalities—including many Italian Austrians—shared this sentiment, so that the war against Italy, the "hereditary enemy," was perceived as necessary and just by all, to an extent that was never true of the conflicts with Serbia and Russia. There was also a tradition of defeating Italians, invoked in Franz Joseph's May 23 manifesto to his troops, issued upon Italy's entry into the war: "The great memories of Novara, Custozza and Lissa, which formed the pride of My Youth, and the spirit of Radetzky, Archduke Albrecht and Tegethoff, which lives on in My Land and Sea forces, guarantee . . . that we will also successfully defend the borders of the Monarchy against the South." Enthusiasm for the war ran especially high in German-Austrian and South Slav areas of the empire, which felt justifiably threatened by Rome's expansionist plans. More than 25,000 volunteers from the German Alpine provinces, most of them teenagers, came forward in May to defend Carinthia and the Tyrol against the invader. Emotions among Slovenes, Croats, and Serbs ran equally high, and the outbreak of war with Italy was greeted enthusiastically. Italian designs on the Littoral and Dalmatia were well known, and few South Slavs—including General Boroević—had any illusions concerning Italian intentions. For the Slovenes in particular, the struggle on the Isonzo was a people's war, a national resistance against the foreign invader. And even the most anti-Habsburg Serbs feared Italian occupation of their territory, and were willing to fight to prevent an Italian invasion of South Slav lands. Slovenes, Croats, and Serbs in Austrian uniform were as determined to hold the Isonzo line as the most ardent Italian volunteers were to redeem *Italia irredenta*.

In the last days of May, General Frugoni's 2nd Army advanced into the upper Isonzo valley without much of a fight. The Austrian XV Corps decided to make its stand not at the frontier, but beyond the river's east bank, in the high Julian Alps. It was precisely these mountains that the Italians had to take. The Mrzli range roughly paralleled the Isonzo, running ten miles from just north of Tolmein almost to Flitsch. Its four main peaks—Mrzli vrh (4,500 ft.), Krn (7,410 ft.), Vrata (6,400 ft.), and Vršič (6,260 ft.)—dominated the upper Isonzo. Cadorna felt that the Mrzli range, particularly its southern half, had to be cleared of Austrian troops before the general thrust across the Isonzo could start; he did not want any threats emerging from the north during his advance. Frugoni ordered his IV Corps, three divisions strong and reinforced by several *Alpini* battalions, to cross the Isonzo and take the Mrzli line. On the early morning of May 24, Italian troops crossed the frontier and seized the river town of Karfreit, gaining an important bridgehead across the Isonzo. By June 1, *Alpini* detachments had likewise taken Vrata and Vršič, virtually without a fight. However, the IV Corps had not rushed into the Mrzli range soon enough. By the end of May, its southern half was occupied by Austrian mountain troops.

The 3rd Mountain Brigade, a polyglot formation, was rushed from the Serbian border to the upper Isonzo in less than a week. Most of the nationalities of the empire—Germans, Czechs, Poles, Ukrainians, Magyars, Romanians—were represented in its five battalions, all veteran mountain units trained and equipped for fighting in difficult terrain. In the first three days of June, the war began in earnest on the upper Isonzo. On Cadorna's orders, the IV Corps made a maximum effort to take Krn and Mrzli vrh. The Italian 8th Division, supported by elite *Bersaglieri*, assaulted the positions of the 3rd Mountain Brigade on Mrzli ridge. Boroević ordered the brigade to hold the ridge at all costs. Despite heroic efforts, the Italians made little headway up the steep mountains and suffered heavy casualties. In just one attack on June 2, the 8th Division's Modena Brigade lost 37 officers and 1,200 men to Austrian machine gun and rifle fire. The reinforcing Salerno Brigade suffered almost as many casualties, and the

12th *Bersaglieri* Regiment lost more than 400 riflemen, many of whom fell off cliffs. When both sides ran out of ammunition, they resorted to throwing rocks, occasionally with deadly results. By June 4, the 8th Division had advanced only a few hundred paces, and both Krn and Mrzli vrh remained in Austrian hands. Austrian losses of a thousand dead and wounded, most of them in the 3rd Mountain Brigade, were steep, but Mrzli ridge had been held. The 3rd Brigade had followed its demanding orders fully. It had no choice: a battalion commander of the brigade's 80th Regiment was court-martialed for losing Hill 1186 near Mrzli vrh. Boroević would not tolerate the loss of a foot of ground without a grueling fight.

In the opening engagements, Boroević's strict policy worked. Italian commanders were frustrated by the lack of progress against such a numerically weak enemy. Some units took their frustrations out on Slovene civilians. Soldiers of the IV Corps destroyed six villages near Mt. Krn, alleging that residents had opened fire on Italian units. In a similar incident, the 42nd Regiment, advancing on Mrzli ridge, claimed that Slovene civilians from a nearby village had killed Italian wounded. Military police took all sixty-one men from the village, lined them up, and shot every tenth man as a reprisal; the survivors, as well as the women and children of the village, were rounded up and sent to internment camps in Italy.

General Frugoni was determined to take Krn, called Monte Nero (Black Mountain) by the Italians. He permitted the IV Corps several days' rest before attempting to wrest the peak from the Austrians. On June 16, six battalions of *Alpini*, led by the Susa and Exilles battalions, executed a predawn surprise attack on the snow-covered, fog-shrouded summit. The Italian troops scaled the 7,410-foot mountain under cover of the moonless night. The defenders, a battalion of the 4th *Honvéd* Regiment just arrived from the Carpathians, were caught completely unaware by the lightning assault. Once his men were near the summit, Captain Vincenzo Arbarello, commander of Exilles' 84th Company, ordered his men to drop their packs and charge the Habsburg positions. The *Alpini* emerged from the thick fog and overwhelmed the dazed Hungarians in hand-to-hand combat, capturing hundreds of defenders. By 4:45 A.M., Mt. Krn was in Italian hands and the survivors of the Hungarian battalion had been taken prisoner. Losses among the attackers were steep: Captain Arbarello was seriously wounded, and all the officers under him also were casualties. Among the dead was Lieutenant Alberto Picco, leader of the company's daring assault group, who was awarded the war's first Gold Medal for Bravery, the highest Italian decoration. The twice-wounded Picco kept fighting until he collapsed, dying in Captain Arbarello's arms. Italy had its first heroic martyr. The *Alpini* were showered with accolades and medals for their seizing of Krn, including thirty-two Silver and seventy-nine Bronze Medals for Bravery. It was Italy's first triumph of the war. The capture of Monte Nero gave Italy an early and inexpensive conquest; no one doubted there would be many such victories to follow. An *Alpini* veteran of the operation gave the army the first of many romantic war songs. It began:

> *O vile Monte Nero*
> *Traditor della patria mia*
> *Io lasciai la mamma mia*
> *Per venirti a conquistar*

> (O contemptible Black Mountain
> Betrayer of my motherland
> I left my own mother
> To come to conquer you)

Mt. Krn would remain in Italian hands until the end of the Isonzo fighting. Its quick capture gave the Italian military and people a dangerously unwarranted sense of optimism.

The Austrian 50th Division occupied Mt. Batognica, the neighboring peak a half-mile southeast of Krn. The Italians had seized Vršič, Vrata, and Krn, but they failed to take Mrzli ridge. In particular, Austrian troops still held Mrzli vrh and the southern third of the ridge. The potential threat to the 2nd Army's advance remained. Even so, Frugoni abandoned the costly efforts the IV Corps on the upper Isonzo in favor of a crossing on the central Isonzo. At the village of Plava, fourteen miles downstream from Mrzli vrh, the Isonzo turns west, and then rapidly east again, forming a bulge. At the center of the bulge is a small mountain, Hill 383 (1,260 ft.), overlooking the town and the river. The Plava bridgehead represented the most direct path to the strategic Bainsizza plateau, as well as the key to Mt. Santo and Mt. Sabotino, the double "gate" of the river just north of Gorizia. The Italians had to take Hill 383, "the key to Gorizia," before they could advance on Gorizia or the Bainsizza. Frugoni gave Lieutenant General Gustavo Reisoli's II Corps the task of crossing the Isonzo at Plava and seizing the hill. Reisoli assigned two of his three divisions to the mission. The 3rd Division crossed the frontier and took the village of Plava without a fight, and on the evening of June 3, under the cover of darkness, Italian engineers built a pontoon bridge across the river to support the impending attack. The 3rd Division prepared its infantry and artillery for the assault. Hill 383's Austrian defenders could only watch and wait.

The six-mile Isonzo sector from Plava to Mt. Santo was held by troops of the 1st Mountain Brigade, recently rushed to the Isonzo from the Balkans. Its battalions were diverse—Silesian, Viennese, Bohemian, and two Transylvanian—but filled with experienced mountain fighters. Its commander, Major General Guido Novak von Arienti, had only recently returned to duty after a long convalescence: he had been wounded in the head while leading the brigade in the Serbian campaign. The fifty-six-year-old Novak, aged for a brigade commander, had considerable experience commanding Alpine units, and was an effective leader of men, having spent his entire career with the infantry. He was a pure line officer, not a desk-bound General Staff type. His brigade was outnumbered six to one, and had only two mountain artillery batteries to support it, but Novak was confident that his troops would hold Hill 383 no matter what the Italians threw against them.

On the evening of June 9, two battalions of the 3rd Division's Ravenna Brigade crossed the Isonzo in boats, under the cover of artillery fire from fifty guns. They established a bridgehead on the east bank and marched up the forested hill, garrisoned by only a single entrenched Austrian rifle company with 200 men. The Italian assault soon faltered in the face of unexpectedly accurate rifle and machine gun fire, and the brigade retired for the night. The next day, June 10, the Ravenna Brigade prepared to attack the hill again. After an intense artillery bombardment, the whole 6,000-man brigade arose from its positions at the base of Hill 383 at 9:30 P.M. as the sun disappeared for the night. The Austrian defenders, now a battalion strong, raised their heads from their trenches as the shelling lifted. Through the dust and clouds of smoke unleashed by the Italian bombardment, they saw the entire 37th and 38th Regiments marching up the hill in waves, yelling the traditional Italian battle cry, "*Avanti Savoia!*"[4] Machine gun nests, undamaged by the bombardment, opened up on the advancing ranks of Italian infantry, and the stunned Ravenna Brigade quickly broke and fled back to their positions at the river's edge.

The next day, while Novak's brigade was repairing its shell-damaged trenches, the 3rd Division was readying itself for another assault on Hill 383. The Ravenna Brigade received replacements to make good its losses of the last two attempts, and the Forlì Brigade was brought forward to reinforce the battered 37th and 38th Regiments. On the morning of June 12 the Italian guns opened up again, and the hill's Austrian defenders took cover. Throughout the day, the six battalions of the Ravenna Brigade charged up the hill no less than seven times. Austrian machine guns took their toll of infantry advancing up 383's now bare hillsides. Each attack brought the Italians closer to the summit, but the capture of the hill eluded them. The Ravenna Brigade's losses that day were 476 dead and wounded in the 37th Regiment and 361 in the 38th. The 3rd Division, now thoroughly exhausted by futile assaults, was taken out of the line. Among its survivors, Hill 383 had earned the title *la collina della morte*—"the hill of death."

The foot soldiers of Novak's 1st Mountain Brigade were just as weary after several days' hard fighting. The defending units were so depleted that a fresh battalion of the 22nd Regiment was sent to hold the summit of Hill 383, now surrounded by hundreds of unburied Italian corpses. Novak told the soldiers, just arrived from the Serbian front, that the hill had to be held at any price. The 22nd Regiment's infantrymen were Croats and Serbs from Dalmatia. For them, this was a personal fight: their home province had been promised to Italy by the Treaty of London. Indeed, their battalion commander, Major Stanko Turudja, was a Dalmatian Serb. He told his men before battle that they were defending not just a hill on the Isonzo, but "Slav earth." On the morning of June 16, the Italian II Corps tried to take it from them. The fresh 33rd Division was committed to battle. Three regiments from the Spezia and Forlì Brigades went over the top, charging across the short distance between the Italian positions and the summit. There was little artillery support for the attack—both sides were now too close together, and Italian batteries would be more likely to kill their own troops than the enemy. The dug-in Dalmatians opened fire with rifles and machine guns at point-blank range, their well aimed rounds ripping through the advancing waves of infantry. Through sheer courage, the Italians reached the summit and forced the 22nd out of its positions. The Italians and Dalmatians fought hand to hand with knives and bayonets until the outnumbered defenders were forced to withdraw down the hill's east face to regroup. The 43rd Regiment had taken the summit. Soldiers of its 2nd Battalion raised the Italian tricolor, and officers and men embraced each other, crying for joy and for all the men who had died to raise the flag on Hill 383. The cost of the final assault on the hill had been high: 1,307 casualties, including 480 dead. Yet the 33rd Division's triumph would be short-lived. In the early hours of June 17, Turudja's 2nd Battalion of the 22nd Regiment regrouped and attacked the Italian-held trenches at the hill's summit. The Dalmatians surprised the sleeping soldiers of the 43rd Regiment, who were enjoying a well deserved rest. The rudely awakened Italians quickly retreated down the hill's west face. By dawn, the 33rd Division had reestablished its positions halfway down the hillside, and Hill 383 again belonged to Novak's 1st Mountain Brigade. The Dalmatians had retaken the summit, the piece of "Slav earth" they had been ordered to hold at all costs, losing 433 officers and men, half their strength.

On June 17, Frugoni ordered the attacks at Plava suspended. Attempts by the II Corps to take and hold Hill 383 had proved too costly, and further assaults would have to wait. This was welcome news for the hill's Austrian defenders, too. The cost of the weeklong tug of war had been exorbitant for both sides. Novak's brigade had lost 2,577 soldiers killed, wounded, and missing in its defense of the Plava bridgehead. Italian losses were probably three times as many. Reisoli's II Corps was severely battered in the fight for Hill 383; a later official Italian account of the initial offensive at Plava would term it merely "the first holocaust." One of the prisoners taken in the Dalmatian counterattack was a reserve second lieutenant, Giovanni Paradotto, a cavalry ordnance officer and member of Italy's parliament. Paradotto revealed that his army's losses were exceptionally high, and that the medical service was appallingly bad. The Italian medical corps was short of everything—doctors, medicines, bandages—and wounded soldiers frequently went untreated. Morale was understandably quite low, according to the captured lieutenant. The first sustained battle for the II Corps, indeed for the whole Italian Army, was a bruising shock. The Austrian 1st Mountain Brigade at least had a victory to justify its suffering: badly outnumbered, it had held Hill 383 against all comers. It had prevented an Italian breakthrough at a decisive point. Novak was rewarded for his energetic and determined leadership. He was presented the Knight's Cross of the Order of Maria Theresia, the highest Habsburg decoration, the first to be awarded on the Italian front.

The 2nd Army's attempts to advance elsewhere on the Isonzo had proved no more profitable than at Plava. The untested VI Corps, facing Gorizia, crossed the Austrian frontier in early June and made several probing attacks in the hills in front of the city. Its 11th and 12th Divisions attempted to break through, but were bloodily repulsed by Dalmatian battalions of the 5th Mountain Brigade. In just one abortive advance on June 10, the Italian 35th Regiment lost 639 soldiers. An effort by the 4th Division to seize Mt. Sabotino was equally unsuccessful. Farther south, the Duke of Aosta's 3rd Army crossed the lower Isonzo without much resistance, its divisions advancing to the edge of the Carso, where Austrian regiments were dug in. They advanced no farther before Cadorna gave the official order to launch his great offensive. By June 20, the Italian Army was ready to cross the Isonzo in strength. Three weeks of preliminary fighting to better position the 2nd Army for its role in the coming offensive had yielded little. They demonstrated only that dislodging well entrenched Austrian units would be difficult and costly. Cadorna's forces admitted to losing 11,000 soldiers in this battle before the battle; the true figure was certainly far higher, perhaps twice as many. Austrian casualties, difficult to determine precisely, amounted to at least 5,000. A month after Italy's declaration of war, Cadorna was ready to start his long-awaited drive across the Isonzo.

On June 21 Cadorna finally issued the formal orders for the general advance toward Gorizia and Trieste, thus beginning the First Battle of the Isonzo. The month's delay in starting the offensive had given the Austrians vital time to reinforce the Isonzo line with men and entrenchments. Cadorna remained typically unconcerned. His main blow was to fall in the Gorizia sector, with major supporting attacks at Plava and on the Carso. He felt that Gorizia had to be secured before his forces could drive on Trieste. Frugoni's 2nd Army was thus assigned the decisive mission. The 2nd Army, totaling 160 infantry battalions supported by 136 artillery batteries, had been strongly reinforced for the offensive. The main effort was in the hands of the VI Corps, four divisions strong, which was ordered to seize the hills before Gorizia, secure the west bank, and then cross the river to take the city. The battered II Corps was to renew its attacks on Hill 383, secure the Plava bridgehead, then advance southeast toward Mt. Santo. In the upper Isonzo valley, the IV Corps, bolstered by numerous *Alpini* and *Bersaglieri* battalions, was ordered to seize the strategic Tolmein bridgehead. On the lower Isonzo, the Duke of Aosta's 3rd Army, sixty-five battalions and seventy-six batteries strong, was to support Frugoni's drive by occupying the western edge of the Carso, the Doberdò plateau. In particular, the 3rd Army was supposed to seize the plateau's northern edge, which overlooked Gorizia. Monte San Michele, 900 feet high, was the highest hill in the sector, and securing it was the task of the XI Corps. The neighboring X Corps, just arrived on the Isonzo, was ordered to occupy the center of the plateau's western edge. Farther down the river, on the Adriatic coast, the VII Corps was assigned the mission of seizing several hills on the plateau's southern flank. Cadorna kept the XIV Corps, two reinforced divisions, as a general reserve to exploit the success of the initial attacks. His plan was straightforward, slow, and methodical. He planned to crush the Austrian defenses with a massive weeklong artillery barrage before he launched the infantry offensive. Italian foot soldiers would then merely have to occupy the shattered Habsburg trenches.

The Austrian troops holding those trenches expected that the long-awaited major Italian effort would start any day. Despite their success holding off the Italians at Plava, there was little cause for optimism. On the eve of the First Battle of the Isonzo, the 5th Army possessed only one-third of the infantry battalions and three-fifths of the artillery batteries of Cadorna's forces arrayed against it. By the numbers, the situation was highly unfavorable, particularly considering the Austrians' chronic shortage of replacements. Cadorna could rebuild his depleted regiments after every failed assault, but Boroević had only a handful of replacement battalions at his disposal to replenish his units. There was virtually no heavy artillery available to support the infantry, and Boroević's shell reserve for all calibers was alarmingly low, far lower than Cadorna's. The 5th Army could not sustain a prolonged defense of the Isonzo line. The determination of the Austrian infantry holding the forward trenches would therefore be the decisive factor.

By late June the riflemen occupying the forward trenches were well entrenched and prepared for the coming Italian onslaught. They did not have enough machine guns and artillery to support them, to be sure, but their weapons were well positioned, and everywhere they held the high ground. Austrian positions literally looked down on the Italian avenues of advance. The troops were confident that they would exact a high price from the attackers. The vital Gorizia sector, the centerpiece of Boroević's defenses, was held by the 58th Infantry Division, another recent arrival from the Balkans. The 58th, raised only in March, was a mountain formation whose soldiers were almost all Dalmatians. The Croats and Serbs of the division were as determined to defend South Slav land as their kinsmen at Plava had been. Although the 58th was not particularly well equipped—half its artillery was obsolete, much of it quite antiquated—it had good leadership. Its two brigadiers were experienced leaders, and the divisional commander was an outstanding officer. Major General

Erwin Zeidler was not a typical Austrian general. He was not from a military family, and he was neither an infantryman nor a cavalryman, nor even a gunner. The fifty-year-old Zeidler had spent his career in the engineers, a studious branch that did not produce many generals. He enjoyed an excellent reputation as a thorough, efficient officer, and was decorated before the war for his excellent construction of fortifications in Bosnia and the Tyrol, experience that would prove invaluable on the Isonzo. Zeidler's first major troop command was in the Serbian campaign, where he led a Croatian division. In the spring of 1915, he was chosen to lead the newly raised 58th Division, and he led it to the Isonzo in late May, where it would remain for the next twenty-nine months and twelve battles.

The terrain of the 58th Division's seven-mile defensive sector extended from Mt. Santo to the Vipacco River. The all-important four-and-a-half-mile front on the Isonzo's west bank was more hilly than mountainous; it included two notable hills, Oslavia and Podgora; the town of Pevma; and, at its northern edge, Mt. Sabotino, the 2,010-foot "gate" of the Isonzo. All these features had to be held to ensure the integrity of the defensive line. Zeidler did everything he could to prepare his division for the coming battle. He persuaded Boroević to give him seven construction companies, more than 1,500 men, to help his troops dig positions. Although building materials were in short supply, the work crews made quick progress; the general personally oversaw the construction of the division's entrenchments. By late June, the 58th's trenches, covering all the hills and especially Mt. Sabotino, were between five and six feet deep, reinforced with wood, and protected by sandbags. Zeidler had replicated the Western front on the Isonzo. His infantry would be shielded from the worst effects of the imminent Italian bombardment.

The artillery of the 3rd Army opened fire in the early morning hours of June 23, and the guns of Frugoni's 2nd joined the bombardment in the afternoon. The major target areas were the Gorizia bridgehead, the Plava sector, and the western edge of the Doberdò plateau. The shelling was heavy but essentially random; Italian batteries were not firing at specific targets, but instead were wreaking general havoc on Austrian positions. The barrage continued steadily all day, tapering off in the evening. There were few infantry actions on the first day, only occasional Italian patrols advancing temporarily to observe the shelling. Austrian positions were hit hard by the bombardment on June 23, but the level of destruction was still relatively low. The next day's barrage was far heavier, however. One of the first areas to be struck was an Austrian observation post on Mt. Santo, overlooking Gorizia. At the summit of the 2,250-foot-high mountain was a medieval monastery. Mt. Santo—called Sveta Gora (Holy Mountain) by the Slovene natives—had been a pilgrimage site for five centuries, and the monastery dated to the 1540s. Sveta Gora was a Slovene national treasure, known for its late Gothic basilica and a portrait of the Virgin Mary that had rested there since 1544. On the morning of June 24, Italian shells exploded near the summit, throwing up fiery clouds of smoke around the basilica. There was barely enough time for the Franciscan brothers to escape down the mountain, taking their holy portrait with them. The Virgin's image was saved and moved to Ljubljana for the duration of the war. But shells ripped through the monastery, destroying the basilica, then the pilgrims' guest houses. By nightfall, Sveta Gora lay in ruins. For the Slovenes, the loss of the monastery was a national tragedy—further proof, if any were needed, that the invading Italians had to be resisted at any price. The poet Simon Gregorčič, a native of the Isonzo valley, expressed his people's sorrow in "Temple":

> A flock of pilgrims rushed to her,
> To seek the peace and comfort the world cannot give.
> But the church is no more!
> The walls, o cruel godless ones, they have been destroyed;
> No tower to see, no bells to hear,
> Neither hymns nor the voices of holy prayers.

The bombardment continued for five more days, sometimes through the night. Each day, more Austrian soldiers were killed or wounded, and their positions were gradually weakened. Movement to and from the front lines was dangerous, but the troops in well built trenches, notably Zeidler's Dalmatians, were reasonably safe. The infantry suffered from a lack of sleep and a shortage of food and supplies, but their positions were not yet in danger.

Cadorna ordered a series of attacks to precede the major push, scheduled for June 30. The Italians made halfhearted attempts to advance on the western edge of the Carso and before Gorizia, but their major effort, as before, was at Plava. The 33rd Division, replenished since the June 16–17 battle, was sent up Hill 383 again. A battalion of Novak's mountain troops still held the summit. On June 24, the 33rd sent its infantry up the north face of the hill eight times, but made no progress. Losses were very heavy, especially among the officers. The following day the II Corps renewed its attack, this time in the middle of a rainstorm, with even deadlier results. Soldiers of the 33rd Division retreated to their dugouts at the base of the hill. On June 26, the Italians attempted to take the summit again, but the exhausted assault regiments gained no ground in the face of concentrated machine gun fire. Hill 383 was still firmly in Austrian hands.

Cadorna's great offensive began in earnest on the morning of June 30. After seven days' artillery preparation, the 2nd and 3rd Armies launched their all-out assaults to breach the Isonzo line. Frugoni's troops started with an infantry attack on Zeidler's 58th Division by the four divisions of the VI Corps. The Dalmatians were tired from a lack of sleep, but their trenches were still intact after the week's shelling and their machine guns were targeted on Italian positions. When regiments emerged from their trenches and began to advance, their lead companies were cut down by torrents of fire from Austrian Schwarzlose machine guns. Italian attempts to take Mt. Sabotino and Podgora soon faltered bloodily and had to be suspended. The 2nd Army had no better fortune on the upper Isonzo. There the IV Corps attempted to take the town of Tolmein and cross the Isonzo to seize the town of St. Luzia, the Austrian railhead for the upper valley. The 7th Division advanced on Tolmein, but was painfully repulsed by Hungarian troops of the 50th Division. A few miles upstream, the 8th Division tried to take Mrzli vrh and expand eastward from its positions on Mt. Krn, but Croatian troops prevented the *Alpini* from breaking out of Krn's summit. Renewed Italian efforts were fought off with grenades and even stones. In all, the 8th Division managed to advance a thousand feet deeper into the high Julian Alps, but it took none of its assigned objectives. By July 4, the 2nd Army's drives were thoroughly halted, having made no notable progress.

The Duke of Aosta's 3rd Army had done somewhat better on the Carso. Repeated attacks by the X Corps on the western edge of the plateau around the town of Redipuglia, a mile east of the Isonzo, achieved minor gains. A two-division attack on July 2 at the town of Sagrado failed, but the defending 93rd Division was forced to yield 300 feet of the Carso at Redipuglia. The next day, the X and XI Corps attempted to push the 93rd even farther back at Redipuglia, to exploit the previous day's advance, but with terrible results. The Austrians surprised the Italians with a five-battalion counterattack that pushed the Italians off the Carso entirely. The disorderly retreat of the X and XI Corps was witnessed by King Vittorio Emanuele, who left his headquarters at Udine to see Cadorna's great battle for himself. He observed his troops' disaster through binoculars from a church tower in the town of Turriaco, three miles west of the Carso. The 3rd Army renewed its offensive on July 4, and the Italians fought their way 200 feet back onto the plateau at Redipuglia. At the plateau's northern edge, the 21st Division advanced up Mt. San Michele at 2 P.M. The Italians were pushed off the hill after a bruising two-hour melee that left both sides exhausted. By the evening of July 4, the tired 3rd Army was stalled on the edge of the Doberdò plateau.

Cadorna was furious with his subordinates. He never accepted less than success from those under him, and he failed to see why his armies had not yet pushed the Austrians out of Gorizia and the Carso. He of course did not travel to the front lines to discover why his carefully planned offensive had bogged down so disastrously. Instead, Cadorna strongly reproached Frugoni and his 2nd Army for their poor performance, claiming that their supporting attacks had been halfhearted. He demanded victory, and ordered both his armies to try again the following day. The exhausted Italian infantrymen, the carelessly used *fanti*, rested for the night. They would need all their strength to push the Austrians out of their trenches.

Boroević's foot soldiers were no less exhausted. Days of almost uninterrupted combat, particularly on the Carso, had left his regiments weak and weary. They had endured a week of shelling followed by a week of infantry assaults. They were tired, hungry, and thirsty—it was difficult to get supplies to the forward trenches in the midst of battle. But Boroević had no reserves left, and no replacements. The understrength battalions in the front line would have to hold out. Boroević was in his own way as obstinate as Cadorna. The commander of the 5th Army felt that not a single position should be surrendered without a fight to the finish, and that any lost trenches would have to be recaptured. Even the insignificant Italian gains at Redipuglia would have to be overturned. The distance to Trieste—less than twenty miles from the western edge of the Carso—was so short that every foot of the battlefield counted. Thus there would be no relief for the infantrymen facing the Italians.

July 5 was the high-water mark of the First Battle. Opposite Gorizia and on the Carso, Cadorna's divisions advanced recklessly on Austrian trench lines. The 2nd Army's VI Corps tried again to push Zeidler's Dalmatians off the Isonzo's hilly west bank. On the heels of a predawn barrage, four and a half divisions fixed bayonets and charged Austrian positions along the entire length of the 58th Division's four-and-a-half-mile front—two Italian infantrymen per foot. Italian officers urged their men forward in dense columns, sometimes at gunpoint. Outnumbered more than six to one, the Dalmatians fired their machine guns and rifles into the screaming waves of onrushing *fanti*. At such close ranges, Zeidler's gunners could not miss. The steady fire of the Austrian machine guns drowned out the cries of "*Avanti Savoia!*" and the screams of the dying and wounded. The mass attack crumbled before it reached the main Austrian positions at Mt. Sabotino, Podgora, and Oslavia. Inspired by their battle cry "*Napred! Na nož!*"[5] the Dalmatians counterattacked, pushing the Italians back to their own positions in disarray. Before they were forced to fall back, troops of the Rè and Casale Brigades got close enough to the river to catch a glimpse of Gorizia; they were the first Italian troops to see the City of Violets. This was as close as Cadorna's men came to taking Gorizia. Zeidler's determined regiments had held their ground. Their well built trenches were surrounded by mounds of Italian corpses. The 29th Division, attacking the southern end of the 58th's trenches, lost 4,000 dead and wounded. The Dalmatians' losses were by no means light. Most of the Austrian casualties were suffered by the 37th Rifle Regiment, which bore the brunt of the defense. Its 2nd Battalion lost over 500 men, two-thirds of its strength, on July 5. The Dalmatians had not lost a single position to the enemy.

The 3rd Army renewed its Carso offensive with vigor on July 5. At 8 A.M., the heavily reinforced X Corps tried to push the Austrians away from Redipuglia. They encountered not the expected 93rd Division, its recent nemesis, but Magyar infantry of the 17th *Honvéd* Regiment, a unit just arrived from the

Carpathians via Carinthia. The outnumbered Hungarians dueled with the Italians for Redipuglia through the day. Casualties on both sides were heavy, but by the evening the town of Redipuglia was again Austrian. Instead of breaking out of its foothold on the Carso, the X Corps had been evicted from its hard-won starting positions. Both the Italians and the Hungarians were utterly exhausted, and neither army attempted to renew the fighting the next morning. There were minor abortive Italian attacks before Gorizia and at Mt. Krn on July 6, but in general the Isonzo front remained quiet. July 7 was the first day of inactivity for either army in several weeks, and by the evening it was clear that the First Battle was at an end. Cadorna had suspended his offensive.

The Italians' "walk to Vienna" had ended in disaster. Cadorna's armies remained essentially where they had been when the battle started. His superiority in men and guns had availed him little. The Isonzo's outnumbered and outgunned defenders had stopped the 2nd and 3rd Armies in their tracks. The Austrian advantages of terrain and battle experience, combined with raw courage, had proved decisive. Cadorna's novice regiments had been brutally repulsed on the Isonzo. Cadorna, of course, did not accept any responsibility for the catastrophe, but the fault was mostly his. His blindness to the realities of the modern battlefield doomed his armies to fight with men against steel and fire. Enthusiasm and courage weighed little against well entrenched machine guns. Perhaps even more damaging was Cadorna's inexcusable monthlong delay before initiating his great offensive. This gave the Austrians four decisive weeks to transform their Isonzo line into an impressive fortification. As a result, after two weeks of shelling and attacking, the Italian Army had taken only two insignificant pieces of the Carso from the Austrians: a thin slice of the plateau near Sagrado, and two villages south of Redipuglia. Neither advance was more than a few hundred paces.

The price of this inconsequential territory was far too high. Neither army admitted the full extent of its losses—Cadorna in particular was regularly fraudulent in his accounting of his casualties—but the numbers of dead and wounded on both sides can be reliably estimated. The Italians admitted to 13,500 casualties, and the Austrians conceded a loss of 10,000. The true Austrian figure was probably at least twice the official count; certainly Italy's losses amounted to no less than 30,000. In any case, the cream of the 2nd and 3rd Armies, the trained officers and men of Cadorna's standing army, fell on the Isonzo in June and early July. For every one who died, another was put out of action permanently. The unexpected defeat also had a serious impact on Italian morale. Instead of marching on to Vienna, as everyone had confidently believed, by the end of the First Battle of the Isonzo it was evident that the Italians would be in the valley for some time to come, and that pushing the Austrians out of their positions would be very costly.

The Austrians naturally prided themselves on their success. Against expectations, the 5th Army had won its first battle. Even more remarkably, during the entire First Battle of the Isonzo it had not lost a single noteworthy position to the enemy. Boroević's unbending doctrine had prevailed. The Austrians fighting under Boroević had shown themselves to be determined and brave soldiers. They gave the hard-pressed empire a badly needed victory. Austria had enjoyed few battlefield successes in the war, and even defensive triumphs were important for morale. Still, the polyglot regiments of the 5th Army were tired, and there were few replacements available to refill the ranks of Boroević's depleted divisions. The occasional replacement battalion arriving on the Isonzo invariably included more teenagers, middle-aged fathers, and returning wounded than well trained, fit men. The lack of reserves was mourned by generals at all levels. Certainly the Italians' weakness offered a tempting target, but there were no spare divisions available. Defending the Isonzo had stretched the army to its limits. Conrad said ruefully as the First Battle came to a close, "If only we had four divisions for a counterattack, the hounds would run to the Tagliamento River," thirty miles west of the Isonzo. Cadorna's wounded armies were unquestionably unprepared for defense, but weakened Austria could as yet offer no offensive threat. Besides, the 5th Army was busy enough preparing for the next Italian offensive, which was sure to come.

FOUR

THE BATTLE OF MONTE SAN MICHELE

The Italian Army was surprised by the failure of Luigi Cadorna's offensive, and shocked by the losses inflicted by the outnumbered Austrians. For the soldiers at the front, the disappointment soon led to disillusionment. Morale remained high in many units, especially those not yet committed to battle, but in the bloodied regiments of the 2nd and 3rd Armies the expectation of a quick victory had evaporated. Politicians in Rome might still speak of resuming the "walk to Vienna," but the riflemen in the line knew better. The *fanti* holding the forward trenches all along the Isonzo had only more grueling attacks to look forward to. They had learned at a terrible cost that the Austrians were not going to be easy to defeat. The peasants who filled the ranks of Cadorna's legions were tough, hardy soldiers, men accustomed to a harsh, demanding life. Yet the prospect of more offensives worried even the most stoic Italian infantry. The conditions of service in the Italian Army were poor: abysmally low pay, inadequate rations, and few diversions for troops when not in the line. The demanding life of the divisions on the Isonzo took its toll on the soldiers' morale, and destroyed any naive enthusiasm. The blistering midsummer heat wore further on the soldiers' fighting spirit. Still, Cadorna's armies remained steadfastly loyal and willing to carry out the orders of the chief of staff.

In the two weeks after the First Battle died away, the frontline regiments were busy absorbing replacements, improving their positions, and readying for the inevitable second offensive. Italy still had enormous manpower reserves, so there was no difficulty rebuilding shattered regiments. The army called up a few more classes of reservists, and Cadorna's armies were again up to strength.

Units absorbed reservists, as well as a smattering of teenaged volunteers and lightly wounded soldiers returning to the front. Hundreds of freshly commissioned lieutenants arrived to take the places of those already fallen on the Isonzo. The regiments rested during the day, when possible, and worked at night to build better entrenchments, to provide more protection against the occasional Austrian shell. Otherwise the infantry waited anxiously for the order to go on the offensive again.

Cadorna did not give his soldiers long to wait. He was anxious to achieve the breakthrough that had eluded him. He gave little thought to the condition of his armies or to the morale of his fighting men. Cadorna remained uninterested in how his regiments were faring; like too many Italian officers, his attitude toward the mostly peasant *fanti* was dismissive. He showed little concern for his soldiers' living conditions, rations, or water supply even in the scorching summer heat. He never visited the front lines to see how his armies were holding up under the strains of war. To Cadorna, the Italian infantry existed only to win his great battle. The soldiers' suffering, though perhaps regrettable, was the natural by-product of war. He had no desire to see it for himself.

Keeping the army motivated to fight and conquer was always a major concern for Cadorna. He believed at the outset that Italy was "morally unprepared for war"; like many Italians—and not just generals and conservatives—Cadorna felt that chronic indiscipline was the "old evil" of the Italian race.[1] For Cadorna, the indomitable individualism of the Italian spirit—to him, slackness and weakness—was as much the enemy as the Austrians were; ordinary methods of maintaining morale would not work. Therefore the fighting spirit needed to achieve victory was instilled through fear, as in the eighteenth century, when infantrymen advanced because they were more afraid of their own officers than of the enemy. Cadorna was never squeamish about stern disciplinary measures, even terror. Indeed, he considered them vitally necessary to win his war. He spoke forthrightly about "the usual discipline of persuasion which is needed in Italy," and he meant what he said. As the count explained to a journalist, "The country was undisciplined, and so was the army; we have taken care of the problem by the usual and proper means, the shooting of the insubordinates to prevent the sparks from turning into a fire." Units that failed to advance far enough were dealt with harshly; for soldiers showing insufficient courage, there was always the firing squad.

The High Command was hardly more lenient with officers who failed to meet Cadorna's exacting standards. He relentlessly dismissed commanders whose units had not advanced as far as he considered necessary. In the face of Austrian machine guns, moving units forward was often impossible at any cost, but Cadorna remained uninterested in tactical realities. He was concerned only with battlefield success. His *siluramento* (torpedoing) of subordinates began just after the end of the First Battle. He abruptly fired commanders of battalions, regiments, divisions, even army corps. The discarded career officers were sent to the rear to sit out the fighting. In the first two months of the war, Cadorna dismissed twenty-seven generals, as well as uncounted more junior officers, and the torpedoing continued unabated for the next twenty-seven months.

Cadorna was accountable to no one, not even to the king. Vittorio Emanuele inevitably deferred to his chief of staff's presumably superior judgment in military matters, and never dared to challenge his orders. Cadorna tolerated no dissent among his staff, and was rigidly closed to any suggestions. A drive across the Isonzo remained the only course of action, despite the catastrophic failure of the First Battle. Certainly he dismissed the politicians out of hand. Cadorna was inflexibly hostile to all politicians, regardless of political stripe. He was especially contemptuous of Socialists and others on the Left whom Cadorna regarded as traitors, but he basically hated the entire political class. In Cadorna's thinking, Rome was at least as much the enemy as Vienna, and he paid no attention to the numerous questions raised by politicians about his strategy and tactics. Once, before a visiting Frenchman, Cadorna ripped up a note from Prime Minister Antonio Salandra to demonstrate his contempt for politicians. The only voice that Cadorna listened to was God's. A devout Catholic, he attended Mass daily, and his personal chaplain never left his side. To Cadorna, the road to victory led through the Isonzo valley as surely as the way of Christ led to the cross. His faith in another offensive appeared as unshakable as his faith in the Holy Trinity.

This irrational belief ignored the obvious and growing strength of the Austrian defenses on the Isonzo. Yet Cadorna continued to maintain that more determined attacks would crack the Austrian line. With more valorous assaults supported by more artillery, the road to Trieste would be forced open. He was ready to renew his offensive on July 18, only eleven days after the end of the First Battle. This time, the brunt of the push would be borne by the 3rd Army. Cadorna had decided that before he could conquer Gorizia, the north edge of the Carso, particularly Mt. San Michele, would have to be taken first. Only then could the 2nd Army successfully restart its drive on Gorizia. To achieve this, the Duke of Aosta was given all available reserves of men and munitions. His 3rd Army, seven divisions strong, was to clear the western edge of the Doberdò plateau of Austrian troops. The main effort was in the hands of the XI Corps, whose three divisions were aimed at Mt. San Michele. Further down the Isonzo, the the VII Corps was to advance past Redipuglia and take Hill 118, Mt. Sei Busi, which overlooked the south-central Carso and the river as it neared the Adriatic. Between the two attacking army corps, X Corps was to make supporting attacks. The Duke of Aosta had a considerable reserve of two infantry and three cavalry divisions at his disposal to reinforce his success on the plateau. General Pietro Frugoni's 2nd Army was relegated to a secondary, supporting role in the Second Battle. The three divisions of the VI Corps were to attack

Austrian positions before Gorizia, the II Corps was to assault the Isonzo line at Plava, and the IV Corps was to renew its efforts on the upper Isonzo. Cadorna had eighteen divisions and 900 guns to break through the Austrian defenses. He expected that heavy shelling, to begin July 18, would so weaken Boroević's defenses on the Carso that the 3rd Army would be able to achieve the strategic victory he had been denied in June and early July.

The Austrian infantry manning the Isonzo defenses knew another offensive was coming. There were signs of enemy movement everywhere, and Italy was surely not going to abandon its attempt to seize *Italia irredenta* after a single failed effort, no matter how costly. So the soldiers in the front lines rested when they could, and spent most of their time improving their trenches. Italian artillery had caused most of the Austrian casualties in the First Battle, and Cadorna was sure to have more, not fewer, guns for his next try. Everywhere Austrian infantrymen, assisted by sappers, worked frantically to deepen, widen, and strengthen their positions. On the Carso, this was especially difficult because the limestone proved a formidable obstacle to digging deeper trenches. The ideal defense against Italian artillery was the *kaverne*, a position blasted ten to fifteen feet into the rock, which was invulnerable to direct hits from even the heaviest shells, none of which could penetrate more than five feet of limestone. Considerable quantities of explosives, building materials, and man-hours were required to construct *kavernen*, including prolonged work by hard-pressed engineering detachments, in addition to intensive labor by the infantry, who did much of the digging and preparation. Thus, despite heroic building efforts, by July 18 there were insufficient *kavernen* even for troops in forward positions. Most Austrian frontline defenses on the Doberdò plateau were simply normal trenches hacked into the stone, reinforced by many sandbags, occasionally protected by steel shields, and surrounded by barbed wire and "Spanish riders."[2] In addition to command emplacements and communication and supply trenches, the trench system included secondary trenches and foxholes immediately behind the front line for infantry reserves, held back to provide badly needed reinforcements at decisive moments to turn back Italian assaults.

The overworked Austrian engineers were equally invaluable for other important tasks. Among these was the impressive civil engineering effort required to keep the troops on the Carso supplied with fresh water. There was little fresh water available on the plateau, and though soldiers went to great lengths to collect rain water, virtually all the water required by frontline infantry had to be piped to them. Nor could the almost barren plateau provide the troops with the considerable quantity of wood required for the construction of sturdy positions, not to mention for cooking and heating, so the engineers also had to keep the fighting units supplied with freshly cut timber. Additionally, the rough terrain and shortage of decent roads made resupply difficult; and, in the opposite direction, casualty evacuation was a prolonged, complicated process frequently involving airborne stretchers, propelled by ropes and pulleys. So the engineers were busy building more roads, too. The almost two-week pause between Italian offensives was used to good effect by Austrian infantry and engineers, but would their defensive preparations prove sufficient to keep the Italians at bay?

The morale of the defending Austrians remained high, despite the heavy casualties incurred during the First Battle. Battalions holding the Isonzo line absorbed what replacements were available, and prepared themselves for the next enemy onslaught. The infantrymen remained convinced of the justice of their cause, and the German-Austrians and South Slavs in particular were steadfastly determined to repulse the coming Italian offensive. Their fighting spirit flourished, undulled by the losses of the recent battle. The riflemen holding the trenches just opposite the Italians, in many cases less than a hundred paces away, knew the odds were against them. Yet they were ready to resist the Italians with all their strength. The mostly peasant infantry's will to fight was bolstered by religious faith and devotion to the emperor. The war against Italy was not just an ethnic war but a religious war, too, even though both armies were overwhelmingly Catholic. For the 5th Army's Catholic soldiers—the vast majority of Boroević's troops—Italians were not just faithless allies and perhaps ethnic foes, but also the jailers of the pope.[3] Troops in the front line, convinced of the righteousness of their cause, commonly wore religious medals on their breasts, and many had crosses sewn into their caps; others carried portraits of Franz Joseph. The Austrian infantrymen were ready to fight and die for God, emperor, and country, as their oath required them to do.

The defensive system devised by Boroević and his staff took advantage of the infantry's stubborn determination to resist the Italians. The idea was basic: no matter how many shells or men the Italians could throw at the Isonzo line, the trenches had to be held at all cost. There was no room to retreat. The essence of Boroević's scheme—"better a wiped-out battalion than a regiment shattered in a counterattack"—was simple and deadly. It meant that units were to be kept in forward positions, without relief, until overwhelmed. Any losses of territory, no matter how minor or inconsequential, had to be redeemed through counterattacks. Cadorna's armies could not be permitted to advance any closer to Trieste than they already were. Boroević's defensive plan was, a survivor later recalled, "a frightful, mathematically precise system, a mill that had to grind economically so as not to languish idle. But woe to the battalion caught between the stones." The defense was based on the assumption that in any assault the Italians would run out of men before the Austrians did.

This assumption was mostly accurate, and the concept had proved effective in the First Battle. Even so, Boroević's tactics were crude and costly, and received much criticism. Boroević—Bosco to his troops and critics alike—was not his army's chief of staff like Cadorna, and had to contend with questions from rival officers and senior generals. The commander of the 5th Army was not much more open to criticism than Cadorna, however, and sometimes showed a similar alarming lack of interest in his soldiers. Confronted by queries about the high casualties his army suffered in the First Battle, Boroević replied laconically that his losses in the Carpathians were worse. Like Cadorna, Boroević refused to visit the front line; his defenders explained that the general could not possibly continue to employ such costly—but necessary—tactics if he saw their results on the infantry with his own eyes. Boroević's many detractors were not as forgiving. Colonel Franz Schneller, head of the Italian intelligence section at the High Command, considered "this army-wrecker" incompetent, and was adamant that his methods were ruining the 5th Army. He informed Franz Conrad von Hötzendorf bluntly, "Bosco has got to go." Boroević made the situation worse by arguing incessantly with rival generals. He particularly detested Lieutenant General Alfred Krauss, chief of staff of the Southwestern front. The fifty-three-year-old Krauss, perhaps the Austrian Army's finest tactician, was contemptuous of Boroević and his crude defensive methods. Boroević returned Krauss's hostility with venomous personal attacks, ridiculing Krauss's "Kaiser mustache" and calling his demeanor "that of a trained poodle." Field Marshal Archduke Friedrich, titular army chief, eventually intervened to make the two rivals overcome their mutual antipathy and work together. Conrad nevertheless continued to support Boroević, although he shared some of the widespread doubts about his methods. In the final analysis, Boroević was the best general to lead a steadfast, unbending defense of the Isonzo line, no matter the cost, and that was what ultimately mattered to the High Command.

On the eve of the Second Battle of the Isonzo, the 5th Army had reached a strength of nine divisions with 103,000 riflemen and 431 guns, about half the size of the forces Cadorna was about to send against it. This considerable increase in men and artillery over the previous battle was attributable mostly to the arrival of the VII Corps from the Carpathians. The Hungarian corps reached the Isonzo at the end of the First Battle, too late to see significant action. Its two divisions, the 17th Infantry and 20th *Honvéd*, were seasoned veterans of the terrible fighting in Galicia and the Carpathians. Its commanding general, Archduke Joseph von Habsburg, was likewise experienced in modern warfare. The forty-three-year-old general had spent most of his life in the army, and received the accelerated promotion enjoyed by all Habsburg archdukes in military service. Yet Joseph was a competent commander, having led the VII Corps on the Eastern front since November 1914. He was also a devoted native-born Hungarian nationalist. Atypically for a member of the House of Habsburg, Joseph was a Magyar chauvinist who regularly espoused the martial virtues of the Magyars. Although this was doubtless offensive to other generals and nationalities, and perhaps even to the emperor himself, the mostly Magyar soldiers of the VII Corps loved their general for it. Just days before Cadorna's offensive started, the VII Corps entered the front line, its two divisions freshly filled with replacements. Archduke Joseph's corps was assigned the all-important defense of the Carso, leaving the XVI Corps to concentrate on the defense of Gorizia and the Bainsizza plateau. The Hungarians assumed their place in the Isonzo line, particularly on Mt. San Michele and Mt. Sei Busi, crisscrossed with freshly dug entrenchments. The 17th and 20th Divisions prepared for combat and waited in their unfamiliar trenches for the shelling to begin. The Second Battle of the Isonzo was to be their fight.

The Italian preparatory barrage began at 4 A.M. on July 18, shattering the pre-dawn stillness with a hail of fire. The shelling engulfed the entire western edge of the Carso, but, as expected, was particularly heavy in the Mt. San Michele and Mt. Sei Busi sectors. Cadorna's artillery, including all the guns of the 3rd Army and the southern end of the 2nd Army, was more accurate than in the First Battle. This time, the guns were aimed at specific targets, rather than firing blindly at the Austrian lines. The intensity of the shelling increased through the morning; it was worse than anything the Hungarians had endured on the Eastern front. The troops of the VII Corps holding the forward trenches on the plateau were soon blinded by clouds of smoke and dust. Heavy shelling destroyed many positions, killing or wounding all occupants; one regiment recorded "the gigantic, hard-pounding hammering of thousands of shells, which no words on God's earth can express." Dazed survivors struggled to find safer trenches as the earth shook around them. The Hungarian soldiers holding Mt. San Michele were hit especially hard. The mountain absorbed more than 2,500 heavy shells that morning; numerous defenders were literally blown to pieces, and many carefully constructed trenches and dugouts were reduced to rubble. One doomed young lieutenant of the 46th Infantry Regiment, holding part of the San Michele sector, recorded in his diary

July 18th. The artillery fire became terrible in the night. It's coming to an end, I think, and I am preparing myself to die bravely as a Christian. It's all over. An unprecedented slaughter. A horrifying bloodbath. Blood flows everywhere, and the dead and pieces of corpses lie in circles, so that

There the subaltern's diary ended; it was found near the body of its author. Casualties among the defenders were severe. The brittle limestone of the Carso made it worse. Every exploding shell propelled hundreds of lethal, razor-sharp rock fragments in all directions. The rock claimed as many Austrian soldiers as the shrapnel did. The number of often fatal head wounds was very high because there were no steel helmets. Worse, the evacuation of the wounded was impossible during the barrage. The Austrian defenders who managed to survive the initial bombardment were stunned by its severity, which far surpassed anything experienced in the First Battle.

At 11 A.M. the shelling ceased on the middle sector of the plateau, and the 14th Division fixed bayonets, went over the top, and charged the Austrian defenses on Hill 118, Mt. Sei Busi. The Italians reached the shell-scarred Austrian trenches, and bitter bayonet and hand-to-hand fighting ensued. At 1 P.M. the shelling on the northern edge of the Carso died away. Soon two divisions of the XI Corps left their trenches and assaulted the Austrian defenses in the Mt. San Michele sector. An hour later, the last Italian batteries fell silent, and the 20th Division attacked Austrian positions around Redipuglia. Everywhere the survivors of the morning's bombardment emerged from their entrenchments to meet the Italian advance. The Hungarian troops of the VII Corps had been ordered to defend every foot of the Carso with all their strength—to the last man, if necessary. The battered *Honvéd* regiments of the 20th Division bore the brunt of the first day's fighting. Their depleted companies held off the Italian onslaught. The Italian artillery performed better than in the last battle, but Cadorna's infantry tactics remained primitive, with lethal effects for his advancing foot soldiers. As in the First Battle, Italian regiments went forward in dense columns, "nearly disorganized crowds," led by officers carrying swords and standard-bearers armed only with large flags. Italian artillery was almost useless during the infantry assault. The Italian guns gave little fire support to the advancing infantry during the all-important last phase of the attack; indeed, communication between the riflemen and gunners was so poor that Italian batteries often inflicted more casualties on their own men than on the Austrian defenders. The tightly packed battalions approaching Austrian positions were cut down in waves by well entrenched machine guns that had survived the preparatory barrage. A single properly placed machine gun was able to hold up a whole regiment and inflict crippling losses on exposed infantry. The Italians fought bravely when they got to the Austrian lines, but too few *fanti* survived long enough to reach them.

Italian progress on July 18 was therefore slight, despite the 3rd Army's courageous efforts, limited to minor gains on the western edge of the Carso. The next day was more productive for the attackers, however. Cadorna vigorously renewed his offensive on July 19. The Duke of Aosta's divisions attacked the Austrian line again, this time with more success. The fighting was particularly heavy around Hill 143, two and a half miles southwest of Mt. San Michele. The weary 20th *Honvéd* Division tried to hold its ground, but was pushed back after hours of vicious melées and heavy shelling. The Hungarians retreated several hundred feet to the east by nightfall, relinquishing Hill 143 to the Italians. Typically, the Italian artillery, not the infantry, had been the decisive factor. The rifle company of the 61st Regiment holding the peak of Hill 143, bloodily repulsed repeated Italian mass infantry assaults with ease. But after several hours of shelling, the hundred survivors of the surrounded company had no ammunition left, and could not be resupplied, so they decided to surrender. Elements of the 17th Division were rushed into the line to halt the Italian advance. The division's commander, Lieutenant General Karl Gelb, was a native of Gorizia, and was determined not to let his home fall into Italian hands. He made sure his troops held their new defensive positions that night, so as not to endanger the Austrian stand on Mt. San Michele, the key to the defense of the northern Carso and Gorizia. The 17th prevented the tired attackers from advancing further. By the evening of July 19, the VII Corps was still maintaining a coherent defense, but it was badly strained. It had lost 5,500 men in two days' fighting, most of them in the shattered 20th Division. The *Honvéd* division entered the battle with 6,000 riflemen; less than forty-eight hours later it had only 2,000 left.

Even with the support of the 17th Division, the drained 20th Division could not keep the Italians at bay. The threat of another push by the 3rd Army to take Mt. San Michele compelled Archduke Joseph to order a counterattack to regain Hill 143 and force the Italians away from San Michele. Boroević, true to form, would not tolerate the loss of Mt. San Michele, and was anxious to regain the lost hill. The Duke of Aosta, however, was planning his own attack for the following morning in the same area. He ordered his X and XI Corps to break through the disorganized Austrian defenses and seize San Michele before noon on July 20. The guns of the 3rd Army readied to fire a five-hour preparatory barrage in the San Michele sector to clear the way for the infantry.

In the early hours of July 20, several battalions of the 17th Division, reinforced by the remnants of the 20th *Honvéd* Division, left their trenches and charged the Italian positions just west of Mt. San Michele. The ill-fated Habsburg infantry walked into the preplanned Italian bombardment, suffering catastrophic losses; the dazed survivors struggled back to their own lines. The Croatian 96th Infantry Regiment, one of the lead elements in the attack, lost more than 600 men to the 3rd Army's guns. At that moment the Italian infantry attacked. The frontline units of the VII Corps, confused by the failed attempt to recover Hill 143, were soon overwhelmed by the aggressive Italian advance. The Italian guns kept constant pressure on the Austrians, making the supply of reserves and munitions all but impossible. In the early afternoon the fighting reached the slopes of Mt. San Michele. The mountain, blanketed by thick clouds of smoke, saw dozens of vicious engagements between Italian and Austrian troops. The battle was disorganized, more a series of close encounters between small units of attackers and defenders than a coherent struggle. The *fanti*, encouraged by their progress, fought with great courage, and the beleaguered Hungarians of the VII Corps resisted with unexampled passion. By 5:30 P.M., troops of the Italian XI Corps had secured the flat upper part of Mt. San Michele, and the Austrians were pushed 300 feet to the southeast. The summit had fallen to the 3rd Army. The Duke of Aosta's infantry had a clear view of Gorizia, five miles to the northeast.

The fall of Mt. San Michele was by far the worst news yet to arrive at 5th Army headquarters. It was the first serious Austrian setback in the Isonzo fighting. Predictably, Boroević, under pressure from the High Command not to lose any positions, was adamant that San Michele must be retaken before dawn on

July 21. However, he had no fresh troops at his disposal; all his units were engaged in combat and could not be sent to the Doberdò plateau. The only reserves available on the entire Southwestern front were two regiments of crack Tyrolean mountain troops, ideal forces for the counterattack, but they were in the Tyrol, two days by train from where they were needed on the Carso. So Boroević decided that the counterstroke would have to be made with the tired and depleted regiments of the VII Corps. He commanded Major General Boog to launch all available battalions against the Italians on the summit before dawn.

Boog collected fifteen battalions from four different formations, a jumble of mostly weary units from all corners of the Habsburg Empire. The most important mission, the recapture of the summit, was given to the 12th Mountain Brigade, which was still relatively fresh. Its five battalions had not yet fought on the Carso, and had so far sat out most of the Second Battle. The lead unit chosen for the attack was the 3rd Battalion of the 2nd Bosnian Regiment. The Austrian Army's four regiments of Bosnian troops were among the empire's youngest, raised in 1894 in the Balkan provinces of Bosnia and Hercegovina, occupied by Vienna since 1878. Yet the novice regiments of Bosnian Serbs, Muslims, and Croats soon developed a reputation for martial prowess. The four regiments of *Bosniaken* proved to be among the toughest Austria produced; they were certainly the most feared by the Italians. The Bosnians were excellent close-in fighters, especially at night. They were aggressive, even brutal, in the attack, liking to close with the enemy to kill with knives and bayonets. Thoughts of fez-wearing, knife-wielding Bosnians gave even battle-hardened *fanti* the shivers.

Fearing that Boroević would attempt his usual counterattack, on the evening of July 20 Cadorna gave the Duke of Aosta his last reserves, the two-division-strong XIV Corps. During the night the fresh troops were moved toward the San Michele sector to repulse any Austrian attempt to retake the mountain. While the Italians were organizing their defenses, the VII Corps was busy preparing its gunners and riflemen for the night attack. The counterattack was supported by every available Austrian gun on the Carso. At 2 A.M. on July 21 the barrage opened up, showering the peak of San Michele with fire. An hour later the 12th Mountain Brigade left its positions and marched on the summit of Mt. San Michele. Major Nikolaus Ružčić led his *Bosniaken* forward, with two companies in the lead and two supporting companies behind. The Bosnians of the 9th and 10th Companies emerged from the darkness and soon reached the Italian trenches, yelling their battle cry, "*Živio Austrija!*"[4] as the terrified defenders attempted to resist. The screaming *Bosniaken*, knives and battle clubs at the ready, jumped into the Italian trenches and overwhelmed the startled *fanti*. The bloody melée continued for more than an hour, and by 5 A.M., after much costly hand-to-hand fighting, the summit of Mt. San Michele was again in Austrian hands.

The general counterattack started at 4 A.M., when the other ten Austrian battalions assaulted the San Michele sector. As at the summit, tired and surprised
Italian defenders retreated before the VII Corps. By 9 A.M., the entire sector had
fallen to Major General Boog's attack, and the Italians were still withdrawing.
The reserve 30th Division of the XIV Corps was thrown into the fight to keep
the Austrians at bay, but to no avail. The 3rd Army's formations on the north
Carso were in disarray. The only reason the Italians were not pushed completely back to the Isonzo was that the Austrians had no reserves left. Boog's
battalions were tired by midmorning and needed a rest. As had happened in the
First Battle, only Austrian weakness staved off a complete Italian catastrophe.

Both sides exhausted themselves that morning, so the afternoon and evening
of July 21 were relatively quiet on the northern edge of the plateau. On the
Carso's southern flank, the Italian VII Corps renewed its attacks around Selz
and Vermegliano, but made no progress. Boroević was pleased with Boog's
counterstroke, but he still wanted to regain all ground lost to the Italians, including Hill 143. On the morning of July 22, the VII Corps tried to push the Italians
farther back. The battered survivors of the 20th Division, hungry, thirsty, and
totally exhausted, went over the top and advanced on Italian positions around
Hill 143, but this time the Italians were ready. The attack was a fiasco. Only
1,200 *Honvéd* riflemen returned. The Carso's defenders were at the end of their
strength. Constant Italian shelling made reinforcement and resupply impossible; the wounded could not be evacuated, and there was no fresh food or water.
The infantry simply waited in their dugouts for the bombardment to stop. Fortunately for the Austrians, the 3rd Army was equally exhausted. On July 23, after
five days of almost constant fighting, the guns fell silent in the San Michele sector. On the southern edge of the Carso, the Italian VII Corps again attempted on
July 23 and 24 to advance in the Selz-Vermegliano area. This won little except
heavy losses for both sides; the Austrian VII Corps suffered nearly 3,000 casualties, and the attacking Italian VII Corps certainly lost far more. On the evening of July 24, the Duke of Aosta ordered his divisions to temporarily cease
their attempts to advance on the Carso. Since July 18, Archduke Joseph's VII
Corps had lost 25,000 soldiers dead and wounded, more riflemen than it had
brought to the Isonzo from the Carpathians. Still, their sacrifices prevented an
Italian breakthrough on the Doberdò plateau.

The Hungarians were not the only Habsburg troops to sustain losses in the
battle's first phase. Frugoni's 2nd Army had been busy supporting the 3rd
Army on the Carso. On July 19, the II Corps, now known as the Plava Corps, assaulted its old nemesis, Hill 383. Yet again, the defending 1st Mountain Brigade held onto its positions at the summit of 383, and the attacking 3rd and 33rd
Divisions were pushed back with heavy losses. Farther down the Isonzo on the
same day, the VI Corps tried to dislodge Erwin Zeidler's 58th Division from its
trenches around Podgora and Mt. Sabotino. The 4 P.M. advance by three divi-

sions ended in disaster, as all the previous attempts had. The Dalmatians successfully defended their line, and the Italians failed to make progress anywhere.

During the morning of the following day, July 20, the VI Corps made minor probing attacks on the 58th's positions to determine their precise strength. This was followed in the early afternoon by a full-fledged corps attack. This Italian offensive, like all the others, was slow and methodical. Artillery plastered the Austrian trenches, and the infantry soon charged in waves. The 4th Division advanced up Mt. Sabotino while the 11th, 12th, and 29th Divisions assaulted Podgora hill. The Dalmatians' machine guns carried the day, as usual, ripping terrible swaths through the dense columns of *fanti*, and by the early evening the Italian effort had faltered. The 58th Division had again prevented the VI Corps from reaching the Isonzo. The Italians advanced anywhere from a few dozen to a few hundred paces, but they managed to take only one small forward observation post from the Austrians, a minor accomplishment. Otherwise the 58th Division's defenses were intact. That night Zeidler's headquarters reported to Boroević that the Dalmatians' entrenchments were surrounded by "mountains of corpses."

Undaunted, the VI Corps repeated its futile attacks on July 21 and 22. The 4th Division made three more doomed charges up the west slope of Mt. Sabotino, and the 11th, 12th, and 29th Divisions launched more heroic and useless attacks up Podgora hill. Again pure courage and fighting spirit failed miserably to overcome concentrated machine gun fire. On July 23, the 58th Division launched a local counterattack that cleared Podgora hill of any Italian infantry. The minor Italian gains of July 19–22 were thereby erased. Italian official sources claim that the VI Corps lost 3,390 soldiers in its five-day offensive, but the true total must have been far higher. The 2nd Army's attempt to advance toward Gorizia to support the 3rd Army ended, like all previous attempts, in utter failure. The last VI Corps action in the first phase of the battle was the inexplicable shelling of Gorizia itself. Italian policy effectively forbade the bombardment of Gorizia, as well as Trieste and other majority-Italian cities and towns in the Littoral—after all, why should the Italian Army attack fellow Italians, those whom it was trying to liberate? But on July 24, the VI Corps artillery dropped incendiary shells on the city, causing fires and killing civilians. The shelling, almost certainly a mistake, has never been satisfactorily explained.

In retrospect, the 2nd Army's attempt to advance in the upper Isonzo valley seems hardly more explicable. As in the May and June fighting, the Austrians, though spread thinly, held strong positions in the dauntingly high Julian Alps. The difficulty of advancing against well entrenched units was compounded by the treacherous terrain. Nevertheless, the IV Corps tried again to push units of the defending XV Corps off Mrzli ridge. The 8th Division's objective was Mrzli vrh itself; the *Bersaglieri* Division, reinforced by elements of the 7th Division, planned to attack from Vrata and Vršič to the north; and two brigades of

Alpini intended to push northeastward from Mt. Krn. On the heels of a heavy preparatory artillery barrage, the *Alpini* began their advance from Krn at 5 A.M. on July 19. One brigade assaulted troops of the 3rd Mountain Brigade holding neighboring Hill 2163 (6,790 ft.), while the other attacked units of the 1st Mountain Rifle Regiment on Hill 2041 (6,720 ft.). The skilled Italian mountain troops advanced bravely, but were beaten back by machine gun fire and a vigorous counterattack by the 3rd Mountain Brigade. The 8th Division's attempt to advance up Mrzli vrh—literally "the cold peak" in Slovene, an accurate name, even in July—and the *Bersaglieri* Division's drive to the north likewise stalled in the face of Austrian firepower. Undeterred by their initial setbacks, the *Alpini* resumed their offensive on July 21 with attacks on Hill 2163 and Hill 1931 (6,350 ft.). Artillery support kept the defenders' heads down, giving the *Alpini* time to reach the Austrian trenches. Intense close combat ensued in an area measuring only 800 feet by 200 feet, resulting in heavy casualties for both sides. The 3rd Mountain Brigade, weakened by the loss of 1,300 dead and wounded in two days, was forced to withdraw from Hill 2163 to another peak, 800 feet to the east. The rest of the Austrian line was intact, however, and the *Alpini* were too exhausted to push the retreating 3rd Brigade farther east.

On the evening of July 22, the Italian mountain troops moved into position to deliver a decisive blow to the depleted 3rd Mountain Brigade. At midnight the *Alpini* launched their surprise attack, which quickly became a confused melee in the dark. The close combat continued through the night, but at dawn the Austrians still held their trenches. The Italians made several smaller efforts over the next two days to force the Austrians to retreat deeper into the Julian Alps, but the defenders would not budge. The brave *Alpini* had proved their courage, and had won another hill in the Mrzli chain, but the IV Corps had otherwise failed to endanger the Austrian hold on the upper Isonzo. The conquest of one peak among hundreds meant little, and the Austrians simply reestablished a secure defensive line a few hundred feet to the east. As in so much of the Isonzo fighting, the minimal Italian gain was certainly not worth the uncounted cost.

To Cadorna, however, the situation looked quite different. The losses his forces had inflicted on the defending 5th Army would prove decisive, he believed; the week of relentless artillery bombardments and infantry assaults had weakened Boroević's divisions to the breaking point. He remained confident that the Second Battle would end with a breakthrough on the Carso. On July 24 Cadorna therefore ordered the Duke of Aosta to renew his offensive with full force, and to take the Doberdò plateau—"at any price," if necessary. The 3rd Army would continue to throw all available shells and men at the Austrian positions on the Carso.

To achieve the long-awaited breakthrough, Cadorna gave the Duke of Aosta the last reserves in the entire Italian Army, the two fresh divisions of the XIII Corps. The attack was scheduled to begin on the evening of July 24, but problems with the 27th Division delayed it until the following morning. At 9:30 A.M. on July 25, the 3rd Army's infantry left its trenches yet again, headed for the Austrian lines. The XI Corps went forward in the San Michele sector, and the VII assaulted on the plateau's southern end, both after two hours' artillery preparation.

Archduke Joseph's VII Corps had no reserves left. The Hungarian soldiers were weak and tired, as Cadorna had anticipated, but they were not yet ready to give up the fight. As in the first phase of the battle, overworked Schwarzlose machine guns claimed huge numbers of Italian attackers, but this time more *fanti* reached the Austrian trenches. The artillery had done its work, wiping out many VII Corps weapon emplacements, destroying machine guns. In several places, the Duke of Aosta's battalions got close enough to use cold steel. The fighting was predictably bitter in the San Michele sector. There, three Italian divisions, reinforced by battalions of *Bersaglieri*, attacked Mt. San Michele from the northwest. The defending Hungarians countered with accurate rifle fire and, when the two sides met, with bayonets and knives. The hand-to-hand fight for the summit was nightmarishly intense. Losses on both sides were heavy. The major general commanding the lead Italian brigade fell at the head of his troops, as did numerous other Italian regimental and battalion commanders, slowing down the pace of the attack. Leaderless Italian infantry fought on regardless well into the night. By 10 P.M., their sacrifices paid off: the summit was again in Italian hands.

As before, the 12th Mountain Brigade was called upon to push the Italians off Mt. San Michele. The brigade attacked at noon on July 26 and again wrested the peak from the weary Italians. The Italian advance was more permanent on the southern flank of the Carso. There, after hours of close combat on July 25, the 3rd Army finally took Hill 118, Mt. Sei Busi, from the Austrians. By 5 P.M., troops of the VII and X Corps pushed the last of the 14th Mountain Brigade off the hill. Mt. Sei Busi was little more than a small rise on the westernmost edge of the plateau, but it was one of the highest points in that area of the Carso; more than that, its capture was at least a psychological victory for the Duke of Aosta and his bloodied regiments.

Both armies fighting on the Doberdò plateau were thoroughly exhausted. Two days' fighting on July 25–26 cost Archduke Joseph's VII Corps 6,000 dead and wounded; casualties in the 3rd Army were at least as many. The crippling losses, coupled with the summer heat and shortages of food and water in the front lines, meant that neither the Italians nor the Austrians were ready to keep fighting. Nevertheless, both Boroević and Cadorna continued to press their soldiers hard. Bosco, as ever, demanded that his army regain all lost ground. To that end, on July 27 he sent the weak 14th Mountain Brigade back into battle to regain Hill 118. The brigade attempted to dislodge the defending 27th Division from Mt. Sei Busi for the next two days, but without success. The Austrians by now were too drained to succeed with their customary counterattack technique. The effort cost the VII Corps 2,500 more casualties, for nothing in return.

The Second Battle had begun to wither away. Cadorna suspended major operations, at least on the Carso, and Boroević had no reserves left to send into battle. Still, the battle was not yet over. Every day both armies continued to fight doggedly to win minor, insignificant gains. The fighting on the Carso became a struggle between battalions and regiments, rather than between divisions and army corps. These efforts did not always succeed, and they were invariably wasteful of human life. In particular, the Italian artillery kept up the fight all along the plateau, and the 3rd Army's guns remained as great a threat to the Austrians as ever. In what Boroević's headquarters considered the "quiet days" between July 30 and August 1, the VII Corps lost 4,000 dead and wounded, almost all of them to nonstop Italian shelling. For the Hungarian soldiers holding the line, life was as dangerous as ever. One of the most hazardous undertakings was moving troops from the front lines to the safe rear areas, and back again, because there were few communication and supply trenches to offer protection from artillery fire. In just one instance, on August 2, a relatively uneventful day on the Carso, a 600-strong battalion of the 96th Regiment, a hard-fighting Croatian unit, attempted to march forward from a rest area to take its place in the line near Mt. San Michele. It was caught in the open by heavy Italian shelling and machine gun fire. Pinned down and raked by shrapnel, in a matter of minutes the battalion lost more than three-quarters of its soldiers. Only 105 riflemen escaped the slaughter, and they were incapable of fighting; the battalion commander observed that his surviving soldiers' morale was "completely ruined."

Fortunately for the exhausted Austrians and their equally worn-out Italian opponents on the Carso, the fighting slowly wound down until Cadorna formally ended his offensive on the plateau on August 7. He reluctantly acknowledged that the Duke of Aosta's attempts were not winning the war, but only adding to the casualty lists. To reassure the irredentists of Trieste that Italy had not abandoned them, the poet and romantic nationalist Gabriele D'Annunzio flew over the city, showering it with leaflets. They encouraged the *triestini* to be patient, reminding them that Cadorna's armies would soon reach the city, and ended, "Courage, brothers! Courage and constancy!" In official accounts, the Second Battle was considered to end on August 10. That is, however, largely a notional date. Low-level combat persisted on the western edge of the plateau and before Gorizia throughout the month. Hardly a day went by without a notable Italian or Austrian raid on the enemy's positions. These small, battalion- or company-sized operations, frequently supported by some artillery, were intended to harass the other side, not to break through. Still, the Second Battle raged quietly on the Isonzo throughout August. Soldiers continued to die every day, despite Cadorna's suspension of the 3rd Army's offensive.

The flames of war burned as brightly as ever on the upper Isonzo. The northern half of the river valley, from Tolmein to Flitsch, had been relatively quiet for much of the Second Battle. The soldiers enjoyed a two-week pause in the fighting after the late July battles for Mrzli ridge. Yet their well-earned rest would be short-lived. Cadorna had suspended his great offensive on the Carso, but he had no intention of giving up the fight on the Isonzo entirely. He decided to attempt another breakthrough in the high Julian Alps. Every Italian effort in the upper valley had stalled with heavy loss of life, due mostly to the difficult terrain: no place on the Isonzo offered more natural obstacles to the attacker than the Tolmein-Flitsch sector. Undaunted, Cadorna ordered a major offensive along the entire twenty-mile front to push the Austrians deeper into the Julian Alps. What this would achieve, and how this would lead to the occupation of Gorizia or Trieste, was not made clear.

The attack was in the hands of the IV Corps, commanded by the Piedmontese Lieutenant General Nicolis di Robilant, one of Cadorna's favorites. The overstrength corps included four heavily reinforced divisions (one of them composed of elite *Bersaglieri*), two brigades of *Alpini*, an extra infantry brigade borrowed from the neighboring Carinthian Group, and five *Alpini* battalions in reserve. The corps had more crack rifle and mountain battalions than the rest of the 2nd and 3rd Armies combined. The defending Austrians were outnumbered, as usual. To hold the line, Boroević had allotted the upper Isonzo three mountain divisions, all understrength in men and guns. There were no reserves available to reinforce the infantry in the line if the Italians achieved a breakthrough. The defense would therefore be based on the well-rehearsed formula of holding mountain positions at all costs, and rapidly counterattacking to retake any lost ground. Still, the defenders enjoyed the inestimable advantage of holding high Alpine defensive positions, some of them nearly impenetrable rock fortresses.

The offensive began on August 12 with a massive artillery bombardment, the heaviest yet seen on the upper Isonzo. Di Robilant's artillery, supported by the heavy guns of the 2nd Army, pounded Austrian positions from south of Tolmein to north of Flitsch. The preparatory bombardment continued, day and night, for two days. The shells rained especially hard on two vital sectors, the Tolmein bridgehead and the Flitsch basin. The Italian infantry did not emerge from their trenches until August 14, after forty-eight hours of hard work by their supporting guns. The major blow fell in the Tolmein area, where the bulk of the IV Corps was committed to battle. The main Italian objective was the town of St. Luzia, on the river's east bank just south of Tolmein, the sole Austrian railhead for the upper valley. Taking St. Luzia, the defenders' supply depot, would render the Austrians incapable of fighting on in the high Julian Alps. To occupy St. Luzia, however, the Italians first had to clear the Isonzo's west bank of Austrian troops. Di Robilant dispatched an entire reinforced division, the 7th, to break through. The distance from the Italian lines to St. Luzia was less than a mile, but between the 7th Division and the railyard stood the 8th Mountain Brigade, holding secure mountain positions.

For five days, the 7th Division tried to push the Ukrainian, Czech, and Croatian defenders back to the Isonzo. The understrength 8th Mountain Brigade held two main positions, the Church of Holy Mary, perched on a hill, and Hill 588, a 1,940-foot peak in the center of the defensive sector. The repeated Italian attacks were aimed at these two positions, where the Austrians were dug in. The brave *fanti* of the 7th Division charged the enemy trenches every day, without success. Despite ample artillery support, the division could not break through the wall of machine gun and rifle fire thrown up around the church and Hill 588. Italian guns killed and maimed hundreds of defenders, but there were always enough survivors to hold the line. Only once, on August 19, did the Italians even seriously threaten the Austrian hold on 588, and the four assaulting battalions were soon pushed back by a vigorous counterattack by a Hungarian battalion. Five days' hard fighting had reduced the 7th Division to a shell of its former self, but had brought no gains worth mentioning. It made one more sustained attempt before the battle ended, launching a determined assault on Hill 588 on the night of August 21–22. The attack soon ended in disaster, like all the others. Undeterred by heavy casualties, di Robilant ordered one more try. From late afternoon until dusk on August 22, the division's artillery, sixty guns strong, pounded Austrian positions on Hill 588, on a front of less than a mile. The 7th's night attack failed again despite the extensive artillery preparation. The 8th Mountain Brigade held its ground, as in every previous attack. A handful of machine guns kept the division in check and inflicted terrible losses. The 7th Division was now too weak and tired to keep attacking.

The other divisions of the IV Corps fighting in the Tolmein area fared no better. Just north of Tolmein, a brigade of *Alpini*, reinforced by a regiment of *Bersaglieri*, failed to cross the Isonzo and reach the town. The 3rd Mountain Brigade, the veteran defenders of Mrzli vrh, stopped the elite Italian units in their tracks. The brigade also prevented the 8th Division from advancing deeper into the Julian Alps. Repeated costly attacks by the division in the third week of August pushed the IV Corps no farther across Mrzli ridge. Even the overstrength 33rd Division could not break the Austrian hold on the eastern Krn sector. Hungarian and Slovak soldiers of the 15th Mountain Brigade kept the Italians from moving more than a few hundred feet beyond the slopes of Mt. Krn. At the end of August, after seven days of relative calm, di Robilant ordered one more effort to break the Mrzli line. On the morning of August 28, the 8th Division, bolstered by rifle and mountain battalions, launched five successive assaults between Mrzli vrh and Mt. Sleme. The depleted 3rd Mountain Brigade held this one-and-a-half-mile front through the day at considerable cost. At 8 P.M., the 8th Division made a final attempt. Four regiments of infantry made a mass charge through the darkness, overrunning the Austrian forward trenches.

The stunned defenders mixed it up with the Italians in vicious hand-to-hand combat, but eventually gave way. The 8th appeared to have finally broken through the Mrzli line, and threatened to pour into the high Julian Alps. Its victory was cut short, however, by a well-timed and daring counterattack by a Bosnian battalion that surprised the *fanti* and threw the division entirely off balance. The knife-wielding *Bosniaken* emerged suddenly from the darkness and pushed the advancing Italians back to their own lines. By the early hours of August 29, the remnants of the 8th Division were retreating to their own trenches, their brave and futile effort collapsed in unexpected defeat. Two weeks of determined attacks left the IV Corps weaker, but no farther eastward into Austrian territory.

Di Robilant's drive on Mrzli ridge ebbed away, but the fighting continued unabated in the Flitsch sector, the northernmost reaches of the Isonzo front. On the southern end of the sector, Austrian *Landwehr* troops prevented a significant Italian advance in the Vršič-Javorček area. A series of courageous attacks by the *Bersaglieri* Division east of Mt. Vršič (6,260 ft.) pushed the 21st Rifle Regiment a few hundred feet deeper into the Julian Alps, but faltered before securing any noteworthy gains. The major fighting in the sector occurred in the Rombon area, just north of Flitsch. The 7,290-foot Mt. Rombon dominates the Flitsch basin and is the highest peak on the Isonzo. It is the summit of the Rombon mountain chain, one and a half miles wide and two and a half miles long, on the river's north bank. Italian troops of the Carinthian Group occupied the town of Flitsch, but their hold was unsure because the Austrians held Rombon. From the summit, Austrian mountain guns shelled the Italians below with impunity. It was therefore imperative that the Italians take the peak before they could advance into the highest Julian Alps, east of Flitsch.

Rombon, the greatest of the Austrian rock fortresses, was garrisoned by one of the hardest-fighting regiments in the Habsburg Army, the 2nd Mountain Rifles. The regiment, the most Slovene in the army, had just arrived from the Eastern front to defend their homeland. Its soldiers, 88 percent of them Slovenes, were determined to keep the Italians at bay. They marched up Rombon singing Slovene nationalist songs and wearing Slovene national insignia on their caps, in violation of army regulations. They would hold Rombon at any price, for their people and for their emperor. There were not enough troops to garrison the whole area, so the main bastion was the peak itself, with smaller units dispersed to several lower mountains in the chain. At Rombon's peak, the Austrian positions were very strong. The defenses consisted of two to four main trenches, as deep as a man and three feet across. They were cut into the barren stone at the summit, bolstered by rocks, wood, and sandbags. Only a direct hit by a heavy artillery shell could destroy the rock entrenchments. The Slovene defenders were supported by well-positioned, presighted machine guns and mountain artillery. It would take an enormous effort to dislodge the mountain troopers from Rombon.

The Flitsch area remained quiet while fighting raged farther down the Isonzo. Di Robilant did not attempt to advance up Rombon until the last week of August, long after his other offensives had faltered. The Carinthian Group, supported by *Alpini*, tried to push past the town of Flitsch, down in the Isonzo valley, on August 24. Five battalions failed to drive the Austrians eastward. The Slovene soldiers on Rombon watched the Italian attacks more than a mile below and waited for the inevitable assault up the mountain. It came on August 27. Before the Italians could secure the peak, they first had to occupy Mt. Čukla, the logical staging point for a drive to the summit. The 5,920-foot Čukla is located three-quarters of a mile southwest of the summit. Rombon's peak was held by just three Austrian companies, and Čukla by only two platoons. A rapid, relentless charge up the mountain might take and secure the defenders' trenches before the Austrians could launch their inevitable counterattack. On the morning of August 27 two *Alpini* battalions, Bes and Val d'Ellero, assaulted Čukla from the south and west under an umbrella of artillery fire. Taking Rombon would surpass even the capture of Mt. Krn in the annals of Italy's mountain troops, and the *Alpini* went forward with dash and determination. They annihilated the two platoons defending Čukla in hand-to-hand combat and continued their advance to the snow-capped summit. By now, the Slovene riflemen were ready, and well aimed machine gun and artillery fire ripped through the charging companies of *Alpini*, exposed on the bare, rocky slopes. A vigorous bayonet charge by the defenders pushed the attackers back to Čukla, and the weary *fanti* began to withdraw. Hundreds of brave Italian mountain troops lay dead and maimed on the southwest slope of Rombon, leaving two *Alpini* platoons stranded on Čukla ridge. The remnants of the Bes and Val d'Ellero Battalions tried another attack on August 29, but this one gained even less ground than the first. The two cut-off platoons repulsed Austrian probes for three days, but were eventually forced to retreat down the ridge. The Slovenes had held their mountain. Still, the issue had not yet been decided. The first Italian attack on Rombon failed with heavy losses, but, like the rest of the Isonzo front, there would doubtless be more offensives to come.

With the last day of August, the Second Battle of the Isonzo ended. A two-week sustained offensive on the Carso, combined with a month of probes on the upper Isonzo, had won precious little ground for Cadorna and for Italy. The 3rd Army had taken Hill 118, Mt. Sei Busi, in the center of the western edge of the Doberdò plateau, but that was about it. Other advances on the Carso, a few hundred paces in some sectors, amounted to little. They in no way affected the outcome of the battle, much less the war. Despite dozens of heroic attacks, Mt. San Michele remained firmly in Austrian hands, and Gorizia—much less Trieste—increasingly seemed an unattainable goal. Similarly, insignificant Italian advances in the Mrzli chain meant nothing to the outcome of the war; Italian efforts proved no more decisive on the upper Isonzo than on the lower.

Even more than the First Battle, the cost of the Second Battle was appalling. The disparity between lives lost and ground occupied had grown alarmingly. The two-week battle for the Carso in late July and the first days of August officially cost Italy almost 42,000 casualties. Certainly by the end of August, Cadorna's butcher bill far surpassed 50,000. Yet, as always, the true number of Italian dead and wounded was doubtless higher still. Boroević's 5th Army admitted to 46,640 casualties, including 6,400 sick, between July 15 and August 15; the total figure probably exceeded 50,000. Incessant counterattacks, often against hopeless odds, added considerably to the numbers of Austrian dead and wounded. In fact, Boroević's losses were, in relative terms, even worse than Cadorna's: nine Austrian divisions lost nearly as many men as eighteen Italian did. For both armies, the totals of dead and wounded far surpassed what had been accomplished.

During the Second Battle, divisions in the line were fed a constant stream of replacements to keep them in the field. The Austrian 17th Infantry Division, part of the VII Corps, successfully defended Mt. San Michele and the northern sector of the plateau. It lost almost 10,000 soldiers in the battle, more than its full rifle strength, but always remained in the fight. For instance, one of the 17th's regiments, the 61st, lost 482 soldiers on August 5 in a bloody skirmish on the slopes of Mt. San Michele, reducing the regiment to just 820 riflemen; but owing to the rapid supply of reinforcements, less than twenty-four hours later the 61st had 1,786 riflemen. The Italians, too, repeatedly rebuilt destroyed regiments and divisions and sent them straight back into battle. Losses among officers and NCOs were always heavy, and the quality of leadership inevitably suffered. Austria could ill afford such casualties, particularly in some of her best divisions. Even Italy was beginning to drain her reserves of trained infantry.

By the end of the Second Battle, the Italian ranks of nationalist volunteers and ardent interventionists had been decimated by Austrian machine guns. The romantic ideals of May and June had been drowned in a sea of blood on the banks of the beautiful Isonzo. Cadorna was sacrificing in vain many of Italy's most promising young men, her future. One of the thousands of Italian soldiers to die in July and August was Lieutenant Renato Serra, a thirty-year-old reserve officer. He was killed on August 20 while leading his men in a charge up Podgora hill. The attack was a suicidal effort and, like the dozens of others assaults on Podgora that summer, was cut down in a hail of fire from the hill's Dalmatian defenders. The attack won nothing, changed nothing except for those killed and maimed in it. Serra was decorated posthumously for his reckless courage.

He had been a promising young writer. A native of the Romagna, he studied classics at the University of Bologna. After his studies he served two years in the army as an infantry subaltern, a duty he performed effectively and enthusiastically. Serra led a sometimes troubled personal life, but became a respected and rising young author. Like most Italian literati, he greeted the coming of the war with enthusiasm, and he believed that Italy's cause would prevail; as he observed shortly before the fighting began, "The sea, the mountains, this theater of history does not change: Italy has time." Sadly, Serra himself did not. His best—and last—work, "Self-Examination of a Man of Letters," was published in late April 1915, several months after he had been recalled to the colors. In it, Serra sounded a note of caution, observing, perhaps in a premonition of his own fate:

What is there, on this tired earth, that will have changed, when it has drunk in the blood of so great a slaughter: when the dead and wounded, the tortured and the abandoned, shall sleep together beneath the ground, while the grass above will have become tender, bright, and new, all silent and luxuriant in the spring sun which returns unchanged?

Still, Lieutenant Serra continued to perform his duty, fighting on the Isonzo until he was killed by an Austrian bullet on Podgora. He lived long enough to see the naive hope of a quick and triumphant war evaporate. Yet, like so many Italian *fanti*, he went stoically, even heroically, to his death, supported by a faith in Italy's ultimate victory. He noted, in what could serve as an epitaph, "The fields of battle are the same, and the roads to them are the same." Renato Serra took part in, and fell victim to, what so many young Italians of his generation experienced: a deep-felt desire for intervention, for glory, which led to an unprecedented slaughter on the Isonzo.

What is remarkable, in retrospect, is that so many Italians and Austrians went to their deaths so willingly. The Second Battle was the end of any dreams of an Italian quick-march on Trieste, or of an easy Austrian defense of the Isonzo line. For both armies, it was the death of all innocence. That the war would continue for a long time now seemed assured. Nevertheless, young Italians and Austrians continued to offer themselves as a sacrifice. Cadorna's methods of discipline were unquestionably harsh, and any soldiers who refused battle would face the firing squad; still, the *fanti* attacked again and again with recklessness and dash, far more than orders required. Such courage alone could not win the battle, but it was an impressive display of Italian heroism and commitment to redeeming *Italia irredenta.*

The Austrians likewise proved enthusiastic soldiers throughout the Second Battle. Habsburg soldiers of all nationalities fought with admirable, and frequently unanticipated, courage. The South Slavs, particularly Slovenes, continued to resist the Italians with unquenchable determination, as did German-Austrians in the ranks. The Second Battle demonstrated that Hungarians could fight as well as any Habsburg soldiers; the battle belonged especially to the Hungarian VII Corps, whose stand on the Carso decided the battle's outcome. Even suspect nationalities fought surprisingly well on the Isonzo. Regiments of Czechs and Ukrainians that fought feebly against the Russians often battled heroically against the Italians. Prague's infamous 28th Regiment, the unit that went over to the Russians in the Carpathians in early April, redeemed itself on the Isonzo. The 28th was disbanded in disgrace after the humiliating Dukla Pass incident, but a battalion of raw recruits remained in service. By midsummer, the situation on the Isonzo had deteriorated, and the High Command reluctantly dispatched the Czech battalion to Boroević; even questionable reserves were better than none. To the army's astonishment, the Czechs fought well on the Carso. The provisional battalion resisted several Italian attacks on Mt. San Michele with great courage, suffering heavy losses. It was praised by the High Command for its "steadfastness," "good spirit," and general soldierly honor, "withstanding the severest test of discipline." The training battalion continued to fight so well that Franz Joseph eventually ordered the 28th reraised around it, rescuing the honor and reputation of the army's Czech troops. Ironically, Vittorio Emanuele had only months before been the 28th Regiment's honorary colonel.[5] The war with Italy, although costly, was genuinely popular in the ranks, and soldiers of all nationalities could be depended on to fight loyally and reliably against the Italian invader.

Despite the admirable determination shown by his polyglot army, Boroević was growing concerned by the end of the Second Battle. His rigid defensive methods had prevailed, but at a terrible, and probably unsustainable, cost. The 5th Army's losses were a shock to the normally imperturbable Croatian warrior. He wrote to István Tisza, the Hungarian prime minister, on August 10, reflecting on the battle: "My losses are severe. . . . It's getting so that one can't bury the corpses. . . . It was the purest Hell." Boroević's controversial tactics had paid off with victory, but the number of dead and wounded had surprised even the normally unimpressed and unconcerned general. Even so, he remained at his headquarters, thirty miles behind the lines, far from the suffering. Boroević was undoubtedly troubled by his army's losses, but not enough to reevaluate his methods. His uncompromising orders to hold every inch of ground at all costs would continue unchanged. His soldiers did not call him "the thick-skinned Croat" without cause.

At his headquarters in Udine, twenty miles behind his own front lines, Cadorna reconsidered some of his assumptions. The 3rd Army's massive offensive on the Carso had ended in disaster. Clearly, numbers of men and courage alone would not prevail against prepared Austrian defenses; the siege-like conditions described in prewar reports from the Western front had been recreated on the Isonzo. More guns and more weight of shell were what Cadorna needed, and demanded, for future offensives. The 3rd Army's shattering preparatory barrage failed to blast a path through the Austrian defenses on the Carso, but next time Cadorna would have even more guns. In this limited sense, Cadorna reevaluated his methods. Otherwise he stuck doggedly to his faith in a drive across the Isonzo into the heart of the Habsburg Empire. Privately, he admitted that the Austrians had to be worn down further before he could reach Trieste; he already expected the fighting to continue through 1916. The objective remained unchanged, even though the frame had been altered considerably. Publicly, of course, Cadorna presented a very different image. Vittorio Emanuele, observing the slaughter much more closely than Cadorna (the king liked to visit the front lines and take photographs), was seriously worried about the war's course; he had begun to doubt that victory was still possible. Cadorna dismissed the queries raised by the king, his nominal superior, and simply lied to politicians and the press. He and his staff systematically concealed the true number of casualties, and even began to manufacture victories when none existed to keep up national morale and public confidence in his generalship. Cadorna perhaps fooled those far from the sound of the guns, but the fighting men in the trenches knew better. But there was nothing they, or anyone else, could do to convince Cadorna to alter his disastrous strategic course.

FIVE

MATERIELSCHLACHT: ASSEMBLY-LINE WAR

With the end of the Second Battle, soldiers on both sides of the Isonzo enjoyed a well-deserved rest before preparing for the next round of fighting. Those who had been fortunate enough to survive the July and August bloodletting unscathed enjoyed the few comforts provided for frontline soldiers. They received a regular supply of food and water, in contrast to during the battle, and were able to bathe and to exchange filthy, tattered uniforms for clean, new ones. There was plenty of work to be done, between sentry watches and the backbreaking improving of trenches, but soldiers were able to catch up on lost sleep, play cards with comrades, and write letters home. There was little else for the troops to do. Luxuries were limited, especially for the Italians; the best the average infantryman, the ordinary *fantaccino*, could hope for was a bottle of strong, army-issue red wine, and, if he were very lucky, a quick, unromantic trip to a field brothel. The Austrians at least had better organized entertainment, with field concerts and ample supplies of alcohol for the troops when they were not in battle. Only the comradeship of the front, uniting men of widely different classes and regions, made life bearable. Still, danger was everywhere, even on the quietest days on the Isonzo. If the Austrians were tormented by the random Italian artillery shell, the Italians lived in fear of Austrian snipers, the dreaded *cecchini*. No Italian soldier who poked his head above the trenches in the forward area was safe, at least during daylight. It was best for the soldiers on both sides of the Isonzo to keep under the cover of entrenchments, and hope fate would keep them safe.

Fortunately for the infantrymen on the Isonzo, Luigi Cadorna gave them their first extended respite from battle. Aware that his forces had suffered grievous losses during the Second Battle, he sought to rebuild his armies with even more artillery before he tried to crack the Austrian defenses again. He fully intended to mount another major effort in the autumn, but his legions needed several weeks to rest and recover. In the first week of September, only days after the fighting on the upper Isonzo had ended, Cadorna was visited at his Udine headquarters by General Joseph Joffre, French chief of staff and architect of Allied strategy on the Western front. By the late summer of 1915, it was evident that the war was not going well for the Allies. The German hold on Flanders and northeastern France appeared unshakable, and developments on the Eastern front appeared even more ominous. The trench warfare that prevailed in the West, from the English Channel to the Swiss border, had reduced the fighting to static and futile attempts to penetrate the German lines in the hope of achieving a strategic breakthrough. Throughout the year, the French Army, sometimes supported by its British allies, had tried to push the German invader off French soil, but without success. A major effort in Flanders from late April to late May cost the Allies 70,000 soldiers, but was notable only for the introduction of poisonous gas as a battlefield weapon. The German use of chemical agents proved to be more an irritant than a practical weapon; the French and British failed to break through anyway. France's early summer offensive in Artois cost another 100,000 casualties, but was no more successful than previous efforts. Despite crippling losses already in 1915, Joffre was determined to evict the Germans from French soil before the year ended. He could expect little effective help from his allies. Britain was still preparing to join the war as a major player; her volunteer army expanded impressively from ten to thirty-seven divisions in 1915, but most units were still poorly trained and untested in battle. The vaunted Russian juggernaut had collapsed in the East. By late summer, the Germans and Austrians had completely evicted the Russians from Galicia, and had taken all of Russian Poland. After losing a million prisoners, the Russians were barely holding on, and were incapable of assisting their French allies. Even the Dardanelles operation, the British effort at Gallipoli that had aroused such hopes of victory, by late August had ended ignominiously. Some of the finest divisions in the British Army had failed to make headway against the entrenched Turks, and the operation had to be abandoned. Undaunted by the prospect of going it practically alone, "Papa" Joffre told Cadorna of his plan to win the war. He had assembled two armies, thirty divisions, to attack the German trenches in Champagne in the last week of September; he expected to break through within three days. Joffre believed that a decisive victory in Champagne would force the Germans into a strategic retreat that could decide the war. He asked for a supporting Italian offensive on the Isonzo in late September, both to distract the Germans and to keep pressure on the Austrians, who would then be unable to supply their German ally with any reserves.

Cadorna considered Joffre's request, but informed his French counterpart that he was not optimistic that his battered armies would be ready to take the offensive so soon after the end of the Second Battle. In truth, Cadorna had little interest in helping the French. There were no long-standing military or diplomatic ties between Rome and her newfound allies, as there were among the French, British, and Russians. Cadorna was unconcerned with France's fate, except where it directly affected his own war plans. In addition, the 2nd and 3rd Armies were unquestionably too weak to undertake a major offensive in late September. Cadorna therefore informed the disappointed Joffre that he would be unable to launch another Isonzo offensive until six more weeks had passed, that is, mid-October. Italian support for the French Champagne offensive would have to wait.

The Austrians used Cadorna's six-week delay to reinforce the 5th Army. To Boroević, the situation still appeared very precarious. Trieste was less than twenty miles from the fighting line on the central Carso, and little more than a dozen miles from the front's southern edge. The city's residents could hear the shelling clearly, and often watched the bombardment of the Carso from their windows. The threat to Trieste was serious; there were not enough Austrian troops available to prevent any Italian breakthrough on the Carso from taking the city. The loss of Trieste would not constitute just a major psychological and political defeat: the fall of the city to the Italians would immediately endanger Ljubljana, western Croatia, and the Istrian Peninsula with its naval bases, all within striking distance of Trieste. To prevent this, the High Command scraped together all available reserve formations and sent them to the Isonzo. Boroević received two fresh divisions in late August and a third in early September. He soon had to send two veteran divisions back to the Balkan front, so his net gain was only a single division. However, two of his newly arrived divisions, the 22nd Rifle and 28th Infantry, made up the III Corps, the "Iron Corps," the finest in the Habsburg Army. Raised from German and Slovene Alpine districts, the hard-fighting Iron Corps took its place in the line on the southern edge of the Doberdò plateau.

Before Cadorna was willing to renew his push across the Isonzo, he wanted to remove any Austrian threat to his left flank. This required pushing the 5th Army deeper into the high Julian Alps. As before, this entailed seizing the Tolmein bridgehead and the Rombon area. Evicting the Austrians from the Mrzli chain and the Flitsch basin had proved impossible in the first two battles, but Cadorna demanded that the IV Corps win the victory that had so far eluded it. He gave it generous reinforcements of infantry and artillery. On the eve of battle, it boasted four strong divisions, an extra infantry brigade, and two brigades of *Alpini*, but it had the actual strength of eight divisions. It was virtually the size of an army. The three defending Austrian divisions had received no notable reinforcements since the end of the Second Battle.

The Italian offensive on the upper Isonzo began with local attacks at the Tolmein bridgehead on September 4 and 5. The 7th Division again failed to dislodge the 8th Mountain Brigade. The next effort was more substantial. At noon on September 9, the heavily reinforced 7th assaulted the Austrian positions at the Church of Holy Mary and Hill 588. The division, twenty-seven battalions strong—fifteen infantry, eight *Alpini* and four *Bersaglieri*—was as big as an army corps. The savage fighting, much of it at close quarters, continued well into the night. The 8th Mountain Brigade still held its ground. Reinforced by two battalions of the elite 2nd Imperial Tyrolean Rifle Regiment, the famed *Kaiserjäger*, the Austrians met the Italians' courage with demonstrations of equal bravery. The best regiments of the Italian and Austrian Armies fought hand to hand all day, producing frightful losses for both sides. When the last guns fell silent after twelve hours' sustained fighting, hundreds of Italian corpses littered the slopes around Holy Mary and 588. The shattered 7th Division needed a rest, but it was back in action, topped off with fresh replacements, within three days. After twenty-four hours of preparatory shelling, the division went over the top again on September 12. Five assaults on Hill 588 still did not push the Austrians off the summit. The Tyrolean troopers, including Italians from the Trentino, helped by Ukrainian and Croatian companies, managed to repulse every Italian attack. Again, the advantages offered by well entrenched machine guns and holding the high ground brutally outweighed Italian heroism.

During the third week of September, the IV Corps devoted its main effort to breaking the Austrian hold on the Flitsch basin. Attempts to take Mt. Rombon failed as they had three weeks earlier. The *Bersaglieri* Division and the Aosta Brigade made more sustained efforts in the mountains just south of the Flitsch valley. Supported by heavy artillery, Italian troops tried to break out of their positions on the summit of Mt. Vršič and push the Austrians off Mt. Javorček, the 5,110-foot peak that overlooks Flitsch from the south. Italian heavy guns pounded the peak, inflicting casualties on the defenders and sapping their morale; the Austrians had no heavy guns to counter the enemy's hard blows. Still, the Austrian *Landwehr* troops were willing to keep fighting, and Italian efforts to evict them proved as trying as ever. Several days' attacking failed to gain even a foot of Austrian territory. The last assault came on the night of September 18.

As usual, the *Bersaglieri* left their positions after dark, headed for the Austrian lines under the cover of their own guns. The hard marching uphill with full packs at high altitudes was difficult for the riflemen, many of whom were recalled reservists and teenaged recruits just arrived to replace the recently killed and wounded. One of the *Bersaglieri* struggling to reach the Austrian trenches that night was Benito Mussolini, who had arrived on the upper Isonzo only hours before. The journalist and rabid irredentist had been recalled to the colors just three weeks earlier. When war broke out, Mussolini, like so many of his nationalist comrades, volunteered to fight to redeem *Italia irredenta*. However, the army refused Mussolini's patriotic request. The *Comando Supremo* remembered Mussolini as a hotheaded Socialist who regularly insulted the army and all other Italian institutions. It certainly did not want him rabble-rousing in the ranks. The War Ministry informed Mussolini, a reservist, that he would have to wait until the rest of his reserve class of 1884 was recalled to the colors. The most vocal of all irredentists thus had to endure a summer of insults and jeers from his political opponents. While Italy's finest young men were sacrificing themselves on the Isonzo, Mussolini watched and waited, taunted endlessly and mercilessly by his Socialist ex-comrades, who blamed him for the war.

It was therefore a relief when Mussolini received his call-up notice on August 31. He immediately reported for duty with his old corps, the *Bersaglieri*. He received just two weeks' refresher training at Brescia, and was then sent directly to the front with a unit of replacements. Although his education entitled him to a place at an officer candidate school, Mussolini went to the Isonzo as a rifleman, an ordinary *fantaccino*. He crossed the old Austrian frontier on September 15, headed for the high Julian Alps. His unit passed through Karfreit, at the foot of Mt. Krn, *il famoso e misterioso Monte Nero*, as he recalled in his diary. They crossed the Isonzo and marched five miles northward into the dark mountains, reaching the freezing Italian trenches 6,200 feet up Mt.Vršič (Monte Ursig to the Italians), in the early evening. Mussolini and the other replacements were exhausted, but they had no time to rest. The regiment to which they had been assigned, the 11th *Bersaglieri*, was going into battle again that night. At 10 P.M., Mussolini's battalion advanced on the Austrian positions, only a hundred paces to the east. The *Bersaglieri*, wearing their distinctive broad-brimmed black hats with green cock feathers, mounted a bayonet charge. Austrian rifle fire almost immediately forced the Italians to seek cover. Both sides exchanged rifle and machine gun fire, and the occasional hail of hand grenades, for two hours. Losses on both sides mounted. Just after midnight, Austrian sappers detonated a mine under an Italian trench section. Mussolini's company occupied those trenches, and he was caught in the confusion. When he realized what had happened, he noticed that more than thirty of his comrades lay dead and wounded. The disorganized fighting on the frozen, snow-covered summit continued until dawn, when both sides broke off the engagement. Italian artillery opened up on the Austrian positions, giving the *Bersaglieri* time to gather survivors and regroup. Mussolini was one of the lucky ones. He had survived his baptism of fire unscathed. His first battle was the last effort by the IV Corps to break through in the upper valley before the Third Battle. Like so many other engagements, large and small, on the upper Isonzo during September, Mussolini's September 18–19 firefight had been bloody and inconclusive. It was notable only for those who were killed and maimed there.

The September fighting around Tolmein and Flitsch illustrated again that courage alone could not overcome firepower. The lessons of the Western front, learned at such a price by the French and Germans in 1914, were now, a year later, evident to the Italians. The Isonzo battles even taught the Austrians a great deal about the importance of fortifications and heavy artillery. Simply put, the Italians needed many heavy guns to break through Boroević's defenses, and the Austrians required strong entrenchments and lots of machine guns to stop them. Heroism alone had been found cruelly wanting. It was no longer a war between men, but a struggle between weapons and technologies. The question remained: Would Cadorna's forces devise a better method of attack faster than the Austrians could find a technical antidote? Austrian Lieutenant General Alfred Krauss, the tactically astute chief of staff of the Southwestern front, coined a term for this new style of warfare, *Materielschlacht*—the battle of matériel, of equipment. There was still a considerable human element, to be sure, but the essential matter was the technical power and proficiency of the armies. The Austrians devoted most of their energy to digging better entrenchments. Major General Anton Pitreich, Svetozar Boroević's chief of staff, took advantage of the lull in fighting and ensured that all available manpower was used to build permanent trenches and caves to protect the infantry from Italian guns. On the Carso alone he had four battalions of highly trained sappers and a dozen of laborers at his disposal to perfect the 5th Army's entrenchments. The workers, many of them Russian prisoners of war, dug and blasted day and night. By mid-October, their task was nearly complete. Three strong defensive lines, trench systems cut into the rock, ran from Tolmein to Trieste; they were ready in the Gorizia and Bainsizza sectors, and nearly finished on the Carso. The engineers had blasted hundreds of *kavernen* into the "stony sea" of Doberdò, the only reliable protection for the infantry. They had also built enough barracks for forty battalions to rest when not in the line, and finished a water pump system to keep the Carso's defenders supplied with water. The technical improvements were remarkable, the result of six weeks of constant laboring, a task hardly less trying than combat. Boroević's infantry was better prepared than ever to face Cadorna's onslaught.

The Austrian artillery shortage proved more difficult to remedy. Clearly the 5th Army needed more artillery, particularly heavy, long-range guns, to protect the infantry from relentless pounding by Italian guns. Yet the Austrians were fighting a three-front war, and had little heavy artillery to spare. The forces in the field would remain short of both modern artillery and a steady supply of munitions for many months to come. Still, Boroević managed to get more guns from the High Command. His artillery counted 462 pieces in August, 62 of them medium and heavy; by mid-October he had 604 guns, including 108 medium and heavy pieces. The heavy guns included four batteries of superheavy mortars and eight 150mm naval guns, ideal weapons for hitting back at

Cadorna's artillery. For the first time, the infantry also had its own artillery, light mortar batteries. Mortars, located just behind the frontline trenches, were short-range but deadly weapons that could respond more rapidly than conventional artillery to changing situations on the battlefield. They represented a considerable increase in Austrian firepower. The Austrian gunners still could not compete on even terms with the Italians, but by the Third Battle at least they had a fighting chance.

One piece of new technology that the Austrians still sorely lacked was the steel helmet. Primitive steel headgear had been in use on the Western front since early 1915, and standardized models were in use in France and Flanders by early autumn. They had proved notably effective at protecting soldiers from fatal head wounds. Here, too, Austrian industry lagged behind. There had been some small field trials, but Austria did not yet have a steel helmet to issue to her infantry. Desperate to decrease the number of head wounds, the 91st Division, fighting in the Tyrol, issued its riflemen a thousand firemen's helmets, with some success. The less fortunate soldiers of the 5th Army would have to wait several more months before receiving protective headwear. Until then, they would have to brave the thunderous Italian bombardments unprotected.

The lack of steel helmets did not damage morale much, however. Most Austrian soldiers did not look forward to more fighting, but their spirits remained high in October. The harsh Alpine winter was coming soon, but Boroević's infantry was prepared to resist all comers, as they had for the past five months. The 17th Infantry Regiment, a battle-tested Slovene unit that arrived on the Isonzo just in time to fight in the Third Battle, was eager to mix it up with the Italians. A soldier-poet in its ranks, traveling from Galicia to the Isonzo, recorded these sentiments:

> Our blood has already flowed on hundreds of battlefields,
> And all our enemies know us well—
> Still we carry rifles and will fight
> For honor to the last drop of blood.

It is a testament to the 5th Army's fighting spirit, and to Slovene Italophobia, that combat veterans could express such romantic feelings after fourteen months of total war. On the eve of battle, Boroević's army had grown to a dozen divisions with 137 infantry battalions, a total of 128,600 riflemen. The Italians had far more men and guns, and Boroević's divisions were short 27,000 men according to officially authorized strengths, but nevertheless the 5th Army had never been stronger in soldiers and equipment. The Austrians had prepared well for the coming *Materielschlacht*. Occupying well placed and well fortified positions, and bolstered by victory in the last two battles, Boroević's infantrymen were prepared to repulse Cadorna's next offensive.

The Italian High Command was similarly aware that the outcome of the Third Battle of the Isonzo would likely depend on the amount of firepower Cadorna's armies could bring to bear on Austrian positions. Artillery was Cadorna's major preoccupation. He scoured arsenals across Italy and collected an impressive artillery park of 1,372 guns for his offensive. Some 305 of them were medium and heavy pieces, vital for shattering Austrian defenses. Cadorna ordered fortress guns removed from outmoded nineteenth-century forts far behind the lines, he received some French superheavy howitzers, and he borrowed several batteries of long-range naval guns to support the next Isonzo effort. Just as important, he amassed a reserve of a million artillery shells (many of them from Britain and France) for the Third Battle—enough, he believed, to blast a gaping hole through the crust of Boroević's defenses. The infantry also received its share of new weapons. By mid-October, the 2nd and 3rd Armies boasted hundreds more machine guns, some new heavy mortars, better hand grenades, new demolitions to destroy Austrian wire and entrenchments, and even protective body armor—the first steel helmets from France, and steel shields for assault detachments. The Italians, too, had realized that the war had become a contest between machines as much as a fight between men.

The gradual reequipment of the Italian Army was no easy task. Italy's prewar economic backwardness made gearing up for total war a slow and painful process, made worse by the habitual bureaucratic complications. To overcome these realities, Cadorna put General Alfred Dallolio in charge of waging the industrial war that made the Isonzo fighting possible. As undersecretary for arms and munitions, and later as head of the Central Committee for Industrial Mobilization, Dallolio organized Italy's fragmented private industries into a united war effort. He oversaw the establishment of joint committees to resolve disputes, increased industrial productivity, improved labor relations, and established hundreds of auxiliary factories to expand Italy's modest industrial base. Dallolio's labors had just begun to bear fruit by October 1915, but he laid the foundation of eventual Italian victory in the First World War.

In the autumn of 1915, however, ultimate victory still seemed very far in the future. Most seriously, a financial crisis threatened to cripple the war effort. War Minister Vittorio Zupelli had grossly underestimated the cost of the fighting, so by October an ominous shortfall in government outlays constrained the army. A shortage of funds produced a shortage of shells. At the outset, Zupelli announced that a billion lire would be needed to purchase the army's munitions for the duration of the fighting. Like nearly all Italian generals and politicians, he had believed that Cadorna would lead Italian forces to a quick and easy victory over Austria. The cost of the war, and the quantity of munitions needed, therefore vastly exceeded the War Ministry's predictions. By the end of 1915, the army would use up six billion lire worth of shells. Only rapid British and French financial assistance prevented an autumn industrial halt in Italy. Cadorna could not wage war without funds to purchase munitions, and he was already dependent on his allies to provide much of the needed credit.

Unconcerned with the financial situation, Cadorna intended the Third Battle to be his long-awaited victory. The objective was Gorizia. The capture of the City of Violets would not be militarily decisive, but it would be a bitter blow to Austrian prestige and morale. His attempt to take the Carso and drive on Trieste had failed, so he now aimed his armies at Gorizia, a far closer and more attainable objective. Cadorna planned a two-phase battle. It would begin with coordinated attacks to the north and south of the city, at Plava and on the northern Carso. These flank attacks would drive behind Gorizia, cutting it off. Then a direct assault on the city would lead to its capture. To achieve this, Cadorna had collected two-thirds of the Italian Army, twenty-nine divisions with 338 infantry battalions, some 350,000 riflemen. The main mission was given to Pietro Frugoni's 2nd Army, with 163 battalions and 654 guns. On the left, its bloodied IV Corps would attack the Austrians again in the upper valley, with the objective of taking Tolmein. On the central Isonzo, the VIII and II Corps would move into the Bainsizza plateau and outflank Gorizia from the north. Across the Isonzo from the city, the VI Corps was ordered to take Podgora and Mt. Sabotino, familiar objectives, and wait for the drive to the river's east bank. The Duke of Aosta's 3rd Army, slightly weaker with 125 battalions and 546 guns, was given the mission of taking Mt. San Michele and making supporting attacks on the central and southern edges of the Doberdò plateau. Cadorna kept two corps with four divisions in reserve to exploit the success of the first phase. By mid-October he was ready.

The Austrians were well aware what Cadorna was planning. The army's intelligence service was efficient, and excelled at deciphering enemy codes; in fact, at the beginning of the Great War, Austria was the only country in Europe besides France to have a signal intelligence service, and experienced Habsburg code breakers rendered sterling service on the Russian and Italian fronts. Boroević's signal intelligence section intercepted numerous Italian messages that indicated an imminent offensive; 5th Army intelligence knew Cadorna's order of battle in almost every detail. At lower levels, Austrian forward positions observed Italian movements all along the Isonzo. Cadorna and his soldiers made little attempt to conceal their actions. Everywhere Italian infantry was on the move, new artillery units were arriving, and in some places Italian engineers made preparations for a river crossing in broad daylight. If this did not make the picture sufficiently clear, as the day of battle approached, some Italian troops sought refuge in Austrian captivity. In the three days before the battle, the Tolmein sector alone collected fifty-four deserters, who were happy to have avoided combat and who provided Austrian intelligence officers with a wealth of information about their units and their orders. The Austrians were thus well prepared when Cadorna began his epic preparatory barrage, signaling the beginning of the Third Battle.

Precisely at noon on October 18, the massed artillery of the 2nd and 3rd Armies opened fire, beginning by far the greatest barrage yet witnessed on the Italian-Austrian front. The shelling blasted Austrian positions all along the Isonzo, from Krn to the Adriatic, a distance of more than thirty miles. The bombardment by more than 1,300 guns continued virtually nonstop through the day and night. The morning of October 19 saw increased shelling, and the first major Italian air attack of the war. The air services of both sides were still in their infancy, and large air operations were a rarity. The early morning raid on the main Austrian airfield, just east of Gorizia, was thus a surprise. Over a hundred bombs fell on the aerodrome, causing few casualties but extensive damage to aircraft; secondary bombing runs on headquarters, reserve positions, and rail stations added to the chaos. Ammunition shortages prevented Austrian guns from responding to the Italian barrage except in a few areas. The infantry stoically had to endure the Italian shelling and wait for it to end. The barrage reduced hundreds of emplacements and trench sections to rubble. Sleep and rest were impossible for the defenders. On October 18, on the Carso alone, Italian guns killed and wounded 5,300 Austrian soldiers. The casualty rate dropped as the shelling wore on, but the impact of Cadorna's great preparatory barrage on Boroević's frontline infantry was terrible.

Except for a few probes, Cadorna's infantry remained in their positions while the guns did their fearsome work. After seventy hours of shelling, the bombardment ceased at 10 A.M. on October 21. Two hours later the first mass infantry attacks began. The offensive's left flank soon bogged down. On the upper Isonzo, the fighting was intense but indecisive. Attempts by the IV Corps to break through the Mrzli chain typically failed. Combat around Vršič and Javorček was sustained and costly for both sides. Repeated Italian assaults up the second mountain proved in vain. The Austrians resisted with all their strength, even resorting to rolling flaming barrels of explosives down the mountainside on the heads of the advancing *Bersaglieri*. These "rolling bombs" were an old tradition on the upper Isonzo; Habsburg defenders had used them successfully against Napoleon's *Grande Armée* in 1809. Italian soldiers, Mussolini among them, continued until midnight to attack what he remembered as "the tragic passes of Vršič and Javorček." Snowstorms and complete exhaustion brought an end to the Italian attempts. Renewed efforts to reach the Tolmein bridgehead also failed. Four major assaults led by elite battalions of *Alpini* and *Bersaglieri* broke apart on the Austrian defenses around Hill 588.

The Italian push on the central Isonzo was equally abortive. On the northern edge of the Bainsizza plateau, troops of the VIII Corps crossed the Isonzo in boats, but were soon repulsed and pushed back to the west bank with heavy losses. Plava continued to live up to its evil reputation. Flanking attacks by the

3rd and 32nd Divisions around Hill 383 were likewise turned back. Later efforts ended disastrously on the hillsides of 383. Everywhere on the northern flank, Austrian forces, much battered by Cadorna's barrage, still managed to keep the Italians in check. The seventy-hour bombardment inflicted heavy losses on the defenders, but always enough machine gunners and riflemen survived to hold the Italians back. Austrian losses were heavy, of course; the XV Corps, defending the upper Isonzo, lost 2,900 soldiers in the first week of the Third Battle, including 650 confirmed killed. Still, Italian casualties were considerably worse.

The 3rd Army's experience on the Carso proved similarly frustrating for Cadorna. The general attack, which began on October 21, soon stalled before Austrian machine gun nests, as before. The first waves of assault troops initially made impressive gains. They emerged from their positions clad in steel, wearing protective helmets, breastplates, even leg guards, looking like resurrected knights of the Middle Ages. Eight infantry regiments charged up Mt. San Michele, on a front little more than a mile wide. The defending Hungarians of the 20th *Honvéd* Division resisted fiercely, and the Italians advanced only on the mountain's west side. An Austrian counterstroke retook even that minor gain from the 3rd Army, capturing more than 500 tired *fanti*. The Italian net gain in the San Michele sector was an advance of a hundred paces. Losses for both armies were unprecedentedly high. The Austrian VII Corps, defending the Carso's northern half, lost 4,600 soldiers in five hours of fighting on October 21. The uncounted Italian casualties likely were higher still. The story was the same on the Carso's southern half, where the III Corps managed not to lose a single important position to the combined attacks of five Italian divisions. The cost was prohibitive, indeed even worse: 5,650 Austrian casualties, including almost a thousand known dead. Italian losses were surely worse, and there were no gains to show for such a sacrifice.

Frustrated by his lack of success, Cadorna ordered an even more vigorous offensive on the Carso the following day, October 22. The artillery opened up again, showering the exhausted defenders of the Doberdò plateau with high explosives. The bombardment was so intense that it could be heard more than sixty miles away. At 11 A.M., the XIV Corps launched another mass attack up Mt. San Michele. It fell apart after a bitter struggle near the summit with bayonets and hand grenades. The Austrian 43rd Regiment, a mostly Romanian unit, maintained its hold on San Michele. Italian efforts on the southern Carso fared no better. A determined counterattack by the 6th Austrian Militia Regiment even managed to retake the summit of Hill 118, Mt. Sei Busi, lost in the Second Battle; bombs dropped from an Italian airship failed to dislodge the militiamen. A brave attack by the Italian 16th Division up Hill 121, a rise less than two miles north of the Adriatic, ended in catastrophe. The division charged into the fire of Austrian machine guns and lost 4,000 soldiers on the hillside, without gaining any ground. The Iron Corps had lived up to its name.

The first phase of Cadorna's Third Battle reached its high point the next day, October 23, on the Carso. Cadorna realized that he could not take Gorizia without first clearing Mt. San Michele of Austrian troops, so he sent his legions back into battle against the apparently impregnable Austrian positions. He reinforced the 3rd Army with fresh battalions and replenished shattered regiments with replacements straight from training depots. Cadorna concentrated his effort on the San Michele sector, aiming three and a half divisions at the mountain. The attack promised to be very costly. The poet Gabriele D'Annunzio observed doomed *fanti* headed for Mt. San Michele. The energetic bard had volunteered to fight as soon as war broke out, and was assigned by Cadorna to 3rd Army headquarters. Despite his years—fifty-two in 1915, an age, he admitted, "fit for slippers and easy-chair"—he participated actively in the war effort. Between daring flights over Austrian territory and other dramatic exploits, D'Annunzio regularly visited the Carso front, which inspired him to write gruesomely romantic poetry. Watching infantrymen at a field Mass, just before entering battle on San Michele, D'Annunzio observed "Heads already touched by Death, marked by the terrible Worker. A mass of meat to be slaughtered." The horrible fate of the *fanti*, the "holy infantry," did not worry D'Annunzio; indeed, he proudly announced, "I am a poet of slaughter." The fight for San Michele would give the warrior-poet all the slaughter he could ask for.

After a brief but intense bombardment, the Italians again charged the Austrian trenches on Mt. San Michele, the first of several mass attacks on October 23. Fighting raged throughout the day, punctuated by more shelling. The battle was vicious and intense, with much hand-to-hand struggling in the Austrian trenchworks. The bayonet and hand grenade decided the day. The fight continued well into the evening, with Austrian attempts to regain lost entrenchments. In the late hours of October 23, both sides, thoroughly exhausted, enjoyed a brief rest. The Romanians of the 43rd Regiment still held Mt. San Michele. The cost of defending the Carso had been terrible. The Hungarian VII Corps was being bled white on San Michele. One of the many to fall on the mountain on October 23 was Colonel Eduard Weeber, commander of the 81st *Honvéd* Brigade, the defenders of the summit. Weeber was the second Austrian brigadier to fall on the Carso in as many days; Colonel Franz Drennig died the previous night defending Hill 121 alongside many of the soldiers of his 19th Militia Brigade. Most regiments were at less than half-strength, but it was difficult to bring replacements into the line. Around-the-clock Italian shelling of Austrian rear areas prevented a steady stream of food, water, and fresh men from reaching the front lines. The Third Battle would be decided on the Carso, on San Michele, as every Austrian soldier from Boroević to the lowliest private knew. The only question was whether the tired, hungry, and thirsty defenders could withstand another Italian attack.

A predawn assault by the Italian 29th Division seized part of Mt. San Michele's north slope. So the VII Corps started October 24 with a 7 A.M. counterattack. The Austrian move pushed the Italians back down the mountainside, but the 3rd Army was not going to give up the fight. At noon, hundreds of Italian guns began shelling the VII Corps. The barrage continued for three hours and was especially heavy on Mt. San Michele. At 3 P.M., another mass infantry attack followed. As many as eight regiments—two divisions' worth of infantry—charged up the mountain, past the countless unburied corpses of comrades fallen in recent days. Surviving Austrian machine guns cut swaths through the advancing ranks of *fanti*, but more savage close combat followed when the Italians reached the Austrian trenches. Hand-to-hand fighting lasted all afternoon, but by the evening the Italians began to withdraw. This attack had stalled like all the others. Austrian infantry soon chased the survivors back to their own trenches. Boroević's first defensive line was still intact. In the last hours of October 24, Cadorna reluctantly ordered the 3rd Army's offensive suspended; it was a pause, not a halt. The Duke of Aosta's divisions needed fresh men and more munitions before they could fight again. For the moment, the Austrians had prevailed. Archduke Joseph's VII Corps had again held all its ground in the face of the fiercest shelling and mass attacks yet seen. The cost had been terrible: in seven days' fighting, the VII Corps lost 13,500 dead and wounded, half its rifle strength; the precise losses of the neighboring III Corps, much less the Duke of Aosta's 3rd Army, can only be guessed at.

The failure of Cadorna's first phase did not deter him from beginning the second, the drive on Gorizia. Although the flanking attacks at Plava and on the Carso made no progress, Cadorna ordered the 2nd Army to assault the Austrian positions before the city. The main objectives of this attack, like all previous ones, were Mt. Sabotino, Oslavia, and Podgora. The mission was assigned to the VI Corps, which had spent so much of its strength during the summer trying to wrest trench lines from Erwin Zeidler's Dalmatians. The corps had a new commander, however, who promised to transform defeat into victory. Lieutenant General Luigi Capello had been in command of the VI Corps for less than a month, but he already had a reputation for toughness and determination. The fifty-six-year-old Capello, although like Cadorna a northerner, was in many other ways quite different from his commander in chief. His father, a bureaucrat in the state telegraph service, encouraged him to pursue a military career. Capello was by all accounts very successful in his chosen profession, with many years in the field with the infantry. He commanded a brigade during the Libyan war, where he earned a reputation as a hard driver of men, an impression cemented by his aggressive command of a division on the Carso during the First and Second Battles of the Isonzo. It was this ruthless determination to win that Cadorna wanted above all in his subordinates. He therefore chose to overlook other aspects of Capello's life that he did not like: the new corps commander was a politically active, high-ranking Freemason, whereas Cadorna was a staunch Roman Catholic who detested politics. Cadorna considered Capello a schemer, *un generale politicante*. The two generals therefore agreed on little save the battlefield tasks at hand. They were never personally less than distant.

Capello had at his disposal more than three divisions, amply supported by artillery. For the first time, the VI Corps had enough heavy and superheavy guns—eleven batteries in the Sabotino sector alone—to blast holes in the Austrian defenses. The Italians were still opposed by the tough and well entrenched 58th Division, now reinforced by a brigade of Poles from East Galicia. The Polish 30th Regiment, new to the Isonzo front, garrisoned Mt. Sabotino, "Snake Mountain" to its defenders because of its long, winding ridges. A surprise night attack by the Livorno Brigade on Sabotino on October 23–24 made little progress. Attempts by the 11th and 12th Divisions to advance on Oslavia and Podgora were no more successful. On October 24, Italian mortars and heavy guns pounded Sabotino mercilessly, blowing apart and burying Austrian entrenchments. Still, a mass bayonet charge by the 4th Division up the mountain's northwestern face was annihilated by the Poles' remaining machine guns and the 58th's artillery, which caught the *fanti* on the bare, treeless slope. The heavy barrage had blasted away any cover for the advancing infantry. The remnants of the 4th Division struggled back down the mountain in the afternoon, chased by counterattacking Poles. The Pavia Brigade's effort two days later likewise collapsed, leaving 3,000 Italian dead and wounded on the mountainside. Capello, unconcerned by these setbacks, concentrated his divisions on the southern half of the sector instead. An assault by ten battalions against Podgora on the morning of October 25 was cut short by Austrian machine guns and mortar fire, as were further bloody attempts on October 26 and 27. By then it was evident that the VI Corps could make no headway. Capello's first offensive as a corps commander ended in frustration. The heavy artillery was successful at cratering the terrain and creating a great deal of noise and smoke, but it was not destroying Zeidler's sturdy defenses, only damaging them. Every attack found plenty of Austrian weapons still before it, enough to inflict grievous losses and block any advance.

While Capello's offensive before Gorizia stalled, Cadorna ordered Frugoni to renew his 2nd Army's drive on the upper and central Isonzo. Between October 24 and 27, the II Corps, the Plava Corps, made repeated attempts to take and outflank Hill 383. All failed. The 3rd and 32nd Divisions lost an additional 2,000 dead and wounded in these futile attacks on "Bloody 383"; the defending 1st Mountain Brigade counted 570 casualties in these struggles with its longtime adversaries. Farther up the Isonzo, the IV Corps tried yet again to occupy the Tolmein bridgehead. The attack, the biggest so far with two strong divisions and two *Alpini* brigades, similarly achieved nothing save a notable addition to the casualty lists. Still, attrition was wearing the Austrians down. The 5th Army was running out of soldiers. The XV Corps, defending the Mrzli chain, on October 26 had to commit its last reserves to stem the Italian tide. They were a regiment of middle-aged German and Slovene militia, armed with captured Russian rifles and clad in ancient dark blue uniforms. Cadorna's bloodletting was not pushing his armies any closer to Trieste, but it was draining the already shallow reservoir of Austrian manpower.

Aware that Boroević's army could not withstand such losses much longer, Cadorna renewed his drive on Gorizia after just a day's pause. He sent the 2nd and 3rd Armies back into battle after only twenty-four hours to rest and absorb replacements. His army, like Boroević's, had become a machine with an apparent life of its own, a ceaselessly running meat grinder that steadily consumed fresh regiments and spewed out their tattered remains. The battle's second phase began with a massive blow by Capello's VI Corps aimed at Zeidler's defenses. It started on October 28 with an attack by the 4th Division on Sabotino. The veteran division was joined by the Grenadier Brigade, the senior unit of the Italian Army, raised in 1659. Its two regiments of Grenadiers—the House of Savoy's famed *Granatieri di Sardegna*—took the tallest recruits in the army, and were renowned for their courage under fire. The six regiments together stormed the mountain, braving machine gun and artillery fire that felled whole companies of charging *fanti*. They did not reach the Austrian lines. Even the tall and strong grenadiers could not prevail against modern firepower. Casualties were very high, among them Colonel Buonamici, commander of the 127th Regiment, who died with hundreds of his troops while leading the futile charge up the north slope. Later in the afternoon, Capello sent the 11th and 12th Divisions into action against Podgora and Oslavia. These attacks also failed to make noteworthy progress. Even the limited gains on Podgora hill were undone by a vigorous counterstroke by five companies of the Dalmatian 23rd Rifles, who charged the Italian-held trenches with bugle calls signaling the attack. The 58th Division suffered too, but it had a good day: it held all its ground and took 500 Italian prisoners.

Despite these painful setbacks, Capello remained confident that his weakened divisions could still capture Zeidler's trench lines. On the morning of October 29 he sent the 12th Division against Podgora hill yet again, accompanied by artillery and mortar barrages. The bombardment was indiscriminate and inflicted minimal losses on the Dalmatians; several stray shells hit Gorizia, causing civilian casualties. The exhausted Italian infantry somehow managed to rise from their trenches and attempted to cross the mere hundred paces between them and the Austrians. A few *fanti* even reached the Dalmatians' positions, and the usual hand-to-hand fighting ensued. The assault was hopeless, however, and the 12th was forced to concede defeat by the afternoon. In a rare display of Habsburg firepower, the Austrian artillery shelled Capello's infantry for hours on end, saving the tired Dalmatian foot soldiers. The withdrawal of the 12th Division to its own lines was welcome news to the Austrians because the

58th was worn out by the fierce brawling. Field Marshal Archduke Friedrich, titular commander of the Austrian Army, observed much of the day's fighting. He was visiting the Isonzo front and wanted to see Zeidler's methods for himself, so he watched the battle from the nearby headquarters of the division's artillery. The archduke was astounded by how close the two sides' trenches were, and by how long and hard the infantry mixed it up with knives and bayonets. Friedrich, like all generals and staff officers who could stomach watching the troops in action, was shocked by the cost of the bloody fighting.

Cadorna was still determined to keep battering the Austrian defenses; after all, he had not seen his tactics at work with his own eyes. The appalling casualty figures that reached his headquarters at Udine—figures he did his best to keep from the king, the government, and the people—represented only numbers on a page, not human lives sacrificed to his hopeless schemes. He committed the Duke of Aosta's 3rd Army to another attack on Mt. San Michele. Hundreds of guns dropped high-explosive shells on the Austrian trenches through the morning of October 28, and the inevitable infantry advance soon followed. Two entire army corps charged the Austrian lines in the San Michele sector between the Vipacco River and Mt. Sei Busi, ninety-six infantry battalions on a front of less than four and a half miles—an Italian foot soldier every two and a half feet. The Austrian machine gunners had more targets than they had ammunition. The Duke of Aosta's infantry fell in the thousands before they reached the VII Corps's trenches, nowhere more than 300 paces to the east. The four divisions that assaulted Mt. San Michele itself made some progress during the day. Only a determined nighttime counterattack by the Hungarian 17th Division pushed the XIV Corps back to its own lines.

The slaughter resumed the following morning. October 29 was filled with Italian charges and Austrian counterstrokes. The Italian XIV Corps, mauled by the struggles around Mt. San Michele, fought throughout the day, but the Romanians of the 43rd Regiment held on to the summit. Both armies were running out of fresh troops. The 3rd Army's offensive was losing steam due to frightful losses, and Archduke Joseph's VII Corps sent its last reserve battalion into the line on October 29. The two sides were now only 100 to 200 paces apart, in many cases much closer. The defenders had had no sleep in six days, rat-bitten unburied Italian and Austrian corpses lay everywhere, and the wounded could not be evacuated. Maimed soldiers sought refuge in *dolinas* and waited for the shelling to end. There had not been fresh food or water for days. Thousands of soldiers in both armies suffered from cholera, brought by Austrian reinforcements from the Eastern front. Even Boroević's rear areas were not safe from Italian shelling. One unfortunate half-company of Austrian militiamen, resting in a *dolina* behind the front, was struck by a large-caliber shell. It left nineteen dead and twenty-six wounded, with the survivors running around insane. The Carso's defenders had reached the breaking point.

Cadorna anticipated that Boroević's army could take little more. He observed, "The time has arrived to pick the fruits of the pressure exerted on the enemy and now to decide to begin the decisive phase of the offensive." Hence he ordered another massed offensive by the 2nd and 3rd Armies to outflank Gorizia and to attack the city head-on. It began on the 2nd Army's northern flank, with an attack on the Plava bridgehead. The objective of the II Corps, as it had been since the beginning of the fighting five months before, was clearing Hill 383 of Austrian defenders and advancing southward down the Bainsizza plateau toward Gorizia. A successful drive would surround Mt. Sabotino and seize Mt. Santo, an important Austrian observation post overlooking the city. The 32nd Division prepared to hit Hill 383 from the north and west while part of the 3rd Division readied to take it from the south. The rest of the 3rd would take the village of Zagora, a mile downstream from Plava. The attack started late on October 31, when Italian infantry emerged from the darkness and charged the trenches of Guido Novak's 1st Mountain Brigade. The 3rd Division struck Zagora especially hard, and the Austrian defenses were severely tested. The Plava Corps continued to push the next morning, with renewed attacks at dawn. The defenders of Zagora began to give way as *fanti* advanced through the rain and fog; the river road leading straight to Gorizia was nearly in Italian hands. Desperate to avert a disaster, the Austrian 18th Division dispatched its only nearby reserve, the 4th Battalion of the 4th Infantry Regiment, to Zagora.

The small but significant battle for Zagora showed the vital role played by individuals even in a *Materielschlacht*. The battalion commander, Emil Fey, was an unlikely hero. The twenty-nine-year-old son of a state insurance official, Fey had served in the army since the age of eighteen, when he enlisted as an officer cadet, and had spent almost his entire career in the supply corps. Casualties among frontline officers were so heavy that Fey was sent to the infantry in March 1915, to the ancient 4th Infantry, the *Hoch- und Deutschmeister* Regiment, recruited in his home city of Vienna.[1] He had successfully traded in his logistical charts for a rifle and bayonet, but Plava would be his first real battlefield test. Fey and his Viennese battalion, 800 strong, arrived at Zagora just in time to meet the Italian breakout. Aware that an Italian victory would mean disaster, Fey led his soldiers in repeated bayonet charges against the onrushing 3rd Division. The Italians and Austrians fought through the day for control of the worthless little village of Zagora, until both sides were exhausted. By the evening the ruins of the village were again in Austrian hands, and the tired and weakened 3rd Division had been firmly contained; there was no longer any danger of an Italian drive down the Isonzo valley. Fey and his troops had saved Gorizia's northern flank, for which the captain was awarded the Knight's Cross of the Order of Maria Theresia, the highest Habsburg decoration. The cost had been steep. Only a quarter of the Viennese battalion survived November 1 unscathed, Fey miraculously among them. Some 600 comrades lay dead and wounded around Zagora, on the banks of the Isonzo.

The opportunity for a quick victory at Plava evaporated with Fey's exploits, but the II Corps continued to throw its infantry at Hill 383. Until November 4, the 32nd and 3rd Divisions waged daily battles to advance up the barren hillside, without success. A strong Austrian counterattack on the evening of November 2 nearly pushed the Italians into the Isonzo. After five days of heavy fighting, the II Corps abandoned its efforts. Its two divisions had been completely destroyed. The defenders suffered notably as well: the 1st Mountain Brigade lost 40 percent of its soldiers dead and wounded, including Major General Novak, severely injured by Italian shrapnel during the November 2 counterstroke. Nevertheless, the brigade still held Hill 383 and Zagora. The Italian gain was limited to the capture of a single Austrian position and an advance of little more than a hundred paces near Zagora.

While the II Corps sacrificed itself at Plava, Capello's neighboring VI Corps restarted its drive on Gorizia. At dawn on November 1, Capello's guns opened up on the 58th Division's whole four-and-a-half-mile front. The 4th Division was so spent by the last attack on Sabotino that its place was taken by the Marche Brigade, assisted by the Grenadiers. The 55th and 56th Regiments advanced up Sabotino's north face while the two regiments of *Granatieri* assaulted the western side. The attacks continued until late on November 2, but captured no Austrian trenches, and the four shattered regiments had to retreat down the mountain. The 11th Division's attempts to take Oslavia also failed bloodily, after some minor early gains. Zeidler committed his last reserve battalion to push the 11th back to its own lines. The 12th Division's effort on Podgora hill was more successful. By November 3, when Capello was forced to cease his attacks because of his troops' complete exhaustion, the 12th still held Hills 184 and 240 west of the village of Podgora. They had been bought at a cost of 10,300 dead and wounded to the VI Corps since October 18, according to official Italian figures. The two hills were militarily insignificant, even useless; they brought the 2nd Army less than a hundred paces closer to Gorizia. But they were the greatest Italian gains during the entire Third Battle. Only in Cadorna's army would such an advance have been hailed as a victory or considered a profitable trade of men's lives for territory.

The 3rd Army had absolutely nothing to show for its eighteen-day battle on the Carso. The blasting of Austrian positions by the Duke of Aosta's guns continued unabated, giving the defenders no chance to rest or regroup. A major two-division attack on Mt. San Michele on November 1 inflicted heavy losses on the 17th Division but gained no ground. The next day's effort produced the same results. A shattering early morning barrage shook the mountain and collapsed many Austrian positions. The 17th Division barely survived the shelling, but, as always, just enough of Boroević's soldiers remained alive to man the machine guns that destroyed the attacking regiments of *fanti*. The 3rd Army launched its final attack of the Third Battle on November 4, but this brave effort likewise won nothing for the Duke of Aosta and his men. Two and a half weeks of powerful blows against the Austrian trenches on the Carso proved utterly fruitless. Heroic sacrifice, bolstered by almost a thousand guns, could not crack the Carso's defenses. The Italians failed to take and hold a single Austrian position on the entire Doberdò plateau.

The failed offensive had cost Cadorna 67,000 soldiers. After the war the Italians admitted to 10,733 killed, 9,624 missing,[2] 44,290 wounded, and 2,351 captured during the Third Battle. All figures are certainly underestimates; the Austrians captured at least 4,000 *fanti*, and there is no reason to think the other categories are substantially more accurate. To win a few positions around Zagora and two hills west of Podgora, Cadorna had sacrificed an entire army, an average of almost 4,000 soldiers a day. Italy still had plenty of fresh men left; Cadorna's methods had hardly begun to tax Italy's manpower reserves. Italy's industries were just beginning to mobilize. Cadorna could keep fighting such futile and sacrificial battles for many months to come without overly straining Italy's warmaking potential. There was enough men and matériel available for many more such offensives. Yet, the morale of the army was being tried as never before. D'Annunzio, a fanatical believer in fighting spirit and redemption through suffering, hailed the catastrophe on the Carso as "the ideal transfiguration of the Italian peasant"; always searching for a poetic metaphor, he compared the "sublimation of the spirit" he witnessed on the Doberdò plateau to Dante's *Inferno*. Doubtless the doomed *fanti*, without literary allusions to comfort them, felt differently.

Cadorna's brutal tactics and unforgiving discipline were at least as great an enemy to the frontline Italian soldier as the Austrians were. The *fantaccino* had to endure not just the virtual certainty of being killed or maimed, but also a deplorable medical system, poor rations, few distractions from battle, and the army's harsh code of justice. Mussolini, a veteran of the Third Battle and what he modestly termed "those days of extreme hardship" on the upper Isonzo, defined morale as "the sense of responsibility, the impulse toward the fulfillment of duty, the spirit of resistance, which an individual possesses." The ordinary Italian foot soldier displayed such qualities in abundance, even during the darkest hours of the Third Battle of the Isonzo. Whole brigades and divisions were slaughtered over and over again, only to return the next day to the same hill, without a mutiny. The Italian Army was holding up surprisingly well to the unprecedented strains of the Isonzo fighting. The elite *Alpini*, *Bersaglieri* and Grenadiers displayed remarkable dash, as the army anticipated, but even regiments recruited in southern Italy, an unmartial region with a poor military reputation, fought bravely. The Sassari Brigade from Sardinia, another region which the *Comando Supremo* believed produced mediocre soldiers, distinguished itself on the Carso.[3] It lost more than 2,500 soldiers, including its commander, during the Third Battle. The ordinary Italian peasant, backbone of Cadorna's infantry, was a very good soldier when well led, recklessly courageous in the attack. He would fight bravely even when poorly led, as was too often the case. Still, how much longer could the 2nd and 3rd Armies be abused in such a fashion without a collapse of fighting spirit?

The cost of the Third Battle for the 5th Army was proportionately even worse. Boroević's forces, ten divisions strong at the battle's end, registered almost 42,000 casualties, including 8,228 killed, 7,201 missing, and 26,418 wounded. The policy of holding every inch of ground had again led to terrible losses. More than half the casualties, nearly 24,000, were sustained by Archduke Joseph's VII Corps—a figure equal to 85 percent of the corps' rifle strength on October 18. The Hungarians' courage and sacrifice had again prevented an Italian breakthrough on the Carso. Their legendary ability to endure endless heavy bombardments assumed its rightful place in the annals of Habsburg military history. Amazingly, infantrymen of all nationalities showed no signs of weakness in the face of repeated Italian attacks. Against all odds, they continued to resist the enemy ferociously. Yet, the cost of the Third Battle in men and matériel raised pessimistic queries at 5th Army headquarters and the High Command. Both Boroević and Franz Conrad wondered how long Austria could sustain such a pounding. Her army and industry, strained by a three-front war, could ill afford such expenditures of scarce infantry, weaponry, and munitions. One *Materielschlacht* was enough; a series of several more beatings at the hands of Cadorna's armies would quickly prove an unbearable burden. The Third Battle signaled the appearance of a new kind of war for the Italians and Austrians, the pattern for all future battles of the Isonzo. The new warfare was called *fabrikliche Krieg*—assembly-line war—by staff officers safely removed from the front lines. In the long run, such bloody industrialized fighting could only favor the Italians, who possibly could still afford it. The tired infantry holding the trenches on both sides of the Isonzo understood only that it meant more artillery, mortars, machine guns, and other highly lethal weapons, and a corresponding ever decreasing life expectancy for themselves.

SIX

"THE SUPERIOR IS ALWAYS RIGHT, ESPECIALLY WHEN HE IS WRONG"

Despite more than five months of war on the Isonzo, many civilians near the front continued to lead a tolerably normal existence. The fighting had shattered the security of prewar life in the Littoral, but much of day-to-day living remained unchanged. In Trieste, safely behind the front lines, residents were able to live reasonably undisturbed by the nearby slaughter. The war had deprived the city of many of its young men and much of its prosperity, both perhaps forever, but the essential patterns of life were able to continue without drastic alterations. Heavy Italian bombardments of the Carso could be heard clearly anywhere in the city, but Trieste had been spared the direct effects of Luigi Cadorna's three great offensives. The same could not be said of Gorizia. The City of Violets had been trapped in the middle of the Isonzo fighting from the beginning. The front line, where Luigi Capello's VI Corps and Erwin Zeidler's Dalmatians dueled ferociously for every hill, ran through its once industrious western suburbs. Still, even many civilians in Gorizia managed to live surprisingly normally while the war took its toll all around them. There were not many Gorizians left in their city, barely 10,000 by November, less than one-third the prewar population. Some diehards, mostly older residents, refused to abandon their homes. Many of them were retired Austrian officers, determined to wait it out no matter the cost or duration. Some residents had stayed behind to greet Cadorna's legions when they arrived in the city; there were not many, however, and by now they were deeply disappointed. Such Gorizians would have many more painful months to wait for their liberation and redemption.

In the meantime, the city's residents enjoyed few luxuries; war-induced inflation and rationing quickly impoverished everyone. Nevertheless, a façade of happier prewar days lived on, and much that was familiar had remained. The city still had its newspaper, and many businesses stayed open. There were few goods in the shops, and even fewer advertisements in the paper, but Gorizians contented themselves with what they had. A handful of schools were still in session, and the ever efficient Austrian postal service kept the mail coming to Gorizia with few delays. Hotels continued to stay open and accept guests, although there were few visitors now. Most important to the city's morale, the cafés were still in operation. Throughout the Habsburg Empire, the café had long served as a refuge from the pressures of day-to-day life, a place where people of all classes could take a break from the world, visit with their longtime friends, and catch up on the day's news, and Gorizia was no exception. Even during the worst fighting, the cafés stayed open. The wartime coffee was of poor quality, and there was little to discuss except the war, but Gorizians had much to forget for a while, and were happy to have their beloved cafés to comfort them. The city's most fashionable café, located in the main square, was as popular as ever. Many of its habitués were officers of the 58th Division, seeking a temporary refuge there from the fighting on Podgora hill, only one and a half miles to the west. Weary officers could walk from the forward trenches to the city's main square in twenty minutes. There they enjoyed a brief glimpse of prewar life, a world destroyed by the endless fighting. They ensured that the café was always full, and it was frequently difficult to find a table. The table at the front window, however, was rarely requested, even during the café's busiest hours; it was in the clear line of fire of an Italian machine gun on Podgora hill, an unpleasant surprise when first discovered.

Still, many Gorizians could be forgiven for forgetting during lulls in the fighting that there was a war going on around them, that Cadorna's army was less than two miles away. It was impossible to sleep during the frequent around-the-clock Italian bombardments, but not many Gorizians feared for their lives. Astonishingly few residents had been killed by the fighting. Cadorna's general policy of not bombarding majority-Italian cities meant that only a handful of shells and bombs had landed in Gorizia itself, despite all the Austrian military positions in and around the city. There were unpleasant exceptions, of course, such as the huge 305mm shell that hit an army repair shop, killing and wounding nearly a hundred workers. So far, however, the Isonzo fighting had proved to be more a hardship than a terror for the residents of Gorizia who had remained in their city for the duration of the war.

The hundreds of thousands of Austrian and Italian soldiers dug in around Gorizia and on the Isonzo were not so fortunate. By November, cold Alpine winds had arrived and late autumn rains turned trenches into seas of mud, making the already primitive living conditions dangerously unsanitary. The filthy trenches, with their limited bathing facilities, cold and damp sleeping quarters, and inadequate latrines, were a haven for infectious diseases; the countless thousands of unburied corpses all along the Isonzo only increased the opportunities for disease to spread among the living. Only the legions of rats that plagued both armies thrived in such surroundings. Without any allegiances, the rodents were free to roam contentedly from trench to trench, across no man's land, growing fat on the flesh of dead soldiers. The soldiers were much less happy, and less adapted to life in such squalor. During the brief lull in the fighting, the toll of seriously ill Italians and Austrians rose alarmingly. Tens of thousands of soldiers in both armies became gravely sick from a number of pervasive maladies—trench foot, skin infections, persistent stomach ailments, and, worst of all, cholera. A major cholera epidemic broke out on the Isonzo in late October and reached its peak in mid-November, taking a heavy toll on both sides. The Italians, poorly prepared to deal with the crisis, were harder hit. Their squalid and overcrowded field hospitals were swamped by *fanti* struck down with cholera, and were unable to cope with the crisis. Thousands of Italian soldiers whom the Austrian bullets had missed were killed by disease; they died needlessly and painfully in dirty army hospitals.

One of the many Italian infantrymen laid low by disease was Benito Mussolini. Like many of Cadorna's fighting men, he feared Italian hospitals more than the enemy. He survived the Third Battle unscathed, and even managed to avoid the cholera epidemic, but in November he was infected with typhus. His condition worsened, and he was sent to an army hospital in Cividale, twenty miles behind the front, where he nearly died. He was eventually dispatched to a larger hospital in Milan to recover. There Mussolini enjoyed an almost three-month convalescence, missing the Fourth Battle entirely. However, like many Italian soldiers, he had not just the enemy and disease to contend with, but also his own army's troublesome bureaucracy, combined in his case with political interference. Before Mussolini fell ill, his colonel offered him a chance to avoid the fighting by becoming the regimental clerk. Certainly the former journalist was better suited to such a desk job than to life in the trenches, where his chances of survival were slim. Mussolini declined the offer: he came to Isonzo to fight, not to type. He did want the chance to become an officer, however. The colonel approved Mussolini's request, which was a normal one, given the ex-journalist's education. Mussolini was immediately promoted to corporal and was soon on his way to an officer training school safely behind the lines. Yet his time as an officer cadet was destined to be short-lived. The *Comando Supremo* soon received word of Mussolini's admission to the school and reacted immediately; citing his "deplorable background," the War Ministry decided without delay that it could never grant such an infamous radical a commission. Prime Minister Antonio Salandra even became involved. He, too, agreed that the officer corps was no place for a troublemaker like Mussolini, no matter what his educational qualifications were. Salandra personally saw to it that the corporal-cadet was dismissed from the school and sent straight back to the Isonzo. After only a week in the rear, Mussolini was again in the high Julian Alps with his *Bersaglieri* comrades, his career as an officer ended before it could begin.

While Mussolini was being shuffled around by the army bureaucracy, and thousands of *fanti* suffered from cholera, Cadorna was at his comfortable head-quarters in Udine, planning his next offensive. The bloody Third Battle had failed to achieve anything of note, but this naturally did not restrain Cadorna from another attempt to break the Austrian hold on the Isonzo. Despite the abundant evidence that Italian firepower and masses of infantry could not yet hope to penetrate Svetozar Boroević's defenses, the count's faith in himself and his methods continued to reign unchallenged by doubts. His obsession with the Isonzo, particularly the drive to Trieste, persisted, undulled by three catastroph-ically failed offensives. Indeed, the terrible cost of the first three battles tragi-cally served to make future battles necessary. Cadorna knew that his frightful butcher bill demanded the capture of Trieste and the redemption of *Italia irredenta;* nothing less could silence his many vocal critics. By November, only a complete and unchallengeable victory over Austria could possibly make his army's sacrifices seem worthwhile. He thus refused to entertain other strategic options: only through the Isonzo valley could Cadorna see victory. A Balkan operation in support of Serbia, recommended by some generals and politicians, might well have delivered notable military and diplomatic gains, at a fraction of the cost of the Isonzo bloodbath; Austria's southern frontier was lightly de-fended, and assisting the Serbs with a few divisions might have produced deci-sive results. Cadorna would hear none of it. He was equally dismissive when the navy, in a rare gesture of interservice cooperation, offered to help Cadorna land troops on Austria's vulnerable Dalmatian coast and islands. An amphibious landing there, or better yet on the Istrian peninsula, would have turned Boroević's southern flank and forced a serious—perhaps fatal—weakening of the 5th Army's hold on the Isonzo. Nevertheless, Cadorna had no interest in such schemes. He could envision only a direct strategy; more indirect methods ap-pealed to his rigid mind not at all. The *Comando Supremo* therefore remained irrevocably committed to the Isonzo front.

To be fair to Cadorna, he was by no means the only Allied general in 1915 who persisted in seeking a breakthrough where none could possibly be achieved. The Allied war effort in the latter half of the year was characterized by repeated dismally failed attempts to dislodge German and Austrian static defenses. In the East, major Russian offensives intended to push the Central Powers back into Galicia gained no ground but suffered grievous losses; by the end of the year the Russians appeared to be barely in the war. Worse, offensives by the Western Allies could not recapture lost ground in France and Flanders at any price. Joseph Joffre's much anticipated late September "war winner" fell apart after only three days. The battle was not over, however; in a pattern that was repeated on all fronts, attacks produced counterattacks, which only led to further futile attacks. By the time the second Champagne offensive sputtered to a halt in early November, the French had lost 145,000 casualties without regaining any French soil worth mentioning. Joffre was certainly no closer to winning the war. The British participated, too, rounding out the Allies' tale of woe by adding a doomed effort in Flanders, what the easily victorious Germans termed *das Leichenfeld von Loos*—the corpse field of Loos. Everywhere the defense reigned supreme. The Allies seemed incapable of evicting the Central Powers from their positions in the East, in the West, or on the Isonzo. Nevertheless, both Joffre and Douglas Haig, the new commander of the British Expeditionary Force, were planning even greater offensives—with more men and more guns—in 1916 to gain the ground they so painfully failed to take in 1915. No general, no army had yet learned how restore mobility to the battlefield, how to overcome the dramatic superiority of entrenched machine guns and artillery over human flesh. That would take time, and countless more lives to achieve. Cadorna was hardly alone in his ignorance.

Even so, Cadorna does stand out as unique for his obstinance and ruthlessness, which were remarkable even by the terrible standards of the First World War. His intolerance of opinions contrary to his own cherished military theories was legendary. Cadorna's favorite dictum, quoted regularly at his headquarters, was the old Piedmontese maxim, "The superior is always right, especially when he is wrong." Commanders in the field who disappointed the chief of staff were quickly "torpedoed," sent to the rear in disgrace. Members of his staff who dared question Cadorna's methods were dealt with far more directly. Talented staff officers who quietly noted the obvious—that Cadorna's strategy was dangerously simpleminded, and his tactics were lethal—were subject to imprisonment for insubordination. Several of Italy's finest military minds were thus thrown in jail for their common sense.[1]

The harsh treatment meted out to officers who disappointed or questioned Cadorna was nevertheless mild compared to the sentences that awaited common soldiers who fell afoul of Cadorna's iron discipline. The chief of staff's brutal understanding of how to motivate his men made no allowances for human frailty. In the best Piedmontese tradition, he made no attempts to inspire his troops to victory; fear and intimidation were always more congenial to his uncompromisingly authoritarian outlook. His infantrymen knew there was no choice but to charge the Austrian lines, no matter how hopeless the odds. Cadorna made sure his men understood that the firing squad awaited those who would not face the enemy's machine guns. During and after every battle, accused deserters and cowards were rounded up and executed publicly, lest any soldier entertain ideas of avoiding combat. By November, Cadorna's disciplinary methods had hardened further still. To make his troops fight with greater determination, Cadorna, like most Italian soldiers an avid admirer of all things Roman, resurrected one of the ancient Roman Army's most loathsome practices, decimation. In this atavistic ritual, regiments that failed to achieve their objectives were taken out of the fighting, lined up in rows, and every tenth soldier was executed, to encourage his comrades to do better next time. The effect of decimation and Cadorna's other cruel disciplinary methods on the Italian Army's morale was understandably corrosive. Yet Cadorna's iron rule ensured that his regiments would not easily desert or refuse battle. It took a very brave soldier to contemplate desertion in Cadorna's army.

Assured that his divisions would advance, Cadorna prepared to send his armies into battle again. He was convinced that Boroević's forces were so weakened by the Third Battle that a rapidly executed follow-up offensive would achieve the gains which so far had eluded him. His battle plan was essentially unchanged. Cadorna intended to refight the Third Battle, almost without modifications—except that this time he was confident the tired and depleted Austrian regiments would not hold their ground. The Fourth Battle, like its predecessor, was aimed foremost at Gorizia, with major supporting offensives north and south of the city. As a month before, Cadorna believed that the 2nd Army could outflank the city from the direction of Plava while the 3rd Army could outflank it from the Mt. San Michele area. To achieve this, Cadorna again had the bulk of Italy's field forces at his disposal. He was fortunate that the army's wartime expansion program was beginning to bear fruit. Months of increased draft calls, coupled with the recall of more classes of reservists to the colors, meant that by November the Italian Army had expanded unprecedentedly, despite the enormous numbers of troops needed to replace Cadorna's losses. The mobilization of Italian industry for the war effort supplied the newly raised units with the substantial quantities of modern equipment they needed. Nine new infantry divisions had been added to the order of battle, and overall the number of infantry battalions had grown by one-sixth. The army's expansion was tailored to the tactical needs of the Isonzo fighting, which demanded specialist mountain troops and sappers, lots of infantry, and, most of all, substantial quantities of heavy artillery. The 1915 expansion program gave Cadorna 181 freshly raised combat battalions: 102 infantry (seventy-two line, plus four *Bersaglieri* and twenty-six *Alpini*), forty-two artillery (four mountain, eighteen heavy, and twenty superheavy), and thirty-seven of combat engineers. At last the army was being reorganized to suit the siegelike requirements of the Isonzo front. Only with an army organized for trench warfare could Cadorna hope to break through.

General Pietro Frugoni's 2nd Army was to bear the brunt of the offensive. It controlled fourteen of Cadorna's twenty-eight divisions on the Isonzo. Its IV and VII Corps were supposed to at last take the Tolmein bridgehead, and the II Corps was ordered to assault the Plava area and roll up the Austrian lines from the northwest. Most important, Capello's VI Corps was given the mission of clearing Oslavia and Podgora of Austrian troops, which had to be done before the 2nd Army could cross the Isonzo and reach Gorizia. Farther south, the Duke of Aosta's 3rd Army, ten divisions strong, was ordered to seize the western edge of the Carso, particularly Mt. San Michele, with its four corps. Cadorna held an additional two corps with four divisions in reserve to reinforce the 2nd Army's drive on Gorizia. By November 9, he was ready to send his armies against the Isonzo line again. His infantry had enjoyed less than a week's rest since the end of the Third Battle. They had had little time to regroup and absorb replacements, the vital human fuel on which Cadorna's war machine ran, and which his tactics consumed so voraciously. Regiments shattered only days earlier on San Michele, Podgora, and Plava were ordered back into the fighting line, to be sacrificed again on hillsides with deservedly evil reputations.

The Austrian infantrymen holding the opposite trenches were hardly more enthusiastic about resuming the fighting. Boroević's troops also had been ravaged by cholera, and had enjoyed less than a week to rest and replenish shattered regiments. The 5th Army was tired and understrength; the Third Battle had pushed the polyglot army to the breaking point. Ten percent of its 150 infantry battalions were too weak to be deployed in the fighting line. Morale had been frayed by months of terrible shelling and costly counterattacks. Still, Boroević had not resorted to shooting his own men *en masse* to keep them in the fighting line. There was strong discipline, to be sure, and a captured Austrian deserter was destined for the firing squad just as his Italian counterpart would be, but on the whole the Austrians continued to fight because they believed in the cause. Naive talk about the ghost of Radetzky and teaching the *Katzel-macher* (cat eaters) a lesson had disappeared months before, but fighting spirit remained high in Boroević's multinational legions, even after three bloody battles on the Isonzo.

The 5th Army was not as strong in early November as it had been in mid-October, but it remained an impressive force. It had nine divisions in the line and a tenth in reserve behind Gorizia; all divisions were short of both men and guns, but they were competently led veteran formations. Every province and region of Austria and Hungary was represented in their ranks. The German-Slovene 44th Rifle Division held the Flitsch basin, and the mixed 50th and 1st Divisions, collections of polyglot mountain battalions from all over the empire, occupied Mrzli ridge and the Tolmein bridgehead, respectively. The Bainsizza plateau, including the Plava bridgehead, was garrisoned by the 18th Division, a multinational formation with a high proportion of Croats and Serbs. As ever, the approaches to Gorizia were guarded by the tough South Slavs of the Dalmatian 58th. The San Michele sector was now occupied by the veteran Alpine German 6th Division, but the much abused Hungarian 17th remained on the northern Carso as well. The central and southern edges of the plateau, the road to Trieste,

were held by the hard-fighting mixed German-Slovene regiments of the 22nd
Rifle and 28th Infantry Divisions. Austria had collected regiments from every
corner of the Habsburg possessions to defend the Isonzo line, including many
soldiers from the empire's most martial races. In all, Boroević's command
promised to offer the Italians as hard a fight as ever; the Austrian infantry was
still determined to exact a frightful price for every foot of the Isonzo front.

The Italians again helped the defenders by not bothering to hide their intentions. As before the Third Battle, the river's west bank was busy with frenetic
activity in the days before the offensive. Signs of an imminent Italian attack
were everywhere. Intelligence officers at 5th Army headquarters monitored the
numerous indications: increased radio traffic, more trains coming from the
west, the arrival of more artillery and large stocks of ammunition, and above all
the delivery of impressive numbers of fresh infantry. Closer to the fighting line,
Austrian positions all along the front observed the unconcealed Italian movements of men, guns, and munitions that promised a Fourth Battle of the Isonzo.
When Cadorna began his renewed offensive where the last had left off, it came
as no surprise to the defenders.

The fourth Italian attempt to break through Boroević's defenses began on
November 10, precisely at noon. Along the entire front, the massed guns of the
2nd and 3rd Armies opened up, pouring tons of high explosive on Austrian positions. As expected, the shelling was particularly heavy in the San Michele,
Podgora, and Plava sectors. The bombardment lasted only four hours, but it
made up in intensity what it lacked in duration. Even battle-hardened veterans
of earlier Italian barrages were shocked by the power of the preparatory bombardment. Many dugouts and trench sections, especially between Podgora and
Oslavia, were flattened by heavy shells. At 4 P.M., Capello's infantry emerged
from their positions, bayonets fixed, and charged the Austrian trenches. The
northern end of the 58th Division's sector was reinforced by a brigade of Poles
from East Galicia atop Mt. Sabotino. The Poles on "Snake Mountain" were attacked by General Montuori's 4th Division. This division, which had already
sacrificed so many men on Sabotino's rocky slopes, mounted a mass infantry
attack up the bare hillsides. Although the Poles lost several machine guns to the
shelling, the infantry charge accomplished nothing; as ever, enough machine
gunners and riflemen survived to stop the *fanti* well before they reached the
Austrian trenches. Capello's corps did somewhat better on the sector's southern
flank. The 12th Division, attempting yet again to take all of Podgora hill,
charged the Dalmatians' trenches, little more than a hundred paces to the east.
On the hill's southern end, the Italians reached the Austrian positions, and vicious hand-to-hand fighting with the Croatian and Serbian defenders continued
until midnight. The neighboring 11th Division's attack in the Oslavia sector
registered one notable gain on November 10. The division's 70th Infantry Regiment evicted the Austrians from the village of Oslavia. In truth, the village no

longer existed; the Italians captured only a few worthless ruins of houses abandoned months earlier. Still, the loss of the village to the Italians was a psychological setback for Zeidler's troops.

The fighting resumed with even greater fury the next morning. All through the day on November 11, the armies dueled for control of Oslavia and Podgora. The Italians and Austrians were now everywhere less than a hundred feet apart, in many places within easy hand grenade-throwing range. The fierce battle was decided with hand grenades, bayonets, and knives. The 12th Division tried in vain to expand its tenuous hold on Podgora hill. Capello sent the 6,000–strong Grenadier Brigade to Podgora to assist the 12th, but despite valorous efforts it, too, failed with heavy losses; only 3,200 *Granatieri* returned to the Italian lines that evening. At Oslavia, the 11th Division mixed it up with the Dalmatians all day in an inconclusive fight until both sides were exhausted. That evening, Zeidler, acting in accordance with Boroević's orders that all lost ground had to be retaken, dispatched his last reserve, the 37th Rifle Regiment, to Oslavia to recapture the ruined village. The counterstroke surprised the tired *fanti*, and by the early morning hours of November 12, Oslavia was again Austrian. The 11th Division had been pushed back to its starting positions on November 10, and Zeidler's troops had captured more than 500 Italian soldiers.

Capello was furious. He was as determined to gain ground as Boroević was loath to lose it. Adamant that his troops must reach Gorizia, he sent the exhausted 11th and 12th Divisions back into combat without any rest. The seesaw battle for Oslavia continued all day and into the evening. By the late hours of November 12, the VI Corps had recaptured the tactically useless ruins. Zeidler's Dalmatians were too tired to mount a counterattack, and there were no fresh troops left in the Gorizia sector, so the night was abnormally tranquil. By morning, however, Zeidler had collected a few half-strength companies to retake Oslavia. This attempt, like the previous one, succeeded in evicting the weary Italians from the village. By November 13, after four days of fighting, the VI Corps had nothing to show for its heavy losses. Capello's divisions had failed to hold their initial minor gains.

The story was much the same in the Plava sector. Only three battalions of the 1st Mountain Brigade occupied the two-mile river front, so the two divisions of the II Corps—twenty-four battalions—should have made considerable progress against the badly outnumbered Austrians. As before Gorizia, November 10 attacks by the 3rd and 33rd Divisions made initial gains up Hill 383. However, a lightning counterattack by a battalion each of the Viennese 4th and Dalmatian 22nd Regiments at dawn on November 11 took all the lost ground and even captured some Italian trenches. Later that morning the 3rd Division, undeterred by the setback, launched a mass infantry assault on the Austrian entrenchments at Zagora, a mile downstream. Battalions from five different regiments charged the village, and nearly overran the weak Austrian defenses. Only rapid action by the Viennese and Dalmatians, reinforced by a battalion of Bosnians, pushed the Italians back. Fire from machine guns overlooking the attackers tore through their ranks, pinning the *fanti* down. Sustained shelling from two supporting Austrian mountain artillery batteries ripped apart the trapped battalions, shattering the 3rd Division's attack. Few survivors returned from the massacre, and for the moment the Italians were too weak to attempt further offensives at the Plava bridgehead. As in every previous effort, the Plava Corps had failed to advance toward Gorizia, and the 3rd and 32nd Divisions were yet again destroyed around "Bloody 383."

The 3rd Army's offensive on the Carso, aimed at clearing San Michele of its Austrian defenders, began on November 10. Attacks by eight divisions failed to make any progress that day or the next. The 6th Division's hold on Mt. San Michele was never endangered by these efforts, which, like so many before, fell apart in the face of concentrated machine gun fire. The Duke of Aosta wanted desperately to attain the objective that had eluded him for the past five and a half months, so on November 13 he sent the XI Corps up the slopes of San Michele again. The noontime attack by several regiments up the mountain's north face started promisingly. But a second, follow-up effort that afternoon to advance closer to the summit was cut short with a vigorous counterattack by the 7th and 9th *Jäger* Battalions,[2] tough Carinthian and Styrian mountain fighters. By dusk the German riflemen had chased the attackers back down the north slope. Attempts by the XI Corps to seize neighboring hills ended just as badly; a victorious company of the 17th Division's 43rd Regiment, garrisoning nearby Hill 143, found itself surrounded by more than 500 dead and dying Italian foot soldiers after a hard fight. The Italians renewed their attacks the next morning. After a three-hour bombardment of the VII Corps' entrenchments, the 29th Division charged up San Michele's north face, where so many attacks had drowned in blood. The defenders, just two companies of the 2nd Bosnian Regiment, were soon overwhelmed by the thousands of *fanti*, and were forced to retreat to the second defensive line. By the afternoon of November 13, the 29th Division held a 600-foot section of the Austrians' main entrenchments, and were close to taking the summit of San Michele.

An Italian advance to the peak had to be prevented at all costs, so the VII Corps commander, Archduke Joseph, ordered a counterstroke by his only nearby units, the survivors of the half-battalion of Bosnians, plus the 7th and 9th *Jägers*. The determined Austrian effort to push the 29th Division back down the hill continued well into the night. Hand-to-hand combat in the Austrian trenches with knives and clubs produced frightful losses for both sides until the Italians broke and ran. By the early hours of November 14, the XI Corps had again been pushed away from San Michele's summit. Retaking their own trenches cost the Austrians 540 dead and wounded; further Italian efforts on November 14 and 15, which lasted until the 3rd Army was completely spent, inflicted 1,750 more casualties on the VII Corps. The price of holding on to San Michele had reached unsustainable heights: from October 15 to November 15, the 17th Division lost 11,700 soldiers, its entire rifle strength. How much longer could the Austrians possibly absorb such losses? Worse, the Fourth Battle was far from over. The Austrian High Command sent Boroević the scant reserves it possessed and hoped for the best.

Italian losses on the Carso were even higher than Austria's frightful casualties, but Cadorna was typically unconcerned. He still had plenty of fresh divisions and reservoirs of replacements left to throw into the fray. He knew that Boroević's troops were exhausted, both in the Gorizia in the Carso sectors, and that there were few Austrian reserves remaining. Cadorna therefore determined that the offensive had to be continued at any cost, without concern for casualties. The breakthrough that appeared so temptingly near would justify his losses. He collected all available reserves and dispatched them to the Gorizia front. The fate of the Fourth Battle was placed in Capello's hands; his VI Corps was assigned the capture of the City of Violets, the 2nd Army's long-awaited goal. On November 17, Cadorna formally ordered a renewed offensive between Mt. Sabotino and the Adriatic, a last push to victory in 1915 before the approaching winter brought an end to major operations on the Isonzo.

Just before dawn on November 18, the combined guns of the 2nd and 3rd Armies began shelling the city of Gorizia. Cadorna, believing the city's civilian population had been almost entirely evacuated, ordered a four-hour bombardment by medium and heavy batteries. More than 3,000 shells rained on the city in the morning alone. A pause in the shelling was followed by a midday air raid that lasted two hours. Italian aircraft bombed Austrian artillery positions, troop concentrations, and supply depots, but inevitably many bombs missed their targets. By the early afternoon, a quarter of Gorizia's 2,000 buildings had been destroyed, and hundreds of civilians had been killed or injured. The Italian miscalculation laid waste to much of the city Cadorna's divisions were fighting to liberate. Some 7,000 of Gorizia's residents now abandoned the city rather than face more shelling; the population was soon reduced to 3,000, less than one-tenth the prewar total.

The artillery preparation soon shifted to the 58th Division's frontline entrenchments. The relentless hammering of Austrian positions on Sabotino, Podgora, and Oslavia continued the next day. By the morning of November 20, the VI Corps was ready to attack. Three entire divisions—a dozen regiments—advanced on a front of a mile and a half, a rifle company of 200 men for every sixty feet of front. On the corps' left flank, the reinforced 4th Division charged in battalion columns up Mt. Sabotino and neighboring Hill 188, a rise between the mountain and the village of Oslavia. General Montuori personally led his division up Sabotino while the Grenadiers assaulted Hill 188. The densely packed ranks of infantry, thick columns of gray-green on the bare brown hillsides, were easy targets for Austrian machine gunners and sharpshooters. Hundreds of *fanti* fell quickly to the 58th Division's machine guns, but the survivors charged bravely forward over their fallen comrades. The Grenadiers were stalled and could not continue their advance, so they were replaced on Hill 188 by the fresh Livorno Brigade. Its 34th Regiment spearheaded the bayonet charge, personally led by Livorno's commander, Major General Count Ferruccio Trombi. The hill's Polish defenders, exhausted after two days' shelling, tried desperately to hold their positions, inflicting heavy losses on the attacking brigade, but eventually they were overwhelmed. Hill 188 fell to the Livorno Brigade, yet the fighting was by no means over; General Trombi was killed by an Austrian hand grenade not long after the hill was captured. Progress up Sabotino was negligible, and the 12th Division's attacks on Podgora hill registered only minimal gains. An Austrian counterattack after dark, led by the Dalmatian 37th Rifles, pushed the tired 12th back to its own lines with heavy losses.

Yet, Capello's troops had managed to wrest Hill 188 from the Dalmatians, a clear, if not overly significant, victory. To reward this feat, Trombi was posthumously awarded the Cross of the Military Order of Savoy, and both his regiments collectively received the Silver Medal for Bravery to adorn their colors. The 58th Division was so tested by the day's combat that it had no reserves left to retake 188. Boroević immediately sent Zeidler a Slovene regiment to recapture the lost hill, but it would not be in position until early on November 22. The inevitable counterattack would have to wait. It was therefore surprising that the Austrians succeeded in recapturing Hill 188 a day ahead of schedule. On November 11, an attempt by Capello's VI Corps to push beyond 188 ended in disaster. In the confusion, a battalion of the 37th Rifles was thrown into the melee. The Dalmatians halted the Italian advance, overran Hill 188, then unexpectedly pushed the dazed *fanti* back to their own lines. Virtually all the Austrian trenches on 188 were thus recaptured, and the hill again belonged to the 58th Division.

Capello's four divisions were too weak and exhausted to try to retake the hill. The next day, however, the Novara Brigade arrived from the Tyrolean front. Capello immediately threw its two regiments against Hill 188 and Oslavia, where they were cut to pieces. Some 270 of the brigade's soldiers were captured, and hundreds more lay dead around the ruined village and the nearby hill. Capello's last available reserve had been sacrificed. His corps desperately needed a rest before it could attack again.

The 3rd Army's offensive on the Carso proved even less successful than Capello's battle. The Duke of Aosta's XI Corps courageously resumed its efforts to take Mt. San Michele. On November 18 it attacked the mountain's north face after an intense early morning artillery barrage. San Michele's defenders, troops of the 6th Division reinforced by the 17th, lost only a few forward positions to the mass infantry assault, and those were soon retaken. The noteworthy counterattack was executed by the 11th Replacement Battalion of the 28th Regiment, the Czech unit that had gone over to the Russians in the Carpathians but fought heroically on the Carso. The battalion of recruits, just arrived on the Isonzo fresh from the training depot, lived up to the brave regiment's reestablished reputation, losing two-thirds of its men in its dynamic counterstroke on San Michele's north slope. The Italians still had plenty of reserves to throw at the mountain, and the next day they tried to advance up San Michele's south face. This attempt was even less successful, so on November 20 the XI Corps advanced up the mountain simultaneously from both the north and the south. The battle-scarred 17th Division bore the brunt of this offensive. Its Hungarian regiments, which had already shed so much blood on San Michele, stopped the two-pronged advance before it made any notable progress. The 3rd Army mounted continuous attacks for the next five days all along the Carso front, particularly around San Michele. They were all in vain, and served only to completely exhaust the attacking divisions.

Everywhere Italian forces had failed to make significant progress against the Austrian defenses. Even mass infantry attacks, amply supported by artillery and enjoying enormous numerical advantages over the defenders, could not advance except on a few very narrow fronts. The Austrians continued to excel at overturning all Italian gains; tired and weakened Italian regiments rarely were able to hold on to hard-won ground. All this terrible fighting was exacting a high price from Boroević's army, one that the Austrians could not afford. That said, the Italian exchange rate of men for ground was as depressingly unfavorable as it had ever been. Such offensives would in time wear the Austrians down, but at current rates it would be many more months—and countless more lives thrown away—before Cadorna's armies would conquer the Isonzo valley. The ill-used *fanti* were utterly exhausted; morale was at an all-time low. The infantrymen of one regiment, the 148th, even staged a mutiny, refusing to reenter the line. A few executions persuaded the rest to do their duty; but it was an alarming portent of things to come. Yet Cadorna, true to form, decided to continue the offensive. It was his last chance to make notable gains before the winter. He continued to believe that his methods would prevail, that his divisions would soon break through Boroević's entrenchments and reach Gorizia.

The Fourth Battle's final phase began neither before Gorizia nor on the Carso, but rather in the high Julian Alps. Cadorna still wanted to push the Austrians deeper into the mountains to secure his vulnerable left flank. So far during the battle, bad weather had prevented the 2nd Army from attacking on the upper Isonzo. Winter arrived earlier in the high Julian Alps than on the Carso, and by November 1 the icy mountains were covered with snow and pelted by frozen rain. The harsh climate made military operations, particularly offensives, very difficult, so during the first week of the battle the Julian front was mostly quiet. From November 10 to 18, virtually nonstop snow- and rainstorms brought all movement to a halt. While Italians and Austrians dueled fiercely for

Gorizia and San Michele, their comrades at Tolmein, and on Vršič, Javorček, and Rombon waited for battle and tried to keep warm and dry. By the third week of November, however, the weather had improved somewhat, and the IV and VIII Corps were able to participate in Cadorna's offensive. On November 25 the guns of the two Italian corps concentrated their fire on Austrian positions at the Tolmein bridgehead and on Mt. Rombon. At dawn the following morning, the 8th Division, strongly reinforced by battalions of *Alpini*, tried to break through the Austrian lines before Tolmein. The spirited attack faltered long before it reached the Isonzo. As had happened so many times before, the Italian assaults broke up on Hill 588, where Austrian machine gunners and riflemen picked off hundreds of advancing *fanti*. Simultaneous efforts by *Alpini* units to move forward in the Flitsch-Rombon sector likewise failed with heavy losses. Two days later the 8th Division was sent back into battle at the Tolmein bridgehead, but this attack proved even less successful than the first. Attacks by the 3rd and 32nd Divisions downstream at Plava were equally abortive. After November 28, the 2nd Army had to suspend operations on the upper Isonzo. The weather had taken a turn for the worse. The severe Alpine winter had arrived, bringing the offensive to a halt. For the next several icy months, both armies on the upper Isonzo would be too busy defending against the snow and cold to waste time fighting one other.

Shortly after the Italian mountain artillery opened fire at Tolmein, Capello's guns began their own preparatory barrage. Throughout November 25, the VI Corps artillery, including heavy howitzer and mortar batteries, hammered away at the 58th Division's trenches around Oslavia and Podgora. The infantry made only limited probing attacks to determine the Dalmatians' strength. The general offensive came the following morning with a two-division attack at Oslavia and an assault on Podgora by the 12th Division. Four courageous mass attacks in the morning around Oslavia failed to push the Italian line forward. Two more attempts in the afternoon similarly made no progress. As usual, Zeidler's few craftily placed Schwarzlose machine guns decided the day. The 58th's machine gunners and riflemen crushed all six spirited advances before they ever reached the Austrian lines. The 12th Division's drive on Podgora also stalled painfully. Unmoved by his infantry's suffering, Capello sent the battered divisions back into the fray the next morning. After a brief predawn artillery barrage, five divisions went over the top between Sabotino and Podgora. The assaulting divisions were heavily reinforced by battalions brought from Plava and crack *Bersaglieri* from Cadorna's special reserve. Capello aimed his major effort between Hill 188 and the ruins of Oslavia, confident that a breakthrough there would be the quickest route to the Isonzo and to Gorizia. The four Austrian battalions holding the sector—Slovenes, Czechs, Croats and Serbs, and Ukrainians—held their ground, repulsing eight bayonet charges in as many hours. The close-quarter fighting, particularly the bitter struggle around the ruins of

Oslavia's church, exhausted both sides by nightfall. The modest Italian gains were rapidly overturned by a determined Austrian counterattack. Capello still had nothing to show for his terrible casualties.

The Italian losses on November 27 were so severe that Capello had to postpone his next attack. The planned offensive, scheduled to begin before dawn the following morning, was delayed until the afternoon, after the arrival of fresh replacements. The effort by the VI Corps on November 28 was by any standards a failure. The capture of Hill 188 and the wrecked village of Oslavia still eluded Capello's shattered divisions. Both his VI Corps and Zeidler's Dalmatians were understandably running out of steam. Regiments of both armies were very understrength, soldiers were tired, and ammunition was running low. Nevertheless, Capello was not yet ready to give up the fight. He felt his ruined corps had enough energy and men left for one more attack on the Gorizia bridgehead. The last major Italian drive on Gorizia in 1915 came at midday on November 29. As he had two days before, Capello concentrated his forces between Hill 188 and Oslavia, a distance of less than a half-mile. The rocky terrain, now devoid of trees and littered with thousands of unburied corpses, offered no cover for the advancing Italian infantry. Capello committed his last reserves to the fight, the rebuilt 32nd Division, just shipped from Plava, supported by the resurrected Novara Brigade. Both formations were filled with teenaged conscripts and middle-aged recalled reservists just arrived at the front. Their bayonet charge came on the heels of a concentrated barrage. The *fanti*, knowing they had no place to seek cover, climbed out of their trenches and ran at top speed toward the Austrian lines, only a hundred paces eastward. The defenders were surprised by the speed of the Italian advance. In several places, the mad dash succeeded and the Italians were in the Austrian entrenchments before the machine gunners could react. The weary Austrians began to give way, and this time there were no reinforcements on hand to push the attackers back. Capello's infantry pressed on, capturing several Austrian positions. By the late afternoon his forward detachments were within a half-mile of the Isonzo. They could clearly see the river, its fast, blue-green waters, and Gorizia just beyond. Yet Capello's soldiers would get no closer to the City of Violets in 1915. The assault divisions had exhausted themselves advancing that far. Zeidler had no reserves left to push the Italians back to their own lines, but neither was the VI Corps able to continue its advance. Both armies were so tired and depleted that the lines stayed where they were. Capello had nearly reached the Isonzo, but it was too late, and he had used up too many good men to secure even these modest gains. He would have to wait until next year, after the winter snows evaporated, to resume his relentless drive on Gorizia.

The 3rd Army made no gains worth mentioning during the final phase of the Fourth Battle. As had happened so often before, brave infantry attacks registered modest advances that were quickly erased by vigorous Austrian counterattacks. The loss of thousands of infantrymen gained only bitter defeat. The Duke of Aosta continued to push his men hard. In the last days of November his XI and XIII Corps, seven divisions in all, tried vainly to capture the San Michele sector. On November 27 the 3rd Army's guns pounded Austrian entrenchments around the mountain, from the Vipacco River to Hill 111, a distance of three and a half miles. As always, the shelling was concentrated on the mountain, especially the north face. The afternoon's infantry attacks failed to gain any ground. The experienced machine gunners and riflemen of the 22nd Rifle and 17th Infantry Divisions cut down repeated bayonet charges. The tempo of the fighting increased on November 28. The Duke of Aosta's gunners shelled the entire VII Corps front, down to Hill 118, Mt. Sei Busi. At noon, four Italian regiments attempted to advance up Mt. San Michele. Austrian batteries caught the dense columns of *fanti* on the bare north slope. Shrapnel ripped through the Italian ranks, felling hundreds, until the attackers broke and fled. The division-sized assault made only slight gains on the north slope, but they were nearly all lost to rapid Austrian counterattacks. The same occurred at the village of San Martino, a mile southwest of the mountain. There, after a bitter struggle, troops of the 21st and 22nd Divisions captured several Austrian positions just west of the village. However, German and Czech militiamen of the 106th Division, returned to the Carso only hours before, pushed the weary attackers back to their own trenches. Cadorna's soldiers still had not learned to be prepared to resist Austrian counterattacks, with frustrating and costly consequences.

The Duke of Aosta prepared his army for one final mass assault on Mt. San Michele. Like Capello, he had enough men and munitions left for one last try on November 29. Yet the VII Corps preempted the Italian push with a predawn battalion-sized attack on San Michele's north face. Czech riflemen of the 28th Regiment's 11th Replacement Battalion mounted a surprise bayonet charge through the darkness toward Italian-held trenches near the summit. The Czech recruits quickly overwhelmed the sleeping Italians, and the positions again belonged to the VII Corps. Only minutes later, at 7 A.M., the 3rd Army's artillery commenced a powerful preparatory barrage. The earth shook between Hill 111 and the Vipacco River as thousands of medium- and heavy-caliber shells crashed around Austrian entrenchments. The troops holding the line ran for cover in dugouts and *kavernen*. During the night Archduke Joseph ordered the replacement of the weary German and Slovene regiments that had successfully defended San Michele. Their places were taken by two fresh regiments of the 20th *Honvéd* Division, the veteran formation that had shed so much blood on the Carso but that so far had been held in reserve during the Fourth Battle.

Two *Honvéd* regiments, the Magyar 1st on San Michele and the mostly Romanian 4th at San Martino, emerged from their dugouts at midmorning when the intense shelling ceased. Soldiers ran to their posts to man machine guns and mortars before the Italians reached their positions. As the Hungarians carefully watched the huge clouds of dust and smoke thrown up by the bombardment, they could hear the Italians' battle cry, "*Avanti Savoia!*" rising from thousands of voices. The blinding clouds slowly lifted, and the defenders caught a glimpse of three divisions' worth of bayonet-wielding Italian infantry climbing out of their trenches, headed for the Austrian lines. The *fanti* suddenly charged, and the *Honvéd* troopers opened fire with machine guns and rifles. Thousands of bullets tore through the advancing Italian columns, cutting down the front ranks. Austrian sharpshooters looked for the conspicuous battalion and company commanders leading their troops. Within a minute, dozens of Italian officers had fallen to the guns of the deadly *cecchini*. Leaderless, the forward Italian battalions became disorganized, and the mass attack began to fall apart. The distraught survivors struggled back to their own trenches. The 1st and 4th Regiments lost not a single position or entrenchment to the 3rd Army.

Disappointed by the morning rout but still determined to keep trying, the Duke of Aosta ordered his divisions to attack San Michele and San Martino again. The XI Corps needed several hours to regroup and to move replacements into the line, so the day's second attempt had to wait until the late afternoon. At 5 P.M. the regiments went over the top again. This time the Hungarians were ready, and the first wave was shattered by bursts of staccato fire from Schwarzlose machine guns. However, the XI Corps, well aware that the lead battalions would be slaughtered, had a second wave waiting nearby in reserve. The follow-up attack was launched before the first had ended, surprising the defenders; in several places, Italian infantry managed to reach the Austrian lines. Nevertheless, the hard-fighting Hungarians pushed the second wave back, too. As night fell, only one Austrian trench section west of San Martino was in Italian hands. The Hungarians had prevailed again. The day's offensive had been a bloody failure. The last major Italian effort on the Carso in 1915 ended disastrously, like all previous attempts, without achieving any gains worth mentioning.

The next morning, before dawn, the 3rd Army made a minor effort to seize the north slope of San Michele, almost as an afterthought. The 6 A.M. surprise assault on the mountain was repulsed easily by rifle and machine gun fire. In retaliation, the VII Corps sent a regiment to retake the lost trench section west of San Martino. The Austrians' well-honed ability to counterattack yet again proved its worth as the Hungarians wrested the position from the Italian 22nd Division. The 3rd Army thus lost the only ground it had gained in the San Michele sector during November. By December 1 the Fourth Battle of the Isonzo was over. Official historians later considered that the battle continued two more weeks, but Cadorna's effort to conquer the Isonzo in 1915 effectively came to an end by the first day of December. The 2nd and 3rd Armies still made local attacks, and soldiers certainly continued to lose their lives on both sides, but the early December attacks were minor and inconsequential. They added to the terrible butcher bill but decided nothing on the battlefield. These mostly small Italian probes, lasting until December 14, proved to be little more than an annoyance to the weary defenders. Italian artillery shelled the Carso sporadically between December 3 and 6, followed by a two-division attack up Mt. San Michele on December 7. The 22nd and 29th Divisions, which had already lost countless thousands of soldiers on the mountain's battle-scarred slopes, tried again to advance up the north face. The attack, far larger than what the Hungarian defenders had anticipated, managed to capture part of the north side, but the inevitable counterattack pushed the Italians back. Renewed efforts by the 3rd Army to take the mountain on December 8 and 9 were even less successful. Through it all, the 1st *Honvéd* Regiment remained the masters of San Michele.

The Gorizia front was by no means quiet during the two weeks after major operations ended. Capello's three divisions holding the front line regularly sent nighttime patrols into no-man's-land, both to conduct reconnaissance and to harass the bridgehead's defenders. These probes gained no ground, but they were an incessant irritant to Zeidler's Dalmatians. Capello's artillery frequently shelled Austrian trenches and rear areas, a constant form of harassment. The on-again, off-again bombardment killed few Austrians, but it prevented the tired Dalmatians from getting a good night's sleep. On December 2 and 4, Italian guns shelled the city of Gorizia; however, by now most civilians had left the city rather than endure more Italian shelling, so the artillery inflicted few civilian casualties.

Capello could not expand his hold on Oslavia. Instead, he sent out patrols to raid Austrian trenches there, as well as on Podgora and Sabotino. Every raid lost soldiers killed and maimed. Occasional daytime attacks tested Zeidler's defenses, but usually were very costly. One of the many Italian soldiers to fall in these raids, these small battles after the battle, was Scipio Slataper. His death was one of the numerous needless sacrifices after the Fourth Battle was really over, a burnt offering in the cooling embers of Cadorna's catastrophic offensive. The twenty-seven-year-old Slataper died on December 3 while taking part in a 12th Division raid on Austrian entrenchments on Podgora.

Slataper was one of hundreds of *fanti* to die on the Isonzo after Cadorna had abandoned his great offensive, but in many ways he was different from his fallen comrades in arms. In the first place, he was a native of Trieste, and therefore an Austrian citizen. Although he was born and raised in Habsburg Austria, his heart had always belonged to Italy. Slataper was only half-Italian by blood (his father was of Slav origin, as his very un-Italian surname indicates), yet from his earliest days he was a fervent believer in Italy's greatness and destiny. His father, a devout nationalist and irredentist, raised the young Scipio on romantic stories of Garibaldi and the *Risorgimento*. His boyhood hero was Oberdan, the fellow *triestino* of Slav origin who became the first martyr for *Italia irredenta*. He hated Austria and the Habsburgs, but he passionately loved Trieste and especially the Carso, where he spent a happy teenage convalescence after a bout of nervous exhaustion. Slataper's fascination with the Carso deeply affected his personality and remained with him all his short life. After completing secondary school, Slataper left Trieste to attend the University of Florence. (There was no Italian university in Austria; Italian youths had to leave the Habsburg Empire if they wanted to study in their mother tongue.) Slataper received his degree in 1912 with a highly praised dissertation on Ibsen. He became a journalist; in his spare time he wrote about the need for Italian liberation of the Littoral. Like virtually all educated and liberal Italians, Slataper believed Trieste was mortally threatened by Slavs, and that union with Italy was the only desirable solution. War to liberate Trieste would be preferable to Austrian domination. He had dramatic premonitions of bloodletting and suffering. His greatest work, *Il mio Carso* (My Carso), written between 1910 and 1912 while he was studying at Florence, was a romantic prose-poem dedicated to his home city and region; it firmly established the young Slataper as one of the most promising figures in Italian literature. In it, he wrote prophetically:

We love Trieste for the restless soul she gave us. . . . She has reared us for struggle and for duty. . . . Trieste is blessed for having let us live without peace or glory. We love you and bless you because we are happy even to die in your fire.

Slataper was in Germany when the First World War broke out. He was determined not to return to detested Austria; under no circumstances would he offer himself as a sacrifice to the Habsburg throne. He traveled to Italy, where he agitated for Rome to declare war on Austria and liberate *Italia irredenta* from the Habsburg yoke. In June 1915, days after Italy declared war, Slataper joined the holy crusade; like hundreds of other "Julian volunteers" who offered to fight their country of birth, he took the precaution of enlisting under a false name— otherwise, he would be shot for treason if captured by the Austrians. Slataper underwent several weeks of infantry training, followed by months of waiting to enter action. He went to the Isonzo and fought in both the Third and Fourth Battles, an experience that caused him to take a more sanguine look at the war he had championed. Shortly before his death, he wrote

War is not in the explosion of grenades or a fusillade nor in hand-to-hand combat. War is not in what, from far off, one believes to be its terrible reality and which, close at hand, turns out to be a poor thing and makes little impression; it is—as Tolstoy realized—to be found in that curious space beyond one's trench, where there is silence and color and where the corn is ripening to no purpose. It is that sense of certain death which lies "beyond," there where the sun still shines on the age-old roads and the peasants' houses.

His promising literary career was cut short on December 3 on Podgora hill, where thousands of comrades had fallen before him, where so many Italian dreams and hopes had been forever shattered. Slataper died within sight of his beloved Carso, a haunting and inevitable death somehow foretold in his romantic writings about his homeland. Like Oberdan, his childhood idol, he offered himself as a willing sacrifice to *Italia irredenta*, a dream of redemption neither Italian patriot lived to see realized.

Scipio Slataper's death was, of course, only one among thousands during the Fourth Battle of the Isonzo. The vast majority of his fallen comrades were not educated men who volunteered to die to liberate Austria's Italian provinces. Instead, they were uneducated, often illiterate peasants who reported for duty because they had no choice; Trieste and the Carso meant nothing to them. Still, they did their duty and died in the tens of thousands to conquer the Isonzo for Rome. Sadly, their enormous sacrifices had brought Italy no closer to victory. Cadorna's net gain after the Fourth Battle amounted to the now nonexistent village of Oslavia, a few trenches on Podgora, and some useless positions on the north face of Mt. San Michele. Tragically, these conquests were tactically inconsequential; they in no way endangered the Austrian hold on the Isonzo. Yet this very modest gain officially cost Italy 49,000 soldiers; unofficially, of course, the total was far higher. Italian losses for the autumn of 1915, the total casualties for the Third and Fourth Battles, were estimated by the army at 116,000 dead and wounded. A later, more accurate count revealed a loss of 170,000 men. In all, Cadorna's four attempts to break the Isonzo line in the second half of 1915 robbed Italy of 230,000 of her sons killed and maimed. They died bravely but futilely. Cadorna's offensives gained almost nothing for Italy. Despite the loss of 230,000 soldiers—twenty divisions' worth of infantry—the Italian Army was really no closer to victory in late December than it had been when Rome declared war in late May.

The terrible cost of the fighting could not be completely concealed by Cadorna and his staff. The general felt no need to answer awkward questions from politicians and journalists, but the sheer magnitude of Italian losses on the Isonzo was obvious. By the end of 1915, almost a quarter of a million Italian families had been notified that a son, father, or brother was dead, wounded, or missing on the Isonzo. Many politicians had already grown restless. One exasperated parliamentarian rued, "The occupation of Rome cost Italy far less than a single square meter of the Carso."[3] Cadorna naturally did not respond to this painful observation, or any others. He continued to believe that his methods would prevail in the end; he was discouraged by the obviously catastrophic failure of his grand schemes, but it in no way caused the stubborn Piedmontese to rethink his strategy and tactics.

Few of the foot soldiers who arrived with the 2nd and 3rd Armies on the Isonzo in early June were still alive and unscathed. Their places had been taken by teenaged conscripts and middle-aged reservists. The constant losses drained regiments and divisions over and over again. The frontline Italian infantryman had hardly any chance of surviving the fighting without injury; *fanti* were virtually guaranteed death or maiming. Lightly wounded soldiers were patched up and sent back into battle until they were killed or crippled. In a typical case, the Bari Brigade fought in the Third and Fourth Battles, suffering its share of casualties. In seventy-five days in the line in the San Michele sector, the brigade lost 7,250 officers and men—120 percent of its authorized strength. Yet such losses were not considered exceptional. The morale of Cadorna's armies was noticeably low by the onset of winter. The chief of staff's ferocious discipline kept his army in the field, but indications of disaffection were everywhere. The 148th Regiment's short-lived mutiny was a sign of things to come. Perhaps even more ominously, the Austrians captured almost 9,000 Italian soldiers during the autumn; clearly many prisoners were only too happy to give themselves up to escape the war. Liberal application of firing squads and decimations assured Cadorna that the majority of his soldiers would remain loyal, but the naive enthusiasm of the summer's volunteers had been permanently replaced by the sober, hard-earned realism of combat veterans, whose sole aim was survival.

Boroević's exhausted veterans at least had another victory to console them. The 5th Army had again prevailed against overwhelmingly superior Italian forces. Raw courage had repulsed innumerable Italian attacks; the fighting spirit of Austrian regiments on the Isonzo was still admirably high. Boroević observed of his battered army, "Every soldier on the Isonzo front deserves the Gold Medal for Bravery." Nevertheless, the cost of victory had been hardly less bitter than defeat. From November 10 to December 1, the 5th Army lost 25,391 soldiers; the last two weeks of skirmishing added another 4,700 men to the casualty rolls. However, the true total was doubtless higher. The Third and Fourth Battles together cost Boroević 95,000 soldiers dead, wounded, and missing. As always, the price of the numerous counterattacks that Boroević demanded had added considerably to the numbers of dead and wounded. Between October 15 and December 15 the 5th Army received almost 120,000 reinforcements and replacements, yet total strength barely rose during that two-month period: almost 100,000 Austrian soldiers were consumed by Boroević's war machine. At the unit level, Austrian losses were often as bad as Italian figures. The 22nd Infantry Regiment, the Dalmatian unit that repeatedly distinguished itself at Plava and before Gorizia, claimed 4,086 dead and wounded soldiers on the Isonzo in 1915. The "Lions of Podgora," the bravest of the brave, lost about 120 percent of their official strength between June and December. They had prevented an Italian breakthrough, but had been destroyed in the process.

The Austrian consumption of munitions was almost as daunting. During the Third and Fourth Battles the 5th Army fired a total of 37 million rifle and machine gun bullets, 706,000 artillery shells, 13,500 mortar shells, and 76,000 hand grenades. It had truly been a *Materielschlacht*. In the long run, the Austrian war machine could not possibly sustain such a consumption of men and munitions. The empire's limited reserves of men, guns, and munitions were strained nearly to the breaking point by fighting a three-front war. Boroević and his soldiers were lionized in the Austrian press and congratulated by senior generals for their heroic defense of the Isonzo line, but the High Command knew that such losses could not be made good for much longer. Boroević's methods had stopped Cadorna in his tracks, but they committed Austria to an endless war of attrition that she could not hope to win. Simply not losing on the Isonzo was not the same thing as victory, particularly at such a price.

Sobering doses of realism did not interest the Austrian infantrymen holding the Isonzo line as winter approached. They knew the odds were not in their favor, but they were happy to be alive. Boroević, now hailed as "the Lion of the Isonzo," saw to it that his subordinates were showered with decorations for their bravery. Erwin Zeidler received the Knight's Cross of the Order of Maria Theresia for his pivotal role in the defense of Gorizia, and thousands of humbler soldiers were rewarded with medals of all classes for their victories over the Italians. The tens of thousands of exhausted Habsburg fighting men living in trenches from Rombon to the Carso celebrated their unexpected triumph; they had prevailed four times against impossible odds. They had stopped Cadorna's armies, thus saving Austria from total defeat. They had little to look forward to, save better rations at Christmas. The harsh Alpine winter had arrived. Snow had fallen everywhere in the Isonzo valley, and the bitterly cold *bora* now lashed their positions mercilessly. Trench life, always unpleasant, was now almost unbearable. At least the winter brought large military operations to a halt; the spring thaw would only bring more Italian offensives, a prospect too dreadful to waste time thinking about. So as 1915 drew to a close Austrian soldiers hoped for the best and in a dozen languages prayed to God for the slaughter to end.

1916

SEVEN

A So-Called Battle

As the Fourth Battle of the Isonzo ebbed away slowly and painfully, the senior Allied generals met near Paris to determine a combined strategy for the coming year. The Chantilly conference was an attempt to craft a joint war effort to defeat the apparently insurmountable defenses of Germany and Austria; only by waging war together, France, Britain, Russia, and Italy finally realized, could they hope to win the war. Luigi Cadorna was too busy with the Fourth Battle to attend, so he sent his trusted subordinate General Porro, subchief of the General Staff, to represent him at the conference, which was to begin December 6. At Chantilly, a glorious Renaissance château, Porro enjoyed the sumptuous surroundings with his Allied counterparts. While their soldiers died and struggled to stay warm on a dozen battlefields across Europe, the generals were wined and dined in the best Parisian fashion; Chantilly, a relic of the *ancien régime*, boasted an English garden, an impressive Temple of Venus, and an Isle of Love where the generals could stroll and ponder strategy. The results of the conference were predictable enough. The French, British, Russian, and Italian representatives pledged to launch massive, coordinated offensives starting in the spring; the planned Allied blows would knock the Central Powers out of France, and possibly out of the war. Porro, speaking on behalf of his anxious superior, argued in favor of simultaneous offensives as soon after the March thaw as possible. Why these attacks would be more successful than those launched in 1915 was not explained.

As 1916 began, and Italian soldiers endured their first winter in the frozen Alps, Cadorna continued to believe that his methods, which had so unmistakably failed four times, would nevertheless prevail in the spring. He steadfastly resisted all attempts to reign in his unlimited powers. In January, Prime Minister Antonio Salandra, alarmed by Italy's terrible losses and negligible gains, requested that Cadorna establish a Council of War, where Italy's other generals and senior politicians might be able to suggest alternative strategies. Cadorna tactlessly rebuffed Salandra's suggestion, arguing that he need answer only to the king, never to mere politicians; of course, Vittorio Emanuele dared not question Cadorna. The count thereby remained a law unto himself, the most supreme of all supreme Allied generals, the sole and unchallenged architect of Italy's war effort.

By early 1916 Cadorna's view of the war encompassed all of his well known beliefs about fighting, modified only slightly by four costly defeats. The half-year of bloodletting on the Isonzo had finally convinced him that the Julian front had become inalterably static, at least for the moment. All the unheeded warnings from his attachés and intelligence officers a year earlier about the Western front now seemed sadly prophetic; trench warfare had emerged on the banks of the Isonzo with a vengeance, a development that even Cadorna could not fail to notice. The rapid battle of maneuver Cadorna and the Italian Army had hoped for had disappeared irrevocably. Italy was now committed to fighting a long, siegelike war of attrition against Austria. The strong entrenchments, barbed wire, machine guns, and ample artillery that covered the Isonzo valley removed all possibility of maneuver. Instead, the war had become a bloody wearing-down process to exhaust the enemy. Only after Austria was worn down much more could Cadorna hope for any kind of decisive breakthrough on the Isonzo. He accepted this reality without reservation, even though it committed him to an almost endless war of attrition, one that would bleed Italy far worse than anything seen in 1915. The chief of staff knew that Austria, slowly collapsing from the pressures of a three-front war, would give in before Italy, and that was enough. The effect of this fighting on Italy's fighting men, who would have to bear the deadly cost of attrition, did not concern him.

Cadorna still saw no need for a coherent set of rules on how to defeat the Austrians on the battlefield. Despite all the tactical changes of the past year, he continued to put faith in numbers of men and guns. He doggedly believed that bravery and weight of shell would eventually vanquish Svetozar Boroević's army. The need for a systematic fighting doctrine—how to plan artillery barrages, how to target the artillery most effectively, how to coordinate the infantry and artillery, how the infantry should advance, for instance—eluded Cadorna; instead, he argued, "It is enough that at the right moment the decisions are taken quickly." Although huge superiorities in men, guns, and shells had availed him little in the first four battles, he nevertheless believed that he needed ever more infantry and artillery to succeed; exactly how they were to be used most effectively did not concern him.

Cadorna pressed the War Ministry, industry, and the government for more men and munitions, and his wishes were fulfilled without argument. The ongoing expansion of the army continued unabated. Cadorna demanded 270,000 more soldiers and hundreds more guns by the spring, to bring his total strength up to 1,340,000 troops in the field, supported by 2,344 guns. The conscript class of 1896 was called early to the colors, as were several more classes of reservists, to bring Cadorna's armies up to strength. The army's service and supply branches were combed out to supply the front with more riflemen. General Alfred Dallolio ensured that Italy's factories worked overtime to provide Cadorna with the thousands of guns and mortars and millions of shells he needed to break through on the Isonzo. In the first half of 1916, Cadorna received a new army headquarters, five new army corps, eight freshly raised infantry divisions, and dozens more heavy and superheavy artillery batteries. In addition, the army's four cavalry divisions were dismounted to provide more infantry. Cadorna could not justly complain that Italy failed to respond to his incessant requests for more men and matériel. Like all generals, however, he inevitably rued that he never had enough soldiers and shells, but in Cadorna's case these criticisms were unrealistic and largely unwarranted. Italy's army had expanded enormously, and her disorganized prewar industries had responded surprisingly well to the needs of the war economy. Italy did not lack men and guns, but ideas of how to use them effectively.

The soldiers who invariably bore the brunt of Cadorna's unrealistic demands were of course the infantry. As in all armies during the First World War, the Italian infantry had declined considerably as an overall percentage of the army's strength; as the war became increasingly an industrial struggle, the supporting and service branches—the artillery and engineers, backed up by the construction, transport, maintenance, signal, and medical corps—took an ever greater slice of the available men. Yet it was the infantry who still did the real fighting, the dirty work in the trenches, and it was always the infantry that suffered almost all the casualties. Despite the impressive technological changes that had irrevocably altered the face of war by early 1916, the war's outcome still depended on the ordinary, unexalted *fantaccino*.

Italy's tired and abused *fanti* holding the Isonzo line enjoyed the rest afforded by the onset of winter. For the first time since the war's beginning, there was no prospect of another immediate offensive. The foot soldiers had time to improve their positions and enjoy a break in the fighting. However, the Italian trenches were nowhere near as well constructed and comfortable as the impressive Austrian entrenchments across the river. Cadorna had shown little concern for the condition of his troops' trenches. He did not expect to be on the Isonzo for long, so Italian trenches were primitive and unsanitary compared to the more permanent positions built by Boroević's engineers. Italian frontline trenches were shallow and uncomfortable, affording little protection against

Austrian shells or the weather. As the Alpine winter arrived and thousands of *fanti* had to sleep outside through snowstorms without overhead cover, it was evident that the army had to make major improvements to the trenches running all along the Isonzo. Although building materials were in short supply, the engineers, assisted by the infantry, began to construct deeper and more comfortable trenches where the foot soldiers could live underground year-round. The ideal trench system included well ventilated shelters underground, safe from shells, where the infantry could live and sleep undisturbed. It would take many months to complete the project, and thousands of Italian foot soldiers would have to endure the winter virtually without shelter, but at least it was a step in the right direction. The Italian Army was going to be on the Isonzo for a long time, and the troops therefore had to have permanent entrenchments.

Cadorna's infantrymen were pleased to be getting better living quarters, but they still had numerous other grievances. Although the winter on the Isonzo was fierce, especially in the high Julian Alps, the army supplied few of its soldiers with adequate winter protective clothing; only the *Alpini* were issued proper winter gear, including mountain boots and thick snowsuits; the rest of the infantry had to make do with normal uniforms, often supplemented with scarves and pelts sent by concerned relatives at home. Soldiers from the South, unaccustomed to harsh winters, in particular suffered badly. The army's medical service remained desperately short of doctors, medicines of all types, bandages, and of course clean hospitals, inspiring little confidence among the fighting men. Rations were usually poor and inadequate; the supply corps was no better at providing the army with fresh meat and vegetables than with medical supplies. Frontline soldiers frequently lacked even cooking appliances to prepare warm rations, a serious problem during the cold winter months; morale inevitably suffered when infantrymen did not get hot food for days on end. As Napoleon once observed, "An army marches on its stomach," and Cadorna's was no exception.

The greatest numbers of complaints, however, centered on the army's shockingly low pay. The Italian private soldier was the worst paid in Europe. The prewar pay rate, only a few *centi* a day, had not been raised, and there was no extra allowance for soldiers at the front. To all soldiers this was an outrage; for married men it represented a severe economic crisis. The army's meager wage was barely enough to support a single soldier, and it was pathetically inadequate to feed and clothe a family. The hundreds of thousands of soldiers with wives and children worried not just about surviving the war, but also about how their families were surviving at home. Home leave was rare, and soldiers who visited home before returning to the front—usually wounded men on convalescence—came home to genuine hardship. The families of fighting men regularly did not have enough to eat, and the government was slow to do anything to remedy this desperate situation. The soldiers' resentment was exacerbated by their hatred of all those who managed to avoid the draft. Men still safe at home—inevitably denounced as shirkers by frontline veterans—incurred the wrath of all those in uniform. Particularly detested were the legions of industrial workers who supported the war economy. Workers who built guns, shells, and other vital matériel were both exempt from conscription and very highly paid; they enjoyed the security of the home front and the inflated wages of war workers while abysmally paid *fanti* died by the thousands on the Isonzo. The workers' role in the war effort was indispensable, but the fundamental inequality of the situation galled the soldiers no end.

Italy's infantrymen therefore had little to comfort them. Yet they did not rebel or desert en masse. Their morale, though by no means high, was nevertheless adequate to keep them in their trenches, waiting for the winter to end and the fighting to resume. What kept the *grigioverdi*[1] in the line was not just Cadorna's willingness to shoot deserters and cowards, but also a deep loyalty to their comrades. Soldiers who shared the extreme hardships of combat invariably developed intense bonds with each other and to their unit; the terrible sufferings of the infantry bred deep affection in its ranks. Their suffering was shared, and before long, combat soldiers felt much more in common with fellow *fanti* than with anyone else, including their families. Units in the rear, safe from the fighting, frequently had serious morale problems, but infantry regiments, brought together by common dangers and hardships, only rarely suffered from severe crises of morale. Mussolini, who returned to the 11th *Bersaglieri* in the snows of Vršič and Javorček during February's bitter winter, observed accurately, "The morale of men in the front line is not that of men in the rear." The educated journalist felt a strong bond with the soldiers in his unit, most of them uneducated peasants.[2] His regiment included men from all over Italy; they shared no common region, dialect, or class to unite them, but they were all *Bersaglieri*, and they were all Italians. Even the insurmountable distance between officers and enlisted men narrowed at the front. The *fanti* frequently got along well with their junior officers, often just out of cadet school, the platoon and company commanders who shared the dangers of combat; it was the staff and more senior officers, safely behind the lines, whom they detested.

The solidarity of fighting men was equally visible on the Austrian side of the Isonzo. In Boroević's army, too, infantrymen developed an intense loyalty to each other and to their units. In Austria's army, this powerful bond was often buttressed by regional or ethnic ties; the Austrian practice of recruiting regiments from a single province or region meant that its soldiers were united by a common language or dialect and a shared local identity. German, South Slav, and Magyar regiments regularly boasted a noticeable ethnic pride. They all hated the Italians, but the sense of frontline unity on rare occasions even managed to transcend the war. At Christmas, a few units on both sides the Isonzo arranged brief unofficial truces, in flagrant violation of both armies' regulations.

Soldiers of the two overwhelmingly Catholic armies stopped shooting at each other for a few hours; in some places they met in no-man's-land to exchange mementos and Christmas greetings.

The morale of the 5th Army was doubtless higher than that of Cadorna's forces. This can be largely attributed to Austria's better care of its soldiers. The Austrian administration was far superior to the Italian, and the Habsburg Army supplied its fighting men with amenities that were lavish compared to those enjoyed by their adversaries. Austrian trenches were permanent and reasonably comfortable, including sleeping areas and other amenities. The rations enjoyed by Boroević's army were acceptable, if not first-rate, and the soldiers' pay was adequate. Most important, Boroević's staff had arranged a system of regular rotation of units in the front lines. Battalions were frequently taken out of the line and moved to permanent rest areas behind the front, where tired soldiers could sleep in real beds, eat fresh meat and bread and drink real coffee, receive rations of beer and tobacco, and enjoy concerts by army bands and other entertainment. Such three-day rest periods proved a vital restorer of morale in infantry units, particularly during the harsh winter months.

When in the line, infantry battalions of both armies were always busy, even during the quiet periods between battles. Very little happened during the day. Movement during daylight hours was too dangerous; the Italians feared the deadly accurate *cecchini*, and the Austrians dreaded surprise Italian artillery barrages. Therefore soldiers slept during the day and did their work at night. Every evening on the Isonzo front, the armies dispatched patrols into no-man's-land to survey the enemy's positions, and sometimes to raid a troublesome machine gun nest. Under the cover of darkness, the sappers improved entrenchments and laid barbed wire, while stretcher bearers stealthily collected the wounded and dead lying between the two sides. Service and supply units were just as busy laying telephone wires, repairing damaged equipment, and bringing fresh rations and ammunition to the forward trenches. Soldiers on both sides soon adjusted to the backward world of working only at night, which proved especially easy during the winter months, when the hours of darkness were extended.

Yet the winter's complications far outweighed its benefits. The cold weather made life unpleasant for sentries and all others who ventured out of their dugouts. Heavy snows and ice storms made the movement of supplies difficult, especially in the high Julian Alps. More ominously, the winter brought avalanches to the upper Isonzo. Throughout the winter, Austrian and Italian infantry garrisoning the Mrzli chain and the Flitsch basin were far more afraid of the "white death" than they were of each other. Both sides did their best to prevent avalanches and to protect their entrenchments, but it was alarmingly easy to cause a mountain of snow to tumble down a slope. Enormous avalanches were caused by explosions of shells and other munitions, or missteps by mountain patrols, and sometimes had no apparent reason. The two armies used avalanche alarms to warn of impending disaster and raised ski detachments to rescue buried soldiers, but losses to avalanches were steep. During the winter of 1915–1916, Austria's Carinthian sector (which included the Vršič, Javorček, and Rombon areas of the Isonzo front) alone lost 600 soldiers killed by avalanches. In one catastrophic incident, on March 8, 1916, an avalanche in the mountains behind Vršič buried six Austrian watchposts and more than a hundred Russian prisoners of war who were working on a road through the mountain pass. Although the pass had avalanche buttresses, the snow completely submerged the road, cutting off traffic to the Vršič sector for several days.[3]

Despite the serious risks posed by the weather, both armies continued military operations, albeit on a much reduced scale. Even on the precarious upper Isonzo, Austrians and Italians dueled sporadically for mountains and ridges. The fighting centered on strategic Mt. Rombon. The 44th Rifle Division, garrisoning the Flitsch basin, feared that Italian positions around Mt. Čukla endangered Austrian troops down in the valley east of Flitsch. Čukla, the 5,860-foot peak southwest of Rombon's summit, was held by a well entrenched *Alpini* battalion, supported by a mountain battery that often rained fire on Austrian positions in the valley below. In early February the 44th sent troops of the Carinthian 1st Mountain Rifle Regiment to retake the positions lost to the Italians in August. The lightning attack began just after midnight on February 12. Two companies of the 1st Mountain Rifles, tough German troops trained and equipped for Alpine warfare, silently advanced a quarter-mile in snowshoes, over man-high snows, down the slope toward Čukla, where they surprised the sleeping defenders. The *Alpini* attempted to mount a defense, but they were soon overrun, and the survivors escaped down the mountain; by 3 A.M. Čukla was in Austrian hands. At a cost of just five dead and thirty wounded, the two companies of Carinthians had captured the Italian fortress along with eighty-three *Alpini* and four machine guns.

Outraged by the loss of Čukla, the commander of the 36th Division (the renamed *Bersaglieri* Division) sent three fresh *Alpini* battalions back up Rombon to retake the lost position. For the next week the Pieve di Teco, Exilles, and Bassano Battalions, seasoned veterans of earlier upper Isonzo battles, launched repeated assaults on Čukla. The withering fire of the three battalions and their supporting artillery batteries blasted the Austrian-held trenches. Losses mounted steadily in the two defending Carinthian companies, but the Italians failed to dislodge them, despite heroic efforts. Appallingly bad weather and accurate rifle fire kept the *Alpini* at bay until February 20, when the attacks were called off. The weeklong fight cost the Italians more than 400 casualties, versus only a hundred for the Austrians. The 36th Division decided to wait until the weather improved before trying again to retake Čukla.

Austrian attempts to regain lost ground during the winter were not limited to the upper Isonzo. Boroević and his staff were particularly worried about the Italian penetration before Gorizia in the last stages of the Fourth Battle; Italian forces on the heights of Oslavia were only a half-mile from the Isonzo. Major General Erwin Zeidler, acting on Boroević's orders, sent units of his 58th Division to retake their former trenches around Hill 188 and the wrecked village of Oslavia. Capello's headquarters did not expect any Austrian counterattacks so soon into the new year, so the heights of Oslavia were garrisoned relatively lightly. On the evening of January 14, under a moonless sky, seven companies of Dalmatians left their positions and charged through the darkness toward the Italian-held trenches. The surprise assault rapidly overran both Hill 188 and Oslavia. Within less than an hour, both positions again belonged to the 58th Division. The startled Italians had not fought very hard; a thousand defenders, including thirty-four officers, were taken prisoner.

Capello, furious at the loss of such hard-won positions, immediately dispatched all available reserves to push the Dalmatians back to their own lines. Troops of the 11th and 27th Divisions moved up and prepared to retake the ruined village and the neighboring hill. They struck on the morning of January 15. Zeidler, fearful of heavy casualties from Italian shelling, withdrew most of the attacking companies, leaving only a few platoons to hold the recaptured positions. The Italian attackers thus found Hill 188 and Oslavia weakly defended. The defenders had several machine guns, however, which took a heavy toll of the advancing *fanti*. The outnumbered Dalmatians were forced to relinquish Hill 188 late on January 15; Oslavia, a day after. The status quo of three days before had been reestablished. This small and indecisive engagement cost the 58th Division 600 dead and wounded, and Italian losses were far higher; officially Capello admitted to 1,500 casualties in the 27th Division and almost 800 in the 11th.

On January 19, under pressure from Boroević, Zeidler decided to try to take and hold the heights of Oslavia one last time. He planned a rapid daytime infantry assault with modest artillery support. He gave his troops several days to rest and prepare for the attack. The 58th Division's guns opened up on the afternoon of January 24, shelling Italian trenches around 188 and Oslavia. After the two-hour long barrage lifted, the three assault battalions climbed out of their trenches and headed for the Italian lines. At 5 P.M., as the sun went down, the Austrian infantry fixed bayonets and marched through thick fog toward Oslavia and 188. The assault was led by platoons of sappers, armed with flamethrowers and explosive charges, newly introduced weapons to destroy sturdy Italian positions. The Italian 27th Division fought back, especially around the sunken road that ran between the hill and the village. The ferocious battle for the road lasted half an hour, inflicting heavy losses on both sides and ending in an Italian retreat. In the darkness the 27th Division began to withdraw in the face of determined Austrian pressure. Zeidler's sappers cleared the way, blowing up and incinerating several Italian machine guns nests and dugouts. Two companies of the Magyar 69th Regiment charged up the cloud-shrouded slopes of Hill 188, overrunning the positions at the summit. Soon after, Dalmatians of the 37th Rifles retook the church at Oslavia. By 7 P.M., the 58th Division had regained the heights of Oslavia and seized all the positions it had lost to the VI Corps. It also took 1,200 Italian prisoners from five different regiments, among them forty-five officers. Many of the prisoners appeared to have been driven temporarily insane by the shelling, explosions, and flamethrowers. They were led eastward across the Isonzo, under close guard. The morale and fighting spirit of Capello's much-abused VI Corps had been shown to be surprisingly fragile. That evening Capello tried to recapture his lost positions, but to no avail. A strong ten-battalion counterattack was bloodily repulsed by Zeidler's machine gunners, and a disappointed Capello had to abandon any hope of retaking Hill 188 and Oslavia for the moment. The day's fighting cost Austria 334 more dead and wounded, and the VI Corps conceded a loss of 2,320 soldiers, many of them captured. The Gorizia bridgehead again quieted down for several more weeks. Both sides needed a rest to recover from the seesaw mid-January battle, which succeeded only in reestablishing the Austrian hold on the inconsequential heights of Oslavia; it decided nothing of any tactical, much less strategic, significance.

Cadorna was planning an attack that he hoped would have strategic consequences. Now committed to a clear policy of attrition, he naturally lowered his expectations; he would be content to make minor gains on the battlefield while inflicting heavy losses on the Austrians. Even so, a decisive breakthrough on the Isonzo remained his ultimate goal. The inevitable Fifth Battle began several weeks ahead of schedule, before the spring thaw. It was the product of Italy's relationship with the Allies, the result of German strategic thinking. Throughout 1915, the chief of the Imperial German General Staff, General Erich von Falkenhayn, pursued an Eastern strategy. Confronted with trench deadlock in the West, he concentrated Germany's offensive forces against Russia while his armies stood on the defensive in France and Flanders. To a considerable degree Falkenhayn's strategy worked: German armies decisively defeated the tsar's forces in Galicia and nearly knocked Russia out of the war. However, by late 1915 it was evident that the Russian colossus, though grievously injured, was not yet dead, and that the Allied threat in the West had increased markedly. Falkenhayn therefore opted for a Western strategy for the new year; he believed that inflicting a major defeat on France was Germany's only way of securing ultimate victory.

The mighty German military machine, though clearly the war's preeminent fighting force, was nevertheless not powerful enough to wage a war-winning offensive against France while still committed to holding the line in the East;

there simply were not enough men and guns to go around. Falkenhayn thus opted for a limited offensive in France; its goal was not winning on the battle-field, but wearing the French military down to the point of utter exhaustion. Falkenhayn accepted the same deadly logic of attrition that Cadorna heartily embraced. He selected the Verdun sector in eastern France for the offensive. The Verdun region, heretofore a quiet part of the Western front, was of consid-erable psychological and political significance to France; Falkenhayn was sure that Joseph Joffre would not part with Verdun, an ancient fortress city, without a hard fight. The Germans planned to launch a limited offensive against Verdun and let the French die in droves trying to take back their lost ground. Falkenhayn's plan was simply to bleed France white.

He put his scheme into practice on February 21, 1916, with an enormous twelve-hour bombardment by 1,400 guns. When the barrage lifted after firing two million shells, the German 5th Army advanced through snowstorms on the fortresses surrounding the city. The Germans made impressive progress at first, but the offensive soon bogged down; as Falkenhayn predicted, the *poilus* were fighting doggedly for every foot of French soil. By the tenth day of the offen-sive, Falkenhayn had begun to entertain doubts about his plan, which he feared might be spiraling out of control. It no longer looked like a limited, controlled offensive. French losses were steep, but so were Germany's, and there seemed to be no end in sight. In one of the most important decisions of the Great War, Falkenhayn cast his second thoughts aside and resolved to continue his scheme through to its conclusion. By the time the fight for Verdun ended nearly ten months later, it had claimed almost a million dead and wounded, cost Falkenhayn his position as Germany's senior general, and helped turn the tide of the war.

For the moment, however, Joffre was merely concerned that Verdun not fall to the Germans. France had already lost so much territory to Germany that she would not willingly surrender any more of it; Verdun thus attained an impor-tance to France and her army that far outweighed its military significance. The battle gave France an epic struggle around which the nation rallied. It also be-came a terrible fight for tiny pieces of ground, with progress measured in feet, not miles—much like the war on the Carso. The French Army indeed was being bled white at Verdun, as Falkenhayn expected, and Joffre appealed to France's allies to take the pressure off by launching immediate offensives against Ger-many and her Austrian ally. Douglas Haig, commander of the British Expedi-tionary Force, for months had been planning Britain's first great offensive for midsummer, and responded that his volunteer divisions could not possibly be ready before then. The Russians were only slightly more accommodating. They answered truthfully that the Tsar's armies were in no condition to launch a major offensive to help the French, but they promised some kind of attack against German positions on the northern end of the Eastern front. Cadorna proved more responsive. He had been planning an offensive on the Isonzo for the spring anyway, and Joffre requested only that Italy move its timetable forward by a few weeks. Cadorna did not value his allies very highly, but he realized that a French defeat at Verdun would have catastrophic consequences for his own war plans, so he agreed to launch the Fifth Battle of the Isonzo ahead of schedule.[4]

Cadorna's objectives for the Fifth Battle of the Isonzo reflected consistent themes. The 2nd Army was ordered to attack Austrian positions at the Tolmein bridgehead, and the 3rd Army (which now included Capello's VI Corps) received orders to assault the Gorizia sector and the western edge of the Carso, with a particular emphasis on the San Michele sector. This was not to be a war-winning blow, even in Cadorna's mind; it was instead supposed to weaken Austria further while rendering assistance to the beleaguered French. The chief of staff planned the offensive to start at the beginning of the second week of March. The winter weather would be a serious impediment to movement, particularly on the upper Isonzo, but Cadorna expected his forces to advance modestly. He assembled an impressive force to strike the 5th Army's positions. By the eve of the offensive, Italian forces on the Isonzo totaled twenty-nine divisions: seven reinforced divisions with Pietro Frugoni's 2nd Army, eleven with the Duke of Aosta's 3rd Army, and eleven more in special reserve in eastern Friulia. In all, Cadorna's armies possessed 350 infantry battalions and nearly 1,400 guns. His orders remained typically vague and imprecise—he told Frugoni and the Duke of Aosta that they should aim their forces at any objective they liked, so long as they contributed "directly or indirectly" to taking Gorizia and Tolmein—but his numerical superiority guaranteed that the offensive would make a considerable impression on the Austrians.

By early March, the Austrian forces holding the Isonzo line were weaker than they had been for nearly a year. The needs of other fronts meant that the relatively quiet Isonzo front had lost several veteran formations during the winter; four crack Alpine divisions[5] departed in February and early March. On the eve of the Fifth Battle, Boroević's army was down to just ten divisions with about a hundred battalions, half of them second-line militia units. In less than a month, the 5th Army had relinquished a third of its 147 rifle battalions, and artillery strength had fallen from 693 guns to 467. Boroević's shell reserve was similarly cut back, and his army had received few of the new, more modern weapons being produced by Austrian arsenals. As long as Cadorna remained on the defensive, the Isonzo was a low priority for the Austrian High Command.[6]

Still, the outnumbered Austrians continued to enjoy the advantages of terrain that strongly favored the defender and excellent entrenchments, two benefits which Boroević's troops had used to such decisive effect since the beginning of the Isonzo battles. In addition, the Austrians knew an Italian offensive was coming. Austrian intelligence noted heavier rail traffic through

Venice and Friulia from early March, and the days before the attack were filled
with all the usual troop movements that indicated an imminent Italian blow.
The 5th Army used the first days of March to improve its defenses and deploy
its reduced divisions to best effect. Starting on March 8, Italian divisions all
along the front sent out reinforced patrols to test the Austrian defenses, another
sure sign of an impending offensive. When Cadorna's preparatory barrage began on March 11, the Austrians were ready.

The combined artillery of the 2nd and 3rd Armies, more than 900 field guns
reinforced by 300 medium and 85 heavy pieces, pounded Austrian defenses all
along the Isonzo, from Rombon to the Adriatic. The powerful bombardment
lasted almost forty-eight hours and destroyed many entrenchments, but its fire
was often indiscriminate. Italian batteries seemed to be aimed at general target
areas rather than specific targets. The barrage was therefore considerably less
destructive than it might have been. Cadorna's infantry attacks began on the
morning of March 13 with actions all along the front and major assaults by the
VI Corps at Podgora and the XI Corps around San Michele. The *fanti* found it
tough going. In the first place, the late winter weather was everywhere against
them. On the upper Isonzo, deep snows made advancing up mountainsides difficult, in some places impossible. On the lower Isonzo, dense fog reduced visibility
almost to zero on the Carso and in front of Gorizia. In such conditions coordinated attacks were impossible, and the offensive soon stalled completely.

The 2nd Army's offensive hardly even happened. Efforts by the IV and VIII
Corps to take their objectives in the Flitsch basin and on Mrzli ridge barely got
off the ground and gained nothing. Similarly, the VI Corps' attempts to advance
on Podgora hill proved abortive. In the thick fog, only one battalion from the
three attacking divisions got anywhere near the Austrian lines, and it was
quickly turned back. The 3rd Army did little better on the Carso. In the San
Michele sector, the XI Corps made concerted efforts to take the mountain and
the neighboring village of San Martino, but the fog and efficient Austrian defenses prevented any possibility of success. At San Martino the 21st Division
launched an attack by a full brigade, but it was repulsed with heavy losses by the
46th Regiment of the 17th Division, Magyar veterans who knew the terrain intimately. Farther downstream, the XIII and VIII Corps, five divisions altogether,
likewise advanced not at all. The two corps managed to mount no determined
attacks in the blinding fog; none of the assaults exceeded regimental strength,
and all were turned back easily by the southern Carso's Czech and German
defenders.

The 2nd and 3rd Armies executed even more halfhearted attacks the next
day. The Austrians held all their ground until March 16, when Cadorna officially abandoned the Fifth Battle. It was obvious that the offensive was getting
absolutely nowhere. It was a poor showing compared even to the dismal records
of the 1915 fighting. For once Cadorna was not reluctant to call a halt to his of-

fensive. He had demonstrated his loyalty to his French ally by attacking the Austrians on the Isonzo; the alliance demanded an effort, not an all-out drive for victory.[7] Cadorna did what duty required, and no more. The five-day Fifth Battle claimed only about 2,000 Italian casualties and an equal number for the Austrians, most of them caused by the preparatory bombardment. Compared to the epic struggles on the Isonzo in the summer and autumn of 1915, the Fifth Battle hardly seemed a battle at all; indeed, the Austrian official account dismissed it as "an attempt by the enemy to pretend there had been a serious battle." Cadorna's brief offensive perhaps appeased the panicked French High Command, but it surely failed to help the beleaguered French forces at Verdun. A five-day minor attack against Austrian positions on the Isonzo could not possibly cause Falkenhayn to reduce his pressure at Verdun. The Fifth Battle, although a near non-event in the history of the Isonzo fighting, nevertheless had one lasting impact on Cadorna's military thinking. It further hardened his belief that what he needed above all else to achieve a breakthrough was more large-caliber guns and shells; as he recalled after the battle, "The Italian Army could not advance victoriously on the Carso or anywhere else until it had been able to increase its resources in heavy artillery." He therefore decided to wait until he had many more big guns to attempt another major offensive on the Isonzo.

Yet the Fifth Battle did not end as tidily or completely as Cadorna's orders demanded, or as official histories portray. Sporadic fighting dragged on for several weeks after the brief battle formally ended. Most of these minor actions were small-scale Austrian attempts to gain minor pieces of ground to improve their defensive position. Combat flared up again on the upper Isonzo despite the deep snows and bitter cold. On the evening of March 17, the 6th Bosnian *Jäger* Battalion stormed forward positions of the Italian 7th Division in a surprise attack at the Tolmein bridgehead. The lightning assault overran Italian trenches just west of the Church of Holy Mary, bagging 558 prisoners and strengthening the Austrian hold on the hill. On the same evening, in the Flitsch sector the 44th Rifle Division launched a surprise attack on Italian positions on Mt. Rombon. Alpine veterans of the 1st Mountain Rifles left their staging area at Čukla after dark and advanced down the mountain through the deep snow. They quickly overwhelmed the surprised defenders, seizing the Italian positions and inflicting 559 casualties (224 of them taken prisoner) to just eleven of their own.

This astonishing local victory outraged the commander of the 24th Division, who now controlled the Italian side of the Rombon sector. He was determined to retake Čukla, which he believed would put an end to Austrian raids on his positions. He decided, however, to wait for the weather to improve before launching his assault. While the Italians waited for spring to arrive, the defense of Rombon passed from the Carinthian 1st Mountain Rifles to the 4th Bosnian Regiment, a unit of equally skilled and courageous mountain fighters. When the Italian attack came on May 10, Čukla was garrisoned by just three companies of Bosnians. The 24th Division's efficient mountain batteries poured fire on the Austrian entrenchments while four battalions of *Alpini* prepared to advance up the mountain. After several hours of shelling, the Italian infantry went over the top, the Saluzzo Battalion first, led by its commander, Lieutenant Colonel Luigi Piglione. The charging *Alpini* braved withering Austrian rifle fire that felled many of their comrades, but soldiers of the Saluzzo and Bassano Battalions pressed on and eventually reached Čukla. Vicious hand-to-hand combat ensued between *Alpini* and *Bosniaken*, the cream of their armies, with heavy losses on both sides. Soon the Bosnians were surrounded and could not escape. Following several hours of costly melées, the Italian tricolor again flew over Čukla after three months of Austrian occupation. Losses on both sides were considerable. The three companies of Bosnians were nearly wiped out, losing 250 men, half of them captured; the *Alpini* suffered 534 casualties, including the brave Lieutenant Colonel Piglione, killed at the head of his victorious battalion. He was posthumously awarded the Gold Medal for Bravery, the coveted *medaglia d'oro*, for his feat, which rivaled the capture of Krn, almost a year before, in the annals of Italy's mountain troops.

Farther downstream, fighting also flared up occasionally as the winter gradually turned into spring. In the days after the end of the Fifth Battle, Boroević tried to exploit Italian weakness by attempting to grab some minor positions before Gorizia and on the Carso. Between March 19 and 21, Austrian regiments conducted small and indecisive raids on the western edge of the Doberdò plateau. The 58th Division's effort on Podgora proved more successful. In a well planned raid, the 37th Rifle Regiment left its trenches on the heels of a two-and-a-half-hour barrage, headed for positions held by the 11th Division on Podgora hill. The surprise assault pushed the Italians out of their dugouts with heavy losses. At a cost of 259 casualties, the Dalmatians inflicted 1,269 losses on the 11th Division, half of them prisoners. The failure of the Italians to resist for long, coupled with the large number of prisoners taken, indicated again that the morale of Capello's VI Corps was low.

Not all Austrian efforts ended in success. On March 26 the 5th Army's air units attempted the first major Austrian bombing raid on the Isonzo front. The Austrian air service was well trained but suffered from a persistent lack of aircraft and spare parts, a further indication of Austria's weak war economy. Large air operations therefore were very much the exception, rather than standard practice. The mass raid, to be conducted by seventy-eight army and navy aircraft, was designed to hinder Cadorna's supply effort by bombing the rail bridges over the Piave River, sixty miles behind the front. It was led by Major Junovicz, commander of all Austrian air units on the Isonzo. The raid began favorably enough, encountering little resistance from Italian air units and antiaircraft batteries; the bomb run appeared to be a complete success, registering several hits on the rail bridges. However, troubles began on the flight home.

Italian fighter squadrons pounced on the returning bombers, shooting down four aircraft and damaging several more. Worse yet, heavy fog had moved in over the Isonzo, and the pilots had great difficulty finding their bases; in the confusion, several more aircraft crashed. In all, the Austrians lost eighteen aircraft and several of their most experienced pilots were killed, including Major Junovicz. Most disturbingly, the raid failed to inflict notable damage on the Piave bridges. The Italians repaired the bomb damage within hours, and the rail bridges were soon operating again at full capacity. Such heavy losses for such modest gains ensured that it would be many months before Boroević would again permit his air squadrons to launch another major raid on Cadorna's rear areas.

More minor engagements followed in late March. On March 28 and 29, the Duke of Aosta's 3rd Army tried to reclaim several positions on the Carso and in front of Gorizia. All attacks failed. The 3rd Army resumed its raiding in the San Michele sector in late April. The armies waged a bitter nocturnal war in no-man's-land, a struggle between sapper detachments and small infantry patrols. Every night the Italians and Austrians sent raiding and mining parties toward the each other's trenches. The nighttime mining grew particularly serious around San Martino. VII Corps sappers placed several large mines under Italian positions, to be detonated before a large raid. The mines usually killed many Italians and blew a significant hole in the XI Corps' entrenchments just west of San Martino. During the night of April 24, 17th Division sappers detonated two large mines, destroying a wide section of the Italian trenches immediately west of the village. In the confusion that followed, the 22nd Division unexpectedly threw an entire regiment into the gap blasted by the mines. The Magyar 46th Regiment, holding the San Martino sector, was completely surprised by this Italian move; worse, it had no reserves on hand to stop it. Several companies of *fanti* charged into the wide gap in the lines and overran the thinly held trenches just a hundred paces to the east. The Italians were only minutes away from capturing the village of San Martino and possibly reaching the Austrians' second defensive line. The breakthrough that ten months of offensives had failed to achieve was now within the reach of the XI Corps.

There was only one company of Austrian infantry anywhere near the Italian penetration, the 6th of the 46th Regiment. The company, held in immediate reserve, was commanded by First Lieutenant Géza Heim, a twenty-five-year-old Magyar. A professional soldier, he had fought on the Serbian front in 1914, and on the Isonzo since the late summer of 1915, becoming an experienced troop leader who knew the Carso well. Receiving orders from VII Corps headquarters to stop the Italian penetration, Heim led his company through the darkness until his soldiers were just a hundred feet from the advancing Italians. He then ordered his infantrymen to fix bayonets and charge the columns of *fanti*. The Magyar company, with Heim in the lead, collided with the Italians full force.

Heim's riflemen, many with *fokó*—the much feared Hungarian fighting knife—in hand and at the ready, attacked the startled Italians ferociously. The regiment had not expected an Austrian counterattack so soon; after a brief firefight and brawl, its forward companies became disorganized and withdrew into the darkness rather than face the *fokó*-wielding Magyars. Soon the whole regiment was in headlong retreat back to its own lines. Within less than an hour the Italian attack evaporated. The 22nd Division's promising effort had turned into a rout. The briefly mortal threat to the San Michele sector had been destroyed by Heim and his lone company. The young officer's rapid action had saved at least the San Martino sector. His corps commander, Archduke Joseph, claimed that Heim in fact saved nothing less than the entire Doberdò position. For his audacity and courage, Lieutenant Heim was awarded the Knight's Cross of the Order of Maria Theresia, a rare honor for so junior an officer.

The skirmishing on the Carso in the early spring, though of great importance to the soldiers involved, nevertheless attracted little attention at the Austrian High Command, far away in the Silesian city of Teschen. Austria's senior generals had for several weeks been focused on the Italian front, but not on the Isonzo. Indeed, since the beginning of 1916 Franz Conrad von Hötzendorf had been able to think of little else but his plans for the Italian front. Conrad, a lifelong Italophobe, had wanted to strike a fatal blow against Italy since becoming chief of the General Staff in 1906. He naturally had had no opportunity before Rome entered the war in May 1915. Since the Italian declaration of war, however, Conrad had pleaded with his German ally to permit him to transfer enough divisions from the East to knock Italy out of the war. Italy's betrayal of its Austrian ally made Conrad and his senior generals even more determined to strike against it. Conrad, often immoderate but always a shrewd strategist, was convinced that an offensive launched from the South Tyrol would quickly bring Italy to its knees. He knew the Tyrolean frontier intimately, having spent many years commanding units in the Tyrol, and believed that the problems posed by the difficult high Alpine terrain were more than offset by the strategic opportunities a Trentino offensive offered to the Central Powers. Conrad argued forcefully that a well planned thrust from the South Tyrol would cut off Cadorna's supply lines to the Isonzo, thus crippling the Italian war effort, and quite possibly knock Italy out of the war entirely. He called his plan the *Strafexpedition*—the "punishment expedition"; it would be an act of revenge against a faithless ally. Conrad's scheme was an excellent example of an indirect strategy, something rarely seen on any front during the First World War, in which blunter methods typically prevailed.

Conrad's strategic concept was very sound, but Falkenhayn remained unconvinced. The Prussian general, unquestionably the senior partner in the Vienna-Berlin alliance, felt that the Italian front was a sideshow of the war. He thus proved unfailingly unreceptive to Conrad's repeated arguments in favor of a Tyrolean offensive. Any major diversion of Austrian effort to the Italian front appeared foolish to German eyes; besides, by early 1916 Falkenhayn was too busy with the Verdun campaign to waste time and troops on Conrad's pet project. He therefore refused to offer any German divisions to Conrad for his offensive; he even denied Conrad a few divisions to take the place of the units Conrad would have to withdraw from the East for his Tyrolean effort. The Austrians would have to go it alone.

Conrad was disappointed by his ally's dismissal of his grandiose scheme, but he preferred the risk of launching the offensive without German help to abandoning what he passionately believed was a war-winning plan. He knew that Austria could not sustain the human and material cost of the Isonzo fighting indefinitely, so a potentially decisive rapid blow at Cadorna's rear offered attractive strategic possibilities. Austrian preparations for the South Tyrol offensive swung into action in the late winter. Boroević was informed on March 3, before the Fifth Battle, that a major offensive against Italy was planned for mid-April, and that it would require the 5th Army to transfer four of its best divisions to the Tyrol. Boroević reluctantly surrendered four of his toughest mountain divisions to Archduke Eugen's assembling army group in the South Tyrol; Conrad also demanded many of Boroević's heavy artillery batteries and numerous supporting troops, a total of 70,000 men. Many more arrived around Trient from the Eastern front. Conrad stripped his Galician defenses of five first-rate divisions and many valuable artillery units. The new army group also received the lion's share of Austria's limited shell reserves for the offensive. Conrad spared no effort for his long-awaited blow against Italy.

By April 10, Archduke Eugen's army group was ready. The Austrian strike force was impressive in both quantity and quality. The two armies, the newly raised 11th and the veteran 3rd, moved from the now dormant Serbian front, totaled fifteen divisions with almost 200 infantry battalions, supported by more than 1,000 guns, including sixty heavy batteries. The force included the cream of the Habsburg Army, tough divisions of veteran mountain troops. The core of Archduke Eugen's assault force was the III Corps, the Iron Corps of German-Slovene Alpine troops, and the XX Corps, the *Thronfolgerkorps* (Heir Apparent's Corps), two divisions of elite Tyrolean and Upper Austrian regiments, commanded by the heir to the throne, twenty-nine-year-old Archduke Karl. Conrad placed his offensive in the hands of his very best troops. The treacherous high Alpine terrain posed limitations on movement and promised difficulties with keeping the advancing troops supplied. In mid-April the South Tyrolean mountains were still snow-covered and dangerously icy, but Conrad believed that breaking through the Italian lines would not overly tax his elite mountain divisions. The attack was amply supported by artillery and included the latest tactical innovations; much of the battle plan was devised by the respected tactician General Alfred Krauss, chief of staff of Archduke Eugen's army group. The offensive's objective was the city of Padua, forty-five miles behind the front lines. It was only twenty miles from the Adriatic coast, and was the easternmost railhead for Cadorna's armies on the Isonzo, the supply source for the Isonzo offensives. There were high Alpine chains and an entire Italian army between Conrad's troops and Padua, but the Austrians were confident of victory.

The Italian 1st Army defended the Tyrolean frontier. It was more than seven divisions strong and included many *Alpini* battalions, in addition to 800 guns. Its very mountainous sector offered daunting natural defenses, as well as extensive entrenchments and fortifications. The 1st Army's commander, Lieutenant General Brusati, oversaw the construction of five defensive lines near the Austrian frontier during the months after the war began. Like Cadorna, he was always fearful of an Austrian offensive, and had organized his forces to defend every foot of their sector. Brusati was in many ways a typical incompetent Italian general—he took no interest in his men, knew little about tactics, and obeyed only the orders from the *Comando Supremo* that he liked—but it cannot be denied that his army occupied solid defenses.

The *grigioverdi* of the 1st Army received an unexpected reprieve when Conrad was forced to delay his grand offensive. The weather in the South Tyrol deteriorated in mid-April; winter returned with a vengeance, bringing deep snows that made an immediate attack impossible. Conrad therefore decided to launch his blow a month later than planned, on May 15. During the four weeks that Archduke Eugen's two armies waited for the weather to improve, Italian intelligence could not fail to detect Austrian preparations for an offensive. Indeed, the *Comando Supremo* had noted heavy rail movement to the Tyrol weeks earlier, but Cadorna refused to believe that the Austrians would dare to launch an offensive from there. He was confident that the 1st Army's defenses were strong enough to repulse any Austrian attack anyway; furthermore, Cadorna feared that the Austrian troop movements were just a feint to distract him from the Austrians' real plan, an offensive on the Isonzo, his worst nightmare. Even so, he was sufficiently disturbed by the plethora of reports about an Austrian buildup around Trient to leave Udine and visit the 1st Army in early May. He was dismayed to find that Brusati had systematically disobeyed repeated orders from the High Command about the proper manning of entrenchments. Of the five Italian defensive lines, only the first two were occupied, and those were poorly organized. The 1st Army was strong, but its defensive scheme had serious defects. Cadorna dismissed Brusati on the spot and ordered the 1st Army's staff officers to improve the defenses immediately. To shore up the defenses further, Cadorna dispatched two divisions from his special reserve to the Tyrolean frontier. He felt that would be sufficient; besides, he could not believe that Conrad would strike from the Trentino.

The beginning of the offensive on May 15 therefore came as an unwelcome shock to Cadorna and his staff. Playing to Cadorna's obsession with the Isonzo, the Tyrolean effort was preceded on May 14 by a minor Austrian thrust on the Carso, enough to distract the Italians. The next morning a thousand Austrian guns opened up on a twenty-mile front in the South Tyrol. Archduke Eugen's two armies then advanced, making impressive gains in several sectors. The 1st Army's undermanned and disorganized defenses offered only sporadic resistance to the Austrian mountain troopers. By the end of the first day, the Austrians had advanced in some places as deep as five miles into Italian territory, an amazing feat by Great War standards. Despite the difficulty of moving quickly in the high Alps, the experienced Austrian infantry maintained its steady forward march for the next several days. Although many Italian units resisted fiercely, few managed to hold their ground in the face of determined and well planned Austrian assaults.

Cadorna reacted to the crisis by shifting considerable forces from the Isonzo; he soon realized that the Tyrolean offensive was no feint but a serious, perhaps mortal, threat to his armies. He reacted surprisingly well to the looming disaster; Cadorna sometimes displayed better qualities of leadership in times of profound crisis.[8] (He later remembered, with typical modesty, "I was never so calm as at that moment.") He began to move an entire army from the Isonzo to the Asiago plateau in front of Padua, transferring the equivalent of eight infantry divisions, numerous battalions of *Alpini* and *Bersaglieri*, and dozens of artillery batteries from the Carso and Gorizia sectors to new defensive positions a hundred miles west. By the end of May he had shored up the Asiago sector with a half-million soldiers from the Isonzo and all over Italy. Cadorna's reinforcements, traveling along interior lines, enjoyed a notable logistical advantage over the Austrians. The arriving units were assembled in a new army, the 5th, whose mission was halting the Austrian drive. Most important, Cadorna appealed to his allies for immediate help.

Cadorna's impressive troop movements at first had little impact on the Austrian advance. Until the end of May the 3rd and 11th Armies continued to move slowly but steadily into Italian territory. By the month's end they had seized the town of Asiago, on the rugged plateau of the same name. The Austrians had advanced fifteen miles—only a third of the way to Padua, but a very impressive achievement nevertheless. However, supply problems mounted as the advancing divisions outpaced their slow-moving logistical columns; moving tons of munitions over the almost roadless high Alps proved frustratingly difficult and impossible to remedy quickly. The Austrian advance therefore slowed its pace to wait for its all-important supplies to catch up. The 5th Army took advantage of the slowdown to build strong defenses on the Asiago plateau, where the next round of fighting would take place.

Far more significant for Italy, though, was the Russian offensive in East Galicia, which began on June 4. Cadorna's plea for help was answered generously by the Russians. The Tsarist High Command was unable to promise a major effort, but it did order General Alexei Brusilov, the commander of the Southwestern front, to launch a limited offensive against Austrian positions in East Galicia. On paper, the Russian attack was doomed from the start: Brusilov's fifty-six divisions barely outnumbered the forty-five Austrian divisions across the lines, and his artillery was hampered by serious shell shortages. Most important, the Austrian defenses in East Galicia, improved throughout the winter and spring, appeared impregnable; indeed, Conrad was willing to strip his forces in the East for his Tyrolean gamble precisely because the Galician defenses seemed so strong. Brusilov responded to his orders to attack the Austrians with novel tactics. Knowing that he had only a bare numerical superiority over the defenders, and that his shell reserve was too limited to allow a sustained preparatory bombardment, Brusilov and his talented staff devised a previously untried solution. The Southwestern front would concentrate its offensive in force in several places, rather than spreading its forces all along the front. Furthermore, because the artillery barrage would have to be brief, it would be very intense and directed at specific vital Austrian targets. In addition, Brusilov innovatively ordered that all his assault divisions be trained realistically for the offensive, including live-fire exercises with mock-ups of the Austrian entrenchments they would attack. He thereby totally contradicted the prevailing tactical wisdom of 1916, which emphasized mass attacks on long fronts, supported by weeklong bombardments. As evidenced on the Western front and the Isonzo, spread-out mass attacks inevitably failed with heavy losses, and extended barrages only served to wreak general destruction and make the ground impassable for the attacker. Brusilov's new tactics avoided such frequently encountered pitfalls.

When the Russian artillery opened fire on the morning of June 4, it blasted carefully selected Austrian troop positions, ammunition dumps, artillery batteries, and headquarters behind the front. The serenely confident Austrians, like Cadorna a month before, had witnessed numerous signs of an impending Russian attack, but they had refused to take them seriously. Stunned by the intense and deadly accurate barrage, the Austrian infantry was unable to resist the determined waves of Russian infantry. Several Austrian divisions simply collapsed in the face of Brusilov's lightning blow; veteran regiments holding solid positions surrendered *en masse* to the advancing Russians. In several sectors the Austrian defenses just crumbled, and a mass withdrawal soon followed. Leadership was lacking, and the retreat evolved into a rout; soon it was a catastrophe. In the first week, Brusilov's advancing armies captured 200,000 Austrian soldiers, an unprecedented feat, and nowhere in East Galicia could Conrad's forces hold their ground. The Russians' limited offensive turned into one of the greatest advances of the war. By the end of June, the Austrians had again lost all of East Galicia to the Russian steamroller, and there was no end in sight for Brusilov's advance. Urgent German assistance was required to halt the Russians. By the time Brusilov's offensive ran out of steam in midsummer, the Austrians had lost half of Galicia and at least 600,000 soldiers, most of them captured. It was the worst defeat in the long history of Habsburg arms, a psychological blow of immense proportions. It changed the balance of power in the East, reducing Austria to a mere German satellite in the war against Russia. Most of all, it dealt the Austrian Army a blow from which it never fully recovered.

For Conrad, it also meant the end of his Tyrolean offensive. His strategic gamble was one of the first victims of Brusilov's victory in East Galicia. Confronted with an unexpected disaster in the East, the Austrian High Command immediately had to transfer several divisions from the Italian front to fight the Russians, thus crippling Archduke Eugen's advance. The offensive ended after advancing fifteen miles; it had been an impressive gain, particularly considering the difficult terrain, but nothing like the war-winning blow that Conrad had hoped to deliver. The South Tyrolean offensive was officially suspended on June 16, several days after it had ground to a virtual halt from a lack of supplies. The enormous effort had gained a bridgehead to nowhere. Still, Cadorna was determined not to let the Austrians keep their useless bridgehead. On the same day that Archduke Eugen regretfully ordered his forces to stop their advance, Cadorna sent his newly raised 5th Army on the offensive. The battlefield was the Seven Communes, a plateau occupied by German-speaking farmers since the Middle Ages, a curious Teutonic island in a Latin sea. Cadorna's attack was a two-pronged advance intended to encircle the Austrians on the plateau; however, the defenders cleverly retreated far enough to avoid being cut off. The Italian push soon devolved into a bitter wrestling match for the frontier hills. Italian tactics were primitive, as on the Isonzo, and the attackers had difficulty retaking lost ground. Casualties mounted. By the time Cadorna called off the 5th Army's three-week drive, it had recaptured half of the territory lost in late May. The cost of the seven weeks of fighting on the Tyrolean border was steep for both sides. The Austrians counted 89,000 casualties, including 26,000 soldiers captured; Cadorna's forces lost 147,000 men—a rare case when the defender's losses were nearly twice those of the attacker. Italian casualties included the alarming loss of 56,000 men and 294 guns in Austrian captivity, a sign that after only a year of fighting, Italian morale had become brittle.

Nevertheless, Italy had turned back Conrad's intended death blow. Of course, Italy's salvation was mostly attributable to the Russians' stunning victory in the East, which cut short the Tyrolean offensive in midstride, but Cadorna and his generals naturally pretended otherwise. Conrad's offensive failed to achieve any strategic gains, but it did succeed in making Italy's political rulers take the war far more seriously than before. The specter of Austrian armies descending on northern Italy frightened the politicians into action. On June 10, Prime Minister Salandra, the man who brought Italy into the war, resigned from office. He and his cabinet were replaced by a government of national unity headed by Paolo Boselli, at seventy-eight the oldest deputy in Parliament. The new prime minister had no visibly outstanding qualities, but he was a badly needed symbol of national cohesion. The cabinet was reshuffled, but Sonnino remained foreign minister, although the home front was now controlled by a new interior minister, Vittorio Orlando. Cadorna, of course, remained chief of staff—no politician yet dared challenge the iron-willed Piedmontese count. So Cadorna's monopoly of military power remained undiminished, and he was still answerable to no one. The only thing Cadorna learned from Italy's close escape on the Asiago plateau was that he should launch another great offensive on the Isonzo as soon as possible. He was eager to inflict the decisive defeat on Boroević that had eluded him for more than a year. Six months had elapsed since the last major Italian attempt to break the Austrian hold on the Isonzo, and Cadorna believed the time had come to try again.

EIGHT

THE BATTLE OF GORIZIA

The Isonzo front was relatively quiet while the Asiago plateau was aflame. There were the typical nighttime patrols and occasional raids, of course, but the Italian and Austrian forces on the Isonzo, both weakened by the need to reinforce the armies fighting a hundred miles to the west, enjoyed a brief respite from battle. Once the fighting died down on the Trentino front, however, the tempo of operations on the Isonzo slowly increased. Beginning in the second week of June, Italian patrols grew larger and more aggressive. On the evening of June 14, the 3rd Army launched a limited but powerful raid on the Carso's southern flank. After several hours of heavy shelling of Austrian positions around Mt. Sei Busi, two Italian divisions advanced through the darkness toward trenches held by the 106th Militia Division. Intense combat followed as the *fanti* and the Czech riflemen of the 11th Austrian Militia Regiment vied for control of the trenches around Hill 118. The three-day fight ended in a nominal victory for the Austrians; they held all their positions, but at a cost of 1,400 casualties for the 106th Division. Italian losses were higher still, but the 3rd Army continued its harassment of the Austrians on the south Carso after a few days' rest. The 106th became involved in another bruising match with the Duke of Aosta's troops in the last week of June. This fight, which dragged on painfully into the first week of July, was as inconclusive as the first, but inflicted a further loss of 4,700 soldiers on the militia division. It speaks volumes about the bloodiness of the Isonzo fighting that both sides considered the latter half of June to be "quiet days" on the front.

While the 106th Division was busy repulsing Italian probes around Mt. Sei Busi, Svetozar Boroević and his staff were preparing for a surprise attack in the San Michele sector. They believed that the recent Tyrolean battles had sufficiently distracted the Italians to permit the VII Corps to launch a successful raid to recapture some lost positions around San Michele and San Martino. Boroević wanted to retake some trenches on the mountain's north face, as well as Hill 197, just north of the village of San Martino. These Italian-held positions were a source of constant concern for 5th Army headquarters; Boroević feared that they would be important staging points for the next Italian attempt to seize Mt. San Michele. He therefore ordered a division-sized raid to retake them before Cadorna had a chance to launch another offensive. The Austrian raid, scheduled for the last week of June, was a typical minor attack, much like a dozen other probes made by both armies in 1916, except for one crucial difference. This time the Austrians were going to use gas.

Poison gas, though widely used on the Western front, had heretofore been unknown on the Isonzo. The Austrian Army had never used gas in battle, and neither had the Italians. Both armies had small units of chemical warfare troops, but so far they had sat idle. The climate and terrain of the Isonzo valley rendered the use of chemical agents difficult. The mountain winds and unpredictable temperature changes made the deployment of poison gas a risky proposition for the attacker. The Austrian idea to use gas on the Isonzo first came in November 1915, when Boroević feared an Italian breakthrough on the Carso, but it was shelved as impracticable. Yet by the following summer Austria's chemical specialists had changed their minds: a gas attack in clear weather conditions might be possible. Boroević eagerly seized upon this idea, believing that the use of chemical agents would give his surprise attack a decisive advantage.

In the first week of June, the VII Corps readied its assault force, a brigade each of the veteran 17th and 20th Divisions. Five battalions of the latter were aimed at San Michele, and four of the former were slated to seize Hill 197. By June 10 the assault troops were ready, but they had to wait for weather conditions ideal for the use of chemical weapons to arrive on the Carso. They waited more than two weeks for the winds to die down; in the meantime, troops of the army's Special Sapper Battalion, the gas experts, delivered 6,000 cylinders of phosgene to forward trenches in the San Michele sector. Late on the evening of June 28, the commander of the chemical battalion informed VII Corps headquarters that the weather conditions for the following morning appeared ideal. Archduke Joseph gave his permission just after midnight, and the gas cylinders were in position by 4:15 A.M. Within an hour the infantry was ready to go over the top.

The gas cylinders were opened at 5:15 A.M., and for the next half-hour waves of phosgene crept westward over the trenches of the XI Corps, only a hundred paces away. The highly toxic gases sank into the Italian positions, choking the forward battalions of the 21st and 22nd Divisions. The *fanti* in the front lines, unprotected by gasmasks, suffocated agonizingly by the thousands. The battalions holding the second defensive line panicked at the sight of the advancing clouds of phosgene and ran away. At 5:45 the Hungarian infantry, wearing gas masks, charged through the dissipating gas clouds to the Italian lines. They found thousands of Italian corpses, and ran over the first trenches without a fight. As they advanced farther, however, they encountered stiff resistance; outraged by the use of gas, poisoned Italian infantrymen fought back fiercely. Still, by 7 A.M. the two Italian lines of entrenchments on San Michele were occupied by the 20th Division, and a battalion of the 17th held the summit of Hill 197. Austrian shelling of the Isonzo bridges behind the XI Corps prevented the 3rd Army from sending reinforcements, and the attackers were able to consolidate their gains before the Italians could respond in strength. The gas attack had been a complete success. At a cost of 1,572 dead and wounded, the VII Corps had taken all its objectives in only an hour and had inflicted grievous losses on two Italian divisions.

Italian casualties were terrible. The XI Corps lost 6,900 soldiers, the vast majority of them suffocated by phosgene. The 10th Infantry Regiment of the Regina Brigade, occupying Hill 197, alone lost 1,666 *fanti*, 90 percent of them dead. They died horribly and slowly, their lungs and eyes burned out by gas. One of the thousands of Italian foot soldiers who died at dawn on June 29 was Ermino Cortellessa, a twenty-two-year-old private serving with the Florence Brigade's 128th Regiment. He was drowned in a sea of phosgene, alongside hundreds of his comrades on San Michele. Private Cortellessa's death was notable only because, in a tragic irony, his older brother had died in almost exactly the same spot nearly seven months before. Twenty-four-year-old Achille was killed in action with the 132rd Regiment on San Michele's north face on December 3, 1915, at the tail end of the Fourth Battle. The loss of a second son was a terrible blow to the Cortellessa family, peasants from Caserta, near Naples, in Italy's poor South. They had already sent their third and last son to the army to fight for *Italia irredenta*. In less than five months, twenty-year-old Luigi would join his brothers in the legions of Italian dead. He fell on the Carso's southern end on December 10, 1916, mortally wounded by Austrian fire. Within twelve months the Cortellessa family lost all three sons on the Carso. Surely there was no more bitter sacrifice to win the barren limestone plateau for Italy.

The gas attack at San Michele was unquestionably an Austrian victory, but in the long run its legacy hurt Boroević's soldiers. The sight of thousands of suffocated *grigioverdi* powerfully affected Italian troops on the Carso. They thirsted to avenge their dead comrades. Italian soldiers became noticeably less willing to accept the surrender of Austrian troops; after June 29, 1916, Boroević's foot soldiers could surrender safely only in large numbers—individuals or small groups trying to give up were likely to be shot. It was this desire for revenge that Luigi Cadorna sought to exploit in his coming offensive.

The Sixth Battle of the Isonzo grew out of the successful Italian defense of the Asiago plateau. Stopping Austria's Tyrolean offensive vastly improved the morale of the Italian military and nation. Sagging spirits on the home and fighting fronts, caused by months of bloody defeats, were bolstered immeasurably by the 5th Army's stand around Asiago. Italy was united as never before by a desire to bring the war to Austria.[1] Cadorna wanted to take advantage of this newfound national unity to launch a decisive blow on the Isonzo. It would be aimed at Gorizia and Mt. San Michele, well known objectives. The *Comando Supremo* believed that the Austrians were tired from their Tyrolean gamble, and would not expect an Italian offensive on the Isonzo so soon after the Asiago battles—an almost flawless analysis of Boroević's predicament. Furthermore, the time had come for a Sixth Battle because the Central Powers were under great pressure on all fronts. July saw by far the greatest Allied offensives of the war: the French had switched over to the attack at Verdun, the British had just started their enormous push on the Somme, and the Russians continued their advance deep into Galicia. Surely the hour had arrived for a massive Italian strike at the 5th Army. The Austrians, collapsing in the East, could afford few reinforcements for the Italian front, and the Germans were far too busy in the West to offer their Habsburg ally any help.

Cadorna therefore ordered a massive shift of forces from the Asiago plateau to the 3rd Army before Gorizia and on the Carso. Starting in early July, the Italian 5th Army was disbanded, and its troops and supplies were moved by rail to staging areas on the Isonzo. In three weeks, Cadorna transported a dozen reinforced divisions, 300,000 men and prodigious stores of munitions, to the Duke of Aosta's sector on the lower Isonzo. The battle-hardened divisions were fresh from victory at Asiago, and were eager to fight the Austrians again. Just as important, this massive movement of men and matériel was undertaken behind a veil of secrecy; the Italians had finally learned to mask their intentions.

The forces that Cadorna had amassed along the Isonzo by late July were impressive. The Italian Army was a third larger than a year before, and the troops were much better armed, enjoying a steady supply of machine guns, heavy artillery, mortars, and other equipment needed on the modern battlefield. Morale was also higher than it had been for many months. The Sixth Battle was in the hands of the 3rd Army, which held the line from Sabotino to the Adriatic; the 2nd Army, now commanded by Lieutenant General Settimo Piacentini, was reduced to a supporting role on the upper Isonzo. The Duke of Aosta's enlarged command included six corps with more than sixteen strong divisions, a total of 220 battalions supported by 1,250 guns and 770 mortars. The two spearhead corps were Cigliana's XI, aimed at San Michele, and Luigi Capello's VI, poised to take Gorizia.

Capello's veteran corps was given the major task of the whole offensive; its six divisions were ordered to clear Sabotino, Oslavia, and Podgora of all Austrian troops and to cross the Isonzo into Gorizia. All efforts for the last fourteen months had failed dismally, but this time Capello was confident of victory. His divisions would be well supported by heavy artillery with ample supplies of shells, and his battle plan had been very carefully assembled. For months, forward detachments had collected information about Erwin Zeidler's defenses. In addition, Capello's talented chief of staff, who actually devised much of the battle plan, believed that the VI Corps would reach Gorizia this time. Capello's number two was newly promoted Colonel Pietro Badoglio, a rising star in the Italian Army. The forty-four-year-old Badoglio had been a lieutenant colonel on the General Staff when Italy entered the war, but he had advanced rapidly in the past year. Although not from a military family, he attended the prestigious military academy at Turin, followed by exemplary service as an artillery officer. He commanded field artillery units in action in Ethiopia in 1895–1896, and again in Libya in 1911–1912; he was universally considered an efficient officer with a promising future. Badoglio served as a staff officer on the Isonzo during 1915, but went to the front in February 1916 as an infantry regimental commander. After just seven weeks in the trenches, he was promoted to chief of staff of the 4th Division, part of the VI Corps. There he caught Capello's eye. The senior general liked the energetic young Badoglio, and soon promoted him to full colonel and chief of staff of his corps. There he proceeded to plan the VI Corps attack on Gorizia.

Badoglio's scheme was simple. First, the VI Corps needed all the heavy artillery it could get; by the eve of the attack it controlled 261 field guns, 210 medium and heavy pieces, and forty mortar batteries, all generously supplied with shells. Italian batteries carefully selected their targets, including Zeidler's ammunition dumps, headquarters bunkers, communication centers, and numerous weapons dugouts along the 58th Division's front. The bombardment would cripple the Austrian defenses before the *fanti* even went over the top. The infantry attack to follow would be rapid and merciless—four whole divisions on a front of just five miles. Badoglio, confident of victory, assembled a maneuver group of eighteen cavalry squadrons and two bicycle battalions to advance rapidly into Gorizia once the Austrian defenses began to falter. The first objective was Mt. Sabotino, which dominated the region. The loss of Sabotino would endanger the 58th Division's hold on the river's west bank, and probably force a retreat to Gorizia. Badoglio therefore concentrated his heavy artillery and fresh infantry on the mountain. He assigned the capture of Sabotino to General Giuseppe Venturi's 45th Division, a war-raised formation new to the Isonzo. Badoglio divided the division into three assault groups. The first two were assembled in storm brigade, to be commanded by Badoglio himself, and the third was kept in reserve to reinforce the success of the initial waves. Capello's double-sized corps was ready to do battle by early August.

Cadorna likewise believed that the hour of victory was nigh. More confident than ever because of his halting of the Austrians on the Asiago plateau, he also felt that he now had enough heavy guns and sufficient shells to crack Boroević's defenses. He explained to the Duke of Aosta that the key to victory was "the bringing together of an imposing mass of artillery of all calibers on the narrowest front," and his armies now had the equipment to do the job. Cadorna was similarly confident of his troops' morale. Many of the divisions had enjoyed several months of relative inactivity, and for once were well rested. Still, there had been some worrying indications of flagging morale even during the victory on the Asiago plateau. One particularly hated divisional commander, General Carlo Giordano, a noted sadist, had been shot by his own troops. In another embarrassing incident, *fanti* of the Salerno Brigade refused to advance again after several failed and costly assaults; some even tried to surrender, so their brigadier called artillery fire onto his own troops, and had the survivors rounded up and executed. Despite these troublesome events, Cadorna was sure that the troops of the 3rd Army could be depended on to take Gorizia and San Michele.

Boroević's skilled intelligence staff had been detecting signs of an Italian offensive for weeks. Espionage revealed considerable Italian rail movements to the Isonzo, and the radio experts and code breakers had reported impressive amounts of wire traffic that indicated some kind of offensive. Italian secrecy extended only so far. Still, Boroević and his staff remained unconvinced by the collected evidence. It was obvious that the Italians were planning an attack on the Isonzo by mid-August, but the Austrians expected nothing more than a repeat of the minor, short-lived Fifth Battle. It seemed impossible that Cadorna could launch a major offensive so soon after waging a major, sustained counter-offensive on the Asiago plateau. The Austrians therefore chose to believe that the coming attack would be small and brief.

Perhaps Boroević and his staff officers simply did not want to believe that a major Italian offensive was imminent. The condition of the 5th Army was unenviable. The Tyrolean campaign and the Galician disaster had stripped the Isonzo front of many men, guns, and supplies. In early August the 5th Army boasted only eight divisions with just 106 infantry battalions and 584 guns and 333 mortars. Its paper strength was barely half that of the Italian forces arrayed against it; most regiments were undermanned, and there were few replacements on hand to bring them up to strength. Boroević was particularly short of heavy artillery; all but four batteries had been sent elsewhere. Even worse, ammunition was in short supply for guns of all calibers. The 5th Army was still an impressive force occupying excellent positions, but it had lost much of the equipment and several of the crack Alpine divisions that had secured its impressive victories throughout 1915. It certainly was in no condition to fight a sustained battle.

The Italian offensive began with a feint to further deceive the Austrians. At 10 A.M. on August 4, the artillery of Tettoni's VII Corps opened fire on the southern flank of the Carso, hammering the Austrian positions around Selz and Vermegliano. Four divisions attacked at 2 P.M., and within four hours they had captured the first line of Austrian trenches. The East Galician 60th Brigade, Poles and Ukrainians who had endured so much on Sabotino during the Fourth Battle, were forced to retreat to the second line of defenses, losing several hundred men. The Gorizia sector remained quiet during the day as Austrian attention shifted to the Carso's southern reaches, almost ten miles downstream from where the main Italian blow would fall.

When the Italian guns opened fire again on the south Carso the next morning, Boroević began to fear the worst. Slowly realizing that the VII Corps probes were not the main attack, but merely a feint, he cabled the High Command to send him heavy artillery and all available infantry reserves at once. The Croatian old soldier at last knew that the long-feared drive on Gorizia was set to begin. Franz Conrad von Hötzendorf was unresponsive; the army was far too hard-pressed in Galicia to give Boroević anything until it was clear that a major Italian offensive had arrived. By the evening of August 5, as the scorching summer sun started to set, 5th Army headquarters knew that the following dawn would deliver calamity. It was too late to do anything but wait for the attack to get under way.

The night of August 5–6 was unnaturally calm. Tens of thousands of *fanti* who would go over the top the next day gathered in forward trenches, making last-minute preparations, securing their gear, cleaning their weapons, writing letters home, and making sure their wills were in order. Sunrise came early, and the temperature began to climb well before the artillery commenced firing at 6:45 A.M. The barrage was deafening, with high-explosive shells raining on Austrian positions from Tolmein to the Adriatic. The bombardment was heaviest on the 58th Division's front, as thousands of heavy shells collided with dugouts, weapons pits, and trench sections. The Dalmatians had never experienced anything like this. While the earth shook continuously around them, they were blinded by dense clouds of smoke and dust thrown up by thousands of explosions. The barrage quickly cut the division's telephone lines, and the frontline infantry lost contact with division headquarters and artillery. The 58th's eighty-seven guns were unable to respond in strength anyway; many batteries were hit by Italian fire, and there was a severe shell shortage. Zeidler's nine battalions holding the line on Sabotino, Oslavia, and Podgora were cut off and isolated almost immediately. There was nothing to do but endure the shattering barrage delivered by Capello's 900 guns and mortars, and wait for the inevitable infantry assault. The Dalmatians' duty was clear, and known to even the lowliest private; they had received Boroević's orders before the wire was cut. The message and mandate were familiar: " not to give up a single foot also this time, and eventually to counterattack and win back any lost ground." For the battleworn 58th, it was to be a fight to the finish.

Mt. Sabotino was held by a reinforced battalion of the veteran 37th Rifle Regiment. At 2 P.M., after over seven hours of unprecedentedly heavy shelling, the dazed defenders watched as the 45th Division sent its first waves of infantry up Snake Mountain's north and west slopes. In the lead was Colonel Badoglio's reinforced brigade, including the 78th Regiment, a battalion each of the 58th and 115th Regiments, two companies of sappers armed with demolition charges, and a mountain battery with light guns to be pushed forward to give the attack direct fire support. Badoglio's five assault battalions had their way cleared for them by the enormous barrage of 220 guns, including 72 heavy and 28 superheavy pieces, which had laid waste to many of the Dalmatian-held positions. The attack was spearheaded by the 1st Battalion of the 78th Regiment, commanded by Major Abelardo Pecorini, who personally led his troops up Sabotino's rugged and barren slopes. Badoglio watched as Pecorini's 800 *fanti*, rifles and bayonets at the ready, ran up the steep mountainside, followed by four more reinforced battalions. The 37th Rifles returned fire where they could, but a sustained defense was impossible. Too many machine guns had been destroyed by the shelling, and there was neither artillery support nor hope of reinforcement. Still, the 78th Regiment suffered heavy casualties in its lead battalion as the doomed Dalmatians kept firing, and *grigioverdi* collapsed dead and wounded on the slopes where so many Italian soldiers had fallen before them. This time, however, there were plenty of fresh companies to keep pushing to the 2,010-foot-high summit.

Within less than an hour, Badoglio's forward platoons had reached Sabotino's peak. They found hundreds of dead and wounded Dalmatians lying in their trenches, killed and maimed by the bombardment. Some Dalmatians continued to resist fiercely, but the battle had been won. After nearly fifteen months of trying, Mt. Sabotino was in Italian hands. The triumphant *fanti* had a clear and commanding view of the Isonzo directly below, and of Gorizia only a mile to the south. Badoglio did not just revel in his victory and wait for the inevitable Austrian counterattack. Instead, he reinforced the summit with his remaining troops, and they tried to clean up any lingering Austrian opposition. More important, in accordance with the detailed battle plan, General Venturi sent his second and third echelons, seven more reinforced battalions, up Sabotino, but they did not stop at the summit. Rather, they kept going, headed for the Isonzo; they would give Zeidler no time to regroup.

Major General Francesco Gagliani's Tuscany Brigade, the 45th's second echelon, reached the summit and ran down Sabotino's southeast slope, headed for the Isonzo below. By the afternoon Gagliani's four battalions had occupied the village of San Mauro and reached the river's banks, the first Italian troops to touch the Isonzo's cool, blue-green waters. They headed for the railway bridge at Salcano, Gorizia's northernmost suburb. A rapid counterstroke by the 58th Division—Zeidler and his staff had watched in horror as the Tuscany Brigade moved unopposed down the mountainside to the Isonzo—seized the bridge first and prevented a river crossing; for the moment. Venturi's division would remain on the west bank. Nevertheless, the 45th Division had conquered Sabotino and reached the Isonzo. Badoglio's attack had unlocked the mountain's defenses at a cost of only 1,186 casualties. Zeidler lost his most important position, exposing Gorizia to a direct assault; without Sabotino, the city could not be held for long, and both Zeidler and Boroević soon knew it. The Italians were busy all day rounding up Austrian prisoners on Sabotino. Hundreds of Dalmatians were trapped in their *kavernen*, unable to escape. Eventually most of the defeated Croats and Serbs were persuaded to give themselves up, but some defiant riflemen were determined to fight to the bitter end. One of the largest pockets of the 37th Rifles left fighting, the remnants of a company cut off in a large *kaverne*, refused to surrender. Badoglio's sappers offered the Dalmatians one more chance to give themselves up, but when no response was forthcoming, they poured gasoline into the cave's entrance and air shafts, then tossed a torch, incinerating the last of Sabotino's defenders. Some 1,200 of their comrades had chosen surrender. By any standards, the capture of Sabotino by Badoglio's assault troops was the greatest Italian triumph of the war yet. Gabriele D'Annunzio, the famed romantic poet and wartime adventurer, composed a few lines to celebrate the triumph:

> *Fu come l'ala che non lascia impronte*
> *il primo grido avea già preso il monte.*

> (A shouted order, fast as wings that do not touch.
> The ground, the mountain, had been taken.)

Venturi's victorious 45th Division proudly took D'Annunzio's words as its motto.

While Badoglio's storm brigade charged up Sabotino, the rest of Capello's VI Corps attacked Austrian positions at Oslavia and Podgora. The 24th Division made little progress at Oslavia. Hill 188 and the ruined village were held by two battalions of Austrian militia, whose shell-shocked soldiers managed to repulse eight Italian battalions all day long. Capello's men did better at Podgora. The 12th Division overran most of the Austrian trenches on Podgora hill, leaving only isolated pockets of resistance. The neighboring 11th Division, attacking between Oslavia and Podgora, succeeded in penetrating the Austrian defenses and reaching the Isonzo's banks near Gorizia. As at Salcano, rapid action by 58th Division reserves blocked an Italian crossing, but the 11th

Division had reached the river in strength. By the evening of August 6, Capello's VI Corps had captured Sabotino and most of Podgora, leaving only cut-off pockets of Austrian resistance. In a matter of hours Zeidler's division had lost the battle for the heights on the Isonzo's west bank, putting Gorizia in mortal danger.

That evening, Zeidler and his staff were only too aware of their precarious predicament. If the division could not retake its lost positions—especially Sabotino—before dawn, a retreat to the Isonzo's east bank would be necessary within twenty-four hours. As a precaution, Zeidler ordered two companies of sappers to prepare to blow up the Isonzo bridges. The 58th Division had only seven weak battalions to launch a counterattack, and there would be scant artillery support available; the XVI Corps and 5th Army headquarters informed Zeidler that they had no reserves to give him. Regardless, Boroević's unbending orders demanded a counterstroke, no matter how hopeless the odds, nor how remote the chances of success. The troops trapped on Podgora had to be saved, too. For a moment when the wind blew the thick clouds of smoke away from the hill, staff officers at 58th Division headquarters a mile away in Gorizia clearly saw calls by signal lamps coming from the surrounded riflemen on Podgora, begging for help. Zeidler dispatched Austrian and Hungarian militia units to relieve the surrounded Dalmatians, and four more battalions to recapture Sabotino. The counterattacks were doomed from the start. Badly outnumbered by the Italians holding the hills, the attackers also had no artillery to clear the way for them. Nevertheless, the Austrians fought bravely through the night, trying desperately to push Capello's troops back. The drive on Podgora made surprisingly good initial progress, but soon stalled from a lack of reinforcements. The ill-fated bayonet charge up Sabotino's southeast slope overran several Italian positions, but it failed to reach the summit. It was not for lack of effort. The 600-strong 2nd Battalion of the 22nd Regiment, the hard-fighting Dalmatian veterans of so many battles on the Isonzo, recaptured the village of San Mauro and continued to push up the mountainside. The "Lions of Podgora" did their duty to the last, charging Italian machine guns; not a single soldier of the 22nd returned to the Austrian lines. Their futile sacrifice could not turn the tide, and at dawn Sabotino was still firmly in Italian hands.

The Austrians suffered an equally bitter defeat on the Carso's northern flank. At 7 A.M. on August 6, more than a hundred Italian batteries opened fire all along the Doberdò plateau; at noon, the fire concentrated on San Michele. At 4 P.M., after the shattering nine-hour barrage had ceased, Cigliana's XI Corps started its well planned assault on Mt. San Michele. The sector was garrisoned by the five-battalion-strong 81st *Honvéd* Brigade; its Magyar veterans of the 1st and 17th Regiments occupied excellent positions and knew the terrain intimately. Yet, as at Sabotino, it was not enough to hold the mountain. More than 500 Italian guns blasted the brigade's entrenchments, burying dozens of machine gun and mortar pits, killing and maiming hundreds of defenders, and covering the mountain in thick clouds of dust and smoke. The double-strength 22nd Division then charged the Austrian lines, only a hundred paces to the east. The four Italian brigades, outnumbering the confused Hungarian defenders nearly five-to-one, quickly overran their trenches. After a brief but bloody melée, the bayonet-wielding *fanti* reached the summit. By 6 P.M., the peak of Mt. San Michele was held by troops of the Catanzaro, Brescia, and Ferrara Brigades. They had succeeded where twenty-six brigades before them had failed. After the loss of 112,000 Italian soldiers on its slopes, Mt. San Michele belonged to the 3rd Army.

The news of the capture of San Michele spread electrically through the ranks of the Duke of Aosta's army, soon reaching army headquarters, and then Cadorna's staff in Udine. Spontaneous celebrations erupted all along the Carso as joyous *fanti* reveled in their long-awaited victory. The fall of San Michele even eclipsed the capture of Sabotino earlier in the day. At last Italy had a tangible triumph, and Gorizia was now surrounded on the north and south by Italian-held peaks. The capture of Mt. San Michele, coupled with the seizing of Mt. Sabotino, surely meant that Gorizia itself would soon follow.

Archduke Joseph, pondering the day's terrible events at VII Corps headquarters, was well aware of this. Like Zeidler, he knew that he must counterattack with the meager resources at his disposal; Boroević, acting on the orders of the High Command, would not permit a withdrawal. Joseph collected just six battalions from the 17th and 20th Divisions, all that could be spared from other parts of the line, and threw them against the Italian-held trenches on San Michele. The battle for the summit raged through the evening as the six Hungarian battalions made repeated charges up the mountain's east slope. The Romanians of the 4th *Honvéd* and 43rd Regiments, alongside the Magyars of the 46th, fought bravely, capturing several hundred *fanti* and some trench lines, but the cause was hopeless. The understrength 5th Army had no troops to spare, and a half-dozen weary Hungarian battalions could not possibly wrest San Michele from the 22nd Division, four times its size. For want of fresh Austrian soldiers, Mt. San Michele would remain Italian.

Zeidler's crisis had reached a decisive point by the morning of August 7: either the 58th Division would achieve the impossible and recapture Sabotino and Podgora in the next twelve hours, or it would retreat across the Isonzo to Gorizia. Boroević was adamant that the exhausted division attempt to retake its lost positions. Because Zeidler had not even a single fresh company left, the 5th Army command sent him all its scant supply of troops and replacements. The 22nd Rifle Regiment, Romanians and Ukrainians from Bukovina, the empire's easternmost province, arrived in Gorizia in the early afternoon, and Zeidler immediately sent its three battalions up Sabotino. Without artillery support—Zeidler's artillery was out of ammunition—the attack was doomed, and the brave battalions suffered severe casualties on the rocky and barren southeast slope, gaining no ground. Likewise, an attempt by the remnants of the Dalmatian 23rd Rifles to seize Podgora collapsed bloodily without producing any results. Capello continued his drive on Gorizia, adding a fresh division to his front line. By the evening, the five divisions of the VI Corps had taken Oslavia and almost all of Podgora; only a few scattered bands of isolated Dalmatians remained on the latter hill. All along the 58th Division's front, Italian infantry had reached the Isonzo.

By the evening, there was no choice but to withdraw all Austrian forces to the Isonzo's east bank. Zeidler's infantry had been all but annihilated, his artillery was out of ammunition, and communication with several units had been lost. No one knew where veteran battalions were, or if they still existed. Yet the tired major general was determined that his retreat would be an orderly one; under no circumstances could the Italians be permitted to take advantage of the withdrawal to Gorizia. Boroević made it clear to Zeidler in a late afternoon communiqué that, regardless of events, "In the worst case, the Isonzo line is to be absolutely held." The actual decision to retreat, and when, was left to Zeidler. He knew that if he did not move his division to the east bank before dawn, there would be nothing left to save. In the late evening, he ordered his engineers to prepare the explosive charges on the Isonzo bridges, and to make sure the second defensive line—behind the city of Gorizia—was ready. Zeidler did not issue the order to withdraw until 2 A.M. on August 8, when he was absolutely sure that there was no other option. The retreat, covered by darkness, was surprisingly orderly. Small parties of machine gunners in the rear guard made sure that the Italians were not aware of what was going on. Before dawn, the 58th Division had completed its retreat to the city of Gorizia, leaving only a small detachment of the 37th Rifles on the river's west bank near Salcano, to block Italian probes across the rail bridge. All the other Isonzo bridges were blown up by engineers of the 9th Sapper Battalion. After more than fourteen months, the 58th Division had relinquished the Isonzo's west bank to the Italians. The Dalmatians had paid a heavy price. Of the 18,000 soldiers Zeidler had on the morning of August 6, only 5,000 reached Gorizia less than forty-eight hours later. Those few tired Croats and Serbs who had survived now had to defend the City of Violets against the might of Capello's triumphant VI Corps.

The Austrian situation appeared just as grim on the Carso. At dawn on August 7, the VII Corps tried again to evict the 22nd Division from San Michele's summit, but the attempt predictably failed. Without artillery support—VII Corps' batteries, like Zeidler's, were out of ammunition—the infantry hardly had a chance. Later in the morning, two fresh Italian regiments pushed the Hungarians even farther from the summit. The remnants of the 4th *Honvéd* and 43rd Regiments evacuated the mountain's east slope and retreated to a temporary defensive line several hundred feet to the east. While the Hungarians were withdrawing, the XI Corps sent the 22nd Division two reserve brigades to push even harder the next morning. Without reinforcements, Archduke Joseph knew that a general retreat to the second defensive line, two miles to the east, would soon be necessary.

On the evening of August 7, the Duke of Aosta savored his victory. His divisions had captured Sabotino and San Michele, and were well on their way to taking Gorizia. He knew the Austrians were tired, and out of fresh men and munitions: Boroević's deadly counterattacks, unsupported by artillery, lacked their usual potency. All that remained to be done was to advance across the Isonzo into Gorizia. For once, he had good news to report to Cadorna. In the late evening, the duke left his headquarters and visited Capello. He wanted to see his troops' accomplishment and the impending fall of Gorizia with his own eyes. The 3rd Army's commander planned to conduct the next morning's river crossing, and he gave the order to renew the VI Corps' offensive at about the same time Zeidler ordered his units to withdraw across the Isonzo.

Boroević wanted to hold on to Gorizia, but for political, not military, reasons. The fall of the City of Violets would be a serious psychological blow for Austria, and a major gain for the Italians—the first Habsburg city to fly the Italian tricolor. Yet, in military terms, defending the city on the banks of the Isonzo made no sense. The second defensive line, the only place where the 58th Division had any hope of making a successful stand, was a mile east of downtown, and two miles from the river's edge. Forcing Zeidler's shattered division to hold the river's east bank was a prescription for disaster: With just 5,000 men, how could the 58th defend a front of eight miles against the assaults of six divisions? Nevertheless, Boroević insisted that the Dalmatians at least attempt to keep the Italians at bay at the Isonzo's edge. The mission fell apart almost immediately. In the late morning of August 8, a battalion of Capello's 12th Division simply waded across the Isonzo[2] and walked up the east bank unopposed. Within a few minutes the *fanti* reached the outskirts of the city. Several more companies of Italian infantry followed, and by noon the 12th Division had established a bridgehead on the east bank. There was nothing Zeidler could do; he had no reserves to push the Italians back, and his artillery was completely out of munitions. By nightfall the 58th's predicament was hopeless. Zeidler informed Boroević that there was now no choice but to withdraw the tattered remains of his division to the second defensive line. At 11 P.M., he ordered the 37th Rifles to abandon their foothold at the base of Sabotino and retreat to the Isonzo's east bank. The Dalmatians withdrew silently in the darkness, then blew up the stone rail bridge connecting Sabotino and Salcano. They then took their place in the second defensive line on Mt. San Gabriele. By dawn on August 9, there were no Austrian soldiers left in Gorizia.

The same occurred on the Carso. The Hungarian troops on the northern half of the Carso continued to fight impressively. The XI Corps attacked the Hungarians all day long around San Michele and San Martino, without much success; the remnants of the 17th *Honvéd* Regiment repulsed no less than nine assaults by the 21st Division at San Martino. Even so, the Austrian situation was hopeless. By the late afternoon of August 8, it was evident to Archduke Joseph that the VII Corps could not withstand further Italian offensives. The 3rd Army's massive reserves of men and munitions meant that the Duke of Aosta could keep attacking for several more days, far longer than the VII Corps could hope to hold out. Without reserves, a withdrawal to the second defensive line was urgently needed. Far better to evacuate the survivors of the 17th and 20th Divisions, the archduke reasoned, than to lose everything in a doomed last-ditch defense. Besides, with the fall of San Michele there was little reason to hold on to the westernmost edge of the plateau. By the evening, Boroević agreed. The 5th Army's commander reluctantly conceded that a withdrawal to the second defensive position was unquestionably necessary within twenty-four hours. Boroević ordered that the Carso's defenders hold out for one more day, to give Zeidler time to establish his own defenses.

At this point, with the 58th Division withdrawing to the second defensive line and the Carso's defenders preparing to do the same, Cadorna should have sent all his forces relentlessly forward. Rapid and determined Italian full-scale attacks at Gorizia and on the Carso would have cracked the feeble Austrian defenses, with strategic results. Hitting the 58th Division and VII Corps before they had time to consolidate their hold on the second defensive line might have been a war-winner for Cadorna. Yet, regrettably for Italy, that was not what Cadorna did. Despite the chief of staff's recklessness in his expenditure of men, Cadorna was, at root, a deeply cautious leader. Confronted with the quick victories of his armies before Gorizia and at San Michele, he seemed not to know what to do. So long accustomed to bruising and indecisive battles of attrition, when he was confronted with a dramatic success and the chance to dash forward, Cadorna failed to seize the opportunity. His vision did not extend beyond the Isonzo's east bank. An immediate direct assault past Gorizia would have been a virtual walkover—a hundred Italian battalions were opposed by only thirteen weak Austrian battalions. Yet, at precisely the moment that Capello could have burst through the weak Austrian lines at Gorizia, Cadorna noted that he had "great doubts about the success of the attack." Capello expected to dash through the city with his mobile group and proceed to the fields beyond, but Cadorna reigned him in. The chief of staff put Capello in charge of the Gorizia Group, with the VI and VIII Corps, then ordered the II Corps to secure Capello's northern flank before the general advance could proceed. Once Cadorna did decide to send Capello's forces forward in strength, the offensive was delayed by numerous technical problems: the need to build pontoon bridges across the Isonzo, traffic tie-ups on the roads, and a general confusion about supplies. The result of all this was the loss of a whole day, twenty-four hours that Zeidler's division used to good effect to prepare itself for the defense of the second line of entrenchments. It was an inexcusable delay that would cost Italy and her army dearly.

The August 9 flanking attacks on the central Isonzo proved much less successful than the earlier offensives before Gorizia and on the Carso. At 7:30 A.M., the II Corps artillery began shelling Austrian positions around Hill 383 and Zagora. The barrage continued through the morning and into the early afternoon, reaching an unprecedented intensity by 1 P.M.. It was the strongest bombardment yet at the Plava bridgehead. After a full twelve hours of heavy shelling, the infantry regiments of the 3rd Division assaulted their old nemeses, 383 and Zagora. The *fanti* launched four determined attacks inside two hours, but all were brutally repulsed. The tough Dalmatian battalion of the 22nd Regiment on Hill 383 and the Magyar battalion of the 52nd Regiment at Zagora kept the 3rd Division at bay, throwing back each assault with heavy losses. By nightfall, the slopes of "Bloody 383" were again strewn with mangled Italian corpses, and the II Corps was no closer to seizing the Plava bridgehead than it had been for the past fourteen months. Plava continued to live up to its evil reputation, and Cadorna's left flank remained vulnerable.

The Duke of Aosta's troops on the Carso were disappointingly inactive on August 9. They turned back an early morning counterattack by the 4th *Honvéd* Regiment, a last, desperate attempt by the VII Corps to regain Mt. San Michele. The Romanian infantry managed to recapture several positions on the mountain's east face, but the effort clearly was hopeless, and was abandoned by midmorning. Instead of taking advantage of this setback, however, the 3rd Army was content to shell the Austrian lines all day. The Italian infantry was astonishingly inactive; the duke, like Cadorna, was damagingly cautious when he should have been audacious. The daylong barrage inflicted casualties on the Austrians, but had no impact on the overall campaign. The three Austrian divisions remaining on the Carso were preparing to retreat to the second defensive position, three miles back, well behind San Michele and the town of Doberdò. When the sun went down, the the VII Corps began its retreat, abandoning all the positions it had held so bravely for more than a year—San Martino, Hill 197, Mt. Sei Busi, Hill 121. Each division left behind parties of machine gunners and snipers to keep the Italians' heads down while the bulk of the troops withdrew silently. By dawn, VII Corps had reestablished its positions on the second defensive line. The Italians, deceived by the work of the rear guard, never noticed the Austrian retreat.

Cadorna, by now dimly realizing what had happened, ordered Capello "to get his troops on their feet" and press on past Gorizia before the Austrians were permanently entrenched. August 10 began with several Italian attacks, starting with Capello's troops. The Gorizia Group, seven divisions strong, advanced unopposed through the city to the eastern suburbs, where they encountered the new Austrian defenses. There the Italian infantry soon stalled. Zeidler's second line of entrenchments, carefully built over months by construction units, were as formidable as anything on the Isonzo's west bank had been, and Capello's regiments made no progress. They were now tired and had received few supplies in the last forty-eight hours, and thus were in no condition to attempt an all-out offensive against strong Austrian positions. The II Corps did no better at Plava. Renewed efforts to clear Hill 383 and Zagora of their tenacious defenders met with no success, despite another heavy artillery barrage. The fighting continued long into the night, but the Austrian hold on Plava was never seriously threatened.

Nevertheless, August 10 was the day the Italians officially took control of Gorizia. Once the city center was secure, the Duke of Aosta rode his favorite mount triumphantly across the Isonzo into Gorizia, formally entering the city at the head of the 3rd Army. He oversaw the official raising of the tricolor over this newest Italian city, and named Major Giovanni Sestili as Gorizia's commissioner, responsible for the well-being of the city's residents. Sestili's first task was feeding the hungry civilians, who had endured several days of heavy shelling, cut off from food and other vital supplies. Italian field kitchens cooked up a serving of pasta for each of the 3,000 residents who were still in Gorizia when the Duke of Aosta arrived. Celebrations followed, but most of Capello's soldiers were too busy to join in. They were already down to the deadly serious business of cracking the new Austrian defenses.

The next day Capello's Gorizia Group (now returned to the jurisdiction of Piacentini's 2nd Army) tried even harder to push the 58th Division out of its new positions. August 11 began with a predawn attack by the 45th Division up St. Katarina, a 1,000-foot peak behind Salcano. The church at the summit, overlooking Gorizia, was surrounded by stone walls dating to the Iron Age and the Roman period. St. Katarina's current defenders, troops of the 37th Rifles, had added considerably more modern entrenchments, including sandbags, barbed wire, and steel shields. After a brief supporting barrage, the Italian infantry charged up the west and south slopes, but were repulsed by accurate machine gun and rifle fire. Further attacks made no more headway, losing many prisoners to the hill's Dalmatian defenders. This time, Venturi's division was stopped in its tracks by the 37th Rifles, eager to avenge their recent defeat. Unlike the fiasco on Sabotino five days before, the Dalmatians now held their ground against the 45th.

There was little Italian activity on the Carso on August 11. The Duke of Aosta's artillery shelled the new Austrian defenses sporadically, but his infantry stayed out of the fight. The 3rd Army needed time to move its troops and supply columns forward more than three miles, nearer to the Austrian second defensive position. The victorious *fanti* marched through the towns and villages on the Carso that had eluded capture for more than a year, especially San

Martino and Doberdò, only to find them abandoned and destroyed by months of Italian shelling. By the time the 3rd Army was ready to attack again on the Carso, twenty-four hours later, it would find the VII Corps thoroughly reentrenched in its new defenses.

On the evening of August 11, Boroević contemplated his army's situation. The Austrian Army had been defeated, to be sure; the loss of Gorizia and the western Carso was a bitter setback. That said, the Italian advance had been inevitable, and the 5th Army had succeeded in retreating to the second defensive line, where it was now ready to fight another sustained battle against the 2nd and 3rd Armies. Boroević's casualties had been very heavy—36,000 dead, wounded, and captured in just five days, more than a third of his rifle strength; the 58th Division's losses were the worst, but the 17th and 20th Divisions had each lost 6,000 soldiers. The tide had begun to turn, however. By August 11, the 5th Army had received a division's worth of fresh troops from the Tyrol, and three more divisions were on their way; the supply of munitions and replacements had increased, too, so that the Isonzo army could keep fighting. Late in the evening, Boroević cabled to the High Command that the worst had passed. The crisis was over, the front had been restored, and the danger to Trieste had evaporated. Cadorna's task now was to break through a line of Austrian defenses as strong as those which had held out for more than a year before Gorizia and on the western Carso. The prospect of an easy Italian strategic victory had disappeared.

This painful reality became evident on August 12. The day began with more attacks by the Gorizia Group. Capello was eager to achieve the breakthrough that had eluded him the previous day. He sent his seven divisions forward toward Zeidler's entrenchments; the main assault was borne by the newly arrived XXVI Corps, which was committed to battle in the center of the sector. Its objective was the capture of Hills 171 and 174, just east of Gorizia. The two hills, occupied by tired Austrian militia battalions of the 121st Brigade, were struck at 3:45 A.M. by the 43rd and 48th Divisions. Bitter fighting lasted for more than twelve hours. The Italians captured Hill 174, but it was retaken in a lightning counterstroke by Dalmatian riflemen. At nightfall both hills were still controlled by the 58th Division. Hill 174 was surrounded by no fewer than 500 dead *grigioverdi;* Austrian losses were not much less, but Zeidler's troops had prevailed. Their defenses remained intact. The same had happened on the division's northern flank. There, the Dalmatians succeeded in maintaining their hold on St. Katarina and the neighboring peak, Mt. San Gabriele. The latter, a 2,140-foot-high peak two-thirds of a mile northeast of St. Katarina, was the linchpin of Zeidler's northern sector. The steep, forested mountain, blanketed with Austrian entrenchments, dominated Gorizia from the northeast. To advance past the city, Capello's divisions would have to capture it just as they did Sabotino. They met with no success on August 12. The 45th Division failed to make any notable gains on either St. Katarina or San Gabriele, which were defended tenaciously by the 8th Mountain Brigade, fresh troops just arrived from the Tyrol.

The 3rd Army finally got on its feet on August 12, though its infantry was hardly more successful. The new Austrian defenses on the northern Carso were dominated by Hill 212, Nad logem, a "beak" protruding west, about two miles directly behind San Michele. Cigliana's XI Corps concentrated its efforts there, beginning with an impressive bombardment. Its 23rd Division then assaulted the hill in strength at noon. The defenders were Ukrainians and Romanians from Bukovina, part of the 59th Infantry Brigade, taken out of reserve to hold the line. The Italian infantry soon reached the Austrian trenches, and hand-to-hand fighting followed. The savage battle raged well into the afternoon, and losses mounted on both sides. By the evening, the Italians held Nad logem, but they were far too weak to exploit their gain. The hill's defenders had been pushed back a few hundred paces, but they had inflicted such heavy casualties on the 23rd Division that it could not advance farther. The depleted 59th Brigade then had enough time to establish a new line of defense behind Hill 212.

The 3rd Army resumed its offensive the next morning. The 23rd Division, topped off with fresh replacements, was sent into battle again to push the the XI Corps past Nad logem. It ran into the 17th Division, rushed into the line during the night on the orders of Archduke Joseph. The Hungarians prevented an Italian breakthrough, both at Nad logem and at the village of Lokvica, a mile and a half farther south. The veteran battalions of Magyars, Romanians, and Serbs battled fiercely with the *fanti* of the XI Corps among the limestone rocks. The fighting was intense and costly, the struggle for each *dolina* or dugout becoming a small but bitter siege. The arduous skirmishing cost the XI Corps dearly and cut short an Italian breakout on the northern Carso. Capello's troops also gained no new ground on August 13. His infantry was too exhausted to attack anywhere on the 58th Division's front. The Gorizia Group relied instead on its artillery, which pounded Zeidler's entrenchments while the infantry received thousands of replacements, rested, and prepared for the next major attack, scheduled for the following morning.

Cadorna was now exasperated by his armies' lethargy. He urged Piacentini and the Duke of Aosta to get their troops moving, ordering a major combined offensive for August 14. It was to be a massive blow by the 2nd and 3rd Armies, directed at the Austrian defensive line from Plava to the central Carso, a final large-scale effort before Cadorna's regiments collapsed from exhaustion. The offensive began before dawn, with a thunderous artillery barrage aimed at the heights north of Gorizia. The VI Corps was ordered to seize St. Katarina, then move on to its higher neighbor, San Gabriele. The bombardment increased in pace and intensity after sunrise, pounding the Austrian positions on St. Katarina mercilessly. At 6 P.M., after more than a dozen hours of shelling by heavy artillery and mortars, the infantry of the 45th and 24th Divisions fixed bayonets and advanced up the now bare hillsides. Troopers of the 8th Mountain Brigade, a thousand feet above, poured ceaseless machine gun and rifle fire into the charging ranks of Italians, felling hundreds on the naked west and south slopes. The first attack faltered, but was soon followed by a second wave of *fanti*, which managed to overrun some of the lower Austrian trenches. A battalion each of Magyars and Ukrainians then charged down the mountainside to push the Italians back, which they succeeded in doing by nightfall. The VI Corps was back where it had started before dawn.

The 48th Division fought hard to evict the Austrians from Hill 171, just east of Gorizia. All morning the guns of the XXVI Corps blasted the hill, but the infantry attack that followed at 1 P.M. was ultimately unsuccessful. The Italians and Austrians vied bravely for 171 through the afternoon, and the 48th eventually seized some of the defenders' positions, but the inevitable Austrian counterattack forced the *fanti* back to their own lines with heavy casualties. The same happened at Plava, where the II Corps tried again to seize the bridgehead and advance down the river road toward Gorizia. The artillery of the Plava Corps shelled the Austrian militia battalions on 383 and at Zagora through the morning, but the 3rd Division's infantry attack at noon got nowhere. Austrian mountain batteries targeted the advancing companies, blasting large gaps in their ranks, and the advance soon collapsed in bloody disorder. The Italian artillery answered with more shelling, which was predictably followed at 3:30 P.M. by another infantry charge up Hill 383. The *fanti* captured a few Austrian gun pits, but held them only briefly before the Austrians pushed them back down the hillside. On August 14, the 2nd Army failed to take and hold a single piece of the new Austrian defensive line.

The 3rd Army accomplished as little on the Carso. The Duke of Aosta's troops attacked VII Corps entrenchments at several points, but made their strongest effort around the village of Lokvica. There, units of the XI and XIII Corps attempted to break through the defenses of the 17th Division on the heels of a supporting barrage. The midday attack failed to gain any ground. Even mass infantry charges supported by Italian armored cars were repulsed by the Hungarians. *Honvéd* troops at the village of Opacchiasella, where Franz Joseph maintained a hunting box before the war, destroyed the armored cars with hand grenades and forced the *fanti* back to their own lines with concentrated machine gun and rifle fire. The 5th Army enjoyed complete success on August 14. Its weary infantry lost none of its new defensive lines to determined Italian attacks. The soldiers' confidence had been restored after the defeats at Gorizia and San Michele; they again believed in their superiority over the Italians. In addition, another division's worth of reinforcements had arrived on the Isonzo in the past two days, a significant and well timed addition to the 5th Army's order of battle. Boroević's troops had good reason to feel self-assured.

Cadorna had enough men and munitions left for one last gamble. He ordered Capello to make another attempt to seize the heights north of Gorizia, and he ordered the Duke of Aosta to try again to break through on the central Carso. The noon attack on August 15 by the Gorizia Group, four divisions on a front of five miles, started promisingly but quickly bogged down in front of the 58th Division's machine gun nests. The Schwarzlose machine gun proved it was still the master of the Isonzo battlefield. The Italian infantry captured a few positions on St. Katarina, but Austrian artillery officers on Mt. San Gabriele directed lethal howitzer and mortar fire onto the swollen ranks of Capello's riflemen. The forward battalions of the VI Corps sustained frightful casualties on the slopes of St. Katarina as the Austrian gunners poured shrapnel and high explosives in their midst. Eventually the *fanti* broke and ran, and the Austrian infantry moved in and recaptured their briefly lost entrenchments. They discovered several hundred dead and dying Italians in and around their trenches and took a hundred prisoners, including the commander of the lead Italian regiment. The 3rd Army's effort on August 15 likewise stalled in the face of dogged Austrian resistance. A mass charge around Lokvica and Opacchiasella by five Italian divisions was cut short by VII Corps artillery and machine guns. The six-hour battle gained nothing for the Duke of Aosta save several shattered regiments; it won not a single Austrian position.

By now Cadorna's divisions were thoroughly exhausted, incapable of further mass assaults against Austria's new defensive line. August 16, the last day of the Sixth Battle, was therefore an anticlimax. North of the Vipacco River, Capello's Gorizia Group was so weary that its infantry did not even leave its trenches. Instead, Capello's artillery shelled St. Katarina through the day, without effect, and soon even the Italian gunnery died down on the Gorizia front. On the Carso, the 3rd Army attempted one last attack against the VII Corps in the Lokvica sector. At 9:30 A.M., the Duke of Aosta's guns began a powerful barrage against Austrian positions along the entire Carso front. Ninety minutes later, waves of *fanti* attacked Hungarian-held entrenchments on the northern flank of the Carso. Relying on their machine guns, the tired troopers of the 17th and 20th Divisions beat back the Italian attack with heavy losses. At 4 P.M., the 3rd Army launched a final mass assault against the VII Corps. Archduke Joseph's gunners were ready, and as densely packed columns of Italian infantry climbed out of their positions, headed for the nearby Austrian lines, hundreds of howitzer and mortar shells crashed among the exposed *fanti*. Entire companies of Italian infantrymen fell dead and wounded on the rocky plateau as VII Corps artillery was joined by the guns of neighboring Austrian divisions. The lethal barrage destroyed the 3rd Army's final large-scale effort in the Sixth Battle. At 9:30 P.M., the Duke of Aosta's infantry tried one last attack, a small probe against the 20th *Honvéd* Division near Lokvica. The Italians were repulsed in a bloody fight with Romanian troops of the 4th *Honvéd* Regiment, and the Sixth Battle of the Isonzo was finally over.

The Sixth Battle was hailed throughout Italy as the first authentic Italian victory of the war. After more than a year of bloody stalemate on the Isonzo, Cadorna's armies at last had crossed the river and occupied Gorizia. The 2nd and 3rd Armies had both triumphed, taking Sabotino and San Michele in lightning attacks in the first hours of the battle. The government in Rome was so elated by the victory that on August 28, a day after Romania entered the war on the Allied side, Italy declared war on Germany. The capture of Gorizia gave Italy and its army the confidence they had sorely lacked and needed so badly.

Of course, the victory had been bought at a high price. Cadorna's armies lost at least 100,000 soldiers in the brief Sixth Battle of the Isonzo. Italy could still afford such frightful losses, but the capture of Gorizia was anything but a bloodless triumph. Roughly 30,000 soldiers died to win the Italian victory—almost exactly the prewar population of Gorizia. Austrian casualties were heavy, too, amounting to no less than 50,000 dead, wounded, and missing, half of Boroević's frontline strength. They included some 8,000 prisoners, many from Zeidler's 58th Division, the largest number of Austrian captives yet taken on the Isonzo. The battle had undeniably been a major defeat for Austria.

That said, Boroević's setback was more a political than a military reverse. The loss of Gorizia was without question a considerable blow to Austrian pride and prestige, but the 5th Army had managed to reentrench itself two or three miles farther to the east. The new positions had withstood every Italian attack. Attrition would therefore continue on the Isonzo. The much feared all-out Italian drive for victory never materialized. After the conquest of Gorizia, Cadorna proved fatally cautious. By refusing to exploit his victory, particularly by diverting fresh troops to the Plava bridgehead on August 9–10, Cadorna had squandered an epic opportunity to achieve a complete breakthrough on the Isonzo—indeed, to win the war. The caution exercised by the *Comando Supremo* immediately after the fall of Gorizia condemned the Italian Army to several more costly battles of attrition on the Isonzo front. Gorizia belonged to Italy, but the heights beyond it, as well as most of the Carso, remained in Austrian hands. Worst of all, Boroević's tired army was again deeply entrenched in front of the Italians all along the Isonzo. Evicting the Austrians from their newly established defenses was Cadorna's next task, and it promised to be just as costly and time-consuming as conquering San Michele and Gorizia had been.

NINE

THE TRIUMPH OF ATTRITION

Knowing that the end of the Sixth Battle represented only a brief pause, rather than a sustained break in the fighting, and that Cadorna would soon try to crack his new defensive line, Svetozar Boroević prepared his tired army to do battle again. He knew it was a race against time, a contest between the Austrian and Italian forces to rest, regroup, and reequip for the next round of Isonzo fighting. The most urgent task for Boroević was strengthening the second defensive position. By early September, the 5th Army had 40,000 construction troops, half of them unarmed Russian prisoners of war, working day and night in the Isonzo valley. They built stone reinforcements, dug deeper trenches, laid foot-high walls of sandbags, placed steel shields and barbed wire in front of entrenchments, and did all the arduous tasks that were required to make the army's positions ready for Cadorna's next attack. They worked especially hard on the Carso, where the next Italian blow was expected to fall. The construction units suffered regular losses to random Italian artillery fire, but they labored doggedly until the second defensive line was ready in the second week of September.

The other indispensable task for the 5th Army was absorbing replacements and reinforcements. The loss of Gorizia convinced the High Command of the gravity of the Italian threat, and Boroević therefore received more new units and replacement battalions than ever before. By mid-September, the Austrian forces on the Isonzo reached an unprecedented strength of almost fourteen divisions with 165 infantry battalions. Boroević also accepted generous artillery reinforcements from the High Command, a dozen battalions' worth—half of them medium and heavy pieces—by mid-September. The battle-worn divisions broken by the Sixth Battle were slowly rebuilt. A month after its destruction, Zeidler's 58th was again at full strength, but its character had changed; only one-third of the division's eighteen infantry battalions were Dalmatian, the rest being new units drawn from all over the empire. The 17th Division was reconstructed to look much like its former self, but its sister division, the 20th *Honvéd*, had suffered so badly that even a month after the Sixth Battle's end it was at half-strength and considered unfit for frontline duty. Nevertheless, Archduke Joseph's VII Corps still held the line on the north and central Carso; the plateau's southern third was garrisoned by Lieutenant General Alfred Schenk's mostly Czech battle group, one and a half divisions strong. In all, Boroević had seven brigades—32,000 infantrymen—on the Carso to beat back the coming Italian offensive.

The Austrians had correctly surmised Cadorna's very predictable intentions. The inflexible count continued to believe that the Carso was the only route to Trieste, and that the only way to secure its capture was by direct assault. After the fall of Gorizia and the 3rd Army's capture of San Michele, the navy again approached Cadorna about a possible amphibious landing on the Istrian peninsula. The landing of a division-sized force behind Austrian lines would have turned Boroević's vulnerable left flank; combined with a general offensive, such a joint army-navy operation might easily have enjoyed strategic success, including the capture of Trieste from the rear. Cadorna had plenty of troops to spare, but he was as uninterested as ever in any plan that was not his own and was not focused solely on the Isonzo front. He had no time for amphibious landings or any other novel ideas, no matter how promising. He was sure that this time his armies would break through the Austrian defenses on the Carso. The Austrian catastrophe in Galicia and the recent entry of Romania into the war on the Allied side only increased Cadorna's faith that the Habsburg Empire was on the brink of collapse.

Like Boroević, he spent late August and early September preparing his weary forces for the Seventh Battle of the Isonzo. His 2nd and 3rd Armies filled their depleted infantry regiments with tens of thousands of replacements fresh from training depots, and the artillery received hundreds of thousands of shells straight from munitions factories to restock its batteries. By early September, Cadorna's legions were again ready for battle, at least on paper. The mass mobilization of peoples and economies brought about by total war meant that Italy, like all major belligerents, enjoyed the unprecedented ability to supply its armies with fresh soldiers and shells even after the worst battlefield losses. Italy's reserves of men were still prodigious, and her industrial mobilization was only just reaching full capacity. The Duke of Aosta's 3rd Army, which would bear the brunt of the upcoming battle, boasted a dozen divisions with 150 battalions, and Abelardo Pecorini's 2nd, relegated to a supporting role at Gorizia and on the upper Isonzo, possessed fourteen divisions with 155 battalions. The duke's dozen reinforced divisions on the Carso, divided among three army corps, were to attack on a front of less than seven miles, backed up by 954 guns and 584 mortars. They outnumbered the opposing Austrians nearly three-to-one in manpower and almost four-to-one in firepower. To reach Trieste—only thirteen miles from the Italian right flank—the 3rd Army had only to blast its way through the Austrians' new defensive line.

The duke's engineers prepared for the offensive during the first week of September, digging assault trenches close to the Austrian lines, but their work was difficult and slow. The weather hampered their efforts as heavy rains fell all week, flooding both armies' entrenchments with mud and rainwater. The Isonzo rose as the rains continued, disabling several Italian pontoon bridges, and slowing the supply of equipment and munitions to the 3rd Army's divisions on the Carso. The weather began to improve on September 7, permitting the Italian sappers to finish their work. Still, Cadorna was forced to delay his offensive for a few days. Unconcerned, he ordered the gunners to begin their preparatory barrage anyway, albeit gradually, while the infantry made final preparations for the attack. The 3rd Army's 1,500 guns and mortars shelled the Austrian lines, especially on the north-central Carso front between Nad logem and the village of Nova Vas, held by Archduke Joseph's VII Corps. The pace and intensity of the bombardment started to increase on September 10 as heavier Italian guns targeted Austrian supply depots and reserve positions behind the front, a sure sign of an imminent offensive. The Hungarian defenders sat in their *kavernen* and waited for the inevitable infantry assaults that followed every prolonged bombardment. On the evening of September 13, the barrage reached a fever pitch, relentlessly blasting positions all along the VII Corps' defensive line, with a squadron of Italian heavy bombers joining in before dark. The veterans of the 17th and 28th Divisions tried to get some sleep, knowing that the coming dawn would bring another major offensive.

As the brilliant late summer sun rose over the Carso on September 14, the 3rd Army's artillery opened the final phase of its barrage, showering the limestone with high explosives from the Vipacco River to the Adriatic. The shelling lasted nine hours, raising enormous clouds of dust and smoke and destroying Austrian communications posts, supply depots, and roads leading to the front lines. Unable to talk with forward units and blinded by the smoke, Austrian divisional and brigade commanders had little idea what was happening in the trenches. The Duke of Aosta launched his infantry assault in midafternoon, after the artillery had had time to do its deadly work. On the northern Carso, the XI Corps' regiments struck Archduke Joseph's positions between Nad logem and Opacchiasella, but gained little ground. An attack by three whole regiments of the 23rd Division on the heights of Nad logem was halted and broken by a determined counterattack from a single battalion of the 61st Regiment, a mixed unit of Magyars, Romanians, Germans, and Serbs. The 22nd Division's advance at Opacchiasella was shattered by concentrated Austrian artillery fire. The *fanti* did somewhat better slightly to the south, where the Austrians were forced to retreat about a hundred paces to the east. Otherwise, all XI Corps gains were overturned by VII Corps counterattacks.

At the Nova Vas salient on the central Carso, a bulge in the line dominated by a 680-foot-high hill, Slovak and Czech infantry pushed back several mass attacks by the XIII Corps. The 19th Division's midafternoon advance was cut short by machine gun and rifle fire, but the 31st Division gained some ground in the evening. Only a surprise counterstroke by the 24th Austrian Militia Brigade saved the village of Nova Vas, but at a high price. By nightfall, the VII Corps still held all its trenches on the central Carso, but its troops were growing tired. On the Carso's southern flank, the VII Corps registered the day's only significant advance for the 3rd Army. The sector's defenders, East Galicians of the 60th Brigade, were spread too thinly, just four battalions for a front of three miles. They repulsed a division-sized advance near the Adriatic coastline, but were overwhelmed by a 6 P.M. assault on Hill 144 by the reinforced 16th Division. After a vicious fight for the 470-foot-high hill, the exhausted and badly outnumbered Poles retreated 200 feet to another trench line. The capture of 144 represented the Italians' only notable progress on September 14.

Italian attacks were not confined to the Austrian front lines. In the evening, as the infantry battle subsided, long-range Italian guns shelled the Aurisina waterworks, the pumping station for the Austrian troops defending the Carso, halfway between the front line and Trieste. The barrage damaged the pumps and threatened to destroy the station entirely, a setback that would have made a sustained defense of the Carso impossible. Only rapid action by the Austrian Navy saved the waterworks; six flying boats took off immediately from Trieste Naval Air Station to find and destroy the Italian battery. They discovered and bombed the heavy guns just as the sun was setting, relieving the threat of dehydration for the hard-pressed infantry on the Carso. Ironically, the night then brought a temporary excess of water. After dark, an intense thunderstorm buffeted the lower Isonzo, adding nature's explosions to the day's shelling and tumult. The storm, combined with an unexpectedly strong gust of the *bora*, frayed the nerves of the tired infantrymen, both Austrian and Italian. Major General Anton Pitreich, Boroević's chief of staff, recalled, "It was a night filled with shivers and fear, which shook the nerves of all combatants in a disproportionate manner, and which on our side as much as theirs at times prevented greater battle capacity."

The poorly rested infantry returned to combat the next morning. September 15 began with another heavy Italian barrage, this time along the entire Isonzo front, from Rombon to the Adriatic. Frightful shelling through the morning wore down the weary Austrian defenders on the Carso, where the bombardment was particularly violent. The battered 17th Division, holding the line east of Nad logem, was hit on two flanks by XI Corps assault infantry. The freshly committed 49th Division rolled up the Hungarians' northern flank, advancing several hundred feet. Its Grenadier Brigade mounted a bayonet charge, seizing the village of San Grado di Merna; the *Granatieri* continued to advance, taking the village church, valuably perched on a hill. The XI Corps was prevented from achieving a major breakout by the vigorous defense of the Romanian 43rd Regiment, yet its four divisions nevertheless succeeded in pushing the 17th Division off the heights of Nad logem, an advance of a third of a mile.

The less fortunate XII Corps failed to make any gains on September 15. Its 19th Division reentered the battle with a mile-wide mass charge between Opacchiasella and Nova Vas. The swollen ranks of *fanti* were torn apart by presighted machine gun and artillery fire long before they reached the 28th Division's trenches. Then a surprise counterattack by a single company of the 11th *Jägers* pushed the dazed Italian survivors back to their own lines. Similarly, the neighboring 31st Division's advance up Hill 208, just south of Nova Vas, was cut short, with heavy losses, by intense Austrian fire and a determined counterattack. An attempt by the Italian VII Corps to expand its hold on Hill 144 likewise failed; six line infantry battalions and two of *Bersaglieri*, supported by artillery and a dismounted cavalry regiment, could not push the Poles of the 60th Brigade away from the summit. In all, September 15 was a failure for the 3rd Army. Despite the modest gains east of Nad logem, its dozen divisions had hardly pushed the Austrians back. Vigorous attacks generously backed by heavy guns achieved little, as had happened so many times before on the Carso. Small numbers of Austrian troops again had succeeded in repulsing entire Italian divisions, and were as capable as ever of inflicting lethal counterattacks against initially promising advances. Attrition had returned to the Isonzo with a vengeance.

Regardless, Cadorna and the Duke of Aosta both wanted to press even harder the next day. Both the Italians and the Austrians were very weary and in no condition to fight another sustained brawl among the *dolinas*. Still, both armies sent their frontline regiments fresh men and munitions during the night and prepared for the next round at dawn. The combat on September 16 was the most intense yet during the Seventh Battle. The 3rd Army's three corps threw themselves at the Austrian defenses again, with minimal results. Only just south of the village of Nova Vas did the attackers gain any ground; the depleted 31st Division managed to wrest Hill 208 from tired battalions of Czech and Slovene militia. Everywhere else on the Carso the duke's offensive stalled bloodily. VII Corps machine guns and artillery prevented any Italian success, adding to the mounds of Italian corpses surrounding Austrian entrenchments all along the Carso. The only alteration in the Italian battle plan from the previous two days was the addition of another attack at the opposite end of the Isonzo front, thirty miles north of the Carso on Mt. Rombon.

Rombon continued to be a thorn in the side of the 2nd Army. The apparently unshakable Austrian hold on the mountain blocked any Italian conquest of the Flitsch basin; the army that occupied Rombon controlled the uppermost Isonzo. Lieutenant General Settimo Piacentini wanted another attempt to push the Austrians off the mountain, particularly before the autumn arrived, a recommendation heartily endorsed by Cadorna. Piacentini ordered the IV Corps to assault Rombon and seize the summit at any cost. The better part of an *Alpini* brigade, including ample artillery support, was in place by mid-September. The well trained mountain troops were eager to prove their mettle and to capture Mt. Rombon, a feat that would eclipse even the glorious conquest of Mt. Krn more than a year before. The only obstacle was the Austrian regiment at the summit.

Since April, Rombon had been garrisoned by the 4th Bosnian Regiment. Two of its battalions had become well established around the 7,290-foot-high peak. (Indeed, the Bosnians had become such a fixture on Rombon that the army built a small mosque, complete with minaret, at the base of the mountain for the regiment's many Muslim soldiers.) The hard-fighting regiment had seen relatively little action over the last five months; the logistical difficulties of sustaining operations at such high altitudes meant that pitched battles were few and far between. That said, the *Bosniaken* were ready to fight. Five companies of the regiment occupied stone entrenchments around Kleiner Rombon, a 6,750-foot-high position lying a quarter-mile south of the summit. The lower position included a single mountain gun, as well as the regimental headquarters nearby. Three reserve companies were kept at the peak. The 4th's commander, Lieutenant Colonel Leo Kuchynka, was confident that his troops could defend Rombon against all comers. The forty-one-year-old Kuchynka, a Czech career officer, had worn the emperor's uniform since entering cadet school at age fourteen; he had fought at the front with his *Vierer Bosniaken* since the start of the Galician campaign in August 1914. He was an experienced leader, widely respected by his men.

Life for Rombon's isolated defenders was frequently unpleasant. Fresh food and water were regularly in short supply, the summit was frozen for most of the year, and there were the ordinary hazards of life in the front lines, and then some; occasional Italian shelling took its toll of dead and wounded, as did lightning, an especially dangerous threat near the summit—in just one month, the regiment had lost six soldiers killed by lightning strikes. Nevertheless, the morale of the *Bosniaken* was admirably high. The tough peasant infantrymen were first-rate soldiers with an outstanding battlefield reputation among friend and foe alike, and they knew it. A burning hatred of the Italians united the regiment, whose Croatian, Muslim, and Serbian soldiers often shared few other common sentiments. They were fierce fighters who particularly liked hand-to-hand combat, when they could wield their deadly battle club, the much-feared *buzdovan*. The Bosnians' morale was especially high whenever they received their twice-weekly alcohol ration. Like all Austrian infantry, they looked forward to their two cups of strong rum every week, the fighting man's privilege. The rum ration was an important boost to morale, even in elite units like the 4th Bosnians. It was particularly prized before battle; the *Vierer Bosniaken* even made up a little rhyme about their feelings toward their beloved rum ration:

> *Ako ima ruma, biće i šturma.*
> *Ako nema ruma, nema ni šturma.*

> (If we have rum, we fight and attack.
> If there's no rum, then there's no battle.)

Once he received word that the Seventh Battle had begun, Colonel Kuchynka made sure every one of his soldiers received his cup of rum.

The Italian attempt to take Mt. Rombon, the third of the war, began precisely at 6 A.M. on September 16 with a thunderous barrage by IV Corps mountain artillery batteries located lower down the mountain and in the Flitsch valley. Large-caliber shells shattered the morning calm, blasting Austrian positions around Kleiner Rombon; as a precaution, Kuchynka had left only small guard units in the forward trenches, so the Bosnians sustained few casualties during the bombardment. Just before 8 A.M., Kuchynka ordered his supporting artillery to hit the Italian troops assembling at Čukla, 1,600 feet southwest of the Bosnians' trenches. Within minutes heavy shells exploded in the midst of the Ceva *Alpini* Battalion, massing to charge the Austrian lines; the battalion lost twenty-nine killed, including its major commanding and the unit's chaplain, before it even went over the top.

Undeterred by the setback, the *Alpini* then advanced up Rombon's steep slope. At 8:15 A.M. *Bosniaken* of the 3rd and 4th Companies, occupying trenches just south of Kleiner Rombon, peered through the thick morning fog and caught their first glimpse of the Italian attack, three battalions strong with the Ceva Battalion in the lead. Austrian machine guns opened up at once, followed by rifle fire, drowning out the Italian battle cry, "*Avanti Savoia!*" *Alpini* in the three forward companies started to fall, but their comrades continued their charge toward the Bosnian-held trenches. Then the lone Austrian mountain gun at Kleiner Rombon joined in, firing at point-blank range over open sights, its 75mm high-explosive shells tearing gaping holes in the Italian ranks. The brave *Alpini* tried vainly to push forward, but staccato fire from Schwarzlose machine guns felled the entire first wave; the second wave attempted to advance, but made no progress. The Italians were stalled well short of Kleiner Rombon, nowhere near the summit. What was left of the *Alpini* brigade soon was running back down the mountainside to its own positions, chased by a Bosnian counterattack as violent as it was sudden. The effort had lasted less than an hour, but Italian losses were grave. The lead battalion alone lost 500 mountain troopers;

only three of Ceva's officers survived the brief encounter with the Bosnians. In all, a mere fifth of the elite attackers made it back to Čukla. The mile-high assault had been a complete fiasco. Two days later the IV Corps tried again, but this second attempt proved even less successful than the first. Colonel Kuchynka and his Bosnians still ruled Rombon.

The 2nd Army abandoned its efforts on the upper Isonzo, but the 3rd Army tried one more time on the Carso on September 17. The Duke of Aosta's attacks seemed halfhearted, however, in comparison even with his divisions' advances just three days before. The artillery continued to pound the Austrian defenses impressively, but the infantry clearly lacked ardor. After seventy-two hours of brawling, the *fanti* were exhausted and needed a rest. As a result, the 3rd Army failed to make any impression on the Austrian defenses on September 17. The XI Corps struck the 17th Division again on the Carso's northern flank, and the XIII Corps hit the 28th Division around Nova Vas, but neither attack gained any ground. By the evening, it was evident even to Cadorna that his infantry was just too tired to keep attacking. He and the Duke of Aosta therefore agreed to a pause in the fighting, at least until the 3rd Army could be restocked with enough fresh men and munitions to resume its offensive on the Carso. With that, the Seventh Battle of the Isonzo ended after only four days.

The 3rd Army registered some minor gains during those four days. It had managed to wrest territory from the Austrians in all three Carso sectors, north, center, and south. Yet, the gains in the center and south were barely noticeable—representing only the peak of Hill 144 and a 200-foot advance around Opacchiasella—and the advance in the north penetrated only a third of a mile into the Austrian defenses. None of the territory was significant, militarily or otherwise, and its loss in no way endangered Boroević's hold on the Carso. The cost of the fighting had been significant, however. The Italians admitted to 17,500 casualties during the four days of the Seventh Battle; the true figure was considerably greater, as always, perhaps two or even three times higher. The true number of Cadorna's dead and wounded will never be known precisely. Boroević's casualties were by no means light: officially about 15,000, more than half the rifle strength of the Carso's defenders; the real figure was doubtless somewhat higher. The Austrian Army had again stopped a major Italian offensive in its tracks, no small feat. Courage and firepower had preserved the new defensive line against the first serious Italian threat. However, Cadorna remained completely willing to fight battles of attrition until the Austrians were forced to give way, and the defenders knew it. The outlook left scant room for optimism in the Austrian trenches on the Carso. The Italians would be coming again soon.

Indeed, the halt that Cadorna ordered late on September 17 did not even represent an official rest period for his armies. It was instead an opportunity for the 3rd Army to consolidate its modest gains, regroup its damaged divisions, and prepare for the Eighth Battle. The exhausted infantry had few opportunities to catch up on lost sleep; the foot soldiers were kept busy digging new trench lines, bringing supplies forward, and accepting thousands of replacements. Cadorna gave his riflemen no time to ponder the hopeless fate that awaited them.

The Italian side of the Carso was filled with frenetic activity during late September as the 3rd Army geared up for the coming fight. This time, the 2nd Army would play a major supporting role. Cadorna ordered its VIII Corps, three divisions strong, to attack the Austrian lines north of the Vipacco River, below Gorizia, to assist the main effort on the northern Carso. The Duke of Aosta again tried to cram as many soldiers as possible onto the narrow plateau. The Eighth Battle's spearhead would be the XI Corps, with five and a half divisions on a front of only two and a half miles—two *fanti* for every foot of front. The duke's two other corps, the XIII and the VII, each boasted three divisions; he also had four divisions in reserve, one of them a fresh formation just sent from the Tyrol to participate in the battle. In all, the Italian attack force included eighteen divisions on a front of only ten miles; many regiments were still short of men because of the Seventh Battle's heavy losses, but the Duke of Aosta's paper strength of 221 infantry battalions was nevertheless very impressive. Quantitatively, the Italian force was even stronger than a month before, but qualitatively, it left something to be desired—after sixteen months of attrition, the infantry endured a permanent shortage of trained officers and sergeants, and unit leadership invariably suffered. Even so, both the duke and the count were confident that their vast numbers of men and matériel would prevail over the weakened Austrian defenses, still reeling from the pounding they absorbed during the Seventh Battle.

The Italian appraisal of Boroević's position on the Carso was one that the Croatian general and his staff would have endorsed. The Seventh Battle certainly had reduced the new Austrian defensive lines to a depressing shambles. The 3rd Army's heavy guns had wrought havoc with the carefully constructed trenches, dugouts, and weapon pits, particularly on the Carso's northern half. What was left was an unimpressive collection of sandbags and stone walls, too weak to withstand another Italian onslaught; Boroević's chief engineer considered the entrenchments after the Seventh Battle to be as bad as the Carso's ramshackle positions had been when the war began. Many of the Austrian casualties had been caused by rock fragments, sent flying lethally through the air by high explosives, a problem that had to be remedied before the next battle started. The 5th Army's first priority, therefore, was the rebuilding of its main defensive line. The Carso's 8,000 laborers worked around the clock to improve the infantry's entrenchments: digging deeper; adding more sandbags, steel shields, and stone reinforcements; and re-laying barbed wire and telephone lines. Some 3,400 of the workers were preparing a third defensive line, running all along the Carso two miles behind the current positions, to which the defenders could retreat to in the event of an Italian breakthrough. By early October, the militia laborers and Russian prisoners had completed their tiring tasks, just in time for the next round of fighting, and Boroević's defenses could again withstand everything the Italians could throw at them.

The 5th Army's staff still worried about the great numerical imbalance between the 3rd Army and their own forces on the Carso. To oppose the eighteen Italian divisions set to attack on the Carso, the Austrians had placed six and a half of their own. They were solid, battle-tested divisions—the Hungarian 17th Infantry and 20th *Honvéd*, the Ukrainian-Romanian 43rd Rifles, the Alpine German-Slovene 28th, the Czech 9th, plus the newly arrived Transylvanian 16th—but they were badly outnumbered by the Duke of Aosta's forces. Against the duke's 221 battalions, the Carso's defenders could produce only 69 (87, including all possible army-level reserves), but most of these were notably short of both men and equipment. The Italian preponderance in artillery was even more pronounced. Boroević knew that another Italian offensive was imminent, and his pleas to the High Command for reinforcements did not go unheeded; Franz Conrad von Hötzendorf, now seriously alarmed by the prospect of an Italian breakthrough on the Carso, had sent the 5th Army what little he could spare. Unfortunately for Austria, in September 1916 that proved to be quite little indeed. Again fighting a three-front war now that Romania had invaded Transylvania, the Habsburg Empire had few regiments and batteries to spare for the Isonzo. Conrad considered the Italian threat to Trieste to be very grave, and he dispatched two more divisions to Boroević, all he could scrape together; the 5th Army could expect no more. After the summer's Galician catastrophe, the Russian threat was clearly greater than the Italian, and the Romanian drive into Transylvania terrified Hungary's ruling classes, who demanded all available troops to turn back the invaders. The Isonzo was therefore accorded the lowest priority by the High Command, despite Conrad's undiminished Italophobia. Boroević's tired army would have to keep the Italians at bay with the forces already at its disposal, a mission that increasingly appeared to be a hopeless task.

Boroević's forces included a new army corps, General Karl Křitek's XVII, with two divisions to hold the Bainsizza plateau between Mt. San Gabriele and the Tolmein bridgehead. The brunt of the battle would be borne by Wenzel von Wurm's battle-hardened XVI Corps, behind Gorizia, and by Archduke Joseph's weary VII Corps on the northern Carso, supported by Alfred Schenk's corps-sized battle group on the southern Carso. Before the Italian infantry joined battle, the Austrians were forced to endure a weeklong barrage. Cadorna wasted no time, and the Italian guns opened up on September 30. Boroević, alarmed by the shelling, believed that the Eighth Battle had arrived and dispatched his last reserves, the 44th Rifle Division, to the Carso. Yet the battle was only just beginning; there were still painful days to wait before the *fanti* came over the top.

The preparatory barrage increased in intensity on October 3, as sustained fire from heavy guns and mortars pounded Austrian positions throughout the day. The pace and severity of the gunnery grew fiercer on October 5. Its impact on the defenders was terrible: in the first five days of October, the Austrians lost 700 dead and 3,000 wounded on the Carso, before the battle officially began. October 6 was an ugly day, with nonstop rain all along the Isonzo and thick fog enshrouding both armies' positions; the Italian barrage slowed and weakened. Greatly relieved by the pause in the pounding, Austrian staff officers hoped that the shelling was just a feint; Archduke Eugen's headquarters in the Tyrol, however, correctly surmised that the Italian guns would remain silent only as long as the weather was bad.

Clearer skies on the morning of October 7 brought ever stronger Italian artillery preparation that continued for nearly forty-eight hours. All along the Carso front, Austrian entrenchments, machine gun posts, and supply lines lay in ruins, and the worst was still to come. Cadorna, broadly aware of the destruction his guns were causing, was, as usual, quite optimistic; amazingly, despite the weeklong barrage, he believed that his infantry would achieve surprise and overrun the wrecked Austrian defenses. He ordered his artillery to commence "annihilation fire" on the entire Carso at 6:30 A.M. on October 9, the last phase of the barrage. More than a thousand guns rained high explosives on the Austrians all morning, followed by probing infantry advances in the afternoon to test the 5th Army's defenses. The main infantry assaults would come the next morning. That evening Boroević no longer doubted that the long-awaited Eighth Battle had begun in earnest.

The following dawn brought a brief but ferocious barrage by the massed guns and mortars of the Italian 2nd and 3rd Armies, a last softening of the Austrian positions before the infantry joined the battle. The shelling rained fire like a wall from Gorizia to the Adriatic, obscuring the battlefield with dense clouds of smoke and dust. Then the *fanti*, D'Annunzio's "holy infantry," fixed bayonets, climbed out of their trenches, and charged the Austrian lines. Everywhere the fighting was ferocious as the infantry emerged from the fog and smoke to overwhelm the shattered Austrian defenses. Soldiers wearing gray-green collided with their opponents, clad in uniforms of drab field gray. The exhausted defenders resisted and died hard, but by the afternoon Cadorna's foot soldiers had made impressive gains in several Carso sectors.

North of the Vipacco River, just south of Italian-held Gorizia, two reinforced divisions of the 2nd Army assaulted shell-shocked Ukrainian and Romanian battalions of the 43rd Rifle Division and pushed them back a mile, an enormous gain by Isonzo standards; within two days the Austrians had regained half their lost territory, but the Italians held on to the village of Sober and its entrenchments. Across the Vipacco the 3rd Army was likewise making impressive gains. On the northern Carso, the XI Corps, more than four reinforced divisions strong, attacked two of Archduke Joseph's entrenched divisions. The Hungarian and Slovene defenders, exhausted and at half-strength from the seven-day battering, quickly gave way. Giuseppe Venturi's 45th Division, the victors at Sabotino, took the lead and nearly seized the village of Lokvica; the XI Corps registered a gain of a half-mile, and the Austrian defenses were in disarray. The situation was even worse for the 5th Army on the central Carso. Three Italian divisions struck the exhausted 20th *Honvéd* Division around Opacchiasella and trounced the weary Hungarians. By nightfall, the 3rd Army had advanced a half-mile and seized the village of Nova Vas, capturing several hundred prisoners. The Italians had gained territory everywhere on a front of almost four miles, and at last the Austrians appeared close to the breaking point. Only on the southern edge of the plateau did the 5th Army manage to hold its ground on October 10.

Indeed, the defenders acquitted themselves very well in Schenk's sector. The Austrians manning the line in the south, facing the Adriatic, were exhausted and outnumbered; the decisive performance of the defenders that day owed everything to individual initiative. The main battle in the south was for Hill 144, where the Italians held the west slope and the Austrians the east. Two Italian divisions advanced past the summit and assaulted the shell-scarred trenches of the 102nd Regiment. The two Czech battalions, reeling from the Italian barrage, were quickly overwhelmed by thousands of charging *fanti*; the defenders' predicament, as everywhere else on the Carso, appeared hopeless. The 3rd Battalion was nearly surrounded and its commander wanted to retreat, and even the regimental headquarters was in danger; by midafternoon the situation was bleak.

One junior officer of the 102nd refused to give in so easily. First Lieutenant Theodor Wanke, a twenty-nine-year-old professional soldier, was held in reserve with his 9th Company, near the base of Hill 144. He watched in horror as the Italian 16th Division overran his regiment's forward positions, knowing the 102nd was close to defeat. Wanke had spent eight years—his entire career—with the 102nd, and had fought with it since the Serbian campaign in August 1914. He knew that even good regiments sometimes broke and ran under severe pressure, but he was determined that *his* regiment would not be one of them. Wanke ignored his battalion commander's sense of impending doom and rallied his company, ordering his Czech riflemen to charge the advancing Italian columns, an apparent suicide mission. His daring counterstroke hit the 16th Division at precisely the right moment, sending a full battalion of *fanti* fleeing back to the summit in panic. Knowing that victory was within his grasp, Wanke then ordered the neighboring 10th Company to join the counterattack. But the tired and scared soldiers were trying to leave the battle, not join it, and refused to accompany the young officer; Wanke then brandished his pistol and threatened to shoot any soldier who did not follow him to the summit. With that, the 10th Company joined the 9th in a general counterattack. Soon the Czech column, with Wanke in the lead, saved both battalion and regimental headquarters, pushing the 16th Division well away from the summit. Wanke kept going, and with just seventeen men behind him captured a hundred *fanti*. The lieutenant demonstrated, as had been done many times before on the Isonzo, the impact of small numbers of determined soldiers on the outcome of battle. By counterattacking at the correct moment, Wanke had turned back an entire Italian corps and saved the southern Carso, the road to Trieste.[1]

Boroević was elated to hear of the impressive local victory in Schenk's sector, but otherwise there was no good news that evening. Inevitably the obstinate general ordered all available forces to counterattack at dawn in a desperate attempt to regain ground and block further Italian progress. October 11 began less bloodily than anticipated, however, due to the arrival of heavy fog banks on the Carso before dawn. The dense clouds prevented the armies from launching any significant attacks. Yet once the clouds lifted in the early afternoon, the 3rd Army's mighty artillery opened fire all along the Carso, as the Italians and Austrians dueled for trench lines from the Vipacco to the Adriatic.

The fighting was vicious, even though both sides were tired and depleted. The few fresh Austrian battalions were committed early in the battle. The beleaguered 17th Division managed to hold its ground only with the help of the Czech 98th Regiment, just arrived from the Eastern front. On the central Carso, where the VII Corps had lost significant ground the previous afternoon, battalions of Hungarians, Slovenes, and Alpine Germans vied for every inch of rocky territory with a half-dozen Italian divisions. By the end of the day, the determined Austrian efforts had blunted all Italian advances and regained some lost trench lines, but at a terrible cost. The fighting was just as bloody on the southern Carso, where Schenk's tired infantry again stalled the 3rd Army's drive on Trieste. In all, October 11 represented a successful effort by the 5th Army. After losing much of its main defensive line on the Carso on October 10, it had managed to prevent any further Italian gains and had wrested some lost trenches back from the Duke of Aosta. That said, the cost had been exorbitant, even by the normally dreadful standards of the Isonzo. Boroević's divisions lost probably 24,000 soldiers on the Carso on October 11, including dead, wounded, and missing; according to Major General Pitreich, the 5th Army chief of staff, the artillery registered a loss of forty-one guns to shelling and capture, almost a whole division's worth of artillery. It was a staggering one-day loss. The 5th Army had again prevailed, but it could not hope to continue such a costly battle for more than another day or two.

Fortunately for Boroević and his soldiers, the Duke of Aosta had lost as many men and guns as the defenders, probably even more. By the evening of

October 11, the 3rd Army was utterly exhausted. The duke, acting in accordance with Cadorna's wishes, ordered his army to ready itself for another attack in the morning, after a few hours' rest. As commanded, the *fanti* went over the top again in the early hours of October 12, but their attacks could not hope to succeed. The offensive ardor of even two days before had evaporated, and the exhausted and depleted battalions made no gains all day, despite repeated efforts. The brave 45th Division tried in vain to make headway on the central Carso, but to no avail; by nightfall, Venturi's proud division counted a loss of 4,200 soldiers in less than seventy-two hours. Additional Italian assaults around the Nova Vas salient likewise failed to gain ground. Everywhere the tired defenders proved just strong enough to stall the weary Italian infantry. In the early evening of October 12, Cadorna called a halt to the brief Eighth Battle of the Isonzo. The *fanti* had done all they could, and needed a rest before Cadorna could launch another major offensive.

By the terrible standards of the Isonzo, and particularly compared to the bitter, unending siege on the Carso, the Eighth Battle was an Italian victory. Everywhere on the northern two-thirds of the plateau the Duke of Aosta had managed to advance—in the Nova Vas sector, a mile into Austrian territory. The Italians were still nowhere near Trieste, but Cadorna had shown again that attrition worked. At a likely cost of 60,000 soldiers, the Italians had cracked the Austrian defenses.[2] Of course, the 3rd Army could not hope to absorb such casualties indefinitely, but doubtless the Austrians would collapse first under such conditions, and that was what mattered to Cadorna. As long as there were enough *fanti* to sacrifice—"offered up in grey-green clothes," in D'Annunzio's telling phrase—the terrible arithmetic of attrition inevitably weighed in Italy's favor.

Boroević and his staff were well aware of this appalling reality. The 5th Army had halted the Italian drive, but just barely. Attrition was grinding the multinational army to pieces, as shown in the casualty figures: the Eighth Battle cost Boroević about 32,000 soldiers. Ominously, this steep number included as many as 8,000 Austrian troops in Italian captivity (3,500 captured around Nova Vas alone). The frightful beating delivered by Italian artillery, compounded by numerous infantry assaults, was wearing down the 5th Army to the point of collapse. One more such battle and Trieste might be lost.

To prevent this, Boroević removed some of his battered units from the front lines. The veteran 20th *Honvéd* Division, reduced to just 3,000 men by the recent fighting, was moved from the central Carso to the army's rear to recuperate; its sister division, the 17th, was similarly replaced in the line to give the infantry time to rest. Boroević nevertheless remained very worried about his army's prospects in the next round of fighting, which was sure to come before winter's arrival. His staff dispatched a report to the High Command just four days after the end of the Eighth Battle, detailing the army's terrible losses and what it needed to prevail in the coming battle. The October 16 report spoke of a crisis caused by heavy casualties and a shortage of replacements. It noted that normal losses were so high that each division required 2,000 replacement troops per month, *not counting* major battles; those, of course, consumed even more fresh soldiers. The 5th Army had lost 100,000 soldiers in eight weeks and had few replacements on hand to flesh out its depleted regiments. In addition to more men, Boroević pleaded with the High Command for more artillery and mortars, as well as ammunition for both. In addition, steel helmets were badly needed on the rocky Carso to prevent fatal head wounds, a frequent cause of death while under Italian bombardment. Conrad was very concerned about an impending Italian breakthrough and promised Boroević more replacements, firepower, and shells—and steel helmets, too, as soon as possible. Conrad wanted to dispatch more divisions to the Isonzo, but that required Berlin's approval. The Germans were habitually uninterested in the Italian front, which they considered a sideshow; but by late October, Paul von Hindenburg, convinced of the gravity of the Italian threat, relented and permitted Conrad to transfer a single Austrian infantry division from East Galicia to the Carso. It would arrive to fight in the Ninth Battle.

On the same day that Boroević dispatched his gloomy report to Conrad, Cadorna ordered the 2nd and 3rd Armies to be ready to launch a major offensive in one week. He knew that the Austrians were near their breaking point, and that one more big push before winter could decide the issue. Aware of the difficulties posed by unpredictable autumn weather, Cadorna permitted the Duke of Aosta to decide exactly when the offensive should begin. The scheme of the attack was as it had been during the Eighth Battle; the 2nd and 3rd Armies were arrayed precisely as they had been three weeks before. Numbers of men and weight of shell, not surprise, mattered to Cadorna. The Italian superiority again was daunting: on the Carso, 221 Italian battalions against ninety-one Austrian (counting all available reserves), and 1,350 guns versus 543.

Boroević accurately guessed his adversary's intention, and his timetable as well; the 5th Army command knew that the next, decisive phase of the autumn campaign could arrive as early as October 23. This foreknowledge was the result of ample evidence of an impending attack: Austrian intelligence officers observed more reconnaissance overflights and more troop trains moving to the Isonzo, and, most important, interrogated many Italian deserters who preferred surrender to a part in the imminent offensive. October 24, the day Cadorna had wanted to start the battle, was plagued by poor weather, so the artillery preparation was postponed. The thunderous barrage began the next morning, under clearer skies, with heavy artillery and mortar fire striking Austrian entrenchments all along the Carso. At midday, however, dense fog and intense rains returned, and the shelling halted. The artillery resumed its deadly task on the morning of October 26, uninterrupted by weather, as long-range guns bombarded Austrian artillery emplacements, reserve barracks, supply depots, and headquarters. The Austrian foot soldiers in forward trenches on the Carso now knew that the Ninth Battle had arrived, and that the *fanti* would attack on the first clear day.

The Austrian gunners tried to protect their infantry brethren by shelling Italian gun and mortar positions and ammunition dumps, but it was an impossible task. The outnumbered and outgunned Austrian artillery was incapable of silencing the Italian barrage, even for a few hours. Boroević's infantrymen could only sit in their mud-filled entrenchments and endure the pounding. The brutal preparatory barrage wrecked Austrian forward and rear positions for the next three days; by October 28 the 5th Army had lost 2,800 soldiers to the Italian guns, including nearly 500 dead. Austrian trenches from Mt. Santo to the Adriatic had been reduced to rubble, burying many of the troops inside. The shelling continued mercilessly through October 31, supplemented by air raids, and was accompanied by infantry probing attacks in the afternoon, as before the Eighth Battle. The following dawn, November 1, the massed guns of the 2nd and 3rd Armies commenced "annihilation fire," the immediate precursor to the infantry assault. Cadorna's ninth attempt to take Trieste was under way.

North of the Vipacco, the Italian VIII Corps made a spirited effort to push the 43rd Rifle Division away from Gorizia. Seven Italian brigades—fourteen regiments—struck the Austrian 41st Regiment, a polyglot unit from the Bukovina, the empire's easternmost province. A division of 12,000 soldiers attacked on a front of a quarter-mile: ten *fanti* for every foot of front. Yet the Romanian, Ukrainian, and Jewish riflemen, relying on their trusted machine guns, bloodily repulsed the daylong Italian attacks, and the 2nd Army made no headway beyond Gorizia on November 1. The 3rd Army was more successful. On the northern Carso in particular, the devastating barrage inflicted such damage on Austrian defenses that several positions fell quickly to the attacking XI Corps. The spearhead, as had become the custom, was the veteran 45th Division, whose intrepid infantry charged the ruined trenches of the 28th Division north of Lokvica. The 45th, reinforced by a brigade of *Bersaglieri*, advanced swiftly and overran the Croatian and Czech defenders. Two more Italian divisions rolled up both of the 28th Division's flanks, pushing back the crack 44th Rifle Division as well. By midday, the 45th Division had taken several hills and annihilated the 21st Rifle Regiment, killing or capturing 1,800 Austrian soldiers, and the VII Corps was on the verge of collapse. Archduke Joseph reluctantly prepared a retreat to the second defensive position, two miles back, but first he wanted a general counterattack to restore the main line of defense if at all possible.

There were scant reserves available, however; by scraping together all his uncommitted companies, Archduke Joseph collected eight battalions by the afternoon. Boroević had no fresh regiments to offer, so the VII Corps would have to attack alone. The counterstroke got off to a bad start, being hit hard by Italian artillery (including gas shells) while assembling for the attack. Nevertheless the Austrian infantry advanced, retaking several positions, and the fighting raged all night along the northern Carso. By dawn on November 2, the VII Corps had recaptured ten major positions lost the previous day and had netted 500 prisoners. Yet the situation remained critical; the VII Corps, weakened further by the overnight skirmishing, could not hope to withstand another major Italian blow. At noon, the 3rd Army delivered the expected second round of the offensive. Under the cover of a punishing barrage, the XI Corps infantry assaulted the Austrian entrenchments. By midafternoon the VII Corps was near complete collapse and without any fresh troops; Archduke Joseph now had no choice but to retreat to the second defensive position, the Kostanjevica line.

The retreat was a bloody melee that lasted well into the night. Austrian and Italian infantry fought doggedly for every hill and *dolina*, and casualties mounted on both sides. By the early hours of November 3, the Kostanjevica line was temporarily secure, but only due to the rapid intervention of the tired 17th Division, which was taken out of corps reserve to stall the continuing Italian drive. Yet, one more major Italian push could easily shatter the second defensive line, and there were no fresh reserves on the whole Isonzo front available to stop them. The situation was hardly better north of the Vipacco. There, Zeidler's 58th Division resisted all Italian efforts to advance past Gorizia, but the neighboring 43rd Rifles fared badly. An assault group of Italian infantry forded the cold, waist-deep waters of the Vertojbica River, a tributary of the Vipacco, and charged trenches held by the weary 41st Regiment. The surprised Austrian riflemen eventually reestablished their defenses, but only after bitter close combat and the embarrassing loss of twenty officers, 400 men, and 7 machine guns captured by the Italians. Under the relentless pressure of attrition, the 5th Army was beginning to lose its fighting edge.

Boroević wanted to counterattack, as usual, but it was simply impossible; merely holding the second defensive line seemed hopeless. The 3rd Army delivered its expected follow-up offensive on the morning of November 3. The cloudy weather and the weariness of the Italian infantry dulled the attackers' spirits, but the *fanti* proved tough adversaries nevertheless. The main Italian blow fell just east of Fajti hrib, at Hill 464, in the center of Archduke Joseph's fighting line. Either the 17th Division would hold Hill 464, the decisive sector, or the Carso at last would be in Italian hands. The Duke of Aosta's spearhead division was, as expected, the 45th, which assaulted the Austrian trenches with three infantry regiments, backed up by generous amounts of heavy artillery and mortar fire. By midmorning the exhausted and outnumbered defenders began to give way, and a major Italian victory was at hand. Only rapid action could save the VII Corps, and there was but a single reserve battalion available on the entire Carso.

That was the 4th Battalion of the 61st Regiment, a mixed unit of Romanians, Germans, Magyars, and Serbs from the Banat in south Hungary. It was an ordinary rifle battalion, led by an apparently ordinary commander, Captain Peter Roósz. The thirty-year-old Magyar career soldier, a native of the polyglot Banat, was the son of a coach builder. Like many junior officers, Roósz had spent his entire career with his regiment, including impressive war service in the Balkans and the East, punctuated by several wounds and decorations. When the 17th Division began to falter in the Fajti hrib sector on the morning of November 3, Roósz received the order to lead his battalion in a last-ditch counterattack, a final effort to turn back the 3rd Army's drive on Trieste. With reckless daring, the captain led his battalion in a headlong rush against the advancing 45th Division, a single Austrian battalion against at least a half-dozen Italian battalions. The two armies collided among the *dolinas*, and savage, disorganized fighting raged with bayonets, knives, grenades, and even rocks and stones; the surprise counterstroke caught the Italians off balance, and the startled 45th Division began to retreat in disarray. After two hours of vicious hand-to-hand combat, the 45th Division, the best Cadorna could offer, had been pushed away from Fajti hrib, and the 4th Battalion of the 61st Regiment owned Hill 464. Captain Roósz, who miraculously survived his courageous charge and the melee that followed, captured eleven officers, more than 500 riflemen, and eleven machine guns from the Italians. Yet again, the actions of a single intrepid and determined junior officer had saved the Austrian hold on the Carso.[3]

On the evening of November 3, after the 17th Division's successful defense of the Kostanjevica line, the Austrian predicament was much improved. That night, the fresh 14th Division—which Conrad had transferred from East Galicia with Hindenburg's permission—began to arrive on the Carso. At last Boroević had the troops he needed to guarantee the integrity of the second defensive line; now he could assure the High Command that Trieste was safe.

The Duke of Aosta's divisions had also begun to demonstrate signs of serious weariness, and were clearly incapable of sustaining another great push. Still, the 3rd Army made one final assault on the Carso before the Ninth Battle was ended. On the morning of November 4, the XI and XIII Corps tried one more drive toward Trieste. The duke's last fresh brigades attacked the Austrian lines on the central Carso, but were soon halted bloodily by accurate machine gun and artillery fire. The Austrian infantry was exhausted, so the gunners stalled the 3rd Army's push, blasting the lead Italian regiments to pieces on the rocky plateau. The fighting struggled on into the early evening, but by nightfall on November 4 the Ninth Battle was finally over.

The Duke of Aosta was able to report to Cadorna that in five days of fighting his divisions had advanced as much as two miles on a front of four and a half miles, an impressive gain compared to previous Carso battles. Yet this advance in no way undermined the Austrian hold on the Carso; the Italians were perhaps two miles closer to Trieste, but there were still fourteen miles to go, and the Austrian defenses in front of them remained formidable. In all three autumn battles, the 3rd Army had exhausted itself before achieving any decisive gains; in every battle, Cadorna was willing to sacrifice countless soldiers at first, but proved fatally cautious about committing his last reserves to achieve decisive success. This curious combination of recklessness and timidity, which proved so damaging in the Sixth Battle, undercut Italy's autumn gains on the Carso. Worse, the losses sustained by the Italians to get two miles closer to Trieste were horrifying. Officially Cadorna admitted to about 36,000 dead, wounded, and missing, but, as always, the real figure was far steeper—perhaps 70,000 casualties. The official Austrian conclusion about the Seventh, Eighth, and Ninth Battles—"the success of the Italians bore no relation to the mighty expenditure in men and matériel that it cost"—was painfully accurate. At such a rate of exchange, the 3rd Army would need a dozen more offensives and a million more men to sacrifice to reach its objective.

That said, the end of the battle brought no rejoicing either in the Austrian trenches or in Boroević's headquarters. The 5th Army had halted a major Italian offensive yet again. Considering the forces arrayed against it, Boroević's army had surrendered very little ground. The Carso remained firmly in Austria's grasp. But the human cost had been frightful: at least 30,000 casualties, among them 9,000 captured. In just two months the Austrian forces on the Carso had officially lost 74,000 soldiers (or 102,000, counting the sick), and that shocking figure was surely an underestimate.[4] Attrition was wearing the 5th Army away; only the onset of winter saved the Austrians from further punishing blows.

As ever, the battle dragged on in a limited but painful manner for several days after it formally ended. The Austrians, in particular, launched a series of minor raids to regain lost ground, often enjoying local success. On November 14 the 58th Division attempted to retake recently lost trench lines on the east slope of Hill 171, a low peak just southeast of Gorizia. Without artillery support, a battalion of the 28th Regiment, Prague's formerly ill-starred *Hausregiment*, mounted a surprise bayonet charge against the soldiers of the defending 48th Division. The spirited Czechs quickly overwhelmed the entrenched Italians, retaking 171's east slope and inflicting grievous losses on the startled *fanti*: 580 killed and 480 captured. The lightning raid accomplished all its objectives; it meant little to the Isonzo campaign overall, but it gave a badly needed boost to flagging Austrian morale.

Austrian morale was low indeed by November, with the harsh winter coming and no prospect of victory in sight. Many of the defending divisions had been so badly mauled that they had to be removed from the line; one of them, the 20th *Honvéd*, which had fought so doggedly on the Carso for well over a year, was in such bad shape that it had to be transferred to the quieter Russian front. Their famed corps commander, Archduke Joseph, soon followed. On November 21 the Habsburg archduke, recently promoted to colonel-general, departed the Isonzo to assume command of a sector on the Eastern front, leaving his beloved VII Corps behind. For sixteen months Joseph and his Hungarian corps had been the core of the Carso's defense, the symbol of Habsburg resistance to Italian aggression. The unflinching Austrian stand on the rocky plateau would continue without Archduke Joseph, but his departure was nevertheless a blow to the 5th Army's fighting spirit.

Far worse was the tremendous loss that the entire Habsburg Army experienced on November 21 with the death of Emperor Franz Joseph. Although he had been ill for many months, Franz Joseph's death in the sixty-eighth year of his reign still came as a profound shock to his subjects. The eighty-six- year-old monarch had reigned for so long, and survived so many personal tragedies, that he had seemed all but immortal. His death was a particularly grave loss for the army. Franz Joseph had been not just the first soldier of the monarchy, a duty he took very seriously until the last day of his life, but also a badly needed symbol of unity; his personality and prestige gave the empire and its fighting forces a cohesion that was vital to survival during a total war, and was perhaps otherwise lacking. Franz Joseph came to the throne in 1848 with the Habsburg Empire in disarray, beset on all sides by crises and with its army fighting the Italians, and he left it two-thirds of a century later in much the same condition. *Cecco Beppe*—as the Italian soldiers on the Isonzo knew him—died in the middle of his empire's fourth war against the House of Savoy during his long reign. Austria and its army required a strong and persuasive monarch to see it through the Great War, but Franz Joseph's successor exhibited neither strength nor persuasiveness. The young Archduke Karl, just twenty-nine in 1916, replaced his great-uncle on the throne; he would be the last Habsburg emperor, a fact that no one knew—but many suspected—during the gloomy winter of 1916. Karl was fundamentally a weak man, controlled to a large extent by his wife, Zita, an Italian princess (a fact that led many generals to suspect—and not unfairly, as it turned out—that she harbored pro-Allied sympathies). How detrimental Karl would ultimately prove to the Habsburg war effort would not be evident for many months, but as the winter of 1916 approached, all Austrian soldiers on the Isonzo felt a sense of loss as Franz Joseph was laid to rest in the Capuchin crypt in Vienna, the ancient burial vault of the Habsburgs.

Death continued to be ever present on the Isonzo, too, as winter arrived. The huge number of unburied corpses and freshly dug graves was the first thing noticed by all newcomers to the Isonzo front, whether Italian or Austrian. Even the virtual cessation of fighting with the first snows brought little relief to the soldiers dug in from Rombon to the Adriatic. Especially in the upper reaches of the Isonzo front, avalanches again became a serious hazard, burying countless unlucky infantrymen of both armies. In just four days in December, Austrian forces in the Julian-Carnic sector (the area around Mt. Rombon) lost 637 killed and 143 wounded to the "white death."

It was this omnipresence of death that struck Sergeant Benito Mussolini when he reached the Carso on December 1. He had fought for a time on the Carinthian front in the first half of 1916, then training courses and leave had kept him away from the Isonzo for many months. His arrival on the bloody Carso thus came as a rude shock to his senses. He announced triumphantly, "By the banks of the Tiber Italy was born, by the banks of the Isonzo she was born again." When he crossed the "sacred river" to reach his regiment on the Carso, he observed the impressive batteries of massed guns and noted in his diary, "We have so many cannons! Advancing will be easy!" The reality of life on the Carso therefore depressed him profoundly.

Mussolini entered the line at Hill 144 on the southern plateau, joining the 16th Division. Life in the trenches was difficult, even disgusting. The cold and wind-swept hill, site of so much fall fighting, was littered with unburied, rotting corpses; dirt and detritus covered the battlefield. Whenever the artillery of the opposing Transylvanian 16th Division shelled Hill 144, the *Bersaglieri* were showered with filth thrown up by the explosions. Disease was a serious concern, too. Cholera was rampant, caused by all the dead bodies and feces in the surrounding ponds. Mussolini wisely decided against bathing in the tainted water, a decision that saved his health but hardly made trench life pleasant. Worse, he was unpopular with most of his comrades. He got on well enough with junior officers, educated men like himself; by and large they liked and respected Mussolini and treated him well, some even deferentially. His comrades, however, were not so well disposed to the former journalist. The workers and peasants who filled the ranks of Mussolini's regiment had little respect for him; many, indeed, positively hated him; they blamed him for the war.

Yet by chance Mussolini enjoyed a pleasant Christmas to finish 1916. A captain serving in a nearby unit had worked with Mussolini—under him, in fact—before the war at *Popolo d'Italia*. Upon hearing that his comrade was on Hill 144, the young captain walked to visit Mussolini and wish him a happy Christmas. He brought a surprise gift, a roasted chicken hidden under his officer's cape. Mussolini was overwhelmed by the captain's kindness; years later *Il Duce* spoke of that Christmas on the Carso with tears in his eyes. Mussolini was one of the very few soldiers on the Carso to receive a pleasant surprise that cold Christmas. He received more good fortune a week later. On New Year's Eve, his company was relieved and sent to the rear for ten days' leave. Mussolini was lucky enough to spend the last hours of 1916 in the relative comfort of the rear areas, safe from the dirt and danger of the Carso. Few of his comrades or enemies on the Isonzo were so fortunate.

Monument "to the defenders of Rombon" at Log pod Mangartom (note Bosnian soldier on left).

Isonzo at Kanal (Canale).

"12,000 unknown" inside the Italian ossuary at Oslavia.

Monument to unknown Italian infantryman at Colle S. Elia (Redipuglia).

Austrian cemetery at Fogliano/Redipuglia.

Town of Sagrado (Carso) at Isonzo's banks.

Monument to Austrian dead at Loče pri Tolminu.

Italian ossuary at Redipuglia.

Isonzo at Sagrado/Gradisca, looking at Mt. San Michele.

Church of the Holy Ghost at Javorca.

Franciscan monastery atop Mt. Santo (Sveta Gora).

Town of Kobarid (Caporetto).

Hungarian monument at Sabotino.

Kavernen on Hill 383, Plave (Plava).

Monument to 4th Honvéd Regiment at Mt. San Michele.

1917

TEN

A Hundred Thousand Shells an Hour

The arrival of 1917, the fourth year of the Great War, brought little good news for the Allies, in Italy or elsewhere. The condition of Luigi Cadorna's tired armies seemed particularly unenviable—after eighteen months of war and nine battles of the Isonzo, Italy had conquered only one Austrian city, Gorizia, and a wrecked one at that—but the same could be said in varying degrees of all the Allied armies. The British and French were no more capable of evicting the Germans from France and Flanders than the Italians were of capturing Trieste; the two major Western front battles of 1916, Verdun and the Somme, cost France and Britain well over a million casualties. Even the Russians, who enjoyed epic successes in East Galicia during the summer, by winter were ailing, beginning to collapse under the weight of total war. Everywhere attrition dominated the battlefield, and the cost of war in men and matériel had grown unbelievably. By 1917 no one, least of all Cadorna, still believed in quick breakthroughs or decisive victories. The war against Germany and Austria had become a fight to the finish, and could be won by only wearing the enemy down to the breaking point.

It was evident to the Allies that only by coordinating their offensives could they hope to decisively wear down the Central Powers during the coming year. In mid-November 1916, the Allies met again at Chantilly to determine a combined strategy for 1917. The Allied commanders—Joseph Joffre and Douglas Haig, as well as Palitsyn for Russia and Lieutenant General Porro, Cadorna's trusted subordinate, for Italy—agreed to coordinate a series of simultaneous offensives on the Western, Eastern, and Italian fronts to deliver a crippling blow to the Germans and Austrians early in the new year. On paper, the scheme was simple enough; it assumed, correctly, that the Central Powers, although still strong and enjoying all the customary benefits of the defense, could not withstand simultaneous major offensives on all three fronts. Berlin and Vienna, too, were weary after so many months of attrition. At Chantilly, Italy agreed to a new offensive on the Isonzo by February.

From the outset Cadorna was skeptical, despite Porro's promise of a late winter push on the Isonzo. In February, the Isonzo front was still frozen and snow-covered, hardly ideal conditions for a major attack. Besides, after the bruising autumn battles on the Carso, the 2nd and 3rd Armies were not ready to undertake another major offensive—and Cadorna wanted the next offensive to be the biggest yet. He also felt that he needed more heavy guns, preferably on loan from France and Britain, to achieve victory. Cadorna therefore decided that he could not follow through on Porro's Chantilly promise.

The Italian chief of staff reiterated this point at the Rome conference in January 1917, when the senior Allied generals met for additional and more detailed strategic planning. Cadorna's argument found a sympathetic audience in David Lloyd George, the new British prime minister. The fiery Welshman was deeply disappointed with Britain's performance on the Western front, and was searching for a new, less direct—and, he hoped, less costly—strategy. He liked the essence of Cadorna's argument, that the surest way to defeat Germany was to topple its weaker partner, Austria: "knocking out the props," as Lloyd George called it. The prime minister did not like generals (Haig especially), and he had no love for the Allies: he described the Chantilly conference as "a pure comedy," and he considered Italy's war leadership to be "talentless"; yet he listened to Cadorna, who promised him decisive results for only a modest commitment of British blood and gold.

Lloyd George proposed a general Allied offensive on the Isonzo early in 1917, with several British and French divisions and hundreds of heavy guns from the Western front to support the Italian Army. The objective was to be Ljubljana, and then Vienna; a combined Allied push would succeed where so many Italian efforts had failed completely. Cadorna was enthusiastic about the prospect of Allied help—he considered that not less than 300 heavy guns and eight divisions from the Western front would be needed to break the Austrian defenses—but he felt that Trieste should be taken before any drive to the east. As ever, Cadorna's personal goals took precedence. Worse, the British and French general staffs were by no means as enthusiastic as Lloyd George about diverting hundreds of guns and tens of thousands of troops from the Western front. To Haig and Joffre, the war's main front was in France and Flanders, and they—rightly—saw Lloyd George's scheme as an attempt to diminish their authority. Besides, the French and British were unimpressed by Italy's military performance so far, and considered a combined offensive on the Isonzo to be a waste of precious resources. Thus the generals balked, and the great Allied push on the Isonzo would have to wait.

Cadorna was disappointed by Haig's and Joffre's refusal to lend his armies the men and guns he needed, but it gave him a convenient excuse to delay his promised offensive, which had been his intention all along. When General Robert Nivelle, the new French chief of staff, visited Cadorna at his headquarters in Udine on February 1, 1917, the Italian bluntly informed his French counterpart that Italy would have to wait until the spring to attempt another offensive on the Isonzo. The army simply was not ready. Nivelle had little choice but to endorse Cadorna's decision, and made vague promises about French and British assistance later in 1917. Cadorna and his armies would spend the rest of the winter preparing for the Tenth Battle of the Isonzo.

It was just as well for Italy and her army that Cadorna delayed the next offensive. War weariness was noticeably on the rise, and hopes of victory had dimmed to the point of disillusionment. Although Cadorna still believed that attrition would eventually win the war for Italy, some of his senior subordinates were no longer sure. Even the Duke of Aosta, whose 3rd Army had borne the brunt of the costly fighting of 1916, now had lost faith in Cadorna's strategy and tactics: by the spring of 1917 he expected to be fighting on the Carso ten years hence. Among lower ranking officers and common soldiers, who were asked to sacrifice themselves on the Isonzo, hopes of victory had given way to despair. Morale had plummeted in almost all units, and there were frequent disturbances. In March, when there was no fighting to speak of, the Ravenna Brigade experienced a mutiny; its doomed *fanti* wanted out of the war. After the usual enforcement of discipline—decimation, *pour encourager les autres*—the brigade was returned to the front.

Morale on the home front was not much better. Workers, although safe and well paid, were nevertheless tired of wartime hours and rationing. Even more, millions of average Italians, especially women, whose husbands and sons did the fighting and dying, and who had to feed and clothe their families on little money and food, were disgusted with the war. Antiwar demonstrations were commonplace by 1917, and even in Parliament deputies dared to openly question the army's needlessly bloody methods. Cadorna, of course, took no notice of these criticisms. He ignored their message, remained content to prosecute the war as he desired, and considered all protest to be sedition. He blamed Italy's war weariness not on the appalling human and economic cost of the Isonzo battles, but rather on socialists, pacifists, and spies. By 1917 Cadorna was obsessed with what he termed "the contagion of the poisonous propaganda of seditious parties." True to form, the remedy he demanded to cure Italy's "weakness" was ever stronger discipline, on the home front as much as on the fighting front.

Although Italy was beginning to show ominous signs of disaffection by the spring of 1917, Austria was doubtless in even worse condition. Defying the hopes of its foes and the fears of its leaders, the Dual Monarchy, which had not been expected to survive more than a few months of the Great War, was still in the fighting, but just barely. Austria's weary army had staged an impressive and unanticipated recovery: its polyglot divisions still held the Isonzo line, had rebounded from the Galician catastrophe of mid-1916, and had decisively defeated Romania's invasion attempt. That said, Austria's outlook for 1917 appeared bleak. The war economy was beginning to suffer worrying setbacks due to the Allied blockade, resulting in shortages of weapons, ammunition, and spare parts. Worse, Austria was running out of men: by January 1917, the army had taken in 7,500,000 soldiers—67 percent of all men between eighteen and fifty—and had lost 2,800,000 to death, crippling wounds, and capture. Still more were unfit for frontline duty. The horrible casualties sustained in Galicia, in the Carpathians, and on the Isonzo could be made good only with great and increasing difficulty.

The Isonzo had by now been accorded the highest priority. Although the army still had more men in the East—of 854,000 Austrian infantrymen at the end of 1916, 452,000 opposed the Russians, 74,000 were in the Balkans, and 328,000 faced the Italians—with Russia's slow demise, the Italian front was now considered to be the most important by the High Command. Certainly Italy now posed a greater threat to the empire than the tired Tsarist state could. In early 1917, newly crowned Emperor Karl dismissed Franz Conrad von Hötzendorf, whom he felt to be a hotheaded and dangerous war leader, not at all the ideal chief of staff for the cautious and pacifist new monarch. Conrad was sent to lead an army group in his beloved Tyrol, his place at the High Command taken by General Arthur Arz von Straussenburg, a Transylvanian officer of no great distinction. Upon becoming chief of the General Staff, Arz took stock of Austria's precarious strategic position. He was particularly concerned with the outlook on the Isonzo, where he felt that Cadorna's strategy of attrition, although bloodier for Italy than for Austria, ultimately would end in Cadorna's favor. He observed, "In this struggle it was inevitable that the Italians would prove successful." The coming battle would prove how correct his assessment had been.

In the meantime, as the harsh winter dragged on, the infantrymen of both armies struggled to keep warm and dodge snipers' bullets and stray shells. Although there were no major engagements on the Isonzo before the spring, skirmishes and especially accidents claimed a steady toll of killed and maimed Austrian and Italian soldiers. One such unfortunate was Benito Mussolini. In February 1917, Sergeant Mussolini was appointed commander of a trench mortar section, a job that he relished and performed most effectively. It was a welcome change from day-to-day trench life on the Carso, which he described as

"Snow, cold, infinite boredom. Order, counterorder, disorder." Mussolini spent his days supervising the shelling of Austrian trenches on the east side of Hill 144. Trench mortars were short-ranged but deadly and much feared weapons, ideal for the close-quarter fighting that prevailed on the Carso. Unfortunately, they were also primitive and prone to malfunction and misfire.

On February 23, Mussolini was supervising his trench mortar section during a routine barrage of the Austrian lines. The nearest officer ordered a mortar to be loaded with one round too many; Mussolini protested, but to no avail. The result was a misfire, and the explosion of the mortar shell while still in the tube. Five of Mussolini's men were killed immediately, and several others were wounded critically by burns and shrapnel. Mussolini was among them. He was knocked unconscious by the powerful explosion, his body perforated by more than forty pieces of shrapnel. He suffered a smashed right collarbone, a serious laceration of his right thigh, a temporarily paralyzed left arm, and dozens of cuts on his legs. He was gravely wounded, but when a comrade tried to move him and asked for assistance, several soldiers refused; they would not help the man who caused the war. Eventually Mussolini was moved to a field hospital safely behind the fighting line, at Ronchi, where he spent the next five weeks in agony. He was too badly injured to undergo immediate surgery. Later he endured a series of painful operations to remove the shrapnel, and suffered high fevers due to infection. It was amazing that Mussolini survived at all. His war was over. Yet his near-death on Hill 144 spared him the fate awaiting his *Bersaglieri* comrades in the coming Tenth Battle.

Although Cadorna did not plan to begin his next offensive until May, he prepared his armies for battle throughout the winter and early spring. His plan of attack was simple. After an extended artillery preparation, the largest yet on the Italian front, his left flank would attack Austrian positions on the Bainsizza plateau and around Gorizia; then his right flank, the Duke of Aosta's 3rd Army, would join the offensive, breaking through on the Carso. The ultimate aim, as ever, was the shattering of the Austrian line and the capture of Trieste.

The first phase of the infantry assault would be borne by a new command, the Army of Gorizia, assembled specially for the Tenth Battle. This new army, with a strength of 146 infantry battalions, 988 guns, and 402 mortars, organized in a dozen divisions and four corps, was under the command of Luigi Capello, heralded as "The Victor of Gorizia" in the press, and known to his troops, who knew him better, as "The Butcher." Capello was a hard driver of men, cut from much the same cloth as Cadorna, who still held faith in the superiority of morale and spirit over steel and fire. He believed that success in battle depended not on machine guns and artillery, but rather on "the work of the heart, mind, faith, enthusiasm, and reason." He felt that the first nine battles fought on the Isonzo, although not necessarily victories in strictly military terms, were nevertheless to be applauded as "spiritual" victories; Capello placed "very great value on the invigorating function of the offensive." The bloodbath on the Isonzo therefore seemed to Capello not a needless sacrifice, but instead a painful foundry where new Italians and a new Italy were being forged. It produced "steely souls able to carry the burden of present and future struggles." Capello was just the general Cadorna needed to launch a ruthless offensive against Svetozar Boroević's forces on the Bainsizza and behind Gorizia. The Army of Gorizia's objective was to take the western edge of the Bainsizza plateau, from Plava to Mt. Santo, and also Mt. San Gabriele, just northeast of Gorizia. Capello's forces outnumbered the Austrians across from them almost three-to-one in men and guns, so his army appeared likely to achieve the victory that had so long eluded the Italians on the Bainsizza.

The second infantry phase of the battle was the responsibility of the 3rd Army. Its commander, the Duke of Aosta, was a more compassionate and realistic general than Capello, but his army faced the same bloody fight to push the Austrians back. The 3rd Army, with a strength of sixteen divisions by early May, an awesome total of 162 battalions backed by 1,250 guns and 584 mortars, was charged with breaking the Austrian hold on the Carso. The duke, like Capello, enjoyed a nearly three-to-one superiority over his opponents in man- and firepower, but he knew it would be a bruising struggle nevertheless. Since June 1915, the 3rd Army had managed to gain a few miles of the Carso at a great cost, and the coming fight promised more of the same. The duke's only hope was that Capello's drive north of Gorizia would draw enough Austrian troops away so that his army could make a major penetration of the 5th Army's defenses.

Besides the daunting power of the defense, with all its machine guns, presighted artillery, and solid entrenchments, there were other reasons for unease in the Italian forces on the eve of the Tenth Battle. Although Cadorna's army had reached an unprecedented size,[1] it was still an immature force in the all-important areas of tactics and doctrine. Despite two years of war, Italian combat methods remained primitive. There was little detailed prebattle planning, and virtually no cooperation between the infantry and artillery, a crucial defect. The infantry was still devoted to mass bayonet charges, and the artillery was content to shell Austrian positions without specific reconnaissance. The two main combat arms, which needed to work together to achieve victory, in practice hardly ever spoke to one another. Field Marshal Sir William Robertson, Britain's chief of staff, observed despairingly after a March 1917 visit to the Italian front, "No system of cooperation existed between the artillery and infantry in attack, in fact the relations between the two arms seemed strained." A coherent, standardized tactical doctrine still did not exist; generals pretty much fought as they thought correct, with Cadorna's blessing. Worse, Italian training methods remained rudimentary, with lethal results on the battlefield; realistic battle preparations were unknown. Too few officers were adequately trained and prepared for the rigors of combat, and the army continued to make scant provision for the welfare of its troops. As a fighting machine, the Italian forces on the Isonzo still left a great deal to be desired. Viewed on paper—as Cadorna and so many other Allied generals remained content to do—the Italian Army appeared impressive, but a detailed examination revealed crucial weaknesses that threatened to undermine its effectiveness and cohesion in disastrous ways.

That said, the mere size of Cadorna's forces on the Isonzo caused Boroević and his staff serious and growing concerns. On a positive note for the 5th Army, by late April the Austrians suspected that an Italian offensive was imminent, and began to make detailed preparations. By May, after several months' rest, Austrian entrenchments from Rombon to the Adriatic were again in first-rate condition, filled with infantry, well provisioned with ammunition, and ready to defend the Isonzo line. The 5th Army had reached a record strength of eighteen divisions, including reserves, five of which had arrived since the end of the Ninth Battle.[2] In all, Boroević had 215 infantry battalions, 1,470 guns, and 434 mortars at his disposal. Yet the 5th Army still had grave weaknesses. Most of the infantry units were well understrength, and all units—especially the artillery—had limited ammunition reserves. The 5th Army, too, looked impressive on paper, but it could sustain only a brief battle; it could not hope to withstand another series of attritional brawls like those which bloodied it on the Carso from September to November. Boroević's divisions were tough, battle-hardened, and determined to hold their own against the Italians, but they had limited staying power. Either his forces would wear the Italians out quickly or disaster would result.

Exactly when the Italian offensive would begin remained a mystery, despite the best efforts of Boroević's efficient intelligence staff. The Austrians expected Cadorna's main effort to come in the south, on the Carso, where his armies had fought so doggedly in the autumn, and by early May, 5th Army headquarters had seen nothing that caused it to revise this prediction. The Italians were now exercising an unprecedented degree of secrecy and caution in their preparations for the coming offensive, so early May proved very quiet on the Isonzo, a lull before the storm. Italian deception methods, including camouflaging troop movements and keeping radio traffic to a minimum, were helped by the weather, which was consistently rainy and foggy, obscuring the movement of Cadorna's guns and supplies to the front lines. When the weather began to clear in the second week of May, Austrian observers could not fail to notice the burgeoning Italian camps and dumps just to the west of the Isonzo, and concluded that the long-awaited offensive was imminent; this conclusion was enhanced by the testimony of numerous Italian deserters, *fanti* who preferred Austrian captivity to a role in the coming assault. Boroević therefore ordered his reserves to be ready to move at any time. But he and his staff were confused when, on May 10, Italian movements and overflights nearly ceased; it appeared that Cadorna had called off—or at least delayed—the Tenth Battle. May 11, too, was an unexpectedly quiet day on the Isonzo. Thus, when at dawn on May 12 Capello's and the Duke of Aosta's massed guns opened fire on Austrian trenches all along the Isonzo, unleashing the most ferocious barrage yet seen on the Italian front, it came as a rude awakening to Boroević and his staff. The Tenth Battle of the Isonzo had finally arrived.

The combined firepower of 2,150 guns and 980 mortars hammered mercilessly at Austrian positions from the northern edge of the Bainsizza plateau to the shore of the Adriatic thirty miles to the south. The shelling continued, virtually without rest, through May 12 and 13, killing and maiming thousands of Austrian soldiers and destroying hundreds of entrenchments, machine gun nests, supply dumps, and command posts. By May 14 the Army of Gorizia was ready to attack. Its main objective was the taking of the "Three Saints"—Mt. Santo, Mt. San Gabriele, and Mt. San Daniele—the three peaks that overlooked Gorizia from the northeast and dominated the lower part of the central Isonzo valley. Yet Capello's army would first have to secure its left flank, the Bainsizza plateau, before it could seize the *Tre Santi*. That meant his troops would have to occupy the Plava bridgehead and two significant peaks due south of it, Kuk and Vodice. In two years of fighting, the Italians had never managed to gain more than a foothold at Plava, despite the sacrifice of several divisions. Breaking through the Austrian lines at Plava was therefore Capello's highest priority.

He entrusted the task to the II Corps, the famed Plava Corps, which was acquainted with the bridgehead and Hill 383 so intimately and painfully. The corps was heavily reinforced for the assault to a strength of four divisions, including many crack battalions of *Alpini* and *Bersaglieri*. To ensure a rapid victory, Capello ordered the II Corps to charge straight up Hill 383 with three full divisions, but the corps commander, Lieutenant General Garoni, protested, arguing that such a frontal assault would lead to a slaughter; instead, he pleaded with Capello to allow the 47th Division to launch a diversionary flanking attack four miles upstream to draw Austrian troops away from Plava. Capello was outraged by Garoni's insolence and fired him without hesitation. On May 13, the eve of the great attack, Capello appointed his trusted chief of staff, Major General Pietro Badoglio, the hero of Sabotino, to lead the II Corps in the offensive. Badoglio, only forty-five and a general officer for just three months, was promoted above much older and more experienced generals, including the four divisional commanders now under him. But Capello knew he could trust Badoglio to act with the determination and ruthlessness that the coming battle required. Badoglio would not disappoint his mentor.

At noon on May 14, on the heels of a forty-four-hour bombardment, II Corps infantry battalions left their trenches near the Isonzo's banks and charged up Hill 383, signaling the beginning of the Army of Gorizia's offensive. The upper half of the Bainsizza, including 383, was defended by the Austrian 62nd Division, led by Major General Guido Novak von Arienti; he had held this piece of land for two years against Italian attacks and was not prepared to give it up now. Every inch of the plateau would be defended absolutely, to the last man if necessary. His division was a diverse and polyglot mix of battalions, many of them militia. Hill 383 was garrisoned by a battalion of the Magyar 52nd Regiment, and the village of Zagora, a mile downstream, was held by a battalion of the Dalmatian 22nd; both were hard-fighting veteran units that could be relied upon to resist to the end of their strength.

The Hungarians on Hill 383 were struck by the full force of five Italian regiments. The 3rd Division, which had fought continuously at Plava since the war's beginning, attacked with its Udine Brigade on the left flank and its Florence Brigade on the right, with the 21st *Bersaglieri* Regiment in support. The Italian charge was executed with great dash, as the weight of fifteen battalions charged up Hill 383, bayonets fixed. The attack illustrated the heroic élan of the ordinary *fantaccino*, even after two terrible years of war. Tragically for the II Corps, the May 14 assault also showed the power of machine guns and artillery against human flesh. Despite all the damage wrought by the fierce preparatory barrage, enough Austrian machine guns survived to stall the 3rd Division's charge. Both brigades were trapped on the bare slopes of "Bloody 383," which lived up to its evil reputation that afternoon. As machine gun and rifle fire felled the first two waves of *fanti*, presighted artillery fire tore frightful gaps in the tightly packed ranks of Italian infantry trying to reinforce the attack. The Udine Brigade's lead battalion, raked by machine gun fire, nearly reached the summit, but not before suffering crippling losses; almost all its officers fell within a half-hour. Battalion command changed hands five times in thirty minutes, as officers were cut down trying to lead the battalion's survivors to the Austrian trenches.

Losses mounted among the defenders, too. By 2 P.M., the exhausted Hungarian battalion around the summit was running out of ammunition, and the incessant Italian artillery fire was so intense that neither reinforcements nor supplies could reach the stranded troops of the 52nd Regiment. The 3rd Division made another attempt at 3 P.M., adding all available reinforcements. This time, weight of numbers prevailed; the remnants of the Udine and Florence Brigades reached the summit and overran the battered trenches. A few survivors of the 52nd Regiment managed to escape down the east slope, but most of the Hungarian defenders lay where they had fallen. After twenty-three months, the 3rd Division and II Corps at last occupied "Bloody 383." The Udine and Florence Brigades both suffered more than 50 percent casualties in the three-hour fight, but they had prevailed; outnumbered fifteen-to-one, the 52nd Regiment never stood a chance of success. Capello's army had reached its first objective.

The story was the same at the ruined village of Zagora, a mile downstream, where the 60th Division's Avellino Brigade stormed the positions of the 3rd Battalion of the Dalmatian 22nd Regiment. Like their comrades on 383, the Croatian and Serb troops resisted ferociously, firing every available bullet into the ranks of the advancing 231st and 232nd Regiments. The Austrian commander, Major Karl Hausser, led his hard-fighting battalion until it was completely overwhelmed, drowned by the onrushing waves of Italian infantry. By midafternoon, the Avellino Brigade occupied Zagora and had annihilated the defenders: not a single soldier of the 22nd Regiment's 3rd Battalion escaped the slaughter. The Dalmatians had defended Zagora to the last man. In the unrestrained close-quarter fighting for the village, Italian losses likewise mounted rapidly. For the 60th Division, the cost of taking Zagora was 3,000 of the 5,000 *fanti* sent into battle.

Two miles downstream from Plava, troops of the VI Corps attempted to seize the summit of Mt. Santo, the closest of the *Tre Santi*. Under the protection of a deadly barrage, a wall of steel, the 10th Division's Campobasso Brigade advanced up the steep slopes of the 2,250-foot-high "Holy Mountain." The shell-scarred summit was held by a battalion of the 25th Hungarian Militia Regiment, a Croatian outfit. The unfortunate militiamen were pounded relentlessly by VI Corps artillery; the barrage was so strong that it literally blew many defenders off the mountain. The Campobasso Brigade's regiments approached Mt. Santo carefully, hiding when possible in the underbrush on the west face, overlooking the Isonzo. When the *fanti* charged the summit, they surprised the Croatian defenders and captured many of them. The summit, with its ruined monastery, was in Italian hands. Elation spread through the VI Corps and then the whole Army of Gorizia as word of the victory reached Capello, and then Cadorna. The joyous news was read to the Parliament in Rome, bringing spontaneous and unrestrained applause. Monte Santo, the unattainable objective, had fallen at last. It was a triumph to rival the capture of Sabotino and San Michele.

Yet, the Italian euphoria proved to be premature. Upon receiving word that Mt. Santo was in Italian hands, the determined Major General Novak ordered all available reserves to retake the summit as soon as possible, at any cost; the defense of the entire Gorizia front depended on it. Not long after nightfall, troops from several Austrian battalions scaled the rugged east slope of Mt. Santo and surprised the Italians dug in at the summit, as only hours before they had surprised the Austrians. The rudely awakened *fanti* were soon retreating in disarray down the west slope. The Campobasso Brigade held on to several trenches near the monastery, but the summit was again solidly in the hands of the 62nd Division. In addition, the lightning counterstroke liberated numerous Croatian troops who had been taken prisoner in the afternoon. By the morning, word of the setback reached Rome. Italy would have to endure several more months and many more bloody attacks before its army could take and hold Mt. Santo.

On May 14, the VI and VII Corps made determined efforts to break through due east of Gorizia. Eleven brigades advanced on Austrian trenches between Mt. San Gabriele and the Vipacco River, but met with no success. The VI Corps made no progress against the 58th Division, which held doggedly onto Mt. San Gabriele and the neighboring peak, St. Katarina; the VII Corps similarly stalled in the face of determined resistance by the Hungarian 14th Division, whose Magyar and Slovak battalions blocked any gains south of Gorizia. In these battles, Austrian artillery proved decisive; although outgunned by the Italians, the defending XVI Corps gunners fired accurately and reliably, inflicting crippling losses on advancing columns of Italian infantry. May 14 ended badly for Capello's army east of Gorizia.

The Duke of Aosta's 3rd Army launched supporting attacks on May 14, in the hope of helping Capello break through beyond Gorizia. Two of the duke's divisions assaulted VII Corps positions just south of the Vipacco, but were soon halted by machine gun and artillery fire. The corps's new commander, Lieutenant General Georg von Schariczer, proved his troops could still stand firmly on the northern Carso. Determined Italian attacks due east of Fajti hrib ended disastrously. Further efforts by the 3rd Army, lasting into the evening, likewise were costly and in vain.

Regardless, Capello was encouraged by his army's successes on May 14, particularly the capture of Hill 383 and much of the Plava bridgehead. The II Corps had not advanced very far, little more than a quarter-mile, but it had accomplished more in an afternoon than it had in the previous two years. Clearly the main task for the Army of Gorizia was to keep hammering the now weakened Austrian defenses, in the expectation of capturing the entire Bainsizza plateau.

Boroević was very worried as May 15 arrived. The objective of the enemy offensive—the capture of the Bainsizza plateau—was now evident, and troubling. The loss of Hill 383, though hardly decisive in itself, nevertheless was an ominous portent; the quick fall of Mt. Santo, though redeemed by a brave counterstroke, still was a nagging concern. Given enough shells and men, the Italians could seize even the most courageously defended positions. The only way to guarantee the 5th Army's hold on the Bainsizza was to have enough fresh men on hand to overturn Italian advances. Boroević gathered all his available reserves behind Ludwig von Fabini's XVII Corps and requested help from the High Command; within hours two divisions were leaving Galicia for the Isonzo. Yet in the few, decisive days ahead, the defense of the Bainsizza would be pretty much in the hands of the troops already there. The staying power of the exhausted and understrength battalions at Plava and on Kuk, Vodice, and Mt. Santo would decide the issue.

On the morning of May 15, as anticipated, the II Corps, replenished overnight with fresh men, launched several attacks around the Plava bridgehead, in the direction of Kuk and Vodice. The Austrian defenders fought back bravely, yet futilely. With the weight of the 3rd, 53rd, and 60th Divisions bearing down on them, the scattered remnants of Novak's 62nd Division had no hope of holding on to their second defensive line. But they died hard. The division's last reserve, the 2nd Battalion of the 22nd Regiment, was thrown into the fray near Zagora, where its sister battalion had been annihilated the day before. The Dalmatians' sacrifice bought a little time, but could not hold the II Corps back: in forty-eight hours, the 2nd and 3rd Battalions of the 22nd lost 2,354 soldiers, virtually every man.

Badoglio's regiments advanced slowly, but they did gain ground. By the evening of May 15, the II Corps had troops near the summit of Kuk, and forward patrols were closing in on Vodice. Victory seemed well within Badoglio's grasp. A minor cross-river assault by the 47th Division at Bodrez and Loga, two miles upstream, helped distract the Austrians. The Isonzo crossing, though not large—including just two battalions of *Bersaglieri* and one of *Alpini*—nevertheless scared the XVII Corps badly, the effect that Capello intended. The commitment of two regiments of Austrian militia, just arrived on the plateau, halted the Italian drive up Kuk and Vodice on the evening of May 15 after savage hand-to-hand skirmishes, but the outlook for the Austrians remained bleak.

Both armies on the Bainsizza were by now exhausted and understrength. The II Corps, tired and overextended, needed a pause as much as the Austrians did. Badoglio's troops therefore spent most of May 16 regrouping and accepting replacements. The capture of Kuk and Vodice would demand the corps's maximum effort, and Badoglio wanted his divisions to be ready. Capello, though encouraged by his army's progress so far, was concerned that his artillery would not have enough ammunition to break through on the Bainsizza, but Cadorna overruled him. The Army of Gorizia would seize Kuk, Vodice, and Mt. Santo, regardless of ammunition supply. Boroević was no more understanding with his subordinates. He had no more reserves on hand to offer the divisions barely holding onto the plateau, but he ordered von Fabini, the XVII Corps commander, to not lose any more mountains, no matter the cost. The Descla-Vodice line had to hold at any price, a death sentence for the scattered remnants of the 62nd Division. Boroević made vague promises to von Fabini about reinforcements in a few days, but the XVII Corps would have to stand and die with the tired forces on hand.

Before Badoglio's divisions could launch an all-out attack on Vodice, the key to Mt. Santo, Kuk had to be taken. The II Corps had already advanced far up the 2,000-foot-high mountain's west face, so the infantry had to advance only a few hundred more feet to reach the summit. In the late hours of May 16, five brigades of the II Corps assaulted the Austrian defenses. The garrison, German and Czech militiamen and some Dalmatian Rifles, was exhausted and badly outnumbered; they had had no food or water in three days. The Italian preparatory barrage blasted the summit mercilessly, destroying the Austrian flanks and cutting off any possibility of retreat. Unable to escape, the defenders resisted as long as possible, well into May 17, until their ammunition ran out. The II Corps finally secured the peak in midafternoon. Kuk was in Italian hands; Vodice was next.

The May 18 offensive was Badoglio's attempt to capture the whole western edge of the Bainsizza plateau, principally Vodice and Mt. Santo, the land bridge to Mt. San Gabriele: it promised to be a triumph as great as the capture of Gorizia nine months before. The II Corps was thoroughly replenished and reinforced for the assault, its shattered regiments filled with fresh recruits. The main role was given to the 53rd Division under Lieutenant General Maurizio Gonzaga, the "Iron General," a commander ruthless even by Capello's standards. Gonzaga was determined to seize Vodice in an all-out push. He assembled two strong brigades and several battalions of *Alpini*, all generously backed up by artillery, for the mission. Seizing the 2,150-foot-high mountain overlooking the Isonzo promised to be a costly task, even considering the poor condition of the defenders, but Gonzaga was confident in his division.

At dawn on May 18 the massed guns of the Army of Gorizia opened fire, cascading high explosives on Vodice and Mt. Santo. A rapid attack up Mt. Santo by troops of the 10th Division soon followed, a diversionary effort, but was cut down in a hail of machine gun and rifle fire. At 10 A.M., after four hours of nonstop shelling, Gonzaga's regiments rose from their positions, bayonets fixed, and charged the summit of Vodice. Their start line was actually 1,300 feet up the mountain, so the division had to advance only 800 feet to reach the Austrian trenches, but the peak was rocky and treeless. There was no cover; it would be a mad dash up the steep, barren slope, straight into the fire of the Austrian guns. The 53rd Division attacked in three columns: the 241st Regiment of the Teramo Brigade on the left, the Levanna and Aosta *Alpini* Battalions in the center, and the Girgenti Brigade's 247th Regiment on the right. The Austrian militia at the summit poured fire into the tightly packed columns of *fanti* as every available rifle and machine gun was brought to bear. The first attack ended disastrously as the advancing waves slowed, then crumbled, cut down in the deadly cross fire.

Undeterred by this setback, Gonzaga sent his second echelon into the fray. He dispatched four fresh battalions of *Alpini*, daring mountain fighters; the "Iron General" knew the "green flames"[3] would not disappoint him. At noon the entire 12th *Alpini* Group charged the Austrian trenches, under the cover of artillery fire. They ran past hundreds of fallen comrades, straight into the withering fire of Schwarzlose machine guns, and succeeded where the first attack had failed, overwhelming the defenders and taking 300 prisoners. Only a rapid and well-timed counterattack by the 32nd Austrian Militia Regiment kept the Italians at the summit. The Polish militiamen fought hand to hand with the *Alpini* for control of the peak and prevented an Italian breakthrough past Vodice. The bloody melée continued through the afternoon, claiming hundreds of men but deciding nothing. By nightfall, Gonzaga's troops occupied the summit, winning the Gold Medal of Bravery for their general, but could advance no further.

At midnight an entire Austrian regiment, the 41st, on Boroević's direct orders stormed the summit in a desperate attempt to regain Vodice. The brave attack failed dismally: 60 percent of the Austrians fell; they could not wrest the summit from the 53rd Division, but they established a solid defensive line, a wall beyond which Gonzaga's troops could not advance. Even so, Boroević was disappointed. May 18 had ended badly for his army. The loss of Vodice was a major setback, even if more psychologically than militarily. The XVII Corps prevented a general Italian breakthrough, but it was little consolation compared to the loss of men and morale that the 5th Army suffered at the hands of Badoglio's II Corps. Emperor Karl was present on the Isonzo during the fighting; he spent May 18 at Boroević's headquarters, his first visit to the Isonzo front. Considering the crisis atmosphere that day, the monarch's visit was ill-timed. Still, he praised his brave forces, and announced that the 5th Army would henceforth be known as the Isonzo Army, in recognition of its heroic two-year stand.

The newly christened Isonzo Army did everything it could the next day to prevent the collapse of the Bainsizza line. May 19 began with a further Italian push in the Vodice sector. The II Corps had already suffered grievous casualties—by May 19 Gonzaga's left flank, the 241st Regiment, which began the day before with more than 2,500 infantrymen, was down to just 149 *fanti*—yet Badoglio, sensing that the Austrians were close to collapse, pushed his corps hard to break through at Vodice. But all Italian efforts failed, despite several brave attacks. Austrian artillery fired accurately all day, inflicting grave losses on II Corps assault units, and the infantry holding Vodice's east slope refused to budge. The surviving Ukrainian and Romanian troops of the 41st Regiment, vanquished the previous night, repulsed numerous Italian charges, not yielding an inch of ground on May 19. The close-quarter struggle was decided with bayonets and grenades, and by evening both armies were thoroughly exhausted.

During the night of May 19–20, a fresh Austrian artillery brigade arrived on the Bainsizza, forty-eight guns strong and amply supplied with ammunition, to turn the tide in favor of the XVII Corps. Badoglio's corps renewed its efforts on May 20, as the last reserve brigades were committed to battle in an effort to seize the peak of Mt. Santo. The Elba and 1st *Bersaglieri* Brigades advanced on the summit, dominated by its ruined monastery. Weight of numbers prevailed as the six battalions of *fanti* overran the thinly spread Austrian defenders, and the ruins were soon in Italian hands. Yet, as had happened so many times before, a determined Austrian counterattack, as violent as it was sudden, threw the Italians off balance, and the ruins were again in Austrian hands by the afternoon. Both armies used their artillery relentlessly, showering the already bare summit with high explosives, yet it did little but cause heavy losses among the infantry, Austrian and Italian alike. When the guns fell silent, the Austrians still occupied the peak of Mt. Santo, "the bloody mountain with the holy name," and the Italians remained where they had been at dawn, in trenches just below the ruins.

Despite such setbacks, Badoglio continued to believe that another ruthless attack would wreck the Austrian defenses and open the door to Mt. San Gabriele. To achieve this, he launched a final assault on the XVII Corps just after dark on May 20. The massive drive included every available battery and battalion, but in the end it achieved little. The Austrians, though exhausted, still held solid positions, and the II Corps was simply too tired and depleted to evict them. This last attack collapsed in bloody failure, reducing Badoglio's weary and ill-used forces to the breaking point. Capello now wisely decided to suspend the Army of Gorizia's offensive. It had accomplished all it could; continued efforts would be futile and costly.

Boroević was greatly relieved by the Italian halt. His forces had prevented a major Italian breakthrough, but only by the slimmest of margins. The Isonzo Army lost Hill 383, Kuk, and the summit of Vodice, but still held Mt. Santo. Boroević had no more reserves, no troops to spare. For Austria, the cost of the weeklong fight for the Bainsizza had been exorbitant: at least 30,000 casualties, more than 12,000 of them suffered by the XVII Corps, representing two-thirds of its rifle strength. In response to the bloodletting, the High Command—with Berlin's assent, of course—agreed to the dispatch of two more divisions from the Russian front to the Isonzo, but they would not arrive for a few weeks. In the meantime, the Isonzo Army would have to defend its positions with the troops it had.

Italian casualties during the weeklong drive on the Bainsizza had also been terrible. Certainly the Army of Gorizia lost more men than the Austrians did, but how many is not clear; it is known that the II Corps lost nearly 12,000 soldiers in the fight for Vodice alone. Gonzaga's 53rd Division, the conquerors of Vodice, no longer existed. Such suffering at least brought some visible gains, particularly the seizure of the Plava bridgehead, Kuk, and the summit of Vodice, victories that had eluded the Italian Army for two years. The Army of Gorizia had failed to capture Mt. Santo—the vital objective—but it had done well enough, and its troops certainly could not be faulted for lack of effort. Yet the end of the Bainsizza offensive represented not the end of the Tenth Battle, but only the completion of its first, northern phase. The second phase, which promised to prove decisive, was set to begin on the Carso. The hope of victory was again placed in the hands of the Duke of Aosta and his 3rd Army.

The second phase of the Tenth Battle of the Isonzo began at exactly 6 A.M. on May 23, when the massed guns and mortars of the 3rd Army opened fire, shattering the morning calm, shelling Austrian positions from the Vipacco to the Adriatic. It was the largest and most powerful barrage ever on the Isonzo, as lethal as any bombardment on any front during the entire Great War. Some 1,250 guns and nearly 600 mortars rained high explosives on every known Austrian entrenchment and position on the whole eleven-mile Carso front. To clear the way for its infantry, the 3rd Army had an artillery piece for every thirty feet of front, shelling almost nonstop. The Italian rate of fire on the Carso was a hundred thousand shells an hour. By the time the barrage lifted at 4 P.M., the 3rd Army had unleashed a million artillery shells at the Austrians, twenty shells for every foot of the front.

The impact of the barrage was devastating, far worse than anything experienced before. The Carso's defenders were well prepared to withstand bombardment, but this pushed many positions, and many soldiers, past the breaking point. As the plateau shook under the thunderous barrage, communications were disrupted and supply routes were destroyed. The Carso's frontline defenders—six divisions in the VII and XXIII Corps—were thrown badly off balance by the shelling, and there was little available to back them up; the Bainsizza battle had drained the Isonzo Army of virtually all its reserves. The battered regiments on the Carso would have to hold the line on their own, an apparently hopeless task.

When the Duke of Aosta's infantry went over the top at 4 P.M., it did so in overwhelming strength. Seventeen brigades advanced in the first wave, with another fourteen in the second echelon. The huge clouds of smoke and dust thrown up by the shelling covered their assault, and many Austrian trenches were overrun immediately. Riflemen and machine gunners tried desperately to resist, and in places took a heavy toll of the advancing *fanti*, but in many sectors the first line of defense began to unravel. Austrian setbacks came quickly on the Carso's southern half, where the Italian effort was particularly strong. Just east of Hill 144, the 16th Division, led by Mussolini's comrades of the 2nd *Bersaglieri* Brigade, overwhelmed the defending Austrian 2nd Infantry Regiment. The Transylvanian troopers, stunned by the barrage, reacted fatally slowly, and the regiment was drowned in the Italian tide. An entire battalion and the regimental headquarters were captured *en masse*.

The attackers suffered heavily, too, of course. In one ill-fated assault, the 4th Division's Barletta Brigade charged the village of Kostanjevica, whose *Honvéd* defenders returned a hail of machine gun and rifle fire. The attack cost the doomed brigade 2,700 dead and wounded in a matter of minutes. Yet the 3rd Army was achieving impressive gains farther south. The southern Carso's defenders, Schenk's XXIII Corps, were under strict orders from Boroević to hold their four defensive lines at any price; the fate of Trieste depended on it. The predominantly Hungarian soldiers resisted heroically but in most cases futilely. A battalion of the 7th Division held its positions against repeated assaults by the whole Italian 33rd Division, including the elite Grenadier Brigade, but in the end had to retreat with just a hundred soldiers remaining. Near the Adriatic coast, the 31st Regiment held on to Hill 77 through several assaults by the 45th Division, but it, too, was eventually forced to relinquish its trenches. A handful of survivors reached the Austrian lines later that evening. The XXIII Corps had no choice by nightfall but to reestablish itself on the third line of resistance, a retreat of a mile and a quarter. Tettoni's VII Corps, with its right flank on the Adriatic shore, registered the most impressive Italian gains on May 24. It forced the Austrians out of two defensive positions, destroyed several regiments, and captured the bulk of the 9,000 Austrian prisoners taken on the first day of the 3rd Army's offensive.

Capello's Army of Gorizia was by no means inactive on May 23. It launched several attacks on Austrian positions in the Vodice, Mt. Santo, and Gorizia sectors. Although its mission was secondary, mainly intended to draw Boroević's reserves away from the Carso, Capello's divisions went forward with determination. The drive enjoyed an impressive artillery barrage to soften its advance, followed by mass infantry attacks northeast of Gorizia. Every Italian effort was turned back with heavy casualties—the southern Bainsizza received powerful reinforcements in the days after May 20—but it served its purpose of drawing Boroević's attention away from the main offensive on the southern Carso.

Although Boroević was unsure where the main Italian blow was falling, he was absolutely sure that no ground should be given up without a fight to the finish. He was, typically, just as adamant that all lost ground be recaptured as soon as possible. To that end, he demanded that Schenk use his last reserves not to firm up his shaky defenses but to regain all lost positions. It was no less than a suicide mission. Hence May 24 and 25 saw huge and bloody fights all along the southern Carso as the armies vied for every trench line, position, and dugout. Austrian counterattacks were met with Italian counterstrokes until both sides were utterly exhausted. The murderous skirmishing achieved little—neither army gained notable ground—but it bled both forces white and drained the will and morale of *fantaccino* and *Frontkämpfer* alike.

On the morning of May 24, the understrength 7th Division attempted to push the Italian XIII Corps away from the town of Selo. The daring attack took several hills and startled the Italians, but stood no chance of lasting success. The Italians marshaled sufficient strength for their own counterattack, then steamrollered over the 7th Division. What little remained of the 7th tried heroically again the next day, but the effort quickly ended in disaster. By the afternoon of May 25, the 7th Division was gone: in forty-eight hours it went from a strength of 6,900 riflemen to just 1,700. The dismal story repeated itself a mile to the south, where the 16th Division, another loyal Hungarian formation, tried desperately to regain the ground it lost on the afternoon of May 23. Northeast of the town of Medeazza, the division sent several battalions forward in an attack against the 45th Division. The counterstroke worked better than most, registering one brilliant success. The 3rd Battalion of the 11th Regiment, a mostly

Czech outfit, advanced with just three understrength companies—240 men in all—under Captain Stanislaus Wieroński, an experienced Polish officer. Charging up rocky hills overlooking the Adriatic, the battalion made up in leadership and spirit what it lacked in numbers, for it quickly overran two weary battalions of *fanti*, netting six officers, 400 soldiers, and six machine guns as prisoners. But Wieroński was not content to stop there. He kept going, leading his battalion deeper into Italian-held territory. The opposing 45th Division, a very fine formation by any standards, was thoroughly exhausted, and hardly bothered to resist. By 6:30 P.M., Wieroński had captured thirty officers, 2,000 men, and nineteen machine guns, an entire regiment. Italian morale was clearly flagging, but the Austrians were in no condition to exploit it. Although Wieroński's counterattack was an impressive feat, one that provided the Isonzo Army with a badly needed boost to its own ailing morale, it did little to change the outcome of the battle. Wieroński's valor earned him a well deserved Knight's Cross of the Order of Maria Theresia, but despite his efforts the XXIII Corps was still barely hanging on. On the southern Carso, the 3rd Army was too tired to keep advancing, but the Austrians were no less exhausted. As a result, after two hard days of inconclusive brawling, both armies slowly ceased fighting.

May 26 saw minor skirmishes, but no attacks larger than battalion-sized, and by dawn of May 27 the fighting on the Carso had ebbed away. Both armies needed time to recuperate before entering battle again. Even so, the embers of the 3rd Army's offensive remained dangerously hot for the thousands of *fanti* in the front lines, and soldiers continued to die in futile attacks. One such was the failed May 26 assault of a battalion of the 45th Division across the narrow Timavo River on the Adriatic coast. The battalion commander, Major Giovanni Randaccio, led his unit in a suicidal charge against the Austrian trenches on the river's east bank. The plan of attack was devised by Randaccio and his assistant, the warrior-poet Gabriele D'Annunzio, who showed up on the Carso in time for the Tenth Battle and persuaded the major, his friend, to let him take part in the effort. The attack called for the whole battalion to cross the river on a single gangplank and rush the Austrian trenches head-on, a corpse-producing scheme if there ever was one. When the battalion's soldiers learned of the plan, they mutinied, shouting, "We no longer want to be brought to the slaughterhouse." The reckless D'Annunzio, outraged by the battalion's rebellion, ordered the unit decimated. The survivors were then led over the gangplank into Austrian machine gun fire, with the disastrous results the *fanti* had foreseen. Although the initial assault took several Austrian positions, it succeeded at great cost, and was soon nullified by the inevitable Austrian counterattack. Hence the battalion's assault gained nothing. Among the many Italian casualties was Major Randaccio, who fell mortally wounded while crossing the Timavo.[4] The southernmost sector of the Isonzo front then fell quiet.

The Tenth Battle was not yet ended, however. Although he now felt that a decisive breakthrough had eluded him, Cadorna still wanted to keep constant pressure on Boroević's tired army. The 3rd Army was utterly worn out, so Cadorna gave Capello the mission of harassing the Austrians with several limited attacks northeast of Gorizia. On May 26, the II Corps undertook a surprise night attack on Vodice, without artillery support. This effort made initial progress but, like all the others, failed to dislodge the Austrians from the mountain's east slope. After a pause on May 27, the Army of Gorizia tried again, sending strong forces against both Vodice and Mt. Santo and suffering serious losses, but this, too, gained no ground. By now forty-one Italian regiments on the Isonzo front had taken more than 50 percent casualties since the beginning of the Tenth Battle on May 13. The Austrians remained where they had been, well entrenched on Mt. Santo and on the eastern half of Vodice.

On May 28, the day that Cadorna called off his offensive, Boroević's forces resumed their attempts to regain their lost ground on the Carso. The Isonzo Army had begun to receive fresh troops from the Eastern front; the first outfit to arrive on the Carso was the Transylvanian 35th Division, which was soon committed to battle. Two more divisions were on the way, although they would not reach the Isonzo in time to fight in the Tenth Battle. A major counteroffensive on the Bainsizza was out of the question: it would require too many troops, and the new Austrian defenses appeared reassuringly solid. Besides, the real threat, as Boroević well knew, lay on the road to Trieste, the southern Carso. It was there that he concentrated his forces in the first days of June.

But first the Isonzo Army made a limited counterattack in the Gorizia area, both to reconquer some lost trench lines and to distract Cadorna's attention away from the Carso. The attack was a small affair, involving a single battalion assaulting a lone hill. The objective was San Marco, a strategically placed 750-foot-high rise immediately southeast of Gorizia. It was occupied by a well entrenched Italian battalion, so the odds of success were poor, at least on paper. Yet on the morning of June 3, the Austrians enjoyed both good fortune and excellent leadership.

The attacking unit was the 4th Battalion of the 39th Austrian Militia Regiment, a veteran Viennese outfit led by an outstanding officer, Captain Gustav Sonnewend. He had been born in remote Czernowitz, capital of Bukovina, thirty-two years before, but he had spent his formative years, including his school days, in Trieste and Gorizia, so he knew the local terrain well. Sonnewend, the son of an army doctor, had opted for a career in the infantry, making him something of an exception in the Habsburg Army: Although there were plenty of Jewish professional officers—the young Gustav had converted to Roman Catholicism, but was still ethnically considered a Jew—they were found mostly in the medical corps, like Gustav's father, not in the combat arms.[5] But Gustav had become a combat officer of great dedication and zeal. While serving with a

Slovak regiment earlier in the war, he fought in three Balkan campaigns and was twice decorated for valor. He came to the Isonzo in the summer of 1916, took over his militia battalion, and developed an excellent reputation: his most recent efficiency report considered him "in every respect an outstanding and efficient officer and battalion commander." He was liked and admired by his Viennese troops, who knew that Captain Sonnewend always led from the front.

Sonnewend and his militiamen in fact had already distinguished themselves during the Tenth Battle. On May 14, the first day of the Italian offensive, the 4th of the 39th was holding a position a mile northeast of Gorizia, where it was struck by a whole Italian brigade. Sonnewend's leadership and his soldiers' courage carried the day, sending the Emilia Brigade reeling back to its own lines in a shambles. The militiamen captured more than 600 prisoners and held every single position, a resounding success on a day that was otherwise grim for the Austrian Army. Sonnewend did even better three weeks later, at dawn on June 3. He led his battalion in a surprise bayonet charge up the slopes of San Marco, directly into the fire of Italian machine guns and rifles. Many Austrians were cut down on the hillside, but Sonnewend led the survivors to the summit, where they jumped into the trenches, grenades at the ready. Many *fanti* fought to the death, but others ran away; and some, after resisting for a time, proved quite willing to surrender. So after a brutal fight, by midmorning San Marco belonged to Sonnewend and his militiamen. The 4th of the 39th captured the hill, and ten officers and 500 men with it, most of the garrison.[6] The seizure of San Marco, though hardly a decisive battle, nevertheless was a valuable boost to the Isonzo Army's morale. Even more important, it revealed that among Cadorna's soldiers the spirit of victory had evaporated, and been replaced by resignation and even defeatism.

The same lesson became evident a day later when the Isonzo Army launched its counteroffensive on the southern Carso. Before dawn on June 4, the massed guns of the XXIII Corps opened fire on Italian positions along a three-mile front between Jamiano and the Adriatic. The barrage lasted just forty minutes, but made up in intensity and accuracy what it lacked in duration. When six Austrian assault battalions fixed bayonets and went over the top just before 5 A.M., they rushed the nearby Italian trenches, finding many of them wrecked and filled with shell-shocked *fanti* unwilling to fight. Although some units resisted, many simply folded. The entire forward line of the VII Corps began to collapse. By midmorning, the Austrians had advanced more than a third of a mile, captured all their objectives, and netted more than 7,000 prisoners. Even where Italian troops fought back with determination, the Austrians ultimately prevailed. Just a few hundred feet from the shores of the Adriatic—very near, in fact, where D'Annunzio led his ill-fated charge nine days earlier—the 28th Regiment assaulted Italian-held hillsides. Major Meergans's Prague regiment, two battalions strong, encountered stiff resistance from the 45th Division; the victors of Sabotino would not give up without a fight. Yet after several daring and costly attempts, the Czech troops crushed the *fanti* and occupied their entrenchments. The victory was bought at a dear price: 308 killed and 891 wounded, two-thirds of the brave regiment's strength. But the 28th had broken the 45th Division, capturing 3,000 men and forty machine guns, the better part of a brigade. The June 4 counterattack, although a local effort, was a resounding success and clearly showed that well led and well supported Austrian troops could overturn hard-won Italian gains: an old story, and for Cadorna an endlessly frustrating one. It also demonstrated that the Italian Army was showing painfully evident signs of strain and exhaustion, the result of so many bloody battles of attrition.

Unconcerned, Cadorna demanded that his armies regain the ground they lost so embarrassingly on June 4. With the approval of the Duke of Aosta, what remained of the VII Corps, helped by two fresh brigades, attacked at dawn. The counterstroke never really got off the ground; the *fanti*, tired veterans and raw recruits alike, went forward unenthusiastically and were repulsed bloodily. The Austrians again took many prisoners, Italian soldiers who simply wanted out of the war. The élan that Italian troops had displayed so many times on the Isonzo, even during the most hopeless attacks, had disappeared. Cadorna was furious. He now stood no chance of recapturing the lost positions. His armies were simply too exhausted and ill-used to keep attacking. Cadorna, of course, did not see that; he blamed defeatism and pacifist subversion instead. Most of all, he blamed his tired troops, who, he observed, "have not attacked as they ought to . . . they had no faith . . . they were indecisive." Even so, he knew he had to bring the battle to an end, to restore his forces back to fighting trim. By the evening of June 5 the Tenth Battle of the Isonzo was over.

The end of the great battle was greeted with profound relief at Boroević's headquarters and throughout the Isonzo Army. Although the Austrians had staged an impressive recovery, capped by daring and successful counterattacks, the overall outlook remained bleak. Defeating Cadorna's greatest offensive yet had nearly ruined the Isonzo Army. Boroević's polyglot legions held on to every strategically significant position, but the cost of resistance had reached new and appalling heights. Some 90,000 Austrian troops were lost from an overall rifle strength of 165,000: a casualty rate of nearly 60 percent. Worse, the casualty figures included 24,000 Austrian soldiers in Italian captivity, by far the largest number taken yet on the Isonzo, most of them captured in the first days of the Italian offensives. Although Boroević was not facing a morale crisis as severe as Cadorna's, there was no doubt that the Isonzo Army had nearly collapsed under the strain of an all-out Italian offensive. The spirit of the Austrian troops on the Isonzo was one not of triumph, but of resignation. Just as alarming, the material cost of the Tenth Battle had strained Austria's resources to the limit. During the battle, Boroević's artillery had fired 37,800 tons of munitions—some 2,000,000 shells. The expenditure of small arms ammunition was just as prodigious. In mid-1917, in the Great War's fourth year, Austria could not afford to keep fighting such *Materielschlachten*. Simply put, in human and economic terms Austria could not sustain many more such battles. One more prolonged Italian offensive, and the Isonzo Army might well break.

Cadorna was sure to deliver another offensive before long, but first he had to tend to his battered armies' many festering wounds and sores. From Cadorna's perspective, from his headquarters in Udine almost twenty miles behind the front lines, the Tenth Battle appeared a success. The May offensive was the closest thing to a victory since the fall of Gorizia and San Michele the previous August; in terms of territory gained, the Tenth Battle was the second most productive Italian effort since the war's beginning. After all, Capello's army[7] had seized the Plava bridgehead, Kuk, and the summit of Vodice, and had nearly taken Mt. Santo. Even the 3rd Army, despite setbacks in early June, had managed to occupy many Austrian positions on the southern Carso. Yet in human terms the Tenth Battle was a catastrophe. Cadorna's forces lost almost 160,000 soldiers—including 36,000 killed, 96,000 wounded and 27,000 captured—by the army's own admission, a figure that was surely an underestimate; the overall loss rate was roughly 60 percent, the same as Boroević's. Ominously, Cadorna's attacking forces lost 3,000 more prisoners than the defending Austrians, an almost unheard-of ratio. It signaled the ailing fighting spirit of the Italian Army. After two years of futile offensives, the Italian forces on the Isonzo were now showing unmistakable signs of widespread disillusionment and disaffection. Italy, fighting a one-front war, could still afford the massive expenditures of men and matériel that Cadorna's attritional offensives demanded. But by the summer of 1917 it was by no means clear that the army was willing to keep paying the appalling butcher's bill which invariably accompanied every offensive. Among the ordinary, doomed *fanti* who were the lifeblood and backbone of Italy's war effort, morale had plummeted to crisis levels, something that even Cadorna dimly suspected. The decisive issue was how much longer Cadorna's armies could be so ill-used before suffering a complete collapse of will. Upon this question the outcome of the war on the Isonzo, and the fate of Austria and Italy, too, ultimately rested.

ELEVEN

BAINSIZZA BREAKTHROUGH

In the wake of the Tenth Battle of the Isonzo, Italy's home front was no less demoralized than the armies at the front. Although Luigi Cadorna preferred to ignore domestic politics entirely, by the summer the situation had deteriorated so badly that even the High Command took notice. The bloodshed and deprivation of war, combined with Italy's perennial class warfare, had produced a volatile and discontented country. Germany's resumption of unrestricted submarine warfare, although principally aimed at Great Britain, hurt the other Allies, too. Italy, which imported so many raw materials and foodstuffs, was vulnerable to commerce raiding, and suffered accordingly. By the summer, coal imports had dropped to half their prewar level, and soon even bread was becoming scarce. This serious decline in basic standards of living inevitably resulted in protests, and eventually riots. Northern Italian cities were shaken by major disturbances, often led by women. In the worst case, rioting broke out in Turin and soon got out of control; to restore order, the army brought in heavy weapons, including machine guns, artillery, and armored cars. By the time order returned to Turin, forty-one protesters lay dead, and hundreds more were injured.

Although some citizens profited greatly from the war—the "sharks" so detested by the majority of Italians—most were impoverished by the seemingly interminable war on the Isonzo. Even industrial workers, who gained substantially (they were exempt from the draft, and had seen their real wages rise 27 percent since 1913), were tired of war-induced shortages. For the peasants, who made up the bulk of Italy's population, and whose husbands and sons formed the mass of Cadorna's ill-used infantry, the war was a disaster. In the face of spiraling wartime inflation, their meager wages evaporated. It was especially bad for the families of soldiers, to whom the war brought hardship, tragedy, and hunger. It was therefore no wonder that by July 1917 even the moderate Socialist deputy Claudio Treves proclaimed, "Out of the trenches before next winter." It would prove a memorable phrase. Even the Vatican spoke out publicly against the war. Pope Benedict XV, worried at the fate of his "beloved Italy" under the rigors of total war, called on August 1 for all belligerents to lay down their arms in favor of a "just and lasting peace." Benedict XV wanted not victory but an end to what he termed the "useless struggle" destroying Europe.

Although he was a devout Catholic, Cadorna managed to ignore even this papal plea for peace. He would listen to none of it.[1] Instead of discontent on the home front, he saw subversion and treason. He demanded that the government put an end to the disturbances before they got out of hand and endangered the war effort. Cadorna blamed the politicians, of course, and called for Rome to change "an internal policy that was ruinous for the army's discipline and morale." He wanted the government to apply the same ruthlessness at home that he had used with shirkers and defeatists on the Isonzo. But the government, led by the ancient and moderate Paolo Boselli, would do nothing of the kind.

Still, Cadorna was sure he could remedy the army's problems.[2] After the Tenth Battle, morale difficulties by no means disappeared. Many thousands of soldiers, aware of their chances of survival and angry at the civilians who sat out the war in comfort, simply wanted out. The number of troubling incidents was substantially on the rise. In July the Catanzaro Brigade, which had spilled much blood on the Isonzo, mutinied. Cadorna blamed the mutiny on socialists, defeatists, and a lack of discipline, and ordered it crushed brutally; the decimated brigade was soon returned to the line.[3] Seeing that, thousands of *fanti* opted for desertion instead of rebellion. The army's desertion rate, just 650 soldiers per month in 1915, rose to 5,500 by midsummer 1917. There was little Cadorna thought to do except enforce ever harsher and more unbending discipline. Terror had kept the army in the field for more than two years, and Cadorna saw no reason to moderate his routine punishments.

In an attempt to shore up army morale and deliver a badly needed victory, Cadorna undertook a local offensive on the Tyrolean front just following the Tenth Battle of the Isonzo. On June 9 the 6th Army attacked Austrian positions around Mt. Ortigara, on the Asiago plateau, the rugged, mountainous border between Austria and Italy. The battle pitted the elites of both armies against each other: the crack Austrian III "Iron" Corps versus several divisions of highly trained *Alpini*. The two-week battle was vicious, fought on a front of little more than a mile, but ultimately inconclusive. Mt. Ortigara changed hands several times, but in the end both armies were pretty much where they had started on June 9. The cost, however, was frightful, even by Great War standards. The Austrian III Corps took 10,000 casualties, but the Italians suffered far more, at least 23,000. The all-*Alpini* 52nd Division was completely destroyed, losing almost 16,000 men on the mile-wide battlefield. The pointless offensive sacrificed thousands of Italy's best-trained troops; among the *fanti*, Ortigara became known as "the calvary of the green flames." Needless to say, the offensive hardly helped army morale.

That said, there were a few positive developments in the Italian Army during the summer of 1917. The most important of these involved the raising of special assault troops to lead attacks. In the spring, the High Command at Udine received word of special Austrian assault detachments. Following her German ally's lead, Austria's army experimented with *Sturmtruppen*, elite companies of selected veteran soldiers. These young and fit volunteers were given more heavy weapons (machine guns, light mortars), improved tactical training, and better rations and pay. Their mission was to lead the way in attacks; their advanced tactics, heavy firepower, and superior training would enable them to overcome stiff resistance. They quickly became the *corps d'élite* of the Habsburg Army. Initial combat experience with these crack units in mid-1917 was very positive, and the program was expanded. By the end of 1917, every Austrian division was scheduled to have its own battalion of *Sturmtruppen*.

Cadorna and his staff were impressed by what they heard about these Austrian assault units. Highly motivated, well trained units of brave volunteers seemed just what the increasingly demoralized Italian Army needed to lead it in battle. As the Austrian experience indicated, such elite companies were worth far more to an offensive than their small numbers suggested. They offered at least a partial solution to the army's morale problems. Therefore in July, Cadorna authorized the raising of a first, experimental unit, the 1st Assault Battalion (*I reparto d'assalto*). It was placed under Luigi Capello's 2nd Army, and selected its men from among the many young, ardent volunteers who came forward to serve in the new unit.

The *reparto d'assalto* was no larger than a conventional infantry battalion, but was much more powerful: it had twice the number of heavy machine guns, and six times the number of light machine guns, as a line unit; and it had many more light mortars, as well as a pair of light infantry guns to provide portable direct fire support. Each of the battalion's three assault companies was armed with eight machine guns and hundreds of grenades. The battalion commander, Major Giuseppe Alberto Bassi, trained his men to be recklessly, even fanatically, brave. The soldiers, soon known universally as the "daring ones" (*arditi*) exuded an aura of courage and violence. Bassi devised a distinct uniform for his elite troops, including special Alpine trousers and a black shirt, tie, and fez. The young soldiers all carried fighting knives (*pugnali*), too, a symbol of their willingness to fight hand to hand. Italy had its newest crack corps, the "black flames," to assist in its struggle against Austria. The *arditi* would not have long to wait to prove their reckless daring.

Cadorna decided to attempt another Isonzo offensive in mid-August. Despite the terrible losses suffered in May, the army continued to grow. The factories turned out weapons and munitions in record numbers, and the early call-up of the conscript class of 1898 gave the army the fresh blood it needed to bring its depleted regiments up to strength. These nineteen year-old *ragazzi de '98* would see an early baptism of fire on the Bainsizza. During the summer Cadorna added six new infantry divisions, as well as dozens of heavy batteries and ample ammunition reserves, to his still-growing legions. The count was confident that the Austrians could not withstand another all-out blow. To crack Boroević's defenses once and for all, in early August, Cadorna sent fifty-one divisions and 5,200 artillery pieces—three-quarters of the entire Italian Army—to the banks of the Isonzo.

There were alliance pressures on Cadorna, too. The spring and summer did not go well for the Allies. In mid-April, France attempted an enormous offensive against German forces along the Aisne River. The new chief of staff, Robert Nivelle, amassed 1,200,000 soldiers for this effort, which he promised repeatedly and publicly would be a war-winner. Yet the Chemin des Dames offensive enjoyed little success, and instead quickly stalled, ending in the stalemate and slaughter that had become commonplace on the Western front and the Isonzo. Nivelle's hollow assurances of victory lowered morale to unprecedented depths. French infantrymen, disgusted at the heavy casualties and ill treatment, revolted. The mutinies spread throughout the army; only rapid intervention by General Philippe Pétain, the hero of Verdun, restored discipline and saved the army from complete dissolution.

The Russian front looked even worse for the Allies. The February revolution overthrew the Tsar and led to a provisional government under Alexander Kerensky. This new regime assured its worried Allies that it would continue the war faithfully. But the provisional government proved too weak and divided to keep the army at the front. Desertion and mutinies became commonplace as tired and hungry soldiers threw down their weapons in disgust. Russia attempted one last offensive in East Galicia in July. It was directed by Alexei Brusilov, who had nearly destroyed the Austrian Army the previous summer. The July push initially went well, forcing local Austrian withdrawals, but Russia was now too strained and divided to sustain a major offensive. Rapid German intervention kept Brusilov's armies at bay in East Galicia, and by August the Russians were in headlong retreat. Soon the Russian Army began to dissolve, leading the Bolsheviks under Lenin to attempt a coup. This first Bolshevik revolt failed, but within four months Lenin and his cohorts would succeed, taking Russia out of the war.

The only optimistic development for the Allies was the entry of the United States into the war on the Allied side on April 6. America's enormous economic might and virtually limitless manpower reserves guaranteed ultimate Allied victory, yet in the short term America's entry meant little. Certainly it would take many months for America to raise, equip, and dispatch an expeditionary force to fight in Europe, and it would be at least a year before an independent American army could take the field in France. Therefore the Allies were still on their own for many months to come. Hence the pressure on Cadorna to act was considerable. Exhausted Russia pleaded with him to launch an offensive on the Isonzo to distract the Austrians from Galicia. France, too, was hoping for a major Italian push to keep the pressure on the Central Powers. By August, Cadorna was ready to go on the offensive again.

The plan of attack, slated to begin on August 18, was simple. Its main goal was the seizure of the Bainsizza plateau, the last obstacle to a breakthrough north and east of Gorizia. Cadorna allowed his two army commanders, Capello and the Duke of Aosta, considerable latitude in their planning: He gave them no written orders, instead leaving the tactical and operational details up to them. The main role in the Eleventh Battle would be played by Capello's 2nd Army. He considered his most important mission to be the capture of the strategically indispensable Tolmein bridgehead, with its railhead. The secondary mission was overrunning the whole Bainsizza plateau and taking Mt. Santo and Mt. San Gabriele. To achieve this, Capello's heavily reinforced 2nd Army possessed six corps with twenty-six divisions, backed up by 2,070 guns (half of them heavy calibers, some of them in British and French batteries loaned to Italy for the offensive) and almost a thousand mortars. This awesome force included numerous crack battalions of *Bersaglieri* and *Alpini* (and the *reparto d'assalto*), and enough ammunition to guarantee a major breakthrough.

The Duke of Aosta's 3rd Army was assigned a secondary mission, as in the Tenth Battle. It was to support Capello's forces by drawing Austrian divisions away from the Bainsizza; naturally, it was to gain any ground on the Carso it could. The duke's *Terza Armata* was reinforced to include twenty divisions and 1,350 guns and 756 mortars, divided among six corps. This was not enough to reach Trieste, but it was surely sufficient to exhaust the half-dozen Austrian divisions on the Carso. Cadorna also had six more divisions in a special reserve, to be committed wherever he decided. In August 1917 the Italian Army suffered from grave morale and discipline problems, but by any standards the Eleventh Battle promised to be a hard fight. The army at Cadorna's disposal— 530,000 infantrymen (1,246,000 soldiers in all) on a thirty-mile front—was almost twice the size of the whole Italian Army in 1915, and nearly four times bigger than Cadorna's forces in the First Battle. The coming epic battle would be one of the mightiest offensives undertaken by any army during the Great War.

It was precisely this numerical imbalance that so worried Svetozar Boroević and his staff at Adelsberg. The Isonzo Army had reached a strength of twenty divisions (fifteen in the line and five held in reserve) supported by 1,526 guns and howitzers. Including all available units and weapons, the Austrians on the

Isonzo were outnumbered almost three-to-one in infantry and four-to-one in weight of shell. Worse, most Austrian divisions were somewhat short of men, and few had adequate ammunition reserves. After the Tenth Battle, three of Boroević's most exhausted divisions (including the 7th and 16th, destroyed on the southern Carso) were sent to the Russian front, their places taken by three new arrivals from the East. Yet these reinforcing divisions were not in first-rate fighting trim, and none of them had any experience fighting the Italians; the coming battle would be their initiation to Cadorna's merciless methods. Boroević also knew that he could expect no help from the High Command. Russia's Galician offensive in July had drained Austria's limited reserve pool, so there was nothing more to send to the Isonzo. Bosco would have to hold off the Italians with the forces he had, a daunting task.

By mid-August the Isonzo Army was sure a major Italian offensive was coming soon. Boroević's intelligence staff, in fact, predicted an Italian push in late July, but it failed to arrive, giving the Austrians three more weeks to prepare. Despite Italian efforts at concealment and deception, it was obvious that the 2nd and 3rd Armies were gearing up for an attack. Austrian observers noted greater troop and rail traffic all along the front, as well as increased Italian overflights by reconnaissance aircraft. Austrian suspicions were confirmed by the confessions of numerous Italian deserters. Starting in early August, dozens of scared *fanti* crossed the lines daily, in a desperate attempt to avoid the imminent bloodletting. These groups of deserters, sometimes whole units reaching the Austrian trenches, were sent to the rear, to safety with the order "*nach Mauthausen*."[4] Examining deserters' accounts and other intelligence, Isonzo Army headquarters correctly anticipated an Italian attack on August 18.

There were other indicators, too. As the start of the offensive approached, Italian air raids grew larger and more daring. There were too few Austrian pursuit aircraft on the Isonzo to defeat the Italian air offensive. On several occasions Italian bombers attacked Austrian headquarters and supply sites, particularly on the Bainsizza plateau, sometimes with devastating results. On August 11 Italian aircraft struck an ammunition dump at Grapa, southeast of Tolmein. The raid destroyed the base, the main Austrian munitions site on the upper Isonzo, causing a huge explosion. The same day, a few miles to the south on the central Bainsizza, Italian aircraft bombed and strafed XXIV Corps headquarters, forcing General von Lukas and his staff to flee from Čepovan to Lokve. Austria attempted to retaliate. Emperor Karl, who regularly meddled in military affairs, this time permitted a large-scale air raid on Italian bases at Venice; he usually forbade any bombing that might endanger civilians.[5] Thirty-eight Austrian bombers took off from bases in the Isonzo valley on August 14, with Emperor Karl's blessing, headed for Venice. Yet fate intervened as the squadrons were beaten and knocked off course by severe winds and unexpected rainstorms. Only eleven aircraft reached Venice, and two of them were shot down. The raid caused no appreciable damage to any Italian bases. In all, for Austria it seemed a bad omen for the impending battle.

The artillery preparation began early on August 18, four hours before sunrise. From Mrzli vrh to the Adriatic, 5,000 Italian guns, howitzers, and mortars cascaded fire on Austrian positions. The noise was deafening, the feeling awesome, as the earth shook all along the Isonzo. Both Cadorna and Boroević clearly heard the explosions at their headquarters, a safe distance from the front lines. Thirty miles of Austrian entrenchments, carefully reconstructed since early June, were torn into ruin as heavy shells ripped through all but the deepest dugouts and positions. Communications and supplies were cut off by the barrage, so it was impossible for Boroević's divisional and corps commanders to gain a coherent picture of what was happening to their units. As the tempo of the bombardment increased with first light, the plight of the Austrian infantry grew grimmer still. Pounded by hundreds of shells a minute, parched by the August sun, the doomed *Frontkämpfer* could only hide in their trenches and wait for it to end, for the real battle to begin.

The lead Italian infantry did not leave their positions until late in the evening, after the shells had done their deadly work. The first wave was the 2nd Army's XXIV Corps, whose mission was crossing the Isonzo and unlocking the northern Bainsizza's defenses. Its commander was the veteran Lieutenant General Enrico Caviglia, an energetic and decisive leader. Its two divisions in the front line, the 47th and 60th, were tough, battle-hardened formations that knew the Isonzo and the Austrians well. Both divisions were backed up generously with artillery—an average of seventy guns per division, plus many more heavy guns and howitzers farther back—as well as engineers for crossing and bridging the fast-moving river. The XXIV Corps knew the sector well, with its steep river banks and numerous Austrian entrenchments on the hills overlooking the east side. But Caviglia had studied the northern Bainsizza rigorously, helped by the revelations of a Czech junior officer who defected to the Italians in early August. Caviglia and his staff knew how the Austrians were arrayed, where their defenses were, and how to defeat them. The diligent corps commander, an exceptional officer by Italian standards, ensured that his assault troops were well trained and prepared for battle. By the early hours of August 19, the XXIV Corps was ready.

The northern Bainsizza's defenders were no match for Caviglia's elite corps. The Isonzo's east bank and the steep hills behind it were the responsibility of Major General Karl Haas's 21st Rifle Division, a recent arrival on the Italian front. The 21st Division had had a bad war. This mostly Czech formation, recruited in western Bohemia, mobilized in July 1914 and was sent to the Serbian front. Through no fault of its own, the poorly trained division was mauled by experienced Serb regiments at the Battle of Valjevo in mid-August 1914. The defeat was a humiliation for Austria, causing a general retreat from Serb soil, and it gave the Allies the first victory of the Great War. Ever after, the 21st Division fought with this black mark on its reputation. The division kept fighting on the Serbian front for the rest of 1914—suffering 120 percent casualties by Christmas—and was then transferred to the East. Like many Austrian formations, the 21st absorbed terrible losses in the frozen Carpathians in early 1915, and again in Galicia in the summer of 1916. Because the Czechs had little desire to fight the Russians, morale sometimes plummeted to dangerously low levels, and desertion was an all too common problem. The battle-scarred Czech division was sent to the Isonzo during the summer of 1917 because Boroević was desperate for troops, no matter their quality. The 21st, about a quarter under strength, was placed on the rugged northern end of the Bainsizza plateau, heretofore a quiet sector due to its steep riverbanks and lack of good roads. The Italian offensive of August 19 therefore came as a rude shock to the tired soldiers of the 21st Division.

Caviglia's two assault divisions crossed the fog-enshrouded Isonzo in assault boats between Loga and Descla, a front of three miles. On the southern flank, just above the Plava bridgehead, the 60th Division made slow progress against the Czech defenders, taking heavy casualties during the river crossing. The 47th Division achieved greater success upstream, quickly overrunning the Austrian defenses near the river's edge, particularly at the town of Canale. The 47th Division, with its two full brigades of *Bersaglieri*, secured the east bank by dawn. The "red flames" lived up to their hard-won reputation for audacity, attacking with their trademark élan and capturing several major Austrian positions and their defenders. By midmorning, the 47th's engineers had built six bridges across the Isonzo, and the victorious *Bersaglieri* were heading uphill into the heart of the Bainsizza plateau.

Major General Haas had little idea what was happening to his division. His telephone lines had been cut by Italian shelling, but he knew something ominous was developing, so he decided to act without any reliable intelligence. He sent his only reserve, the 28th Rifle Regiment, to the Isonzo, in the desperate hope of restoring the front line. The all-Czech 28th Rifles fought hard through the day in a doomed effort to keep the XXIV Corps at bay, but by the evening of August 19 the cause was lost. The 21st Division sustained such heavy losses so early that it stood no chance of re-forming and fighting again on the Bainsizza. Isolated companies of the 28th Rifles resisted through the night, until the early morning of August 20. In the end they were surrounded on all sides by *Bersaglieri*, and then annihilated. After just twenty-four hours, the 21st Rifle Division was no more, and the northern edge of the Bainsizza plateau was in Italian hands.

Yet Capello's offensive was not successful everywhere. Divisions to the north and south of Caviglia's victorious XXIV Corps encountered stiff Austrian resistance. Immediately upstream from the 47th Division, the 22nd Division had managed to secure the Isonzo's east bank, but only at a great cost. The sector was defended by just two undermanned and overstretched Hungarian militia battalions, but the river crossing proved trying. The first wave included troops of the 1st Assault Battalion. Major Bassi's intrepid *reparto d'assalto* went into battle for the first time and garnered a reputation for valor and efficiency. The *arditi* crossed the Isonzo successfully, capturing several Austrian trenches and 500 prisoners, but the rest of the 22nd Division had a hard fight. By midday on August 19, it was across the river securely, after taking heavy losses, but its march inland proved arduous.

Farther upstream, Capello's divisions fared worse. The 2nd Army's first objective was the Tolmein bridgehead, but the strong Austrian defenses there showed themselves to be as resilient as ever. The attacking Italian army corps, the XXVII, had been raised only in late July under Lieutenant General Vanzo, and had enjoyed little time to organize and prepare itself for battle. It had plenty of men and artillery, including 326 guns and 131 mortars, but it fought clumsily, and Vanzo showed himself to be an indecisive leader. The 19th Division assaulted the tiny Tolmein bridgehead, but won no ground. The division was stalled by accurate machine gun and artillery fire, suffering grave casualties while winning no noticeable gains.

The story was the same on the lower Bainsizza, where Pietro Badoglio's II Corps attempted to break out of the recently conquered Plava bridgehead and seize the summit of Mt. Santo. Just east of Hill 383, the 3rd Division tried to advance. This division, which fought impressively in May, went forward with its Udine Brigade on the left and the Florence Brigade on the right, exactly as at the outset of the Tenth Battle. This time the Italian attack ended in disaster. Determined Austrian militia companies of the 106th Division cut down repeated waves of *fanti*, and Badoglio's drive met with complete failure. The 3rd Division incurred crippling casualties; the neighboring Girgenti Brigade lost 2,000 soldiers on August 19 alone. It was a black day for the II Corps, a sad contrast with its celebrated success in May. Similarly, the 8th Division charged up the slopes of Mt. Santo at dawn in a determined and costly assault on the ruins at the peak, yet its Avellino and Forlì brigades failed to reach the summit. East of Gorizia, Capello's divisions met equally stiff resistance. The weight of the VI Corps failed utterly to make any impression on the Austrians at the summit of Mt. San Gabriele, and the VIII Corps likewise stalled before Erwin Zeidler's tenacious 58th Division. Despite valiant efforts and a decisive numerical superiority, except on the northern Bainsizza, Capello's army made little progress on August 19.

On the morning of August 19, the Duke of Aosta's four army corps joined the battle. A dozen reinforced Italian divisions assaulted the Carso's defenses, supported generously by heavy artillery, including several efficient British batteries. Most of the 3rd Army's attacks were blunted by the strong Austrian defenses, but on the central Carso the Austrian line was soon in danger. The central sector, immediately west of the village of Selo, was defended by Major

General Stanislaus von Puchalski's 12th Division, another recent arrival on the Isonzo. Up to mid-1917 this mostly Polish division had spent the entire war fighting the Russians. In general the West Galician 12th had performed competently, save for an embarrassing collapse during Alexei Brusilov's breakthrough in July 1916. The 12th Division never fully recovered from this defeat, and it arrived on the Italian front a year later short of trained officers and men. On the morning of August 19, the West Galicians were hit by two strong divisions of the XXIII Corps, and the 12th soon began to lose ground. It bravely tried to hold the front line, but the effort was hopeless; by midday the shell-shocked division had retreated to its second defensive position. An afternoon counterattack to restore the line collapsed bloodily, wiped out by torrents of Italian artillery and machine gun fire. By evening the scattered remnants of the 12th Division had retreated to the third defensive position. Selo was lost. Austrian troops on the southern Carso were harassed by intense shelling by long-range heavy batteries. The bombardment caused considerable damage, including the destruction of the main coastal rail line, which ran from Trieste to the front. The barrage was assisted by British and Italian ships that fired through the day at numerous Austrian coastal targets, including Trieste. Austrian coast artillery returned fire but was unable to silence the Allied guns, either at sea or on land.

Boroević was alarmed by the Italian success on the northern reaches of the Bainsizza plateau, but as August 19 came to a close, he was relatively optimistic. Except for the retreat of the 12th Division before Selo, his forces on the Carso had held their ground and inflicted heavy casualties on the attackers, as had his divisions northeast of Gorizia. Even the unenviable fate of the 21st Division did not seem particularly dramatic or decisive. Boroević had little information about the poor condition of the 21st, and was unaware how critical the situation on the northern Bainsizza had become. He sent some of his precious and scarce reserves to the Bainsizza to reestablish the first line of defense, but not with great alarm.

Only on the morning of August 20 did Boroević realize how serious the crisis had become. The battle's second day began with more Italian shelling, concentrated heavily on the northern Bainsizza. The hammer blows of hundreds of Italian guns and mortars finished off what little was left of the 21st Rifle Division. The crushing Italian barrage also prevented reserves from reaching the Czech riflemen, so the shaky Austrian front line collapsed on the upper plateau. Only a thin line of scattered and diverse battalions was left on the northern half of the Bainsizza, barely enough to hold on to the ramshackle second defensive line and certainly too little to overturn any Italian gains. Yet, for the moment these troops were enough to stop any Italian breakthrough. Capello, who was often so reckless in his expenditure of human life, at this moment chose to be cautious. Like Cadorna, the commander of the 2nd Army was sud-

denly overcome by caution, and decided to wait and consolidate his forces before launching an all-out drive on the Bainsizza. On August 20, when there was
little to stop them, Capello's divisions advanced slowly and cautiously.
Caviglia's XXIV Corps, which easily could have marched into the very center
of the plateau, instead spent the day mopping up Austrian resistance and securing its flanks.

Capello's other corps achieved even less on August 20. At the strategic
Tolmein bridgehead, XXVII Corps units again failed to advance, and the II
Corps gained precious little ground on the central Bainsizza. Badoglio's divisions could not advance past Vodice's summit, and made no headway on Mt.
Santo. Although all these failed efforts cost many Italian lives, August 20 was a
lost day for Capello, and for Italy. The 2nd Army squandered one of the greatest
opportunities of the whole Isonzo fighting, indeed of the entire war. Capello's
fatal caution—a decision that Cadorna supported—deprived his army of a
rapid and decisive victory, and gave the Austrians badly needed time to shore
up their creaking defenses.

The Duke of Aosta threw away several opportunities on the Carso, too. August 20 was another day of harsh fighting on the Carso, begun with both Italian
assaults and Austrian counterstrokes. The 3rd Army's renewal of its offensive
won little ground, but it destroyed all of Boroević's attempts to regain lost positions. A dawn counterattack by the tattered 12th Division ended catastrophi-
cally, disrupted and then annihilated by a simultaneous Italian attack. The last
elements of Puchalski's 12th Division retreated in chaos, causing units of the
neighboring 48th Division to withdraw, too. A counterattack by the 35th Division on the southern Carso was likewise cut short, crushed by heavy Italian
coastal artillery and naval gunfire (including shelling by two Royal Navy moni-
tors). Yet the 3rd Army took no advantage of the potentially decisive Austrian
setbacks. The Duke of Aosta, though not as fatally cautious as Capello, still
failed to convert these Austrian reverses into Italian gains. Nowhere did 3rd
Army units charge into the growing gaps in the creaking Austrian lines; the Italians still had not learned the art of the counterattack, a well honed—and frequently decisive—Austrian tactic. Timidity, not audacity, again prevailed, with
disastrous consequences for Italy and her army battling on the Isonzo.

Indeed, the Italian forces on the Isonzo were clearly in difficult circumstances. By the evening of August 20, Boroević's beleaguered divisions had
captured 5,600 Italian prisoners. These captives, taken from forty different brigades, were a shocking indication of the fragility of Italian morale: it was unknown for an attacking army to lose so many prisoners so early in an offensive.
Even so, Boroević was in no position to take advantage of his enemy's weakness. On the evening of August 20, his own predicament appeared precarious
enough. He was already out of reserves, and he could not expect that Capello's
cautiousness would last much longer. Boroević and his staff knew that another

major Italian drive was imminent, and there was nothing to stop it but raw courage.

Fortunately for Boroević and for Austria, the Isonzo Army still displayed courage in abundance. Even against hopeless odds, platoons, companies, and even whole battalions fought to the last man, denying the Italians an easy victory. The dogged Austrian resistance continued undulled on August 21, when the 3rd Army attempted to break through on the Carso at several points. The main Italian drive was aimed at several hills on the southern plateau, the last natural obstacles between the 3rd Army and Trieste. The greatest of these was Mt. Hermada, "the unconquerable beast," a 1,060-foot-high rise overlooking the Adriatic, dominating the whole southern edge of the Carso and crisscrossed with Austrian entrenchments. So far, the 3rd Army had enjoyed no success here, but on August 21 the duke's divisions pushed hard up against the rocky, barren slopes of Hermada. Throughout the day, two Italian corps mixed it up with troops from three Habsburg divisions in vicious fighting; the battle raged between the first and third Austrian defensive positions, with neither army gaining a decisive advantage. The last remnants of the 12th Division were wiped out in this fight around Flondar, so the West Galicians' place in the line was taken by the Czech 9th Division after nightfall.

By then the Austrian main line of resistance had been restored, thanks to the efforts of the Transylvanian 35th Division. Its 63rd Regiment, a three-quarters Romanian unit, bore the brunt of the battle and helped turn the tide in the Austrians' favor.[6] The 63rd had been punished badly by the Italians for three days, losing several positions around Hill 146 and taking notable casualties. Its companies were weak and scattered, many of them out of contact with regimental headquarters.

The 17th Company was one of these. It had been struck very hard for several days, virtually without rest, by Italian infantry and artillery. The company had lost two *kavernen* on Hill 146, where many of its soldiers were trapped. Worse, it was surrounded on three sides by *fanti*, completely out of contact with regimental headquarters, and down to just thirty men, less than a platoon. But the 17th Company was not ready to give up. Its young commander, First Lieutenant Friedrich Franek, was unwilling to surrender and remained determined to rescue his trapped soldiers.

Fritz Franek, though only twenty-six years old, was a very experienced officer and company commander. The son of a Viennese baker, Franek graduated from infantry cadet school in 1910 and joined the 63rd Regiment in 1913 as a junior lieutenant. He had fought with his regiment since the beginning of the war, and was gravely wounded in the first weeks of the 1914 Galician campaign, receiving a near-fatal bullet wound to the neck and mouth during the battle for Lemberg. After several months' convalescence, Franek returned to the 63rd, leading his company through the Carpathians, and was again wounded, taking a bullet to the head. Yet Franek miraculously survived, indeed recovered, and was back on the Russian front by the fall of 1915. He was laid low by typhus early in 1916, requiring another extended hospital stay. The battle-scarred lieutenant had garnered a reputation for heroism, demonstrated by the several decorations he had already received, and resumed command of his company, the 17th, in June 1916. Franek accompanied it to the Isonzo a year later, and the Eleventh Battle was his baptism of fire against the Italians. It began badly enough, with his company and his regiment overrun by Italian assaults, but Franek kept a cool head and saved his trapped men, as well as the entire Flondar position, by acting on his own initiative and leading his depleted company against the entrenched Italians. The odds seemed hopeless, but the surprise attack caught the *fanti* off balance, and the panic-stricken Italians soon began to retreat before the thirty bayonet-wielding Romanians and their Viennese lieutenant. The daring counterstroke freed the 17th Company, and by the afternoon, after hard fighting with grenades and bayonets, Franek had retaken the two lost *kavernen* and liberated his trapped soldiers. By the time the Italians regrouped and reacted, the 63rd Regiment had restored its defenses on Hill 146. Flondar, the gateway to Hermada, was again securely in Austrian hands.[7]

Franek was not the only Austrian soldier to win the coveted Knight's Cross on the Carso that fateful day. Three miles to the north, in the VII Corps sector, the veteran 17th Division was barely holding on in the face of repeated Italian attacks. The Austrian defenses depended, as usual, on the control of several hills. The most important of these in the 17th Division's sector was Hill 378, near Fajti hrib. There, tired troops of the Hungarian 46th and 39th Regiments, which had lost so many men on the Carso for more than two years, fought to preserve the line. The peak of 378 was in the hands of the 4th Battalion of the 39th Regiment, led by Major Konstantin Popovici. The forty-five-year-old major, a Romanian from south Hungary like many of the men under him, had been a soldier most of his life. Popovici had served the Habsburgs for nearly thirty years, but his career had been rather ordinary; certainly there was nothing in his service record to suggest any greatness. Yet, on August 21 Konstantin Popovici led his beleaguered battalion with remarkable courage and tenacity. All day, Italian regiments of the XXV Corps assaulted Hill 378, the center point of the Italian offensive, and each time they were repulsed with heavy losses. Popovici ensured that his men stayed in their positions, even under the fiercest shelling, and he was always visible. Each failed Italian attack was met with a sudden Austrian counterstroke led by Popovici. By the end of the terrible day, the Italians were exhausted, and the shell-scarred Hill 378, draped with Italian corpses, still belonged to a much depleted and very weary battalion of the 39th Regiment. Popovici's leadership prevented a 3rd Army breakthrough on the upper Carso, a feat that entitled the major to wear the Order of Maria Theresia. Twice on the Carso on August 21, Boroević's outnumbered troops yet again demonstrated the decisive impact of outstanding leadership and courage on even the most technology-dominated battlefields.

Capello's army was more successful north of Gorizia, showing that the Italians, too, could fight bravely and victoriously. On the morning of August 21, the Forlì Brigade assaulted the Dol saddle, a 1,500-foot-high rocky bridge between Vodice and Mt. Santo. The defenders, a battalion each of Croats and Slovenes, fought hard, but were badly shaken by sustained Italian shelling and aerial bombardment. In the afternoon, after savage hand-to-hand fighting, the Austrians abandoned the Dol saddle, and the Italians controlled the land bridge between Vodice and Mt. Santo. The latter peak remained in Austrian hands, but the loss of the saddle severely undermined the Habsburg defenses. It was now only a matter of time before Capello's troops marshaled sufficient strength to overrun Mt. Santo and push past Vodice.

Capello ordered another major push on the upper Bainsizza for August 21. It promised to be the all-out drive he failed to execute twenty-four hours before. Caviglia's XXIV Corps, brought up to strength with two fresh brigades, would attack, assisted by Badoglio's II Corps, both backed up by considerable heavy artillery. After a thunderous early morning bombardment, the offensive got off to a slow start due to poor infantry-artillery cooperation. However, once coordination was restored by midmorning, the Italians advanced rapidly. The northern Bainsizza's defenders, mainly isolated companies of Austrian militia, as well as some scattered survivors of the 21st Rifle Division, soon gave way. Against so many Italian men and guns, there was no hope. The new Austrian defensive line was an extended mountain ridge a little more than a mile behind the Isonzo. The 2,200-foot-high forested ridge offered excellent natural defenses, but General Lukas's XXIV Corps had too few troops to hold it. Capello's reinforced divisions were now firmly across the Isonzo, and there was little to stop them. By midafternoon most of the Austrians had been forced from the ridge, blasted off by Italian guns and pushed aside by onrushing battalions of *fanti*. As night approached, the northwest Bainsizza plateau belonged to the Italians, and the gap in the Austrian lines was nearly a mile wide.

Ironically, General Lukas was not overly concerned. He remained calm, unaware of how grave the crisis now was, and fully confident that the line could be restored. Boroević had sent him a fresh reserve division from the Carso front, the 73rd, an experienced mountain formation. But, because of a shortage of trucks, the 73rd would not reach Lukas's front lines until the early hours of August 23. The mountain troops were marching to the plateau on tired feet, up the Bainsizza's narrow mountain paths. The journey took more than twenty-four hours. By then it would be too late to save the Bainsizza.

Capello also was rushing reserves to the northern Bainsizza. He knew that at last he had torn a gaping hole in the Austrian defenses, a success that demanded fresh troops to reinforce victory. Capello ordered his reserve, the XIV Corps, two divisions strong, into the gap. The two fresh divisions would exploit the 2nd Army's success and drive into the heart of the Bainsizza plateau. Significantly, Italy's automotive industry had supplied Capello with hundreds of Fiat trucks, enough to move the XIV Corps into the line far quicker than Austrian reserves could arrive to stop it. Hence, by the morning of August 22, the XIV Corps had taken its place in the fighting line, just north of Caviglia's XXIV Corps, and was ready to march on Čepovan, on the eastern edge of the Bainsizza plateau.

August 22, the decisive day of the Eleventh Battle, started with a very potent Italian bombardment of the Bainsizza plateau. The withering barrage sapped the strength of the hopelessly outnumbered Austrian defenders. When Capello's infantry advanced, after the artillery had completed its deadly work, it met only scattered resistance. Several surrounded Austrian battalions fought back with undulled determination, but most units either retreated or surrendered. Indeed, in many places the Italians encountered only trenches filled with hundreds of Austrian dead and wounded. The defenders of the central plateau, the 106th Militia Division, were exhausted from four days of hard fighting, and were unable to hold their wrecked positions. By the afternoon, Capello's forward detachments had overrun the entire Austrian front line, had captured thousands of prisoners, and were moving far inland, into the very center of the densely forested plateau.

By the evening of August 22, Boroević knew he was facing his greatest crisis of the war, the first genuine Italian breakthrough on the Isonzo front. After twenty-six months of trying, Cadorna's forces had finally ripped a gaping hole in the Isonzo Army's main defenses. Even compared to the capture of Gorizia, the imminent loss of the Bainsizza was of far greater significance; the former, although a serious political defeat, in no way undermined Austria's strategic position, whereas the latter threatened to unravel Boroević's entire front. Bosco had spent the fateful day pondering his choices. There seemed to be little to do but abandon the Bainsizza plateau and reestablish a defensible line about five miles to the east. Certainly Boroević had too few troops available to attempt a major counterattack, the only way to retake the Bainsizza. Therefore a general retreat by the XXIV Corps seemed a regrettable but unavoidable reality. Boroević informed Emperor Karl of this on the morning of August 22. By coincidence, the monarch was visiting the Isonzo front that day, and stopped at Boroević's headquarters. In a two-hour confidential meeting, Boroević informed the emperor that the strategic situation was deteriorating, and that a withdrawal was imminent. Karl then went to the front to see for himself. His party arrived on the Ternova plateau, just east of Mt. San Gabriele, at midday. From a safe distance, Karl observed the bloody battle raging around San Gabriele; in the afternoon, disturbed by what he had witnessed, the emperor returned to Ljubljana. In a second coincidence, the same battle was observed by King Vittorio Emanuele. The king, who liked to visit the front regularly to take pictures, observed the Ternova fighting from the west bank of the Isonzo, almost directly opposite Emperor Karl. For the last time in European history, opposing monarchs watched as their armies battled before them. Surely Vittorio Emanuele, whose regiments were advancing, had more reason to enjoy observing the battle than his Habsburg counterpart did.

By nightfall, as further indications of the debacle on the Bainsizza reached Adelsberg, Boroević had no choice but to order a withdrawal from the plateau; to do otherwise would needlessly sacrifice what remained of Lukas's XXIV Corps and endanger the whole Isonzo front. Only by retreating to secure positions east of the Bainsizza could the Isonzo Army expect to stand firm. Caviglia's forward elements had taken the town of Bate on the central plateau, two miles east of the Isonzo, and it was evident that all attempts to resist Capello's onslaught had failed. One Austrian survivor recounted, "The human wall that had withstood ten battles has burst." Therefore, at 9 P.M. Boroević met with his two senior staff officers, Lieutenant General Aurel Le Beau and Major General Anton Pitreich, and officially decided to abandon the Bainsizza plateau. The order did not reach field units until 9 A.M. on August 23, and the retreat was not scheduled to begin until late that evening, but the fateful decision had been made. Boroević pleaded with the High Command for fresh divisions to hold the new line running along the Čepovan valley, but he could not expect reserves for several more days. Indeed, Paul von Hindenburg responded quickly to Arthur Arz von Straussenburg's plea to release troops from the Eastern front, permitting the Austrians to transfer four and a half divisions from East Galicia, but none of them would arrive in time to fight in the Eleventh Battle. The weak and tired Isonzo Army would have to stand and fight with what it had.

The night was quiet, but dawn on August 23 was met with a hail of artillery barrages, both Italian and Austrian. Capello's gunners shelled their usual targets, and their Habsburg counterparts took aim at Italian troop concentrations and artillery positions to protect the impending retreat. The Austrian bombardment came as a surprise, and was unexpectedly heavy. For once, Boroević's artillery took a notable toll of Italian guns, as counterbattery fire struck Italian batteries around the Bainsizza, a revenge for all the shelling the defenders had endured. Italian and Allied heavy batteries awoke to deadly accurate Austrian salvos, a most unwelcome and unusual greeting to the day. One British battery, a recent arrival on the Isonzo, was hit by a large-caliber shell that killed a sergeant and two gunners. The sergeant was blown into pieces; one rested on top of the officers' mess, and another landed in a gun pit 450 feet away.[8]

While the Austrian artillery was hard at work, headquarters staffs prepared to execute the retreat, which promised to be a complex and trying operation. The nocturnal withdrawal appeared so risky that several corps and divisional commanders protested, claiming that Boroević's plan of retreat was too ambitious. Indeed, even Boroević himself had second thoughts. Capello's troops were sluggishly inactive during August 23; the exhausted Italian divisions used the day to rest and regroup. Boroević therefore pondered whether the high point of the battle had already passed, and considered canceling the retreat. Cooler heads prevailed, though, and the great retreat began shortly after dark. Boroević then received word that he had been promoted to army group commander: on the orders of the High Command, the very large Isonzo Army was divided into two separate armies, with Boroević as the overall commander of Army Group Isonzo.[9] It was poor compensation for the loss of the Bainsizza.

The retreat was performed cleverly, with troops left behind to cover the withdrawal and to deceive the Italians. As a result, the complex operation proceeded smoothly, and the following morning Capello's regiments were astonished to discover that the XXIV Corps had retreated to the other side of the plateau. Austrian troops also abandoned the southernmost mountains on the plateau, including Vodice and Mt. Santo. With the Bainsizza now in Italian hands, there was no longer any reason to hold on to these famed peaks, once the very symbol of Austrian resistance. So on the morning of August 24, as the hot late summer sun rose over the Isonzo valley, Austrian infantry cautiously relinquished their battle-scarred entrenchments on Vodice and Mt. Santo.

Capello ordered his troops to immediately take the abandoned summits, particularly Mt. Santo, which the 2nd Army had been attempting to wrest from the Austrians since June 1915. The 8th Division hastily sent reinforcements to the mountaintop. The regiment closest to the peak and its ruined monastery, with forward trenches just forty yards from the summit, was called forward by its colonel, who leaped to his feet and led his *fanti* to the highest point of the mountain, 2,250 feet above the Isonzo and Gorizia. The ecstatic colonel then shouted, "My soldiers, let us cry aloud in the face of the enemy. Long live Italy! Long live the king! Long live the infantry!" His *fanti* cheered in riotous approval, and word spread down the mountain, through the ranks of the 2nd Army—"Our tricolor is waving from the summit of Monte Santo!" The news was greeted everywhere with an enthusiasm not witnessed since the fall of Gorizia a year before. No one seemed to notice or care that the capture of Mt. Santo was really an anticlimax. News of the great event soon reached Cadorna, and then Rome, where Parliament was informed, for the second and final time, that Mt. Santo was now Italian soil. After so long, after so many unanticipated disappointments and costly failures, victory on the Isonzo now seemed to be within Italy's grasp.

Yet, Capello and Cadorna again failed to exploit their obvious success on the Bainsizza. Rather than send victorious divisions inland with all possible speed, they let them advance slowly, cautiously toward the new Austrian defensive positions. This ponderous pursuit gave Boroević's exhausted and depleted units ample time to reestablish their main line of defense. The XXIV Corps was soon dug in on a fourteen-mile front, from Loga to Mt. San Gabriele.[10] The entrenchments were shallow and unimpressive, but the weary survivors of the Bainsizza

fight were just glad to be alive, and particularly relieved that they were now beyond the range of Capello's heavy guns. The fourteen-mile Austrian line was
defended by only fifty-two battalions, many of them at less than half strength—
far too few troops to hold the line against a major Italian assault. But that offensive never came.

Instead, Cadorna decided that he would wrest Mt. San Gabriele from the
Austrians; the cautious count felt that an all-out drive for victory on the central
Isonzo would inflict terrible losses on his armies and push their already fragile
morale past the breaking point. Therefore San Gabriele was the Italian Army's
new objective. In a perverse way, it was the fight for Monte Santo all over again.
Capturing "Holy Mountain" had in fact decided nothing; the battle just shifted
to Mt. San Gabriele, the second of the *Tre Santi*, less than two miles southeast of
the ruined monastery. The steep-sloped San Gabriele was not one mountain but
two: the summit, 646 (2,130 ft), and a lower peak, 526 or Veliki hrib (1,730 ft),
immediately to the west. The Austrians held both peaks and were especially
well entrenched at the summit. San Gabriele was the last significant mountain
overlooking Gorizia that still belonged to the Isonzo Army. It promised to be a
fierce struggle, with Cadorna as determined to take it as Boroević was to keep it
out of Italian hands. Capello, however, was so confident of a quick victory that
he brought a mounted cavalry division and three bicycle battalions to the front
to exploit his imminently anticipated breakthrough on San Gabriele. The horse-
men and bicyclists still had long to wait.

The first major Italian assault on San Gabriele came on August 24. The
Palermo Brigade was sent up the west face of the mountain all day, but met with
no success. It was not for want of bravery: the *fanti* of the 67th and 68th Regiments charged the positions of the 9th *Jägers* twelve times in twelve hours, each
assault being repulsed with heavy casualties. Again the Schwarzlose machine
gun, the backbone of the Austrian defense, won the battle. The daylong effort
was a bitter taste of the enormous struggle for San Gabriele that was to come.

The Austrian troops charged with holding on to the mountain were some of
the best soldiers available in the Habsburg realm. The 18th Brigade included
the Alpine German 9th *Jäger* Battalion, recruited in north Styria, and the
three-battalion-strong 87th Regiment, a Slovene outfit from south Styria. Both
were crack veteran units with an excellent fighting record against the Italians,
their "hereditary enemy." The German and Slovene *Frontkämpfer* were prepared to defend San Gabriele—which they called "The Inferno"—to the last
man. The brigade's commander, Colonel Vladimir Laxa, was likewise a seasoned campaigner. The forty-seven-year-old Croatian officer had extensive experience in both staff and line positions, and was an exemplary officer in all
respects. His mission was the most important on the whole Isonzo front as the
Eleventh Battle entered its second phase. The loss of San Gabriele would force

a withdrawal off the Ternova plateau, and probably a general retreat eastward, away from the Isonzo.

Capello's 11th Division fought hard the next day, August 25, and achieved some minor gains on San Gabriele's west face, winning a few trench lines on the lower peak. Still, the mountain remained securely in Austrian hands. Capello launched a major coordinated effort on August 26, a three-pronged attack on Laxa's positions, generously backed up by hundreds of guns and mortars. The 11th Division again charged up San Gabriele's west and south faces, and the 8th Division attacked from the north, from Mt. Santo. These conquerors of the "Holy Mountain" assaulted San Gabriele via the Dol saddle, the 1,500-foot-high land bridge running parallel to the Isonzo, which extended from Vodice to Mt. San Gabriele. The saddle was the easiest avenue of approach for the Italians, and it was stoutly defended by troops of the 87th Regiment. The Italian advance was eventually cut short with notable losses, but nevertheless it seized some Austrian positions. The bitter fighting raged into the late evening, a merciless brawl among the quarter-mile-high rocks, illuminated only by shell explosions and the moonlight.

The *fanti* battling and dying around San Gabriele on the night of August 26 received an unexpected morale boost when a military band situated at the summit of Mt. Santo began playing martial and patriotic tunes. The music was clearly audible, and it brought cheers from thousands of Italian troops in the area. The mystified Austrians tried to stop the battle's musical accompaniment by shelling the ruins at the peak of Mt. Santo, but they could not silence the Italian concert.

The oddly placed band was directed by none other than Arturo Toscanini, the world-famous conductor. The fifty-year-old Toscanini was an ardent patriot and irredentist, a passionate believer in Italy's cause. He had been raised on romantic nationalist and martial tales told by his father, who had fought with Garibaldi in the wars for unification and against the Austrians in both 1859 and 1866. From the war's beginning, the renowned musician had been a vocal champion of the war effort. He traveled to the Isonzo in August 1917, ostensibly to visit his nineteen-year-old son Walter, a junior artillery officer serving with the 2nd Army. While near the front, he persuaded General Capello to permit him to form a band to play for the soldiers. Capello liked the idea, and soon Toscanini was leading his handpicked band in open-air concerts for the troops of the 2nd Army. On one occasion, Walter Toscanini heard the band playing and was sure his father was conducting it, but could not believe it. Upon hearing that Mt. Santo had at last been taken, the patriotic Toscanini demanded the right to take his band to the summit and play for the victorious soldiers of the 8th Division. On the afternoon of August 26, the conductor and his musicians, carrying their instruments, struggled up the 2,250-foot-high mountain while the 8th Division tried to fight its way to San Gabriele across the Dol saddle. By the evening Toscanini's band was in place at the summit, beside the ruins of Mt.

Santo's monastery, in the open, protected only by a rock. As the *fanti* of the 8th Division fought less than a mile to the southeast, Toscanini's band played patriotic tunes loudly and clearly. After each piece the conductor shouted "*Viva l'Italia!*" The troops loved it and responded with euphoric shouts of approval, so the band kept playing long into the night. Austrian artillery tried to silence Toscanini's band, and the summit was struck by numerous shells. Austrian snipers across the valley took aim, too. Yet Toscanini refused to take cover, and although the bass drum was ripped by shrapnel, no musicians were injured. His dramatic concert was widely hailed in the army and throughout Italy, and Capello personally awarded Toscanini the Silver Medal for Bravery for his conducting in the field.

Unfortunately for Capello, enthusiasm was not enough, and the Italian assaults on San Gabriele continued without success. On August 27, the mountain was shelled relentlessly through the morning, as the firepower of nearly a thousand guns and mortars blasted Laxa's entrenched troops; Cadorna in fact considered the artillery preparation on San Gabriele to be the greatest of the entire war. Yet the noon-hour infantry attack that followed the barrage faltered in the face of accurate and sustained Austrian machine gun and rifle fire. Successive waves of *fanti* were cut down by the staccato fire while trying to make their way up the steep and rocky slopes, now blasted completely barren by all the shelling. Word quickly spread among Capello's troops that Gabriele was "worse than Santo." Although the Italian bombardments invariably exacted a high price among Laxa's Styrian defenders, in every case just enough troops remained alive to man the machine guns and light mortars that formed the basis of the Austrian defense.

A further Italian effort on August 28 met a similar fate, despite the tons of high explosives dropped on the mountain to clear the way for the infantry. The next morning, Capello added several brigades to the assault force, regiments of fresh and well rested infantry. But these units similarly failed to advance more than a few hundred feet up the mountain. By the evening of August 29, when Cadorna called a temporary halt to the offensive after four days of heavy fighting, the 2nd Army had succeeded in capturing a single Austrian trench line on 526, the lower peak. Otherwise, Laxa's defenses remained intact.

By the end of August, even smaller Italian attacks on the eastern edge of the Bainsizza plateau were meeting with scant success. Austrian tenacity had returned after initial setbacks on the Bainsizza, and many units continued to resist fiercely, even against daunting odds. In the countless skirmishes that smoldered all along the Isonzo in the waning days of the Eleventh Battle, it was the willingness of junior soldiers to fight on that weighed decisively in Austria's favor. On the morning of August 27, an Italian assault on Hill 830 on the Bainsizza threatened to break through the still-shaky Austrian defenses. The only unit available to plug the gap, a company of the 4th Bosnian *Jäger* Battalion, did what Austrian units were supposed to do—it counterattacked. Although the odds looked hopeless, the veteran 4th Bosnian *Jägers* were no ordinary unit. The battalion had arrived on the Isonzo front only the day before, and the 4th Company was soon hit hard by constant Italian shelling, losing many soldiers, including its commander. Yet a young corporal took the initiative and wrested Hill 830 from the Italians.

Corporal Rustan Kapetanović, though only twenty-one years old, had been at the front for nearly two years and had twice won the Silver Medal for Bravery; the native of northwestern Bosnia had in fact been recently appointed a probationary officer cadet in recognition of his prowess. When Corporal Kapetanović saw his company commander fall wounded on the hillside, he immediately took charge of not just his own platoon but the entire company, leading its *Bosniaken* in a headlong rush into the advancing Italians, right through an artillery and mortar barrage. Confronted with an unexpected counterattack, the *fanti* retreated, abandoning their gains. Although many Bosnian soldiers had fallen in the counterattack, it was a resounding success, illustrating yet again how decisive a role individual initiative still had to play on the machine-dominated battlefield.[11]

The Austrian victory on San Gabriele and elsewhere was the triumph of men over machines. Again Boroević's infantry had withstood incredible hardships; veteran *Frontkämpfer* had refused to give in, even when shelled ceaselessly by nearly a thousand heavy guns and mortars. High morale and fighting spirit were far more reliable in the defense than in the attack, and the Austrian soldiers' martial qualities and hatred of the Italians decided the struggle for San Gabriele. As Field Marshal Archduke Eugen, commander of the Southwestern front, observed of the 18th Brigade, "The heroic spirit of such troops is the surest guarantee of victory." Although Laxa's brigade was massively outnumbered, short of food, water, and ammunition, and unable to rest, it emerged triumphant, at a cost of three-quarters of its men. Colonel Laxa was instrumental in his troops' success: he unfailingly stayed with his men and was frequently in the front lines, issuing orders.[12] As the Italians had learned so many times before on the Isonzo, it was supremely difficult to evict determined Austrian infantry from well constructed mountain positions. Nowhere did Cadorna's armies learn this lesson more painfully than on the slopes of Mt. San Gabriele in late August 1917.

Indeed, Boroević was so buoyed by his army's success at San Gabriele that he ordered a large-scale counterattack on the southern Carso. He remained concerned that the Duke of Aosta's right flank was dangerously close to Mt. Hermada, the last natural obstacle before Trieste. Therefore the XXIII Corps attacked Italian positions west of Hermada on the morning of September 4. The infantry assault was preceded by a craftily prepared and executed predawn artillery barrage: a brief, heavy bombardment, then a ten-minute pause to deceive the Italians, followed by a devastating half-hour "annihilation barrage." When the riflemen of the 28th and 35th Divisions went over the top at 5:30 A.M., they encountered little resistance; in most places the shell-shocked *fanti*, stunned by the surprise attack, proved only too willing to surrender. Within an hour, the XXIII Corps had retaken virtually all the positions it had lost in the Eleventh Battle and had captured 6,700 Italian officers and men, most of a division. It was a humiliating defeat for the 3rd Army, a startling indication of how fragile Italian morale had become.

That said, on the same morning Capello's infantry demonstrated their tenacity and courage on the slopes of San Gabriele. The Italians launched their own surprise attack at dawn on September 4, the beginning of a clear and bright day, as several fresh brigades fought their way to the summit of San Gabriele, now known to all *fanti* as *il monte del morte*, "the mountain of death." This renewed offensive brought unexpected results. The Italian assault, spearheaded by Major Bassi's celebrated *reparto d'assalto*, quickly overran several Austrian trench lines. San Gabriele's defenders were no longer Laxa's elite mountaineers, but a brigade of the 106th Militia Division. The 106th, destroyed on the Bainsizza earlier in the Eleventh Battle, had been taken out of the line and given drafts of recruits to bring its broken regiments up to fighting strength. Two of its militia regiments, the 6th and 31st, relieved Laxa's tired battalions on San Gabriele. However, these two regiments were at less than half strength—they mustered only 2,500 rifles between them—and were unacquainted with the mountain; indeed, they arrived at San Gabriele only hours before Capello's offensive restarted.

The inexperienced and outnumbered polyglot regiments of German, Czech, and Polish militiamen soon collapsed when attacked by vigorously led Italian infantry. Bassi's hand-picked *arditi*, fresh from their triumph on the Bainsizza, led the way, seizing 546, the lower peak, and then charging toward the summit. By late morning, Capello's infantry had taken 646, too, and captured more than a thousand Austrian defenders. San Gabriele now belonged to the 2nd Army.

The only nearby Austrian reserve, the Czech 25th Militia Regiment, was hastily dispatched to the summit, where it executed a sudden counterattack. The Austrian drive unexpectedly retook the summit, 646, by noon, but was unable to push the Italians down the mountain. A bitter stalemate resulted, with the Austrians entrenched around the summit and the Italians dug in immediately to the west. The 106th Division's last fresh troops, the Polish 32nd Militia Regiment, were fed into the vicious fight around the summit on the morning of September 5, and Capello committed all the fresh regiments he had to the battle. Each side was supported by fearsome amounts of heavy artillery, which paralyzed movement near the peak. The cost was frightful as the forces dug in around the summit were bled white by the carnage. Neither army was strong enough to push the other back, but both armies had enough firepower to inflict grievous casualties. On September 5, Boroević reported to the High Command that due to heavy losses, Mt. San Gabriele probably could not be held much longer.

Nevertheless, Boroević never gave the order to retreat from the peak, and his regiments continued to fight hard against Capello's entrenched infantry. The battle raged through September 6 and 7 as each army tried to keep constant pressure on the other. The fighting was always at close quarters, and in many areas the Austrians and Italians were no more than thirty feet apart, well within grenade-throwing range. The opposing entrenchments were so close together that one night an Austrian soldier accidentally brought his battalion's mail delivery to the neighboring Italian positions. As casualties mounted, both armies—especially Capello's 2nd—sent an endless stream of reinforcements up San Gabriele. "The Butcher" was determined to take the mountain, so he sent regiment after regiment of fresh troops into the cauldron. Few of the *fanti* sent up the mountain would ever return. Regardless, the vicious combat resolved nothing, and both armies remained unshakably entrenched around the summit of *il monte del morte*, which had more than lived up to its evil name.

Frustrated by his infantry's lack of progress, Capello ordered his mighty artillery to blast the summit of San Gabriele away. Through September 8, 9, and 10, the 2nd Army's guns fired nonstop at Mt. San Gabriele, reducing most of the Austrian positions to shambles. In three days, 45,000 Italian shells struck the summit, killing and wounding hundreds of soldiers. In the process, the peak of "the Inferno" was reduced by some thirty feet. Still, the battered *Frontkämpfer* would not budge. On the morning of September 11, the Foggia and Girgenti Brigades charged the Austrian trenches surrounding the summit and encountered unexpectedly stiff resistance. After halting this Italian attack, the defending 106th Militia Division was finally replaced on San Gabriele; a week of battle had reduced it to only a thousand infantrymen, and its trenches were taken over by the 14th Infantry Regiment, first-rate fighters from Upper Austria.

That night two reinforced companies of the elite 14th Regiment, efficiently backed up by a whole brigade of *Honvéd* artillery, assaulted the Italian trenches on the exposed northwest slope of San Gabriele, facing Mt. Santo. The blow took the exhausted Italians by surprise, and by dawn the 14th had captured more than 600 prisoners and retaken nearly the whole mountaintop, pushing the *fanti* far from the summit. All the Italian gains of the past week had been overturned. Capello responded with an attack of his own, but it was too late. The Foggia and Girgenti Brigades advanced up the slopes, now littered with uncounted rotting corpses, but made scant progress. One last try on September 13 similarly failed to win back the lost positions, and Mt. San Gabriele remained securely occupied by the 14th Regiment. Capello's troops were worn out; between September 4 and 14, his lead division, the 11th, alone lost 10,000 *fanti*. Both armies were far too exhausted to keep fighting, and to everyone's relief the Eleventh Battle of the Isonzo was officially declared ended.

Boroević and Cadorna each proclaimed the Eleventh Battle a victory. It had been the largest and bloodiest Isonzo battle to date, and both armies were eager to portray their performance in a favorable light. The Austrians pointed not to the loss of the Bainsizza, but to their epic stand on Monte San Gabriele. After suffering an admitted defeat on the plateau, the Isonzo Army redeemed itself by winning a strategic victory at San Gabriele. The new Austrian defenses on the Isonzo front had proven strong, and the Italians were hardly closer to Trieste than before the Eleventh Battle. For their part, the Italians naturally celebrated the capture of the Bainsizza, an advance of six miles on an eleven-mile front. By Great War standards, this was indeed a noteworthy gain, precisely the kind of victory that had eluded Italy for more than two years.

Still, Cadorna and his tired armies were nowhere near accomplishing their goals of evicting the Austrians from the Isonzo valley and conquering Trieste. After twenty-seven months and eleven battles of the Isonzo, the 3rd Army had advanced less than seven miles on the Carso—only one-third of the way to Trieste. Cadorna's frightful strategy of attrition was winning, in a sense, but at such a slow pace and at such a high cost that ultimate victory seemed impossibly remote. Worse, Cadorna and Capello had again squandered a strategic and decisive victory by exercising caution at the precise moment when audacity was called for. The Italian generals' fatal operational timidity deprived Italy of a war-winning opportunity on the Isonzo, and not for the first time.

And the shocking cost of the Eleventh Battle far outstripped whatever had been gained by either side. In less than four weeks, the armies on the Isonzo together lost 300,000 soldiers. Italy conceded a loss of 166,000 *grigioverdi* between August 18 and September 13, including 40,000 dead, 108,000 wounded and 18,000 missing. The cost of Cadorna's "victory" was 25 percent greater than Nivelle's disaster on the Aisne in April, and this was according to official Italian figures! No less, by the end of the Eleventh Battle the morale of the much abused *fantaccino* had clearly descended to new depths. Even so, Austria had no cause to rejoice. Boroević's losses came to 110,000, among them roughly 15,000 dead, 45,000 maimed, 30,000 missing, and 20,000 seriously ill. Most alarmingly, nearly 30,000 of the Isonzo Army's soldiers—three whole divisions—were in Italian captivity, a disturbing sign that Austria's morale, too, was dangerously low. Hardly less disturbing were the equipment losses the Austrians suffered, including more than a third of the Isonzo Army's artillery, either destroyed or captured by the Italians. Boroević's multinational army had again withstood an enormous Italian blow, indeed one of the mightiest offensives of the Great War.[13] However, the staying power of the Austrian Army was clearly in doubt. The Eleventh Battle had nearly defeated Boroević's forces, and another full-fledged Italian blow would surely shatter them entirely. As autumn approached, the decisive question, then, was when Cadorna would again unleash a major offensive on the Isonzo. Without doubt, the Twelfth Battle promised to decide the fate of the entire Isonzo campaign.

TWELVE

CAPORETTO

As soon as the Eleventh Battle ended, Luigi Cadorna was eager to unleash another offensive against Svetozar Boroević's weakened army. However, several significant factors could not be overlooked. In the first place, Cadorna felt that another push would have to come soon, in the next month: he believed that the imminent arrival of the harsh Alpine winter would prevent any offensive after mid-October. Therefore his armies would have to advance again in less than a month, and that looked unlikely on several grounds.

Second, he estimated that seizing Hermada and Mt. San Gabriele, the last significant natural obstacles in front of his armies, would cost not less than 150,000 casualties and two million heavy artillery shells. Even to Cadorna these were steep figures. So soon after the bloodletting on the Bainsizza, Cadorna knew he could not put his *fanti* to such a severe test; their morale was dangerously close to the breaking point already. Since May, the Italian Army had lost 720,000 soldiers, including those incapacitated by illness, and even Italy's ample manpower reserves no longer seemed limitless. The more than 300,000 battle casualties from the Tenth and Eleventh Battles still had not been fully made good. One more major offensive on the Isonzo in 1917 promised to cost more than Italy could afford in men, in matériel, and in spirit.

Cadorna might have been able to achieve victory with help from the Allies, but he knew that he could expect little assistance from Britain and France. Haig's divisions were bogged down in a costly and ultimately inconclusive fight in Flanders, the ill-starred Passchendaele offensive, and France's weary *poilus*, still embittered by Nivelle's springtime debacle, were in no condition to attempt another major offensive on their own soil, much less on the Isonzo. The Allies might have offered Cadorna more heavy artillery to use on the Isonzo, but even that seemed unlikely in mid-September.

On September 11, as the Eleventh Battle drew to a close, Cadorna received two important British officials at his Udine headquarters: Lord Derby, minister of war, and Major General Frederick Maurice, director of military operations. They came to the Isonzo front to survey the possibilities for major British involvement there. Lloyd George was ever eager to divert Britain's armies from the futile slaughter of the Western front, but he had little confidence in Cadorna's abilities. This sentiment was reinforced by the Udine visit. Derby and Maurice returned to London unimpressed, feeling that Cadorna could promise few results, whether or not he received substantial numbers of British men and guns; they recommended only the bare minimum of British assistance to Italy, and Lloyd George's scheme of a major Allied front on the Isonzo died, stillborn. The British made vague promises of dispatching 160 heavy guns to Cadorna, leaving the Piedmontese count disappointed and angry. He was now even more convinced that another offensive against the Austrians in 1917 would be a mistake.

Therefore, on September 18 he ordered Luigi Capello's 2nd Army and the Duke of Aosta's 3rd to suspend all offensive planning and prepare for the defense. With winter approaching, the Italian Army began digging in and readying to wait out the long, cold months ahead, holding on to its hard-won positions on the Isonzo, just as it had for the past two war winters. From Cadorna to the lowliest *fantaccino* on the Carso or the Bainsizza, none of the million Italian soldiers on the Isonzo front expected to fight a major battle again until the spring of 1918.

Austrian officers soon had ample evidence that the Italians were digging in and hunkering down for the winter. This ought to have been precisely the relieving news that Boroević had been waiting to hear. In a sense it was—at last, he knew his tired army had a reprieve until the spring—but in other ways it worried him all the more. The Isonzo Army was now so weary and depleted that perhaps a winter to rest would not prove sufficient; another Italian offensive in 1918, maybe with considerable Allied—perhaps even American—help, would shatter his army all the same. Boroević's tried-and-true tactic of keeping the front line strong and retaking all lost ground at any price had worked for two years. But the Eleventh Battle demonstrated that it no longer was the key to success; instead, it guaranteed only further attrition, an equation that the much stronger Italians in the end would certainly win. Indeed, a senior Austrian general remarked after the loss of the Bainsizza, "20,000 unwounded prisoners were the sign that no soldiers could be abused endlessly in such a fashion." More than ever, Boroević wished that for once he had enough troops and guns to launch an offensive of his own, a major push to drive the Italians away from the Isonzo and restore Austria's strategic position.

Fortunately for Boroević and his soldiers, Austria's most senior generals had begun to think the same thing. Franz Conrad's South Tyrolean offensive in the spring of 1916 came close to achieving strategic results, but was cut short by a lack of men and munitions and the Russian attack in East Galicia. Since then, the Austrian High Command had been convinced that another major offensive against Italy could win the decisive victory which Conrad came so close to claiming in May 1916. The endless attrition on the Isonzo was, in the end, a losing proposition for the Habsburg Empire, as Arthur Arz and his staff at Teschen feared. More ominously, the Eleventh Battle's heavy losses—particularly in prisoners—were but a foretaste of what the Austrians could expect from the next Italian offensive, in the spring of 1918. Arz knew that the time had come to act, to launch a major attack against Italy before it was too late.

In strategic terms, another Trentino offensive appeared unpromising, principally because the winter arrived early in the steep Tyrolean Alps. Taking climate into consideration—as both the Austrians and the Italians always did—a Habsburg effort on the Isonzo was a better option. The Austrian problem, as it always had been, was a lack of men, guns, and munitions. Even with Russia collapsing, the Austrians alone could not muster sufficient strength to deliver a knockout blow to Cadorna's armies. Any Austrian offensive would inevitably require German assistance, in the form of soldiers or heavy artillery, and probably both.

Initial Austrian inquiries about German help had been refused out of hand. Arz first mentioned the subject to Hindenburg in late July 1917, even before the debacle on the Bainsizza, but met with no success; the Germans preferred to concentrate their efforts against ailing Russia. The Germans, including Emperor Wilhelm II, typically remained uninterested in Austria's war with Italy; for them it remained a sideshow of the war, of little strategic concern.

The unexpected loss of the Bainsizza made the Germans reconsider. In Berlin, Italy's first major success in a year raised concerns about a general Austrian collapse. By September, the Germans were willing to compromise, particularly when Emperor Karl personally requested help from Wilhelm, his fellow monarch. The Austrian plan, developed in conjunction with the German General Staff, called for a major attack on the uppermost Isonzo, north of the Tolmein bridgehead. Although the high Alpine terrain made movement difficult, the Austrians correctly surmised that Italian defenses there, at the leftmost flank of Capello's 2nd Army, were relatively weak. No less important, an Austrian offensive on the upper Isonzo would be the last thing Cadorna and his staff expected. The Germans agreed, and soon a German army (the 14th, under General Otto von Below) was en route to the Isonzo, under the greatest secrecy; it included seven German divisions[1] with 460 guns and 216 mortars, a powerful force of veteran formations. On September 17, the Austrian High Command informed Boroević that it intended to launch an offensive on the Isonzo in late October. It would be the first Austrian offensive on the Isonzo, after eleven major Italian efforts. The Twelfth Battle promised to deliver the decisive blow against Italy that Boroević and his generals had always longed for.

With winter coming soon, the Austrians and Germans had no time to waste, and the planning and preparation for the offensive began immediately, assuming a frenetic pace. The breakthrough force for the offensive was the German 14th Army, under the Prussian Otto von Below, whose chief of staff was Germany's foremost Alpine warfare expert, the Bavarian Lieutenant General Krafft von Dellmensingen. The 14th Army included two German and two Austrian corps, with a total of five Habsburg and seven German divisions, all of them crack fighting forces with ample combat experience. Although von Below's army was nominally German, its spearhead force was the Austrian I Corps, whose mission was breaking through the Italian lines between Rombon and Krn, the roughest terrain on the whole Isonzo front; von Below's three other corps were to break through around the Tolmein bridgehead. The commander of the I Corps was General Alfred Krauss, perhaps the finest tactician in the whole Habsburg Army, and an exemplary choice to lead the Austrians in their greatest offensive of the war.

The fifty-five-year-old Krauss, the son of an Austrian army officer, had devoted his life to serving the Habsburgs, and enjoyed an exemplary career in the emperor's service. An infantryman by training, Krauss spent much of his career on the elite General Staff, including time as an instructor of tactics at the Theresian Military Academy; later he was commander of the prestigious War School, which trained General Staff officers. He was a stern and dedicated officer who demanded excellence from his subordinates. In addition, Krauss was an unusually scholarly general who had studied modern tactics in detail; two of his written works dealt with Austria's 1866 war with Prussia and the Russo-Turkish war of 1877–1878. Krauss served as a divisional commander in Serbia and Galicia in the first year of the Great War, then went to the Italian front in mid-1915, as chief of staff to Archduke Eugen, commander of the Southwestern front. Krauss took over the I Corps in May 1917. His knowledge of modern tactics and the Italian front was unsurpassed in the Austrian Army.

The force at Krauss's disposal for the coming offensive was outstanding in all respects. Besides the crack Prussian *Jäger* Division, his I Corps included two Austrian divisions of Alpine mountain fighters from Styria, Tyrol, and Salzburg, the 22nd Rifle Division, and the 3rd "Edelweiss" Infantry Division. There was also the 55th Division, including two regiments of Bosnian troops. The 55th Division had the most important mission of all: piercing the Italian defenses between Javorček and Krn and crossing the Isonzo at the main bridgehead, the town of Karfreit (Caporetto to its Italian defenders). The 55th Division's commander was Major General Felix, Prince zu Schwarzenberg, an experienced field commander and scion of one of Austria's oldest noble families. The Schwarzenbergs had served the Habsburgs in the army and the civil service for centuries, frequently with considerable distinction. The family was one of the great ancient Bohemian magnate clans, neither German nor Czech but distinctly *böhmisch* in the old, anational sense (Prince Felix spoke both German and Czech). The fifty-year-old prince had enjoyed a successful career in the emperor's service, including many years with the Bohemian 14th Dragoons, a decidedly aristocratic regiment. Yet Major General Schwarzenberg was not the average wealthy cavalry officer; he had attended the War School and had served with distinction with staffs and other units. His war record was equally good, including command of a brigade, and then a division against the Italians. He was a brave officer and an astute tactician well versed in Alpine warfare.

Schwarzenberg was also popular with his troops, including the 7th Infantry Regiment and the 2nd and 4th Bosnian Regiments. The 7th was a centuries-old unit of tough Carinthian mountain soldiers, known to the Italians as the "brown devils." The Bosnian regiments, although raised only in the late nineteenth century, had, if anything, an even more distinguished fighting record against the Italians. Both of the 55th Division's Bosnian regiments boasted considerable combat experience on the Isonzo (the 4th were the famed defenders of Rombon), and the legendary 2nd Regiment was the most decorated Habsburg unit of the whole war, its soldiers winning forty-two Gold Medals for Bravery.[2] In addition, the Carinthians and Bosnians were born mountain fighters imbued with a deep hatred of the Italians, ideal troops to lead Austria's Isonzo offensive. The 55th Division was also provided with two high mountain companies, elite units of handpicked veterans who knew the Julian Alps intimately. Just as important, Schwarzenberg's division included the 55th Assault Battalion (*Sturm-bataillon*), whose young Bosnian and Carinthian volunteers, generously equipped with machine guns, mortars, and flamethrowers, would lead the attack.[3] The over-strength 55th Division counted 138 guns and howitzers, as well as a full battalion of sappers, to break through the Italians' mountain defenses. Major General Schwarzenberg commanded one of the finest and best equipped Austrian divisions of the entire war, indeed one of the most powerful divisions in any army during the Great War.

Krauss ensured that his assault divisions were well equipped and provisioned for the coming offensive, and had adequate transportation to advance deep into Italian-held terrain without running out of supplies. The Austrian Army was the world's foremost practitioner of Alpine warfare, as it had been since the mid-nineteenth century,[4] and its preparations for the Twelfth Battle of the Isonzo were especially thorough, thanks in large part to Krauss's efforts. In fact, Krauss later recounted that the arduous buildup to the great offensive constituted "for us the hardest and bitterest time of the entire operation." His first task was securing enough firepower for his corps to break through, and that meant getting as many guns and shells as possible; Krauss, who understood the tactical realities of static fighting and the vital role of artillery better than anyone, stated bluntly, "The extent of blood that our infantry would have to shed to achieve victory depended in direct proportion on the amount of artillery." Simply put, the more guns and munitions he had, the fewer *Frontkämpfer* Krauss would have to sacrifice to achieve a breakthrough. Therefore Krauss demanded 500 guns to execute a successful assault. In the end, his I Corps was allocated 433 artillery pieces, including 328 field and mountain guns, eighty-five medium and heavy guns, and twenty superheavy guns, as well as forty-eight heavy mortars, a generous portion of the nearly 2,000 additional guns and howitzers brought to the Isonzo for the offensive. It was an unprecedented amount of firepower for a single Austrian corps.

Just as important for the success of the offensive was the stocking of generous shell reserves, particularly for the heavy guns. By scouring depots on the quiet Transylvanian and Russian fronts, as well as hinterland arsenals, the forces on the Isonzo were supplied with considerable ammunition stocks. For the initial push, the divisions of the I Corps were each granted a thousand rounds per field and mountain gun, 500 per medium gun, 800 per heavy howitzer, and 200 for each superheavy piece, more than enough to achieve a breakthrough.

The most laborious task confronting the I Corps before the offensive was the positioning and placement of its artillery in Alpine terrain. This proved especially difficult because the nearest railhead was twenty miles behind the front line; the only available routes were poor roads through the Julian Alps, some of them 6,000 feet high. To assist the 55th Division's artillery, the High Command gave it particularly lavish logistical assistance, because its mission was so vital. To supplement its normal complement of transport units, Schwarzenberg's division received two additional pack animal detachments of 150 animals each, and three motor transport companies, each with seventy trucks.[5] In addition, the division's artillery was assigned 1,200 construction troops to help with the movement of guns and munitions to the battle area. Even so, the placement of the division's heavy and superheavy batteries proved an arduous task. To avoid Italian observation, weapons of 150mm and greater were moved only at night, over high mountains, in some cases to within a quarter-mile of Italian forward positions. Yet no artillery movement was ever detected by the opposing Italian IV Corps, despite nightly shelling by Italian illumination mortars.

For this offensive, the Austrians took extensive security precautions. As the attack's scheduled start day of October 22 approached (it was delayed to October 24 by bad weather), infantry units were moved to the front slowly and carefully, at the rate of one or two battalions per division every night; march discipline was excellent, and the Italians detected very little. More modern methods were also used to ensure that the offensive would be a surprise. The Austrian signal troops performed invaluable service in the weeks leading up to the battle, both constantly monitoring Italian transmissions and enforcing strict communications security on Austrian formations on the Isonzo. Signal units also disguised the Habsburg buildup on the upper Isonzo through the sending of false and deceptive messages. Thus the signalers gained an accurate assessment of Italian dispositions through signal intercepts while keeping the 14th Army's massive troop movements hidden from hearing as well as sight.

The Austrian air service likewise played a key role in the planning for the great offensive. The small, often ill-equipped Austrian air forces had had a hard war; much like the army as a whole, the airmen found themselves fighting on too many fronts to regularly marshal sufficient strength against any one enemy. The maximum effort for the Twelfth Battle was a rare exception. Still, by late 1917 the Habsburg air service was efficient and manned by veteran personnel, who performed sterling service both before and during the offensive. The I Corps was generously provided with four air companies,[6] augmented by a German squadron, some sixty aircraft in all. The air units undertook vital missions: artillery observation, radio interception, general reconnaissance, and the protection of Austrian airspace; the last was a particularly high priority mission, because Italian overflights had to be prevented both to protect the corps from air attack and to preserve the element of surprise.

The air companies' artillery reconnaissance was all-important. It gave Krauss's gunners the information they needed about where Italian guns were located. All the Austrian guns and shells would be useless without confirmed targets to destroy, and by the eve of the offensive, the I Corps artillery knew the precise location of hundreds of Italian guns, thanks to the aviators' hard work. Krauss's fire plan, the first act of the offensive, called for the barrage to begin at 2 A.M., with gas shelling directed against Italian artillery positions; the 55th Division was assigned its own chemical company for this mission, equipped with a new, highly lethal combination of chlorine and phosgene. The use of poisonous gas in mountainous terrain was invariably precarious because of the unpredictability of wind patterns and abnormal temperature variance. Nevertheless, gas shelling was considered necessary to paralyze Italian batteries and forward defenses. By 4:30 A.M., the gas barrage would be finished, followed by a conventional bombardment of Italian trenches at 6:30, then mortar barrages from 7 A.M. These would continue until 9 A.M., when Austrian infantry would advance, led by the storm troopers. The artillery would fire a rolling barrage, keeping pace with the infantry advance, to protect the Austrian foot soldiers. Once Krauss's I Corps reached Karfreit on the Isonzo, and the 14th Army's other corps breached the Italian lines west of Tolmein, the rest of the Austrian troops on the Isonzo—Army Group Boroević, twenty divisions strong—would attack and retake the Bainsizza, Gorizia, and the western Carso from the retreating Italians, if all went according to plan.

Fortunately for the Austrians, their chances of success were greatly improved by Italian incompetence. If the preparations for the Twelfth Battle brought out the best in Austria's army and officer corps, they surely showed Italy's forces in the worst light. On the eve of the great Austrian attack, Italy's armies on the Isonzo were riddled with slackness, overconfidence, and sheer laziness, not to mention sagging fighting spirit. In the aftermath of the Eleventh Battle, and expecting a quiet winter, Cadorna's forces dug in from Rombon to the Adriatic were weary and wholly unready for the unexpected blow Austria was about to deliver.

That said, Cadorna's armies still looked very impressive on paper. Opposite the Austro-German forces massing east of the Isonzo, Cadorna possessed some thirty-four infantry divisions at the front, plus another seven infantry and four cavalry divisions in nearby reserve. In fact, the Italians had more men on the Isonzo than the Austrians and Germans did: 570 infantry battalions versus 383. The Duke of Aosta's nine-division-strong 3rd Army, dug in on the Carso, occupied defensible positions, and was prepared to meet any Austrian attack.

Capello's 2nd Army, however, which would have to absorb the main Austro-German blow, was another case altogether. In the first place, Capello's army was unmanageably large. It was huge, with twenty-five divisions in nine corps, covering a front of thirty miles, from the Vipacco River at the Carso's edge north to Mt. Rombon. In size and scope the 2nd Army was nearly three times bigger than a normal field army. The defensive tasks of such a large and unwieldy force spread out on such a long front would have taxed the most meticulous commander. To make matters worse, the impetuous Capello was uninterested in defense, and took little care to ensure that his army was well positioned and provisioned for the great defensive battle to come. Indeed, the 2nd Army's defenses were thoroughly inadequate, particularly on the upper Isonzo, where the Austrians and Germans were set to attack. Its entrenchments were relatively strong in the Rombon and Krn sectors (where the 55th Division would attack), but decidedly weak at Tolmein and especially on the newly occupied Bainsizza. There the Italian forces were poorly dug in; only at the old front line—at the Isonzo's edge—were the 2nd Army's entrenchments strong enough to guarantee a vigorous defense.

Despite Cadorna's decision in the third week of September to switch to the defensive for the winter, Capello had done very little to prepare his divisions to fight a defensive battle. After so many months of attacking, the Italians had scant experience with defensive tactics, and Capello's formations on the upper Isonzo were woefully unready to protect their sectors against a determined Austrian assault. Italian defensive techniques were primitive and vulnerable to attack. In particular, Capello concentrated the overwhelming majority of his units in the front line, a thin belt of mountain entrenchments running from Rombon to Krn, down Mrzli ridge, across the Bainsizza past Mt. Santo to the edge of Mt. San Gabriele. Although these high altitude positions were well situated and protected by machine guns, there was little behind them; 231 of Capello's 353 infantry battalions were in the front line. There was no defense in depth, and there were few operational reserves. The large artillery arm was ill prepared to protect the infantry in a defensive battle; it was also placed well forward, and therefore vulnerable both to Austrian artillery fire and to infantry attacks. Thus the 2nd Army was arrayed to defend its long and exposed front line, and nothing else. There were practically no reserves on hand to stage counterattacks to restore the front line. If the Austrians managed to achieve a major breakthrough, cracking the thin crust of Italian defenses, Capello's army would be doomed.

Cadorna became aware of the poor state of Capello's defenses. Alarmed by the weakness of the 2nd Army, especially on the upper Isonzo, on October 10 Cadorna ordered his subordinate to reduce his forces on the Bainsizza and move his heavy artillery back west of the Isonzo. It was a sensible defensive measure that might have helped the 2nd Army considerably in the battle to come. Yet, in a manner all too typical of the Byzantine world of Italian military bureaucracy, Cadorna's directive was never carried out. Capello disliked Cadorna,[7] and often followed only the orders he liked or happened to agree with, believing that his own defensive ideas were correct. So Capello simply disregarded a direct order from the *Comando Supremo*, and the 2nd Army stayed where it was. Capello's disobedience would soon bring awesome strategic consequences.

In fairness to Capello, Cadorna had already done a great deal to wreck the Italian Army from within. His ideas about how to wage war and keep an army's offensive spirit high had done seemingly irreparable damage to the forces in the field. By October 1917, the *fanti* were exhausted and plainly sick of the war; many simply wanted the senseless fighting to end. Ordinary soldiers were fully aware of how few gains eleven offensives on the Isonzo had won for Italy, and how demoralized the home front had become. Cadorna had inevitably failed to protect his armies from domestic political "contamination." Decimations and executions, liberally applied, might keep an army in the field through terror, but they signally failed to maintain fighting spirit. Just as devastating for the army, Cadorna had relentlessly continued his policy of "torpedoing" commanders who disappointed him. By October 1917, he had dismissed hundreds of senior officers for a "lack of offensive spirit": 217 generals, 255 colonels, and 355 battalion commanders, in all.[8] Coupled with heavy casualties among field officers, this meant that most Italian infantry units were now led by woefully inexperienced—and sometimes obviously incompetent—commanders. Willingness to sacrifice their men's lives, rather than tactical proficiency, was Cadorna's main test of an officer's ability. Needless to add, such shortsighted policies only served to lower the already poor state of the Italian infantry's morale and fighting prowess.

The army's evident tactical and morale problems were made immeasurably worse by the *Comando Supremo*'s shocking inability to predict the Austro-German offensive. It amounted to an intelligence failure of epic proportions. Although Cadorna had been obsessed with a fear of a major Austrian offensive ever since the war began on the Isonzo—a concern much compounded by Conrad's South Tyrolean offensive in the spring of 1916—by the autumn of 1917 he was absolutely convinced that the Austrians could not launch an offensive so late in the year. Cadorna was serenely confident that a late autumn offensive was impossible, particularly in the snow-covered Julian Alps. In fact, he was so sure that his armies were safe from attack that on October 4 he left Udine for a two-week holiday away from the front. He planned to spend the winter writing his memoirs, recording his outstanding contribution to the Great War, a task that occupied his mind much more than any fears of an Austrian offensive.

Despite Austria's best efforts at deception, there was still ample evidence available to the Italians that an offensive was coming, but Cadorna and his staff simply refused to believe it. By mid-October, Italian military intelligence had collected impressive and convincing information that Austrian and German forces were massing on the upper Isonzo. Signals intelligence, diplomatic espionage, aerial observation, and Austrian deserters' accounts all pointed to only one possible conclusion: the first Habsburg offensive on the Isonzo was imminent. Even so, Cadorna remained obstinately incredulous. On October 19, an Italian intelligence report noted accurately that several German divisions had passed through Ljubljana, headed for the Isonzo, in the past two weeks, and that since mid-September a thousand Austrian guns had arrived to reinforce Boroević's army group. Yet on the very same day, two senior colonels on Cadorna's staff assured him that there were no signs of any impending Austro-German offensive. Cadorna accepted this news unquestioningly; after all, he had always said that no large-scale offensive was possible on the Isonzo after late September, least of all in the high Julian Alps. On October 23, only hours before the Austrian and German guns were scheduled to open fire, Italian signal units overheard an Austrian telephone message which indicated that the artillery was prepared to commence its barrage at 2 A.M. on October 24. Still, the Italians dismissed this, and did nothing to react or prepare. In truth, it no longer mattered. It was already too late.

At exactly two hours past midnight on October 24, Austrian and German artillery opened fire on the upper Isonzo. From the northern Bainsizza to Rombon, Italian artillery batteries were struck by thousands of gas shells. Many Italian soldiers, awakened by the barrage, found their French gas masks useless against the new chemical agents, and died or were burned terribly within minutes. In the dark mountain valleys, thousands of Italian soldiers drowned in the dense, lingering clouds of chlorine and phosgene. The 14th Army's artillery, 1,700 guns strong, kept up its lethal work until dawn. Then the infantry readied to go into battle. As the sun rose, soldiers of the I Corps were read a message from General Krauss, in the troops' many languages, that epitomized the Austrian determination for victory: "Soldiers of the I Corps! For the second time in this war we are going on the attack against Italy! For you this phrase counts: No calm and no rest until the Italians are crushed. Forward with God!" With this message the 55th Division entered the fight.

It was hard going at first. Much of Krauss's sector was hit by an unexpected snowstorm and heavy fog that lasted for hours. The weather was particularly bad in the Vrata-Vršič area, where the 55th Division was set to advance. In addition, Schwarzenberg's opponents, the Italian 43rd Division, included good troops—three line regiments, a regiment of *Bersaglieri*, and another regiment's worth of *Alpini*. As a result, the Bosnians and Carinthians, hampered by difficult weather, made comparatively little progress on October 24. While the rest of the 14th Army advanced pretty much according to schedule, capturing 30,000 *fanti* in the first twenty-four hours, Schwarzenberg's division and the neighboring 22nd Rifle Division to the north advanced slowly. Even the Bosnians had difficulty advancing up 6,000-foot-high peaks through waist-high snowdrifts. Yet the 4th Bosnian Regiment fought effectively, repulsing an Italian night counterattack, and capturing a battalion of the 43rd Division. The only one of Schwarzenberg's battalions to secure all of its assigned objectives for October 24 was the 4th of the 7th Regiment, led by Captain Eduard Barger. The 900-man Carinthian unit advanced daringly through the Mrzli line, but even Barger admitted that victory at that point in the offensive was mostly a matter of chance: "If at this moment . . . even one Italian machine gun had opened up on our attack, we all would have been killed." But the "brown devils" were lucky, and they took all their objectives, losing only twenty dead and eighty wounded on the offensive's first day.

Undaunted, Krauss ordered the 55th Division to attack even more energetically toward Karfreit on the morning of October 25. The snowfall had ceased and the heavy fog had lifted, so Schwarzenberg's soldiers now advanced easily. The 43rd Division, crippled by the Austrian guns, had exhausted itself in futile counterattacks, and was now incapable of sustained resistance. The 7th Regiment, led by *Strumtruppen*, tore a large gap in the Italian line, and the Italian defense began to crumble. By midmorning, both of the 55th's brigades had descended from Mrzli ridge toward the Isonzo valley, and Karfreit, captured by the Italians in the first weeks of the war, was again in Austrian hands by noon. The 43rd Division had evaporated, and the IV Corps's reserve, the 34th Division, which should have launched a counterattack against Krauss's advancing regiments, had been badly bruised in the recent fight for San Gabriele and wanted only to surrender. Schwarzenberg's forward units secured Karfreit's stone bridge over the Isonzo, the most important objective. Although the cold, fast-flowing Isonzo was only three feet deep at Karfreit, Austrian artillery and supply units required a sturdy bridge to cross the river. By midday on October 25 they had it. Soon Schwarzenberg entered Karfreit (Caporetto to the Italians), the river town that would give the great offensive its name.

The triumphant 55th Division continued its advance through the afternoon, encountering no appreciable Italian resistance. Indeed, like its sister formations in the I Corps, the 55th Division found itself inundated with Italian prisoners. Once the IV Corps's first line of defense gave way, morale collapsed and the will to resist disappeared. Many *fanti* surrendered enthusiastically to the Austrians. A platoon of the 22nd Division, fighting on the northern flank of Schwarzenberg's troops, captured a whole entrenched Italian company on October 25 without a shot being fired. Some 140 Italians came out of their mountaintop trenches crying, "*Evviva l'Austria, la guerra è finita.*"[9] One Italian officer was so relieved to be out of the war that he kissed the hand of the Austrian platoon commander. The jubilant Italians were sent to the rear with the words they wanted to hear, "*Nach Mauthausen.*" For them the long and terrible war was over.

Such incidents became increasingly common as the 2nd Army melted away before the advancing Austrian and German divisions. Nowhere on the upper Isonzo was Italian resistance prolonged or successful. Italian generals were caught completely unaware by the Austro-German blow north of Tolmein. Even after hearing early reports of the offensive, on October 24 Cadorna pronounced his "perfect serenity and complete confidence." Capello was not even at the front. On the eve of the offensive, seriously ill, he left the Isonzo for rest in Turin; his place was taken by General Montuori, commander of the II Corps, who inherited the unfolding disaster. Not that it made any difference. The 2nd Army's precarious defenses shattered quickly and never recovered. Chaos reigned as the 14th Army broke through in both the Rombon-Krn and Tolmein areas. Even the 2nd Army's powerful artillery proved no help; on October 24, battery commanders all along the upper Isonzo waited in vain for orders to open fire that never came, and were simply overwhelmed. On October 26, Cadorna at last realized that something had gone dreadfully wrong. The 2nd Army had folded, especially on the upper Isonzo. From Rombon through the Bainsizza, Italian resistance had evaporated, exposing the rest of the Italian Army to lethal encirclement. The *Comando Supremo* had lost all contact with several divisions north of the Bainsizza. No one knew where General Villani, commander of the 19th Division, was; his division, holding the strategic Tolmein bridgehead, had disappeared. In fact, Villani was dead, a suicide. So on October 27, with Austrian and German divisions racing toward his headquarters in Udine, Cadorna reluctantly ordered a general retreat from the Isonzo, before his entire army was lost.

While the Italians were paralyzed by inaction and confusion, the Austrians and Germans continued their advance at an awe-inspiring pace. One of the most successful drives into the Italian rear was executed by the Württemberg Mountain Battalion, an elite unit of veteran Alpine troops. Its objective was Mt. Matajur, a 4,500-foot-high peak four miles southwest of Karfreit. This snowy peak straddled the Austrian-Italian frontier and was the last significant mountain before reaching the Friulian plain. General von Below, commander of the 14th Army, was so eager to capture Matajur that he promised the *Pour le Mérite*, the coveted "Blue Max," Prussia's highest decoration, to the officer whose unit seized it.

The young officer who led the German advance to Matajur was twenty-six-year-old Erwin Rommel, a first lieutenant soon to be promoted to captain. A career infantry officer, Rommel served with distinction in the French campaign of 1914, then helped raise the Württemberg Mountain Battalion in September 1915. He fought with this crack new unit in the Vosges, then in Transylvania, winning a reputation for daring and cunning on the field of battle. He came to the Isonzo with the German *Alpenkorps* to take part in the great offensive; he had been wounded by a Romanian bullet only ten weeks before, but was eager to be part of the coming fight. He was particularly eager to win the Blue Max.

His command was the Rommel Detachment, with three mountain rifle companies and a machine gun company in support, a full battalion in strength. (Major Sprosser's Württemberg Mountain Battalion was nearly the size of a regiment, with eleven companies.) Rommel's detachment began October 24 by breaking through Villani's ill-fated 19th Division due west of Tolmein, just after 8 A.M. By noon, Rommel and his men were in the Italian rear, and there were no forces before them, so they continued their advance toward Matajur. They marched up 3,500-foot-high Kolovrat ridge, just south of the Isonzo, the quickest route to Matajur, but encountered little Italian resistance; the 2nd Army had already begun to collapse. The marching was arduous for Rommel's heavily laden mountain troopers, each man carrying enough ammunition and supplies to last several days, eighty pounds of equipment in all. Rommel's men hardly rested that night, instead continuing their steady march across Kolovrat. By October 25, the Rommel Detachment had captured 1,500 Italian prisoners. The next objective was the village of Luico, three miles east of Matajur. Rommel took it by leading a surprise charge straight into the village. The stunned Italian garrison surrendered *en masse*: a hundred *fanti* and fifty vehicles were added to Rommel's haul. Just beyond Luico, Rommel and his men pounced on the surprised 4th *Bersaglieri* Regiment. The Italians fought back initially, but surrendered once they were surrounded; 2,000 more troops—the whole regiment—entered German captivity.

Major Sprosser, receiving word that Rommel had reached Luico, ordered the enterprising lieutenant to halt and wait for reinforcements. Rommel would hear none of it, and instead led one of his companies toward Matajur, in violation of Sprosser's direct order. On the way to Matajur, Rommel and his forward detachment, a hundred men with six machine guns, captured the whole Salerno Brigade. One of its regiments, 1,500 strong, simply ran out of its positions, shouting "Long live Germany!"; the second regiment resisted briefly, but then gave up, too, adding 1,200 more *fanti* to Rommel's burgeoning column of captives. Rommel, anxious to keep going, sent the prisoners to the rear and continued to advance. By the morning of October 26, he and his company were at the foot of Matajur. The advance to the summit was arduous, ending with a mad 400-yard dash over rocky ground to Matajur's peak. At 11:40 A.M., Rommel fired signal flares from Matajur's almost mile-high summit to indicate that he had taken it.

The last of the Julian Alps was in German hands, and the 2nd Army was doomed. In fifty-two hours of almost nonstop advancing, Rommel had captured 9,000 Italian soldiers, at a cost of less than twenty casualties of his own. He justly received his *Pour le Mérite* (as did Major Sprosser, who forgave Rommel for his insubordination), thus bringing to prominence one of the greatest and most legendary soldiers of the twentieth century.[10]

Although Rommel's feat was the most dramatic, in many places on the upper Isonzo small units of Austrian and German troops managed to capture entire companies, battalions, even regiments of weary Italian soldiers without a fight. The 2nd Army's will to resist had disappeared when confronted with the first Austrian offensive on the Isonzo. That said, in places Italian infantry resisted fiercely, even against hopeless odds, inflicting heavy losses among advancing Austro-German forces. The fight for Rombon was especially vicious and costly. The Edelweiss Division succeeded in pushing the Italians off the mountain on October 25, but only after nearly two days of bruising close combat. Some of Krauss's best regiments, including the 2nd Imperial Tyrolean Rifles (*Kaiserschützen*)[11] took heavy losses in the battle for Rombon, an exception to the generally light casualties suffered by the I Corps during the breakthrough phase of the Twelfth Battle. One of the Austrian casualties was First Lieutenant Franz Janowitz, a twenty-five-year-old officer of the 2nd *Kaiserschützen*, who led his company in the October 24 attack on Rombon.

Janowitz, the son of a prosperous Bohemian Jewish family, had studied philosophy at Leipzig and Vienna, and was serving as an officer cadet when the war began. He fought with his regiment on the Russian front through 1916, when he was transferred to the Italian front. He often wrote poetry between battles, a favorite pastime; indeed, Max Brod had published fourteen of Janowitz's poems in his *Arcadia* yearbook in 1913. Janowitz's works grew increasingly dark and brooding as the war dragged on, and by October 1917 he had collected a folio of fifty-one poems, many dealing with the war, that he hoped to publish.

One of the best was "Be, Earth, True!" ("*Sei, Erde, Wahr!*"), composed in Galicia during the summer of 1916. It focused on what Janowitz had witnessed:

> You star of war, now cover up your flood,
> rise up in spheres in a ball of blood!
>
> As smoking, as you smoke, appear in shame!
> Hang out your sign, let murder be your name!
>
> A raging eye, you gaze on nothingness,
> to every child of light you bring distress.
>
> A wandering sign announcing mothers' woe,
> you at the head, the world must die below.

Janowitz, leading his men into battle, was struck by an Italian bullet on Rombon. He survived the difficult stretcher ride down the 7,290-foot-high mountain, but died in a field hospital on November 4. Franz Janowitz lived long enough to know that the offensive had succeeded, that the Italians had been thoroughly thrashed, but he did not live long enough to see his war poems in print. That came only two years later, when the noted Viennese journalist Karl Kraus, a friend of Janowitz's brother Otto, persuaded a publisher to put out the dead soldier's poems. The collection, *On the Earth* (*Auf der Erde*), which appeared in 1919, was praised but never reprinted.

By the morning of October 28, the Italian Army was in headlong retreat away from the Isonzo. With the collapse of the 2nd Army's left flank, its right flank east and northeast of Gorizia, as well as the Duke of Aosta's 3rd Army, were forced to withdraw across Friulia. It was bitter news, especially for the 3rd Army—"the undefeated"—which had managed to repulse all Austrian attacks on the Carso. Objectives that had been bought at such cost in Italian blood— Gorizia, Plava, Mt. Santo, Mt. San Michele, Sabotino, Podgora, Oslavia—were relinquished without a fight. The 8th Division, the recent captors of the summit of Mt. Santo, left the ruined monastery, aware that they had not been defeated, merely outflanked by the collapse of the 2nd Army on the upper Isonzo. Officers and men wept openly as the army abandoned Gorizia and the Carso, now crowded with hundreds of thousands of Italian graves. The retreating Italian soldiers could do nothing except promise to return again in victory.

On the heels of the Italian retreat, the 1st and 2nd Isonzo Armies reoccupied all the terrain they had lost since June 1915 and the First Battle of the Isonzo. Some 60,000 Italian prisoners were already in Austrian captivity. On October 28, the black-yellow standard of the Habsburgs was again raised over Gorizia, and Boroević's troops crossed the Isonzo and were soon marching past the shell-scarred battlefields of Podgora and Oslavia, headed across the Italian frontier into Friulia.

The Italian retreat was a shambles. Although the 3rd Army, led energetically by the Duke of Aosta, withdrew in good order, showing admirable march discipline, the 2nd Army hardly existed anymore. Even those divisions which escaped the Austro-German breakthrough soon fell apart. Without leadership, the defeated army was reduced to a rabble; thousands of *fanti* just wanted to surrender, and countless others chose to desert. Everywhere the 2nd Army abandoned its equipment—guns, munitions, vehicles, and all.[12] The great *ritorno a casa* had begun. The masses of Italian troops heading westward through Friulia were more a mob than any kind of fighting force. Cadorna might have gone to considerable lengths to save the situation by exercising inspiring leadership in the hour of crisis, but that had never been his style of command. Instead, he spent the early days of the great retreat blaming others—the soldiers, the politicians, the press, the socialists, everyone but himself—for the debacle. He told Antonio Gatti, his adjutant, "What could I do? The army was swarming with worms." Cadorna's official communiqué of October 28, in which he wasted no time pronouncing the defeat "perhaps the greatest catastrophe in history," explicitly blamed the soldiers for the retreat: "The failure to resist on the part of units of the 2nd Army, which cravenly withdrew without fighting or ignominiously surrendered to the enemy, has allowed the Austro-German forces to break through our left flank on the Julian front." Of course, nowhere did Cadorna hint at any command failures, or why the once intrepid Italian infantry had broken so easily; he did, however, repeatedly blame his favorite nemesis, "the internal enemy," for the battlefield reverse. The tactless communiqué was watered down by the government when it reached Rome, but it was published abroad in its original form. By then the political damage was done. Cadorna's military career was probably finished on the morning of October 24, when the 2nd Army started to fall apart, but his dishonest pronouncement four days later confirmed his demise.

While Cadorna was busy composing his communiqué, the Austrian and German armies advanced deeper into Italy. By October 29, the 14th Army and the 1st and 2nd Isonzo Armies stood firmly on Italian territory; the next day Udine, Cadorna's hastily abandoned headquarters, fell without much of a fight.[13] Nowhere east of the Tagliamento River could retreating Italian divisions offer prolonged resistance, and Austro-German forces soon occupied all of Friulia. The next major Austrian goal was crossing the Tagliamento, thirty miles west of the Isonzo. By seizing a bridgehead across the river, the Austrians would cut off what remained of the 2nd and 3rd Armies. It was imperative that Habsburg forces reach the Tagliamento before Italians could blow all the bridges. The 55th Division spent October 28 marching toward the town of Cornino, which possessed the only surviving bridge across the Tagliamento. Although Italian resistance was neither stiff nor prolonged, the marching pace of nearly thirty miles daily was exceptionally arduous. The advancing Bosnians and Carinthians regularly outpaced their supporting artillery and logistical columns, causing ammunition and other supply problems. Regardless, Schwarzenberg's lead companies reached the Tagliamento late on October 29, found the bridge at Cornino intact, and readied themselves for a contested crossing.

At Cornino the river was the better part of a mile wide and apparently unfordable. There was also a large island in the Tagliamento at Cornino, Colle Clapat, which was connected by two wide bridges to each bank. The unit Schwarzenberg chose for the assault was the 4th Battalion of the 4th *Bosniaken*. Schwarzenberg wanted to lead the cross-river attack personally, but was dissuaded by his cooler-headed staff. Although the Bosnians were exhausted from the long march across Friulia, the veteran battalion responded enthusiastically to the chance to decide the campaign's outcome; the breaching of the Tagliamento line would force a general Italian retreat to the Piave River, more than thirty miles farther west. For this reason, the defenders of Colle Clapat, two companies of the 33rd Regiment supported by sixteen machine guns, were equally determined to hold their ground.

The battalion commander, Captain Emil Redl, volunteered to lead the assault. The forty-year-old Redl, a native of Gorizia, had spent his career as a line infantry officer in Croatian and Bosnian units; he had fought with the 4th Bosnian Regiment through the war, commanding first a company, and then a battalion. He led his battalion's 15th Company forward at 4 A.M. on October 31, under the cover of darkness and rain and heavy machine gun fire. Tenacious Italian resistance prevented a predawn victory as the Bosnians stalled on the sandy shore of Colle Clapat. But by midmorning, when the 16th Company entered the fray, the *fanti* began to lose ground. The flat, marshy island offered little natural cover, and losses were heavy on both sides. An Italian counterattack by reserve elements of the 33rd Regiment was repulsed, including a probe across the bridge by armored cars, which the *Bosniaken* destroyed at close quarters with machine gun fire and hand grenades. Redl's troops also found a small ford on the Italians' flank and rushed fresh infantry into the battle, turning the tide. By the end of October 31, Redl's tired companies had secured Colle Clapat, in the process capturing most of the 33rd Regiment—more than 1,500 *fanti*, thirty-one machine guns, and six artillery pieces.[14] Although the Bosnians had suffered heavy casualties in two companies, a further advance to the west bank of the Tagliamento was halted only by the blowing of the second bridge by retreating Italian engineers.

The following two days, both sides prepared for the inevitable Austrian crossing attempt. The remnants of the 33rd Regiment were reinforced and ordered to hold their ground on the Tagliamento's west bank at any cost. The Italians were entrenched in and around the town of Cornino, which overlooked the Tagliamento and was surrounded by steep hills that offered excellent fields of fire for the defender. Schwarzenberg was still confident that his division could cross the river, and he sent Captain Redl a company each of sappers and construction engineers to help the Bosnians reach the west bank. The three-battalion-strong 2nd Bosnian Regiment was also moved forward to exploit Redl's success in the coming assault. The 55th, having lost only 1,655 casualties since October 24 (only 157 of them killed in action, many of them on Colle Clapat), was in excellent fighting trim.

At 6 A.M. on November 2, supported by machine gun and artillery fire, the 55th Division engineers began to construct a temporary bridge over the collapsed span. They were soon followed by two *Sturm* platoons and the 13th and 14th Companies of Redl's battalion. Through sheer courage and determination, by noon the lead companies forced their way across the unstable bridge against withering Italian fire, taking heavy casualties in the process. In the afternoon the rest of Redl's battalion crossed, followed in the evening by a fresh battalion of the 2nd *Bosniaken*. During the night the Bosnians advanced through the town of Cornino, capturing one house at a time, scaling the steep hills above the village. The 33rd Regiment, overrun by the fearsome Bosnians, began to surrender as Austrian reinforcements entered the fray, surrounding Cornino and taking nearby hills. By the early dawn hours of November 3, the Cornino bridgehead firmly belonged to the 55th Division, a whole regiment of 2,500 *fanti* had been captured, and the Austrians had secured a nearly mile-deep hold on the Tagliamento's west bank. The rest of Schwarzenberg's victorious division soon followed to exploit the Bosnians' hard-fought victory.

The success of Captain Redl and his *Bosniaken* proved to be the decisive action of the entire offensive. As Emperor Karl said to Redl when presenting him the Order of Maria Theresia, "You gave our offensive fresh momentum." Unable to hold the Tagliamento line, the Italians began a disorderly strategic retreat toward the Piave. By now, Austrian and German forces had captured a quarter of a million Italian soldiers, as well as 2,300 artillery pieces—essentially the whole 2nd Army. Another 40,000 Italian soldiers were out of action, killed or wounded since October 24. Many more Italian units were rounded up before they reached the Piave; on November 6, the 22nd Rifle Division captured the entire Italian XII Corps, two divisions strong. Countless Italian units, scattered and confused by the retreat, surrendered without a fight. Feeble attempts to maintain national and personal dignity in the face of catastrophe were commonplace. In one instance, an officer cadet of the 7th Regiment, leading an eight-man patrol nearly twenty miles west of Cornino, accepted the surrender of a fully armed battalion of 500 Italians. The *fanti* were cheered by the end of their war, exclaiming "*Mama mia*" while being led into captivity. The major commanding the battalion, however, did not want to be captured by a mere officer cadet and eight men, so some haggling was required to save face. In the end, though, the battalion was disarmed and marched eastward, *nach Mauthausen*, like hundreds of other Italian units captured whole in the days after the initial Austrian breakthrough at Karfreit.[15]

By now the extent of the Italian disaster was evident to the army, to the government, and to the Italian people. Vittorio Emanuele, horrified by the collapse of his beloved army, wrote in his diary, in English, "What caused it all?" He contemplated abdication for a time, but instead resolved to lead his people in resistance to the foreign invader. One of Vittorio Emanuele's first acts in the aftermath of defeat was the dismissal of Cadorna, the architect of catastrophe. Capello was almost immediately sacked, but Cadorna apparently expected his career to survive Caporetto. The first indication of Cadorna's irrevocable withdrawal into unreality was the Rapallo conference. On November 5, the political and military leaders of Italy, Britain, and France met in emergency session to discuss the recent Italian defeat on the Isonzo, and to coordinate an Allied grand strategy to counter the Austro-German victory. Cadorna did not bother to attend, sending his second in command, General Porro, in his place. At Rapallo, Porro claimed that thirty-five German divisions had participated in the offensive—five times the actual number—and, as expected, blamed the soldiers and the politicians for the defeat, as Cadorna no doubt wished. At Peschiera on November 8, at a meeting of British, French, and Italian generals to discuss the details of Allied planning, Vittorio Emanuele, in excellent English, explained his country's predicament; he formally requested help from the Allies, and explicitly blamed Cadorna and the generals for the debacle. Cadorna was outraged. At first he refused to resign, believing himself to be above even the king. He pointedly criticized "the notorious ingratitude of the House of Savoy." He had finally gone too far.

Vittorio Emanuele dismissed Cadorna as head of the *Comando Supremo*, although he did not force him to retire altogether. Cadorna, the director of Italy's war effort from the outset, was out of office, and a replacement was needed quickly to reassure both the army and the public, particularly in such an hour of crisis. The cabinet, and the Allies, wanted the Duke of Aosta to become the new chief of the General Staff. The duke, after all, was Italy's most accomplished general—he had saved the 3rd Army from defeat only two weeks before—and he was popular with the troops. Yet Vittorio Emanuele balked at the idea. Always jealous of his glamorous and dashing forty-eight-year-old cousin (when the unassuming Vittorio Emanuele became king in 1900, he nearly convinced his father to permit him to renounce the throne in favor of the duke), Vittorio Emanuele, never very self-confident, now feared that appointing the Duke of Aosta as Italy's senior general would give him a platform to make the king even less popular. Therefore Vittorio Emanuele suggested a compromise candidate.

The man who took Cadorna's place at the *Comando Supremo* on November 8 was Armando Diaz, a fifty-five-year-old general with an impeccable service record. He was cut from very different cloth than Cadorna, or indeed than most of the Italian officer corps. In the first place he was a southerner, a Neapolitan, from a family of Spanish origins. Diaz was an artillery officer by training, but spent most of his career on staffs—he stayed a total of sixteen years in Rome. But Diaz nevertheless possessed ample knowledge of fighting. He commanded an infantry regiment before the Great War, including time in battle in Libya; he was very popular with his *fanti* because he believed in light discipline and was genuinely concerned for the welfare of his troops. Diaz returned from Libya in 1912 with battle wounds, decorations for valor, and a reputation for humanity and common sense as well as courage. Needless to say, compassion and sensibility were not valued qualities in Cadorna's army, but Diaz nevertheless rose quickly during the Great War. He commanded an infantry division on the Carso for ten months, beginning in mid-1916; again he demonstrated a concern for his troops' welfare and longevity. He was also tactically astute: Diaz managed to conquer more ground, at a lower cost in lives, than other generals on the Carso. He assumed command of the XXIII Corps in April 1917, leading it to victories in the Tenth and Eleventh Battles; indeed, his XXIII Corps captured Selo in August, the only success for the 3rd Army in the last Italian offensive on the Isonzo.

Diaz's appointment as *capo dello stato maggiore* heralded a new era for the Italian army. Unlike Cadorna in virtually every way, Diaz personally understood what the *fantaccino* had endured on the Isonzo. He knew why the 2nd Army had collapsed so quickly and so totally. Diaz assumed his new post with a threefold mission before him: to resist the Austrian invasion, to restore and rebuild the army, and to win the war at the lowest possible cost in Italian lives. Beginning on November 8, Diaz devoted himself completely to attaining these goals. He was helped considerably by the new assistant chief of staff, Pietro Badoglio. Only eighteen months before, Badoglio had been a young and obscure regimental commander; in November 1917, after a meteoric rise, he was the second in command of the Italian Army. Although Badoglio had, in fact, been partly responsible for the Caporetto disaster—his poorly arrayed XXVII Corps had fallen apart almost immediately when struck by Austro-German assault divisions—Vittorio Emanuele did not know this, and felt the enterprising Badoglio could help rebuild the army. This he did effectively, thus redeeming himself for his failure on the upper Isonzo. Badoglio's specialty was rewriting Italian tactical doctrine, particularly defensive doctrine, a glaring Italian shortcoming. He would guarantee that Caporetto could not happen again.

Before the army could be rebuilt, though, the Austrians had to be stopped. By the second week of November, the Italians had decided to make their stand on the Piave. This mile-wide river, which began in the highest of the Carnic Alps, on the Austrian frontier, flowed past the Dolomites, then meandered through the coastal plain, reaching the Adriatic less than twenty miles northeast of Venice. The Piave was the last natural obstacle before the heart of Venetia and Venice itself. Either the Austrians would be stopped at the Piave, or north-eastern Italy would be lost. Diaz hastily dispatched all available reserves to the Piave; it did not amount to much, but by mid-November, most of the Piave line was defended by the 3rd Army. The Duke of Aosta's *Terza Armata* was anxious to inflict a punishing defeat on the Austrians, revenge for the loss of the Carso and the Isonzo. The 1st Army, still in good order, defended the Asiago plateau, and the understrength 4th Army was wedged between them, in the center of the Italian line.

The Austrians tried to breach the Piave line before winter arrived, but it was a logistically impossible task. The Austrian armies had suffered trifling casualties during the Twelfth Battle of the Isonzo compared to the magnitude of their victory, but maintaining a continuous advance was asking too much of the over-extended supply services. The fighting troops were still willing to keep going, but their vital stores of ammunition and matériel could not keep pace. By mid-November, the 1st and 2nd Isonzo Armies had reached the Piave in strength, and the 14th Army was at edge of the eastern Asiago plateau. Army Group Boroević had advanced sixty miles or more since late October 24, an amazing gain by the standards of the Great War. Still, the march into Venetia taxed the Austrian logistical system to its limits; it took weeks for supply columns to reach the Piave in adequate numbers. By then the Italians were firmly established on the river's west bank.

On November 16 the Austrian 29th Division attempted to establish a bridgehead across the Piave, but the effort failed with heavy losses. The Italians resisted tenaciously, meeting the Austrian river crossing with a determined counterattack. The few Austrian survivors swam back to the east bank and safety. The story was the same on the Asiago plateau. There, Austrian divisions—it was by now almost entirely a Habsburg affair, the Germans having headed for home—tried to break through the plateau's rugged mountain defenses. A hodgepodge of Italian units of the 4th Army, undefeated in battle, fought back furiously, and the Austrians advanced only slowly and painfully. Even Krauss's I Corps managed to gain little ground against the Italians there. The 55th Division, fresh from its victories at Karfreit and Cornino, met unexpectedly strong resistance when it tried to clear the highlands south of the city of Feltre, on the Piave. The division fought a vicious battle for Mt. Tomatico, a 5,200-foot-high snowy peak defended by a regiment of *Alpini*, a fight that exhausted even Schwarzenberg's crack division. The veteran 7th Regiment soon called Tomatico "our mountain of death"; the summit fell after several days of costly failed attempts, and then the 55th Division received a well-earned rest from action.

By any standards the Twelfth Battle and its aftermath represented an unprecedented catastrophe for Italian arms. By November 20, Italy had lost some 800,000 soldiers. Perhaps 50,000 were dead and wounded, not less than

300,000 were in Austrian captivity, and the remainder—as many as 400,000—had deserted in the chaos and confusion. By the end of November, Diaz had disbanded much of the lost army: forty-six regiments of infantry, four of *Bersaglieri*, fifteen *Alpini* battalions, and numerous support units. Italy's equipment losses were equally terrible: 3,150 guns, 1,732 mortars, 3,000 machine guns, and 300,000 rifles. In less than a month, the Italian Army shrank from sixty-five divisions to just thirty-three. In stark contrast, Austrian and German battle losses amounted to only 30,000 soldiers. It was an epic defeat. The magnitude of the disaster that befell the Italian Army on the Isonzo in late October 1917 surpassed even the Austrian catastrophe of mid-1916 in Galicia.

Yet Italy was still in the war, though if just barely. The conscript class of 1899 was called to the colors ahead of schedule in mid-November to replace the army's unparalleled losses, and Diaz rushed 300,000 ill-trained replacements and weary convalescents to the front in December to save the remnants of the Italian Army. In addition, help came quickly from the worried Allies: five British and six French divisions, well equipped and veterans of considerable fighting, were shipped immediately from the Western front to the Piave and the Asiago plateau to stave off collapse. Most important, perhaps, was the dramatic change that the Caporetto disaster brought to Italy. Austrian armies now occupied much of northeastern Italy, and total defeat seemed dangerously close. The Caporetto debacle nearly destroyed Italy's armies, and it completely altered Italian feeling about the war. In a few short weeks, the Great War was transformed in Italian eyes from an offensive struggle on the Isonzo to liberate *Italia irredenta* into a defensive fight on the Piave for national survival. Antiwar sentiment evaporated overnight as the Austrians stood at Venice's door; even those Socialists who had long criticized Cadorna's "imperialist war" now sounded militantly patriotic. In the words of newly appointed Prime Minister Vittorio Orlando, who formed a government of national unity after Caporetto, "The people must know that when the nation is in danger, we are all united." Thus the terrible defeat at Caporetto gave Italy the common purpose and unity of spirit that Cadorna's eleven calamitous offensives on the Isonzo had failed to produce.

The Austrians naturally did not notice this yet. The whole Habsburg Empire was still in the grips of a euphoria that transcended national lines. At last the hated Italians, Austria's faithless former allies, had been punished for their betrayal. The "Caporetto miracle"—*das Wunder von Karfreit*—was hailed as the greatest victory and most successful offensive of the Great War, at least in Western Europe, and indeed it was. The Austrian Army, after stoically enduring twenty-eight months of Italian attacks on the Isonzo, finally struck back. Boroević and his armies had brought the war to Italian soil. The army of the Habsburgs had never fought better. It had shown itself to be tactically skilled and imbued with excellent fighting spirit. Soldiers of all nationalities, including some that had failed to fight effectively on other fronts, battled bravely and victoriously on the Isonzo, and marched across Friulia and Venetia. Although Germany had lent her Habsburg ally considerable help with men and equipment, the Caporetto victory was unquestionably an Austrian triumph.

As 1917 drew to a close, the Central Powers appeared tantalizingly close to complete victory. For Austria, after more than three years of bruising total war, a victorious end was finally in sight. Serbia, the Habsburgs' original foe, had been crushed long ago, and Romania had more recently been knocked out of the war. Even Russia, Austria's deadliest opponent, was effectively out of the war, torn asunder by an emerging bloody civil war and Bolshevik revolution. Of Austria's enemies, only Italy remained, and she had been almost fatally weakened by the Caporetto offensive. The war that had begun and raged so long on the Isonzo had moved deep into northern Italy. As the Austrian Army ended 1917, its triumphal year, it could look forward to continuing a one-front, popular war against a nearly defeated foe.

1918

THIRTEEN

AN ITALIAN RENAISSANCE

The future of the Habsburg Empire and its army seemed brighter at the beginning of 1918 than at any point since the outbreak of war. Austria, which started the Great War poorly prepared to fight compared to its adversaries, had survived three and a half years of total war. Costly battles of attrition had worn down the Austrian Army, but the often strategically indecisive campaigns in Galicia and on the Isonzo had in a sense begun to pay off: of Austria's enemies, only Italy remained, and the Italian Army, recently shattered at Caporetto, appeared unlikely to stage a recovery soon.

As the war's last year began, the Austrian Army deployed forty-four divisions against the Italians, including all its elite formations. The Italian front was far and away the main Habsburg front; the Russian and Balkan theaters were now mere sideshows in comparison. Austria's remaining thirty-seven divisions, most of them understrength, were deployed in dormant theaters, more as occupation forces than as combat divisions.

Offsetting such encouraging developments, however, were many grave problems. None was more serious than Austria's increasing lack of soldiers. Ironically, casualty rates had been falling since the beginning of the war: 1917 had been, in fact, the best year yet, but Austria still lost 1,481,000 soldiers during the year, counting those hospitalized for illness. Even though the army's overall loss rate was in decline, the total number of Austrian casualties by 1918 was enormous. Of the 8,420,000 men called to the colors by the end of 1917, a staggering 4,010,000 had been lost to the army permanently, including 780,000 dead, a half-million invalided due to wounds, and over 1.6 million taken prisoner. The unavoidable reality confronting Austria was that the empire was rapidly running out of men. By 1918, Austria had already called more than 70 percent of its available men to the colors.

To make matters worse, the number of soldiers in the front lines had declined precipitously. The *Etappe*, the rear areas so detested by combat troops, including training and replacement depots, convalescent units, and ever growing support echelons, had expanded enormously since 1914 to meet the unprecedented manpower and matériel needs of total war. Thus, of 4,912,000 Habsburg soldiers of all kinds in uniform at the beginning of January 1918,[1] 1,661,000—one-third—were garrisoned in home districts, safe from the combat zone. However, even among the 3,251,000 Austrian soldiers constituting the field army, less than a million were actually combat soldiers.

By the last year of the war, repeated comb-outs of rear area units and industry could produce only limited numbers of men for the war machine; nearly all the fit and able men had long before been dispatched to the front. Even the use of volunteer "female assistant helpers" for service and administrative duties, of whom there were some 90,000 in early 1918, did comparatively little to ameliorate the shortage of Austrian fighting men. The army was especially lacking in infantrymen. The infantry, only 38.7 percent of the army's overall strength, accounted for roughly 95 percent of its casualties. The pool of available infantry replacements had begun to dry up. By January 1918, Austria could dispatch only 100,000 replacements to the field army monthly, versus a quarter-million in earlier years; infantry replacement battalions totaled on average only 500 soldiers, compared to a thousand or more previously. Worse, most of the replacements were convalescents returning to the front, not fresh men. As a result, most infantry regiments were well below strength, filled with weary older men and half-trained teenagers.

No less alarming for the Austrian war effort was the empire's sharp decline in industrial and agricultural output. The poor condition of the transportation system and the increasing shortages of raw materials, coupled with the loss of many industrial workers to the army, steadily took their toll on the war economy. The production of weaponry and munitions, which peaked in the first half of 1917, declined dramatically in the first half of 1918. For instance, Habsburg arsenals provided the army with 2,285 artillery pieces in the first six months of 1917, but only 1,296 in the first six months of the following year. The output of other vital war matériel exhibited a similar pattern of marked decline: artillery shell production fell by almost half (750,000 as opposed to 1,476,000 shells per month), and rifle manufacture dropped by nearly 80 percent (617,000 rifles in the first half of 1917, compared to but 130,000 in the first half of 1918). Even uniforms and accoutrements were increasingly in short supply.

Food, too, was a growing problem for the army, thanks to the Allied blockade and the conscripting of so many peasants. By 1918, the soldier's daily ration had fallen to ten ounces of flour for combat troops and seven for rear area troops, and meat was virtually nonexistent. Fodder was also scarce, and horses often went hungry, too. The army's pool of horses, so vital for all operations, was likewise shrinking: 459,000 by mid-1918, compared to nearly a million in 1916.

The army's paltry rations worsened the already grave impact of disease. The number of troops withdrawn from the front due to illness, always high, rose dramatically: in the last year of the war, a million Austrian soldiers were incapacitated by sickness. Cholera and malaria, prevalent in Italy and the Balkans, were particularly lethal, the latter being especially feared for its ability to cripple whole formations in a very short period of time. In one instance, the 47th Infantry Division, garrisoned in distant Albania, lost 10,000 men almost at once—virtually its entire strength—to malaria; a quarter of them died. The food crisis during the winter of 1917–1918 was severe for Austria, notably in Vienna, Lower Austria, and Bohemia. In late January the High Command ordered two dozen infantry battalions from the Balkan front into the Hungarian countryside—the empire's breadbasket—to assist with food requisitioning, a duty that eventually would absorb whole divisions of already scarce combat troops.

Materially, life on the empire's home front was hardly better than in the combat zone, and in some respects appreciably worse. By early 1918, workers' rations had fallen to five ounces of bread per day. Civilians were dissatisfied with war-induced increases in inflation and taxation; at root, the population was simply growing tired of the war, as in all belligerent countries. In the third week of the new year, civilian frustrations exploded in a series of strikes across the monarchy. The strikes were basically antiwar in character, although some were overtly Bolshevik or nationalist, or both. The dynasty and army were frightened by the strikes, which seemed to threaten internal collapse. Emperor Karl appealed to his army for assistance, and rapid action brought seven divisions of loyal troops from the front to put down the strikes in German Austria and Bohemia; a military government seemed a genuine possibility. Fortunately for the tired empire, the strikes were short-lived and nearly bloodless, and the army was not called upon to take power. Nevertheless, this need for combat troops to maintain order on the home front was merely the beginning of a mission that would absorb increasing numbers of frontline units as the war headed to its conclusion.

The military, of course, was far from immune to civilian ideas and pressures, so it was perhaps inevitable that the strikes would spread to the armed forces. Indeed, the threat of mass nationalist and socialist uprisings in the ranks, although failing to materialize during the first four years of the war, remained a major concern for many Austrian generals. The first incident was a mutiny at Cattaro, a major naval base on the southern coast of Dalmatia, on February 1, 1918. Some 4,000 sailors, many of them Italians and Croats (the navy, recruiting heavily from Istria and Dalmatia, was disproportionately Italian, Croatian, and Slovene), revolted over their poor rations and living conditions. The mutiny was quickly and easily put down by loyal army and navy units, and the mutineers returned to their posts without further incident. The brief Cattaro revolt in fact had little to do with nationalist agitation, the generals' greatest fear; rather, it was a sailors' mutiny similar to those in the German and Russian navies of the period, inspired by stern shipboard discipline and abysmal living conditions. Even so, the incident frightened the High Command, which worried it was the precursor to wider nationalist mutinies in the armed forces. Although Cattaro was a social, not ethnic, protest—and a mild one, at that—it ushered in rear area unrest which would plague the Austrian Army later in 1918.

Fortunately for Austria, frontline army units of all nationalities were still relatively immune to the increasing unrest in the rear areas. Divisions in the field, and particularly those in Italy, still exhibited high morale and combat effectiveness. As spring arrived, however, the Austrian Army's vulnerable rear experienced its first major disturbances of the war. The problem centered on the *Heimkehrer*, Habsburg prisoners of war who were repatriated from Russia following the signing of the Treaty of Brest Litovsk in March; as part of the new Bolshevik regime's concessions, Austria's many prisoners in Russia were returned home. At first, this filled the High Command with optimism; at last it would have the replacements it so badly needed. And the numbers of returnees was staggering: 517,000 by the summer, nearly 700,000 before the war's end. Yet many of the *Heimkehrer* were in poor health due to the abysmal living conditions in Russian prisoner of war camps. As many as a quarter of all Austrian prisoners in Russia died from disease and starvation, and many of the survivors were sick and tired upon their return to Austria. Worse, both the Imperial Russian authorities and their Bolshevik successors had proselytized among their Habsburg captives; the former propagandized among "Entente" prisoners (Serbs, Romanians, and Italians), as well as "brother Slavs"; the latter added a Communist element to the indoctrination. Although few Austrian prisoners returned home convinced radicals of any kind—most were merely happy to be alive—there was a dedicated cadre among the *Heimkehrer* determined to agitate upon their return to Austria.[2]

Upon repatriation, the army dispatched physically fit *Heimkehrer* to depots for retraining, to be followed by reassignment to field units. Army authorities promised the returnees both leave and back pay before sending them to the front. Yet, in a muddle only too typical of the strained Habsburg bureaucracy, many returnees were sent back to their regiments with neither back pay nor leave. Mutiny was the inevitable result. Revolts broke out at rear area depots across the empire in May and June. They involved troops of all nationalities, although Czech, Slovak, and Serb troops were especially active. In most cases, the mutineers quickly returned to their posts when confronted by military authorities, but in a few cases blood was shed when loyal troops put down the mutinies with deadly force.

None of the mutinies was explicitly nationalist in origin. Although claims of ethnic discrimination and persecution were included in the lists of mutineers' complaints, dissatisfaction with material conditions featured far more prominently. Most mutineers just wanted the back pay and leave they had been promised; they revolted against the army's slack and insensitive bureaucracy, not against the Habsburg Empire itself. Significantly, none of the mutinies involved combat units at the front. The High Command was quick to place blame on poor administration and the declining quality of officer leadership; its official report on the mutinies observed, "The blame falls in the first place on the officers." After years of heavy losses among field officers, the abilities of the army's leadership cadres had declined demonstrably. Yet there was little the army could do, except reinforce the concept of discipline.

January's civilian strikes, combined with the late spring's military uprisings, led to the establishment of permanent military security battalions. The High Command raised these special units—the equivalent of seven divisions by the summer—to aid civil authorities in the event of further unrest, military or civilian. The support battalions were taken from hard-pressed line regiments, with German, Magyar, Croatian, and particularly Bosnian soldiers being favored by the High Command for their political reliability. These units proved exceptionally successful at countering any threats to internal order in the empire, even up to the last days of the war. However, internal security was one more mission that the ailing Austrian war machine was ill-equipped to perform. Simply put, there were just not enough battalions and soldiers in the Austrian Army to fulfill all the missions it was given. Throughout 1918, the High Command and the War Ministry argued over unit deployments, the former emphasizing the needs of the front, the latter being more concerned with the threat of revolt and revolution at home.

To make matters worse, the army was additionally called upon to help the Hungarian government requisition foodstuffs to feed the hungry cities. Indeed, by spring, famine seemed a possibility in the empire. In March, Budapest requested 50,000 additional troops to help bring the crops in; soon after, the High Command ordered three whole *Honvéd* divisions and a number of smaller units into the Hungarian hinterland, putting large sections of rural Hungary under military occupation. This further drain on the army's emaciated manpower reserves only worsened conditions at the front. Equally significantly, the huge military requisitioning effort served to alienate many peasants, who heretofore had been mostly loyal subjects of the empire, as well as the backbone of its infantry.

In the spring of 1918, confronted by material and psychological crises on the home front, the Austrian Army sought above all to maintain the fighting spirit of the army in the field. The High Command was sufficiently unsettled by disturbances in the hinterland, and concerned enough about the effect of Allied propaganda, to begin a campaign of explicit political indoctrination of the troops. The prestige of the dynasty and its army and the support of the church, traditional sources of Habsburg strength, were found wanting when confronted with the demoralized *Heimkehrer*, so in late March the army established the Enemy Propaganda Defense Organization to combat Bolshevik and nationalist subversion. Its program of "patriotic instruction" borrowed heavily from Erich Ludendorff's propaganda methods in Germany, and was developed with the assistance of loyal politicians and academics, with the aim of stimulating greater loyalty to the dynasty and the army. It used lectures, journals, pamphlets, placards, and even films to carry home the message that the war was nearly won, and that peace would bring an era of prosperity and liberty to the peoples of the Habsburg Empire. Though this considerable propaganda exercise may have ameliorated the army's condition somewhat, it remains doubtful whether its long-term effects were very great. Austria's dwindling supply of men, machines, and food, the essential military problem, could not be overcome by words. Indeed, many generals were pessimistic about the campaign's utility. Colonel-General Wenzel von Wurm, commander of the Isonzo Army, commented, "The beautiful words of the patriotic lessons could not convince anyone, for an empty stomach and revolutionary ideas supersede stronger arguments."

By the war's last spring, increasing numbers of Austrian soldiers, dissatisfied with the declining conditions of wartime service, were deserting. Many returning prisoners of war, as well as a fair number of other soldiers, chose to leave the army rather than stage revolts inside it. There were likely 100,000 deserters by the late summer of 1918, 35,000 in Galicia alone. Some of them formed bands of armed thugs and thieves, known as the "green cadres"; these groups were particularly strong in the mountainous forests of Croatia and Bosnia, and some of them were politically motivated. The largest bands even had machine guns and artillery. The army proved incapable of eliminating the "green cadres" because there were too few troops available in the hinterland to do more than harass armed deserters. In some areas, bands of deserters were a serious threat to Habsburg authority: when Karl visited Sofia and Constantinople in May, special security precautions had to be taken as the emperor's train moved across the Balkan countryside.

On the whole, though, despite numerous and growing problems, the fighting condition of the Austrian Army in the first half of 1918 was certainly adequate for defensive purposes. The tranquillity that prevailed on all fronts gave field units a chance to rest and absorb what few replacements were available. The Piave line remained strong, and soldiers of all nationalities were determined not to give any ground to the Italians. The army in the field was still largely untouched by the political turmoil that gripped the rear areas and the home front. The army in fact spent the first six months of 1918 undergoing a tactical reorganization. This entailed a rationalization of divisional structure, with each of the army's sixty-five divisions to have one artillery and two infantry brigades, as well as numerous support units. This organization, and the tactical understanding that accompanied it, reflected the maturity of the Austrian Army as a fighting force; it included all the hard-won lessons of total war, especially the need for heavy firepower, close infantry-artillery cooperation, solid aviation, engineering, signal, and logistical support, and coherent tactical doctrine at all levels. In the last months of the Great War, the Austrian Army emerged as a first-rate fighting force, well adapted to the static, firepower-heavy combat that prevailed on most fronts. Unfortunately, many of these vital lessons were learned too late, and by mid-1918 Austria was materially far too weak to equip a first-rate army. Most of the weapons required by the new organization never came from the factories. The Austrian Army would have to fight its last battles with the tired and worn-out men and equipment it had on hand.

The condition of the Italian Army in mid-1918 provided a significant and unanticipated contrast to Austria's precipitous military decline. The Caporetto catastrophe had finally forced Italy to fight the war with all its strength and determination. Rather than bringing Italy to its knees, the disastrous performance of its fighting forces in the Twelfth Battle of the Isonzo instead gave rise to a desire in all quarters to repel the Habsburg invader and win the war. Diaz and Badoglio were fortunate enough to take command when the entire nation wanted, even demanded, resistance and victory. They wasted no time remaking the army. From the tattered remains of the divisions destroyed on the Isonzo, they would raise a wholly new army, one that could defend the Piave line and eventually evict the Austrians from Italian soil. They perceived two major defects that had caused the debacle on the upper Isonzo in late October: outmoded tactics and poor morale. Armando Diaz and Pietro Badoglio spent the first half of 1918 rebuilding the army both in body and in spirit, to enable it to win the war.

The army's tactical deficiencies were numerous and widespread; they were, in fact, the major cause of the debacle between Flitsch and Tolmein. From mid-1915 to late 1917, the army had learned very little, despite years of terrible fighting. Luigi Cadorna was no tactical visionary, so his forces remained wedded to simple, outmoded fighting methods that rarely won victories but always produced high casualty rates. Diaz and Badoglio would no longer tolerate either. Badoglio, whose embarrassing role in the autumn's defeat was forgotten,[3] was particularly concerned with remolding the army's tactical doctrine, which he knew would be necessary to defeat the Austrians in the battles to come. No longer could the army rely on inaccurate extended barrages or costly mass infantry charges in the attack; just as significant, the use of a strong, single defensive line had been found badly wanting, and was in need of revision. To hold the Piave line, Badoglio mandated new defensive techniques that emphasized mutually supporting strong points instead of a continuous line, defenses in depth rather than a single trench system. The Italians also learned to use counterattacks to bolster the defense, a technique that the Austrians had used so successfully on the Isonzo. Infantry tactics were modified, centered around firepower—notably machine guns and mortars—rather than manpower, particularly the human wave attacks that had failed so dismally on the Isonzo. Perhaps most important, Badoglio helped develop a new artillery doctrine to make the gunners more flexible and responsive to the infantry's needs, as well as more accurate and deadly in their shooting. Above all, Badoglio standardized the army's tactical doctrine and ensured that all officers were acquainted with it; no longer would commanders be permitted to fight as they pleased, as Cadorna had been content to do. By mid-1918, the Italian Army had advanced remarkably in its fighting methods, having at last learned the painful battlefield realities of the Great War. It was not yet the tactical equal of its Austrian adversary, but it bore little resemblance to the forces that had been defeated so thoroughly in the Twelfth Battle of the Isonzo.

No less significantly for Italy and her army, Diaz and Badoglio spent a great deal of effort rebuilding the morale and fighting spirit of the much abused *fanti*. They knew that the horrible battles of attrition on the Isonzo could never be repeated, and that the *fantaccino*, the backbone of the army, expected reasonable conditions of service and a decent chance of success before the Italian Army could again go on the offensive. Given good leadership, sound doctrine, and fair treatment, the Italian soldier could be relied upon to fight bravely and effectively. The army's new leaders at last gave Italy's fighting men the decent wages, food, and benefits that Cadorna had denied them. The *Comando Supremo* increased the soldiers' pay, improved their rations, and granted more leave. It also gave each soldier a free life insurance policy, and promised generous postwar benefits from the new Ministry of Pensions and Army Welfare. In a similar vein, the government imposed a special tax on workers exempted from war service, and improved the sad lot of the peasants. The peasantry especially bore the brunt of the war—providing the army with half its infantry, as well as 61 percent of war orphans—and in Rome the politicians finally took steps to lessen the peasants' poverty and suffering. They were promised land reform after the war, and the National Veterans Organization, with a capital base of 300 million lire, bought smallholdings to distribute to peasant soldiers upon their return from the front. No longer would the families of fighting men have to go hungry. After three years of war, the Italian soldier at last had the material comforts that had been provided to the soldiers of other belligerent armies long before.

Diaz and Badoglio also worked hard to improve the army's flagging morale. The Caporetto defeat proved a painful shock, and clearly fighting spirit had to be restored. The *Comando Supremo* did this through a program of intense indoctrination. The army's new information service bombarded the troops with messages about why they were fighting. These messages, conveyed through speeches, leaflets, and an armywide newspaper (Italy's first), portrayed the Austrians as barbarian invaders, Teutonic hordes assaulting northern Italy. Reconquering the lost territories of eastern Venetia and Friulia, as well as *Italia irredenta*, was the new national crusade. Although perhaps half of the *fanti* were illiterate, and therefore unable to read the propaganda material printed for them, all Diaz's soldiers understood that the Habsburgs, Italy's old nemesis, had to be expelled from Italian soil.

Devotion to victory likewise now extended to the home front. In the aftermath of Caporetto and the occupation of the Northeast by the advancing Austrians, Italy's once vocal antiwar protests fell silent. Only the most radical socialists and pacifists still spoke out against the war, and they soon wound up in jail. Vittorio Orlando, formerly a strong defender of civil liberties, refused to tolerate antiwar protest—in his eyes, defeatism—in Italy's hour of crisis. For the overwhelming majority of Italians, whatever their political allegiance, the war was now a just struggle in defense of the homeland. Patriotism flourished even in the most unlikely quarters. As the moderate Socialist leader Filippo Turati was careful to point out, socialism was not "a doctrine of cowardice." A genuine spirit of national resistance spread throughout Italy in early 1918, transcending the recently insurmountable barriers of class, caste, and region.

Strikes, too, disappeared, and industrial productivity rose dramatically. Increasing the output of war matériel was vital to make good the army's massive equipment losses of October and November. Italy's war economy, bolstered by improved labor relations and a streamlined bureaucracy, performed superbly in the first half of 1918. The army lost 3,500 guns as a result of the Twelfth Battle, half its artillery park, but arsenals quickly provided thousands of replacements. By mid-April the army had 5,900 guns, and 6,300 by the onset of summer. Production of all types of weaponry rose appreciably: by 1918 the army received 1,200 new machine guns per month, compared to just twenty-five in 1915. The output of ammunition, just as vital to the war effort, similarly increased: shell production reached 88,400 a day in the last months of the war, nine times the number available at the war's beginning. The army soon put these shells to good use: during the ten months of war in 1918, Italian guns fired more munitions than they had from May 1915 to the Caporetto retreat. Still, the Italian war economy remained weak in some areas—during the winter of 1917–1918 Italy received wheat stocks from British Army depots in France to ward off hunger—but, with Allied help, it managed to reequip the army after Caporetto, an impressive accomplishment.

Diaz and Badoglio used the freshly made guns and equipment to raise what was, in effect, a second army for Italy. The necessary manpower came from several sources. Convalescents and soldiers on leave were dispatched to the front, as was the teenaged conscript class of 1899. In addition, the army made determined efforts to round up the hundreds of thousands of soldiers who deserted in the aftermath of Caporetto. Many were eventually caught, and those deemed reliable were sent back into the line; the unreliable ones were imprisoned, and 60,000 others went to France, where they served in labor units. With this diverse collection of men, the *Comando Supremo* raised 25 infantry divisions by late February 1918 (the equivalent of more than 120 infantry regiments), more than 30 artillery regiments and two dozen sapper battalions, as well as hundreds of supporting units. Dozens of new support regiments and battalions, including heavy artillery and engineers, likewise were added to the order of battle. Just four months after the Twelfth Battle of the Isonzo began, Italy had already made good most of its enormous losses of men and equipment.

Some of the most important increases in troop strength in early 1918 came with the expansion of the army's special assault units. The first battalion of *arditi* had distinguished itself during the Eleventh Battle of the Isonzo, and the second unit fought equally well in raids later in September 1917; both battalions fought bravely, if hopelessly, during the Twelfth Battle. Impressed by the *arditi*'s accomplishments, the *Comando Supremo* ordered nineteen more battalions raised as soon as possible, for a total of twenty-one, one per army corps. There was no shortage of volunteers. Thousands of ardent young men came forward, many of them sons of the middle classes, anxious to take revenge on the hated Austrians. They were notable for their recklessness and violence, as well as their cultivated aura of danger and courage. Well armed and trained to attack and conquer at any price, the young volunteers, clad in black shirts and fezzes, had a standard arrogant response to all outsiders, *me ne frego*—I don't give a damn. They even replaced the army's traditional chant, "Hip, hip, hurrah!" with their own self-absorbed cry: "*A chi l'onore? A noi!*"[4]

With their obvious valor and apparent idealism, the *arditi* became national heroes. Their ferocious enthusiasm was widely admired, even adulated. Indeed, the brave and dedicated "black flames" seemed to many to be just the kind of soldiers Italy needed to win the war. They quickly became the darlings of the nationalists and the Right. One of their loudest champions was Benito Mussolini, who extolled their "sublime heroism." After recovering from his near-fatal wounds received on the Carso, Mussolini was demobilized from the army, unfit for further duty. He returned to journalism, to *Il Popolo d'Italia;* from there he ceaselessly urged the government and the army to prosecute the war ruthlessly until complete victory was won. To Mussolini, Caporetto only confirmed how deeply sick liberal Italy was, and the *arditi* with their cult of violence offered the badly needed cure. He hailed them in print, claiming, "We should pin our faith to those men who make war with conviction and passion." A more sanguine staff officer on the *Comando Supremo* sounded a quiet cautionary note, wondering what peacetime role there would be for the *arditi*, for "these people who no longer know the value of human life." In early 1918 most Italians were, however, more cheered than worried by the rise of the *arditi;* in fact, the army planned to raise even more assault battalions in the second half of the year.

The *arditi* and other Italian infantry saw action in the first half of 1918, even though Diaz was determined to maintain the strategic defense for the foreseeable future. A stand on the Piave did not mean a totally passive role, however, and through the winter and spring the army undertook a series of local counterattacks against Austrian positions on the Asiago plateau. They were intended both to retake some important hill positions and to keep the army's fighting edge sharp. The Italians enjoyed some notable and well publicized small victories in these battles; at the least, they proved that the *fantaccino* was still capable of fighting bravely. One of the best known of these engagements occurred at Sasso Rosso, snow-covered peaks on the eastern Asiago plateau. On January 28, the Monte Baldo *Alpini* Battalion launched an attack on the Austrians entrenched there to recapture the nearest hill, Col d'Echele. The attack largely failed, but was noted for the courageous fighting of the *Alpini* against hopeless odds. The most celebrated event happened on the east slope of Col d'Echele, where the battalion's *arditi* platoon tried vainly to advance. The suicidal charge into Austrian fire was led by a seventeen-year-old Jewish volunteer, Roberto Sarfatti (who was, incidentally, the only son of Mussolini's mistress, Margherita Sarfatti). He was quickly cut down by Austrian machine gun fire, but his heroic deed was hailed throughout Italy as an example to follow. Sarfatti became the youngest Italian soldier to receive the Gold Medal for Bravery. His socially prominent mother, clad in black, accepted his *medaglia d'oro.*

The Italian Army was content to remain on the defensive overall. Diaz and Badoglio knew their newly raised army was too inexperienced and too lacking in self-confidence to take on the Austrians on anything like equal terms. They would not attempt a major offensive until they were absolutely sure of victory, and that promised to be several months. Diaz might have agreed to an offensive had more help from his Allies been available; there were, to be sure, a half-dozen French and British divisions in Italy, along with many support units, but nowhere near enough to break the Austrian defenses on the Piave. The exhausted Allies were now pinning their hopes of victory on the Americans anyway. By the spring of 1918, there were half a million American troops in Europe, preparing to turn the tide of the war, but virtually none of them had reached Italy. General John J. Pershing was adamant that the main American effort would be in France, and almost the entire American Army was concentrated there.

There were, of course, some American troops in Italy by early 1918, but few of them were destined to fight against the Austrians. There were only a few scattered air and support units, and they were in Italy mostly to show solidarity with the Italian cause.[5] Certainly they would not be much help in breaching the Piave line. There were several well publicized American ambulance units serving at the front. They counted among their ranks the nineteen-year-old Ernest Hemingway, who left his job at the Kansas City *Star* in April to join the Allied war effort. He soon found himself working as a frontline ambulance driver with the American Red Cross in the Dolomite foothills, opposite the Austrian 10th Army. Hemingway was eager to enter combat, and as it turned out, he would not have long to wait. But a handful of ambulance drivers and some pilots on speaking tours was not the American help Diaz had hoped for. As the war's last year continued, he became increasingly disenchanted with the Allies—the whole American field army was gathered in France. He pleaded for more help, notably in the form of American divisions to fight on the Piave, but all his requests were rebuffed. Diaz used this as an excuse to refuse to assist the French and British in their hour of greatest need, which soon arrived.

After Caporetto, the British and French had learned to be understanding about Italy's military weakness; certainly neither London nor Paris wanted to provoke another Caporetto-style debacle. Yet, this Allied sympathy evaporated as soon as a serious German threat arose on the Western front. In late March, the Germans undertook a massive attack on British positions in the Somme area. It was the greatest German offensive since 1914, intended to win the war before the Americans could arrive in sufficient strength to alter the balance irrevocably in the Allies' favor. The "Peace Offensive," launched in three stages and backed by the very best German assault divisions, made alarming gains; by April, the British 5th Army had been thoroughly wrecked and Ludendorff's armies had advanced forty miles. The Germans seemed perilously near a breakthrough to Paris, and the Allies were plunged into a crisis worse than any since the Battle of the Marne in September 1914.

At Rapallo in early November 1917, in the aftermath of Caporetto, the Allies had agreed to a Supreme War Council and a unified strategy, so Italy was bound to help her British and French allies in their time of peril. French Marshal Ferdinand Foch, the Allied generalissimo, soon began requesting all available help from Italy to stem the German tide. By May, as successive German drives pounded the French as well as the British, Foch pleaded with Diaz to undertake an offensive—any offensive—against the Central Powers. Diaz refused. Meeting the Allies' demands would involve a major offensive on the Piave, an all-out drive to win the war, and the *Comando Supremo* was unwilling to undertake that until it was supremely confident of victory. His carefully rebuilt army was not yet ready. Diaz and Badoglio told the Allies that an Italian offensive would be too risky; it could mean, they cautioned, "another Caporetto," so the Western front would have to hold without any help from Italy.

Regrettably for Austria and her army, the Habsburgs were not as good at rebuffing the demands of their indignant allies. The immense strains of four years of total war had made Austria wholly dependent on the German Empire for her survival. The attack on Serbia in August 1914, the spark that ignited the Great

War, had been started by Vienna as a last-ditch attempt to maintain the Habsburg Empire's status as an independent great power, so it was a supreme and bitter irony that by the war's end Austria had become so militarily, economically, and politically reliant on Berlin, more a German satellite than an ally.[6] In the middle of the war, German intervention had saved Austria in the East and in the Balkans, and by 1918 Austria was inalterably tied to Germany, for good or ill.

But somehow Emperor Karl managed not to see things that way. Karl was a well intentioned monarch whose deepest desire was peace, and with it the saving of his multinational empire, but he was hopelessly naive. He had, in fact, been conducting secret peace negotiations behind Berlin's back. His envoy was Prince Sixtus of Parma, his brother-in-law and an officer in the Belgian Army. Karl surmised that the Germans were losing the war and that Berlin's demise would drag the Habsburg Empire down with it. He therefore wanted a separate peace, the only way he saw to avoid the collapse of his family's centuries-old empire. He arranged for his brother-in-law to contact the Allies, and Karl's peace feelers were met with a mixture of interest and skepticism; exactly how he planned to take Austria out of the war was far from clear. It all ended when Karl's secret mission was discovered by the Germans. Germany's military and diplomatic leaders, and Emperor Wilhelm II, were outraged by their ally's disloyalty.

Karl wasted no time repenting for his sins. Visiting the German High Command on May 13, he concluded a series of agreements with Germany that tied his empire to Berlin more closely than ever before. Austria was now theoretically joined with Germany in all matters of military, political, and economic cooperation: Karl had essentially signed away the sovereignty of his realm, submitting to the authority of a German-directed *Mitteleuropa*.

To make matters worse, in an attempt to assuage his guilt and reassure Germany of Austria's sincerity, Karl committed his tired army to a major offensive against the Italians as soon as possible. By May, Ludendorff's "Peace Offensive" had begun to stall with heavy losses, and with the seemingly limitless numbers of Americans reaching France, Germany's strategic situation began to appear bleak. The Germans were thus elated to accept Karl's offer of an offensive to take Allied pressure off them in France. But for Austria it was hardly less than a suicidal gesture. The Habsburg armies in Italy were strong enough to hold their defenses in the Piave and Asiago areas for some time, but a major offensive was far beyond Austria's military means. It could not win the war, yet it promised to wreck Austria's weary field forces.

The prospect of an offensive horrified many senior Habsburg generals. Significantly, the highest ranking opponent was Svetozar Boroević, recently promoted field marshal and commander of one of the two Austrian army groups in Italy. Boroević believed that the war would be lost before the end of the year, even without the offensive, and that the army must conserve its waning strength for the coming domestic tumult. He was willing to agree to a limited offensive, albeit with great reluctance, but was adamantly opposed to a general two-pronged push on both the Piave and the Asiago fronts. But this strategic concept, based on Franz Conrad von Hötzendorf's prewar planning, was precisely what Karl's concessions to Berlin promised. Boroević, ever loyal to the emperor, in the end had no real choice but to go along with the operation that he knew would destroy the last remaining Habsburg army in the field.

The plan of attack, set to begin June 15, committed virtually the entire frontline strength of the Austrian Army to the offensive, a total of fifty-three divisions plus an additional ten in reserve. Conrad's army group on the Asiago plateau contained some twenty-eight divisions, and Boroević's army group on the Piave boasted eighteen more. Despite the impressive numbers, the combat readiness of the Habsburg forces left a great deal to be desired. The paper strength of the field army was 2,800,000, but there were actually only 946,000 troops at the front. Furthermore, several of the divisions recently sent to the Piave front from the Eastern and Balkan theaters had no experience fighting the Italians, and were of questionable value in the coming offensive.[7] The deteriorating condition of the war economy meant that the troops were short of virtually everything. Many divisions were mere shells, with only a third or half of their prescribed numbers of riflemen. The supply of replacements had dwindled to near nonexistence. In early June, on the eve of the offensive, the 29th Infantry Division on the Piave, a typical infantry formation preparing to attack, received a replacement battalion: in the past such a unit would have been a thousand strong, but even on paper it came to just 302 soldiers; there were actually only 166 troops on strength, once those on leave were counted. A third of Austrian artillery batteries had no draft horses, and there was no fuel for tractors; ammunition, too, was increasingly scarce. Shortages of spare parts crippled or damaged worn-out equipment. The soldiers themselves were badly malnourished. The daily combat ration was now so meager—infantrymen were fortunate to receive seven ounces of meat per week and mostly subsisted on small portions of corn bread and occasional boiled vegetables—that the average body weight of an Austrian frontline soldier had fallen to just 120 pounds. Clothing and accoutrements were in equally short supply, and such "luxuries" as underwear and decent boots were but a memory in most combat units.

Even so, the majority of Austrian infantrymen were still willing to fight against the detested Italians. Tactical planning for the offensive developed quickly. The brunt of the battle would be borne by Colonel-General von Wurm's Isonzo Army; its four corps with fourteen divisions, backed up by 1,770 guns, had the mission of penetrating the defenses of the Italian 3rd Army, dug in on the lower Piave before Venice, from Papadopoli island to the Adriatic. Only nine Italian divisions stood between the Isonzo Army, and Venice and the northern Italian heartland. To break through, Wurm's army would rely upon careful artillery preparation. In its last offensive, the Austrian Army enjoyed a sophisticated artillery fire plan, beginning with mortar barrages at 3 A.M. on the day of the attack, followed by a general barrage of gas shells to prevent Italian shelling. The Isonzo Army intended to launch the assault elements of its four corps across the Piave at 7:30 A.M., with mountain batteries attached to forward battalions for direct support. Divisional artillery would commence rolling barrages after the initial penetration was achieved, jumping forward 200 yards every four minutes to provide advancing infantry units with constant supporting fire. The detailed artillery fire plan, based on all the tactical lessons of the past four years of fighting, was made possible by the effective use of army aviation. The hard-pressed Austrian air arm performed sterling service in the weeks leading up to the offensive, providing detailed reconnaissance about Italian dispositions, particularly about Italian artillery batteries, and protecting the movement of Austrian troops and supplies to forward staging areas.

Infantry divisions spent the first two weeks of June gradually moving their combat and supply echelons toward the banks of the Piave, a few companies at a time, always under the cover of darkness. To maintain surprise, construction units devised complex camouflage schemes to hide the burgeoning supply depots just behind the Piave front. By mid-June, the army was ready to attack. The months of comparative quiet on the Italian front meant that Austria's combat divisions, although short of rations, clothing, weapons, and munitions, nevertheless were well rested and self-confident. Habsburg soldiers of all nationalities, although tired of the war, wanted to inflict a final defeat on Italy, their last remaining enemy. Such a victory would bring an end to the war. General August von Cramon, chief Prussian liaison officer to the Habsburg Army, observed, "The troops' offensive spirit, confirmed to me on all sides, was the best. Officers and men burned, as in the first months of the war, to compete against the Eyeties." It cannot be doubted, though, that some of the troops' offensive ardor was inspired by hopes of plundering the more generously provisioned Italian trenches.

The offensive began, as scheduled, on the morning of June 15. After an impressive artillery bombardment, the Isonzo Army's infantry assaulted the Piave line, crossing the river with the optimistic battle cry "To Milan!"[8] But Italian defenses proved stronger than anticipated, and few Austrian divisions made notable progress on June 15. The flat Venetian plain offered the Italians comparatively few natural defenses, but the *fanti* fought back surprisingly hard. All of Wurm's nine divisions in the first wave reached the Piave's west bank on June 15, but only two of them penetrated more than a mile into Italian-held territory. The next day the Isonzo Army's divisions continued to advance, but only slowly and with heavy losses. The story repeated itself on the more mountainous Asiago front, where Conrad's army group encountered firm Italian resistance. Austrian casualties mounted as entrenched Italian units fought with unanticipated vigor; their many machine gun nests, in particular, well dug in and positioned, took a heavy toll of Austrian troops and proved difficult to overcome. The Duke of Aosta's "undefeated" 3rd Army, rebuilt and retrained since the Caporetto retreat, held the Piave line, resisting the attacks of the *Isonzoarmee* with determination and skill.

On June 17, the Isonzo Army poured reinforcements into the small bridgeheads it held on the Piave's west bank, but made scant progress. Fresh Italian reserve divisions began to arrive on the Piave, further stalling the Austrian drive.[9] By the evening, despite heroic efforts, the veteran Isonzo Army's best divisions had advanced little more than two miles westward, and the rest remained stuck just beyond the river's edge. Wurm watched the likelihood of a major breakthrough dwindle during the day, and therefore committed his last remaining fresh divisions to the fight that evening, a final attempt to tear a significant gap in the Italian defenses and expand his small bridgeheads. June 18 saw more attempts by the Isonzo Army, particularly its VII and XXIII Corps, to breach the Italian defenses, but the day's advances totaled only a few hundred yards. During the night, fresh Austrian battalions crossed the Piave, and were sent into battle by midday on June 20. Again the 3rd Army fought back with surprising grit, and the Austrian drive stalled with heavy casualties. To make matters worse for the Austrians, the 3rd Army's artillery was active, inflicting losses on forward units; the Isonzo Army's gunners, running out of ammunition, failed to respond.

On the Asiago front, the 11th Army continued to meet equally dogged Italian resistance. There, too, Austrian assault divisions attacked with bravery and tactical skill, but the natural strengths of the defense, bolstered by machine guns and artillery—many of them manned by first-rate British and French troops—carried the day. Army Group Conrad found it impossible to gain ground on the rough, mountainous Asiago plateau. It was not for lack of effort; everywhere Austria's tired *Frontkämpfer*, anxious to win a decisive victory, battled hard. Even when the offensive stalled and the chances of a breakthrough dimmed, officers and men kept trying, always at a heavy cost. One such determined soldier was a young artillery lieutenant of the 5th Division, fighting on the upper Piave. He was Ludwig Wittgenstein, son of a wealthy German-Austrian industrialist. In a few short years he would achieve international fame for his innovative and controversial philosophical concepts, but at the moment he was wholly absorbed in soldiering. Wittgenstein had been an avid supporter of the Austrian cause from the war's beginning, donating considerable sums of his inherited fortune to buy weapons for the army. After receiving a reserve commission in the artillery, he had tried for two years to get into battle, but had spent many boring months in the East, supervising the repair of damaged guns. Now at last he had his chance to see some action. He served as a forward observer with the frontline infantry, marching with them into battle, calling down artillery fire by field telephone to support their advance into Italian territory. It was demanding and dangerous work, but Wittgenstein relished it. Although the offensive soon bogged down, Wittgenstein performed his duty successfully and bravely, following the infantry into battle against British troops several times during mid-June. Miraculously he returned unscathed from every mission. His efforts alone could not bring victory, of course, but they did win him the Silver Medal for Bravery.

Austrian soldiers of all nationalities similarly fought courageously, even as any chance of victory disappeared slowly but inexorably. By the morning of June 21, the Isonzo Army command realized plainly that the offensive had stalled without achieving more than limited tactical gains, and that the threat of a general Italian counteroffensive was very real, indeed increasing. Already the Italians had committed reserve divisions to battle, frequently led by *arditi* battalions, pushing the Austrians back toward the river. After losing so many men and guns during the abortive offensive, the army's power to resist a determined Italian assault appeared dangerously weak. Ammunition shortages continued to worsen, leaving the infantry without much artillery support in the face of continuous Italian barrages. Machine gun ammunition reserves, too, were dwindling. Even rifle ammunition was growing scarce, with regiments in the field reporting a reserve of only 110 bullets per rifleman. Worst of all, Austrian formations were depressingly vulnerable to Allied air attack; by now the Italians, British, and French had concentrated their reserve squadrons on the Piave, pushing the depleted Austrian air service from the skies. Despite heroic efforts to protect the troops on the ground, Austria's pilots, short of everything, were unable to blunt the increasing Allied air attacks on the Piave. Allied pilots strafed and bombed Austrian troops at will. The cost of air attacks on frontline units was bad enough, particularly with respect to morale; the toll on rear echelon units was devastating, as supply depots and columns were attacked incessantly during daylight hours. Eighty percent of Austrian bridging across the Piave was destroyed by Allied air and artillery bombardment.

After six days of the offensive, Austrian positions were growing more precarious by the hour. Fearing a debacle, especially with the threat of tanks looming, General Wurm at Isonzo Army command ordered a general withdrawal to the east bank of the Piave late on June 21. Units in the field received the order in the evening, but the retreat did not begin at once; the Italians could not be permitted to turn the Austrian withdrawal into a strategic rout. No less, the retreat of an entire army was a prodigious logistical undertaking, requiring twenty-four hours of arduous engineering preparations. Thus Austrian divisions on the Piave's west bank continued to resist Italian probes during the night of June 21–22 and the following day, as construction units readied the few remaining bridges and ferries for the retreat. Austrian units in the front line began to withdraw after dark on June 22, always leaving a covering force behind to deceive the Italians. The Isonzo Army's cumbersome service and logistical units crossed first, followed by the artillery, with the infantry bringing up the rear. By dawn on June 23, the last units of the tired and defeated Isonzo Army had reached the Piave's east bank. Austria's last offensive was over.

The ill-fated gamble on the Piave at least ended on a positive note, showing the army's ability to execute a strategic retreat under fire, one of the most difficult military tasks. But there could be no doubt the Habsburgs' final offensive had been a catastrophe. The army suffered grievous losses of men and equipment that it could not hope to make good. As Boroević and others had feared, the "starvation offensive" had achieved nothing but the wrecking of the last Austrian army in the field. The depleted divisions of the Isonzo Army, short of men and guns even before June 15, were now incapable of any offensive action; even their defensive potential now seemed questionable. The six-day battle cost Austria 118,000 dead, wounded, and missing soldiers[10]—nearly 60,000 in the Isonzo Army alone. The defeat cost the army even more than the bloody Eleventh Battle of the Isonzo, and that terrible struggle had at least ended in a draw. The army had nothing to show for its sacrifice on the Piave. Morale among the shell-shocked survivors plummeted as the last hope of victory ebbed away. All the Austrian troops holding the Piave line could do was wait for the inevitable Italian offensive. No one knew when the Italians would launch a major offensive, a decisive push to win the war, but there could be no doubt that it would come.

The Austrian Army had failed in its last offensive. The defeat was not for want of effort; soldiers of all nationalities had fought doggedly but futilely on the Piave and on the Asiago plateau. The sacrifices of the infantry in particular were enormous among all ranks; four colonels, leading their brigades and regiments from the front, were among the dead. Yet it was not enough. The Prussian General von Cramon offered a brief epitaph for the Piave offensive: "In truth this army deserved a better fate." The painful reality was that by mid-1918, weary Austria could not support a major offensive against even one enemy. The war economy was a shambles, and the army was too short of men. Bravery could not compensate for the massive shortfalls of weapons, ammunition, and equipment of all types. As the Italians had learned so bitterly on the Isonzo so many times, courage alone could not deliver victory. Emperor Karl had hastened his empire's impending demise with his foolish offensive. Now all he and his army could do was wait for the Allies' next move.

For Italy, the stand on the Piave was an epic triumph, proof of a military and national renaissance. Seven months after the Caporetto disaster, the Italian Army had held its ground and won a major defensive victory, saving the northern Italian heartland from Austrian invasion. The *fantaccino* had shown that, properly armed and led, he could fight potently indeed. The *arditi* fought especially well, demonstrating their trademark tenacity and recklessness in turning back Austrian assaults.[11] Badoglio's rebuilding efforts had proven successful, for the new army resisted the Austrian drive with both determination and skill.

The artillery in particular, long an Italian weak point, had proven decisive in crippling the Austrian advance. General Roberto Segre, architect of the artillery's defensive fire plan on the Piave, was hailed as a national hero.[12] There had been significant French and British help, to be sure, but the defense of the Piave had unquestionably been an Italian victory. Italian casualties were hardly less than the Austrian, but Italy could still afford such losses. June's victory greatly restored the morale of the fighting forces, very low since Caporetto, and gave the *fanti* the self-confidence they needed to go on the offensive again. Diaz was still cautious, though, and it would be several months before he would be willing to risk a major offensive. In the meantime, the Italian forces on the Piave rested and waited for battle, regularly shelling the Austrian defenders on the opposite bank, a foretaste of the great bombardment to come.[13]

FOURTEEN

"AUSTRIA IS IN YOUR CAMP"

The Austrian defeat on the Piave was soon compounded by German disasters in France. Erich Ludendorff's spring offensives, Germany's final bid to win the war, had run their course by July. They demonstrated Germany's impressive staying power, as well as her army's awesome tactical prowess, but they had failed to win the war. Like so many German efforts, the "Peace Offensive" had proven tactically triumphant but strategically indecisive. The British and French, much helped by John J. Pershing's burgeoning American Army, were growing stronger by the day. By 1918, after four years of total war and a crippling Allied blockade, Germany, like her Austrian ally, could not hope to materially support a war-winning blow; and Emperor Wilhelm, like Karl, was rapidly running out of soldiers for his army.

The Allies survived the German spring offensives, losing many men but wearing away Ludendorff's armies all the same. By July, it was time for the Allies to attempt a massive counteroffensive, a first step to pushing the exhausted Germans out of France and Belgium. It began with the French, who had weathered the spring offensives somewhat better than their British allies. On July 18, the French Army attacked German defenses in the Marne sector, backed up by many guns and 300 tanks, the largest collection of armor yet on any battlefield. This effort, the first large-scale French push since Robert Nivelle's catastrophic offensive in April 1917, made early progress. Several German divisions began to give way before the fresh *poilus* and their fearsome tanks; many tired German soldiers were happy to surrender. By early August, the Aisne-Marne offensive, with some American help, had cracked the German defenses on the central part of the Western front. The war was far from over, but the formidable German Army began to show unmistakable signs of low morale, even defeatism.

Worse news for Ludendorff came on August 8, when the British launched their own offensive to complement the French effort on the Marne. The center of Douglas Haig's push was at Amiens, in the Somme sector, a front all too well known to the British Army. The British struck the German positions in the Amiens salient with twenty-seven divisions—including four Canadian and five Australian divisions, Haig's crack colonials—supported by 2,000 guns and 600 tanks. The tank was still a mechanically crude weapon, and tactics for its use were limited; all the same, the Germans had virtually no tanks of their own, and their infantry was profoundly unnerved by the appearance of hundreds of imposing steel beasts. The result was a débâcle, as the German front line cracked at Amiens. On August 8, several shell-shocked German divisions fell to pieces and British infantry advanced as deep as nine miles past the German front lines. Ludendorff considered it the German Army's "black day" of the war.

By mid-August, Germany was visibly losing the war, and this was even before the American Army had really made its presence felt in France. Pershing was still waiting to employ his fresh divisions *en masse* on the battlefield. Ludendorff's once invincible armies were losing ground in the West, and there was no prospect of relief in sight; the war was not yet ended, but there was little the Germans, exhausted and running out of even the most basic war matériel, could do to stave off ultimate defeat. Germany's decline would quickly bring the Central Powers—including Austria—down with her. During the war, the Habsburgs had come to rely on the Hohenzollerns for battlefield survival, and a Prussian defeat would unavoidably cause the Austrian war effort to collapse.

The Austrian High Command was well aware of Berlin's rapid military decline and its implications for Vienna, but by the late summer it was, if anything, more worried about the empire's increasing domestic tumult. Discontent on the home front had reached dangerous levels, and nationalist insurrections—the dynasty's and the army's oldest worry—seemed imminent. Indeed, the Allies had begun to court the disgruntled nationalities, encouraging them to revolt against the Habsburgs. The dissolution of the Habsburg realm along ethnic lines was a recent addition to the list of Allied war aims, accepted more for tactical than for practical or moral reasons. The Italians were the most vocal supporters of the nationalities' rights, so long as they corresponded to Italy's territorial ambitions. In April 1918 the Congress of Oppressed Nationalities convened in Rome, a well publicized event at which Czech, Polish, Romanian, and South Slav representatives denounced the Habsburgs and demanded national states carved from the empire. This was followed in June by official Italian (and French) recognition of the American-based Czechoslovak Committee and its right of self-determination, although no one was exactly sure who the "Czechoslovaks" were, and precisely what "self-determination" meant.

In truth, these representatives of the nationalities spoke for very few Austrian subjects. They were politicians and academics living in exile, frequently with little idea of what was actually happening in Austria, but they received Allied backing for their perceived propaganda value. By 1918, the Allies were anxious to weaken the Austrian war effort by any means available. The Czech delegation in particular, the most belligerently anti-Habsburg, led by the Prague professor Tomáš Masaryk, succeeded in portraying its cause as just and democratic, a legitimate beneficiary of liberal Allied largesse, even though many of their arguments were self-serving and dishonest. Although there can be no doubt that many Czechs living under the Habsburgs were deeply discontented by 1918, Masaryk and his educated clique spoke for very few of them.

Certainly the exiles had enjoyed little success recruiting armies to fight the Habsburgs. The Poles by mid-1918 had three divisions fighting in France, but most of the soldiers were Prussian and Russian, not Austrian, Poles; and the Polish national movement was relatively sympathetic to the Habsburgs. Even the Czechoslovaks, despite ample enticements, managed to recruit but a single division to fight against the Austrians in Italy. From the hundreds of thousands of Czech and Slovak prisoners in Allied captivity, Masaryk persuaded less than 10 percent to join the national struggle, even though he offered good pay and rations, as well as a way out of the filthy prisoner of war camps. The Slovene, Croatian, and Serbian nationalists—lately restyled as "Yugoslavs"—managed to persuade even fewer ex-Austrian soldiers to fight under their united banner.

Most Austrian soldiers, whatever their nationality, were determined to stay the course, to see the war through, even after the Piave defeat. Some deserted, of course, but few went so far as to take up arms against the Habsburgs. Many Allied leaders were skeptical of the nationalities. Italian politicians, and especially generals, were wary of exploiting the ethnic issue too much. The army was well aware that Slovenes, Croats, Serbs, and Bosnians in Habsburg uniform had been the backbone of the Austrian stand on the Isonzo. No less, Yugoslav territorial claims included the Littoral—including Gorizia and Trieste—and all of Dalmatia, the very land of *Italia irredenta* that Italy had entered the war to liberate. Nevertheless, the Allies, and Italy in particular, desperate to win the war, were making far-reaching political promises to Austria's disgruntled minorities, writing postdated checks which they hoped would never be cashed.

The exploitation of the nationalities issue, though it did not raise many troops to fight on the Allied side, did succeed in terrifying Austria's political and military elites. The specter of Czechs or any other minority taking up arms against the empire sent chills down the backs of the Habsburg officer corps and bureaucracy. There had still been no widespread ethnic disturbances on either the home front or the fighting front, but the High Command was convinced that they were coming. Indeed, in mid-August, as the German Army was reeling from Allied blows in France, the Austrian chief of the General Staff, Arthur Arz von Straussenburg, informed Ludendorff that Austria had to leave the war by the end of 1918, and that its divisions in northern Italy would be required on the home front. Arz told his senior partner bluntly, "The army will be required for the maintenance of order and to help resolve different internal political questions." Ultimately the preservation of the ancient Habsburg realm and dynasty far outweighed the need to keep the Italians at bay. By August 1918, with final defeat drawing ominously near, the Germans were too absorbed with their own impending collapse to take much notice of Austria's internal dilemma.

While the High Command in Teschen was consumed with domestic political questions, the army in the field was busy preparing for the coming Italian offensive. Armando Diaz was cautious, the Austrians knew, but surely he would launch an all-out offensive on the Piave once the war appeared truly lost for the Central Powers. The Habsburg divisions in Italy spent the summer and autumn preparing to meet the expected Italian blow. Isonzo Army intelligence anticipated that the Italian drive across the Piave would be well supported by prodigious quantities of both artillery and aircraft. Aware of the depleted condition of all frontline divisions, the High Command believed that a prolonged defense of the Piave line would prove impossible; operational planning instead centered on a brief holding action, followed by a withdrawal to the Tagliamento. Perhaps there the Austrians could make their stand.

The Isonzo Army planned to fight a mobile defensive battle, with tactics reflecting the hard-learned lessons of the entire war. Colonel-General Wenzel Wurm's staff envisioned a defensive scheme reflecting late war German Army doctrine: a main line of resistance based upon machine gun positions, thinly held but supported by presighted artillery fires; and a second line, dedicated to brief, intense counterattacks to repulse Italian penetrations. These plans required a high degree of cooperation between infantry and artillery, as well as between ground and air units. A mobile defense, unlike the static defense that was the norm during the war, also placed considerable demands on the army's strained signals service. Communication between units would be difficult once the Italian offensive got under way.

Far more ominous in the Austrians' minds, though, was the threat of Allied tanks. The Austrians had no experience fighting tanks, and Italian armored units loomed large in Habsburg fears. The supply of a limited number of British and French tanks to the Italians during the summer of 1918 created a panic in Isonzo Army headquarters, particularly after the Germans suffered their "black day" at Amiens on August 8. The Austrian fear of Allied armor was especially acute because Habsburg forces had no tanks of their own, and few effective antitank weapons in their arsenal. The Isonzo Army's rapidly assembled antitank doctrine, borrowing heavily from German experience, emphasized both tank traps and antitank mines, as well as the use of antitank rifles and field guns firing over open sights to destroy Italian armored vehicles. However, antitank mines, rifle bullets, and armor-piercing shells were in short supply, like everything else, and Austrian frontline formations were forced to dig numerous antitank ditches across roads, in the hope of delaying advancing enemy tanks. The flat Venetian coastal plain offered few natural obstacles to tanks. The Austrians' only chance to stop an Italian armored thrust seemed to lie with bridges: the numerous spans across the Piave, Tagliamento, and other rivers were too weak to support British and French heavy tanks.

One of the more than two dozen Austrian divisions garrisoning the Piave line in the late summer was the 29th, a North Bohemian infantry division. Its defensive sector included Papadopoli island, a flat, marshy island in the Piave, four miles long and just over a mile wide. It was a strategically significant position, astride the most direct route to Friulia and the Isonzo, one of the most important sectors on the whole Austrian front. The 29th Division was a solid, battle-tested formation with an admirable fighting record. It was more than three-quarters German in composition, the remainder being mostly Czechs. Its regiments, recruited in the heavily industrialized towns and cities of the mountainous northern fringe of Bohemia, had proven themselves loyal and tenacious in battle; three were overwhelmingly German, and only one had a bare Czech majority. The Habsburg Army's regiments of Bohemian Germans enjoyed a combat record second to none. Nowhere in Austria did national, indeed racial, pride burn more brightly than in the solidly German districts of Bohemia. The Teutonic fringe of northern and western Bohemia, what would later be popularly known as the Sudetenland, had developed an early regional consciousness, after centuries of German settlement in the Czech lands. During the latter half of the nineteenth century, however, this distinctly *böhmisch* identity had been transformed into race-centered German nationalism. The result was the German Workers' Party, formed in 1904, a forerunner of Hitler's National Socialists. In the decade before the Great War, German nationalism grew increasingly popular and virulent in Bohemia among all classes, becoming a major political force as well as a significant obstruction to parliamentary rule in Vienna.

Yet, when war came, the Bohemian Germans responded with an enthusiasm they maintained throughout the struggle. Fighting against Slav enemies such as Russia and Serbia, a cause that repelled many of their Czech neighbors, invigorated German-Bohemian soldiers, anxious to defend Germandom. They fought with equal determination against the hated Italians in defense of German Alpine territory. No less important a motivator, however, was the Vienna-Berlin alliance. Waging war alongside Germany proved a very popular cause among the intensely nationalist Germans of North Bohemia. Hence the German-Bohemians fought with unparalleled vigor in the Imperial-and-Royal Army, sacrificing themselves in huge numbers on all fronts. Purely German areas of

Bohemia had among the highest wartime loss rates in all the Habsburg Empire.[1] The 29th Division's infantrymen were tired but excellent fighters, among the best Austrian soldiers. They could be relied upon to resist the coming Italian offensive with all their strength.

The 29th Division's commander was equally determined to hold the Piave line as long as possible. Lieutenant General Otto von Berndt was a German-Bohemian himself, the son of a prosperous industrialist. The fifty-three-year-old Berndt, like his fellow *Deutschböhmer* but unlike most Habsburg officers, was a convinced German nationalist. He had enjoyed a distinguished career in the emperor's service, beginning as a subaltern of dragoons and including service on the prestigious General Staff. His excellent war record included lengthy service in the East, commanding first a cavalry brigade, and then a division against the Russians. He reached the Italian front only in the summer of 1918, after the Piave offensive, to assume command of the 29th Division. Berndt was a talented tactician and inspiring leader of men in battle. The coming battle for the Piave promised to be the division's—and the army's—last, but it would be Berndt's first on the Italian front. Even so, he was an excellent choice to lead his homeland's division in its final struggles.

Berndt knew that a prolonged defense of the Piave line would be impossible in the face of a major Italian offensive. His defensive plan therefore intended to hold Papadopoli island long enough to permit an orderly withdrawal across Venetia to the Tagliamento. Three of the division's infantry regiments were in the front line, and a fourth was held back as a counterattack force. The 29th's infantry regiments were experienced, but short of men: each of Berndt's two brigades maintained a reserve of one sixty-man company, and the divisional reserve consisted of three 60-strong companies—300 reserve troops for the whole division. In the final analysis, the fate of the *Isonzoarmee*, indeed of the entire Habsburg realm, depended on the quantity and quality of the soldiers of all nationalities who filled the understrength rifle companies of the last Habsburg army in the field.

No army can be sustained for long without a constant stream of fresh soldiers, but by the Great War's last season both the quantity and the quality of Austrian replacements were seriously deficient. The empire's manpower shortage, acute since the beginning of 1918, had approached a critical stage by the summer's end. Desertion and disease took a steady toll of the few fresh men available. Just as ominously, the level of training given to recruits was lower than ever. The months of tumult in the rear areas, including strikes in recruit depots and the use of so many battalions on internal security missions, had distracted training units from their vital task of preparing soldiers for combat. Many recruits arriving at the front were untrained in even the most rudimentary tactical skills. Line regiments now regularly accepted teenaged replacements who did not even know how to fire their rifles. In late September the Isonzo

Army tried to counter this by instituting special divisional training depots to give conscripts the battle survival skills that rear area depots had failed to provide. It was a well intentioned attempt to remedy the increasing deficiencies of the military bureaucracy, but it came too late in the war to prove its benefits, or to notably improve the condition of the army in the field.

Nevertheless, the Austrian Army's gravest difficulties as the summer turned to autumn had nothing to do with its soldiers, but instead centered on the rapidly dwindling ability of the Habsburg Empire to stay in the war. A High Command report on material conditions in the field noted in late August, "The war has taken on the character of nothing less than an economic struggle for existence," one that Austria was losing. By the last months of fighting, the army was running out of everything required to sustain a force in the field, from the most modern weaponry to the most mundane items of clothing. The army could no longer even keep its fighting men in shoes, and many soldiers wore tattered shoes—even on the Alpine front—or, increasingly, no shoes at all. All items of clothing were in short supply, and in frontline units underwear and socks were rare. Field laundry units had been nearly forced to shut down due to a lack of soap. The Austrian Army in its last campaign was thus clothed in tattered, dirty, ill-fitting uniforms, a stark contrast with the smartly dressed regiments of 1914.

More detrimental to fighting power was the impending collapse of the army's medical system. The numbers of trained medical personnel declined ominously during the last two years of the war: there were 7,392 doctors serving in the field at the beginning of 1917, but only 5,399 a year later, and only 4,870 by the end of April 1918; by the onset of autumn the total had fallen to half the early 1917 figure. It was no longer possible to provide a doctor for each infantry battalion and field artillery and cavalry regiment, as prescribed in army regulations. The supply of medical instruments and medicines likewise declined, and a pervasive shortage of ambulances made casualty evacuation difficult. Compounding these lacks with grossly inadequate nutrition and the unsanitary conditions of frontline service caused the health of Austrian fighting men to continue to plummet, and there was little the army's medical service could do.

Disease, particularly malaria, became a crippling problem on the Italian front. The Piave line remained mostly quiet as autumn began, except for occasional Italian barrages, but Austrian losses rose steadily. During the tranquil month of September, the 29th Division lost 973 men (only six killed), of which fully 966 were due to illness, mostly malaria. Illness, much more than the Italians, was eroding the strength of the Isonzo Army. In early July, after the disaster on the Piave, the 29th Division could muster a rifle strength of 7,394, but after three peaceful months of disease and a dearth of replacements, the division boasted but 4,905 riflemen. None of its four infantry regiments could muster even 1,400 effectives, and one (the 94th) had been reduced to only 841 officers and men in the fighting line.

By October, the army's losses of men to nonbattle causes had outpaced even its material decline. Still, the paper strength of the Isonzo Army was impressive, mostly because infantry battalions that were desperately short of men managed to maintain a fair share of their crew-served weapons—machine guns and mortars—which were the basis of the defense. The same was true of the artillery, which kept its numbers of functioning guns—but not gunners—respectably high even during October. The problem was the supply of ammunition. Counting all possible stores and depots, the Isonzo Army could collect enough munitions of all calibers to keep its divisions fighting for only four days. After that, divisions like the 29th would be out of bullets and shells, and the war would have to end.

By October, Field Marshal Svetozar Boroević, commander of the forces on the Piave, was deeply concerned about the fate of his armies and his soldiers. He was not as optimistic as many of his superiors in Vienna; he knew that an all-out Italian offensive, and with it final defeat, were imminent. But Boroević had no doubt that the dynasty and the army would survive, and that the soldiers' sacrifices would therefore be justified. After more than four years of total war, Austria's—and his—struggle was nearly at an end. Boroević's main concern now was getting his army out of Italy in good order. On October 17, the tired Croatian soldier exhorted his troops on the Piave to defend vigorously with a brief but powerful message: "This must be known by every single soldier. Our honor and the salvation of our fatherland demand that we preserve the foundations of an honorable peace."[2]

Sadly for Austria and her army, by mid-October the Central Powers were headed irrevocably for nothing less than total defeat. The German Army in France had begun to come apart at the seams. The process of final dissolution began with an American offensive in France on September 12. This was the Battle of St. Mihiel, the first large-scale American operation, undertaken by the 1st U.S. Army. The novice Americans encountered only sporadic German resistance; the Germans, like the Austrians aware that defeat was nigh, were now mostly interested in retreating or surrendering. Pershing's forces soon secured all their objectives and captured 15,000 prisoners. Greater still was the Meuse-Argonne offensive, a massive Franco-American push that began on September 26. The Allies boasted 220 divisions, 160 of them in the line; to stop this awesome force, Germany had but 197 divisions (113 in the line), only 50 of them still battleworthy. The offensive began just west of Verdun, near the epic battlefields of 1916, and soon spread to the Argonne forest. Pershing added a newly raised American army, the 2nd, to the battle. Many German regiments resisted bitterly, but the cause was already lost. By mid-October, the French and Americans had broken the back of the German Army in France.

The British accomplished the same thing in Flanders. Haig's great offensive, timed to complement the Meuse-Argonne push, started September 27. Soon

British, Canadian, and Australian divisions overran the once invincible German defenses, and the remnants of Ludendorff's armies were in headlong retreat. By late October, the British reached the fields of Flanders where their divisions had entered the war in the summer of 1914—but this time it was they, not the Germans, who were advancing victoriously. The long-anticipated final defeat of Imperial Germany was now at hand.

Austria's plight was worsened by the simultaneous defeat of her other allies. Bulgaria had spent the war keeping the French, British, and Serbs bottled up at Salonika, ensuring that Austria's southern flank was secure, but in late September, Sofia opted out of the war. Allied forces wasted no time advancing northward, toward south Hungary, and Vienna had no troops left to stop them. A further psychological blow came with the collapse of Turkey in October, under British pressure on several fronts. The final demise of the Ottoman Empire, for centuries Austria's greatest rival but in this war an ally, seemed an ominous portent for the Habsburgs and their ancient, ailing realm.

The time for Diaz to launch his long-awaited offensive had arrived. The Central Powers were on their knees, and weary Austria surely could not withstand a major Italian push on the Piave. Yet, even now Diaz and Pietro Badoglio were cautious, fearful of a debacle. In August, Ferdinand Foch had again pressured Diaz to launch an offensive as part of a combined Allied effort on all fronts. Diaz refused, claiming that he needed twenty-five American divisions to defeat the Austrians. Naturally Foch balked at this request, and Italy remained on the defensive while the French, British, and Americans were busy winning the war in the West.

The reluctance of the *Comando Supremo* to attack the Austrians until absolute victory was assured was fully supported by the government and by Vittorio Emanuele. No one wanted to risk another Caporetto-style defeat, and no one wanted to sacrifice more *fanti* than absolutely necessary. Still, by mid-October it was obvious to even the most faint-hearted Italians that the Central Powers, in retreat on all fronts, were headed for imminent defeat. Indeed, some Italian politicians, observing the rapid demise of Germany, grew fearful that if Italy did not act soon, she might be deprived of the just fruits of an Allied victory. Foreign Minister Baron Sidney Sonnino, in particular, was worried that Italy's timidity was ultimately harmful to her war aims; he wanted the Allies to postpone any armistice until Diaz could arrange a last-minute offensive against the Austrians. The Allies of course refused, but Diaz and Badoglio acted quickly, preparing the army for the anticipated "victory offensive," its last battle of the war.

The army had had many months to ready itself to attack and evict the Austrians from Italy and win the war. By mid-October, its overall strength was impressive: fifty-one Italian divisions, three British, two French, and one Czecho-Slovak, 700 battalions in all, supported by 7,700 guns with six million shells, and 569 aircraft. Allied superiority, both on the ground and in the air, was total.

In addition, all the Allied divisions were at full strength in men and equipment and were well rested, wholly unlike the Austrian units they were to face. The army now also had almost fifty battalions of *arditi* to spearhead the offensive, many of them collected in a special Assault Army Corps, two *arditi* divisions strong. The victorious stand on the Piave had reinvigorated the Italian Army, and the infantry, its ranks fleshed out with the recently conscripted class of 1900, was ready for battle. Diaz overcame his caution and set the date of the long-awaited "victory offensive" for October 24, a year to the day after Austria had launched the Twelfth Battle of the Isonzo.

While the Italians were busy preparing to attack on the Piave, the Habsburg Empire entered its terminal phase. By mid-October, well before Diaz's offensive, Austria had begun to disintegrate. The large numbers of combat troops on the home front—some seventy-five battalions, heavily concentrated in the Czech lands and in the Vienna area—although a drain on the empire's emptying manpower pool, proved remarkably successful at preventing domestic revolution. An abortive coup by Czech nationalists in Prague on October 14 was quickly and easily put down by the local garrison, and no Czech soldiers at the front revolted in sympathy. Indeed, the collapse of the Habsburg Empire was brought on not by the actions of nationalist agitators, much less by military disloyalty, but rather by disastrous political decisions made in Vienna.

Emperor Karl, desperate for peace since assuming the throne, and now aware that the war was lost, appealed for peace with the Allies on September 14 and again on October 4. The Allies might have welcomed a separate peace with Austria a full year earlier, but by the autumn of 1918, with complete victory at hand, the triumphant Allies were in no mood to negotiate. Again Karl's feeble attempts at diplomacy were rebuffed. Even worse was his last-ditch attempt to placate internal and external foes by federalizing the empire. On October 16, Karl unexpectedly issued an imperial manifesto that proclaimed the Austrian half of the monarchy a federal state with complete self-government for the nationalities. This did little but cause general confusion and undermine the remaining legitimacy of Habsburg rule. The manifesto, like Karl's peace feelers, might have helped save Austria a year earlier, but by October 1918 the ardent nationalists were preparing to leave Austria anyway. Karl was undeniably sincere in his desire for peace and the salvation of the Habsburg realm, but his actions in the last months of the war only served to hasten the defeat of his army and the demise of his empire.

The army in particular was left confused by the imperial manifesto. The emperor seemed to have dissolved the empire, and the High Command, facing an imminent Italian "victory offensive," did not know what to do. The Hungarian government, deciding its own fate because Hungary had been excluded from the imperial manifesto,[3] began to take steps toward independence, the lost dream of 1848. All over the empire, nationalists stepped forward to begin assembling national governments in Prague, Cracow, Zagreb, Ljubljana, and even Vienna; some Habsburg Romanians and Serbs prepared to join their conationals among the Allies. On October 21, nationalists declared Czecho-Slovak independence, and the Yugoslav National Council soon followed. What all this meant for the Imperial-and-Royal Army, no one seemed to know.

Major happenings on the home front could not be kept from the soldiers in the field for very long, despite the High Command's best efforts. Individual Austrian soldiers began to leave the Italian front soon after the October 16 manifesto, headed for home. Some Magyar troops started to march eastward toward now independent Hungary on October 22. They went as individuals or in small groups, not as units. Most of the deserters were from rear area or reserve units; very few abandoned the front line. The first mutinies on the Italian front occurred the next day, October 23. Three divisions held in strategic reserve in the Belluno area, at the northern end of Boroević's army group, experienced serious problems that day. Two Croatian regiments of the 42nd *Honvéd* Division refused to enter the fighting line. Czech troops from three regiments of the 21st Rifle Division also refused to return to the front; some Czech infantrymen of the 25th Rifle Regiment opened fire on nearby Magyar troops. Even two veteran battalions of the 55th Division's crack 4th *Bosniaken* revolted, and had to be disarmed by comrades in arms of the Carinthian 7th Regiment. These initial mutinies reflected an omnipresent war weariness, exacerbated by the ill-timed imperial manifesto. The traditionally loyal 4th *Bosniaken*, the heroes of Caporetto and Cornino a year before, wanted to leave the war because Karl had "forgotten" them: the October 16 manifesto made no mention of their homeland, Bosnia-Hercegovina. The mutinies had not yet reached the front line, but without central authority in Vienna, the staying power of the field army was increasingly in doubt.

The Isonzo Army's divisions on the Piave remained essentially unaffected by civilian and rear area disturbances. In the 29th Division, the soldiers' morale was unquestionably low, due in large part to the appalling conditions of service. Desperately hungry, dressed in tattered uniforms, and ravaged by malaria, the troops of the 29th simply wanted the war to end so they could go home. Nevertheless, Berndt's men were almost without exception willing to hold out to the end. Even the division's Czech troops—one-quarter of overall strength—remained loyal; the abortive October 14 coup in Prague had no noticeable impact on the division's Czech soldiery.

Dug in on Papadopoli island, on the northern flank of the XVI Corps, the riflemen of the 29th Division awaited the coming Italian offensive. The division received its last replacements of the war on October 23, a company of the 74th Regiment. Dramatizing the collapse of the Austrian war economy and military bureaucracy, the half-strength company, filled with half-trained teenaged recruits, arrived at the front without a single round of ammunition.

The next morning the Habsburg Army on the Italian front experienced its first frontline mutiny of the war. Two neighboring Hungarian divisions of the 11th Army, holding the line in the mountainous Asiago region, abandoned their positions and headed for home. Soldiers of the Magyar-Slovak 27th Infantry and Magyar-Romanian 38th *Honvéd* Divisions mutinied, simply leaving their trenches and walking east, leaving a considerable gap in the Austrian front line. Units of many other nationalities would soon follow the Hungarians' example. Worse yet, the mutiny of the 27th and 38th divisions coincided with the beginning of Italy's much anticipated "victory offensive," the greatest Italian effort of the war.

On the morning of October 24, the troops facing the 29th Division across the Piave were not Italian, but British. The Italian 10th Army (under the command of the British General Lord Cavan) included two corps, the Italian XI and the British XIV. The latter was dispatched to Italy in the aftermath of Caporetto, and included two experienced, well equipped infantry divisions, the 7th and 23rd. Veterans of considerable fighting in France, they were better trained, equipped, and led than any Italian divisions, and were generously supported by eighty-three batteries of artillery, all amply stocked with ammunition. The British XIV Corps was a formidable and confident adversary, and its mission— breaking through on the central Piave, the shortest route back to the Isonzo— was suitably important.

Across the Piave, the Austrian XVI Corps had scant hope of holding off the British for very long. Berndt's 29th Division faced the 23rd Division, and a few miles south the mostly Magyar 7th Division opposed the British 7th Division. The corps's only reserve was the 201st Austrian Militia Brigade. Like the 29th Division, the 7th Division and the 201st Brigade were tired, hungry, understrength formations incapable of prolonged combat. Once the Piave line was breached, the XVI Corps would have no choice but to retreat to the Tagliamento as quickly as possible.

The great offensive began on the early morning of October 24, revenge for Caporetto a year before. The British attack on Papadopoli started with a tremendous artillery barrage that inflicted crippling losses on forward elements of the 29th and 7th Divisions, as well as on Habsburg batteries behind the front line. The efficient Royal Artillery delivered a heavier and more accurate bombardment than anything the Italian Army had ever achieved, killing and wounding many XVI Corps soldiers in exposed positions. The first British objective was the capture of Papadopoli island. It was held by forward detachments of both Austrian divisions. The defenders occupied two relatively shallow trenches running from the northwest to the southeast of the island; Papadopoli was flat, sandy, and marshy, crisscrossed by numerous small streams, offering little natural cover. The thunderous British shelling wrecked the Austrian entrenchments, so by midday on October 24, the XVI Corps was retreating eastward off the island. Austrian resistance was bitter but brief because of ammunition shortages. The loss of the island seriously weakened the Austrian line, as well as the 29th and 7th Divisions. The British captured 3,600 prisoners and fifty-four machine guns on Papadopoli island, most of them from the Magyar division.

Early on October 25, General Berndt decided to attempt a counterattack to retake Papadopoli, or at least to stall the British advance. All four of the 29th Division's regiments participated, led by their *Sturmtruppen* and backed up by all available batteries. The assault was effectively coordinated and bravely undertaken, but soon faltered in the face of massive British firepower superiority. Machine gun fire tore through advancing Austrian companies, the Royal Artillery silenced Berndt's batteries across the Piave, and Royal Air Force fighters strafed the division's rear areas. The 29th Division's last attack therefore gained nothing, and only weakened its rapidly dwindling supply of men and munitions.

By October 26, the fate of the Habsburg dynasty and its army had been decided, not on the Piave but in Vienna, Budapest, and numerous other cities throughout the empire. In general the Italian "victory offensive" was so far proving a disappointment to the *Comando Supremo*. The first three days of the attack produced few impressive advances, and unexpectedly heavy casualties. Many Austrian divisions continued to fight back effectively, and everywhere Italian units attacked sluggishly, some ineptly. Despite months of preparation, Italian tactics were still not as effective as the Austrian (and certainly not the British), and infantry-artillery coordination remained inadequate.[4] The long-awaited offensive seemed to be evolving into a costly battle of attrition like those which had raged so long on the Isonzo.

While Austrian regiments in the field kept fighting, even if hopelessly, the centers of Habsburg legitimacy at home began to dissolve without serious opposition as national councils all over the empire asserted their newfound authority. Naturally some tired *Frontkämpfer*, confused by events on the home front and wanting out of the war, simply deserted. Formations of all nationalities experienced mutinies—whole platoons, companies, in some cases entire regiments opting out of the war and heading home. Still, many divisions continued to fight on, regardless of national composition. It was a scene even more complex and confusing than the chaos that had erupted in the retreating Italian armies after Caporetto a year before. In truth, there were numerous examples of both dereliction of duty and heroic sacrifice among all Austria's national groups. Among the regiments praised by the High Command for their early performance in resisting the Italians were German, Magyar, Polish, Romanian, and Croatian units. Effective officers proved able to keep their men fighting, regardless of nationality, whereas indecisive officers watched whole divisions disintegrate; the problem was one of leadership, not ethnicity, as it had always been.

Lieutenant General Berndt was one of those effective Austrian leaders who proved capable of keeping his exhausted division in the field and ready for battle. In recognition of this, he was appointed commander of the XVI Corps, one of the Habsburg Army's last battlefield promotions. Berndt was in command of the corps, with the remnants of the 7th and 29th Divisions and the 201st Militia Brigade, as well as the mostly Czech 26th Rifle Division, when the next Allied blow fell. In the late evening of October 26, all along the front, Italian, British, and French divisions renewed their offensive. It was Diaz's attempt to break the deadlock that had recently developed. The British XIV Corps in particular made notable progress against Berndt's troops. The Yorkshiremen of the 23rd Division assaulted the Piave's east bank early on the morning of October 27, crossing from Papadopoli. Their advance was lavishly supported by the Royal Artillery, but the Austrians resisted with determination, pouring machine gun and mortar fire into the ranks of British infantry fording the Piave, inflicting heavy losses on the 23rd Division's assault troops.[5] Even so, Berndt's position was hopeless, and the 29th Division's right flank soon gave way. As the division's 57th Brigade retreated, a gap opened between the North Bohemians and the faltering 7th Division.

As darkness approached, the 57th Brigade launched a counterattack near the village of Tezze, on a tributary of the Piave, in an attempt to close the gap between the two Austrian divisions. The attack was barely supported by artillery (Berndt's batteries were running out of shells), and British gun and mortar fire broke up several Austrian assaults. Units of the 201st Militia Brigade were added to the attack, but to no avail. By the end of the evening, the 29th Division's right flank had been pushed more than two miles back from the Piave's banks, and one of its brigades had been shattered: between them, the 57th Brigade's 92nd and 137th Regiments could muster only six officers and 448 riflemen.

As October 28 began, Berndt, seeing the sorry state of his troops, had no choice but to withdraw his corps to the Tagliamento, to establish a new defensive line. The 29th Division's first objective was to retreat to the Livenza River, ten miles east; securing the Livenza line would give the division enough time to reach the Tagliamento in a more orderly manner. Berndt no longer had the 7th Division under his control. It had suffered badly on Papadopoli island and its remnants had scattered, many soldiers heading for home. Berndt's corps still contained the 26th Rifle Division and the 201st Brigade in addition to the 29th; these were tired and weak formations—together they constituted less than a complete division—but they remained in good order and willing to fight, even in retreat.

Elsewhere on the collapsing Italian front the condition of the retreating Austrian Army was less orderly. Most of Wenzel von Wurm's Isonzo Army was still in the field, under its own commanders, but numerous Austrian divisions in the Belluno and Asiago regions were dissolving, even without Allied pressure. Everywhere, however, Habsburg units of all nationalities continued to fight back, and the Allied advance was proceeding slowly. The Italians had just started to achieve a major breakthrough, near Vittorio Veneto, the city that would give its name to the great Italian victory. But the Austrian retreat had not yet deteriorated into a rout. Nevertherless, the High Command was fully aware that an armistice had to be achieved immediately, if the Habsburg dynasty and realm were to be saved from complete internal collapse. On October 28, Arz instructed General Weber to contact the Italians immediately. The High Command informed the unfortunate Weber, "Every stipulation would be acceptable that does not infringe upon the honor of the army or constitute an outright capitulation." But the High Command's overture was already too late.

The 29th Division spent October 29 retreating toward the Livenza. The 26th Rifle Division covered the 29th's retreat, fighting a series of vicious melees against the advancing British throughout the day. Austrian counterattacks failed, costing the 26th over 2,600 men, including 524 killed, but they bought invaluable time for the rest of Berndt's corps to reach the Livenza. Sappers slowed the Allied advance by blowing bridges, destroying water pumps, and felling trees across roads. The North Bohemians were retreating faster than the British could pursue them. Italian cavalry and armored cars were a major concern, but the most serious threat facing the division was air attack. RAF fighters and bombers, uncontested by the now nonexistent Austrian air service, freely strafed and bombed roads crowded with retreating Austrian units. In this manner the 29th lost much of its artillery and transport. Ironically, the merciless air attacks slowed the Allied offensive: many roads were so clogged with wrecked vehicles, wagons, and guns, and dead horses and men, that British forward units had to halt and clear them before resuming their advance.

The next day the 29th Division continued its retreat to the Livenza, covered by its few remaining machine guns and artillery pieces. The tired infantry kept marching eastward, and by the end of the day most of Berndt's foot soldiers had reached the Livenza's east bank. Yet this was not far enough. As the Austrian military situation deteriorated, the Isonzo Army lost its anticipated rest on the Livenza; instead, it had to withdraw as soon as possible to the Tagliamento. The 29th Division's last act on the Livenza was blowing the bridge at Brugnera, one of the main spans across the deep and swift thousand-foot-wide river. The Livenza could not be forded, so the destruction of the bridge before British reconnaissance patrols arrived in Brugnera late on October 31 bought the 29th a few more hours.

On the last day of October, the 29th Division could muster a rifle strength of only ninety officers and 1,285 men—one and a half battalions. The weakened 26th Rifle Division and 201st Brigade together added only 4,500 more infantrymen to Berndt's command, so the XVI Corps contained the rifle strength of a brigade. Berndt's battle group was still in the field, though, and he was determined to get his men home in orderly units, not as a rabble. His exhausted soldiers remained willing to follow orders; they were concerned with doing their duty and getting home, not the current chaos overwhelming their homeland. In one of the division's ethnically mixed regiments, "The Czechs as much as the Germans protested against the raising of the issue of the future political system." Few others in the dying Dual Monarchy were able to put aside the national question in the tumultuous days of late October.

Isonzo Army command was also busy on the last day of October. Field Marshal Boroević, assisted by Wurm and his trusted chief of staff, Colonel Theodor von Körner, was attempting to save the Isonzo Army, the strongest element in his army group, by bringing it across the Tagliamento intact. The war was evidently lost, but the Isonzo Army's divisions would be needed to restore order at home. Boroević, in faraway Friulia, was unaware how far the situation had deteriorated in Vienna and across the empire.

In the last week of October, the process of dissolution, begun in midmonth, followed its logical course. Throughout the Habsburg Empire, local nationalists were taking power with little or no resistance from military or civil authorities, who in many cases had disappeared. Local nationalists declared sovereignty in Bohemia and Galicia on October 28, and in Slovenia, Croatia, and Bosnia a day later. Leading Slovene and Croatian politicians, fearing an Italian invasion of South Slav lands, petitioned victorious Serbia for help. On October 29, the Budapest garrison agreed to support Mihály Károly's provisional government, which promptly took Hungary out of the war. Two days later, Béla Linder, the new Hungarian war minister, ordered Hungarian troops under Imperial-and-Royal authority to lay down their arms and come home. From Trient to Czernowitz, the imperial eagle was hauled down, and the Dual Monarchy, the last manifestation of the ancient Habsburg realm, had effectively disappeared in a matter of days.

Army garrisons all over Austria, often out of contact with Vienna, were declaring their support for new leaderships. On October 26, the Budapest garrison counted 70,000 troops under arms; by October 31, none remained. The commander of the Budapest Military District observed, "There was not a single soldier . . . one could have used in a suppression of the movement." With the Habsburg realm in dissolution, soldiers began to follow new leaders, flags, and nations. The same happened to the Imperial-and-Royal Navy. The emergent Yugoslav National Council laid claim to the navy, harbored in Istria and Dalmatia. At sunset on October 31, the red-and-white Austrian naval ensign was lowered for the last time at Pola, headquarters of the *k.u.k. Kriegsmarine*, and the new Yugoslav flag was raised in its place. The defunct fleet's commander, Rear Admiral Nicholas Horthy von Nagybánya, took the Imperial-and-Royal ensign under his arm and left Pola, headed for his native Hungary.

At the High Command, Arz tried to delay the total collapse of the state and army, but there was little he and his staff could do. On October 29, the chief of the General Staff was informed that the 3rd Edelweiss Division, perhaps the army's finest division, an elite formation of loyal Alpine Germans, had refused to reenter the line; Arz knew then that the cause was lost, and he informed Emperor Karl that the Italians could not be stopped. After several hours of delay, on October 31 the Italians agreed to let Weber's armistice commission cross their lines, but the fighting raged on, and the Allies continued to advance. At last, the Italians had broken through on both the Piave and the Asiago fronts, and nothing was going to stop them. Caporetto had to be avenged. In the last hours of October, as Arz tried to get Austria out of the war, and after the emperor had effectively abdicated, Field Marshal Boroević was planning to save the dynasty. But like Luigi Cadorna a year earlier, he had to abandon his headquarters in Udine. The Italian Army was coming, and his staff feared attacks by armed Italian civilians. The old Croatian soldier took his staff and headed for the safer hills of Carinthia, where he set about preparing to restore collapsing Habsburg authority, as the legendary Field Marshal Joseph Radetzky had done seventy years before.

For Berndt and his men, as November began, Allied strafing and shelling still remained a more serious concern than the collapse of the home front. Berndt's corps marched toward the Tagliamento bridges, and safety, as quickly as possible during November 1. The 29th Division was outrunning Allied forward detachments, thanks to the destructive work of its sappers, but it could not so easily escape Allied air attacks, and divisional columns were strafed and bombed repeatedly during the day. Despite the inevitable losses and delays, the North Bohemians reached the river by nightfall, and did not pause to rest. Berndt's troops raced across the Tagliamento bridges under the cover of darkness; the last riflemen reached the east bank at 2 A.M. on November 3, and the last supply wagons crossed by 3:30 A.M. The soldiers were exhausted, having marched thirty miles under enemy attack in thirty-six hours. The 29th Division had outrun the Allies and had been saved from captivity by Berndt's energetic leadership; his men would be able to return home.

Berndt permitted his tired and hungry regiments a brief rest before resuming the march to the east. His message to his soldiers was typically blunt: "We still have long marches through the mountains before us." He ordered his units to abandon all but a very small number of horses, an unnecessary burden through the Alps. Unit commanders were instructed to streamline their organizations and supply columns, and to bring home only what was truly necessary: weapons, munitions, and supplies, in that order. Berndt explained lucidly that the 29th Division had to retain its discipline, structure, and weaponry in the coming days in order to carry out its new mission, "the reestablishment of the wickedly disturbed order at home."

While Berndt was rallying his regiments, General Weber and his armistice commission, meeting with Italian representatives at Villa Giusti, were trying to achieve an end to the fighting. In truth, the Italians did not want the fighting to end yet; after more than three years of setbacks and defeats, the Italian Army was finally winning an epic triumph, and the armed forces, king, government, and people alike demanded nothing less than total victory. Late on November 1, the Italian delegation provided an informal statement of Allied terms: an immediate cessation of hostilities, complete and immediate Austrian demobilization, prompt evacuation of all Italian territory (including, significantly, both the South Tyrol and the Littoral), Allied occupation rights in Austria, and a right of passage for Allied troops through the Austrian lands. The terms were those of a complete surrender, not an armistice. Karl, although desperate to end the war, refused to accept the Italian diktat. On November 2, the Italians delivered Weber an ultimatum, demanding acceptance of their terms within twenty-four hours. If any of the Habsburg realm were to be saved, peace with Italy had to be achieved at once, and the High Command reluctantly agreed to accept the terms. At 11:30 P.M. on November 2, Karl stepped down as commander in chief of the armed forces, leaving Arz to sign the humiliating armistice (as General Ludwig von Benedek had done for Franz Joseph in 1866, after the army was trounced by the Prussians in Bohemia). The Italians were informed of the acceptance of their terms, and Arz ordered all Austrian units on the Italian front to cease fighting at 3 P.M. on November 3. The Habsburgs' last war thus officially ended.

The war had not yet ended for hundreds of thousands of Austrian soldiers facing the advancing Allies. Many commanders, particularly in the Isonzo Army, had managed to preserve some of their divisions, and wanted to bring them home in good order. Berndt was by no means defeatist, as he expressed in his order of November 3 that military operations must progress. At three in the afternoon, there were no Allied units near the 29th Division, and the North Bohemians resumed their march back to their homeland. Berndt and his staff were already more concerned about the Slovenes than the Allies. The division had no real idea what was happening to the east, and was prepared to encounter armed resistance beyond the Isonzo. Berndt was determined to get his men home in time to restore domestic order, and was fully prepared to fight his way back to Bohemia, if necessary; that was why he had so strictly ordered his troops to keep their weapons.

Most Austrian soldiers on the Italian front were not as fortunate as those serving in Berndt's corps. At midafternoon on November 3, dozens of Austrian brigades and divisions all along the front laid down their arms, as ordered by the High Command. The Italians did not cease their advance, however, and proceeded to round up entire regiments as captives, a clear violation of the armistice terms. The *Comando Supremo* disingenuously claimed that it required twenty-four extra hours to inform all its formations to cease fighting; of course, the Austrians had not been told this. Unarmed Habsburg units were rounded up en masse, often without resistance, and dispatched to Italian prisoner of war camps. By the time the Italians actually stopped their advance on November 4, almost 360,000 Austrian soldiers, a total of nineteen divisions and countless smaller units, had been taken into Italian captivity. Among the lost units were the headquarters of four corps, ten divisions, and twenty-one brigades, complete with their staffs and general officers. Every nationality was represented among the prisoners. There were 108,000 Germans, 83,000 Czechs and Slovaks, 61,000 South Slavs, 40,000 Poles, 32,000 Ukrainians, 25,000 Romanians, and even 7,000 Italians in Austrian uniform; ironically, the great majority of the captured men were considered "allies of the Entente." Sadly, more than 30,000 of these last captives would die in Italy due to poor treatment, disease, and malnutrition.

While the victorious Italians rounded up the remnants of the Austrian divisions at the front, Emperor Karl prepared to end centuries of Habsburg rule through abdication. He was, in fact, merely formalizing his realm's dissolution, the logical culmination of the process he had helped to begin. The military collapse was by now so total that the High Command grew concerned about the safety of Karl and his family. When Empress Zita asked Arz how many troops would be available to protect her husband, the chief of the General Staff reluctantly, but truthfully, responded, "Not a single battalion, Majesty." The High Command was forced to collect cadet companies from the Military Academy at Wiener Neustadt and the artillery school at Traiskirchen to guard the imperial palace at Schönbrunn from revolutionary mobs.

There was, however, a force prepared to protect the Imperial-and-Royal family and ready to restore the Habsburg monarchy. Field Marshal Boroević and his staff were waiting in Klagenfurt for the order to arrive from Vienna calling them to bring the Isonzo Army to the capital to impose order. Boroević had attempted to preserve the Isonzo Army, with some success, so that it could be used to save the empire from complete collapse. The divisions of the famed *Isonzoarmee* represented the last significant force under Imperial-and-Royal authority, depleted and tired but still loyal to Boroević and the dynasty. They were certainly stronger than the forces of civil unrest on the home front. The ghosts of Radetzky, Alfred Windischgrätz, and Josip Jellačić, the generals who had saved the empire seven decades before, were alive in the hearts of Boroević and many other Habsburg officers. As in 1848, the monarchy had collapsed entirely, Hungary and many other crown lands were in revolt, and the emperor was preparing to leave Vienna. And, as seventy years earlier, only the ancient multinational army remained steadfastly loyal, the only guarantor of Habsburg survival. Again, a loyal army in northern Italy was waiting to save the House of Habsburg.

In 1848, the Viennese playwright Franz Grillparzer celebrated Radetzky's victories in Italy with a memorable poem dedicated to the eighty-two year-old Czech soldier, "Austria Is in Your Camp" (*"In deinem Lager ist Österreich"*). It included the following lines:

> *In deinem Lager ist Österreich,*
> *Wir andern sind einzelne Trümmer.*
> *Aus Torheit und aus Eikelheit*
> *Sind wir in uns zerfallen,*
> *In denem, die du führst zum Streit,*
>
> *Lebt noch ein Geist in allen . . .*
> *Die Gott als Slav und Magyaren schuf,*
> *Sie streiten um Worte nicht hämisch,*
> *Sie folgen, ob deutsch auch der Feldherrnruf,*
> *Denn: Vorwärts! ist ungrisch und böhmisch.*[6]

Seven decades later, a multinational Austrian army in northern Italy, led by another Slav field marshal, was preparing to restore the dynasty.

Boroević repeatedly cabled his monarch in Vienna, informing him that the Isonzo Army was ready to march on the capital at the emperor's order. But Karl never responded. Never strong-willed, by early November he had lost any desire to use force to preserve his family's ancient empire. The Isonzo Army would never be used to restore the dynasty and the realm; Boroević would never be a new Radetzky. The collapse in 1918 was more total than seven decades before, and the foreign threat was far greater. Most of all, Boroević was unprepared to be either independent or insubordinate, like the heroes of 1848 who acted without (and in some cases actually against) imperial dictates to save the House of Habsburg. For several days the old field marshal waited in Klagenfurt for an imperial response that never arrived. By November 9, the dynasty, the monarchy, and its army belonged to history, and Boroević reluctantly disbanded his headquarters.

While the staff of Army Group Boroević was waiting in Klagenfurt for orders from Vienna, Berndt and his men continued their march eastward toward the former Austrian frontier and the Isonzo. During November 4, the 29th Division managed to outpace advancing Allied patrols, even though Italian cavalry and bicycle-mounted *Bersaglieri* were often within a quarter-mile of the division's rear guard. That day, the 42nd Regiment briefly exchanged fire with an Italian cavalry troop, the last shots fired by the North Bohemians in the war. Over the next two days the division reached former Austrian soil and passed through the Isonzo valley. The 29th's journey across numerous battlefields was unpleasant, even dangerous. In wrecked Gorizia, local Italian nationalists had taken over, and some natives taunted the retreating Germans and Czechs. Worse, Slovene deserters from the 2nd Mountain Rifle Regiment sniped at

Berndt's men, their former comrades in arms, as they headed through the shell-scarred Isonzo valley. The Littoral was filled with Austrian soldiers of all nationalities trying to get home. A senior staff officer recognized a former comrade marching past, a Croatian soldier of the much decorated Dalmatian 22nd Regiment, the "Lions of Podgora." The regiment that had fought so heroically on the Isonzo for so long was no more. The dirty and exhausted soldier told the staff officer, "Sir, we're not heroes anymore, just beggars," and kept marching back to distant Dalmatia.

The 29th Division also kept marching home. Berndt was anxious to prevent fighting with Yugoslavia, so he and his staff met with representatives of the Yugoslav National Council at Gorizia, where he explained that his men simply wanted to return home, emphasizing that his units were in good order and represented no threat to Slovene sovereignty. Throughout November the Slovene lands were inundated with retreating Austrian soldiers; in just two weeks more than 800,000 Austrian soldiers passed through Slovenia on their way home. Considering the unstable political climate, the journey across the Slovene lands was surprisingly tranquil. The 29th Division experienced no notable disturbances during its long march to Ljubljana.[7]

The division reached the Slovene capital on November 9, giving the tired soldiers their first rest in several days. Berndt soon realized that the Habsburg Empire no longer existed, and communication from Boroević's disbanding headquarters made it clear that an imperial restoration was out of the question. Berndt's only remaining task was to get his weary soldiers home. The 29th Division remained intact, with just over 7,000 officers and men, but fewer than half of them were combat troops. Like the army as a whole, the division's multinational character persisted to the end: among the combatants there were 2,310 Germans, 571 Czechs, 103 Magyars, and 290 other Slavs, mostly Poles. The large number of Czechs and other nationalities that had recently revolted against Austrian rule indicated the power of effective leadership and comradeship forged in battle, even during the greatest hardships. As one soldier recalled, "Our Czech comrades also stayed with us obediently. We stuck together in ancient loyalty."[8]

Getting the troops home proved to be no simple task. There were so many units trying to leave Ljubljana by train that the 29th was forced to wait several days to board; even though, on average, thirty-two trains departed Ljubljana every day filled with demobilizing soldiers, there were still more troops than places in cars. On November 12, shortly after hearing that Germany, too, had quit the war, the first 29th Division units began to board trains for the long, slow ride home. At least they no longer had to march. Berndt and his staff reached Vienna on November 16. Seeing the extent of the collapse, the general quickly reboarded and headed for his North Bohemian home, now in the newly declared Czechoslovakia. He reached it the next day, delivered a final speech to his soldiers praising their efforts, and went home. Otto Berndt's long war had finally ended.

While General Berndt was demobilizing the division, its final contingents were still journeying home. The 94th Regiment was the last element of Berndt's command to leave Ljubljana, departing the Slovene capital on November 15. Its meandering five-day train ride took the remnants of the veteran regiment through Styria, Upper Austria, Bavaria, Saxony, and finally home to the Sudetenland, reaching Reichenberg, the now defunct divisional depot, at three in the afternoon on November 20.

Like all the hard-fighting Habsburg regiments that survived the Great War, the 94th received no final review, no Imperial-and-Royal march-past to commemorate its achievements, not even a telegram from Vienna thanking it for its service. Many veteran regiments marched home in good order, arriving to find disorder and chaos, receiving only the thanks and praise of the officers who had led them through the costliest, bloodiest war ever seen. The 94th was fortunate, for Berndt had saved his division from captivity, and had gotten his weary soldiers back to North Bohemia. Yet fewer than 200 soldiers of the 94th Regiment made it back to Reichenberg. The regiment's 1st Battalion, once a thousand strong, was represented by six officers, two sergeants, and thirty-eight other ranks; only two soldiers from its 1st Company came home. The proud 94th, which had seen so much fighting in the hills of Serbia, the peaks of the Carpathians, the plains of Galicia, and finally the valleys of Venetia, received kind words from its last commander and demobilized, stacking its arms and marching into history.

Long before the last Austrian troops made it home, however, the Italian Army had picked the fruits of a long-awaited victory. The *Comando Supremo*, elated by the victory at Vittorio Veneto and Austria's total military and civil collapse, ordered its divisions to occupy *Italia irredenta* immediately. *Alpini* seized the South Tyrol, entering Trient on November 4, and the Duke of Aosta's victorious 3rd Army raced across Friulia, crossing the Isonzo and reaching Gorizia a day later. For the second time in the war, the Italian Army entered Gorizia in triumph, and this time it would stay for good.

The real prize, though, was Trieste, as it always had been to Italian nationalists. The military wasted no time ensuring that Trieste was firmly in Italian hands; the generals were particularly afraid that armed Slovene irregulars would overrun the city before the 3rd Army could reach it. The *Comando Supremo* therefore took no chances. Local irredentists had raised the Italian flag over City Hall as early as October 30 (as well as, temporarily, the red flag of revolution), but the Italian military had to arrive for the city to be irrevocably and securely Italian territory. In midafternoon on November 3, the destroyer *Audace* appeared in Trieste harbor. On board were General Pettiti di Rosito and a landing party, arriving to officially annex Trieste to Italy. A crowd of ebullient nationalists, ecstatic that the long-delayed hour of victory had come at last, gathered at the pier to greet the liberators; among them was the normally mild-mannered writer Italo Svevo. At 4 P.M., the destroyer docked and the triumphant *Bersaglieri* came ashore and raised the Italian tricolor over the city. Three years, five months, and eleven days after Italy declared war on Austria to liberate *Italia irredenta*, after eleven failed offensives on the Isonzo, the Italian Army finally occupied Trieste.

EPILOGUE

FIFTEEN

SINCE THEN

In November 1918, in the immediate aftermath of such a long-awaited victory, Italy was gripped with nationwide euphoria. After so long, the Austrians had been defeated, the hated Habsburgs deposed, and the unredeemed provinces joined to the Italian motherland. The army was hailed in all quarters, and the *Comando Supremo* showered generals and many lowlier soldiers with decorations to celebrate the army's triumph.[1] A dozen entire brigades were collectively awarded the *medaglia d'oro* for their outstanding heroism throughout the struggle, among them the Tuscany, Aosta, and Sassari Brigades, which had spilled so much blood on the Carso. The *fanti*, Gabriele D'Annunzio's "holy infantry," finally received the grateful thanks of the nation for their awesome sacrifices on the Isonzo and numerous other battlefields.

But the cost of victory was appalling, and the enormity of the price Italy had paid to liberate *Italia irredenta* was only slowly being fully realized. In material terms alone, the cost of the war was daunting. The Treasury calculated the final cost of the war with Austria at 148 billion lire, equivalent to twice the Italian government's total expenditures from unification in 1861 to the eve of war in 1913. The war was financed in large part with foreign loans, leaving the victorious nation with a notable debt and lingering inflation as well. They ensured that prosperity would be slow to return. The baleful economic consequences of the Great War would remain with Italy for years to come.

Far worse, though, was the human cost of Italy's Pyrrhic victory. In forty-one months of fighting, the armed forces called twenty-seven conscript classes to the colors. Some five and a half million men donned a uniform during the struggle with Austria; two-fifths of them became casualties—killed, wounded, captured, or seriously ill. It took the army a full generation to make an accurate accounting of its losses. The final numbers revealed that Italy sacrificed 689,000 of her sons to redeem the Littoral and the South Tyrol. Another million Italians were seriously wounded, half of them permanently disabled. The overwhelming majority of Italy's casualties fell on the Isonzo, far and away the greatest and bloodiest campaign of the Italo-Austrian war.[2]

The Duke of Aosta's 3rd Army, the "undefeated" *Terza Armata* that fought so long on the rocky Carso, counted a total loss of 1,269,061 soldiers: 140,462 killed, 680,595 wounded, and 448,004 missing (most of them dead)—the vast majority of them fallen on the Isonzo.[3] Italy's mountain infantry and artillery, the famed *Alpini* who did so much of the fighting on the upper Isonzo, alone had 166,881 casualties, more than half of them killed. In all, Italy lost no less than 1,100,000 soldiers on the Isonzo from June 1915 to October 1917, at least 95 percent of them in Luigi Cadorna's eleven futile offensives, twenty-eight months of failed attacks that brought the Italian Army only a third of the way to Trieste. Even by the terrible standards of the Great War, it had been an awe-inspiring and needless sacrifice. Nothing like it had been seen in the history of warfare.

Unsurprisingly, the enormous and unprecedented Italian casualties on the Isonzo demanded adequate compensation. The conquest of the Littoral and the South Tyrol no longer seemed enough to offset such a shedding of Italian blood. Rome soon demanded more. Crudely put, Italy wanted a better return on her frightful investment in Italian lives on the Isonzo's banks. Vittorio Orlando's government pressed the Allies for greater territorial concessions. The lands promised to Italy in the Treaty of London—the Littoral, the South Tyrol, and northern Dalmatia—were not enough. Rome now wanted Fiume, too, an Adriatic port southeast of Trieste. The majority of Fiume's residents were indeed ethnic Italians, but the city had always been part of Hungary and had no connection at all to Italy. More important, giving Fiume—and Dalmatia, for that matter—to Italy would be a mortal offense against the new Kingdom of Yugoslavia. When the British and French promised Dalmatia to Italy in 1915, it had been an Austrian province, but now it was part of Yugoslavia, one of the victorious Allied powers. In British and French eyes, Yugoslavia, a Habsburg successor state, was just as entitled to the Adriatic coastline as Italy; indeed, more so, because Dalmatia was almost wholly South Slav, with hardly any Italians living there. Why, reasoned London and Paris, should the Yugoslavs be deprived of South Slav territory just to satisfy Italian greed?

The Italians were furious. After all, had they not entered the Great War to save Italian lands from the South Slavs? Worse, Italy's generals remembered well the pivotal role played by Austria's South Slav regiments in the defense on the Isonzo. Now they were being asked to surrender their claim on Dalmatia—promised to them in 1915—to satisfy the desires of the Serbs, Croats, and

Slovenes, many of whom had recently been fighting the Italians with vigor. When the Versailles peace conference convened on January 19, 1919, the Italian delegation was determined to wrest Dalmatia and Fiume, too, from the Yugoslavs. Only then would the peace settlement be just in Italian eyes. Indeed, Prime Minister Orlando arrived in France with only one object: collecting on his nation's debts, the blood debts incurred on the Isonzo. Italy had entered the war on the grounds of *sacro egoismo*—sacred egotism—and now Orlando came unashamedly to collect. He faced a tough diplomatic fight. Italy's allies, who had supported her and bankrolled much of the war with Austria, were uninterested in further Italian land claims. The land that was firmly in Italy's grasp, the Littoral and the South Tyrol, had large numbers of South Slavs and Germans; why cede even more territory, all of it almost purely Slav, to Rome? President Woodrow Wilson's notions of national self-determination, which guided the Versailles conference intermittently, certainly recommended against any further land grants to Italy, particularly at the expense of Yugoslavia. Italy was only a second-rate Allied power, far below Britain, France, and America in might and prestige, and her attempted grab of Dalmatia and Fiume was doomed to fail. It was therefore with resignation that the Orlando government accepted the Versailles settlement. In June 1920, the treaties of St. Germain and Trianon, which divided up Austria and Hungary, respectively, gave Italy the Littoral and the South Tyrol, as expected, but ceded Dalmatia and Fiume to Yugoslavia.

The response in Italy was fast and furious. The peace treaties were vehemently denounced. Millions of Italians, especially those on the Right, believed that Italy had been robbed of land she deserved and had bought with Italian blood. They demanded a revision of the postwar settlement in Italy's favor. Actually, dissatisfaction with the war's outcome had emerged almost immediately after the guns fell silent; the treaties were merely the final insult. As early as November 24, 1918, while the troops had only begun to demobilize, D'Annunzio wrote an article in *Corriere della Sera*, Italy's most prestigious newspaper, about the end of the war. In it he rued that Italy would not get what she deserved, and coined a memorable phrase: he called it a "mutilated victory."

D'Annunzio spoke for many Italians who felt that Italy had won the war but somehow lost the peace. The dashing fifty-five-year-old poet and war hero was disappointed by the war's end and lacked a sense of purpose. He seized on the revisionist cause with all his energy; and his usual weakness for self-dramatization and theatrics came to the fore. D'Annunzio, who had done so much to turn popular opinion toward intervention in 1915, now demanded annexation of South Slav lands: "Dalmatia belongs to Italy by divine right as well as human law, by the Grace of God who has designed the earth in such a way that every race can recognize its destiny therein carved out. . . . It was ours and shall be ours again."

D'Annunzio soon had followers. Many of them were disgruntled veterans, unable to find their place in society now that peace had returned. Many, too, were angered by crippling postwar inflation and unemployment; the Italy they came home to was not the idyllic place they had been promised by the government. *Arditi* veterans were notably prominent among the revisionists. As many as 50,000 soldiers served in special assault units during the war, and many of them could not adjust to civilian life. War had brutalized them. They felt that Italy no longer appreciated their heroism and patriotism, and that the government had sold out them and their fallen comrades by accepting the Versailles settlement.

D'Annunzio was not the only political figure courting the *arditi*. Mussolini, too, was looking to recruit disenchanted veterans for his cause. Mussolini also was appalled by the treaties, and he was determined to do something about it. He had argued for war in 1915 not only to defeat Austria and liberate *Italia irredenta*, but also to radicalize the nation, to bring a revolution. But postwar Italy looked much as it did before. The elites that ruled Italy in 1915, the staid, liberal bourgeoisie, were still in charge; worse, Italy was now threatened by the Left. After Russia's Bolshevik Revolution, all Europe was fearful that the Red contagion would spread. Mussolini was perhaps the greatest worrier of them all; he believed that if he did not act, the revolutionary Left, his mortal Socialist enemies, would seize power.

With this political message, Mussolini started down his road to power. On March 23, 1919, he founded the *Fasci di Combattimento* in Milan. These nascent groups of ultranationalists were named for the ancient *fasces*, symbol of the Roman Republic, and soon gave a name to Mussolini's rising movement and ideology—Fascism. Their first chairman, significantly, was a former *arditi* captain. Out-of-work *arditi* filled the ranks of the movement; their violence, elitism, black shirts, and fighting knives appealed to Mussolini and gave his movement a well defined image. Mussolini continually emphasized that veterans like himself and his followers, the men who had fought the endless battles of the Isonzo, were the rightful leaders of Italy: "We, we alone have the right to the succession, because we, we were the men who forced the country into the war and into the victory." His essential message was interconnected and threefold: revise the treaties, revolutionize the country, and defeat the Left. This heady brew of nationalism and radicalism included pretty much the same themes Mussolini had advocated in 1915, only now they were made much more virulent by the cost of the war and the "mutilated victory."

Yet Mussolini was soon upstaged by D'Annunzio. Frustrated by the government's acceptance of the treaties and eager to act, on September 12, 1919, the writer led a motley band of a thousand armed ultranationalists into Fiume. D'Annunzio and his followers marched into the city under the "banner of Randaccio," the flag that had adorned the corpse of Major Giovanni Randaccio, the poet's friend mortally wounded on the Carso during the Tenth Battle of the Isonzo. The legion raised the banner and the Italian tricolor and claimed the city for Italy, a flagrant violation of the peace settlement. D'Annunzio established himself as local ruler, leading an odd life that mixed idealism with debauchery. Nevertheless, D'Annunzio's daring act electrified the ultranationalists. Soon thousands of volunteers flocked to Fiume to join the cause.

In fact, D'Annunzio's action was illegal, and the government in Rome should have evicted the warrior-poet and his strange legion from the city. But not only did the government fail to move against the Fiuman adventurers, but the occupiers actually received considerable military assistance from the army. The senior general in the region was Pietro Badoglio, commander of the 8th Army, garrisoning the northeast and the Littoral. Like many senior officers, Badoglio was sympathetic to the revisionists and lent covert aid to D'Annunzio's forces at Fiume. The government demanded a blockade of the rebel city, but its execution was halfhearted and it failed to damage D'Annunzio's cause. For a time the warrior-poet threatened to fatally destabilize the government in Rome, but the adventure came to an abrupt end after more than a year.

In November 1920, following lengthy negotiations, Prime Minister Giovanni Giolitti's government reached an agreement with Yugoslavia: Belgrade got Dalmatia and Fiume was declared a free city, belonging to neither Italy nor Yugoslavia. The government, anxious to settle the issue, now wasted no time getting rid of D'Annunzio and his adventurers. D'Annunzio pledged resistance to the death, promising Fiume would be "the city of total sacrifice." Obsessed with his memories of the Isonzo, he exhorted his legionaries to defend Fiume to the last man: "This is the August of the torrid battles, of the desperate victories. There is Sabotino with its long gray back reshaped by explosions. . . . There is the Oslavia gully choked up by stagnant smoke. Here is Podgora, reddish like a blood clot. Here is San Michele . . . that saw thirty-two assaults, watered with more blood than that drunk by all the votive altars in the course of the centuries. Where has that blood gone?" Yet D'Annunzio's lurid, religious-sounding battle cry was hollow. When an Italian battleship appeared in Fiume's harbor and fired a single shell, wounding the bard slightly, D'Annunzio hastily fled. He moved into retirement, and the revisionist torch passed to Mussolini.[4]

Mussolini had been busy building his political base. His core of support remained the veterans, but he managed to gain the admiration of many Italians from diverse groups. Many Italians of the Right and Center feared the Bolshevik threat, and a great many wanted an end to postwar inflation and unemployment, which Mussolini promised. No less, millions of Italians of all political stripes detested the treaties and demanded that Italy gain her rightful territory. The Fascists also gained support in the army; this was indispensable because the military was the only force strong enough to block Mussolini's rise. Badoglio, appointed chief of the General Staff to replace Armando Diaz in 1920, was pro-Fascist, as was the Duke of Aosta, the army's most esteemed general. Count-less more junior officers responded favorably to Mussolini's nationalist cries for revision and reform.

The Fascists did not rely on campaigning and persuasion alone, however, to gain recruits and deter their political enemies. From the beginning there was a boisterously thuggish element of the movement. Many former soldiers had de-veloped a taste for violence in the trenches and saw no reason not to use similar tactics against real or imagined opponents of Fascism. Mussolini's party mili-tia, the "Black Shirts," adopted the black uniforms and violent outlook of the *arditi*. Ex-*arditi* gave Fascism a disciplined street-fighting army and a justifi-ably bad image. Fascist violence was particularly brutal against ethnic minori-ties, especially South Slavs. In the recently annexed Littoral, Italy pursued anti-Slav policies even before the Fascists rose to power. Slovenes and Croats, the "Slav barbarians" denounced by D'Annunzio, were persecuted by Rome. Their language and culture were all but outlawed; even the most anti-Austrian Slavs in the Littoral soon missed the Habsburgs. To make matters worse, Fascist toughs routinely beat up Slovenes with impunity. Many of the Slovenes in Trieste were members of the Socialist Party, and they were frequent victims of Fascist thug-gery. Mussolini's Black Shirts liked to abuse Socialists anyway, so finding a vic-tim who was both a Socialist and a Slav was, no doubt, doubly rewarding.

Liberal Italy proved feeble in its attempts to thwart Mussolini's rise to power. By 1922, the Fascist movement had gained significant momentum; to many Italians it was the only force strong enough to resist the radical Left and gain Italy's rightful territorial inheritance. In October, Mussolini planned a March on Rome. It was more a propaganda exercise than an actual grab for power. Mussolini in fact had only 20,000 Black Shirts coming to Rome to sup-port him (and riding trains, not marching, as it turned out), surely not enough to pose a threat to the army. Decisive action by the military and the king would have easily crushed the March on Rome, but Vittorio Emanuele was unwilling to risk a civil war. Earlier in October, Diaz and Badoglio informed the king that the military was sympathetic to the Fascists, and could not be used against Mus-solini and his supporters. Vittorio Emanuele was also afraid that his pro-Fascist cousin the Duke of Aosta, whom he "cordially hated," would depose him with Black Shirt support and assume the throne himself. Therefore the king caved in when confronted with Mussolini's demands for power. No violence marred this bloodless coup. Vittorio Emanuele requested that Mussolini form a govern-ment immediately. The Fascist leader, now *Il Duce* of all Italy, arrived in Rome on October 31, 1922, the new prime minister at age thirty-nine.

From the beginning, the Fascist regime was deeply imbued with the spirit of the trenches. Mussolini himself was a veteran of the war on the Isonzo, and the upper ranks of the Fascist movement were filled with former *grigioverdi*. The Great War had been the most formative experience of Mussolini's life, as it had been for millions of other Italians. He would build a new, stronger Italy, a country reborn in war. Italy's new ruling class, Mussolini promised, would be *una trincerocrazia*—a trenchocracy. Significantly, Mussolini's first official act as prime minister was to pay homage to Italy's unknown soldier of the Great War.

Il Duce's dealings with the army were complex. He was always careful not to alienate the army, the only potential rival and threat to the Fascists. He appointed Armando Diaz war minister and made him a marshal of Italy, the new highest rank. Diaz had an excellent reputation as the savior of the army and the nation after Caporetto, and Mussolini was careful to court his favor. But Diaz was a dying man. He had contracted chronic bronchitis on the Carso and suffered from pulmonary emphysema. Diaz died in Rome in February 1928, aged sixty-six.

His predecessor at the *Comando Supremo*, Luigi Cadorna, outlived Diaz by only ten months. Cadorna's career was ended and his reputation stained by the Caporetto disaster, but he achieved an almost phoenixlike resurgence under Fascism. After the war, Cadorna busied himself writing books, including his self-serving war memoirs and a biography of his father, the occupier of Rome in 1870. He played no political role. Yet, in November 1924, Mussolini promoted the retired count to marshal of Italy, simultaneously with Diaz. Mussolini was sympathetically inclined toward the Piedmontese general, and saw his promotion as a token to the army; his raising of both Cadorna and Diaz to marshal permitted Mussolini to appease both major factions in the officer corps. Cadorna then was back in official favor, a position he maintained up to his death at seventy-eight, in Pallanza, his birthplace. To the end of his life Cadorna remained wholly unrepentant for his deeply flawed generalship on the Isonzo.

The fate of Luigi Capello was less happy, and somewhat less deserved. Like his superior, Capello's reputation was ruined by the collapse of the 2nd Army on the upper Isonzo. Capello, too, tried to justify his failures after the war in print, but met with little success. Mussolini detested Capello, not because he was "the Butcher" of the Isonzo front but because the general was a staunch Freemason. *Il Duce* both hated and feared the Masons, whom he believed were part of an international conspiracy to weaken Italy. Capello's Masonic affiliations denied him any role in Mussolini's Italy, and ultimately doomed him. The general was arrested in November 1925 on trumped-up charges of plotting a coup against the government. He endured a special trial in 1927, Mussolini's method of humiliating Capello and eliminating him from political life. It decayed into a political circus that Mussolini exploited for cynical purposes, and it ended with a thirty-year sentence for the old soldier. Capello was too feeble to serve his time in a regular prison and spent much of his sentence in more pleasant penitentiaries. He was released on compassionate grounds in 1936 and died, forgotten, in Rome five years later, at the age of eighty-two.

The Duke of Aosta maintained smoother relations with the Fascist regime. An early admirer and supporter of Mussolini and his movement, the duke enjoyed privileged status under Italy's new order. He spent much of his time in retirement near the Isonzo battlefields, at Miramare Castle, built for the Habsburg Archduke Maxmilian. For six years the duke enjoyed lengthy stays at the beautiful castle, overlooking the Adriatic just west of Trieste. When he died in 1931, aged sixty-two, the Duke of Aosta was buried on the Carso, at Redipuglia, among the fallen *fanti* of his beloved *Terza Armata*.

One general from the Isonzo front who benefited greatly from Fascist rule was Pietro Badoglio. As already mentioned, he was appointed chief of the General Staff in 1920, only forty-nine years old. Badoglio was ennobled, named the Marquess of Sabotino to commemorate his great deeds of August 1916. He proved as loyal a servant of Mussolini as he had been of the king. During the 1920s and 1930s he played an instrumental role in Mussolini's ambitious military expansion and preparation for war. He commanded Italy's bloody pacification campaign in Libya, as well as the much larger and more brutal invasion of Ethiopia in 1935. Badoglio became intimately associated with the Fascist regime and its military. No Italian general played a greater role in readying Mussolini's armies for the Second World War.

When Badoglio was regional commander of the northeast and the Littoral during 1919–1920, his troops began the herculean task of constructing monuments to the dead of the Isonzo. First, though, Italy had to find and identify the remains of hundreds of thousands of *fanti* still listed as missing in action on the Isonzo front. Many thousands of Italian soldiers had no known grave; countless others had been buried hastily in hundreds of small, temporary cemeteries scattered throughout the Isonzo valley. For twenty years after the war's end, the Italian Army painstakingly searched for bodies and relocated them in larger, central cemeteries. The majority of Italy's dead on the Isonzo were never identified. The years of static fighting blew thousands of corpses to pieces, and decomposition did the rest. Italy built three massive ossuaries—one at Caporetto on the upper Isonzo, another at Oslavia before Gorizia, and the largest at Redipuglia on the western Carso—where the dead were collected. The ossuaries were enormous, moving, churchlike edifices, national shrines built both to remember the dead and to glorify the sacrifice on the Isonzo. Mussolini conducted several propaganda visits to the Isonzo, his old battleground, and in 1938 personally dedicated the ossuary at Caporetto, near where the Austrians had crossed the Isonzo in late October 1917.

The Fascist regime regularly cited the Isonzo battles as an example of Italian valor and willingness to sacrifice for the nation; needless to say, the government never tolerated criticism of the army or its generals for the prosecution of the war against Austria. Mussolini wanted to reap glory, not criticism, from the catastrophe on the Isonzo. Italy permitted the Austrians few monuments along the

Isonzo, and were especially careful not to let the Slovenes use war memorials as nationalist symbols. As a result, the Italians refused to permit the Slovenes to rebuild Sveta Gora, the monastery at the peak of Mt. Santo destroyed by Italian shelling during the war's first month. Instead, the Italian Army erected its own war monument in its place, incurring the undying resentment of the Slovenes.

For many years, the building of ossuaries and war memorials was the only construction taking place on the Isonzo. The entire valley had been wrecked by the twenty-eight months of fighting. Gorizia was mostly in ruins, many smaller towns like Flitsch and Tolmein were equally damaged, and dozens of rural villages had been obliterated. The Fascist regime was perennially short of funds and reconstruction came slowly. Gorizia was rebuilt between 1934 and 1937, almost a generation after the war. The first government reconstruction project was Gorizia's cathedral, dating to 1570 and reassembled beginning in 1927; the city's early fourteenth-century castle was rebuilt by the mid-1930s. Trieste was more fortunate, because the fighting front never got near the city. After the war her buildings were intact, but her economy lay in ruins nevertheless. The collapse of Austria was a disaster for Trieste and her citizens. The Adriatic city was a well integrated part of Austria's economy, her greatest port and a major rail center. Austria's demise reduced Trieste to second-rate economic status. The Great War dissolved Central Europe's economic system no less than its political stability. As part of Italy, Trieste now had to compete with Venice, her ancient trading rival, without the benefit of Austria's protective tariff and favored trade status. Trieste's economy quickly fell into a decline from which it never recovered; no longer was it a leading Adriatic port, much less the eighth busiest port in the world, as it had been in 1914.

Austria's collapse therefore left the residents of the Littoral notably poorer. The chaos and damage inflicted by the Isonzo fighting had been bad enough, and postwar economic instability only worsened matters. Even many Italians living in Trieste and Gorizia were soon disgruntled; the oppressed Slovenes and Croats living under Italian rule did not even have a lingering sense of wartime triumph to comfort them. Italo Svevo, Trieste's most eminent writer, died in September 1928. He lived to witness the annexation of his home city to Italy, a goal he had waited decades to see realized. But he had also lived to see Italy bring not prosperity and liberty to Trieste, but impoverishment and Fascism. Political redemption by Rome, it turned out, was no panacea.

Most of the rest of the world soon forgot about the Isonzo fighting and its painful aftermath. The battles on the Italian front had been well covered by English-language newspapers during the war, but after 1918 Americans and Britons quickly lost interest in the Isonzo. Interest in the English-speaking world was rekindled for a time with the 1929 publication of a celebrated novel by Ernest Hemingway, the American ambulance driver wounded on the Piave. *A Farewell to Arms* was set on the Isonzo, and much of the story takes place in

Gorizia during 1917; the novel also includes graphic descriptions of the Italian retreat after Caporetto. Yet, despite appearances, it was not an autobiographical book: Hemingway reached Italy a half-year after Caporetto, and never laid eyes on the Isonzo and its beautiful valley before he wrote his novel. All the same, the book became an international best-seller, winning Hemingway considerable royalties and universal acclaim. Still, interest in the Isonzo waned. By the 1930s, there were more pressing matters on the world stage, and another war began to loom large in European fears. Except in the countries whose sons died on the Isonzo, the dozen great battles fought there quickly became a mere footnote to history.

The Austrians naturally maintained their interest in the Isonzo. The Habsburg Empire's losses there, although less than Italy's, were nevertheless frightful, amounting to probably 650,000 dead, wounded, and missing. The Austrian Army counted some five million soldiers lost to death, wounds, illness, and capture during the war, the worst loss rate of any major belligerent; Austria's casualties on the Isonzo front were, in fact, far lower than those incurred against the Russians. Even so, the Isonzo occupied a special place in Austrian memory. The soldiers remembered the terrible Isonzo for the merciless and futile slaughter that raged there from June 1915 to October 1917. No less, though, Austria's soldiers and many civilians remembered the Isonzo front with pride: Habsburg arms acquitted themselves superbly there, and the fighting included the Caporetto breakthrough, the greatest triumph in Austria's long history of battles. In 1918 the war, the dynasty, and the army all came to an end because of the Italian front, and the Isonzo therefore stayed fresh in the memory of numerous former Habsburg subjects.

Many senior Habsburg generals were stranded by the empire's sudden collapse in October 1918. Soldiers who had spent their entire lives serving the multinational monarchy watched their world dissolve virtually overnight, and many soon found themselves literally men without a country. Foremost among them was Svetozar Boroević. The battle-worn field marshal was startled by the speed and thoroughness of the Habsburg demise. His efforts to save the dynasty had failed through no fault of his own. Worse, both as an Austrian general and a Croatian patriot, he was horrified by Italy's final victory and annexation of the Littoral. Soon after the Austrian Army dissolved, Boroević contacted the new Yugoslav government and offered his services; he wanted to lead Croatian, Serbian, and Slovene soldiers in defense of the Littoral and Dalmatia, to protect South Slav lands from the Italian invader. The Serb-led Yugoslav government and army balked at the suggestion; soon they even denied Boroević, a Serb, the right to set foot in his Croatian homeland. Belgrade feared Boroević. The Yugoslav regime knew he was hailed as a war hero by many South Slavs, and was revered in Croatia. The Serbian dynasty and army wanted no rivals in their new Yugoslav state.

Turned away from his homeland (the Yugoslav government even confiscated all his personal possessions in Croatia), Boroević decided to stay in now-independent Austria. He and his wife settled close to Klagenfurt, near the Italian and Slovene frontiers and the Isonzo. Rampant inflation ate away the field marshal's modest pension, and the old soldier and his wife found themselves penniless; they lived simply off the kindness of loyal fellow officers, settling in a rented two-room cottage. Yet "the Lion of the Isonzo" did not long outlive the dynasty and army he had spent his life serving. The sixty-three year-old Boroević suffered a stroke while swimming and died on May 23, 1920, five years to the day that Italy declared war against Austria.[5]

The Republic of Austria, the German Alpine rump of the defunct empire, was an unstable creation from the start. A small country of just seven million, it was burdened with Vienna, a capital of two million, overlarge for such a tiny Alpine republic. Worse, its economy had been badly damaged by the war, and its politics proved dangerously volatile. Red Vienna was pitted against more the conservative Alpine provinces, resulting in political deadlock and eventually violence.[6] Most Austrians had desired union—*Anschluss*—with Germany in 1918, but the victorious Allies had strictly forbidden it. Successive governments in Vienna tried hard to bring stability and prosperity, but it was a hopeless task.

Austria's politics were frequently marred by violence. Both the clerical Right and the socialist Left maintained large and well armed party militias, filled with disgruntled veterans, which fought openly in the streets. One of the most powerful of the paramilitary forces was the *Heimwehr* (Home Guard), the armed wing of the Right. The commander of its Vienna detachment was the retired Major Emil Fey, the hero of Zagora in 1915. Active in ex-officers' circles, the Viennese Fey soon rose to prominence in Austrian politics. He benefitted greatly from the dominance of the Right in Austria by the 1930's. The leader of the anti-Socialist bloc was Engelbert Dolfuss, like Fey an ex-Habsburg officer and decorated veteran of the Italian front, who was determined to preserve an independent and conservative Austria. The Dolfuss regime was certainly rightist, but much more traditionalist than Fascist, although, ironically, it courted the favor of Mussolini's regime. Rome's support was needed to stave off aggression on both sides—the ultra-Right and ultra-Left. Radical Socialists were naturally regarded as enemies of the Dolfuss state, yet the threat from the far Right was even greater. From Hitler's assumption of Germany's chancellorship in late January 1933, Austria was in mortal danger. To the National Socialists, an independent Austrian state was a fiction; Austria—Hitler's homeland—was regarded as an inseparable element of the greater German nation.

Both German and Austrian Nazis began to destabilize Austria with propaganda and violence. At this point, Dolfuss should have rallied all anti-Nazi forces, including the Socialists, in defense of the state, but in fact he did just the opposite. In February 1934, in response to a Socialist coup attempt, the Dolfuss regime, with the backing of Fey, the Vice-Chancellor, reacted vigorously. The Socialist putsch was drowned in blood as the army brought artillery into Vienna to blast away apartment buildings occupied by left-wing militants. Habsburg Army veterans fought each other bitterly in the streets of Vienna. The threat from the far Left was crushed, but so was any willingness among the moderate Socialists to defend the Dolfuss state against Nazi aggression. Hitler wasted no time. In July 1934, Austrian Nazis, trained in Germany and acting on Berlin's orders, gunned down Chancellor Dolfuss in his office. Significantly, Vice-Chancellor Fey did nothing to stop the assassination.[7]

With Dolfuss out of the way, the Germans prepared to occupy Austria. Tiny Austria's army was too weak to defend the Alpine republic, and it was by no means clear that many Austrians wished to fight Germans, their wartime allies and racial kin. What prevented a Nazi invasion in July 1934 was Mussolini; unwilling to see Austria—Italy's northern frontier—occupied by Germany, *Il Duce* moved several divisions to the Brenner Pass. Mussolini was still wary of the Nazis, and he was outraged by Dolfuss's cold-blooded murder; the dead chancellor's wife and children had been visiting Mussolini at the time of the assassination. Hitler got the message and backed down for the moment.

In the long run, though, an independent Austria was doomed. The new chancellor, Kurt von Schuschnigg (another ex-Habsburg officer and veteran of the Italian front), wanted to maintain Austria's independence, but his cabinet was soon infiltrated by homegrown Nazis who ardently desired *Anschluss*. Emil Fey was reduced to a mere minister without portfolio. Some former Habsburg officers played an active role campaigning for union with Hitler's Germany. Still, few officers of the old army became National Socialists. The Habsburg Army's multinational ethos and outmoded values were the antithesis of all that the Nazis, with their virulent racialism and anarchic violence, stood for. However, some retired officers were so dismayed by the collapse of the empire that they gravitated toward radical Right circles. Foremost among them was Alfred Krauss, architect of the Caporetto miracle.[8] After the war, Krauss regularly and loudly voiced his view that Austria's defeat was the result of treason and betrayal by the army's Slav soldiers—a uniquely Austrian "stab in the back" legend. As early as 1920, he agitated for *Anschluss*, and his campaigning grew more determined after the rise of Hitler. Krauss, like most German nationalists in Austria, saw the little Alpine republic as hopelessly weak, and looked forward to salvation through absorption into Greater Germany.

Krauss was one of the most vocal champions of *Anschluss*, and he was greatly pleased when it arrived in March 1938. Almost four years after the Dolfuss murder and the first Nazi attempt to take Austria by force, Hitler succeeded. The difference was that by 1938, Mussolini was no longer willing to challenge Berlin on the issue of Austrian independence. Rome now saw the Nazis as allies, and without Italian help, Austria was doomed. The outnumbered Austrian Army, acting on the government's orders, offered no resistance to the German invasion. It was a bloodless coup. Hitler returned to Linz and Vienna, the two cities where he spent his youth, in triumph.

The seventy-six-year-old Krauss was a dying man, but he lived long enough to be made a general in Hitler's army and sit for a formal portrait in his new, bemedaled German uniform. When he died in September 1938, just six months after the *Anschluss*, he was heralded in Austria's Nazi-run press as "a courageous champion of National Socialism." His highly publicized state funeral, "the German People say good-bye to General Krauss," ended with the old Habsburg soldier's casket, draped with the swastika, borne by senior Nazi Party and SS men.

Many other ex-Habsburg soldiers met a less pleasant end after the *Anschluss*. Emil Fey, unpopular with the Nazis because of his failure to back the Germans in 1934, was gotten rid of. Four days after the German invasion, the bodies of Fey and his wife and children were found in their Vienna home, riddled with bullets. The official verdict, released by the Nazi authorities, was suicide. Death awaited other ex-Habsburg officers, too. The Germans quickly absorbed Austria's military into the *Wehrmacht*. Numerous career officers were dismissed, including those believed to be hostile to National Socialism, and especially all Jews. Austria's Jewish officers, many of them decorated veterans of the Great War, were immediately discharged from the service. A worse fate still awaited them.

One of those dismissed just after the *Anschluss* was Gustav Sonnewend, the Jewish hero of the Tenth Battle of the Isonzo. Sonnewend enthusiastically opted for Austria in 1918, married an Austrian wife, and began a successful career in the army of the Austrian Republic. He rose to command a battalion, and was a full colonel when the Germans invaded. He was forcibly retired, despite his many decorations and years of service. Sonnewend and his wife settled in Vienna and watched the Second World War begin, a conflict far more terrible than the slaughter Sonnewend witnessed on the Isonzo. He also saw thousands of Jewish veterans of the Habsburg Army rounded up and sent to concentration camps by the Nazis. Colonel Sonnewend, protected by his Order of Maria Theresia, was safe for the moment.

Ex-Habsburg soldiers of all backgrounds fared better in neighboring Hungary. The first two years after the Great War were terrible for Hungary. The Allies erased Hungary's ancient borders and deprived defeated Budapest of two-thirds of her territory, leaving millions of Magyars trapped in Romania, Czechoslovakia, and Yugoslavia. Worse, the end of the fighting brought no peace to Hungary. The liberal government of Mihály Károly, which came to power at the war's end, was well intentioned but naive and inept; instead of saving Hungary, it exposed it to Allied invasion. It was soon succeeded by a short-lived but brutal Communist regime under Béla Kun, a former *Honvéd* lieutenant. The abortive Communist dictatorship was crushed by the Allies, but not before it wrecked the already ailing economy and left an enduring hatred of Communism among most Hungarians.

The new anti-Communist government was led by Rear Admiral Nicholas Horthy von Nagybánya, who pulled down the Imperial-and-Royal Navy's colors at Pola at the war's end. Under Horthy, who stayed in power until late 1944 as regent, Hungary again became a nominal kingdom; as many observed ironically, Hungary, a land lacking both king and coastline, was ruled for a generation by a regent who was an admiral. There were several attempts at a Habsburg restoration in Budapest, but all failed. Archduke Joseph von Habsburg, the Carso's defender and a vocal Magyar patriot, tried to restore the monarchy, but was undermined by Herbert Hoover, head of America's Commission of Relief; Hoover threatened to deprive starving Hungary of food if a Habsburg returned to power in Budapest. Archduke Joseph then contented himself to live in Horthy-dominated Hungary.

More serious were two attempts in 1921 by dethroned Emperor Karl to reassume his kingship in Hungary. Karl found himself unwanted in Austria, or anywhere else in his former empire, after the war. He tried to claim his throne in Budapest on two occasions, but was met with hostility from the Horthy regime. Although numerous Hungarians, and particularly army officers, were favorably disposed to Karl, many could not forgive his incompetence at the war's end. Horthy wisely felt that Karl was unable to run Hungary but perfectly able to destabilize it. He therefore opposed his ex-sovereign with force. A near civil war resulted, with Hungary's military dividing into pro-Habsburg and pro-Horthy camps, but the dethroned emperor was ultimately persuaded to back down. He died in exile in Madeira a year later, a broken man at the age of thirty-five.

Karl's former soldiers fared well in Horthy's Hungary. Postwar Hungary's army kept the uniforms, medals, and traditions of the old army, as well as many of its officers. Habsburg veterans of the Great War crowded the higher ranks of Horthy's military through the Second World War. Géza Heim, who as a young lieutenant had saved the Carso, according to Archduke Joseph, was ennobled with the title "von San Martino del Carso" after his name. He remained in Horthy's army, dying at his post as a major general and brigade commander in Budapest in 1942.

Habsburg veterans of the Isonzo were less welcome in other successor states. Czechoslovakia, although comparatively fair in its dealings with its large German and Magyar minorities, remained implacably hostile to ex-Habsburg soldiers. Even Czechs who served the Austrians were treated with suspicion; the new state's military was dominated by those who took up arms against Vienna in the last year of the war. Ethnic Germans who fought for Austria were shunned by the Czechoslovak military. A few German career soldiers entered the new army, but were treated poorly. Theodor Wanke, the hero of the Eighth Battle of the Isonzo, was a German-Bohemian who pledged loyalty to the new Czechoslovak state and accepted a commission in its army. Yet prejudice prevented this highly decorated and efficient soldier from being promoted above captain in the Czech-dominated forces. Wanke resigned in disgust.

Romania, too, was suspicious of soldiers who had served the Habsburgs. Few Germans and Magyars received commissions in the Romanian Army, and even ethnic Romanians who fought for Vienna were viewed skeptically; the army, like the state, was led by Austrophobes who battled against the Habsburgs during the war. Even Konstantin Popovici, the Romanian officer who won the Order of Maria Theresia during the Eleventh Battle of the Isonzo, was promoted to colonel, but no higher, in Romania's army. Peter Roósz, who won the Knight's Cross for his exploits in the Ninth Battle, was a Magyar who chose retirement over service in Bucharest's military. Yugoslavia was even less inclined to promote its subjects who bore arms for Austria. The emergent Yugoslav state was run as simply an enlarged Serbia; its army had no room for the impressive martial traditions of the Croats, who had fought bravely under Habsburg colors for centuries. The Yugoslav military by and large refused to promote Croats, Slovenes—even Serbs—who once wore Habsburg uniforms. As a result, Belgrade's forces remained in the hands of Serbs from Serbia, and few veterans of the Isonzo could be found in their ranks.

The only Habsburg successor state that courted ex-Habsburg soldiers was Poland. Renascent Poland, led by the former Austrian subject Józef Piłsudski, viewed the defunct empire sympathetically, and many veterans of the Isonzo made successful careers in the Polish military. Indeed, ex-Austrian officers built the new Polish Army and led it to victory in the war with Soviet Russia in 1919–1920. In a typical case, Stanislaus Wieroński, who received the Order of Maria Theresia for his heroism during the Tenth Battle of the Isonzo, entered the Polish Army in 1918, reaching the rank of major general and divisional commander before his retirement in 1935. In fact, thousands of ex-Austrian soldiers in Polish uniform fought against their former Habsburg comrades when Germany invaded Poland on September 1, 1939, beginning the Second World War.

Violence and suffering returned to the Isonzo because of Mussolini's bellicose policies. *Il Duce* believed that only fighting would bring Rome glory and win Italy her rightful place in Europe and the world. With Pietro Badoglio's help he built a large and imposing military, at least on paper. He sent the army into battle in Ethiopia in 1935–1936, and soon after in Spain, on the Nationalist side in the bitter civil war. Italian forces acquitted themselves respectably, though not as well as Mussolini wanted, in both conflicts; divisions of the MVSN, the "Black Shirts" of the Fascist Party militia, wore the uniforms of the legendary *arditi*, but displayed little of their enthusiasm. Mussolini decided to enter the Second World War on the side of his German ally in May 1940, during the Nazi invasion of France; he expected easy territorial gains. But Marshal Badoglio cautioned *Il Duce* against intervention. The old soldier explained that the army was simply not ready for a major war: despite years of Fascist preparations, the military was poorly trained and equipped. It certainly could not expect to take on a major power on equal terms. Yet Mussolini did not want to listen to words of warning—he had begun to believe his own bellicose propaganda—and Italy entered the Second World War anyway. Badoglio fell from official favor.

The result was a débâcle. The Italian Army performed badly in France, and even worse in Greece, where the outnumbered but spirited Greek Army repulsed all Italian invasion attempts. The army was, if anything, less ready for a major war in 1940 than it had been in 1915, and the *fanti* generally displayed little of the determination that their fathers had shown so often on the Isonzo. Mussolini had failed to make the Italians the conquering martial race of his dreams. Further evidence came from Russia, where Mussolini disastrously sent an ill-fated army to fight alongside the Germans. Worst of all was North Africa, where small numbers of British troops managed to shatter Italy's best divisions. By 1942, the Fascist war effort was entering its terminal phase.

The one notable Italian success came in Yugoslavia. A combined German-Italian invasion quickly crushed the ramshackle South Slav state in April 1941, and Italy formally took possession of Dalmatia, the land she had been deprived of by Versailles. Italy also annexed half of Slovenia and enjoyed de facto sovereignty over Montenegro, as well as half of Croatia and Bosnia. But Italy's triumph was destined to be short-lived. No sooner had the army occupied Italy's new territories than their Slav inhabitants arose in revolt. Slovenes, Croats, and Serbs alike took up arms against the hated Italians. Nowhere was local resistance more bitter than in the Littoral. Slovenes living on the Isonzo, disgusted by a generation of Italian repression, formed local guerrilla units in the Julian Alps to fight the Fascist occupiers. The Slovene partisans established base areas on the upper Isonzo, particularly in the rugged Tolmein-Karfreit area, and by 1942 the northern Littoral was Italian territory in name only. Italian Army units that entered the upper Isonzo valley were subject to vicious attack by bands of Slovene irregulars hiding in the steep, dark mountains overlooking the river.

By mid-1943, Italy was all but defeated by the Allies. By the summer, the Italians and Germans had been evicted from North Africa, and British, American, and Canadian troops were landing in Sicily. Mussolini's policies, particularly his alliance with Germany, had led to disaster. The army leadership, including Marshal Badoglio, wanted to get Italy out of the war before it was too late. On July 15, Mussolini agreed to a meeting of the Fascist Grand Council, the first since 1939. The session, which took place July 24, resulted in the Fascist Party hierarchy agreeing to depose Mussolini. After twenty-one years in power, *Il Duce* was unceremoniously dumped by the party he had founded. He was soon imprisoned on a mountaintop in southern Italy by Badoglio, who was named head of a new provisional government to negotiate Italy's way out of the war. Badoglio wanted to avoid German occupation, but it was a hopeless task. On September 8, 1943, German troops brutally occupied Italy, their recent ally. Four days later, SS commandos under Major Otto Skorzeny rescued the imprisoned *Duce* in a daring glider raid on his mountaintop jail. Mussolini, a nearly broken man, was taken to see Hitler and given a Fascist fiefdom, the Italian Social Republic, in German-occupied northern Italy. Still, Italy's Fascist experiment, born on the Isonzo, was essentially over. The Allies occupied the southern part of Italy, and Mussolini's statelet was a mere puppet of the Germans.

The Germans had good reason to be dissatisfied with Mussolini and the Fascists. After all, on several inconvenient occasions the Germans were forced to devote significant numbers of troops to save Italy's ailing armies, much as Berlin had done for Vienna during the Great War. The largest German bailout of Italian arms came in North Africa, where in 1941 a whole German tank army was dispatched to save Mussolini's legions from total defeat at the hands of the British. Hitler's expeditionary force, the famed *Afrikakorps*, was led by Erwin Rommel, the outstanding hero of the Caporetto victory. In a strange twist of fate, Rommel found himself with thousands of Italians, his former enemies, under him in the Western Desert. Rommel inflicted embarrassing defeats on the overconfident British, nearly taking the Suez Canal. The British admired their talented and wily foe, whom they dubbed the "Desert Fox." Rommel was likewise lionized at home, where Hitler made him a field marshal. Even the Axis reverse at El Alamein in October–November 1942, followed by a retreat across North Africa, failed to tarnish Rommel's great martial reputation.

Rommel was then made commander of an army group in France. His outnumbered and outgunned forces were defeated by the Allied invasion of June 1944, but Rommel did not live long enough to be blamed for the disaster. He was critically injured by a British air attack on his staff car on July 17, 1944. His career was over, a verdict confirmed by a nearly successful attempt on Hitler's life three days later. The failed bomb plot, engineered by Colonel Claus von Stauffenberg, led to a purge of all *Wehrmacht* officers suspected of a role in the assassination scheme. Rommel's name came up, not as an actual conspirator but as a leading general whom the coup plotters trusted and considered to be an ideal representative for Germany in negotiations with the Allies after Hitler's death. That was sufficient evidence to seal Rommel's fate. The celebrated field marshal was forced to commit suicide. Hitler did not want a public trial for the great soldier, and announced that he died of wounds received in the British air attack. The Nazis thus kept Rommel's esteemed image clean.

Other heroes of the Isonzo likewise met an unenviable fate serving in Hitler's armies. Thousands of ex-Habsburg officers fought for the Nazis on all fronts. One of them was Fritz Franek, who as a lieutenant won the Order of Maria Theresia on the Carso during the Eleventh Battle. He stayed in the Austrian Army after the war's end and became a respected military historian, receiving a Ph.D. from the University of Vienna and writing parts of the Austrian official history of the Great War. He returned to active service after the *Anschluss*. Franek led a battalion of mountain troops during the invasion of Poland, where he fought against former comrades in arms and took part in the battle for Lemberg, where he had fought a quarter-century before in Habsburg uniform. Franek, promoted to colonel, then commanded a regiment in France in 1940 and in Russia a year later. He led his regiment courageously on the Leningrad front. He was gravely wounded by two shots to the head, the third time he had been shot by Russians during his career, and was awarded the Knight's Cross of the Iron Cross, Germany's highest decoration, for his valor. Franek was therefore one of the most decorated Austrian soldiers in both world wars. He recovered and was promoted to general in October 1942. He commanded a division in the field until mid-1944, when he was captured by the Red Army and sent to Siberia.

Erwin Zeidler, the hero of Gorizia, died peacefully a few months later. Zeidler retired from Austrian service in 1918, but was named a general (retired) of the *Wehrmacht* in 1940, in honor of his outstanding command of the 58th Division on the Gorizian front from 1915 to 1917. He settled in the quiet Carinthian town of Villach, little more than a dozen miles from the Isonzo's source high in the Julian Alps. He died there in January 1945, nearly eighty, as the Third Reich headed rapidly to defeat, just months before Allied armies occupied Carinthia.

Sadly, many Jewish soldiers who once served the Habsburgs, on the Isonzo and elsewhere, met a cruel end at the hands of the Nazis. Although the Nazis initially exempted Austrian war veterans, especially those who were decorated for bravery, from persecution, in time many Jewish war heroes were exterminated as part of Hitler's "Final Solution." Some of them were killed at Mauthausen, a concentration camp just outside Linz, the only death camp on Austrian soil. During the Great War, Mauthausen had been a prisoner of war camp where Italian captives were sent to wait out the fighting; to thousands of *fanti*, Mauthausen meant life, a refuge from the ceaseless slaughter on the Isonzo. Yet during the next war, the name Mauthausen meant death, genocide. There, hundreds of thousands of Jews, Slavs, and other "subhumans" were mercilessly exterminated by SS Death's Head units. Luckily, Gustav Sonnewend was not among them. As both a convert to Roman Catholicism and a Knight of the Order of Maria Theresia, Sonnewend managed to avoid the hangman. When the war ended, he was one of the very few Viennese Jews to survive the slaughter, the greatest of all pogroms.

The Nazis practiced their evil methods along the Isonzo, too. When Italy left the war in mid-1943, Berlin annexed Austria's lost territories, the South Tyrol and the Littoral. Long-forgotten Habsburg civil servants, German, Italian, and Slovene, returned to power as the Isonzo valley was again called *Küstenland.* Germany's annexation of *Italia irredenta* proved short-lived but vicious. The persecution of Trieste's large and well established Jewish population was the worst legacy of Nazi rule. Mussolini had enacted anti-Semitic laws in July 1938, an attempt to court Hitler's favor, but they were mild compared to Nazi repression; under Fascism, Italy's Jews were hounded out of the army and bureaucracy and suffered countless indignities, but none were killed. Indeed, the Italian Army protected thousands of Jews from German persecution, not just in Italy but in occupied Yugoslavia and France as well. Even so, the Jews of the Littoral were doomed once the Nazis took control in mid-1943.

German executioners, aided by Italian collaborationists, rounded up Trieste's Jews. Soon Trieste had its own concentration camp, San Sabba, where, by the war's end, as many as 5,000 Jews, Partisans, and other "undesirables" had been murdered. Trieste ended the war as a battleground, with many of its sons and daughters dead. In a typical case, of the Triestine novelist Italo Svevo's three grandsons, two died in Russia serving in Mussolini's army, and a third was killed in the fighting for Trieste at the war's end; worse, Svevo's Jewish niece and nephew were exterminated by the Germans at San Sabba. The Second World War proved even more costly for Trieste and the Littoral than the Great War had been.

With the Third Reich's complete collapse in the spring of 1945, Yugoslav Partisans occupied much of the Isonzo valley. The irregular army, made up of all of Yugoslavia's diverse peoples, was led by Tito, the former *Honvéd* corporal. He took up arms in 1941 to evict the German invader from South Slav lands, and in the latter half of the war began to enjoy success. The Partisans received considerable British military assistance, and by 1944 the tide had begun to turn against the outnumbered Germans. Tito's ranks were swelled with volunteers from all over Yugoslavia. A few Habsburg veterans, like Tito, fought with the Partisans. Yet some ex-Austrian soldiers initially sided with collaborationist regimes in occupied Yugoslavia. The *Ustaša* dictatorship in Croatia actively recruited former Habsburg officers. The "Independent State of Croatia" was, in fact, a German puppet regime, led by the virulent racist Ante Pavelić. The *Ustaša* actually enjoyed little support in Croatia (and Bosnia-Hercegovina, which it annexed as part of "Greater Croatia"), and even that diminished once the Pavelić regime began exterminating hundreds of thousands of Serbs, Jews, and other unwanted citizens. The commander of the Croatian Army at the time was Vladimir Laxa, the hero of Monte San Gabriele. He was named a general in the spring of 1941, when the Croatian puppet state was established. The respected Laxa quickly rose to become chief of staff of the army. Yet he was appalled by the *Ustaša* regime's brutal treatment of its minorities, and spoke out against Pavelić. This ensured his dismissal, and Laxa was pensioned in June 1942. He sat out the rest of the war while Tito's Partisans gained strength, and despite his opposition to the excesses of the Pavelić regime, the old soldier was executed by the victorious Communists at the war's end, aged seventy-five.

Slovene irregulars expanded their hold on the Isonzo valley throughout 1944, so that by the war's end, local Partisans were well positioned to seize Gorizia and Trieste. Slovene patriots, who had suffered so long under Italian rule, demanded the complete annexation of the Littoral, as did Tito, a South Slav nationalist and Italophobe as well as a Communist. The Allies, however, were ambivalent about the Isonzo issue; they did not want to reward the Italians, their recent enemies, but neither did they want Trieste in the hands of Tito and his Communist army. The result was a race between the British and the Partisans, ostensibly allies, with the 2nd New Zealand Division crossing the Isonzo and reaching Gorizia at the war's end. On the first day of May 1945, the Slovene 9th Partisan Corps descended from the surrounding hills of the Carso and occupied Trieste, the real prize.

The Slovene Partisans occupied Trieste for forty days. The victorious Communist troops executed many Fascists and other prominent Italians; they were taking their revenge for all the oppression the Slovenes had endured under Mussolini. Yugoslav occupation of Trieste was short-lived, mercifully for the city's Italian majority. The Allies, worried that Trieste would become Tito's—and therefore Stalin's—Adriatic port, demanded that the Partisans withdraw. Soon the city and its environs were garrisoned by American and British troops, there to ensure that the Yugoslavs stayed behind their side of the demarcation line. There were occasional firefights between Trieste's Allied Military Government and the Yugoslavs, recent allies, but the last Allied troops left the city on October 26, 1954, when sovereignty was formally returned to Italy. After Tito and Stalin split irrevocably in 1948, Yugoslavia drifted back into a pro-Western orientation, and Tito's regime was viewed favorably by the British and the Americans.

The 1954 settlement established the Isonzo valley's current borders. Slovenia (then a Yugoslav republic) received the whole upper valley and the eastern third of Gorizia, as well as a slice of the northern Istrian Peninsula (Croatia received the rest, and Fiume—Rijeka to the Croats—too). Italy was given Trieste, its suburbs, much of the Carso, and most of Gorizia. The international frontier ran through many former battlefields. Trieste was relieved to rejoin Italy. The new Italy was a wholly different country than the old Fascist state. After Mussolini's demise, ending in his execution by Italian Partisans at the war's end, the monarchy tried to reestablish its authority, but with scant success. Vittorio Emanuele III, who had reigned since 1900 and led Italy through two world wars and two decades of Fascism, died in 1947. His son, Umberto II, assumed the throne, but only briefly; the ancient House of Savoy had tainted itself through its relationship with Fascism, as indicated in a 1946 referendum, which defeated the monarchist cause. Umberto soon headed for exile in Portugal. The new Italian Republic was led by Prime Minister Alcide de Gasperi, a former Austrian subject from the Trentino and a onetime parliamentarian in the Viennese *Reichsrat*. He led Italy toward postwar prosperity and membership in NATO, and restored Italy's international reputation, so badly tarnished by the Fascist experiment. Trieste slowly rebuilt and recovered some of its long-lost stability and prosperity under de Gasperi in the 1950s.

Tito, too, was busy reconstructing his country, ravaged by war and occupation. The Isonzo valley was painstakingly rebuilt during the 1950s. The Slovene part of Gorizia, a divided city, was renamed "New Gorizia"—Nova Gorica to its inhabitants. The new city included Gorizia's monastery, railroad station, and eastern suburbs. These were gradually restored, and Tito, always conscious of his image, constructed large, unsightly apartment blocks in Nova Gorica; from the air they spelled TITO. Less drab and dull was the Yugoslav reconstruction of the monastery atop Monte Santo (Sveta Gora to the Slovenes). The pilgrimage site, blown apart in 1915 by Italian guns, was rebuilt by Titoist Yugoslavia beginning in 1949. First the Yugoslavs destroyed the Italian war memorial placed at the summit after the Great War. The beautiful late medieval church was reassembled, again a monument to Slovene national pride; the Communist regime, though officially atheist, was always aware of the political value of national symbols. By the 1960s, the Slovene part of the Isonzo valley was again peaceful and stable, and in places quite pleasant to look at.

By then the veterans of the war on the Isonzo were old men. Few of the officers and generals who led both armies in battle were still alive. The last surviving senior Italian commander was Pietro Badoglio, the Marquess of Sabotino. He died in late 1956, aged eighty-five. His pivotal role in both world wars left a controversial legacy of courage and opportunism. Marshal Badoglio was soon followed by the last living Austrian generals, his former adversaries. Otto von Berndt, the decorated Bohemian divisional commander, died in Vienna in 1957, aged ninety-two. Berndt, a convinced German nationalist, supported the Nazis and was forced to leave his native land when the Communists came to power in Czechoslovakia in 1948 and the country's Germans were forcibly expelled. He spent his last days in Vienna, the onetime imperial capital. Also living out his final years in Vienna was Archduke Joseph von Habsburg, the commander of VII Corps in the epic battles for the Carso. The rise of the Communists in Hungary[9] after the Second World War forced the elderly archduke to flee to Austria, leaving his beloved Hungary forever. The former general and hero of the Isonzo died in Vienna in the summer of 1962, less than a month before his ninetieth birthday.

By then, Austria was a wholly unrecognizable place. Occupied by the Russians, Americans, British, and French at the war's end, Vienna negotiated its independence in 1955, in exchange for neutrality in the Cold War. The State Treaty reestablished an independent Austria free of foreign occupation, setting the stage for the Alpine republic's postwar stability and prosperity, a marked contrast with the sad history of Austria after the Great War. The State Treaty was negotiated by Chancellor Julius Raab, a Habsburg sapper lieutenant in the Great War decorated for valor on the Carso in 1916; Austria's president in 1955 was Theodor Körner, a respected ex-Habsburg colonel, confidant of Field Marshal Boroević, and the last chief of staff of the Isonzo Army. Vienna, destroyed by Allied air raids and bitter street fighting, was slowly and tenderly rebuilt. One of the veterans of the Isonzo who lived to see Vienna's rise from the ashes of defeat in 1945 was Gustav Sonnewend. He miraculously survived Nazi persecution and spent his last years in Vienna, dying in 1960 at age seventy-five, the next to last Knight of the Order of Maria Theresia for service on the Isonzo.[10]

From the 1960s through the 1980s, while the last veterans of the war on the Isonzo died natural deaths, unlike so many of their fallen comrades, the Isonzo valley remained pleasingly quiet. The valley was the most demilitarized East-West border during the Cold War, and traveling from Gorizia and Nova Gorica was easy. In fact, many Italians from Gorizia and Trieste regularly drove across the frontier to fill their cars with cheaper Slovene gas. Old animosities were forgotten; six months after the fall of the Berlin Wall, the Italian mayor of Gorizia and the Slovene mayor of Nova Gorica jointly called for their twin cities to realize their vocation as "a laboratory for the common European house." By the early 1990s, however, as Europe's postwar equilibrium dissolved, the Isonzo valley was again tense with military activity. After Tito's death in 1980, his Yugoslav state entered a terminal decline. The national antagonisms submerged forcibly by Communism again came to the fore, with added fervor from being pent up so long. Slovenia, the most prosperous and western of Belgrade's six republics, saw no future in an ailing, Serb-dominated Yugoslavia. Slovenes remembered that their long history tied them to Austria and Central Europe, not to Serbia and the Balkans. On June 25, 1991, Slovenia's democratically elected government formally seceded from Yugoslavia, the first act of open rebellion against the dying Titoist state. The result was war.

Belgrade was determined to prevent Slovene secession and to seize all border crossing points, sources of desperately needed hard currency for the Yugoslav government. The Serb-dominated Yugoslav People's Army, the successor to Tito's Partisans, sent its tanks into Slovenia, into the Isonzo valley. It had been fully two generations since the last war, and more than three since the great bloodletting on the Isonzo's rocky banks. The Yugoslav invasion came as a rude shock, but the Slovenes were ready. Local home guards were called out;

they were equipped with few heavy weapons, but as in 1915 they were fighting for their own soil, and resisted the foreign invader with vigor. Yugoslav aircraft dropped bombs on Flitsch and Tolmein (now Bovec and Tolmin), upper valley towns that had seen so much suffering during the Great War. Yet the ragtag Slovene militia triumphed. Their courage won the day, turning back the halfhearted Yugoslav attack. After a few days, Belgrade's offensive fizzled out; the Slovenes would be a tough opponent, and the army was unwilling to waste its resources on a peripheral target. Instead, Belgrade sent its armies against Croatia, and then Bosnia, beginning the bloodiest European war in a half-century.

Perhaps the decisive battle in Slovenia in late June 1991 was the fight for Nova Gorica. The Yugoslav military sent an armored column to Nova Gorica to seize the border crossing point in the heart of the old city. Tanks rolled into the city, which had seen so much fighting during the Great War; the Slovene home guard was waiting. The poorly armed militiamen fought back hard, destroying several tanks, killing the Yugoslav commander, and capturing several tank crews. One of the prisoners taken, a Serbian tank driver, was asked by his captors why he had come to assault the peaceful city on the Isonzo. The confused soldier responded that his unit commander had told the troops that the city was under Italian attack.

SIXTEEN

THE BATTLEFIELD TODAY

The Isonzo is again peaceful, one of the loveliest valleys in all Europe. It is difficult to believe that there was ever any fighting along the beautiful blue-green
river, surrounded by impressive snowy peaks and dotted with charming
white-washed Alpine villages. Yet, the evidence of the war almost nine decades
earlier is easy to find for the determined explorer. The valley, from the Slovene
frontier to the Adriatic coast, is rich with monuments, cemeteries, and battle
sites, many long forgotten but together a moving tribute to the immense sacrifice on the Isonzo early in the last century. Regrettably, there are few survivors
of the dozen battles still living; hardly anyone of any nationality remains who
personally witnessed the terrible carnage on the Isonzo.[1] Nevertheless, the valley today offers the traveler much sad testimony about the European tragedy
that transpired on the Isonzo from 1915 to 1917. This section is intended as a
guide for anyone who wishes to see the Isonzo front as it is today.

The starting point, traveling from the north, is the Italo-Slovene border
crossing point at the Predel Pass, coming on *Strada statale* 54 from Tarvisio, off
the E55 *Autostrada*. The high Julian road into Slovenia soon reaches the village
of Log pod Mangartom, nestled among the clouds and mountains, some of
them nearly 8,000 feet high. The rugged Predel area has seen much fighting: the
Austrians battled Napoleon's armies here in 1809, and during the Second
World War, German troops burned Log pod Mangartom as a reprisal for Partisan activities. But the village is significant for the Isonzo battles of 1915 to
1917 because it contains an Austrian cemetery. Habsburg authorities built numerous military cemeteries throughout the valley during the Great War, but

they fell into disrepair after the empire collapsed. The remote Austrian cemetery at Log pod Mangartom, undisturbed by the twentieth century, is the last to
remain much as it was during the war. Located behind the village's civil cemetery under a forested mountain, it contains 1,328 graves of Austrian troops
killed in the fighting for Mt. Rombon. They are largely German, Slovene, and
Bosnian soldiers, nearly all of their graves marked with a black steel cross bearing a simple inscription: NEPOZNANI (unknown). In the very back row, at the
forest's edge, is the grave of Franz Janowitz, the Bohemian Jewish poet and officer of the 2nd *Kaiserschützen*, who died of wounds sustained on Rombon during the Twelfth Battle of the Isonzo. The cemetery is guarded by a large
monument, the work of the Prague soldier and sculptor Ladislav Kofranek. It
portrays two Austrian soldiers, one a mountain rifleman, the other a Bosnian
soldier wearing a fez, and is dedicated "To the Memory of the Brave Defenders
of Rombon" in German, Serbo-Croat, and Slovene.

Five miles down the main road, heading into the upper Isonzo basin, is the
town of Bovec (Flitsch), under the shadow of Rombon to the north; to the south
are Javoršček and Vršič, where Mussolini received his baptism of fire in 1915.
Just before the town is another Austrian cemetery containing several hundred
dead from the battles for Rombon and Čukla; the nameplates, unfortunately,
are long gone. Across the road is a monument to the Austrian defenders of Bovec
from 1915 to 1917. The town itself was mostly destroyed during the Great War,
when it was held by the Italians. After the war, Bovec, temporarily renamed
Plezzo, was reconstructed by the occupying Italians. Therefore, with its white
stucco walls and red tiled roofs, it has a distinctly Mediterranean appearance. It
is the major town on the uppermost Isonzo (Soča to the Slovenes) and the center
for Isonzo water sports, principally white-water rafting and kayaking. The
Isonzo, here a cold, fast-flowing Alpine river, runs just south of the town.

Bovec includes an excellent private museum, *Zbirka iz 1. Svetovne Vojne*
"87. Polk" (First World War Collection "87th Regiment"), run by Vera and Ivo
Ivančič. The collection consists entirely of items found in the area, principally
on Mt. Rombon. In Bovec there is a group of amateur hiker-historians who regularly climb the surrounding mountains looking for artifacts; the small museum showcases their findings. Everything from weapons and unit insignia to
radio sets and machine guns is on display, found on the peaks overlooking the
town. Rombon (7,290 ft.) is still remote (the summit is snow-covered throughout the year), and there are many weapons and unexploded shells at or near the
peak. The Bovec group also frequently discovers Austrian and Italian dead,
who are buried in the town. Because climbing Rombon is arduous and dangerous for the inexperienced mountaineer, a trip to the Bovec museum is strongly
recommended instead.

Following the Isonzo road south, toward Gorizia, the next town of any size is
Kobarid (Karfreit, Caporetto). The ten-mile drive follows the river past the

hamlets of Žaga and Srpenica, between steep, often cloud-covered Julian Alps. Kobarid remains much as it was in 1917 when victorious Austrian soldiers of Prince Felix zu Schwarzenberg's 55th Division passed through it. It is nestled on the west bank of the Isonzo, on a plain, overlooked on all sides by steep blue-gray mountains; to the southwest is Mt. Matajur, where Erwin Rommel earned his Blue Max. The greatest of the surrounding peaks is Krn (7,410 ft.), four miles to the east of Kobarid, across the Isonzo.[2] Just north of Kobarid, on the hill of Saint Anthony overlooking the river, is an Italian ossuary. The octagonal memorial, designed by Gianni Castiglioni and Giovanni Greppi, was opened by Mussolini in 1938 and contains the bones of 7,014 Italian dead who fell between Rombon and Tolmin. It includes stations of the cross and offers an impressive view of Kobarid and the surrounding valley.

The town itself, rebuilt in the 1920s, boasts a museum dedicated to the Great War. Located in a restored eighteenth-century house, the Kobarid Museum, opened in October 1990, has numerous displays about the Isonzo fighting, particularly the Twelfth Battle. The impressive collection includes excellent maps, photos, documents, and displays of weapons and uniforms from both armies. It justly received the European Community's award for European Museum of 1993.

Continuing down the Isonzo road, the next stop is Tolmin (Tolmein), the major town on the upper Isonzo and the county seat. Eight miles southeast of Kobarid, it is on the Isonzo's east bank, just south of the imposing Mrzli ridge. The hub of Austrian resistance on the upper Isonzo, Tolmin never fell to the Italians during the fighting, yet it is surrounded by a wealth of historical monuments. At the river's edge is a walled German ossuary, where the Imperial German dead from the Twelfth Battle and the fighting for the Tolmin bridgehead are buried. The impressive building, completed in 1936, was constructed from stones imported from Germany; its indoor mosaic includes the names of all Germany's dead on the Isonzo. Immediately east of Tolmin, at Loče, is a major Austrian cemetery, where as many as 7,000 dead from the battles for Krn and Mrzli ridge are buried. The overwhelming majority are unknown, but some graves are marked with ornate, privately purchased headstones and monuments. Many of the dead are Poles of the 3rd Mountain Brigade. Two miles northwest of Tolmin, near the Isonzo's banks and under the shadow of Mrzli vrh, is the village of Gabrje. There, a small shop, formerly a barn, which was found to have been an Italian military chapel with an accompanying cemetery during the war. The dead, *Alpini* from the 1915 battle for Krn, were moved to Kobarid, and the chapel was forgotten.

Also north of Tolmin is the beautiful Church of the Holy Ghost. It is located east of Mrzli ridge at Javorca, in a remote cattle pasture 3,500 feet above sea level. To get there, follow the road to Zatolmin, just north of Tolmin, then take the dirt track uphill, hugging mountainsides for some four miles. It is a daunting

trip, but well worth it. The church, nestled on a foggy crest overlooking the
Tolminka valley, was built between April and November 1916, by soldiers of
the Austrian 3rd Mountain Brigade, the defenders of Mrzli ridge. It was designed and constructed to commemorate its dead by the architects, artists, and
stonemasons in the ranks of the brigade. The church remains undisturbed after
more than eight decades, receiving only a small number of mostly local visitors. It is a magnificent dark wood and white stucco building with a gray stone
base, complete with painted coats of arms representing the provinces of the empire. Inside it is even more impressive. (The key can be obtained from the old
woman in the neighboring farmhouse.) The interior is finished in tones of blue,
including marble, and the walls are covered with the 3rd Mountain Brigade's
"Book of the Dead," wooden panels inscribed with the names, painted in black,
of every Austrian soldier who fell in the fighting for Mrzli ridge. Hidden in the
Julian Alps and far removed from civilization, the aptly named Church of the
Holy Ghost is one of the best preserved and most moving monuments to the war
on the Isonzo.

Two miles south of Tolmin, straight down the Isonzo, is the town of Most na
Soči (St. Luzia), the wartime Austrian supply depot and railhead on the upper
Isonzo. The determined Austrian defense of the Tolmin bridgehead is commemorated with a stone plaque: *"Hier Kämpfte das XV. Korps"* (the XV Corps
fought here). Just across the Isonzo lies the village of Modrejce, which contains
an Austrian cemetery on the river's edge. It holds 2,750 mostly unknown dead
from the 1916 fighting for the Tolmin bridgehead.

Continuing down the main Isonzo road, which here runs parallel to the river
near the water's edge, the Bainsizza plateau rises ahead. The first major town is
Kanal (Canale), where Enrico Caviglia's XXIV Corps broke the Austrian defenses during the Eleventh Battle. Kanal is perched handsomely on the Isonzo's
east side, its white stucco houses adorning the steep, rocky river bank. It is an
ideal starting point for exploring the rugged, thickly forested, and still sparsely
populated Bainsizza plateau (Banjšice to the Slovenes). There are numerous
minor roads, most no more than dirt tracks, running through the plateau, and
few show any obvious signs of the Great War. Still, several villages contain
large Austrian graveyards. The town of Bate on the central Banjšice possesses a
now abandoned cemetery with 5,000 unknown Austrian dead, none of them
with gravestones. Likewise, the village of Ravnica has an Austrian burial site,
once a cemetery but now just a meadow, adorned only with a cross and a stone
pyramid. The tiny village of Lužarji's Austrian cemetery is *dolina* filled with
some 300 Habsburg dead, many with small headstones. The town of Čepovan
on the plateau's eastern edge once had a large Austrian cemetery, but now only
a stone pyramid remains; the gravestones were removed after the Great War by
peasants looking for building materials to reconstruct their wrecked homes.

The Austrian cemeteries on the Banjšice are filled with the dead from several Isonzo battles, predominantly the Eleventh.

To explore the lower plateau and Gorizia, return to Kanal and continue south on the Isonzo road. Little more than three miles downstream is the village of Plave (Plava), and opposite on the Isonzo's east bank looms Hill 383, the site of so many failed Italian offensives. Despite the huge losses sustained by the Italians in two years of attacks at Plave, there are no official monuments here. The terrible sacrifice of the II Corps apparently has been forgotten. Yet, close examination reveals several poignant reminders of the terrible fighting. At the base of 383, along the road overlooking the Isonzo, a half-dozen *kavernen* remain blasted in the rock, where doomed *fanti* waited to go over the top in 1915. They are just as they were then. Slightly up the hill, hidden behind trees and underbrush, are two stone faces where doomed Italian infantrymen carved their names and regimental numbers into the rock before assaulting the Austrian trenches; they are all that remains of the thousands of soldiers of the 3rd Division who were sacrificed on the slopes of "Bloody 383." The hillsides also contain a few overgrown trench sections, and shell casings are strewn everywhere.

Continuing downstream on the Isonzo road, now on the river's east bank, Kuk and Vodice appear on the left. The valley here is a near chasm, surrounded by high ridges on both sides; the river, too, has changed, becoming deeper, slower, greener. Vodice, two miles southeast of Plave, has a monument at its hard-to-reach summit dedicated to Maurizio Gonzaga, the "Iron General," whose 53rd Division captured the 2,150-foot-high mountain in 1917. Just beyond Vodice is Sveta Gora (Monte Santo), which again has a monastery at its peak. The Slovene government maintains the restored pilgrimage site and its holy portrait of the Virgin Mary, saved from Italian guns in 1915. The 2,250-foot-high summit is accessible by car, a long and twisting ride. The view of the central Isonzo valley, the surrounding mountains, and Gorizia from Sveta Gora's peak is unsurpassed. The buildings at the summit now include a museum, opened in 1989, which highlights the history of the monastery and the bitter fighting for the mountain. It boasts an impressive collection of paintings and posters relating to the Isonzo front.

At the southern foot of Sveta Gora, in the shadow of Škabrijel (Monte San Gabriele), lies the village of Solkan (Salcano). The town borders Nova Gorica and includes a major rail bridge across the Isonzo. There is a Habsburg cemetery near the river's edge, behind and below the town's main burial ground. It was damaged by Allied bombardment of the rail bridge during the Second World War, but eighty-five stones remain. Most of the dead are Hungarians, killed in the fight for Sabotino. That mountain (Sabotin to the Slovenes) is directly above Solkan on the Isonzo's left bank. The international frontier straddles Sabotino, so that the north and east faces are in Slovenia, and the summit and south and west slopes belong to Italy. The mountain, officially designated a *zona sacra* (sacred zone) by the Italian government, is permanently scarred with stone entrenchments, but they are difficult to reach.

The border similarly runs through Gorizia/Nova Gorica, but most of the historical sights are in Italy. There is a city museum, opened in 1934, that highlights the history of Gorizia and the Isonzo battles fought around it. Otherwise, comparatively little remains there of the terrible fighting. Many streets are named in honor of generals and units made famous by the Isonzo front—Cadorna, Capello, Brigata Sassari, Brigata Aosta—but not much else in Gorizia stands as a reminder of the frightful cost paid by the Italian Army to win the city. It is much larger than in Habsburg times, and its suburbs have overrun former battlefields. Nova Gorica, built mostly since 1945, is newer still; largely drab and dull, it contains even fewer memories of the battles of the Isonzo.

One must look across the Isonzo to find graphic evidence of the six bloody offensives Italy undertook to occupy Gorizia. At the village of Oslavia, less than a mile west of the river, is an Italian ossuary. The awe-inspiring mass grave, perched on a 500-foot-high hill facing Gorizia, has the shape of a mighty white fortress. Designed by the Roman architect Ghino Venturi, the imposing circular ossuary was finished in 1938, just before Italy's next major war. It contains the remains of 57,201 Italian soldiers of the 2nd Army killed in the fight for Oslavia, Podgora, and Gorizia. (There are also 539 Austrian dead in the ossuary.) Some 20,700 of the dead *fanti* are identified and interred separately, but 36,440 others remain unknown. In each of the ossuary's three underground corners there is a simple, haunting stone in the floor with a brief inscription: "12,000 Unknown." The central tower of the ossuary contains the graves of thirteen soldiers who won the Gold Medal for Bravery. A hundred yards in front of the Oslavia mass grave is a monument to fifty-five "Julian volunteers," Austrian subjects who died fighting to redeem *Italia irredenta*. One of the names on the marble tablet is Scipio Slataper, the Triestine writer who fell trying to liberate Podgora for Italy.

South of Gorizia, across the tiny Vipacco River, rises Monte San Michele. Its 900-foot-high summit, only a mile east of the Isonzo, has become a monument to Italian bravery and sacrifice. San Michele, an official *zona sacra* since 1922, has an observation deck from which to survey the battlefield, as well as monuments to several of the twenty-nine Italian brigades that fought to win the peak, at a cost of 112,000 Italian killed and maimed. The most prominent of these unit memorials is the "iron grenade" symbol of the Grenadier Brigade, the famed *Granatieri di Sardegna*. There is a small museum at the summit to commemorate the six battles fought around Monte San Michele between June 1915 and August 1916.

The western Carso belongs to Italy, and it retains much of the look it had during the fighting. It is easy to imagine the bloody campaigns that drowned the Carso in blood for more than two years. The battlefield has become overgrown in many places, since the harsh and uninviting "world of rock" remains sparsely populated. There are villages, but no major towns, in the heart of the plateau. There are dozens of Italian, and some Habsburg, monuments scattered throughout the Carso. Many of them mark the site where a brave soldier won the *medaglia d'oro*, usually posthumously. Others are unit memorials, dedicated to regiments and brigades sacrificed on the stony sea of Doberdò. One such is the monument near San Michele to the 4th *Honvéd* Regiment, defenders of the mountain; unlike most Habsburg memorials, it is still in good repair and is visited regularly by Hungarian groups. They come to commemorate Hungary's terrible sacrifice on the Carso more than eighty years before. Much of the plateau remains too hazardous to explore safely. Years of bombardments left countless unexploded shells strewn all over the Carso—Slovenia removed nearly 30,000 pounds of unexploded munitions from its portion of the Isonzo battlefield in 1995 alone. Even after so long a time, they are a lethal threat to the unwary explorer. The plateau boasts hundreds of trench sections carved into the limestone, but many are too risky to merit a visit. Fortunately, the Italian Ministry of Defense has plainly marked areas that represent an unacceptable risk.

The village of Doberdò on the central Carso, which gave its name to many of the costly battles, is now just a mile and a half from the Slovene frontier. The village was wholly destroyed during the Carso campaigns, clear evidence of the savage fighting that engulfed it during the Great War. Villages across the border in Slovenia are much the same. They have been entirely rebuilt since the Carso battles. The villages of Kostanjevica, Opatje Selo (Opacchiasella), and Lokvica, made infamous during 1916, have reemerged, but they reveal little about the bitter battles waged there. All that remains are Austrian cemeteries, and few of them are still noticeable. The maintenance of Austrian grave sites has never been a high priority with any of the Carso's occupiers since 1918, whether Italian Fascists, Yugoslav Communists, or Slovene nationalists. There are several Habsburg grave sites, but most are small; some have been lost entirely. Even the larger ones are frequently in poor shape. A nameless cemetery on the Renče-Žigoni road, a mere quarter-mile from the Vipacco (Vipava in Slovene), still boasts a main monument, but the gravestones themselves are no longer visible. The graveyard at Volčja Draga has an impressive pyramid monument to the 76th Regiment, a mostly German unit from western Hungary. The large cemetery at Štanjel, a dozen miles east of the Italo-Slovene border, was finished in 1918 with the help of Russian prisoners of war. It was the site of a wartime hospital, and the Austrian soldiers buried there died of wounds sustained on the Carso. Few of the headstones at Štanjel remain intact. Time and neglect have taken their toll, and the Austrian sacrifice on the Carso has been largely forgotten.

The same cannot be said of Italy's enormous sacrifice on the Carso. Indeed, the losses of the 3rd Army are amply recalled in many memorials on the western edge of the plateau.[3] The greatest of these is the enormous ossuary at

Redipuglia, the "Park of Remembrance," hardly more than a mile east of the
Isonzo. There, on the west face of Hill 118, Monte Sei Busi, the Italian Army
built an imposing monument to the dead of the "undefeated" 3rd Army. The
oversize memorial was designed by Giovanni Greppi and Gianni Castiglioni,
who also planned the Kobarid ossuary. The imposing Redipuglia ossuary, the
final resting place of 100,000 Italian soldiers, stretches all the way to the summit of Monte Sei Busi. The 39,857 known dead are interred in the twenty-two
terraces that lead to the peak. Some 60,330 unknown *fanti* are buried in two
large common graves on each side of the votive chapel at the top of the ossuary.
At the base of the ossuary lies Emanuele Filiberto di Savoia, the Duke of Aosta.
He was buried at Redipuglia among his soldiers in 1931, under a seventy-
five-ton monolith of porphyry.

The votive chapel at the peak of the ossuary is a touching monument to the
enormity of Italy's sacrifice on the Carso. It includes a small museum of personal artifacts dug up on the plateau—crosses, rosaries, pins, buttons, and the
like—belonging to fallen *fanti*. There are also pictures of dead and missing soldiers, among them the three Cortellessa brothers who fell on the Carso within a
year. Achille, Ermino, and Luigi, the oldest just twenty-four, appear in a small,
faded photograph in the chapel, all that remains of the three doomed brothers
from Caserta.

At the base of the hill, on the right, is a stone trench section, a relic of the bitter 1915 fighting for Monte Sei Busi. It is a fully covered stone entrenchment,
used by the Austrians to protect their infantry from Italian shelling. Across
Strada 305 are more Italian monuments. The site, carefully maintained by the
Ministry of Defense, rests on the east slope of the Hill of St. Elia. Here was the
original Italian monument at Redipuglia; today it boasts memorials to all the
combat arms and services, as well as several Italian artillery pieces employed in
the fighting. There is also a simple monument to the countless thousands of
fanti who fell on the Isonzo but have no known grave; they are commemorated
with a haunting phrase inscribed in marble:

UNKNOWN SOLDIER
What does my name matter to you?
Cry to the wind
ITALIAN INFANTRYMAN
And I will rest in peace

Alongside there is the Casa "Terza Armata," devoted to the history of the 3rd
Army and its role in the Great War. It offers numerous maps, photos, and
weapons from the war on the Carso, a tribute to the sacrifices of the *Terza
Armata* on the rocky plateau. There is also a café where tourists can rest and
ponder the terrible memories they have witnessed. Most of the Carso's few

visitors today are elderly, and no doubt need a coffee break after climbing the immense ossuary.

All these memorials and battle sites are tenderly maintained by troops of the Italian Army, who guard and keep up the graves of their great-grandfathers. The rest of the world, including most Italians and Austrians, may have forgotten the sacrifice on the Isonzo, but the troops at Redipuglia have not. The Italians also maintain an Austrian cemetery a half-mile up the road from Redipuglia, at Fogliano. This is the only notable Austrian cemetery on Italian soil. It holds the remains of 14,406 Habsburg soldiers killed on the Carso. Only 2,406 of the dead are in marked graves; the rest remain unknown, buried in one mass grave of 7,000 at the head of the cemetery, and 2,500 more in each of the two rear corners. The entrance to the Fogliano gravesite reads: "*Im Leben und im Tode Vereint*" (United in Life and Death). The Austrian dead who have found their final resting place here—Germans, Magyars, Czechs, Poles, Romanians, Ukrainians, Slovaks, Croats, Bosnians, Slovenes, Serbs, even Italians—indeed remain united in death, a little more than eight decades after the Habsburg Empire disappeared forever. The cemetery at Fogliano stands as a fitting tribute to their poignant sacrifice in a lost cause.

The cemetery is beautifully maintained by the Italians, Austria's bitter enemies on the Isonzo. The grave sites are colored by evergreen flower beds and rows of cypresses that flourish among the mostly nameless dead. After more than three-quarters of a century and a Second World War that brought Europe bloodshed and terror far worse even than anything experienced during the Great War, Italians and Central Europeans can look back at the Isonzo with sadness and regret, not bitterness and hatred. It is a tribute to Europe at the beginning of a new century that Italians and Austrians, members of the European Union, can now hardly imagine that more than eight decades ago their forefathers fought each other so viciously in an obscure Alpine river valley for twenty-eight months. Indeed, Italian President Oscar Scalfaro and his Austrian counterpart, Thomas Klestil, met at Gorizia on October 4, 1995, for a memorial ceremony, including the joint dropping of a wreath into the Isonzo, to heal the last wounds lingering in their countries from the fighting. Yet, the hundreds of thousands of dead from the dozen battles of the Isonzo, resting in cemeteries from Rombon to the Adriatic, are there to prove that the unprecedented slaughter indeed happened, that a European tragedy took place here. But the care shown by Italian soldiers for the graves of their once hated foes buried at Fogliano stands as moving evidence that the Isonzo front has not been entirely forgotten, and that it will never happen again.

Notes

CHAPTER 1

1. According to Pliny, Julia, the wife of Emperor Augustus, attributed her vitality and longevity—she died at eighty-seven at nearby Aquileia—to the Carso's wine.

CHAPTER 2

1. Hence the correct term for the Habsburg Empire after 1867 was Austria-Hungary; this work frequently refers to just "Austria" for brevity and convenience; the Austrian and Hungarian halves are referred to separately where required, and "Austria" is used to describe the empire as a whole.

2. Among the dead was twenty-three-year-old Herbert Conrad von Hötzendorf, a lieutenant of dragoons, the son of the chief of the General Staff.

3. One of them was the *Seebataillon Triest*, sailors from the naval base at Trieste sent to the Carso front to hold the line.

CHAPTER 3

1. Prime Minister Antonio Salandra later admitted that had Italy been aware of the impending Austro-German offensive, Rome might not have intervened at all.

2. From the Serbo-Croatian term for the Military Border, *Vojna Krajina*.

3. One of the most important tasks the 5th Army had to complete was the construction of new roads through the Julian Alps. There were few decent roads for supplying the troops, so construction of a major road to supply the upper Isonzo valley via

the 5,000-foot-high Vršič pass began in May. The work was done by 12,000 Russian prisoners of war.

4. "Forward Savoy!"—from the house of Savoy, Italy's ruling dynasty.

5. "Forward! With the knife!"

CHAPTER 4

1. Indeed, so pervasive was the despair about Italy's "moral delinquency" that even the philosopher Benedetto Croce believed that the army was fighting on the Isonzo not just to defeat the Habsburgs, but also for "nothing less than . . . redeeming definitively the Italian people from a fifteen-centuries-old guilt."

2. *Spanische Reiter*, named after Vienna's famous Hofburg riding school, were high wooden supports for masses of concertina wire, intended to block the advancing Italian infantry.

3. Not exclusively Roman Catholics, however: many were Greek Catholics or Uniates, Eastern Christians in communion with Rome. Greek Catholics formed the second largest denomination in the Habsburg Empire and were well represented in the army, particularly in regiments from Galicia, eastern Hungary, and Transylvania.

4. "Long live Austria!"

5. The office of honorary regimental colonel, an ancient institution, was commonplace in European armies before the First World War; it was usually held by distinguished generals or foreign royalty. Vittorio Emanuele naturally resigned as the 28th's titular commander once Italy declared war on Austria, as he did with the three Imperial German Army regiments in which he held similar posts.

CHAPTER 5

1. This regiment, raised in 1696, was descended from the medieval Teutonic Knights, established in the end of the 12th century. Its honorary colonel, the *Hoch- und Deutschmeister* (High and German Master), was the head of the order. In 1915 the post was held by Archduke Eugen, commander in chief of the Italian front, who was destined to be the last *Hoch- und Deutschmeister*.

2. "Missing" includes the thousands of dead soldiers with no known grave or whose bodies were blown apart; hence even the official Italian death count likely exceeded 20,000.

3. This brigade, like its sister Cagliari Brigade from Sardinia, had an advantage over other Italian units: its soldiers' native dialect, difficult for mainland Italians to understand, was utterly incomprehensible to the Austrians; thus the Sardinians could communicate on field telephones and radios without using code.

CHAPTER 6

1. One such unfortunate staff officer was Colonel Giulio Douhet, the brilliant airpower theorist and later prophet of strategic bombardment, who wound up in jail for daring to raise awkward questions about Cadorna's fighting methods.

2. The Austrian Army's three dozen *Jäger* (hunter) battalions, like Italy's *Bersaglieri*, were an elite force descended from nineteenth-century light infantry units.

3. This was a particularly biting comment because Cadorna's father, Count Raffaele, had captured Rome in 1870.

CHAPTER 7

1. Literally "the gray-green ones," from the color of the Italian field uniform.

2. Not that Mussolini was universally popular with his comrades in arms, many of whom blamed him for getting Italy into the war.

3. A total of 12,000 Russian prisoners were used by the Austrians to build the 5,300-foot-high Vršič pass. The poorly clothed Russians suffered badly during the winter months, and hundreds succumbed to illness and the weather.

4. Relations between Paris and Rome were never ideal. The French Army, remembering Italy's need of French troops to defeat Austria in 1859, consistently rated Italian arms poorly, and Cadorna displayed no love for Joffre and his generals.

5. These were the three-division-strong Iron Corps and the elite 18th Division, whose mountain troops had so stoutly defended the Bainsizza plateau throughout 1915.

6. The Austrian command structure had been reshuffled during the winter: the XV Corps, defending the upper Isonzo from Tolmein to Rombon, now was under General Franz Rohr's newly raised 10th Army; however, because Boroević was commander of all Austrian forces on the Isonzo, this three-division corps has been counted in the totals for the 5th Army.

7. Cynics have suggested that the British were at least honest enough to admit to Joffre that they would do nothing to help France until the summer. The Russians' March offensive at Lake Naroch was pursued with considerably more vigor than the Italian effort on the Isonzo. The Russian drive ended disastrously with the loss of over 100,000 soldiers while inflicting only one-fifth as many casualties on the Germans; it did little or nothing to relieve the French at Verdun.

8. The crisis did not change Cadorna that much, however; fearing the worst, Prime Minister Salandra again requested a Council of War to determine Italy's course of action. Cadorna brushed this suggestion off as rudely as he had dismissed Salandra's first request.

CHAPTER 8

1. Naturally not all Italians shared this view; in an inexplicable message sent by Vittorio Emanuele to fellow monarch and ally George V in March, the king stated that Germany was the real enemy (even though Italy had not declared war on Berlin), and that the Isonzo was only a secondary front! Cadorna, of course, thought differently.

2. In many places the Isonzo was fordable, except during the spring, when melting snows significantly deepened the river. Artillery and supply units, however, needed bridges.

CHAPTER 9

1. For this feat, First Lieutenant Wanke justly received the Knight's Cross of the Order of Maria Theresia.

2. The official Italian count was little more than 25,000, but independent estimates have ranged as high as 69,000. Certainly the latter figure is much closer to the truth.

3. Roósz was rewarded with the Knight's Cross of the Order of Maria Theresia. He had inflicted crippling losses on one of the finest Italian divisions; in just three days in the Fajti hrib area, its Tuscany Brigade lost 2,634 soldiers, most of them to the 61st Regiment's counterattack.

4. Archduke Joseph's VII Corps bore the lion's share of the casualties, as usual.

CHAPTER 10

1. In May 1917, the Italian Army boasted fifty-nine infantry divisions, twenty-one regiments of *Bersaglieri*, eighty-eight battalions of *Alpini*, and four cavalry divisions, supported by 8,200 machine guns, 3,000 field guns, 2,100 heavy guns, and 1,500 heavy mortars.

2. Three on the upper Isonzo, two on the Bainsizza, two behind Gorizia, seven on the Carso, and four in army reserve.

3. *Fiamme verdi*, so called because of the green collar that adorned the mountain troops' uniform; the *Bersaglieri*, the army's other elite corps, wore red collar patches, and were known colloquially as "red flames" (*fiamme rosse*).

4. Giovanni Randaccio died an agonizing death in a Monfalcone field hospital, D'Annunzio at his side. The warrior-poet managed to turn his friend's meaningless end into a gruesomely patriotic and romantic tale, which he recounted at Randaccio's funeral. The Duke of Aosta liked D'Annunzio's speech so much that he had it reprinted and distributed to the men of the 3rd Army, to assist the "moral preparation of the combatants."

5. Indeed, the Jewish regimental doctor was something of a cliché in the Austrian Army. Many distinguished Jewish physicians had done their service in the army, among them Lieutenant Dr. Sigmund Freud.

6. As befitted his act of heroism and daring, Captain Sonnewend received the Knight's Cross of the Order of Maria Theresia for his leadership on June 3, 1917.

7. On June 1 redesignated the 2nd Army.

CHAPTER 11

1. He believed—rightly—that the Vatican's sympathies lay more with the House of Habsburg than with the House of Savoy.

2. Antonio Gatti, Cadorna's adjutant, recalled frankly, "I never heard him speak about the men and about using them economically."

3. Gabriele D'Annunzio, observing the bodies of twenty-eight soldiers of the Catanzaro Brigade shot for cowardice, penned a gruesome poem, "The Dead Sing with Dirt in Their Mouths" (*"Cantano i morti con la terra in bocca"*).

4. Mauthausen, located on the Danube in Lower Austria, seventeen miles east of Linz, was the largest Austrian prisoner-of-war camp.

5. The zealously humanitarian and religious Karl also denied his generals the use of poison gas in battle without his permission, another gesture that helped to make the monarch decreasingly popular in military circles. He was better liked by civilians; to *triestini* the young emperor was Carlo Piria—"Charles Funnel"—so called for his well known love of wine.

6. The 63rd Infantry Regiment, with its depot at the medieval market town of Bistritz, recruited in the dark and wooded Carpathian valleys of northeastern Transylvania, where two decades earlier Bram Stoker had set his famous novel, *Dracula*.

7. Franek received the Knight's Cross of the Order of Maria Theresia for his heroism and leadership. Many years after the event, when asked about his daring on August 21, particularly his rescue of his trapped soldiers, Fritz Franek modestly retorted, "What else could I have done?"

8. The unlucky sergeant's mangled corpse was buried incomplete; the missing body part, a leg, was found four days later, when the smell of rotting flesh reached the gun positions. The severed limb was discovered resting in a ravine overlooking the battery, covered with blackflies.

9. The 1st Isonzo Army (the Carso and lower Isonzo regions, including the XXIII, VII, and XVI Corps) was assigned to Colonel-General Wenzel von Wurm; the 2nd Isonzo Army (the XXIV and XV Corps, from Mt. San Gabriele to Rombon) was under General Henriquez.

10. Two of its shattered divisions, the 21st Rifle and 106th Militia, had already been officially sent to the rear to regain their strength.

11. For this Corporal Kapetanović received the Gold Medal for Bravery, the highest decoration bestowed on Austrian enlisted soldiers. He paid a terrible price, however; he was among the numerous *Bosniaken* struck by Italian shrapnel during the charge up Hill 830, and was permanently blinded in both eyes.

12. For this, Colonel Vladimir Laxa was awarded the Knight's Cross of the Order of Maria Theresia.

13. In terms of ethnic composition, in September 1917 Army Group Boroević, comprising the 1st and 2nd Isonzo armies, was 60 percent Slav (Polish, Czech, Slovak, Ukrainian, and a large number of South Slavs), 16 percent Magyar, 13 percent German, and 11 percent Romanian. Boroević's army group, even more than the Habsburg Army as a whole, was a Slavic force.

CHAPTER 12

1. Three from Galicia, two from Transylvania, and two from France; Austria added two divisions of her own from the Russian front.

2. The rough Austrian equivalent of the Medal of Honor or Victoria Cross; the 7th Infantry Regiment was the army's second most decorated regiment, with thirty-six *Goldenen* to its credit.

3. In all, the lavishly equipped *Sturmbataillon* boasted eight heavy and a dozen light machine guns, a pair of 37mm light cannons, a dozen light mortars, and its own pioneer platoon with a half-dozen flamethrowers as well as demolitions—the fire-

power of an entire regiment in a single battalion; just as significant, the assault unit's tactics were innovative, indeed revolutionary, emphasizing flanking (not frontal) attacks, rapid exploitations of success, and keeping the momentum of the offensive.

4. Indeed, when early in the war Germany first raised mountain units of its own, it turned to Habsburg staff officers for advice on tactical, organizational, and logistical issues, a rare exception to the general rule of Austrian dependence on its ally's battlefield expertise.

5. Through the war, Austria's mountain troops were well equipped with special Alpine motor vehicles for the movement of troops, artillery, and supplies at high altitudes, many of them designed by the Daimler-Werke at Wiener Neustadt, whose chief engineer and general director was Ferdinand Porsche, later world-famous for his automotive pioneering.

6. One of which, Air Company 39D, was assigned directly to the 55th Division for the battle.

7. The feeling was mutual; Cadorna feared that Capello, a better politician than himself, was trying to depose him at the *Comando Supremo*.

8. The 144th Infantry Regiment, on the Isonzo on the eve of the Twelfth Battle, had recently received its forty-first colonel commanding since the war began.

9. "Long live Austria, the war is over!"

10. The future "Desert Fox" was initially a victim of his own bureaucracy. His hard-won Blue Max was first mistakenly presented to a brother officer, which made Rommel explode with rage.

11. The three elite regiments of *Kaiserschützen* were the Austrian *Landwehr*'s equivalent of the *k.u.k. Armee*'s four regiments of *Tiroler Kaiserjäger*.

12. Even the British artillery units on the Isonzo were ordered to retreat and abandon their guns and huge ammunition reserves; fortunately for the war effort, the British headquarters at Gradisca did manage to save its large stash of liquor and cigarettes from the advancing Austrians.

13. One of the few attackers killed during the capture of Udine was the German General von Berrer, commander of the LI Corps, who took his staff car into the city too quickly and was gunned down by retreating *Carabinieri* on horseback.

14. With this, the total of Italian men and equipment captured by Krauss's I Corps by October 31 reached 45,000 soldiers, 340 guns, and hundreds of machine guns.

15. The officer cadet and his "brown devils" celebrated their bloodless triumph with a three-day drunk in a nearby castle, where they appropriated an Italian general's abandoned stock of vintage wines.

CHAPTER 13

1. Some 300,000 less than the army had in mid-1917.

2. Among the *Heimkehrer* were many future Central European Communist notables, the best known of them Corporal Josip Broz of the 25th *Honvéd* Regiment, later famous by his nom de guerre, Tito. Future Hungarian Communist leaders Béla Kun, Imre Nagy, and Mátyás Rákosi were likewise converted to the Marxist-Leninist faith in Russian captivity.

3. The military's official report on the Caporetto defeat, released in 1919, was highly critical of the army's generalship, Badoglio included (although, significantly, it did not blame politicians or defeatism on the home front); however, the thirteen pages that explicitly blamed Badoglio were tactfully excised.

4. "Who gets the honor? We do!"

5. One of their number was Captain Fiorello La Guardia, U.S. Army Air Service, who had resigned his New York congressional seat to join the struggle. La Guardia regularly addressed Italian troops about America's willingness to help its ally win the war and redeem *Italia irredenta*, and he was doubtless sincere: his mother was a Triestine Jewess.

6. Austrian resentment at the Dual Monarchy's dependence on Berlin ran deep, especially in military circles; Conrad, in fact, on numerous occasions referred to the Germans as "our secret enemies."

7. The typically blunt Field Marshal Boroević informed officers of the 8th Cavalry Division as they arrived on the Piave from the Eastern front in the spring of 1918, "Gentlemen, you haven't been in Italy, you don't know what war is."

8. There had been bad omens, however. On June 11, the Austrian battleship *Szent István* was sunk by an Italian torpedo boat forty-five miles southeast of Pola during a routine Adriatic patrol. It was the worst Austrian naval loss of the war.

9. Diaz's field force counted fifty-six infantry divisions to defeat the Austrian offensive (including three British, two French, and one Czecho-Slovak), of which thirty-seven were at the front on June 15 and nineteen were held in reserve; the Italians also had 7,043 guns and 2,406 mortars of all calibers to resist the Austrian drive.

10. Or 142,550, counting the sick.

11. The *Comando Supremo* organized a whole division of *arditi* just before the battle (with six battalions of *arditi* and four of *Bersaglieri*, as well as mountain artillery and assault engineers), and it acquitted itself so well on the Piave that the army decided to raise a second immediately.

12. Segre was a Jew, as were fifty other Italian wartime generals. Italy's tiny Jewish community was decidedly overrepresented in the officer corps, and they performed well. One of them, Emmanuele Pugliese, was the most bemedaled general in the army, and all told not less than a thousand Jewish soldiers were decorated for valor during the Great War.

13. The Austrians were short of ammunition, but they occasionally responded, claiming unlucky Italian victims. One of them was Ernest Hemingway. Eager to see action, he demanded transfer from the tranquil Dolomites to the more fiery Piave front in late June, and soon found himself driving ambulances for the 3rd Army. His frontline career was brief, however, cut short by an Austrian mortar barrage on July 8 at Fossalta di Piave, a dozen miles from the Adriatic coast. Hemingway was struck by shrapnel and sent to the rear to recover, never to see the front again.

CHAPTER 14

1. The German-Bohemian wartime death rate was 34.5/1,000 inhabitants, compared to an Austrian average of 26.7, a German-Austrian rate of 29.1, and a Czech-Bohemian rate of 26.7. The highest rate in the whole empire was in the German belt of

southern Moravia, which registered a loss of 44/1,000 residents; the second highest loss rate, not far behind, was found in Muslim districts of Bosnia-Hercegovina.

2. Arz, the chief of the General Staff, was similarly pessimistic about the prospects for a successful Austrian stand in Venetia; on October 5 he ordered General Victor Weber von Webenau to form an armistice commission in Trient, in preparation for the impending need to sue for peace.

3. Following Hungary's detailed constitutional understandings, Karl could not divide Hungary along ethnic lines, as he could the Austrian half of the empire.

4. Noting his ally's pervasive inability to coordinate artillery and infantry, Lord Cavan said, "I can tell you privately that they simply will not go in for the scientific side of accurate shooting."

5. In the dawn attack, the lead British battalion, the 11th Northumberland Fusiliers, lost every officer above subaltern, including the lieutenant colonel commanding, who was killed on the Piave's east bank.

6. "Austria is in your camp,/While we others are solitary ruins./Through foolishness and deceit/We have crumbled and decayed,/But her spirit lives still/In those you lead to battle . . . /Those whom God created as Slav and Magyars/Do not quarrel spitefully over words,/They follow, even when the warrior's call is German,/For 'Forward!' calls to Hungarian and Czech alike."

7. Other units were not so fortunate. In one of the worst incidents, a November 10 argument between Graz police and returning Ukrainian and Czech troops led to a firefight in the train station, complete with machine guns, that left eight dead.

8. Even an unrepentantly nationalist German-Bohemian regimental history declared, perhaps reluctantly, "To be fair to the honor of our Czech officers and soldiers, it must be admitted that they remained loyal to their units at all times."

CHAPTER 15

1. Italy's new war minister, appointed in February 1919, was Enrico Caviglia, whose shock troops captured the Bainsizza in August 1917.

2. In a sad irony, Italy's population gain from annexing the Littoral and the South Tyrol almost exactly offset her enormous casualties in the Great War.

3. The 3rd Army also boasted 47,601 bravery medals: 274 gold, 18,467 silver, and 28,860 bronze.

4. D'Annunzio's last years were a pathetic reflection of his valorous war service, with gluttony and sexual excess replacing patriotism and daring exploits. The increasingly feeble bard died in March 1938, aged seventy-five, shortly before Italy's next great war.

5. He was soon followed by Colonel-General Wenzel von Wurm, last commander of the Isonzo Army, who died in Vienna less than a year later.

6. The republic was also burdened with many retired officers who opted for Austrian citizenship upon the empire's demise but remained diehard monarchists; one such was Guido Novak von Arienti, the hero of Plava, who until his death in Vienna in 1928 was active in conspiratorial circles planning a Habsburg restoration.

7. Emil Fey's role in the Dolfuss murder still remains ambiguous, although it is clear that his sin was one of omission, not commission.

8. Otto von Berndt was another.

9. Led by Mátyás Rákosi and then Imre Nagy, both ex-Habsburg soldiers.

10. The last Knight of Maria Theresia for service on the Isonzo was Fritz Franek, who returned from Soviet captivity and died peacefully in Vienna in 1976. The very last Knight of Maria Theresia was Gottfried von Banfield, "the Eagle of Trieste," a former Habsburg Navy lieutenant and Austria's leading flying ace during the war; he received the Knight's Cross in August 1917 for his exploits while leading flying boat squadrons from Trieste Naval Air Station. He stayed in Trieste after 1918, becoming an Italian citizen, marrying into a wealthy shipping family, and establishing a reputation as a maritime salvage expert; he led the clearing of the Suez Canal in 1956 after Nasser's attempts to block the waterway. In time, Banfield became a cherished Triestine fixture (his son, Baron Raffaele de Banfield, won laurels as a noted composer and the director of the Trieste Opera), and when he died in September 1986, aged ninety-six, Trieste knew that an age had ended.

CHAPTER 16

1. A notable exception, as of this writing, is Luigi Berlot of Plave (Plava), born in 1908, who witnessed the opening battles for "Bloody" Hill 383 as a seven-year-old boy. His father was an Austrian soldier, so the young Luigi watched the fighting with great interest. He speaks Italian and Slovene, lives on the Isonzo's west bank, and is very happy to discuss his memories of the battle with anyone who inquires.

2. The summit of Krn is still crisscrossed with stone entrenchments, but its Italian war memorials were long ago destroyed by lightning strikes.

3. Perhaps the most poignant and haunting is an unofficial memorial left by the *fanti* themselves: an inscription carved into the limestone face of Hill 98, above Monfalcone—"*La pace vogliamo* [We want peace]—1917."

MAPS

Map 1
Austria-Hungary, 1914

Cities and regions shown on the map:

Czernowitz, Bukovina, (Transylvania), Nagyszeben, Lemberg, Galicia, Kolozsvár, Przemyśl, Nagyvárad, Temesvár, Kassa, Ujvidék, Cracow, Osijek, Sarajevo, Silesia, Teschen, HUNGARY, Budapest, Mostar, Bosnia-Hercegovina, Ragusa, Olmütz, Moravia, Pozsony, Leitmeritz, Brünn, Upper Austria, Zagreb, Prague, Bohemia, Vienna, Croatia, Budweis, Graz, Dalmatia, Pilsen, Linz, Styria, Klagenfurt, Laibach, Carniola, Zara, Lower Austria, Carinthia, Istria, Salzburg, Görz & Gradisca, Trieste, Salzburg, Innsbruck, Tyrol, Trient, Vorarlberg

360

Map 2
Italy, 1914

Map 3
The Austrian Littoral, 1914

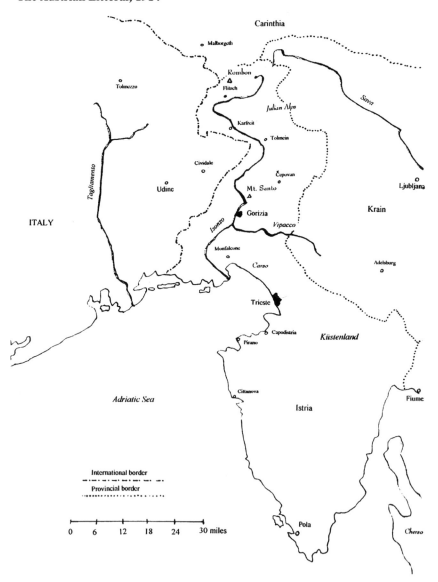

Carinthia

Malborgeth

Rombon

Tolmezzo

Flitsch

Julian Alps

Sava

Karfreit

Tolmein

Cividale

Čepovan

Ljubljana

Udine

Mt. Santo

Gorizia

Krain

Isonzo

Vipacco

Monfalcone

ITALY

Tagliamento

Carso

Adelsburg

Trieste

Capodistria

Küstenland

Pirano

Adriatic Sea

Cittanova

Fiume

Istria

International border

Provincial border

0   6   12   18   24   30 miles

Pola

Cherso

Map 4
The Austro-Italian Front, 1915–1918

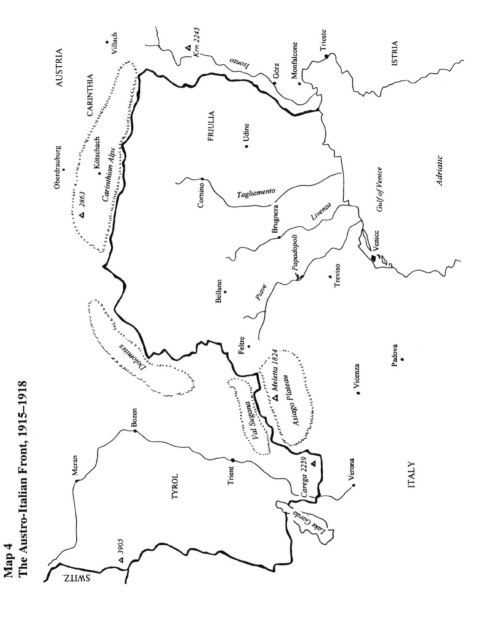

Map 5
The Gorizia-Carso Front

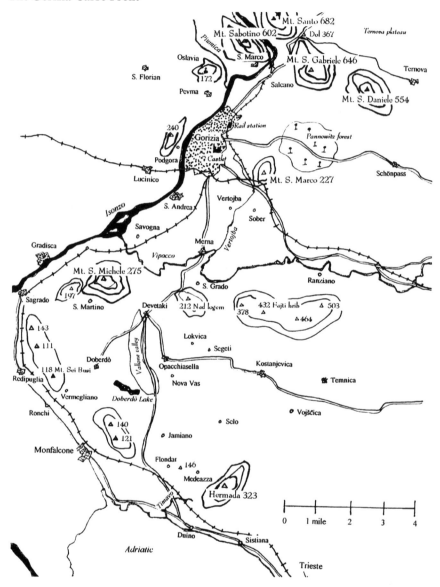

Mt. Santo 682

Mt. Sabotino 602

Dol 367

Ternova plateau

Oslavia

Piumica

S. Marco

Mt. S. Gabriele 646

Ternova

S. Florian

172

Salcano

Pevma

Mt. S. Daniele 554

240

Rail station

Gorizia

Pannowitz forest

Podgora

Castle

Schönpass

Lucinico

Mt. S. Marco 227

Vertojba

Isonzo

S. Andrea

Sober

Savogna

Vertojba

Gradisca

Merna

Vipacco

Ranziano

Mt. S. Michele 275

S. Grado

△ 197

432 Fajti hrib   △ 503

Sagrado

S. Martino

Devetaki

212 Nad logem

378

△ 464

△ 143

Lokvica

△ 111

Segeti

Doberdò

Opacchiasella

Kostanjevica

118 Mt. Sei Busi

Redipuglia

Nova Vas

Temnica

Vermegliano

Doberdò Lake

Ronchi

Vojščica

△ 140

Sclo

△ 121

Jamiano

Monfalcone

Flondar

△ 146

Medeazza

Timavo

Hermada 323

0   1 mile   2   3   4

Duino

Sistiana

Adriatic

Trieste

364

Map 6
The Central and Upper Isonzo

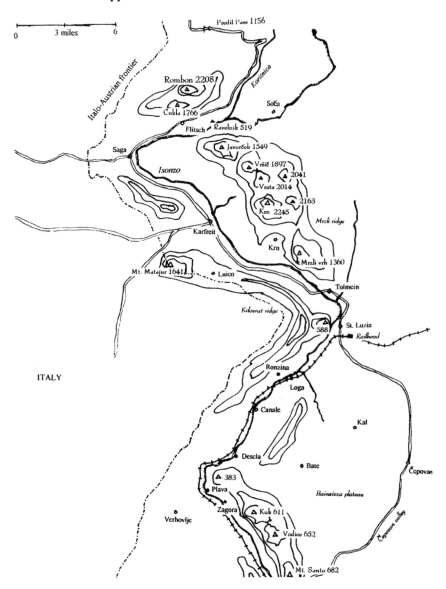

0   3 miles   6

Predil Pass 1156

Italo-Austrian frontier

Rombon 2208

Koritnica

Cukla 1766

Soča

Flitsch

Ravelnik 519

Saga

Javoršek 1549

Isonzo

Vršič 1897

2041

Vrata 2014

2163

Krn 2245

Mrzli ridge

Karfreit

Krn

Mt. Matajur 1641

Mrzli vrh 1360

Luico

Tolmein

Kolovrat ridge

St. Luzia

588

Railhead

ITALY

Ronzina

Loga

Canale

Kal

Čepovan

Descla

Bate

383

Plava

Bainsizza plateau

Zagora

Kuk 611

Čepovan valley

Verhovlje

Vodice 652

Mt. Santo 682

365

Map 7
Italian Territorial Gains, 1915–1917

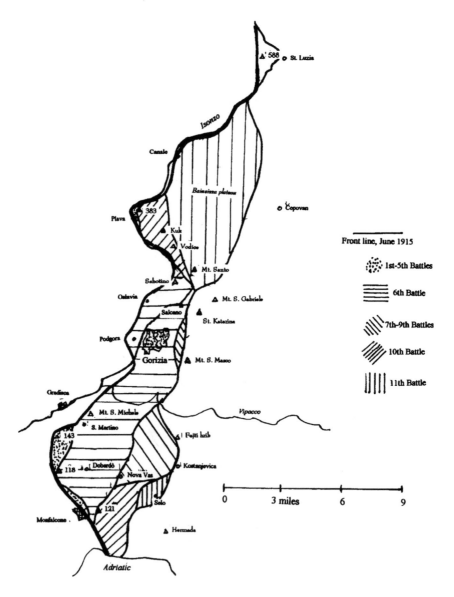

Front line, June 1915

1st-5th Battles

6th Battle

7th-9th Battles

10th Battle

11th Battle

0   3 miles   6   9

Map 8
The Isonzo since 1918

Carinthia (AUSTRIA)

Tarvisio

Rombon
△

Bovec

Isonzo/Soča

Sava

Kobarid

Tolmin

Cividale

Udine

Plave

★
Ljubljana

Venezia-Giulia

Tagliamento

Cormons

Gorizia/Nova Gorica

SLOVENIA

Vipava

Carso

ITALY

Trieste

Koper

Adriatic Sea

CROATIA

Rijeka

Austrian frontier
·—··—··—··—·
post-Second World War border
··········
post-Great War border
+ + + + + + + + + + + +

Istria

0   6   12   18   24   30 miles

Pula

Cres

A Note on Names and Pronunciations

The names of many cities, towns, and rivers mentioned in this book have changed several times since 1918, so finding a standard method to choose the form used has been difficult; this has been particularly trying with the multilingual Habsburg Empire. In general, I have referred to places on the Isonzo battlefield as they were known at the time to the Austrian Empire and Army. This often produces an eclectic mix of German, Italian, and Slovene terms (i.e., Vipacco rather than Vipava; Karfreit, not Kobarid or Caporetto). The current Isonzo place-names are found below. For the Habsburg Empire, I have by and large relied upon post-1918 names, except where this would lead to needless confusion; hence, Ljubljana rather than Laibach, but Lemberg, not L'viv, L'vov or Lwów, for instance. I have used English equivalents where they exist (Vienna, Prague, Cracow). I have also not translated several perhaps untranslatable military terms where I felt appropriate, such as *Bersaglieri, Arditi, Alpini,* or *Honvéd* and *Kaiserjäger.* Any mistakes I have made, or offense I have caused through apparent prejudice, are unintentional and mine alone.

This book therefore includes a diverse array of foreign names and terms. Although the pronunciation of Italian and German is well known in the English-speaking world, exact pronunciation of some names in other languages may be unfamiliar to readers. Therefore I have included this brief guide to assist the reader with pronouncing some names of places and persons encountered in this book.

Serbo-Croat and Slovene

c is pronounced	ts
č	tch (as in "catch")
ć (Serbo-Croat only)	like tch, but thinner and softer sound
dj (Serbo-Croat only)	similar to j (as in "jam")
j	y
lj	ly (as in "colliery")
š	sh
ž	zh

Hungarian

á, é, í, ó, ú	are pronounced as extended long vowels
ö, ü	are pronounced like German umlauted vowels (oe, ue)
c	ts
cs	ch
gy	a soft, extended d
s	sh
sz	s
zs	zh

GUIDE TO PLACE-NAMES

The Littoral

Current Place-name	*Alternate Place-names*
Banjšice (*Sl*)	Bainsizza (*I/G*)
Bovec (*Sl*)	Flitsch (*G*), Plezzo (*I*)
Čepovan (*Sl*)	Chiapovano (*I*)
Doberdò (*I*)	Doberdob (*Sl*)
Gorizia (*I*)	Görz (*G*), Gorica (*Sl*)
Kanal (*Sl*)	Canale (*I/G*)
Kobarid (*Sl*)	Karfreit (*G*), Caporetto (*I*)
Koper (*Sl*)	Capodistria (*I*)
Most na Soči (*Sl*)	St. Luzia (*G*)
Opatje Selo (*Sl*)	Opacchiasella (*I/G*)
Plave (*Sl*)	Plava (*I/G*)
Pula (*S-C*)	Pola (*I/G*)
Rijeka (*S-C*)	Fiume (*I/G*)

Sabotin (*Sl*)	Sabotino (*I/G*)
Soča (*Sl*)	Isonzo (*I/G*)
Solkan (*Sl*)	Salcano (*I/G*)
Tolmin (*Sl*)	Tolmein (*G*), Tolmino (*I*)
Trieste (*I*)	Trst (*Sl*), Triest (*G*)

Austria-Hungary

Bratislava (*Sk*)	Pozsony (*M*), Pressburg (*G*)
Brno (*Cz*)	Brünn (*G*)
Černivtsyi (*U*)	Czernowitz (*G*), Cernăuţi (*R*)
České Budějovice (*Cz*)	Budweis (*G*)
Cieszyn (*P*)	Teschen (*G*), Těšín (*Cz*)
Cluj (*R*)	Kolozsvár (*M*), Klausenburg (*G*)
Dubrovnik (*S-C*)	Ragusa (*I*)
Košice (*Sk*)	Kassa (*M*), Kaschau (*G*)
Ljubljana (*Sl*)	Laibach (*G*)
L'viv (*U*)	Lemberg (*G*), Lwów (*P*)
Novi Sad (*S-C*)	Újvidék (*M*), Neusatz (*G*)
Olomouc (*Cz*)	Olmütz (*G*)
Plzeň (*Cz*)	Pilsen (*G*)
Sibiu (*R*)	Nagyszeben (*M*)
Timişoara (*R*)	Temesvár (*M*)
Zadar (*S-C*)	Zara (*I*)

Guide: G—German, *I*—Italian, *M*—Magyar, *Sl*—Slovene, *S-C*—Serbo-Croat, *Cz*—Czech, *P*—Polish, *U*—Ukrainian, *Sk*—Slovak, *R*—Romanian

ESSAY ON SOURCES

This book is based on extensive research in a variety of sources in several languages. Although there are many historical works, principally in Italian and German, which touch on the Isonzo fighting, comparatively few exist which deal solely with the war on the Isonzo. Certainly the Isonzo remains very underreported compared to other costly Great War campaigns such as Verdun, the Somme, or Passchendaele. Literature has likewise neglected the Isonzo; the Carso and Rombon have not found either their *All Quiet on the Western Front* or their *Storm of Steel*. Even Hemingway's vivid *A Farewell to Arms*, which includes graphic descriptions of the Gorizia and Plava fronts, is far from autobiographical.

Much of the information in the text, particularly concerning the Austrian Army, is taken from primary sources found at the Österreichisches Staatsarchiv/Kriegsarchiv in Vienna. The impressive Viennese War Archive boasts a formidable collection of First World War documents. I have relied heavily on divisional records taken from the New Field Records section, as well as divisional and regimental accounts taken from the Battle Reports section. In addition, I have examined several special collections and the personnel files of many Austrian officers who served on the Isonzo. Austrian documents form the basis of my portrayal of the Habsburg Army.

Official histories of the war on the Isonzo reveal much interesting information, even allowing for their obvious prejudices. Vienna's weighty seven-volume account of the last Habsburg war, *Österreich-Ungarns letzter Krieg*, in many ways stands as a model of history-by-committee. To be sure, the authors of the Austrian work, former Habsburg General Staff officers, were careful to protect sacred reputations, especially that of Field Marshal Franz Conrad von Hötzendorf; no less, the Austrian volumes tend to blame ethnic disloyalty, rather than incompetent generalship, for battlefield defeats. That said, the Austrian official history is less biased than most works produced by ex-staff officers after the Great War; indeed, Basil Liddell Hart, no respecter of "official" viewpoints, considered the Austrian work to be "probably the best and most unbiased of the General Staff histories" to come out of World War One. Although *Österreich-Ungarns letzter Krieg* should be approached with a degree of caution, it remains indispensable for anyone studying the war on the Isonzo.

The Italian official history, *L'esercito italiano nella grande guerra, 1915–1918*, is just as ponderous as its Austrian counterpart, but considerably less serviceable. Most of the government-issue accounts emanating from belligerent armies after 1918 concealed as much as they revealed, and the Italian work is a notable example in this respect. Written during the heyday of Fascism, it is careful to neither criticize nor to disparage Italy's failed efforts on the Isonzo. Nationalism and glory replace wisdom and honesty in most chapters. The result is an official history that, although useful at times, must be read with a high degree of skepticism. The British official account, *Military Operations, Italy 1915–1919* (London, 1949), is better.

Many of the warnings about official histories apply just as strongly to memoirs. Although personal reminiscences are highly valuable to the historian, they must be read with great care. As a general rule, the level of mendacity increases as one progresses up the chain of command. Conrad's lengthy five-volume account of his years as Austria's top general, *Aus meiner Dienstzeit* (Vienna, 1921–1925), is always intriguing, if not always true. Similarly, Luigi Cadorna's apologia for his war work, *La guerra alla fronte italiane* (Milan, 1921), is self-serving to the point of dishonesty, precisely the kind of memoir one would expect from someone with an ego as all-consuming as Cadorna's. Luigi Capello's belabored explanation of his innocence in the disastrous Twelfth Battle of the Isonzo, *Caporetto: Perchè* (Turin, 1967), ultimately conceals more than it reveals and fails entirely to convince.

Among senior generals' memoirs, Alfred Krauss's account of his I Corps's victory at Caporetto, *Das Wunder von Karfreit* (Munich, 1926), is perhaps the most interesting. It is detailed and informative, even if tempered by the author's German nationalist viewpoint. Regrettably Field Marshal Svetozar Boroević left no memoir of his momentous years on the Isonzo. Unsurpassed for gaining an insider's view of Austria's army at war, on the Isonzo and elsewhere, is the often critical *Unser österreichisch-ungarischer Bundesgenosse im Weltkrieg* (Berlin, 1920), by August von Cramon, chief Prussian representative at the Austrian High Command.

Lower ranking soldiers also wrote accounts of their service on the Isonzo. Foremost among them is *Il mio diario di guerra* (Milan, 1922), penned by the ex-*Bersaglieri* sergeant Benito Mussolini. The war diary includes much bravado and myth-making, as befitted the future *Duce*, but the core remains intriguing. Mussolini frankly recalls many unpleasant hours on the Isonzo from the viewpoint of the *fantaccino;* for this reason alone it deserves attention. Another soldier's account, *Caporetto: Note sulla ritirata di un fante della III armata* (Gorizia, 1987) by Mario Puccini, a reprint of a 1918 memoir, includes unforgettable portrayals of the Italian Army's bizarre retreat across Friulia after the Twelfth Battle. Shortly before the Second World War, Erwin Rommel wrote his account of his famous conquest of Mt. Matajur; it appears in his *Infanterie greift an* (Potsdam, 1937). It offers a fascinating glimpse of the Great War through the eyes of a superefficient junior infantry officer.

Because the Isonzo front has been so unjustly neglected by historians, there are comparatively few biographies that illuminate the lives of the leading soldiers who fought there. David Fraser's *Knight's Cross* (London, 1993) is a very readable account of Erwin Rommel's long career; the Twelfth Battle of the Isonzo is treated in a relatively brief but thorough manner. Pietro Pieri and Giorgio Rochat profiled the life of one of Italy's senior soldiers in their *Pietro Badoglio* (Turin, 1974), which explains a great deal about both Badoglio and the Italian Army during the Great War. Gianni Rocca's *Cadorna* (Milan, 1985) is less interesting and revealing than its subject demands. There is only one, very brief biography of Boroević, Ernest Bauer's *Der Löwe vom Isonzo* (Graz, 1985), an overwhelmingly sympathetic account of this controversial general. Bosco awaits his definitive biographer. Another regular on the Isonzo is profiled in Alfredo Bonadeo's recent *D'Annunzio and the Great War* (London, 1995). Bonadeo explains much about this fascinating warrior-poet, his motivations, and his militantly heroic exploits during the war with Austria.

Unit histories are another potential source for military historians, although one fraught with many potential complications. Inevitably the "regimental history" style, although sometimes offering a rich vein of otherwise lost knowledge, more often replaces balance with boasting. After all, no unit likes to admit a defeat. However, there are some serviceable unit histories available that deal with the terrible war on the Isonzo in admirable detail; the more recently written ones are usually better. Several of these are found in the bibliography. The chapters of this book draw upon a diverse mix of sources. Some of the best of them are mentioned below, for the benefit of future researchers.

THE ROAD TO WAR

Chapter 1

For a general overview of Italy on the eve of the Great War, including the irredentist question, see Christopher Seton-Watson's sympathetic *Italy from Liberalism to Fascism, 1870–1925* (London, 1967); or, in a more general way,

Dennis Mack Smith's *Italy: A Modern History* (Ann Arbor, MI, 1969). The sad state of Italy's armed forces going into the First World War is chronicled admirably in John Gooch's *Army, State and Society in Italy, 1870–1915* (New York, 1989), which focuses on civil-military relations; the same author's "Italy Before 1915: The Quandary of the Vulnerable," in *Knowing One's Enemies* (Princeton, NJ, 1984), goes a long way to explaining the army's confusion during the first year of the Great War. Rome's slow slide to war in pursuit of *sacro egoismo* is recounted briefly in William Renzi's "Italy's Neutrality and Entrance into the Great War: A Reexamination," *American Historical Review* (June 1968). A view of Trieste before the war, especially its vibrant literary culture, is found in John Gatt-Rutter's *Italo Svevo: A Double Life* (Oxford, 1988).

Chapter 2

The best short explanation of the Habsburg Empire in its last decades is Alan Sked's *The Decline and Fall of the Habsburg Empire, 1815–1918* (New York, 1989); for a longer version, with special attention to the nationalities question, see Robert Kann's excellent two-volume *The Multinational Empire* (New York, 1952). A revealing, more skeptical viewpoint is found in Oskar Jászi's *The Dissolution of the Habsburg Monarchy* (Chicago, 1929); the comments by the author, a great Hungarian sociologist, on the Habsburg Army are highly interesting. Austrian military questions are detailed in Gunther Rothenberg's masterful *Army of Francis Joseph* (West Lafayette, IN, 1976), unquestionably the definitive one-volume work on the subject. A broad overview of military-political matters up to the war is Christoph Allmayer-Beck's "Die bewaffnete Macht in Staat und Gesellschaft," in *Die Habsburgermonarchie: Bd.V.* (Vienna, 1987). The unique multinational army is recalled vividly through its officer corps in István Deák's *Beyond Nationalism* (New York, 1990). The best quick review of Austria's odd, ill-equipped army before its last war remains Norman Stone's provocative "Army and Society in the Habsburg Monarchy, 1900–1914" in *Past and Present* (April 1966). The empire's failed and costly war effort is recounted superbly in a book by an eminent Austrian historian, Manfried Rauchensteiner's *Der Tod des Doppeladlers* (Graz, 1994), the best single-volume account in any language. Budapest's troublesome political machinations during the Great War are reviewed in József Galántai's *Hungary in the First World War* (Budapest, 1989).

1915

Chapters 3–6

A few books recount the Isonzo fighting as a whole. Among more recent works, the best is *Isonzo 1915–1917: Krieg ohne Wiederkehr* (Bassano, 1993), by Walther Schaumann and Peter Schubert, even though its pictures are better than the rather formulaic text. Pietro Maravigna's *Le undici offensive sull'Isonzo* (Rome, 1929) is both biased and dated; the same can be said of Fritz Weber's colorful *Menschenmauer am Isonzo* (Leipzig, 1932), as well as his three short works, *Isonzo 1915, 1916*, and *1917*, which tell the Austrian point of view. Much better is Antonio Sema's two-volume *La grande guerra sul fronte dell'Isonzo* (Gorizia, 1997), which also has some good photos. The Slovene side of things is told rather dryly in Ivan Hmelak's *Soška fronta* (Ljubljana, 1968), the first Slovene popular history of the Isonzo battles, and better in Vladimir Gradnik's *Krvavo Posočje* (Koper, 1977), and especially in Vasja Klavora's extremely detailed *Plavi križ: Soška fronta: Bovec: 1915–1917* (Koper, 1993), which deals with the war on the upper Isonzo (and is available in German translation). The Magyar viewpoint can be found in an article by Márton Farkas about the Hungarian struggle on the Carso, "Doberdo: The Habsburg Army on the Italian Front, 1915–1916," in *War and Society in East Central Europe*, vol. 19 (New York, 1985); or, in Magyar, in László Szabó's *Doberdo, Isonzo, Tirol* (Budapest, 1980). A moving war memoir of a Hungarian soldier on the Carso, serving in Archduke Joseph's VII Corps during the terrible fight for the "stony sea" of Doberdo, is Joseph Gál's bitter *In Death's Fortress* (New York, 1991).

The bloody fighting at Plava in 1915 is recounted in Gustavo Reisoli's *La conquista di Plava* (Rome, 1932); although the author was the commander of the II Corps in the fighting for Hill 383, this patriotic book is nevertheless revealing about the determination of Austrian soldiers to defend the Isonzo line. Italian military shortcomings throughout the war are dealt with frankly in John Gooch's article, "Italy During the First World War" in *Military Effectiveness*; vol. 1, *The First World War* (Boston, 1988), a very good summary of Italy's martial weaknesses, especially in leadership. The complex and contested issue of nationalities in the Austrian Army, perhaps the greatest historical debate about Habsburg arms at war, is explained succinctly in Rudolf Kiszling's "Das Nationalitätenproblem in Habsburgs Wehrmacht 1848–1918," in *Der Donauraum* (1959). A longer and far more detailed evaluation of this vexing question is found in the Viennese *Kriegsarchiv* in *Nachlass* Robert Nowak, B/726, "Die Klammer des Reichs: Das Verhalten der elf Nationalitäten in der k.u.k. Wehrmacht 1914–1918," an exhaustive multivolume recounting of the nationalities question in the wartime Habsburg military.

1916

Chapters 7–9

The high point of the 1916 fighting on the Isonzo was the Sixth Battle, particularly the Italian capture of Gorizia. This great Italian victory is explained in an official account, *La conquista di Gorizia* (Rome, 1925) by Francesco Zingales. It contains excellent information about Italian dispositions, but ought to be approached carefully. More even-handed is Pietro Pieri and Giorgio Rochat's *Pietro Badoglio* (Turin, 1974), which explains its subject's meteoric rise and role in the planning of the triumphant Sixth Battle. Conrad's daring but ultimately failed South Tyrolean offensive of May–June 1916, one of the foremost what-ifs of the Great War, is explained in two main works: Kurt Peball's "Führungsfragen der öst.-ung. Südtiroloffensive im Jahre 1916," in *Mitteilungen des österreichischen Staatsarchives* 31 (1978), and Gerhard Artl's *Die österreichisch-ungarische Südtiroloffensive* 1916 (Vienna, 1983).

1917

Chapters 10–12

The Tenth Battle of the Isonzo is elucidated from the Italian viewpoint in Rodolfo Pinchetti's biased but informative *Isonzo 1917: Kuk-Bainsizza, Carso, Carzano* (Milan, 1934). Cadorna's strategy and alternative Allied proposals are covered in *1917: Lubiana o Trieste?* (Milan, 1986) by Giulio Primicerj. Mario Silvestri's *Isonzo 1917* (Milan, 1971) is a serviceable overview of Italian efforts during this pivotal year. The rise of the *arditi* and the assault troops' enduring military and political legacies are explained in Giorgio Rochat's solid *Gli arditi della grande guerra* (Milan, 1981). Enrico Caviglia, whose assault divisions broke the Austrian line on the upper Bainsizza at the beginning of the Eleventh Battle, produced *La battaglia della Bainsizza* (Milan, 1930). This book, like all Italian accounts penned during the Fascist era, minimizes Italian casualty figures and presents an overly favorable view of Italian arms, but is interesting all the same.

The Twelfth Battle of the Isonzo and the epic Austrian victory that followed have received more attention than all other aspects of the Isonzo fighting combined. The main English-language account remains *The Battle of Caporetto* (Philadelphia, 1966) by the British military historian Cyril Falls; his work is flawed—like nearly everything written in English about Caporetto, it gives too much credit to the Germans—but worth reading. The Austrian achievement on the upper Isonzo in late October 1917 is chronicled carefully in Alfred Krauss's aforementioned memoir, *Das Wunder von Karfreit*. A noteworthy Italian investigation of the disaster is Mario Silvestri's *Caporetto: Una battaglia e un enigma* (Milan, 1984). Also revealing is *La relazione Caraciocchi sulla battaglia di Caporetto* (Salerno, 1982) by Piero Astengo, which chronicles and explains the collapse of the 2nd Army on the upper Isonzo in admirable detail. Erwin Rommel's daring exploits on Kolovrat ridge are recounted both in his *Infanterie greift an* and in David Fraser's biography, *Knight's Cross*. An interesting English-language memoir that includes much about the Caporetto defeat is *With British Guns in Italy* (London, 1919) by Hugh Dalton, a Royal Artillery subaltern who witnessed the disaster unfolding.

1918

Chapters 13, 14

Austria's alarming material decline, rising domestic turbulence, and military disorder during the last year of the war are explained masterfully by Richard G. Plaschka in *Cattaro-Prag: Revolte und Revolution* (Graz, 1963), and, with Horst Haselsteiner and Arnold Suppan, in *Innere Front* (Vienna, 1974). The Piave offensive in June 1918 is detailed from the Austrian perspective in Peter Fiala's frank *Die letzte Offensive Altösterreichs* (Boppard am Rhein, 1967), and from the official Italian side in English translation in *The Battle of the Piave* (London, 1919). Emperor Karl's incompetent efforts at secret diplomacy in 1918, and their baleful consequences for his empire, are covered by the eminent historian Robert Kann in *Die Sixtusaffäre und die geheimen Friedensverhandlungen Österreich-Ungarns im ersten Weltkrieg* (Munich, 1966). Mussolini's wartime activities are dealt with intelligently in a biography of Margherita Sarfatti, his longtime mistress, by Philip Cannistraro and Brian Sullivan: *Il Duce's Other Woman* (New York, 1993). Hemingway's nebulous war record, the subject of much myth-making, mostly by "Papa" himself, is laid bare in *Hemingway's First War: The Making of A Farewell to Arms* (Princeton, NJ, 1976) by Michael S. Reynolds.

A revealing account of Austria's last battle can be found in Otto von Berndt's memoir, *Letzter Kampf und Ende der 29.ID* (Reichenberg, 1928); similarly, the last days on the Piave, seen by a lower ranking German-Bohemian soldier, are recounted in Karl Bergmann's *Am Niemandslande* (Reichenberg, 1930). The Allied perspective is explained well in E. C. Crosse's *The Defeat of Austria as Seen by the 7th Division* (London, 1919), which recounts the experiences of one of the British divisions that broke the Piave line at Papadopoli. Last, Italy's deceitful and deadly grab of Austrian prisoners at the war's end is elucidated in Emil Ratzenhofer's "Der Waffenstillstand von Villa Giusti und die Gefangnahme Hunderttausender," in *Ergänzungsheft 2 zum Werke ÖUlK* (Vienna, 1932); or, in English, in R. Wayne Hanks, "Vae Victis! The Austro-Hungarian Armeeoberkommando and the Armistice of Villa Giusti," in *Austrian History Yearbook* 14 (1978).

EPILOGUE

Chapters 15, 16

Italian postwar diplomacy at Versailles, the question of Fiume and Dalmatia, and the complex origins of the notion of Italy's "mutilated victory" are explored thoroughly in H. James Burgwyn's *The Legend of the "Mutilated Victory"* (Westport, CT, 1989). The intricate details of border revision, Italian administration of the Littoral, and Germany's "Habsburg revenge" in 1943–1945 are explained lucidly in Dennison Rusinow's *Italy's Austrian Heritage, 1919–1946* (London, 1969), an intriguing overview of an often overlooked subject. Information about the creation and development of Nova Gorica, up to the 1991 Slovene war for independence, can be found in the first chapter of Mark Thompson's solid *A Paper House: The Ending of Yugoslavia* (London, 1992).

Few guides to the Isonzo region mention the war in any detail. By far the best is Petra Svoljšak's *Die Isonzofront* (Ljubljana, 1994), which is thin but clearly written and well put together, and includes excellent photographs: a must for the tourist. There is one very interesting Italian guidebook, the haunting *Sentieri di guerra: Le trincee sul Carso oggi* (Trieste, 1991) by Lucio Fabi, which boasts first-rate photographs and maps of the Carso's limestone battlefields as they were more than eighty years ago and are today.

BIBLIOGRAPHY

UNPUBLISHED SOURCES

Österreichisches Staatsarchiv/Kriegsarchiv (Vienna)

Neue Feld Akten: k.u.k. 12.ID, 17.ID, 29.ID, 55.ID, k.k. 21.SchD.

Gefechtsberichte: k.u.k. I.Korps, XVI.Korps, 12.ID, 17.ID, IR.3, IR.7, bh.IR.2, bh.IR.4, k.k.21.SchD, KSchR.III.

Sammlung Balaban: k.u.k. 12.ID, 17.ID, 29.ID, 55.ID, 57.ID, 58.ID, k.k.21.SchD.

Qualifikationsliste: FML Otto Ritter von Berndt, FM Svetozar Boroević von Bojna, Mjr. Emil Fey, FML Karl Gelb von Siegesstern, FM Erzherzog Joseph von Habsburg-Lothringen, GdI Alfred Krauss, Obstlt. Leo Kuchynka, FML Aurel LeBeau, FML Guido Novak von Arienti, Mjr. Eugen Redl, FML Felix Prinz zu Schwarzenberg, Obstlt. Gustav Sonnewend, GdI Erwin Zeidler von Görz.

Nachlass Robert Nowak: B/726, Nr.1/I, II, III: "Die Klammer des Reichs: Das Verhalten der elf Nationalitäten in der k.u.k. Wehrmacht 1914–1918."

Public Record Office (London)

War Office

106/1513, C17/477, 7.7.17: "Evidence of war-weariness and desire for a separate peace in Austria-Hungary."

106/1513, Very Secret, MO2 Gen. Staff, 24.6.17: "Causes of the lack of success in the recent Italian operations on the Carso."

DISSERTATIONS

Hanks, Ronald Wayne. "The End of an Institution: The Austro-Hungarian Army in Italy, 1918." Ph.D. diss., Rice University, 1977.

Hecht, Rudolf. "Fragen zur Heeresergänzung der gesamten bewaffneten Macht Österreich-Ungarns während des Ersten Weltkrieges." Ph.D. diss., University of Vienna, 1969.

Schindler, John Richard. "A Hopeless Struggle: The Austro-Hungarian Army and Total War, 1914–1918." Ph.D. diss., McMaster University, 1995.

MEMOIRS

Arz von Straussenberg, Arthur. *Zur Geschichte des großen Krieges 1914 bis 1918* (Vienna, 1924).

Bardolff, Carl von. *Soldat im alten Österreich: Erinnerungen aus meinem Leben* (Jena, 1938).

Barnett, George H. *With the 48th Division in Italy* (London, 1923).

Bergmann, Karl. *Am Niemandslande: Fronterleben bei einem sudetendeutschen Regimente* (Reichenberg, 1930).

Berndt, Otto von. *Letzter Kampf und Ende der 29.ID.: Meine Erinnerungen aus der Zeit des Zusammenbruches* (Reichenberg, 1928).

Blasković, Pero. *Sa Bošnjacima u svjetskom ratu* (Belgrade, 1939).

Broucek, Peter (ed.). *Ein General im Zwielicht: Die Erinnerungen Edmund Glaises von Horstenau*, 2 vols. (Vienna, 1980).

Cadorna, Luigi. *La guerra alla fronte italiane* (Milan, 1921).

Capello, Luigi. *Caporetto: perchè* (Turin, 1967).

Caviglia, Enrico. *La battaglia della Bainsizza* (Milan, 1930).

Conrad von Hötzendorf, Franz. *Aus meiner Dienstzeit 1906–1918*, 5 vols. (Vienna, 1921–1925).

Cramon, August von. *Unser österreichisch-ungarischer Bundesgenosse im Weltkrieg* (Berlin, 1920).

Crosse, E. C. *The Defeat of Austria as Seen by the 7th Division* (London, 1919).

Dalton, Hugh. *With British Guns in Italy: A Tribute to Italian Achievement* (London, 1919).

Fadini, Francesco. *Caporetto dalla parte del vincitore: Il general Otto von Below e il suo diario inedito* (Milan, 1992).

Frescura, Attilio. *Diario di un imboscato* (Milan, 1981).

Fritz, Hans. *Bosniak.* (Waidhofen a.d. Ybbs, 1931).

Gál, Joseph. *In Death's Fortress* (New York, 1991).

Goldsmid, Cyril H. *Diary of a Liaison Officer in Italy 1918* (London, 1920).

Habsburg, Joseph von. *A világháború amilyennek én láttam* (Budapest, 1928).

Krauss, Alfred. *Die Ursachen unserer Niederlage* (Munich, 1920).

———. *Das Wunder von Karfreit: Im besonderen der Durchbruch bei Flitsch und die Bezwingung des Tagliamento* (Munich, 1926).

Martinek, Rudolf. *Kriegstagebuch eines Artillerie-Offiziers* (Vienna, 1975).

Mussolini, Benito. *Il mio diario di guerra (1915–1917)* (Milan, 1922).

Novottny, Karl. *Die 29.ID in der Juni-Piaveschlacht 1918* (Reichenberg, 1929).

Powell, E. Alexander. *With the Italians and the Allies in the West* (London, 1917).

Puccini, Mario. *Caporetto: Note sulla ritirata di un fante della III armata* (Gorizia, 1987).

Rommel, Erwin. *Infanterie greift an* (Potsdam, 1937).

Ronge, Max. *Kriegs- und Industriespionage: Zwölf Jahre Kundschaftsdienst* (Zürich-Leipzig-Vienna, 1930).

————. *Meister der Spionage* (Vienna, 1935).

Trenker, Luis. *Sperrfort Rocca Alta* (Munich, 1982).

Triska, Jan F. *The Great War's Forgotten Front: A Soldier's Diary and a Son's Reflections* (New York, 1998).

Váchal, Josef. *Malíř na fronte: Soča a Italie 1917–18* (Prague, 1996).

Vitalis, Alojz. *Doberdob, slovenskih fantov grob* (Celje, 1936).

Zanantoni, Eduard. *Die Geschichte der 29.ID im Weltkrieg 1914–1918* (Reichenberg, 1929).

UNIT HISTORIES

Ajtay, Endre. *A volt cs. és kir. 46. gyalogezred világháborús története 1914–1918* (Szeged, 1933).

Alpini: Storia e leggenda, 2 vols. (Milan, n.d.).

Apostata, Dr. (pseud.) *Pětatřicátníci ve světové válce a na Slovensku* (Plzeň, 1921).

Das bosnisch-herzegovinische Infanterie-Regiment Nr. 2 im Weltkrieg 1914 bis 1918 (Vienna, 1970).

Caricat! Volòire!: 150 anni di artiglieria a cavallo (Milan, 1981).

Chirra, Giuliano. *Trattare ka frates, kertare ke inimicos: Il cammino dei Sardi nella Grande Guerra* (Sassari, 1996).

A cs. és kir. 34. magyar gyalogezred története 1734–1918 (Budapest, 1937).

"Dreihundert Jahre IR.7: Das Jägerbataillon 25." *Das Rote Barett* (1991).

Feuerbereit! Kriegsalbum des Feldartillerieregiments Nr. 104, Wien (Vienna, 1919).

Finke, Edmund. *K.(u.)K. Hoch- und Deutschmeister: "222 Jahre für Kaiser und Reich."* (Graz, 1978).

Flaischen, Hugo. *Die württembergischen Regimenter im Weltkrieg 1914–1918, Vol. 2, Die württembergische Gebirgs-Artillerie 1915–1918* (Stuttgart, 1920).

Fois, Giuseppina. *Storia della Brigata Sassari* (Venice, 1981).

Hegenbarth, Hans. *Furchtlos und treu: 300 Jahre Infanterie-Regiment Nr. 27* (Graz, 1982).

Hoen, Max. *Geschichte des ehemaligen Egerländer IR. Nr. 73* (Vienna, 1939).

Hubka, Gustav von. *Geschichte des k.u.k. IR. Graf v. Lacy Nr. 22 vom Jahre 1902 bis zu seiner Auflösung*, 2 vols. (Vienna, 1938).

IR. 94 im Weltkriege (Reichenberg, 1929).

Lépés, Gyözö, and Artur Mátéfy. *A cs. és kir. 39. gyalogezred világháborús története* (Debrecen, 1939).

Linzer Hessen 1733–1936 (Linz, 1937).

Matčič Ivan. *Skozi plamene prve svetovne vojni* (Ljubljana, 1966).

Motzo, Leonardo. *Gli intrepidi Sardi della Brigata Sassari* (Cagliari, 1980).

Rasero, Aldo. *Tridentina Avanti! Storia di una divisione alpina* (Milan, 1982).
Rochat, Giorgio. *Gli arditi della grande guerra: Origini, battaglie e miti* (Milan, 1981).
Sandilands, H. R. *The 23rd Division 1914–1919* (London, 1925).
Schachinger, Werner. *Die Bosniaken kommen: Elitetruppe in der k.u.k. Armee 1879–1918* (Graz, 1989).
61 in Waffen: Kriegsalbum des k.u.k. IR. 61, 1914–1917 (Budapest, 1918).
Storia del 3. Reggimento bersaglieri (1861–1975). (Brindisi, 1980).
Vogelsang, Ludwig von. *Das steirische IR. Nr. 47 im Weltkrieg* (Graz, 1932).
Wagner, Richard. *Geschichte des ehemaligen Schützen-Regiment Nr. 6* (Karlsbad, 1932).

OFFICIAL SOURCES

Bardolff, Carl von. *Der Militär-Maria Theresien-Orden: 1914–1918*, 2 vols. (Vienna, 1943).
The Battle of the Piave (June 15–23, 1918) (trans. M. Pritchard-Agnetti) (Italian *Comando Supremo*; reprinted London, 1919).
Berkó, István. *A magyar királyi honvédség története 1868–1918* (Budapest, 1928).
della Volpe, Nicola. *Esercito e propaganda nella grande guerra (1915–1918)* (Rome, 1989).
Edmonds, James. *History of the Great War: Military Operations, Italy 1915–1919* (London, 1949).
Ehnl, Max. "Die öst.-ung. Wehrmacht nach Aufbau, Gliederung, Friedensgarnison, Einteilung und nationaler Zusammensetzung im Sommer 1914." *Ergänzungsheft 9 zum Werke ÖUlK* (Vienna, 1934).
L'esercito e i suoi corpi, vols.1, 3 (Rome, 1971).
L'esercito italiano nella grande guerra, 1915–1918 (Rome, 1927).
Franek, Fritz. "Die Entwicklung der öst.-ung. Wehrmacht in den ersten zwei Kriegsjahren." *Ergänzungsheft 5 zum Werke ÖUlK* (Vienna, 1933).
———. "Probleme der Organization im ersten Kriegsjahre." *Ergänzungsheft 1 zum Werke ÖUlK* (Vienna, 1930).
Gallinari, Vincenzo. *L'esercito italiano nel primo dopoguerra 1918–1920* (Rome, 1980).
Glingenbrunner, Franz. "Intendanz im Gebirgskriege." *Ergänzungsheft 8 zum Werke ÖUlK* (Vienna, 1933).
Österreich-Ungarns letzter Krieg, 7 vols. and 7 supp. vols. (E. Glaise von Horstenau, ed.) (Vienna, 1930–1938).
Pieri, Piero. *La prima guerra mondiale 1914–1918: Problemi di storia militare* (Rome, 1986).
Ratzenhofer, Emil. "Verlustkalkül für den Karpathenwinter 1915." In *Ergänzungsheft 1 zum Werke ÖUlK* (Vienna, 1930).
———. "Der Waffenstillstand von Villa Giusti und die Gefangnahme Hundert-tausender." In *Ergänzungsheft 2 zum Werke ÖUlK*. (Vienna, 1932).
Reisoli, Gustavo. *La conquista di Plava* (Rome, 1932).

Schäfer, Hugo. "Die Kriegspläne Italiens gegen Österreich-Ungarn." *Ergänzungsheft 2 zum Werke ÖUlK* (Vienna, 1932).

Schäger, Albin. *Vaterländische Vorträge für Soldaten* (Vienna, 1918).

Veith, Georg. "Die Isonzoverteidigung." *Ergänzungsheft 3 zum Werke ÖUlK* (Vienna, 1932).

Wrede, Alphons. *Geschichte der k.u.k. Wehrmacht: Die Regimenter, Corps, Branchen und Anstalten von 1618 bis Ende des XIX. Jahrhunderts* 5 vols. (Vienna, 1898–1903).

Zingales, Francesco. *La conquista di Gorizia* (Rome, 1925).

UNOFFICIAL SOURCES

Acerbi, Enrico. *Le truppe da montagna dell'esercito austro-ungarico nella Grande Guerra 1914–1918* (Vicenza, 1991).

Alexander, Alfred. *The Hanging of Wilhelm Oberdank.* (London, 1977).

Allmayer-Beck, Christoph. "AOK und 'Armeefrage' im Jahre 1918" *Österreichische Militärische Zeitschrift* (1968).

———. "Die bewaffnete Macht in Staat und Gesellschaft." *Die Habsburgermonarchie 1848–1918*, vol. 5, *Die bewaffnete Macht* (A. Wandruszka and P. Urbanitsch, eds.) (Vienna, 1987).

———. "Heeresreorganization vor 50 Jahren." *Österreichische Militärische Zeitschrift* (1967).

———. *Die k.(u.)k. Armee 1948–1918* (Munich, 1974).

Angetter, Daniela Claudia. *Dem Tod geweiht und doch gerettet: Die Sanitätsversorgung am Isonzo und in den Dolomiten 1915–1918* (Frankfurt/Main, 1995).

Ara, Angelo. "The 'Cultural Soul' and the 'Merchant Soul': Trieste Between Italian and Austrian Identity." In *The Habsburg Legacy: National Identity in Historical Perspective* (R. Robertson and E. Timms, eds.) (Edinburgh, 1994).

Artl, Gerhard. *Die österreichisch-ungarische Südtiroloffensive 1916* (Vienna, 1983).

Astengo, Piero. *La relazione Caraciocchi sulla battaglia di Caporetto* (Salerno, 1982).

Auffenberg-Komarów, Moriz. *Aus Österreich-Ungarns Teilnahme am Weltkriege* (Berlin-Vienna, 1920).

Banac, Ivo. " 'Karl Has Become a Comijadji': The Croatian Disturbances of Autumn 1918." *Slavonic and East European Review* 70, no. 2 (April 1992).

Bauer, Ernest. *Der Löwe vom Isonzo: Feldmarschall Svetozar Boroević de Bojna* (Graz, 1985).

Bertoldi, Silvio. *Badoglio* (Milan, 1982).

Bonadeo, Alfredo. *D'Annunzio and the Great War* (London, 1995).

Broucek, Peter. "Aus den Erinnerungen eines Kundschaftsoffiziers in Tirol 1914–1918." *Mitteilungen des österreichischen Staatarchives* 33 (1980).

Brusatti, Alois, and Gottfried Heindl. *Julius Raab: Eine Biographie in Einzeldarstellungen* (Linz, 1986).

Burgwyn, H. James. *The Legend of the "Mutilated Victory": Italy, the Great War, and the Paris Peace Conference, 1915–1919* (Westport, CT, 1989).

Cannistraro, Philip V., and Brian R. Sullivan. *Il Duce's Other Woman* (New York, 1993).

Cavigioli, Riccardo. *L'Aviazione austro-ungarica sulla fronte italiane 1915–1918* (Milan, 1934).

Cervi, Mario. *Caporetto: I documenti terribili* (Milan, 1974).

Croce, Benedetto. *L'Italia dal 1914 al 1918: Pagine sulla guerra* (Bari, 1965).

Cross, Tim. *The Lost Voices of World War I: An International Anthology of Writers, Poets and Playwrights* (London, 1988).

Czermak, Wilhelm. *In deinem Lager war Österreich: Die Österreichisch-ungarische Armee, wie man sie nicht kennt* (Breslau, 1938).

Deák, István. *Beyond Nationalism: A Social and Political History of the Habsburg Officer Corps, 1868–1918* (New York, 1990).

———. "Pacesetters of Integration: Jewish Officers in the Habsburg Monarchy." *East European Politics and Societies* 3, no. 1 (Winter 1989).

Destrée, Jules, and Richard Dupierrieux. *To the Italian Armies* (London, 1917).

Dizionario biographico degli italiani (Rome, 1960).

Donia, Robert. *Islam Under the Double Eagle: The Muslims of Bosnia-Hercegovina, 1878–1914* (New York, 1981).

Elliott, Lawrence. *Little Flower: The Life and Times of Fiorello LaGuardia* (New York, 1983).

Fabi, Lucio. *Gente di trincea: La grande guerra sul Carso e sull'Isonzo* (Milan, 1994).

———. *Sentieri di guerra: Le trincee sul Carso oggi* (Trieste, 1991).

Falls, Cyril. *The Battle of Caporetto* (Philadelphia, 1966).

Farkas, Márton. "Doberdo: The Habsburg Army on the Italian Front, 1915–1916." *War and Society in East Central Europe*, vol. 19, *World War I* (B. Király, N. Dreisziger, and A. Nofi, eds.) (New York, 1985).

———. *Katonai összeomlás és forradalom 1918-ban. A hadsereg szerepe az Osztrák-Magyar Monarchia felbomlásában* (Budapest, 1969).

———. "Die politische Erziehungsarbeit in der Armee am Ende des ersten Weltkrieges." In *Die Auflösung des Habsburgerreiches: Zusammenbruch und Neuorientierung im Donauraum*. (R. G. Plaschka and K. Mack, eds.) (Vienna, 1970).

Fejtö, François. *Requiem pour un Empire défunt: Histoire de la destruction de l'Autriche-Hongrie* (Paris, 1988).

Fiala, Peter. *Die letzte Offensive Altösterreichs: Führungsprobleme und Führerverantwortlichkeit bei der öst.-ung. Offensive in Venetien, Juni 1918* (Boppard am Rhein, 1967).

Fraser, David. *Knight's Cross: A Life of Field Marshal Erwin Rommel* (London, 1993).

Gabriel, Erich. "Die wichtigsten Waffen der öst.-ung. Armee 1918." *Österreichische Militärische Zeitschrift* (1968).

Galántai, József. *Hungary in the First World War* (Budapest, 1989).

———. *Der österreichisch-ungarische Dualismus, 1867–1918.* (Budapest-Vienna, 1990).

Gallian, Otto. *Der österreichische Soldat im Weltkrieg: Die Legende vom "Bruder Schnürschuh"* (Graz, 1933).

Glaise-Horstenau, Edmund von. *Die Katastrophe: Die Zertrümmerung Österreich-Ungarns und das Werden der Nachfolgestaaten* (Vienna, 1929).

Gatt-Rutter, John. *Italo Svevo: A Double Life* (Oxford, 1988).

Gooch, John. *Army, State and Society in Italy, 1870–1915* (New York, 1989).

———. "Italy before 1915: The Quandary of the Vulnerable." In *Knowing One's Enemies: Intelligence Assessment Before the Two World Wars* (E. May, ed.) (Princeton, NJ, 1984).

———. "Italy During the First World War." In *Military Effectiveness*, vol. 1, *The First World War* (A. Millett and W. Murray, eds.) (Boston, 1988).

Gradnik, Vladimir. *Krvavo Posočje*. (Koper, 1977).

Griesser-Pečar, Tamara. *Die Mission Sixtus: Österreichs Friedenversuch im Ersten Weltkrieg* (Vienna, 1988).

Gudmundsson, Bruce I. *Stormtroop Tactics: Innovation in the German Army, 1914–1918* (New York, 1989).

Halpern, Paul G. *A Naval History of World War I* (Annapolis, MD, 1994).

Hanks, R. Wayne. "Vae Victis! The Austro-Hungarian Armeeoberkommando and the Armistice of Villa Giusti." *Austrian History Yearbook* 14 (1978).

Hartcup, Guy. *The War of Invention: Scientific Developments, 1914–1918* (London, 1988).

Hebert, Günther. *Das Alpenkorps: Organization und Einsatz einer Gebirgstruppe im Ersten Weltkrieg* (Boppard am Rhein, 1988).

Herwig, Holger. "Disjointed Allies: Coalition Warfare in Berlin and Vienna, 1914." *Journal of Military History* 54 (July 1990).

Hmelak, Ivan. *Soška fronta* (Ljubljana, 1968).

Hrvatski biografski leksikon (Zagreb, 1989).

Hrvatski narodni preporod u Dalmaciji i Istri (Zagreb, 1969).

Jászi, Oskar. *The Dissolution of the Habsburg Monarchy* (Chicago, 1929).

Jedlicka, Ludwig. "Die Tradition der Wehrmacht Österreich-Ungarns und die Nachfolgestaaten" *Österreichische Militärische Zeitschrift* (1968).

Jeřabek, Rudolf. *Potiorek: General im Schatten vom Sarajevo* (Graz, 1991).

Kann, Robert. *Die Sixtusaffäre und die geheimen Friedensverhandlungen Österreich-Ungarns im ersten Weltkrieg* (Munich, 1966).

Kennett, Lee. *The First Air War 1914–1918* (New York, 1991).

Kerchnawe, Hugo. *Der Zusammenbruch der öst.-ung. Wehrmacht im Herbst 1918* (Munich, 1921).

Kiszling, Rudolf. *Die Kroaten: Der Schicksalweg eines Südslawenvolkes* (Graz, 1956).

———. "Das Nationalitätenproblem in Habsburgs Wehrmacht 1848–1918." *Der Donauraum* 4, no. 2 (1959).

———. *Österreich-Ungarns Anteil am ersten Weltkrieg* (Graz, 1958).

Klavora, Vasja. *Plavi križ: Soška fronta: Bovec: 1915–1917* (Koper, 1993).

———. *Schritte im Nebel: Die Isonzofront, Karfreit/Kobarid, Tolmein/Tolmin: 1915–1917* (Klagenfurt, 1995).

Leed, Eric J. *No Man's Land: Combat and Identity in World War I* (Cambridge, 1979).

Lichem, Heinz. *Gebirgskrieg 1915–18,* Bd. 3, *Karnische und Julische Alpen* (Bozen, 1982).

Macartney, C.A. *The Habsburg Empire, 1790–1918.* (London, 1968).

Maravigna, Pietro. *Le undici offensive sull'Isonzo* (Rome, 1929).

McGuinness, Brian. *Wittgenstein: A Life. Young Ludwig, 1889–1921* (London, 1988).

Meregalli, Carlo. *Grande guerra: Tappe della Vittoria* (Bassano del Grappa, 1993).

Moritsch, Andreas, and Gudmund Tributsch (eds.). *Isonzo Protokoll* (Klagenfurt, 1994).

Morrow, John H. *The Great War in the Air: Military Aviation from 1909 to 1921* (Washington, DC, 1993).

Neubauer, Franz. *Die Gendarmerie in Österreich 1849–1924* (Graz, 1925).

Österreichisches biographisches Lexikon 1815–1950 (Vienna, 1972).

Pagnini, Maria, and Sandra Bagno. *Guide d'Italia: Friuli-Venezia Giulia (Trieste e il Carso, il Friuli e la Carnia)* (Milan, 1986).

Paschall, Rod. *The Defeat of Imperial Germany, 1917–1918* (Chapel Hill, NC, 1989).

Peball, Kurt. "Führungsfragen der öst.-ung. Südtiroloffensive im Jahre 1916." *Mitteilungen des österreichischen Staatsarchives* 31 (1978).

———. "Um das Erbe: Zur Nationalitätenpolitik des k.u.k. Armeeoberkommandos während der Jahre 1914 bis 1918." *Österreichische Militärische Zeitschrift* spec. iss. (1967).

Pichlík, Karel. "Rozpad rakousko-uherské armády na podzim 1918." *Historie a vojenství* (1963).

———. *Vzpoury navrátilců z ruského zajeti na jaře 1918* (Prague, 1968).

Pichlík, Karel, Bohumír Klípa, and Jitka Zabloudilová. *Českoslovenští legionáň 1914–1918* (Prague, 1996).

Pieri, Pietro. *L'Italia nella prima guerra mondiale (1915–1918)* (Turin, 1971).

Pieri, Pietro, and Giorgio Rochat. *Pietro Badoglio* (Turin, 1974).

Pieropan, Gianni. *Ortigara 1917: Il sacrificio della sesta armata* (Milan, 1974).

Pinchetti, Rodolfo. *Isonzo 1917: Kuk-Bainsizza, Carso, Carzano* (Milan, 1934).

Pitreich, Max von. *1914: Die militärische Probleme unseres Kriegsbeginnes* (Vienna, 1934).

Plaschka, Richard Georg. *Cattaro-Prag: Revolte und Revolution* (Graz, 1963).

Plaschka, Richard Georg, Horst Haselsteiner, and Arnold Suppan. *Innere Front: Militärassistenz, Widerstand und Umsturz in der Donaumonarchie 1918,* 2 vols. (Vienna, 1974).

Primicerj, Giulio. *1917: Lubiana o Trieste? Le ultime spallate di Cadorna viste "dall' altra parte"* (Milan, 1986).

Pust, Ingomar. *Die steinerne Front: Auf den Spuren des Gebirgskrieges in den Julischen Alpen von Isonzo zur Piave* (Graz, 1980).

Rauchensteiner, Manfried. *Der Tod des Doppeladlers: Österreich-Ungarn und der Erste Weltkrieg* (Graz, 1994).

Regele, Oskar. *Gericht über Habsburgs Wehrmacht: Letzte Siege und Untergang unter dem Armee-Oberkommando Kaiser Karls I* (Vienna, 1968).

Renzi, William. "Italy's Neutrality and Entrance into the Great War: A Reexamination." *American Historical Review* 73, no. 5 (June 1968).

Reynolds, Michael S. *Hemingway's First War: The Making of A Farewell to Arms* (Princeton, NJ, 1976).

Rocca, Gianni. *Cadorna* (Milan, 1985).

Rochat, Giorgio, and Giulio Massobrio. *Breve storia dell'esercito italiano dal 1861 al 1943* (Turin, 1978).

Rothenberg, Gunther E. *The Army of Francis Joseph* (West Lafayette, IN, 1976).

———. "The Croatian Military Border and the Rise of Yugoslav Nationalism." *Slavonic and East European Review* 17, no. 100 (December 1964).

———. "Toward a National Army: The Military Compromise of 1868 and Its Consequences." *Slavic Review* 31, no. 4 (December 1972).

Rusinow, Dennison I. *Italy's Austrian Heritage, 1919–1946* (London, 1969).

Sachs, Harvey. *Toscanini* (London, 1978).

Sarfatti, Margherita. *The Life of Benito Mussolini* (trans. Frederic Whyte) (London, 1925).

Schaumann, Walther, and Peter Schubert. *Isonzo 1915–1917: Krieg ohne Wiederkehr* (Bassano del Grappa, 1993).

Schindler, John R. "A Hopeless Struggle: Austro-Hungarian Cryptology During World War I." *Cryptologia*, October 2000.

Schmidl, Erwin A. *Juden in der k.(u.)k. Armee 1788–1918* (Eisenstadt, 1989).

Scrimale, Antonio, and Furio Scrimale. *Il Carso della grande guerra: Le trincee raccontano* (Trieste, 1995).

Sema, Antonio. *La grande guerra sul fronte dell'Isonzo*, 2 vols. (Gorizia, 1997).

Seth, Ronald. *Caporetto: The Scapegoat Battle* (London, 1965).

Seton-Watson, Christopher. *Italy from Liberalism to Fascism, 1870–1925* (London, 1967).

Silvestri, Mario. *Caporetto: Una battaglia e un enigma* (Milan, 1984).

———. *Isonzo 1917* (Milan, 1971).

Sked, Alan. *The Decline and Fall of the Habsburg Empire, 1815–1918* (New York, 1989).

Slataper, Scipio. *Scritti politici* (Milan, 1954).

Smith, Dennis Mack. *Italy: A Modern History* (Ann Arbor, MI, 1969).

———. *Italy and Its Monarchy* (New Haven, CT, 1989).

Sondhaus, Lawrence. *In the Service of the Emperor: Italians in the Austrian Armed Forces, 1814–1918* (New York, 1990).

———. *The Naval Policy of Austria-Hungary, 1867–1918* (West Lafayette, IN, 1994).

Speed, Richard B. *Prisoners, Diplomats and the Great War: A Study in the Diplomacy of Captivity* (New York, 1990).

Spence, Richard B. "*Die Bosniaken kommen!:* The Bosnian-Hercegovinian Formations of the Austro-Hungarian Army, 1914–1918." In *Scholar, Patriot, Mentor: Historical Essays in Honor of Dimitrije Djordjević* (R. Spence and L. Nelson, eds.) (New York, 1992).

Spinosa, Antonio. *D'Annunzio: Il poeta armato* (Milan, 1987).

Steiner, Jörg C. *Schematismus der Generale u. Obersten der k.u.k. Armee: Stand 31. Dez. 1918* (Vienna, 1992).

Stöckelle, Gustav. "Die Südtiroler Offensive gegen Italien." *Österreichische Militärische Zeitschrift* (1966).

Stone, Norman. "Army and Society in the Habsburg Monarchy, 1900–1914." *Past and Present* no. 33 (April 1966).

———. *The Eastern Front 1914–1917* (New York, 1975).

———. "Die Mobilmachung der öst.-ung. Armee 1914." *Militärgeschichtliche Mitteilungen* 16, no. 2 (1974).

Švajncer, Janez. *Svetovna vojna 1914–18: Slovenci v avstro-ogrski armadi* (Maribor, 1988).

———. *Teritorialna obramba Republike Slovenije* (Ljubljana, 1992).

———. *Vojna in vojaška zgodovina slovencev* (Ljubljana, 1992).

Svoljšak, Petra. *Die Isonzofront* (Ljubljana, 1994).

Szabó, László. *Doberdo, Isonzo, Tirol* (Budapest, 1980).

Thayer, John. *Italy and the Great War: Politics and Culture, 1870–1915* (Madison, WI, 1964).

Thompson, Mark. *A Paper House: The Ending of Yugoslavia* (London, 1992).

Tóth, Sándor (ed.). *Magyarország hadtörténete*, 2 vols. (Budapest, 1985).

Urbański, August von. "Spionage und Gegenspionage bei den Mittelmächten vor dem Weltkriege." In *Die Weltkriegspionage* (Munich, 1931).

Weber, Fritz. *Isonzo 1915* (Klagenfurt, 1933).

———. *Menschenmauer am Isonzo* (Leipzig, 1932).

Whittam, John. *The Politics of the Italian Army, 1861–1918* (London, 1977).

Winkler, Wilhelm. *Die Totenverluste der öst.-ung. Monarchie nach Nationalitäten* (Vienna, 1919).

INDEX

About the Author

JOHN R. SCHINDLER, a historian specializing in modern European and military history, is a researcher at the American Enterprise Institute in Washington, D.C., and Adjunct Professor of history at the University of Maryland, Baltimore County. His research interests include multiethnic states and ideologies, military theory, and the history of intelligence. He holds three degrees in history: a B.A. and M.A. from the University of Massachusetts and a Ph.D. from McMaster University. His writings have won numerous awards and have taken him to several countries.